ROCKET INTERCEPTORS
1941–1947

ROCKET INTERCEPTORS
1941–1947

JUSTO MIRANDA

First published in Great Britain in 2026 by
Fonthill
An imprint of
Pen & Sword Books Ltd
Yorkshire – Philadelphia

Copyright © Justo Miranda, 2026

ISBN 978-1-78155-955-0

The right of Justo Miranda to be identified as Author of this work has been asserted by him in accordance with the Copyright, Designs and Patents Act 1988.

A CIP catalogue record for this book is available from the British Library.

All rights reserved. No part of this book may be reproduced, transmitted, downloaded, decompiled or reverse engineered in any form or by any means, electronic or mechanical including photocopying, recording or by any information storage and retrieval system, without permission from the Publisher in writing. NO AI TRAINING: Without in any way limiting the Author's and Publisher's exclusive rights under copyright, any use of this publication to "train" generative artificial intelligence (AI) technologies to generate text is expressly prohibited. The Author and Publisher reserve all rights to license uses of this work for generative AI training and development of machine learning language models.

Typeset in SabonLTStd 10/13 by
SJmagic DESIGN SERVICES, India.
Printed and bound in the UK by CPI Group (UK) Ltd, Croydon, CR0 4YY

The Publisher's authorised representative in the EU for product safety is Authorised Rep Compliance Ltd., Ground Floor, 71 Lower Baggot Street, Dublin D02 P593, Ireland.
www.arccompliance.com

For a complete list of Pen & Sword titles please contact

PEN & SWORD BOOKS LIMITED
George House, Units 12 & 13, Beevor Street, Off Pontefract Road,
Barnsley, South Yorkshire, S71 1HN, England
E-mail: enquiries@pen-and-sword.co.uk
Website: www.pen-and-sword.co.uk

or

PEN AND SWORD BOOKS
1950 Lawrence Rd, Havertown, PA 19083, USA
E-mail: uspen-and-sword@casematepublishers.com
Website: www.penandswordbooks.com

Contents

1	First Flights	7
2	Daytime Combats Over the Reich	14
3	The Gleitjäger Concept	23
4	Verbrauchsflugzeug Competition	29
5	Solid-Propellant Rockets	36
6	The Bordjäger Concept	38
7	Rammschussjäger Specification	44
8	Turbojet/Rocket Mixed Power Plant	62
9	Combat Rocket-Planes	96
10	Chasing the Mach One—German Supersonic Projects	118
11	The Strahlrohrjäger Concept	130
12	Objektschutzjäger Programme	160
13	Towed Projects	162
14	Trolley-Launched Projects	166
15	Ramp-Launched Projects	173
16	Conventional Landing Gear	183
17	Ejector Seats	191
18	Bi-Propellant Rocket Engines	194
19	Projekt Natter	197
20	Air-to-Air Spin-Stabilised Rockets	209
21	Air-to-Air Fin-Stabilised Rockets	211
22	Wernher von Braun Rockets	217
23	Russian Rocket-Planes	242
24	Cold War	270
25	American Rocket-Fighters	275
26	Japanese Rocket-Fighters	285

1
First Flights

The development of rockets in Germany during the 1920s was financed by the automobile builder Fritz von Opel as an advertising medium.

In 1927 engineer Max Valier designed several rocket-powered cars and trains for Opel, in order to obtain funding for his own projects. These solid-propellant rockets were manufactured at Sirius plant-Wessermünde under the supervision of pyrotechnic engineer Friedrich Wilhelm Sander.

Experiments and advertising displays began in 1928.

In March, Opel bought a canard sailplane designed by Alexander Lippisch from glider builder Rhön-Rositten Gesellschaft.

This aircraft, designated RRG Ente (Duck), had been successfully tested in 1926 at the AVA Göttingen wind tunnel.

The intention of the team of Opel, Valier and Sander was to transform the Ente into a rocket-plane capable of taking off on its own powered by a Sander rocket with 360kg peak-thrust and then keeping it in flight with the help of an auxiliary rocket with 22.67kg thrust.

The designer objected that the excess power could damage the fragile structure of the sailplane and it was decided to carry out the launch from the Wasserkuppe facilities by means of a rubber catapult using only two 22.67kg rockets that would ignite sequentially during the flight.

Both rocket-motors are mounted in the tail, counterbalanced by nose ballast.

The RRG Raketen-Ente took off on 11 June 1928, piloted by Friedrich Stamer, and continued to fly smoothly for 1,500m.

RRG Raketen-Ente Technical data: Wingspan: 11.94m. Length: 4.31m. Height: 1.76m. Wing area: 20.3sq.m, aspect ratio: 7.

In July 1929, the sailplane builder Gottlob Espenlaub mounted two Sander rockets on the centre wing section of an Espenlaub EA.1 glider (tethered to the ground for tests) and found that the main wing spar could not withstand the forces imposed by the rockets' thrust.

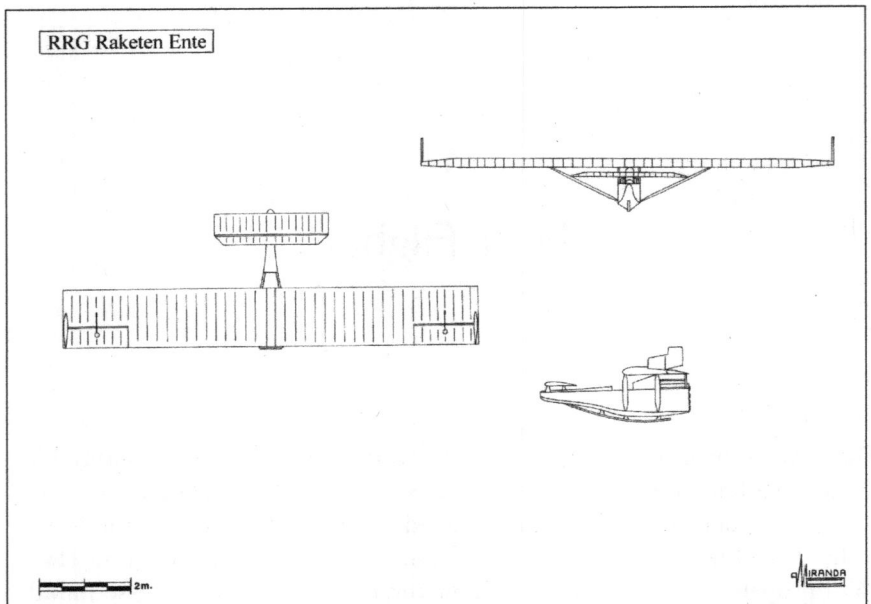

After the destruction of Ente, when one of the rockets exploded during its second flight, Opel commissioned the design of a more conventional aircraft from glider builder Julius Hatry.

On 10 September 1929 the Opel/Hatry RAK.1 was flown at Rüsselsheim powered by sixteen Sander rockets of the 22.67kg class.

The new rocket-plane flew for 75 seconds reaching a distance of 1,400m.

OPEL/HATRY RAK.1 TECHNICAL DATA: Wingspan: 11m. Length: 5.41m. Height: 2m. Wing area: 11.2sq.m. Maximum weight: 270kg. Maximum speed: 150km/h.

On 22 October 1929, the Espenlaub E-7, a reinforced version of the EA.1, flew powered by two Sander rockets mounted in staggered configuration on the central section of the wing.

On 20 April, Espenlaub received a contract from the Studiengesellschaft für Raketen eV institute to build a tailless rocket sailplane with an 18-degree swept wing.

On 4 May 1930 the new aircraft, named Espenlaub E-15, was towed to an altitude of 20m before igniting the first pair of 80kg thrust rockets mounted side-by-side over the central section of the wing. To keep on flying the pilot activated the second pair of 9kg thrust rockets reaching 100km/h.

ESPENLAUB E-15 TECHNICAL DATA: Wingspan: 12m. Length: 3.9m. Height: 1.9m. Wing area: 17sq.m.

None of these propaganda flights achieved practical results applicable to the future of aviation, but they inspired a 12-year-old boy named Wernher von Braun to begin the conquest of the Moon.

In June 1927 the Verein für Raumschiffahrt (VFR) society was founded in Breslau with the aim of demonstrating the superiority of liquid-fuelled rockets over solid-fuelled rockets, theorised by Hermann Oberth in 1923.

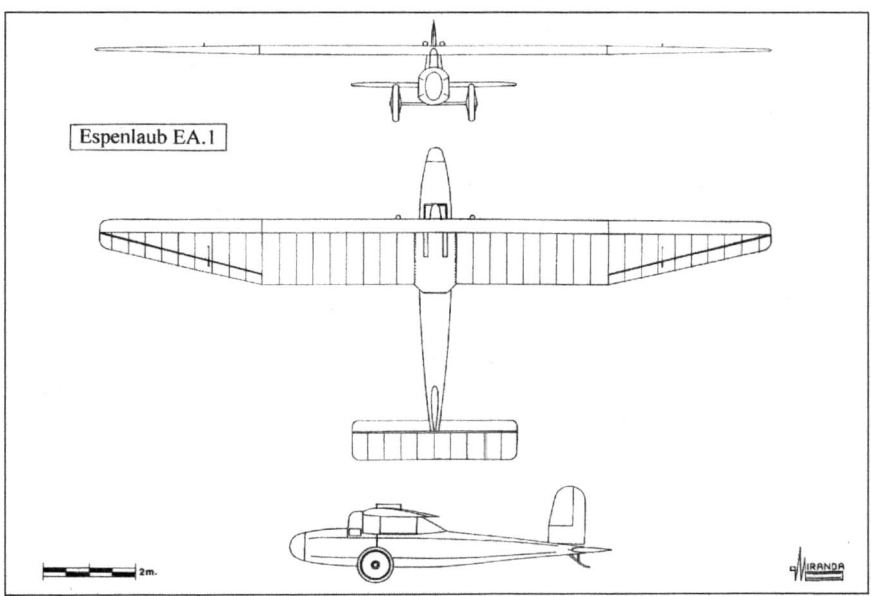

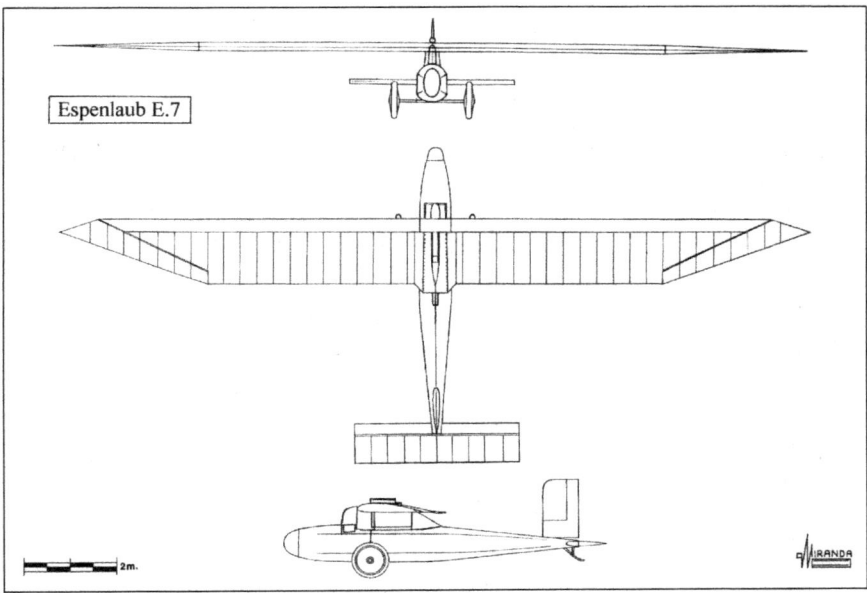

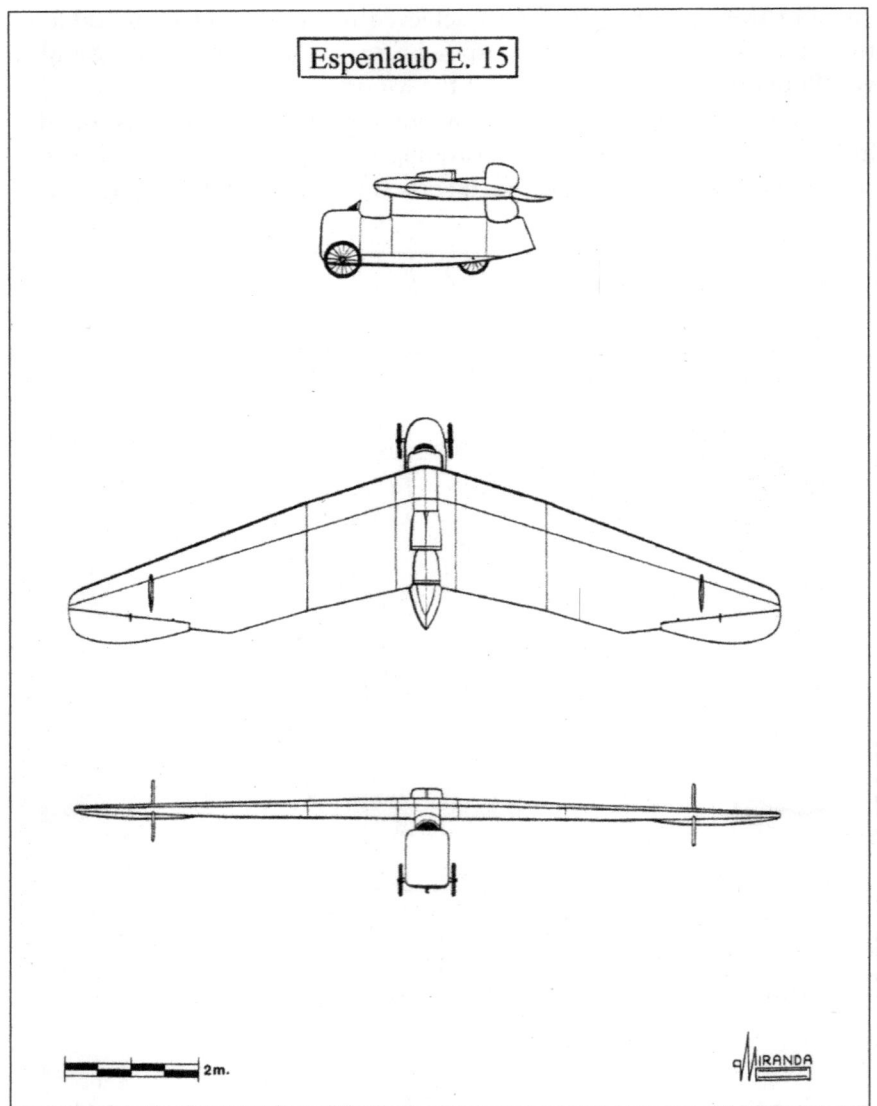

Among its early members were Max Valier, Willy Ley, Hermann Oberth, Johannes Winkler, Klaus Riedel and Wernher von Braun.

In 1929 they built the first liquid-fuelled rocket engine, the Kegelduese, which was successfully tested at the Chemisch-Technische Reichanstalt facilities on 5 August 1930.

Kegelduese ran on gasoline and liquid oxygen, generating 7kg thrust.

The next prototype, Mirak, designed by Klaus Riedel, used carbon dioxide as a gasoline pressuriser.

In 1930 the VFR began to be financed by the Armaments Department of the German Army (Heereswaffenamt), which gave up one of its training grounds (which later became known as Raketenflugplatz) for rocket testing.

In 1931, tests began on the Repulsor rockets, designed to solve the problem of overheating the Mirak's combustion chamber, using water as coolant. During testing, a Repulsor reached an altitude of 1,600m.

In 1933 the Heereswaffenamt created a special section for research into long-range artillery 'A' rockets powered by methanol and liquid oxygen.

Wernher von Braun designed and helped build the A-1 rocket, rated at 300kg peak-thrust.

In December 1934, an A-2 launched from Borkum Island reached an altitude of 2,400m.

The A-3, which used nitrogen as a pressuriser, was not ready until the summer of 1937 for flight tests at Greifswalder Oie.

The development of the A-4 ballistic missile, which would be mass-produced as the EMW V-2 (Vergeltungswaffe-2), continued at Peenemünde.

While these powerful bi-propellant rockets were being developed, engineer Helmuth Walter was experimenting with hydrogen peroxide monopropellant at the Germania-Werft-Kiel Company facilities.

In 1936 Walter built a small 40kg thrust rocket called the HWK R.1, with the help of the Versuchsanstalt für Luftart institute and the Electrochemische Werke-Munich Company.

In January 1937 Heinkel became interested in the project and loaned a small He 72 training biplane and a Focke-Wulf Fw 56 (D-DNYJ) advanced trainer for flight trials of the new propulsion system.

After learning the results of the tests, Heinkel decided to build a rocket-plane capable of flying at 1,000km per hour to impress the Luftwaffe's technical officers.

The new aircraft was designed at the end of 1937 by Dipl.-Ing Hans Regner and built at the Rostock-Marienehe works as He 176 V1.

The 900kg thrust engine that von Braun was developing would not be available until 1939 and Heinkel decided to use a Walter HWK RI 203 rocket with 600kg thrust for the first prototype.

Several ground tests carried out in Peenemünde proved that the small wings of the prototype lacked sufficient lifting power to achieve a take-off with the available power, and it was necessary to suspend the tests and manufacture wings with a larger surface area; these arrived in Peenemünde in the spring of 1939.

On 20 June 1939, the He 176 V1 flew for 50 seconds at 270km/h, but Göring was not at all impressed with the demonstration.

After the He 176 flight, the new power system could not be ignored anymore, although it attracted the Reichsluftfahrtministerium (RLM) attention in the worst sense. The Luftwaffe had not forgiven the Heinkel He 51 fiasco during the Spanish Civil War and had already decided that the main fighter provider onwards would be Messerschmitt and that the new rocket engine was ideal to power a high-altitude interceptor.

The development of the R I 203 rocket by the firm Walter Werke K.G. was considered Geheime Kommandosache (Top Secret) and was controlled by the RLMs Sondertriebwerke (Special Propulsion Systems Development Office).

From the beginning of 1937 the Lippisch/DFS 194 (classified as 'Projekt X') was being developed under great security measures.

The authorisation to build the He 176 V2 was denied and the V1 was sent to the Berlin Air Museum.

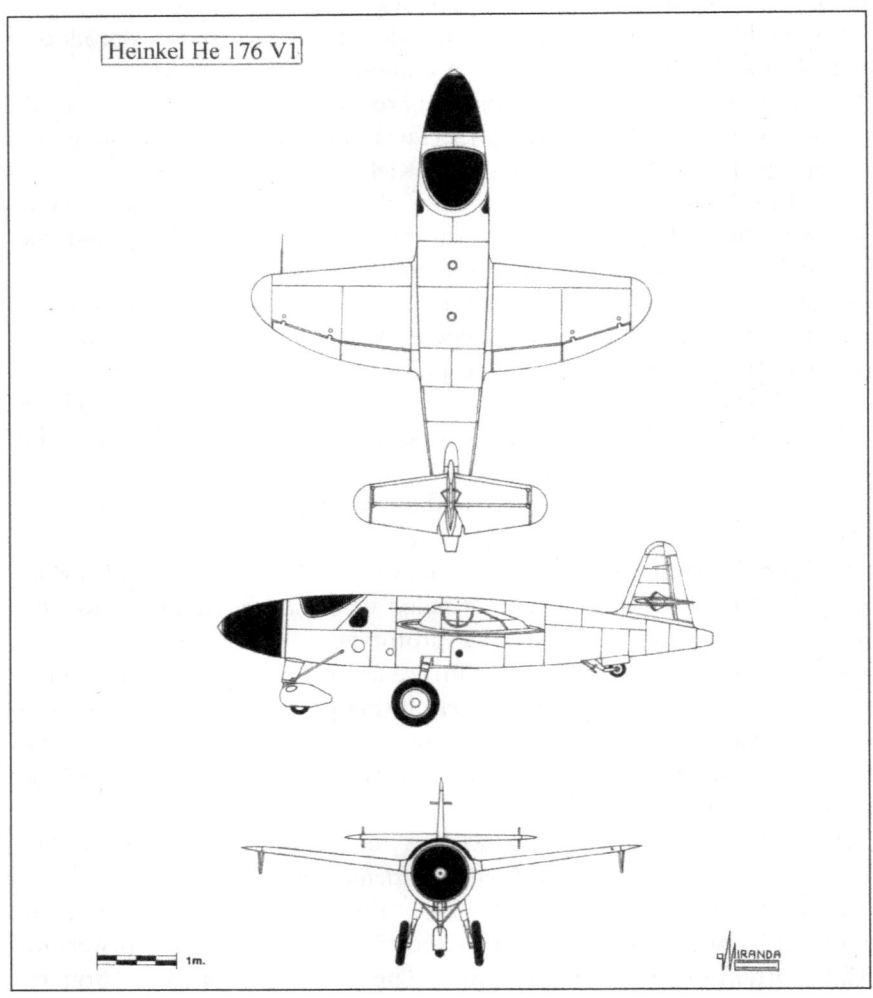

Seventy-three days later, the Second World War began and German industry concentrated all its resources on the construction of conventional piston aircraft.

HEINKEL HE 176 V1 TECHNICAL DATA: Wingspan: 5m. Length: 6.2m. Height: 2.4m. Wing area: 5.4sq.m. Maximum weight: 1,620kg. Maximum speed: 270km/h. Power plant: one Walter HWK RI 203 rocket rated at 600kg thrust.

HEINKEL HE 176 V2 TECHNICAL DATA: Wingspan: 5m. Length: 5.2m. Height: 1.44m. Wing area: 5.5sq.m. Maximum weight: 2,000kg. Maximum speed: 750km/h. Service ceiling: 9,000m. Power plant: one Walter HWK RI-203 rocket rated at 690kg thrust.

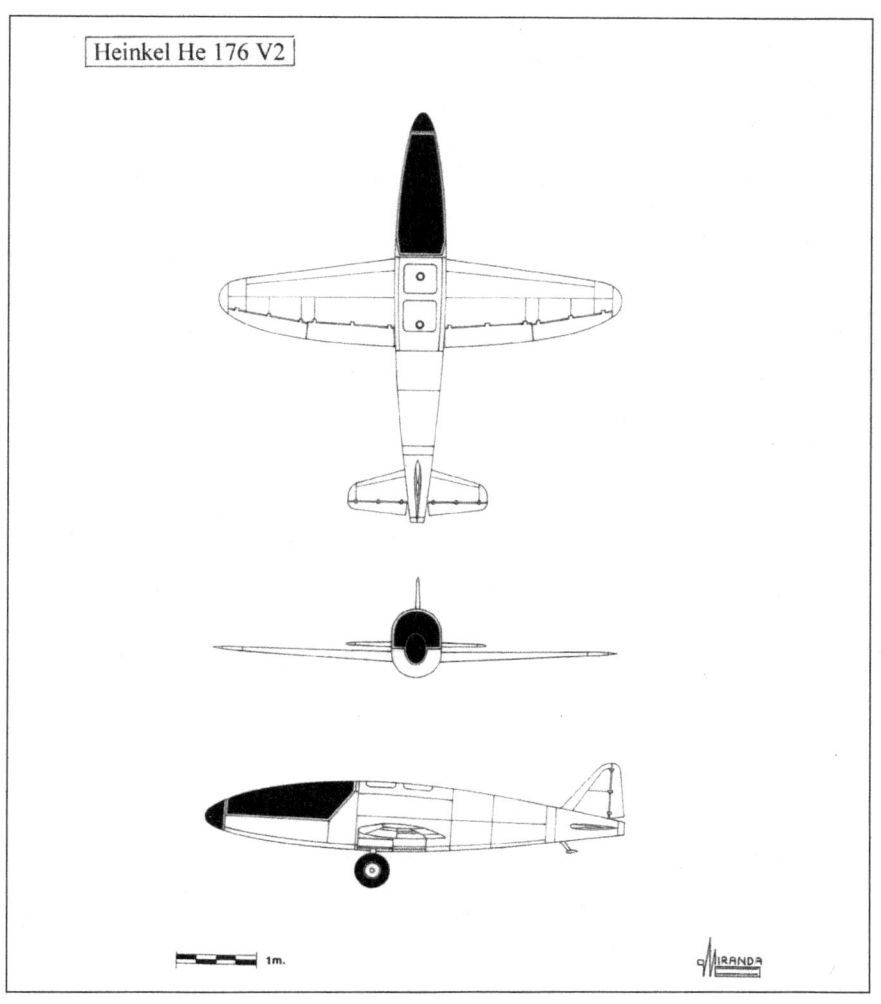

2
Daytime Combats Over the Reich

By mid-1942, American bombers B-17 and B-24 were much better armed than their British counterparts and their crews had been trained to fly in self-defence formations only a few metres apart from each other. The rules of air combat determined that an attacker fighter would not risk flying through such a compact formation, having to choose between shooting from far away and deviating at the last moment, exposing their ventral surfaces to the powerful defensive crossfire of American gunners, who were considered statistically lethal from a distance of a thousand yards.

A lonely fighter attacking a 'box' got in the gunsight of as many as forty Browning M2 heavy machine guns. The Germans tried many different Pulkzerstörer (formation destroyer) tactics to break the 'boxes' without having to get too close. The four-engine bombers, which they called Viermots or Dicke Autos, were attacked from a distance of 1,800m by Messerschmitt Me 410 A-2/U4 heavy fighters, fitted with Rheinmetall-Borsig BK.5 cannons of 50mm that were capable of dismantling a B-17 with a single hit. But this made the Me 410s so heavy that they could not escape the bombers' P-51 Mustang escorts.

The Viermots were attacked from 1,300m with W.Gr.21 rockets of 210mm, launched from specially modified aircraft: Messerschmitt Bf 110 G-2/R3, Focke-Wulf Fw 190 A-7/R6 and Messerschmitt Bf 109 G-6/R2. However, this type of spin-stabilised rocket was very inaccurate and, after the attack, the launcher plane could not release the launch tubes in flight, which considerably diminished its speed.

From 900m range, some Junkers Ju 88 P-2 and Messerschmitt Bf 110 G-2/R1 fired their Rheinmetall-Borsig 'Flak 38' of 37mm, an anti-tank cannon with a low rate of fire that was too heavy to be installed on a single-seat fighter and which, used in air-to-air mode, was a failure.

The Luftwaffe also tested various air-to-air bombing techniques in the summer of 1943, using Messerschmitt Bf 109 G-4 fighters that flew at 1,000m over the 'stream bombers' throwing AB 50 containers, each one loaded with thirty-four standard infantry fragmentation grenades. The Focke-Wulf Fw 190 A-4/U3 of the I./JG1 launched SC 250 bombs and AB 500 containers (loaded with 370kg of H.E. and fitted with time fuses) over the 'boxes' without achieving success.

At the beginning of 1944 there were already designs and prototypes of air-to-air missiles created to solve the 'thousand yards problem', but until they reached service status, the Luftwaffe was forced to fight the Viermots using Sturm (assault) fighter units specialised in *schnauze auf schnauze* (frontal attacks) combat. The advantage of a head-on pass was that the fighter remained only 5 seconds in the thousand-yards area, and took another 9 seconds to cross the 'box', if it was lucky enough to not collide with any bomber. The downside was that the aircraft crossed so quickly that the fighter barely had time to fire. And many shots were needed to shoot down a Viermot!

Major Hans Georg von Kornatzki proposed the Oberkommando der Luftwaffe (OKL) to use saturation tactics by which a group of at least thirty fighters simultaneously attacked a 'box' to avoid the concentration of defensive fire against a single fighter.

Kornatzki did not get the thirty fighters but he obtained approval from the general Adolf Galland to test new tactics with a section of fifteen aircraft that was named I./JG1 Sturmstaffel 1. The tests began in Achmer-Osnabrück in late 1943 using Focke-Wulf Fw 190 A-6 fighters in mock combat against a Focke-Wulf Fw 200 bomber.

Further analysis of the films made with the EK16 gun cameras served to determine that the optimal firing distance with the MG 151/20 rapid fires cannon was of 200m, approximately when the four engines of the bomber appeared to be in the target circle of the Revi 16B gunsight. The Sturmstaffel 1 became operational in February 1944 under command of major Kornatzki with eighteen Focke-Wulf Fw 190 A-6 aircraft based in Dortmund.

His combat method consisted in carrying out a head-on pass with twelve aircraft flying wing-tip to wing-tip in a broad arrow formation, called Breitkeil by the Germans and 'Company Front' by the Americans. Upon receiving an order from the *staffelführer* all aircrafts simultaneously fired their cannons.

In a typical head-on pass, the four cannons of an Fw 190 (with a rate of fire of 780rpm) could make 160 shots launching between 960 and 1,760 grams of H.E. against the target, depending on the type of ammunition used.

According to statistics from the Luftwaffe, at least 400 grams of H.E. were required to destroy a B-17 with a 95 per cent certainty, therefore the attacking fighter should hit the target with thirty-six shots of M-Geschoss, or sixty-seven shots of MX-Geschoss ammunition.

In a frontal attack, the punch of the MG 151 was increased thanks to the combined speed of both aircraft on collision course. In those combat conditions, the radial engines, the Perspex nose and the cockpit windshield of the bomber were very vulnerable.

After the head-on pass all Breitkeil aircraft broke left and right and organised to repeat the attack until breaking the cohesion of the 'box'. When this was achieved, in the resulting panic the bombers were individually attacked by fighters of other units which had kept at a distance during the Pulkzerstörer combat.

These Sturm tactics were so effective that in early May the Sturmstaffel 1 became a Sturmgruppe within the JG3.

In December 1943, the Focke-Wulf Company began manufacturing a series of eighty Fw 190 A-7/R2 aircraft, specially modified for the Sturm combat, replacing the two MG 151s mounted outboard of the wings by other more powerful cannon MK 108/30, called Kurzgerät by the pilots.

In February 1944, the 2./JG11 started operational testing with these aircraft, testing head-on pass tactics as they flew into a shallow dive of 15 degrees to increase attack speed.

In April, the 5./JG1 made operational tests with the new MK 108 cannon, attacking from the rear of the 'box'. They noted that the low range and high-dispersion fire factor of the Kurzgerät required firing at from less than 100m from the target to obtain results. From this distance, the attacker fighter should make at least fifty-two shots to achieve the three impacts that, statistically, would cause the destruction of the Viermot.

The Fw 190 A-7/R2 could carry only 110 shells of the Minengeschoss 30 x 90 RB type, so in a classic attack from the rear, the pilot should start shooting from 90m, reaching up to 30m from the target before breaking contact.

The casualties of the 'Sturm' units were terrible, The Sturmstaffel 1 pilots boasted of 'not shooting until you see the whites of the eyes of the tail gunner'. This phrase became the slogan of the unit and was materialised in a couple of eyes painted on the flying jackets.

The arrival of numerous US fighters to British bases multiplied the number of aircrafts of the Eighth Air Force by four, altering the course of the war over the Reich in favour of the Allies.

German losses increased even more when the American heavy bombers began being escorted by large groups of long-range Mustangs.

Some Staffeln lost a third of their members in each combat, and in August 1944 the Sturmgruppen were losing one fighter by every bomber that was shot down. During its existence, the I./JG1 withstood a 350 per cent loss of pilots, the IV./JG3 a 200 per cent, and the II./JG4 lost seventy-two pilots in six months.

All of the Reich air bases were within reach of the Mustangs and were regularly bombed to keep the runways unusable.

From September 1944, it became necessary to increase the armour of the fighters transforming them into a new type of aircraft called Sturmböck (assault rammer).

The Fw 190 A-6, A-7 and A-8 of the standard series had a 6.5mm-thick armoured ring to protect the oil cooler and another of 5.5mm ring for the annular oil tank located in the front of the engine cowling. This armour was necessary to prevent that an impact of 12.7mm ammunition would provoke an oil leak that completely obscured visibility through the windshield.

The standard protection for the pilot consisted of a 12mm armoured head-rest, an 8mm armoured seat and aft plating of 5mm.

Subsequently, the field modification Rüstsätze 7 was undertaken in some aircraft. This modification included 5mm vertical armour plating in front of the instrument panel and 4mm horizontal plating under the MG 131 weapons bay. This additional armour was deemed necessary to protect the stomach and legs of the pilot against defensive fire from the Sperry and A-13 ventral turrets of the American bombers.

In the Sturm aircraft the windscreen was replaced by a 50mm-thick armoured glass and the triangular side panels by 30mm glass. The front and left windscreen panels would be electrically heated.

The lateral protection of the hood was also increased using 30mm-thick Plexiglas plates called Scheuklappen (Blinkers), but this modification was quite unpopular among pilots due to the formation of ice at altitude which resulted in a dangerous loss of side view. To protect the cockpit against crossfire, 5mm bolt-on Panzerplatten (armour plates) were screwed onto the fuselage sides. All these field modifications were called Sturmjägeransrüstung, and often included the elimination of the nose-mounted MG 131 machine guns to save some weight.

The extra armour was primarily in front for protection during the assault pass but the fighter was vulnerable to attack from the rear. From January 1945 onwards, the Sturmjägern began to be attacked by British fighters armed with 20mm Hispano cannons that were more powerful than the M2 machine guns of the American fighters.

The Fw 190 armour plating headrest had to be reinforced to 14mm thick and the Plexiglas hood was replaced by a metallic one with side windows and a canopy explosive-jettison system. The explosive shells for the MK 108 cannons stored inside the wings were also protected with 4 and 20mm armour plates.

In November 1944 the armour of a Sturmböck weighed 256kg, making it 25 per cent heavier than the Fw 190 series, and a sure prey in dogfight for the Mustangs.

The excess of weight also affected the climb rate and the pilots had to use Methanol-Water MW 50 power boost to reach the flight level of the bombers in a reasonable time. Some aircraft were fitted with

VDM 9-12157 H-3 propellers (taken from the Fw 190 F-9 and D-9 series) with Holzblättern wide wooden blades, more effective on altitude than the old VDM 9-12176 A-3 metallic blades.

The extra weight also resulted in doubling the fuel consumption rate so the Sturmböcke should use an ETC 501 under fuselage rack with a 300l droppable fuel tank which gave them a flight endurance of 150 minutes.

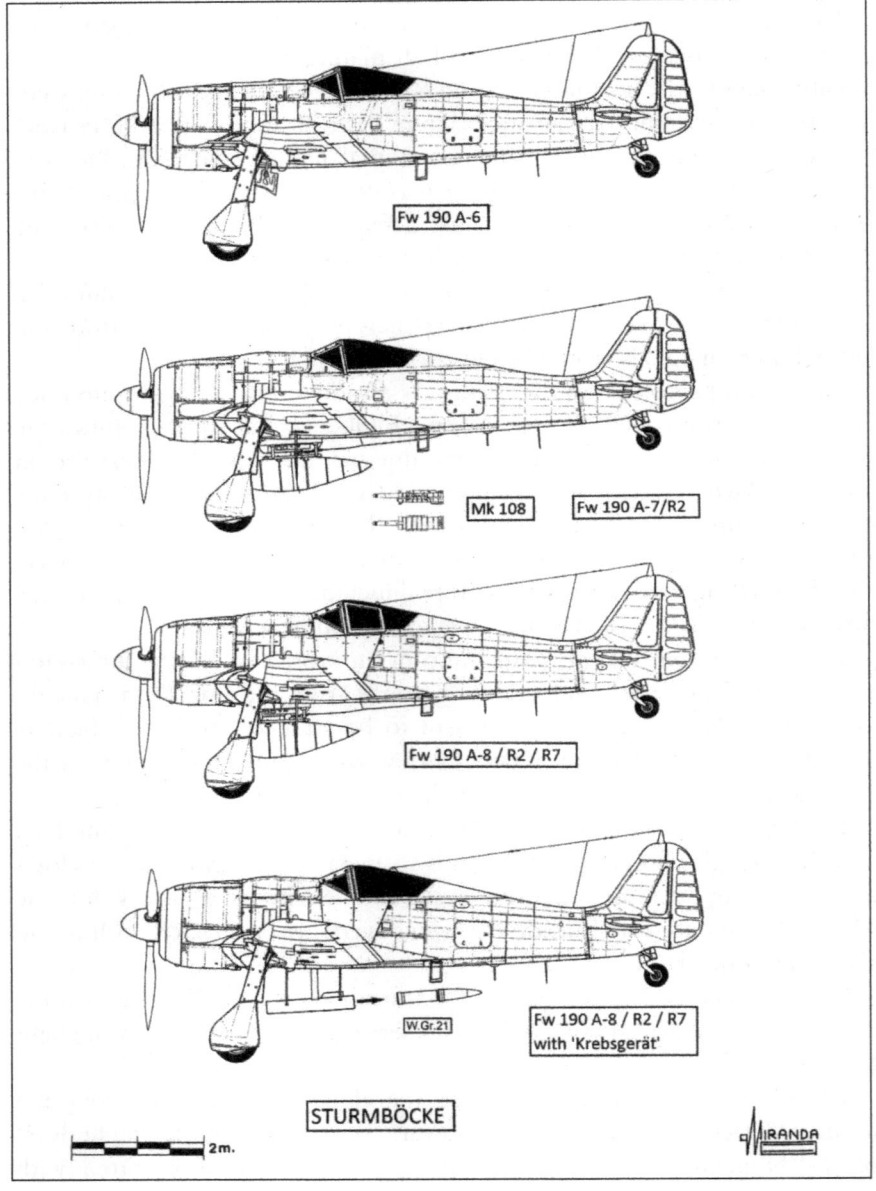

In November 1944 the Focke-Wulf Company began to use the name Rüstsätze 8 (at an administrative level only) to refer to those Fw 190 A-8 that had received the field modifications Rüstsätze 2 and Rüstsätze 7.

As compensation for all the inconveniences, the armour of the fighters allowed them to attack the bombers from behind, ignoring the defensive fire. The slow approach allowed the fighters to shoot more accurately, for

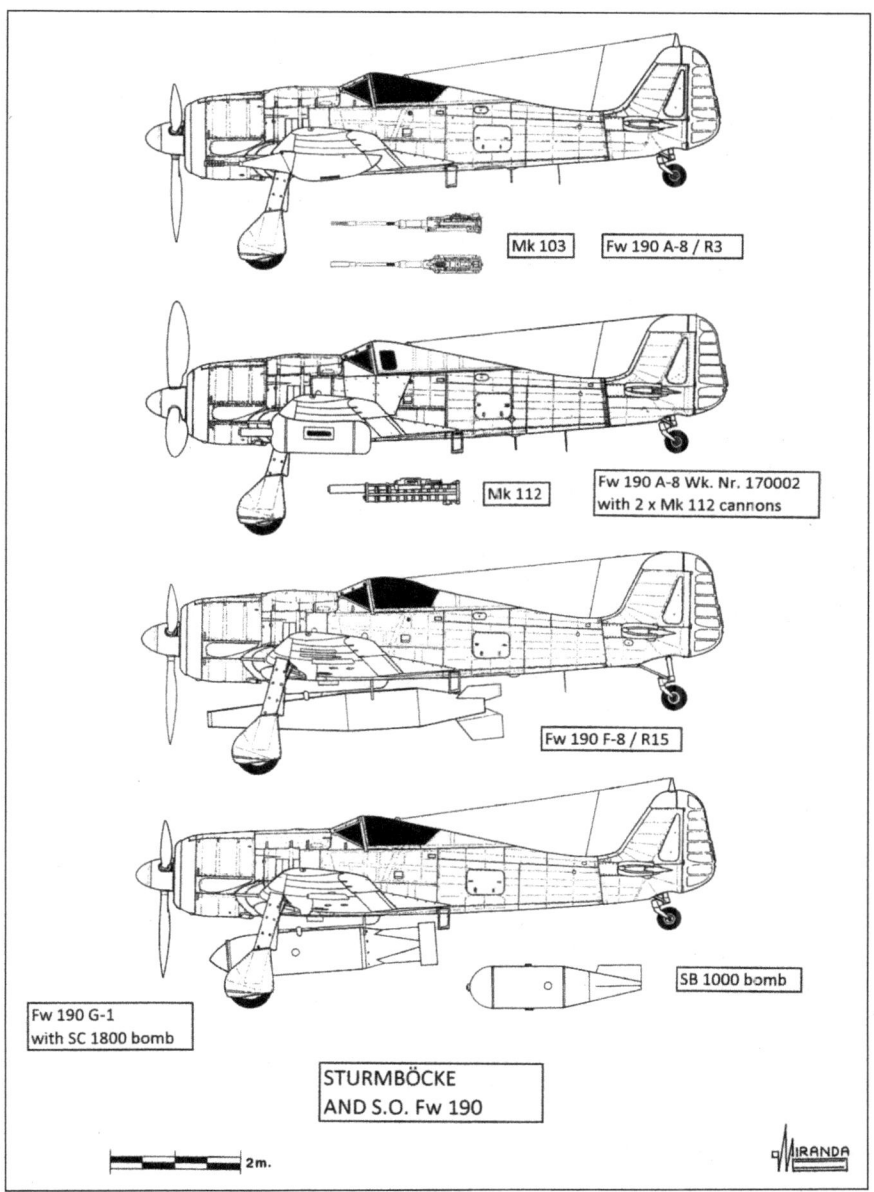

STURMBÖCKE AND S.O. Fw 190

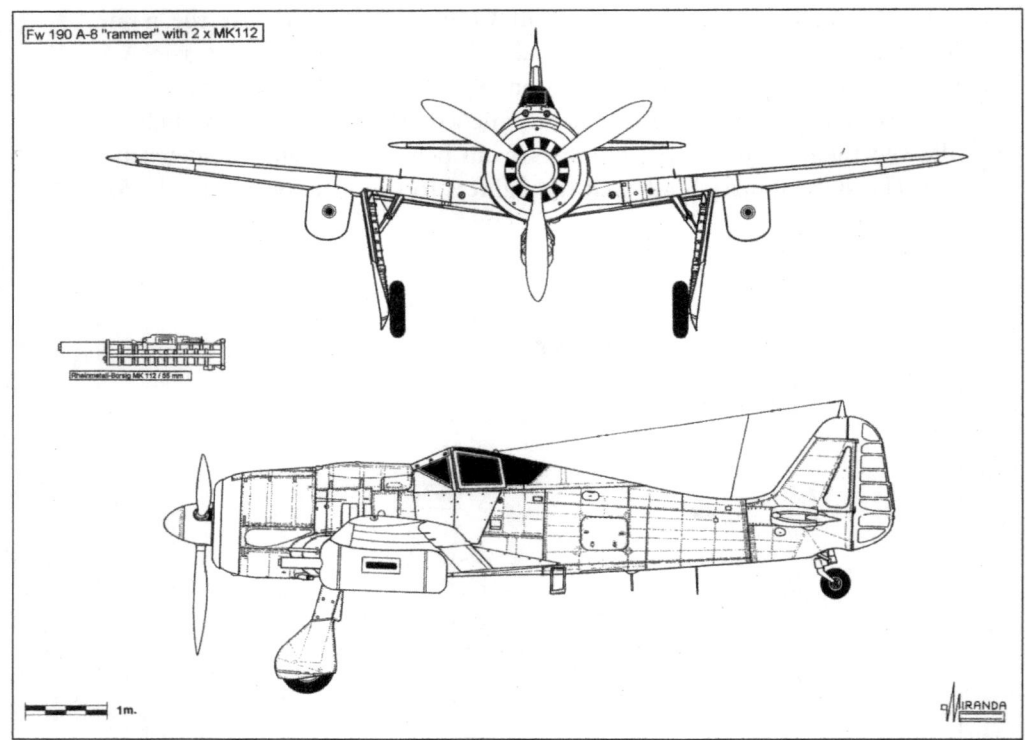

a longer time and with more chances of shooting down the enemy bomber. The greater effective range of the MG 151/20 was very useful in these conditions to neutralise the 'Cheyenne' tail turret of the B-17, reserving the MK 108/30 to shoot from the shortest possible distance.

From August 1944 onwards, the procedure attack from the rear, followed by a head-on pass, became widespread among the Sturmgruppen.

The Americans had many losses caused by the Sturm units and reacted installing in their bombers armoured windshields, chin turrets and two additional machine guns in the nose of the B-17s. They also gradually increased the number of escort fighters until the relative proportion to the German fighters came to be 20/1 at the end of 1944. Groups of fifty to a hundred Mustangs, Lightnings and Thunderbolts protected the sides of the 'bomber stream', preventing the Sturmböcke from regrouping and forming a 'Company Front'. Having greater range than the German fighters, they could pursue them to their bases when they were short of fuel, attacking them during landing or when they were replacing fuel and ammunition.

After the liberation of France, Spitfire and Tempest fighters of the RAF also joined the combat, operating from bases in the Continent, thus putting the Luftwaffe at a greater disadvantage. In 1945 the 'bomber streams' became so great that the escort fighters could not cover its entire length; some Groups were left without any protection and the Reischjägerwelle organisation directed its fighters against them.

The objective of the Sturm attacks was not only to destroy some bombers in the initial confrontation, but also to achieve a Pulkzerstörer effect. Sometimes, panic forced the bombers to break up their cohesion and therefore the integrity of the combat 'boxes', exposing individual aircraft to conventional fighter attacks. The Germans called this tactic situation Herausshuss.

The efficacy demonstrated by the Sturmstaffel 1 led the OKL to create the Sturmgruppe IV/Sturm/JG3 formed by the 10/JG3, 11/JG3, 12/JG3 and the expert survivors of the Sturmstaffel 1. The Sturmgruppe was equipped with new aircraft, Fw 190 A-8/R2/R7 with MK 108/30 cannons and full armour.

The training programme began in April 1944 in Salzwedel, under command of Hauptmann Wilhelm Moritz, simulating fighting against some captured Mustangs from the 2/Versuchsverband der OKW. The new unit became operational with sixty-eight pilots in May. This same month, the II/Strum/JG4 was formed also with the Fw 190 A-8/R2/R7, under the command of Major von Kornatzki. After losing seventy-two pilots in just three months, this unit lost its Sturm condition and their aircraft were retrofitted to the standard type.

In the autumn of 1944, the life expectancy of a Sturm pilot was just ten flying hours.

Between May and September 1944, the US Eighth Air Force made eleven attacks on Leuna-Merseburg, the main production plant for ersatz petrol (synthetic hydrocarbons), stopping its activity. In November the Allies launched a bombing offensive against the hydrogenation plants of Nordstern-Gelsenkirchen, Nordstern-Wesserling, Scholven, Homberg, Wanne-Eickel, Sternkrade, Gastrop, Kamer, Bottrop, Dortmund, Hannover, Hamburg, Misburg, Bohlen, Zeitz and Lützendorf. RAF Bomber Command dropped 13,000 tons of bombs, and the Eighth Air Force 14,000 tons. The US Fifteenth Air Force, based in Italy, attacked the plants located south of the Reich in Florisdorf, Moosbierbaum, Blechhammer South, Korneuberg, Vienna-Lubau and Linz.

By December, German fuel production fell to 151,000 tons of first grade gasoline (Grade C3, 96-octane), aviation base gasoline (Grade B4, 87-octane), gasoline-middle oil (B4 + motor oil) and J2 heavy kerosene for turbojets. The production most affected was that of the C3 and B4 used in piston engines of the fighters, with 25,000 tons only, compared to the anticipated 107,000 tons. Many small plants, also dedicated to the production of Benzol, were destroyed during the bombing attacks by zone, randomly made by the Bomber Command over industrial areas. During the last year of war in Europe, the RAF attacked forty-two hydrogenation plants with 63,000 tons of bombs, and the Eighth with 45,000 tons, finally achieving the collapse of the production system.

The German industrial capacity had been irreversibly eroded by the long naval blockade and continued bombardment. The situation was particularly serious for the piston engine manufacturers, who had already exhausted the chrome and molybdenum reserves needed to harden the steel. There was also a lack of special Schmierstoff lubricants and B4 fuel.

The shortage induced aircraft manufacturers to compete for available turbojets and rocket engines, but only two firms had access to the scarce number of 'Class I' turbojets Jumo 004. One of them was Messerschmitt, to power the Me 262 jet-fighter and the other was Arado, for the Ar 234 jet bomber.

3
The Gleitjäger Concept

From late 1943 several designers were working on parasite fighter projects, the kind of plane that would finally give the opportunity to hundreds of available glider pilots to enter combat.

In its simplest version, Gleitjäger (glider fighter) was a small plane with an armoured cockpit and minimum frontal section. It would be towed to the vicinity of the bomber stream by a conventional fighter and launched from a height sufficient to perform a single attack using one MK 108/30 cannon or several combinations of unguided air-to-air rockets RZ 65, W.Gr.28 and R4M.

Blohm und Voss P.186

By mid-1943 it was quite evident that the Luftwaffe could not prevent the Allied bombers from carrying out punishment missions where and whenever they wanted. The powerful American four-engine bombers specialised in accurate daylight attacks and operated in self-defensive formations, which allowed them to support each other using the concentrated crossfire of their heavy machine guns. Statistically, this was lethal to the target of 1.53sq.m represented by a standard fighter Focke-Wulf Fw 190 in a frontal view at a distance of 1,000 yards.

Theoretically, the solution consisted in reducing the frontal area of the fighter. In practice, this meant eliminating the engine and redesigning the aircraft as an armoured glider. The Germans had much experience in the construction of sailplanes and numerous projects of Gleiterjägern emerged during the last two years of war in Europe.

By placing the pilot in a prone position, they could manufacture an aircraft with a frontal area of just 0.5sq.m, but this modification required numerous studies.

With the widespread use of dive bombers during the first months of the Second World War, the crews of Stukas began to falter. After making a certain number of missions, some of them experienced a black-out phenomena and others fainted, losing control of their aircraft. According to studies by the Luftwaffe Aviation Medicine Branch (LFM), this was caused by insufficient blood pressure in the brain, a consequence of the G-forces that tended to accumulate blood in the legs.

Experiments with centrifuges reaching 14G in 1936 showed that a pilot lying in prone position could better retain consciousness than in a seated position, as the heart was at the same height as the brain.

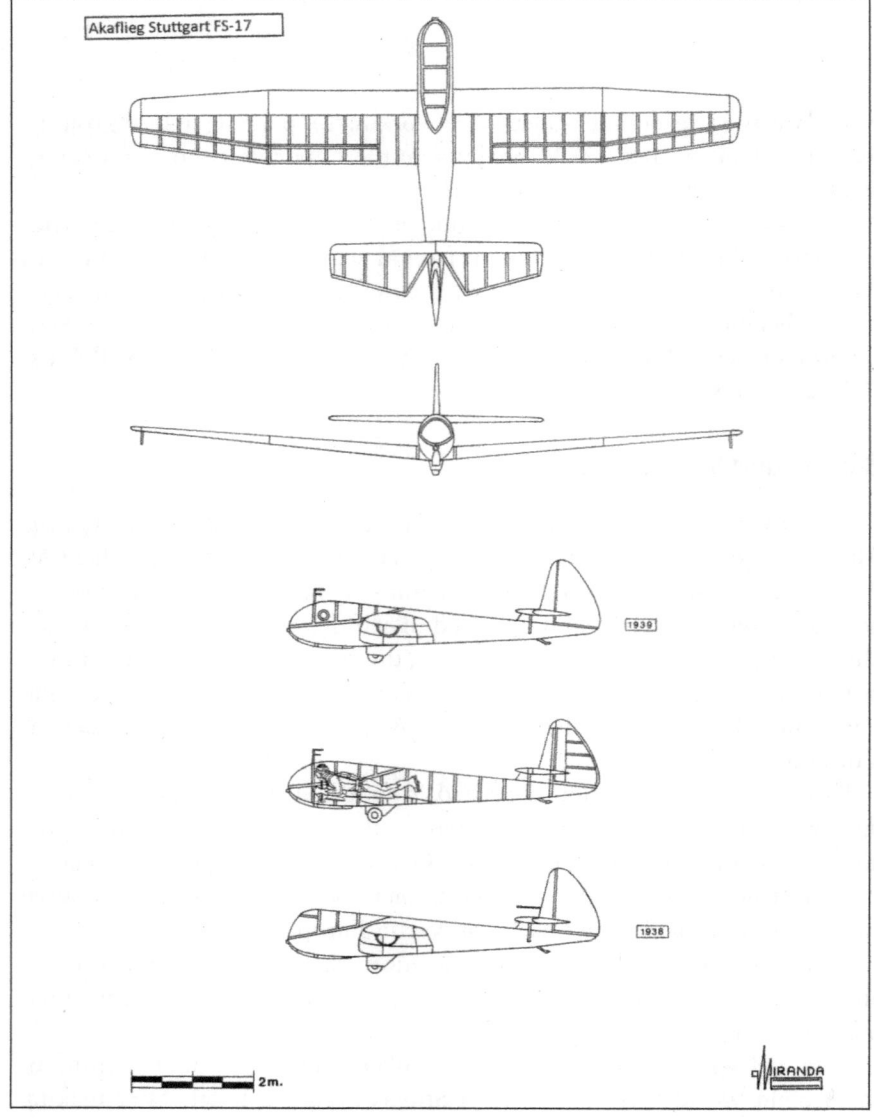

The Gleitjäger Concept

To gain some experience, the LFM used an Akaflieg FS-17, a single-seat glider, and a specially modified DFS Kranich II to place a second pilot in the nose, in prone position.

However, upon reaching a certain level of G-force, the structural strength of the gliders began to fail.

Therefore, to continue experimenting, the company Akaflieg built the Berlin B9, a small twin-engine experimental aircraft capable of supporting up to 22G in flight. In the spring of 1943 the scientists were able to prove that a pilot in prone position could recover in a few seconds after a dive at 8.5G.

During the summer, this information was used to design the Blohm und Voss P.186, an armoured Gleitjäger designed to perform a single attack.

This little fighter should be towed by a Messerschmitt Bf 109 G and released near the bomber stream, but it was found that, being slower than the bombers, the Gleitjäger could only be placed in an attack position by diving from about 1,000m above the stream to gain speed.

However, sometimes the towing plane lacked the power to reach the appropriate flight level in time for the interception and the P.186 was cancelled on 30 October 1943.

BLOHM UND VOSS P.186 TECHNICAL DATA: Wingspan: 5.5m. Length: 3.96m. Height: 1.34m. Armament: Two MK 108/30 cannons over the cockpit.

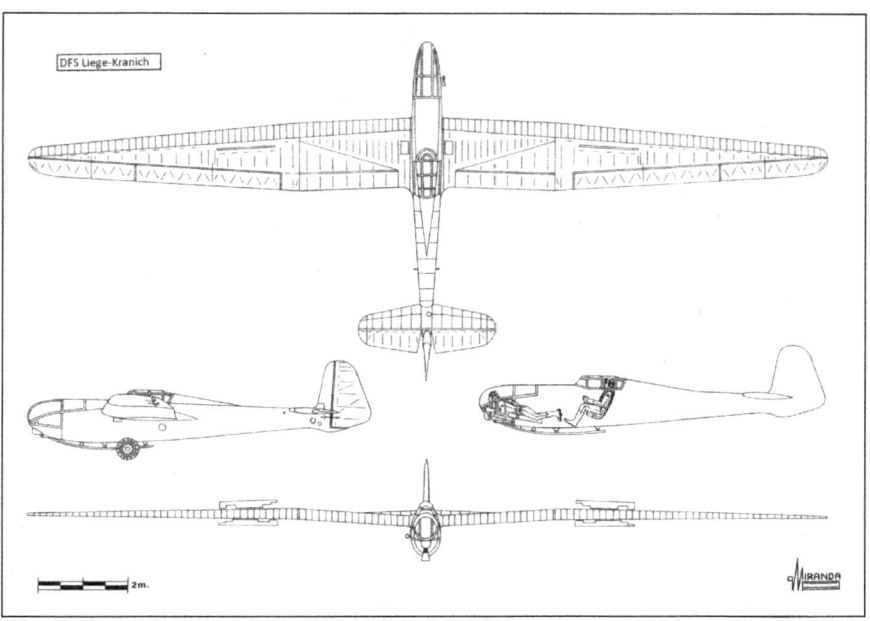

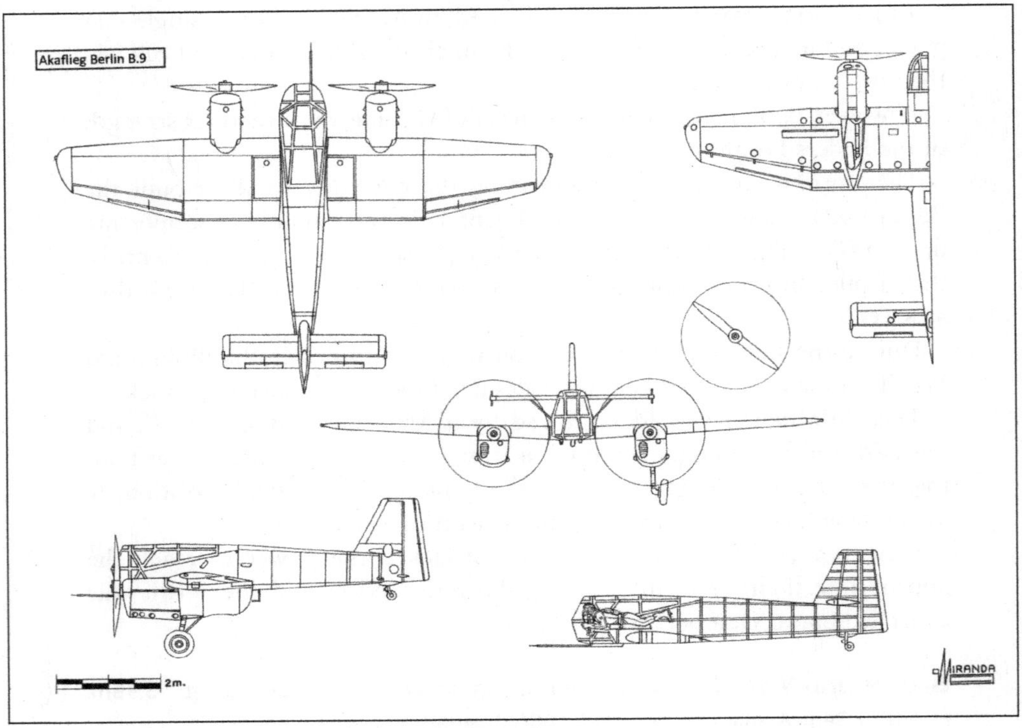

26 Rocket Interceptors: 1941–1947

Akaflieg Berlin B.9

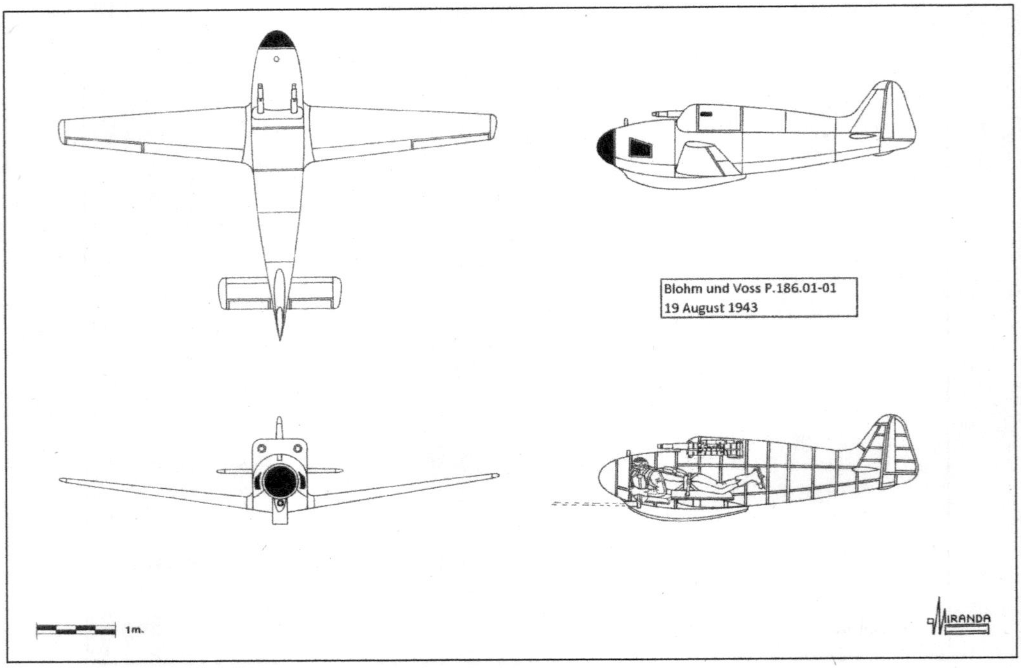

Blohm und Voss P.186.01-01
19 August 1943

Blohm und Voss BV 40

In December 1943 the demand for flying boats, the main aeronautical product by Blohm und Voss, was virtually non-existent; Dr Ing. Richard Vogt designed a heavy armoured Gleitjäger called BV 40 and received authorisation from the RLM for twelve of the aircraft to be built as a pre-series.

The armoured cockpit, virtually invulnerable to the impact of US 12.7mm machine guns, weighed 300kg and was made of welded steel plates. The prone pilot was frontally protected by a 120mm-thick windscreen. The rest of the airframe was built in wood/plywood.

The BV 40 took off from a detachable dolly towed by a Bf 109 G by means of a 30m-long rope, reaching 10,000m in 25 minutes. The launch took place 1,200m ahead of the 'bomber stream' and 500m over its flight level. With a dive angle of 20 degrees, the BV 40 reached an attack speed of 475km/h and the 'bomber stream' cruise speed was 360km/h. The armament initially proposed consisted of a MK 108/30 cannon installed under the port wing root and a towed explosive *paravane* bomb of 2kg called Gerät Schlinge mounted under the starboard wing.

At a distance of 400m from the target, the pilot made a first attack with the gun and then he used the momentum built during the dive to gain altitude for a second attack, with the Gerät Schlinge, on the 'boxes' located in the central section of the 'bomber stream'.

To that purpose, the *paravane* detached from its position under the wing, being linked to the plane by a 20m cable and kept in stable flight 7m under the fighter thanks to its special aerodynamic design. The pilot should just fly over the bomber 'boxes' until the Gerät Schlinge collided with one of the Viermots.

The system did not work properly during testing and the Technical Office of the Luftwaffe (Technicsches Amt) suggested doubling the firepower by installing a second MK 108, replacing the *paravane*.

The BV 40 prototype (PN + UA) was flight-tested on 27 July 1944, but the project was cancelled in October after the bombing of the B&V factory in Wenzendorf in which all prototypes and some pre-production aircraft that were in different stages of construction were destroyed.

The armoured Gleitjäger was very heavy and slow manoeuvring, diving at 900km/h it would have been impossible to use the ailerons owing to flutter.

The Flieger-Stabsingenieur Tilenius proposed using the BV 40 as air-to-air bomber equipped with four AB 250 sub-munition containers. But the idea was rejected in favour of the Me 262s of the Kommando Stamp that used SD 500 bombs and AB 500 containers with acoustic fuses for these attacks.

Blohm und Voss BV 40 (13 December 1943) technical data:
Wingspan 7.77m. Length: 5.70m. Height: 1.62m. Wing area: 8.90sq.m. Maximum Weight: 950kg. Maximum speed (towed): 553km/h. Maximum speed (diving): 900km/h.

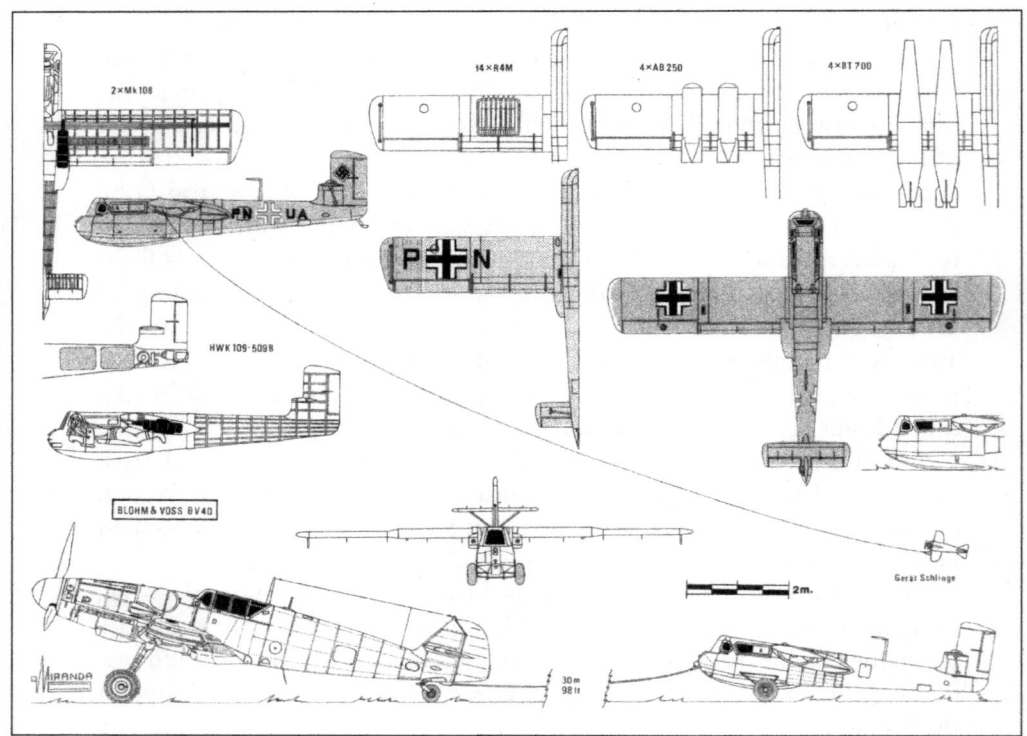

4

Verbrauchsflugzeug Competition

In the summer of 1944, Technisches Amt began evaluating designs of midget interceptors submitted by DFS, DVL and Zeppelin for the Verbrauchsflugzeug contest, which demanded an expendable fighter capable of making two attacks per mission powered by solid-propellant rockets.

DFS Eber Entwurf II

Because of the modification of the Rammschussjäger specification, the rammer Eber Entwurf I had to be equipped with an engine capable of catching up with the bombers. DFS then proposed a second version powered by two Rheinmetall-Borsig 109-505 solid-propellant rockets, with

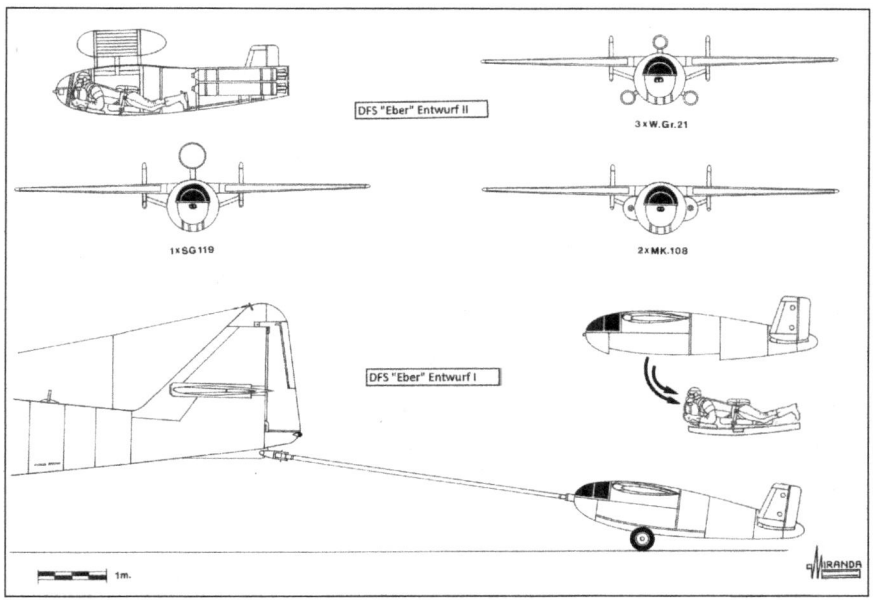

500kg peak-thrust each and 6 seconds of life. After detaching from the towing plane, the Eber used one of the rockets to make the first attack with air-to-air rockets, reserving the second 109-505 to climb between 700 and 1,000m of altitude over the 'box', gaining momentum for the second attack or for escaping the escort fighters, as were the circumstances of combat.

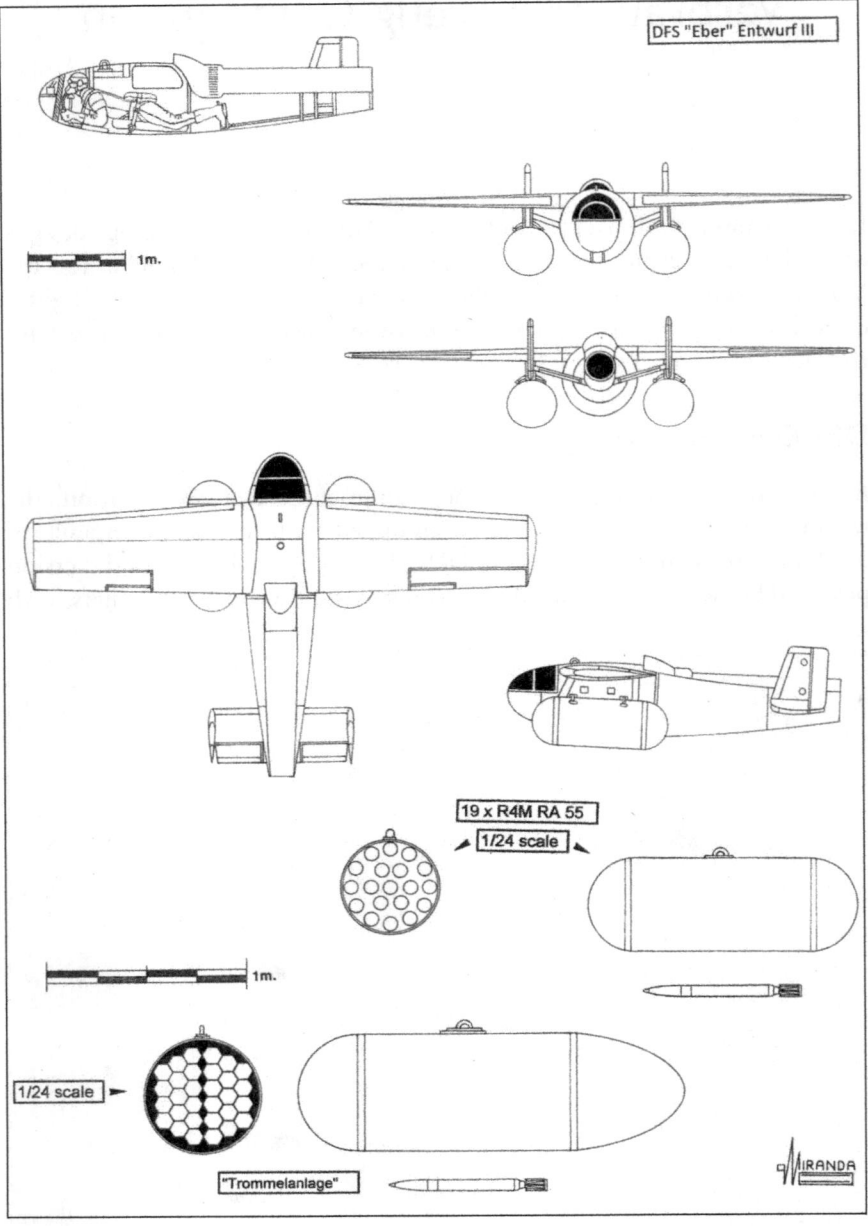

After consuming the rocket propellant, the Eber could fly at 360km/h only in gliding mode, being an easy prey for the Mustangs. Therefore, the DFS decided that the pilot should leave the plane instead of trying to land, without flaps, at too high a speed.

The armament of two MK 108/30 cannons was considered too valuable to lose with each expendable fighter. The installation of three tubes AG 40 Abschussgerät, to launch spin-stabilised W.Gr.21 rockets of 210mm, was also considered but it was a very imprecise weapon that only elite pilots could use to good effect.

Dipl-Ing. Schieferdecker, of the DFS Dept. A3, then proposed to use the Sondergerät SG119, an experimental multiple-shot battery composed of forty-nine barrels of MK 108 cannons, with a rate of fire of 9,900rpm that could dismantle a B-17 in 1/5 sec. The SG119, which was initially developed as the main armament of the Heinkel P.1077 Julia rocket-fighter, was installed on the back of the plane in an aerodynamic pod called Rohrbatterie.

DFS EBER ENTWURF II TECHNICAL DATA: Wingspan: 5.18m. Length: 3.36m. Height: 1.018m. Fuselage diameter: 0.87m. Wing area: 3.7m. Maximum speed: 650km/h.

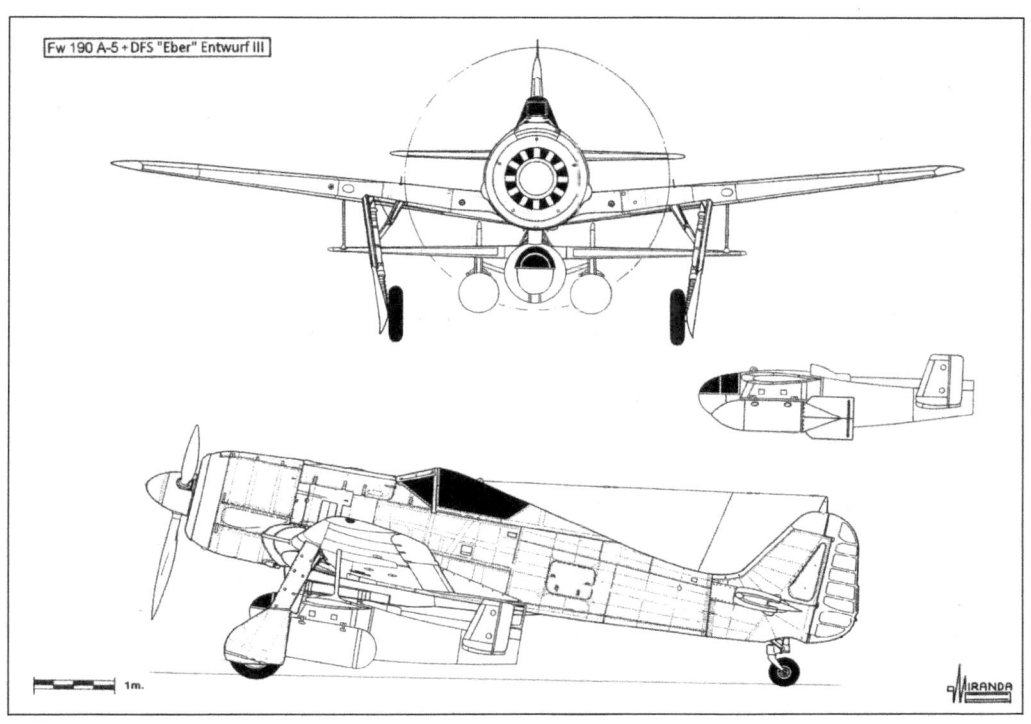

Fw 190 A-5 + DFS "Eber" Entwurf III

DVL Jagdsegler Entwurf II

In order to meet the Verbrauchsflugzeug requirements, the Jagdsegler Entwurf I was modified with the installation of one Reinmetall-Borsig 109-505 solid-fuel rocket engine rated at 500kg peak-thrust.

It was armed with six spin-stabilised RZ 65 rockets housed in two protuberances on either side of the fuselage.

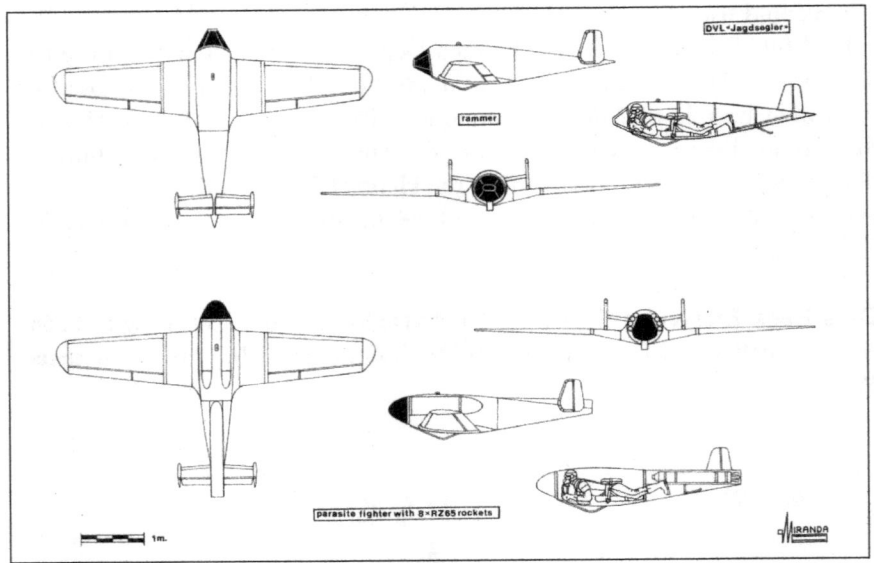

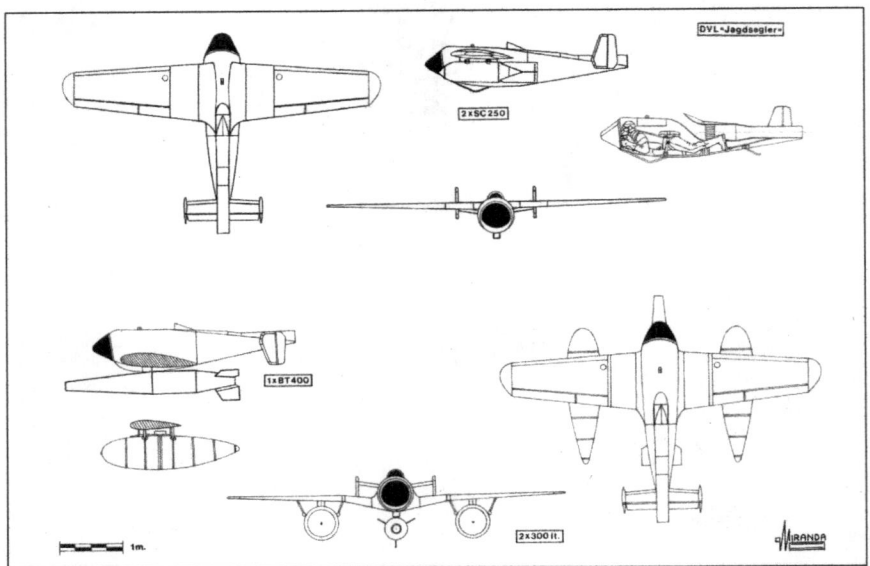

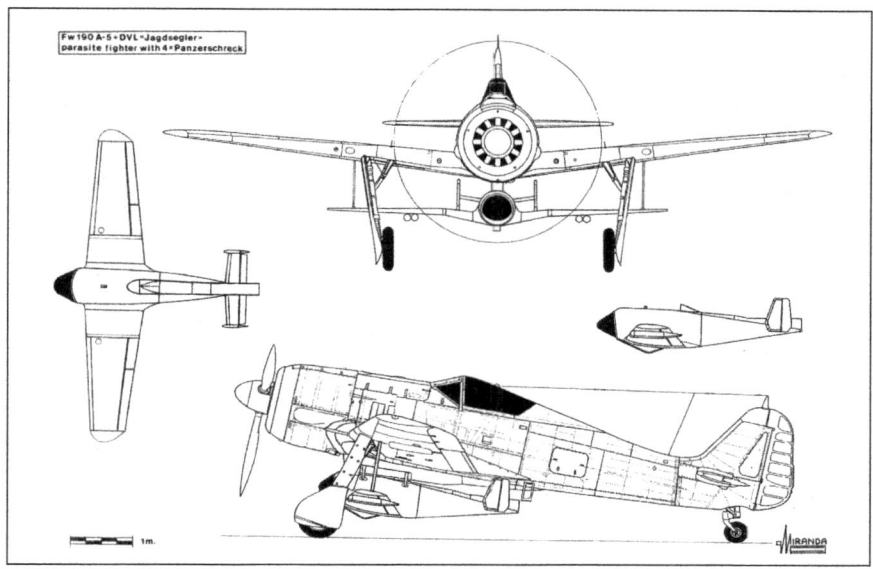

DVL Jagdsegler Entwurf II technical data: Wingspan: 5m. Length: 3.19m. Height: 0.96m. Fuselage diameter: 0.63m. Wing area: 3sq.m. Maximum speed: 650km/h. Armament: six spin-stabilised RZ 65 rockets of 73mm.

Zeppelin Fliegende Panzerfaust

The Starrschlepp system for towing gliders consisted of one rigid pole with articulated ends.

After the launch of the glider the piston fighter that carried it had to detach from the pole before entering combat, but sometimes the mechanism did not work properly and the plane was forced to land with the pole fixed to the tail, damaging the tail surfaces.

To solve the problem and avoid a waste of resources the design team of Flugzeugbau Zeppelin Company, led by Dipl.-Ing. Arthur Förster, proposed the construction of a miniature fighter with shoulder wing, butterfly tail and a nose-mounted towing pole that also served as support for a retractable skid. In the summer of 1944 the project was proposed to the OKL under the code name Fliegende Panzerfaust.

To adapt it to the technical specifications of the Verbrauchsflugzeug competition, the aircraft was designed to carry out two attacks and was completely expendable. But it was also equipped with flaps to land conventionally to suit the Bordjäger formula.

The fuselage was to be built of steel, wood, plastics and light alloys. The armoured cockpit housed the pilot lying in prone position with 120mm-thick windscreen.

The forward section of the fuselage contained the Starrschlepp pole and four launch tubes for 73mm RZ 65 rocket projectiles with a system for laterally discharging the gases produced during shooting, called Abgasleitung openings, located on either side of the cockpit.

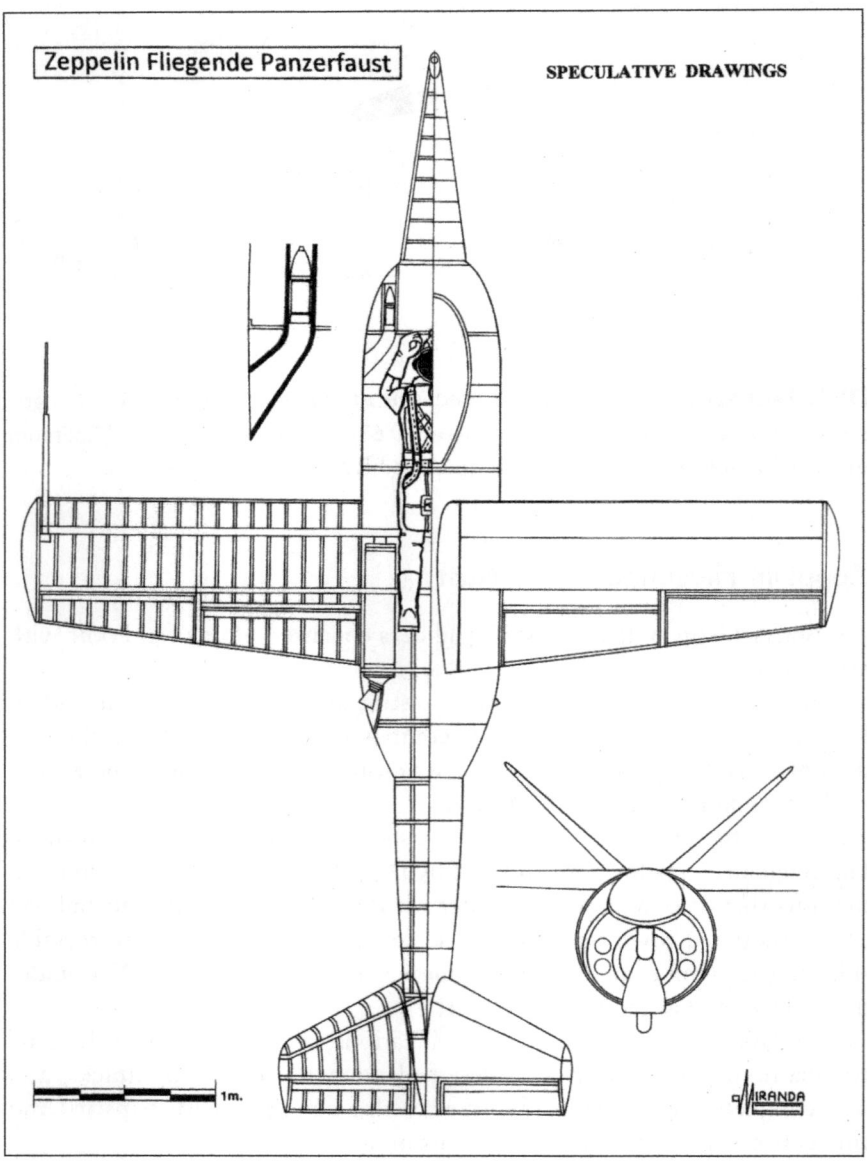

The centre section of the fuselage contained six Schmidding 109-563 rocket engines with 26-degree angled nozzles and a single central wheel that protruded from the belly.

The rear section of the fuselage, constructed of light alloy, served as support for the wooden butterfly tailplane.

The wood/plywood shoulder wing was only 120mm thick and contained the ailerons and flaps.

This midget fighter was to be towed into battle by one conventional interceptor Messerschmitt Bf 109 G.

The separation mechanism and the devices for deploying the skid and flaps were manually operated by the pilot.

After separating from the towing plane, the Fliegende Panzerfaust made a first attack on the 'bomber stream', firing two RZ 65 projectiles, then the pilot ignited two Schmiddings to regain altitude. The second attack had to follow the same scheme and the third pair of Schmiddings was reserved to flee from the allied escort fighters.

One mock-up was completed at Friedrichshafen in January 1945.

ZEPPELIN FLIEGENDE PANZERFAUST TECHNICAL DATA: Wingspan: 4.5m. Length: 6m. Height: 1.5m. Wing area: 3.75sq.m. Maximum weight: 1,200kg. Maximum speed: 850km/h. Armament: four 73mm RZ 65 spin-stabilised rocket projectiles. Power plant: six Schmidding 109-563 rocket engines with 500kg peak-thrust each.

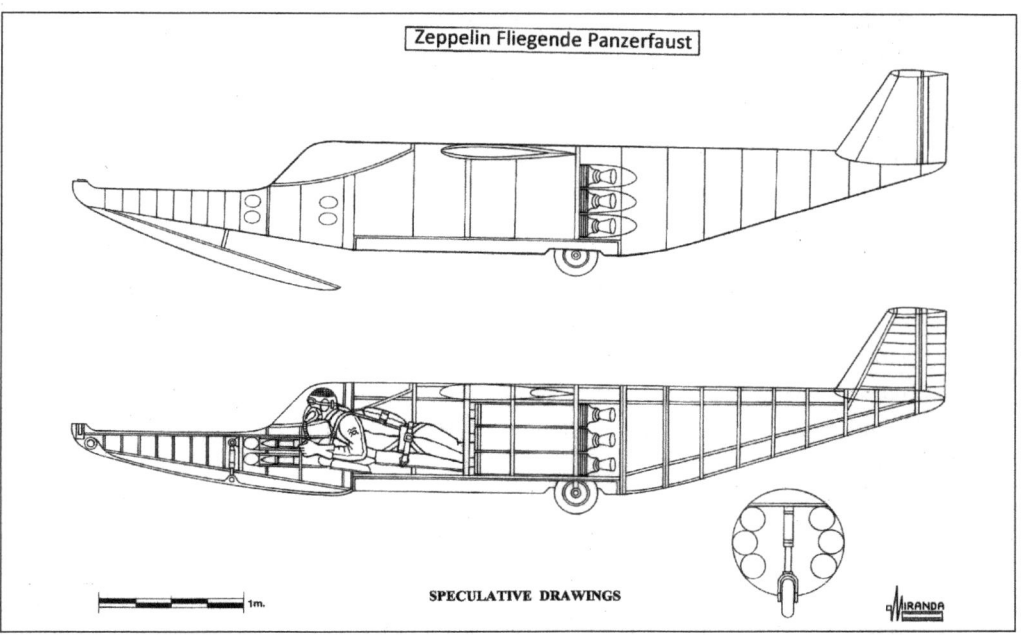

SPECULATIVE DRAWINGS

5
Solid-Propellant Rockets

All three German manufacturers of RATO rockets used the same solid propellant produced by Westfählische-Anhalt Spengstoff (WASAG): Diglycoldinitrat, formed by a mixture, by weight, of nitrocellulose (63%), diethylene glycol nitrate (35%), carbamite (0.5%), wax (0.2%) and graphite (1.2%).

Schmidding 109-513, 1,000kg peak-thrust, 2,220mm length and 350mm diameter, used in the Henschel Hs 293H and Hs 298 gliding bombs.

Schmidding 109-533, 1,000–1,200kg peak-thrust, 1,540mm length and 255mm diameter, used in the Bachem Natter, the Heinkel He 162 A-10/A-11, Heinkel P. 1077 Romeo I & II, Heinkel P.1077 Julia, Junkers EF 126 Elli, DFS Eber II and DVL Jagdsegler II rammers, in the Zeppelin Fliegende Panzerfaust and in the Zeppelin Rammer.

Schmidding 109-543, 150kg peak-thrust, 810mm length and 178mm diameter, used in the air-to-air missile Henschel Hs 298.

Schmidding 109-553, 1,750kg peak-thrust, 2,370mm length and 168mm diameter, used in the anti-aircraft missile Henschel Hs 117.

Schmidding 109-563, 500kg peak-thrust, 990mm length, 168mm diameter, used in the Messerschmitt P. 1103 rammer.

Schmidding 109-573, underwater launch tests.

Schmidding 109-593, 750kg peak-thrust, 990mm length, 168mm diameter, RATO.

Schmidding 109-603, 150kg peak-thrust, designed for the Ruhrstahl-Kramer X-4 air-to-air missile, project only.

Rheinmetall-Borsig 109-502, 600–900kg peak-thrust, 1,270mm length, 178mm diameter, RATO.

Rheinmetall-Borsig 109-505, 500kg peak-thrust, 1,270mm length, 178mm diameter, used in the anti-aircraft missile Rheinmetall-Borsig Feuerlilie 25.

Rheinmetall-Borsig 109-515, 4,000kg peak-thrust, 1,470mm length, 324mm diameter, used in the anti-aircraft missile Rheinmetall-Borsig Feuerlilie 55.

Rheinmetall-Borsig 109-525, 7,500kg peak-thrust, 1,300mm length, 510mm diameter, used in the anti-aircraft missile Rheinmetall-Borsig Rheintochter R1.

Rheinmetall-Borsig 109-535, 16,000kg peak-thrust, used in the anti-aircraft missile Rheinmetall-Borsig Rheintochter R1.

Rheinmetall-Borsig 109-545, 14,000kg peak-thrust, used in the anti-aircraft missile Rheinmetall-Borsig Rheintochter R3.

WASAG 109-506, 69kg peak-thrust, used in the Ruhrstahl-Kramer X-7 anti-tank missile.

WASAG 109-512, 1,200kg peak-thrust, used in the Hs 293 gliding bomb.

WASAG 109-522, RATO.

WASAG 109-532, 69kg peak-thrust, RATO used in the Messerschmitt P. 1104.

6

The Bordjäger Concept

Some Gleitjägern designs aspired to use the auxiliary combustion chamber of the HWK 109-509 B-1 (HWK 109-509 B). With only 300kg peak-thrust, this engine was not enough to perform a conventional take-off but could propel a small Bordjäger to more than 900km/h. By mid-1944, at least four Bordjägern projects were competing for the bi-fuel rocket engine: Arado E 581, Blohm und Voss BV 40 and Messerschmitt P.1103 (12 September 1944).

Arado E 381 Kleinstjäger

During flight tests in July 1944 with the Blohm und Voss BV 40 towed by a Bf 109 G, it was discovered that the parent aircraft took 25 minutes to reach the 10,000m of altitude needed to launch the parasitic fighter. The OKL objected that in a real combat situation the Bf 109 pilot had to use the MW 50 power boost to reach the flight level of the bomber stream in a reasonable time.

The extra weight also resulted in doubling the fuel consumption rate so the parent aircraft used one 300l droppable fuel tank.

In addition, both aircraft were very vulnerable to Allied escort fighters during the climb.

In order to improve the range and the chances of survival of the Gleitjägern, the Arado Flugzeugbau Company designed a series of midget rocket-fighters that could be transported to the combat zone suspended under the belly of an Ar 234 C-3 bomber.

The Kleinstjäger was fastened to the bomber by means of three suspension slips, the intercom connection and the heating circuit.

The Ar 234 C could climb 6,200m in 7.7 minutes and flew at 820km/h.

When the parent aircraft reached an altitude 1,000m higher than the upper 'boxes' of the bomber stream the fighter pilot had to activate the release mechanism and perform the attack propelled by the HWK 109-509 B rocket engine.

The small plane had a glide range of 100km after exhausting the propellants and could land on a retractable skid.

To simplify the construction of the wing, the designers eliminated the flaps by replacing them with a brake parachute 3m in diameter housed in the rear section of the fuselage.

The prone pilot was protected against the US 12.7mm shelling by a 15mm-thick armoured cockpit and by a 140mm armoured glass windshield.

This armour allowed the Kleinstjäger to attack the 'boxes' from behind, ignoring the defensive fire of the bombers.

The slow approach allowed the fighter to shoot more accurately for a longer time.

At the end of 1944, three configurations were proposed to the OKL, under the code name E 381.

The wings and tailplane were made of steel, using the technology developed for the V-1 missile, and the rear part of the fuselage was built in wood/plywood.

The E 381 project was rejected because the unavailability of parent aircraft and rocket engines.

ARADO E 381-01 (31 NOVEMBER 1944) TECHNICAL DATA: Wingspan: 5m. Length: 5.6m. Height: 1.6m. Wing Area: 5sq.m. Maximum weight: 1,200kg. Maximum speed: 885km/h. Service ceiling: 8,000m. Armament: six wing-mounted RZ 65 rocket projectiles and two fuselage-mounted 13mm MG 131 heavy machine guns. Power plant: one HWK 109-509 B rocket engine with 300kg peak-thrust. Propellant tanks: one with 111l of T-Stoff behind the cockpit (separated by a bulkhead) and two with 27l of C-Stoff, each inside the cockpit placed on both sides of the pilot.

ARADO E 381-02 (31 OCTOBER 1944) TECHNICAL DATA: Wingspan: 4.46m. Length: 4.72m. Height: 1.28m. Wing Area: 4.56sq.m. Fuselage diameter: 66cm. Maximum weight: 1,265kg. Maximum speed: 900km/h. Service ceiling: 8,000m. Armament: one wing-mounted MK 108/30 heavy cannon with 45 rounds carried on the port wing or one dorsal launch tube Werferrohr containing one 1,250mm W.Gr.21 spin-stabilised rocket. Power plant: one HWK 109-509 C rocket engine with 400kg peak-thrust. Propellant tanks: one with 150l of T-Stoff behind the cockpit (separated by a bulkhead) and two with 35l of C-Stoff each inside the cockpit placed on both sides of the pilot.

ARADO E 381-03 (1 DECEMBER 1944) TECHNICAL DATA: Wingspan: 4.9m. Length: 4.95m. Height: 1.24m. Wing Area: 4sq.m. Fuselage diameter: 72cm. Maximum weight: 1,500kg. Maximum speed: 895km/h. Service ceiling: 8,000m. Armament: one wing-mounted MK 108/30 heavy cannon with 60 rounds carried on the port wing. Power plant: one HWK 109-509 C rocket engine

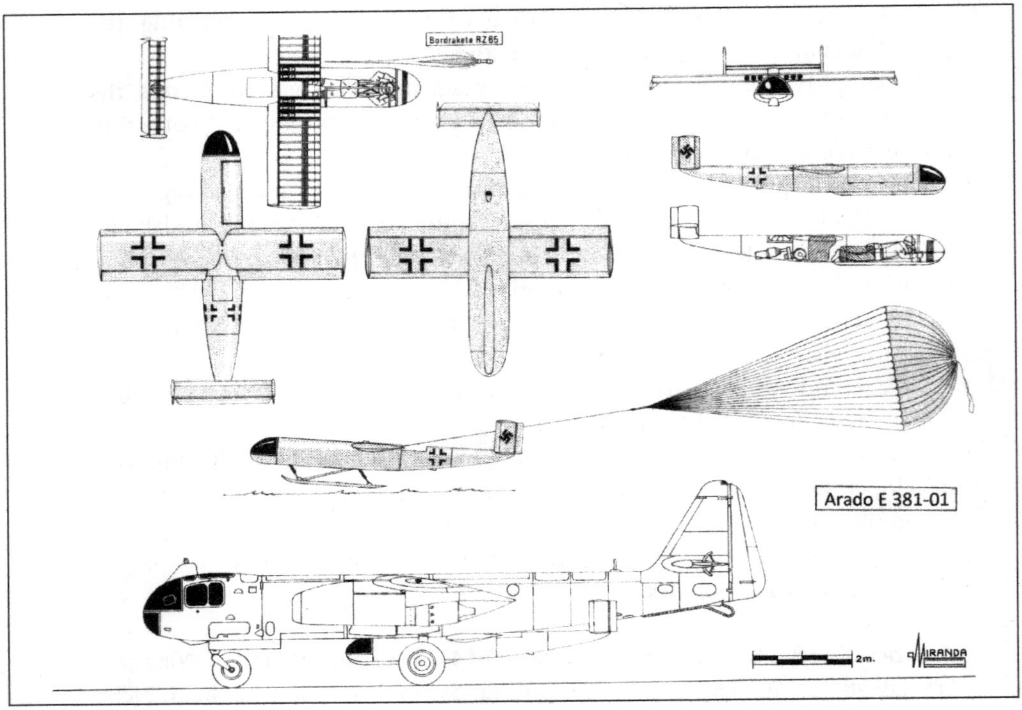
Bordrakete RZ 65
Arado E 381-01
2m.
MIRANDA

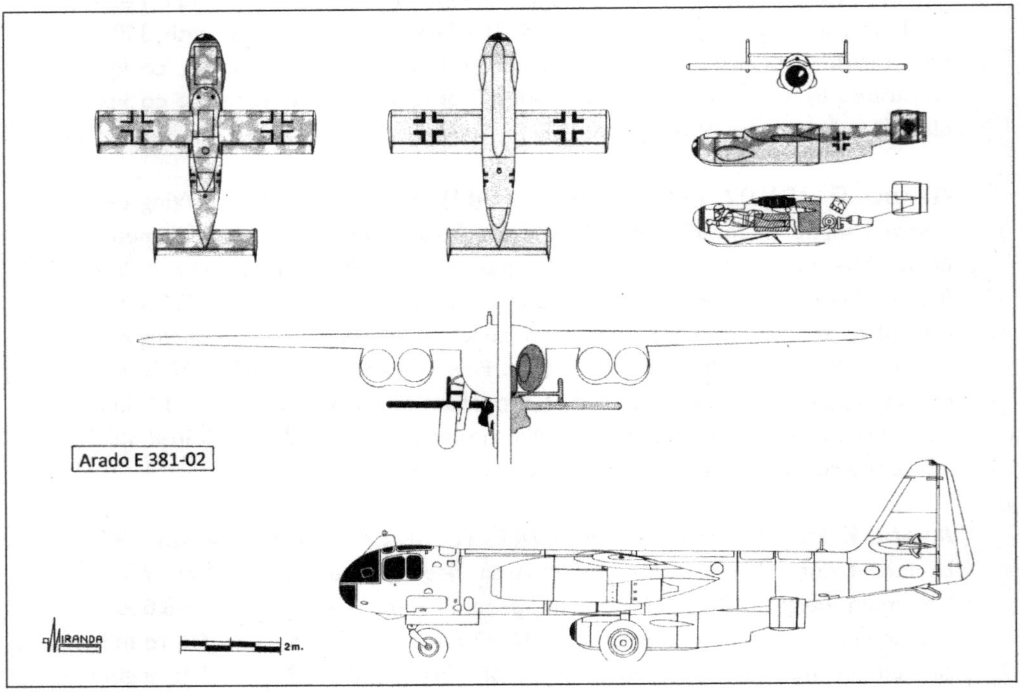
Arado E 381-02
MIRANDA
2m.

Arado E 381-03
2m.
MIRANDA

MK 108 - Kleinstjäger
unter Ar 234C
SKE - 381 - 071

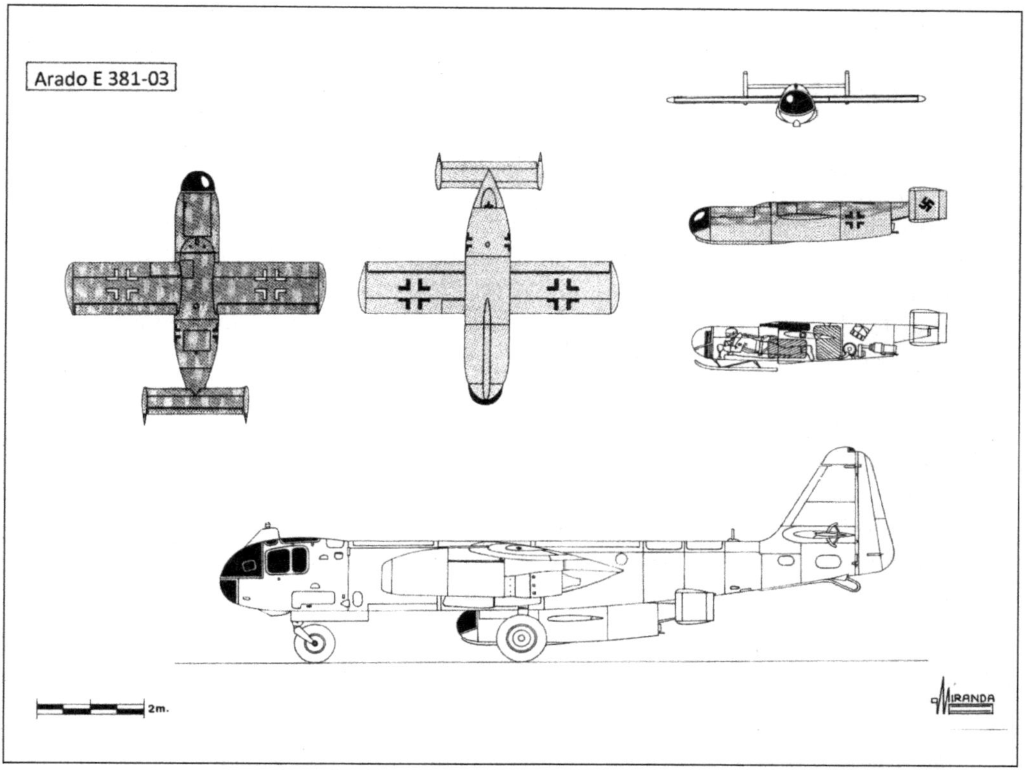

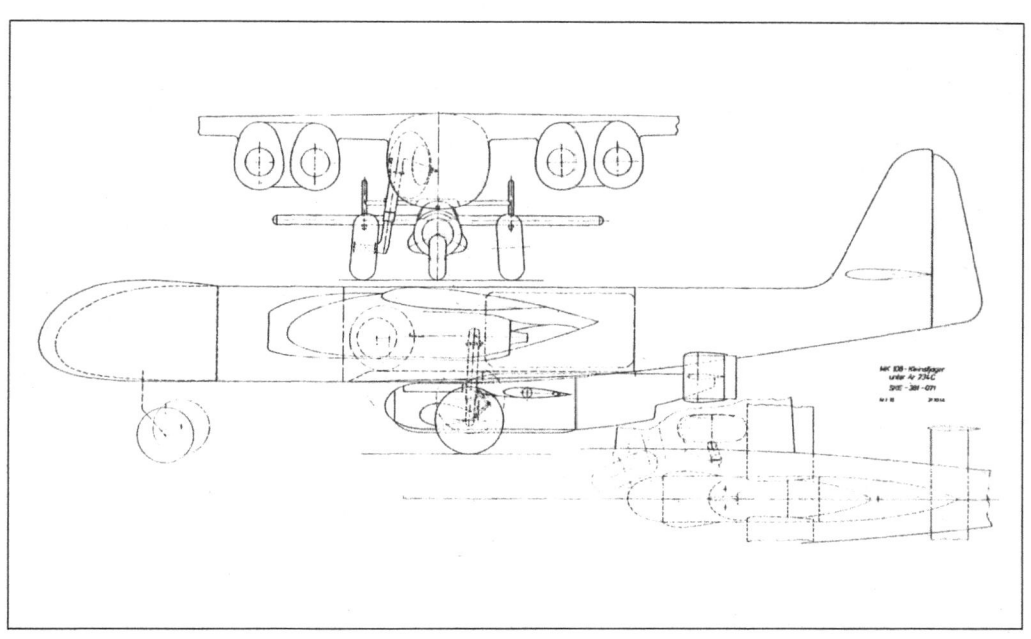

with 400kg peak-thrust. Propellant tanks: one with 150l of T-Stoff behind the cockpit (separated by a bulkhead) and two with 35l of C-Stoff each inside the cockpit placed on both sides of the pilot.

Blohm und Voss BV 40 (with HWK 109-507)

To save the project, in September 1944, Dr Vogt proposed the conversion of the BV 40 into a rocket-fighter by installing a HWK 109-507 bi-fuel rocket engine with 400–600kg thrust (in production for the Henschel Hs 293 missile) that would provide enough speed to make attacks from behind the bombers. Its armament could later be replaced by air-to-air rockets of the R4M type.

After the attack, the plane should land on a ventral folding skid, reducing its speed to 118km/h using flaps.

An anti-ship version was also planned, armed with four BT 700 torpedo-bombs that would be towed by a Heinkel He 177 bomber to the proximity of an Allied fleet. The prone position allowed the pilot to withstand up to 14G, when recovering its flight level after a dive attack, to throw the bombs as close as possible to the warship.

It was decided that the BV 40 could use a little DFS pulsejet for the return flight.

BLOHM UND VOSS BV 40 (SEPTEMBER 1944) TECHNICAL DATA: Wingspan 7.77m. Length: 5.70m. Height: 1.62m. Wing area: 8.90sq.m. Maximum Weight 3,750kg. Maximum speed: 900km/h.

Messerschmitt P.1103 (12 September 1944)

Bordjäger designed by the Oberbayerische Forschungsanstalt Institut to compete for the HWK 109-509 B-1 engine. It was a small rocket-fighter with 10mm-thick armoured cockpit and the pilot seated. The wings and tail planes were built from those of a Fieseler Reichenberg manned missile. It would make the take-off on a detachable twin wheel dolly, towed by a Me 262 jet-fighter in Deichselslepp configuration, and landing with the help of flaps, a retractable skid and a tailwheel.

After separating from the mother-plane, it made a first attack, in shallow dive, against the 'bomber stream', with its ventral gun MK 108/30.

ME P.1103 (12 SEPTEMBER 1944) TECHNICAL DATA: Wingspan: 5.3m. Length: 5m. Height: 1.58m. Wing Area: 5.8sq.m. Fuselage diameter: 80cm. Maximum weight: 1,100kg. Maximum speed: 930km/h. Power plant: one Walter HWK 109-509 B-1 rocket engine with 300kg peak-thrust. Propellant tanks: one

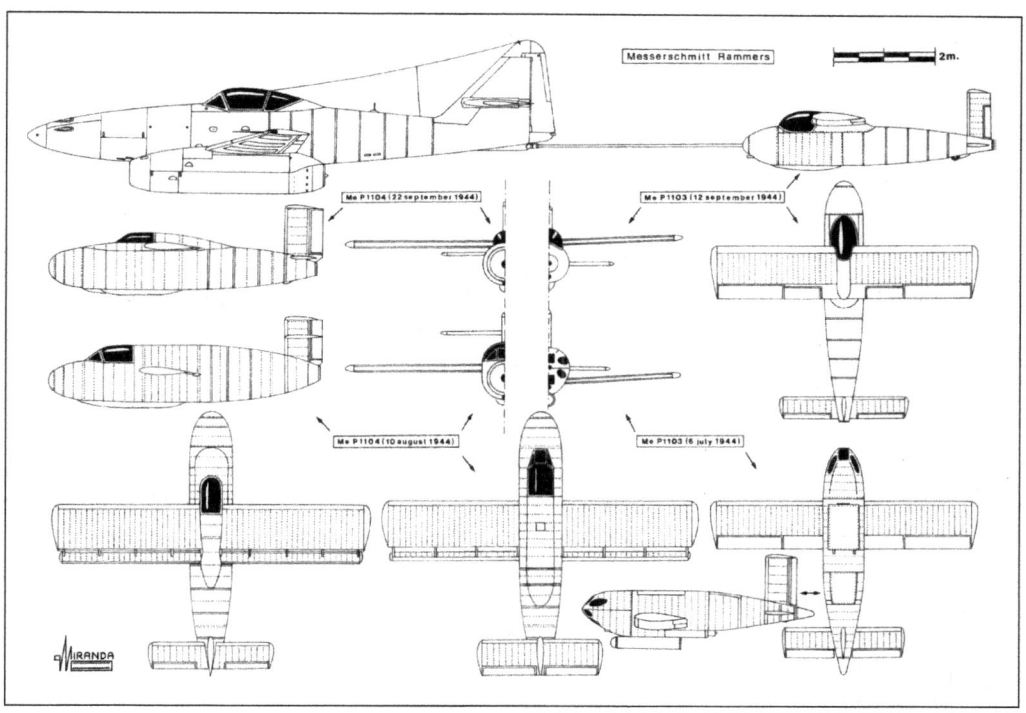

with 167l of C-Stoff mounted behind the cockpit and one with 40l of T-Stoff in the central section of the fuselage. Armament: one nose-mounted MK 108/30 heavy cannon with 100 rounds.

7
Rammschussjäger Specification

Between 17 April 1943 and 20 April 1945, twenty-six cases of ramming were registered, performed by German fighters of Messerschmitt Bf 109 type, nine by Focke-Wulf Fw 190, four by Messerschmitt Me 262s one by Messerschmitt Bf 110 and another by Messerschmitt Me 410.

The ramming sometimes happened accidentally, due to the miscalculation of distances by the pilot of the attacking aircraft, or because the pilot had been injured or killed by the defensive fire of the attacked aircraft. At other times it was a desperate measure due to the malfunction of arms in a conventional attack made from behind. The impact used to occur at low speed because both aircraft were flying in the same direction, with the propeller of the attacking plane acting as a circular saw on the tail surfaces of the attacked plane. The rammer usually suffered damages in the propeller, engine bearings and engine cowling and the survival rate of the pilot used to exceed 50 per cent with a good chance of making a glide landing.

The four-engine American bombers were particularly resistant and some managed to survive a ram attack. Even smaller aircrafts like the DH Mosquito and the Grumman Bearcat managed to return to their bases after a mid-air collision following the loss of part of a wing.

When ramming large aircraft, it was more effective to target the fuselage section between wing and tail plane to sever control cables, but the side-attack manoeuvre required a very precise calculation of relative speeds that only very expert pilots could perform. The impact, between 300 and 450km/h, used to boot a wing of the attacking aircraft that fell into an uncontrollable flat spin; the pilot was thrown violently in the opposite direction to the damaged wing, being wounded or shocked, and with survival possibilities below 25 per cent because the fuselage airframe tended to deform, rendering the opening of the cockpit very difficult.

In early 1944, the technological superiority achieved by the Allies already allowed them to interfere with German radio control systems. This particularly affected the development programs of anti-aircraft

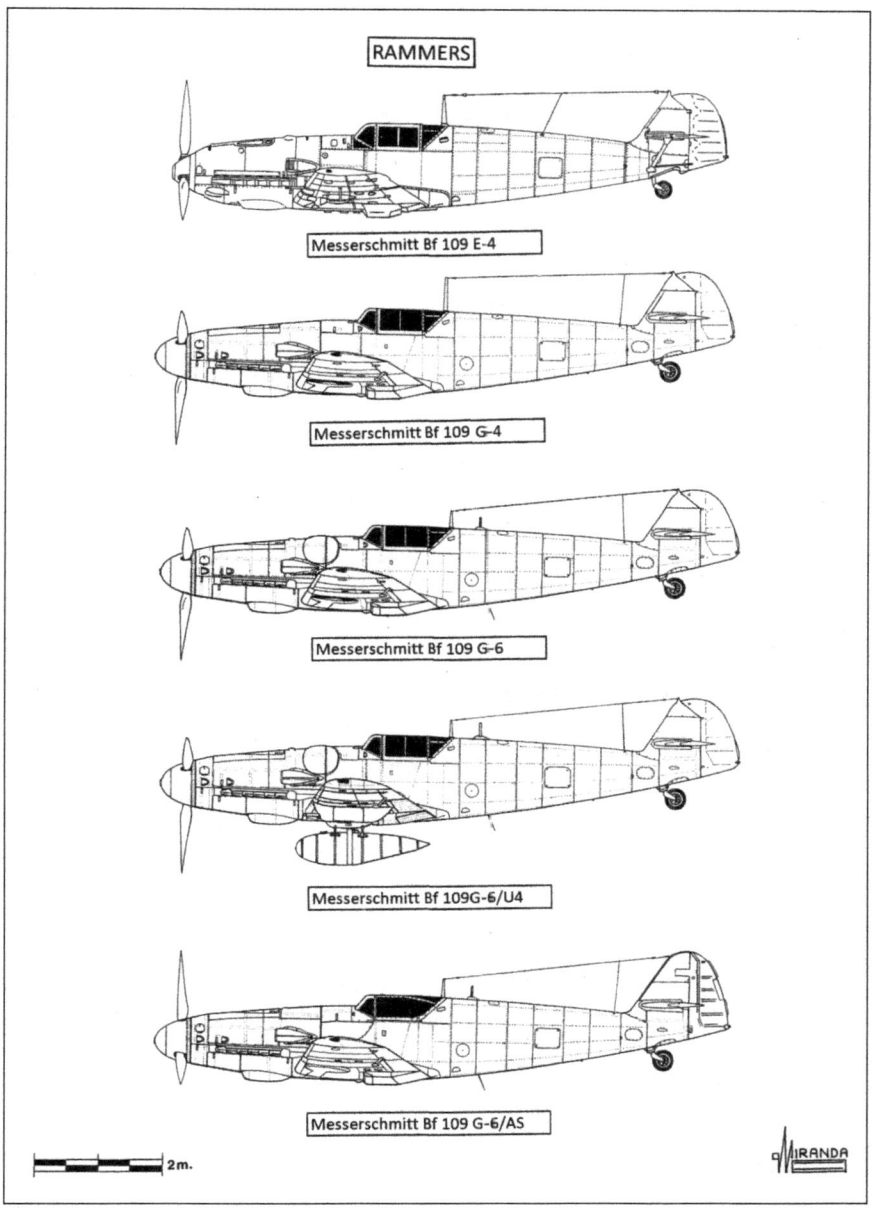

missiles Enzian, Schmetterling, Feuerlilie and Rheintochter in a stage of the war when German fighters were unable to contain the offensive bombardment that increased in intensity day after day. The Me 262 proved to be a poor dogfighter against the Allied Tempests and Mustangs, the Komet killed more German pilots than the enemy and the RLM began to receive proposals for the manufacture of *rammjägers* and piloted missiles.

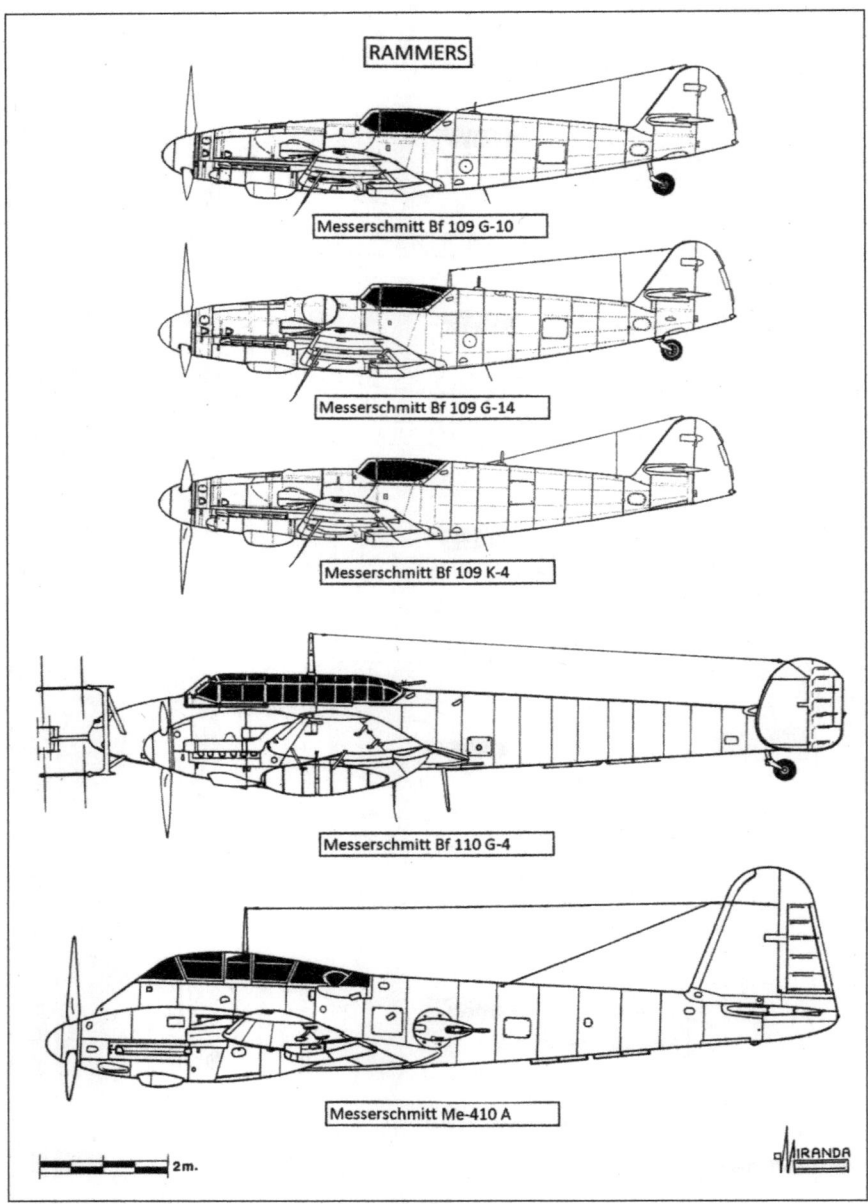

Rammjägers were designed as planes specialised in collision tactics, attacking from behind the bombers and ramming their tail surfaces. To reach the proper impact velocity, they used one or two solid-propellant rockets Schmidding 533/553 or Rheinmetall 515.

The Rammschussjäger RLM specification was published by the end of January 1944.

In February 1945, the Führer had decided to authorise the creation of some units specialised in aerial ramming tactics. He argued that the Luftwaffe was already losing 200 fighters a month in combat, against large formations of enemy bombers that were escorted by numerous Mustang and Thunderbolt fighters, without achieving significant results. According to the theories of Wing Commander Hans-Joachim Hermann, these 200 obsolete aircraft could be used as rammers in one massive attack that, according to the principle of concentration of forces, would cause such damage to the enemy that would generate important political consequences.

The Eighth Air Force was able to afford the loss of 200 heavy bombers by ramming in every mission, bombers that American industry could replace within a week. But neither General Spaatz nor public opinion could ignore the loss of 1,600 crew members in 7 minutes of combat, especially as the war in Europe drew to a close. Perhaps this would be the weakness of democracies; maybe a series of well coordinated *rammstoss* attacks succeeded in altering the relentless bombing offensive on the Reich, offering Göring the opportunity to attempt a First World War style negotiated peace.

On 8 March 1945, all of the Luftwaffe wing commanders were ordered to recruit SO pilots (an acronym for Selbstopfermanner, 'self-sacrifice men'), for a new fighter unit specialised in ramming that was called Sonderkommando Elbe.

Despite the rejection expressed by most senior officers of the Luftwaffe, some volunteer pilots began to concentrate at the Stendhal airfield, to follow a training program of two weeks that began on 24 March.

Bachem Rammers

These expendable rocket-fighters were designed to be built entirely with non-strategic materials and launched vertically from any location using minimum ground equipment. The first sketches, dated 16 June 1944, represent a very simple plane partially built in concrete, a technology that the firm Blohm und Voss had been developing to build the wings of the anti-ship missile BV 246 Hagelkorn.

Nose and cockpit were made of one piece of concrete designed for ramming. To make it lighter, the cockpit height was reduced by placing the pilot in a semi-prone position. Forward viewing was provided by a channel in the nose, and an armoured windshield was fitted into the rear end of that channel. The wings, rear fuselage and tail surfaces were made of steel. The engine would be a solid-fuel rocket of unspecified type and the armament one air-to-air 158mm rocket RZ 15/8.

The initial project evolved into the BP-20 Berak-I (*bemannte rakete projekt*) from 9 August 1944, powered by a ring of eight solid-fuel rockets of the Schmidding 109-563 or 109-553 types, installed around a central

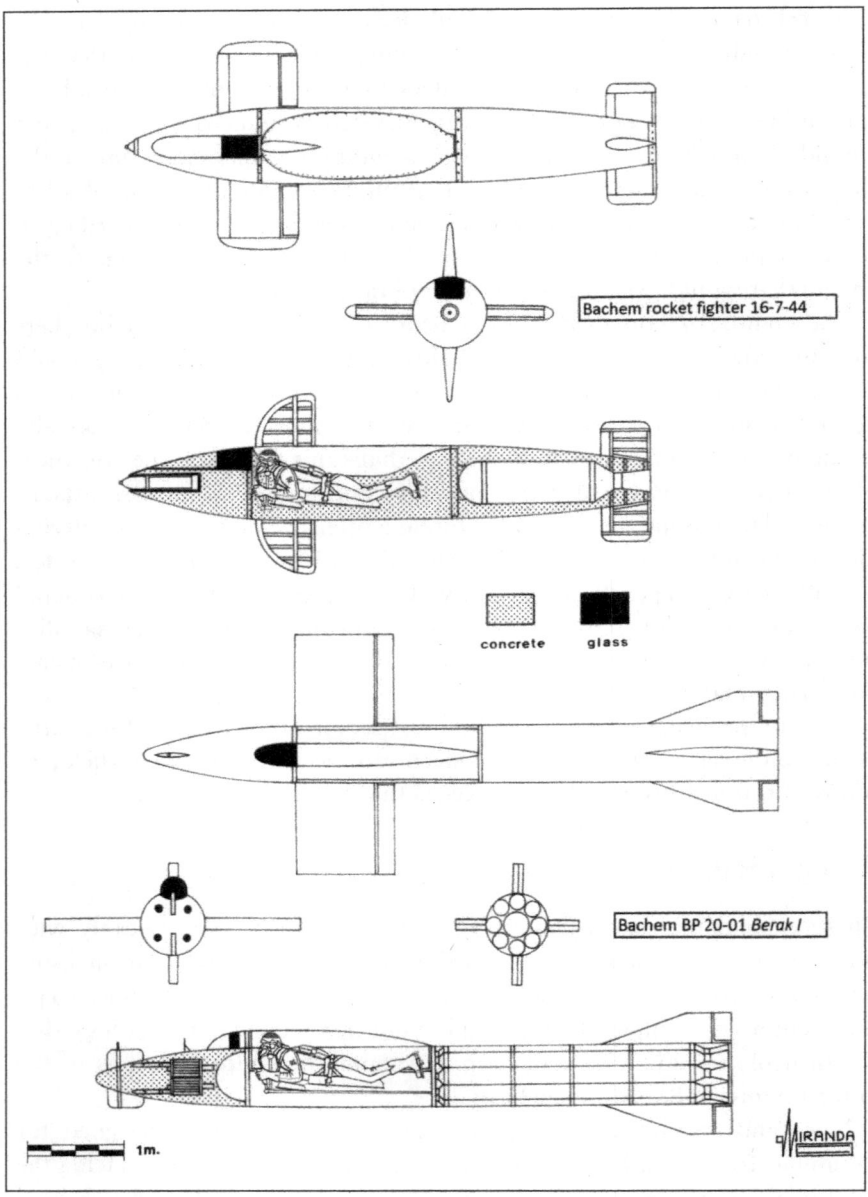

rocket of the Schmidding 109-533 type. The concrete nose cone contained four automatic rocket launchers Trommelgerät of 73mm with capacity for up to thirty-two air-to-air spin-stabilised RZ 65 rockets.

The fighter would take off vertically, firing a devastating salvo against the belly of the enemy bombers. Afterwards, it would continue its ascent until exhausting the power of its thrusters at an altitude of 12,000m. During the fall, it could reach a maximum speed of 800km/h and ram another bomber. Before the impact, the pilot could leave the plane through a hatchback. Berak-I would have a wingspan of 2.6m, a length of 6.5m and a fuselage diameter of 0.6m and weighed 1,230kg at take-off.

BACHEM ROCKET-FIGHTER (16.7.44) TECHNICAL DATA: Prone pilot. Wingspan: 3.24m. Length: 8.1m. Height: 2.8m. Power plant: one solid-propellant rocket-motor. Armament: one spin-stabilised 158mm rocket RZ 15/8. Airframe: steel and concrete.

BACHEM BP-20 BERAK I TECHNICAL DATA: Prone pilot. Wingspan: 3.8m. Length: 9.7m. Height: 1.8m. Power plant: nine solid-propellant rocket-motors. Armament: four Trommelgerät automatic rocket launchers with 32 spin-stabilised 73mm rockets RZ 65. Airframe: wood/plywood and concrete.

DFS Eber Entwurf I

In August 1944 the DFS Institut-A proposed to the OKL the building of an expendable rammer Verbrauchsflugzeug called Eber. This type of small size aircraft had the advantage of using non-strategic materials like steel, wood and plastics. Nor was it necessary to train their pilots in landing manoeuvres, thus saving time and fuel.

Eber was a minimal aircraft, with a length of 3.36m and 640kg of weight only, most of which was armour. It took-off from a detachable twin-wheel dolly towed aloft behind a Messerschmitt Me 262 by a Starrschlepp pole-tow system. After reaching the combat area, the Eber was released from an altitude of 300m above an enemy bomber formation to make a frontal attack. Eber had a front area of only 0.63sq.m. (compared with 1.53sq.m. of a Focke-Wulf Fw 190) with the pilot in prone position, well protected against the defensive fire of the bombers by an armoured windshield and steel plates.

The front ramming was questioned by medical researchers of the Luftfahrt Forschungsanstalt München (LFM), who established that the human body cannot withstand impacts over 16G, while the OKL estimated that in a frontal collision against a heavy bomber the rammer would be submitted to about 100G. The DFS technicians then suggested the possibility that the pilot could be extracted from the rammer before impact by a small braking-parachute.

The original ejection system was designed to loosen the ventral section of the fuselage, dropping the pilot, still attached to the couchette that also contained the oxygen equipment. When the braking-parachute slowed to between 40 and 25 m/sec, the pilot detached the couchette and completed the descent using his own parachute. The RLM rejected the idea because it did not 100 per cent ensure either the impact nor the survival of the pilot, and recommended the construction of rammers specialised in destroying only the tail surfaces of bombers, attacking them from behind at low speed.

DFS EBER ENTWURF I TECHNICAL DATA: Wingspan: 5.18m. Length: 3.36m. Fuselage diameter: 0.87m. Wing area: 3.7sq.m. Maximum gliding speed: 360km/h. Maximum weight: 640kg.

DVL Jagdsegler Entwurf I

On 30 June 1944, Dipl. Ing. U. Kaiser, of the DVL Institut für Flugmechanik, designed a parasite fighter called Jagdsegler that was very similar in size and configuration to the DFS Eber.

Originally conceived as rammer, with the pilot in prone position, Jagdsegler had to be transported to the combat zone suspended under a Focke-Wulf Fw 190 A-5 using an ETC 502 bomb rack. The launch would occur at an altitude of 750m over the bomber stream and 5km ahead of the first bombers (thanks to its glide ratio of 11:1) to make a frontal attack with a speed of 300km/h. Striking a bomber that flew in the opposite direction at 480km/h ensured its destruction.

Following the publication of the results of the studies conducted by doctors Ruden and Schapitz, on impact protection devices at a high number of G-forces, the original purpose of Jagdsegler had to be abandoned because its small size did not allow the installation of shock absorbers and ejection devices. The project was modified with the installation of a Rheinmetall-Borsig 109-505 solid-propellant rocket engine and was proposed to the RLM in four versions by the end of 1944: two parasite fighters and two parasite bombers.

DVL JAGDSEGLER ENTWURF I TECHNICAL DATA: Wingspan: 5m. Length: 3.2m. Height: 0.96m. Fuselage diameter: 0.63m. Wing area: 3sq.m. Maximum speed: 300km/h.

Focke-Wulf Rammjäger

The mass production of Fi 103 (V-1) flying bombs that had been entrusted to the Fieseler and Volkswagen firms, was expected to reach 2,000 units in December 1943, 6,000 in May and 9,000 in September 1944.

However, it was soon made evident that even with the highest political priority, the manufacturing capacity of both firms in their factories at

Fallersleben, Montagewerk Meissen, Montagewerk Cham, Kassel, Kassel-Rothwesten, Wolfsburg and Mittelwerke-Dora would not be enough to achieve the forecasted manufactured units. This circumstance was not ignored by the rest of the aeronautical firms of the Reich that rushed to present their own projects based on the V-1.

The Arado firm presented the *deichselschlepp*, *startwagen* and *huckepack* systems for the transport and launch of the V-1 from the Ar 234 C bombers. The DFS Institut used a V-1 airframe to build the SG 5041 fuel tank that could be towed by the Ar 234.

Heinkel modified some He 111 H-16/H-22 to transport and launch both the V-1 and the manned missiles of the Reichenberg series. Blohm und Voss proposed a transport and launch system, to be used from the U-boats Type XXI, able to reach New York. Gotha worked in a *gleitboot* anti-ship version with float. Porsche designed the Typ 300 detachable turbojet with a superior performance than the Argus 1c9-014.

Messerschmitt designed a *startwagen* device that allowed the transport and launch of the V-1 by the Bf 109 G-6. Its team also designed the P.1103 and P.1104 rocket interceptors using some parts of the V-1. The Zeppelin firm designed a rammer using the wings and tail surfaces of the V-1. Henschel was specialised in the construction of Reichenberg prototypes.

But nothing was known about the projects proposed by the Focke-Wulf company until the French historian Paul Malmassari published his article *Découverte de quelques projets autour du V-1* in *Le Fana de l'Aviation* in September 2000. He describes the Brummer project developed by DFS so that an Fw 190 could transport one V-1 missile in *startwagen* configuration. He also refers to a rammer design proposed by Professor Conradis of the Bad Eilsen Institute in September 1944. The concept behind this design was to install an armoured nose instead of the warhead of a V-1 and a pilot cockpit with armoured windshield and ejector seat in the space usually occupied by the compressed air bottles.

One unspecified bi-fuel rocket replaced the Argus pulsejet, which was not right for high-altitude flight, and the rammer would be launched from a Heinkel He 111 bomber, to save rocket fuel.

There are no drawings of this project, the author has therefore taken licence to reconstruct this design based on Malmassari description, with the warning that any error should be credited to the author, and not to Malmassari. It also seems reasonable that Focke-Wulf would have used the armoured windshield and clear canopy of the Fw 190 A-8/R2 Sturmbock and the wings and control surfaces of the Fieseler Reichenberg manned missile. The engine should have been one solid-fuel Schmidding 563 RATO rocket or one HWK 109-509 B bi-propellant rocket with 300kg peak-thrust, already used by the firm in the designs of the Fw Projekt V and Projekt VI. It could be installed behind the cockpit in a light downwards angle without

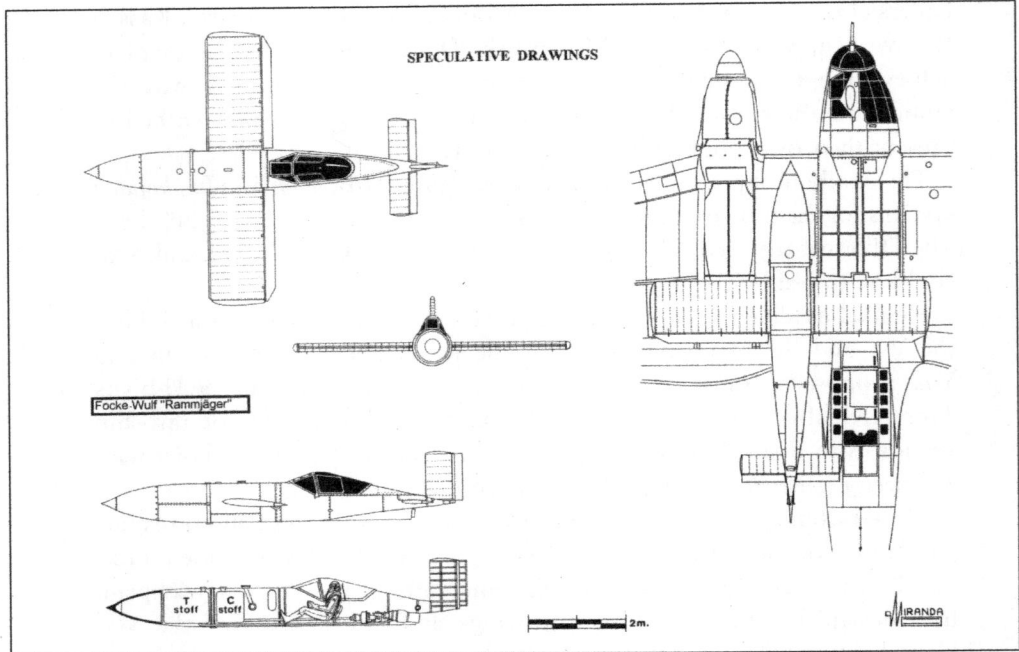

interfering with the control cables of the tail surfaces. The propellant tanks of T-Stoff and C-Stoff could be installed behind the armoured nose.

Some V-1 missiles carried Kuto-Nase (cable-cutter) devices in the wing leading edges, possibly also a useful device in the rammer. We do not know about the type of seat used, except that the Focke-Wulf firm had carried over some experiments with an ejector seat installed in an Fw 190 and with a special type of explosives.

Per Malmassari's story, the ejection happened after the impact. This suggests an anti-shock device installed in the seat like the one in the Gotha P.54.

FOCKE-WULF RAMMJÄGER SPECULATIVE TECHNICAL DATA: Wingspan: 5.8m. Length: 7.5m. Height: 1.5m. Wing area: 6.8sq.m. Estimated maximum speed: 800km/h.

Gotha P.54/I and P.54/II

On 10 October 1944, Gothaer Waggonfabrik AG proposed to the RLM a sophisticated rocket rammer designed by Dipl. Ing. Walter Wundes. Unlike other projects of ramming aircraft already rejected by the Technisches Amt, the new rammer was endowed with several anti-shock devices to improve the chances of survival of the pilot after the impact.

Two versions are known:

The Gotha P.54 Entwurf I was designed to destroy the tail surfaces of a bomber, attacking from behind to minimise the impact speed. It was towed to the combat zone by a Focke-Wulf Fw 190; the mother plane located after the formation of bombers to carry out the launch and the rammer used a Schmidding 109-553 rocket engine to reach the last aircraft of the most delayed 'box' hitting the tail surfaces of one of them at an estimated speed between 160 to 200km/h.

The Luftwaffe Aviation Medicine Branch had established that a pilot could endure up to 20G for 0.1 second, but only when using a vertical launched ejector seat. It was estimated that the impact of Entwurf I against the bomber would last 0.04 second and Gotha designers devised a seat that rotated 90 degrees backward at the time of impact, aligning the spine of the pilot with the fuselage axis. Additionally, the seat base was equipped with a powerful sprung shock-absorbing device.

The entire system was mechanically activated by a trigger located to the extreme nose of the rammer. The pilot stayed in an armoured artillery shell-shaped capsule, attached to the main wing spar by another shock-absorbing device. After impact, the armoured cockpit was detached from the airframe by the action of various explosive bolts and freely fell to 3,000m. The pilot then left its protection, completing the descent by means of his own parachute.

The variant Entwurf II was designed to impact laterally against the fuselage of a bomber in the area between the bomb bay and the tailplane, in an angle close to 90 degrees, in order to cut the control wires. This type of ramming attack was considered difficult due to the relative speeds of both aircraft and possible evading manoeuvres of the bomber. The special configuration of Entwurf II allowed two types of attack: if the impact was produced against the fuselage of circular section of a B-17 bomber, the lower section of the rammer crushed against the bomber, while the pilot capsule was released and *jumped* over the B-17 fuselage to freely fall while the bomber exploded.

If the target was a B-24 bomber, the fuselage of which was deeper and with flat sides, it was planned that the armoured capsule could get through it almost without any resistance. A small explosive charge with impact fuse was installed in the extreme nose for that purpose. It fractured the light alloy structure of the bomber, thus allowing the penetration by the capsule that had already detached from the rest of the airframe with the impact. It was estimated that thanks to the gained momentum before impact, the capsule would completely go through the B-24 with a minimal loss of speed, while the rest of the rammer completed the destruction.

The 'blunt nosed' configuration of the lower element seems to suggest that contained a warhead. According to this hypothesis, Entwurf II would have a dual use as Rammer and as Pulkzerstörer (formation destroyer). If the attacked B-24 was in the centre of the 'box', triggering the explosion of their bombs could achieve a Herausschuss effect, breaking the cohesion of the box, damaging other bombers and exposing them to the action of the conventional German fighters during the return flight to their bases.

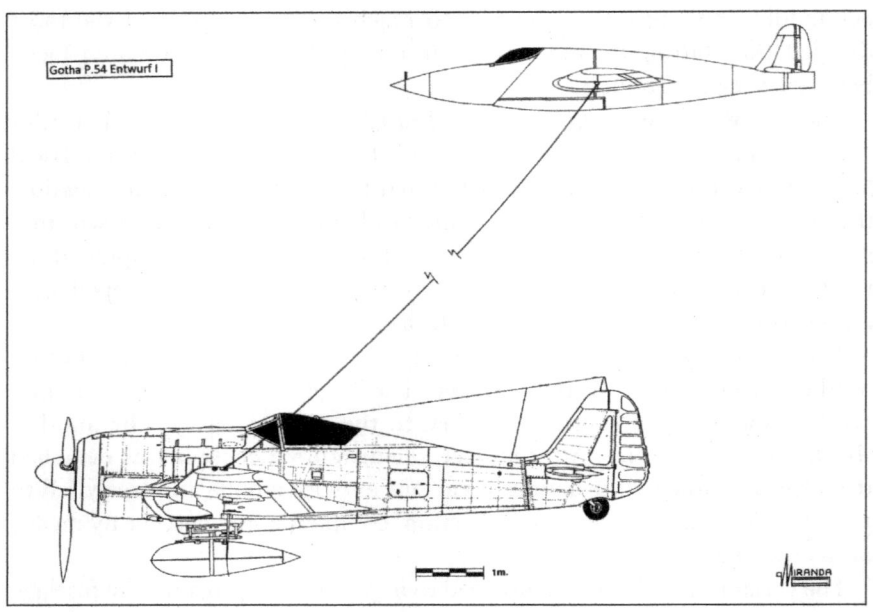

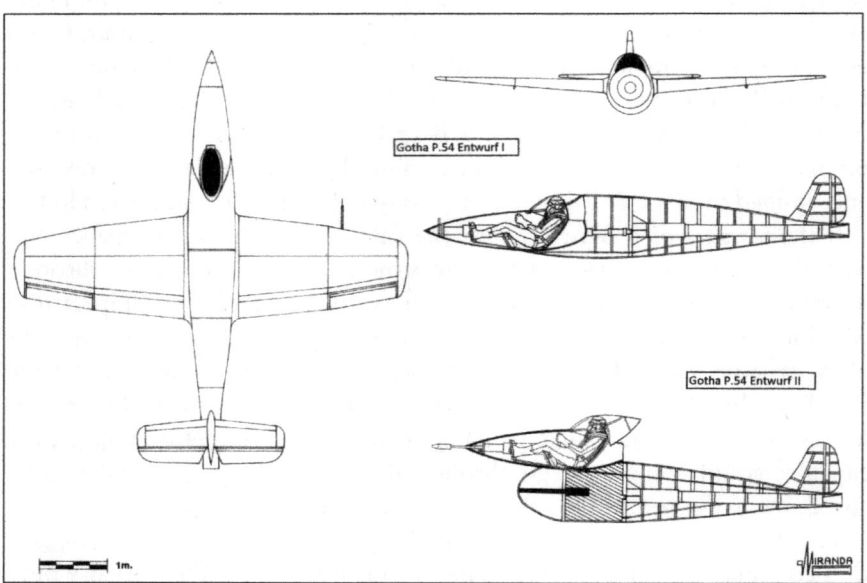

During the Second World War, the DFS Institut performed numerous aerodynamic experiments looking for the most effective method for towing aircraft.

The system usually used for sailplanes was a long wire known as Langseilschlepp, that proved inadequate for the flight at high speed. Great fuel consumption of jet engines was tried to solve by a winged fuel tank towed by a Me 262 by a rigid pole of articulated ends, called Starrschlepp.

The DFS devised a system called Tragschlepp for the Junkers Ju 87 that having been originally designed as short range dive bomber, could perform long flights over the sea.

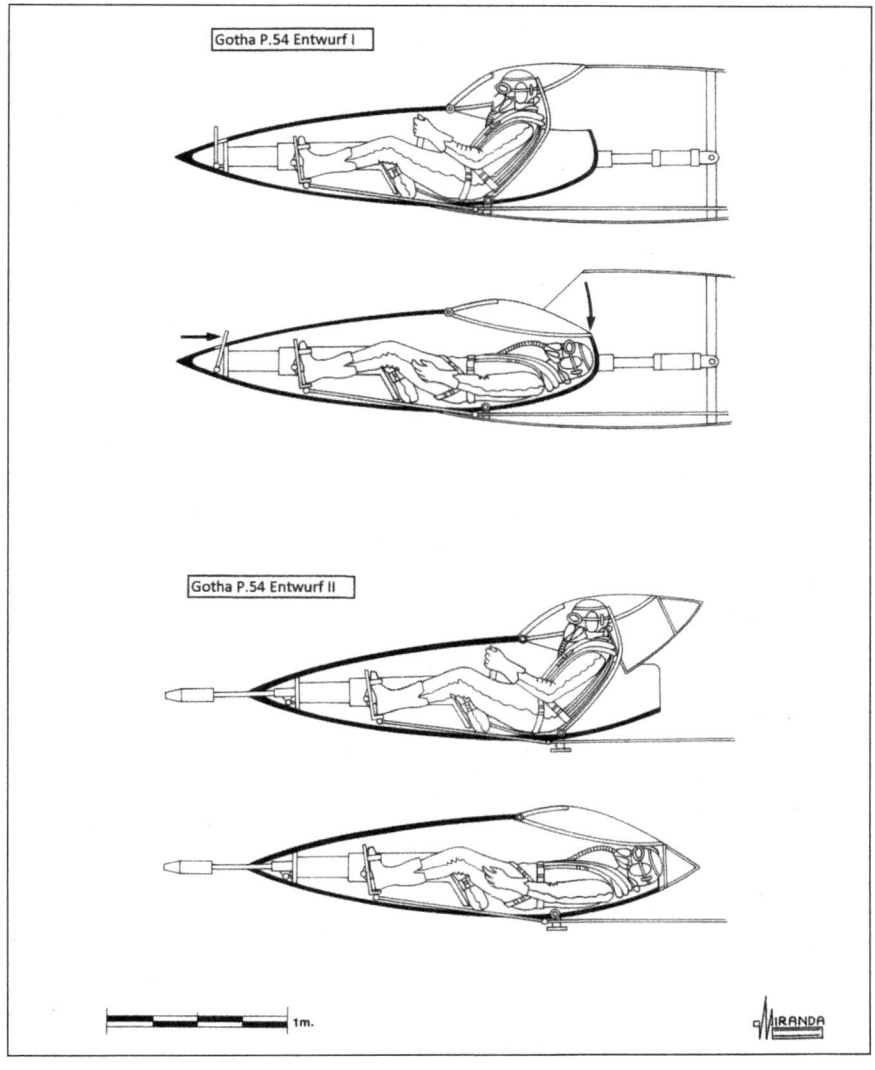

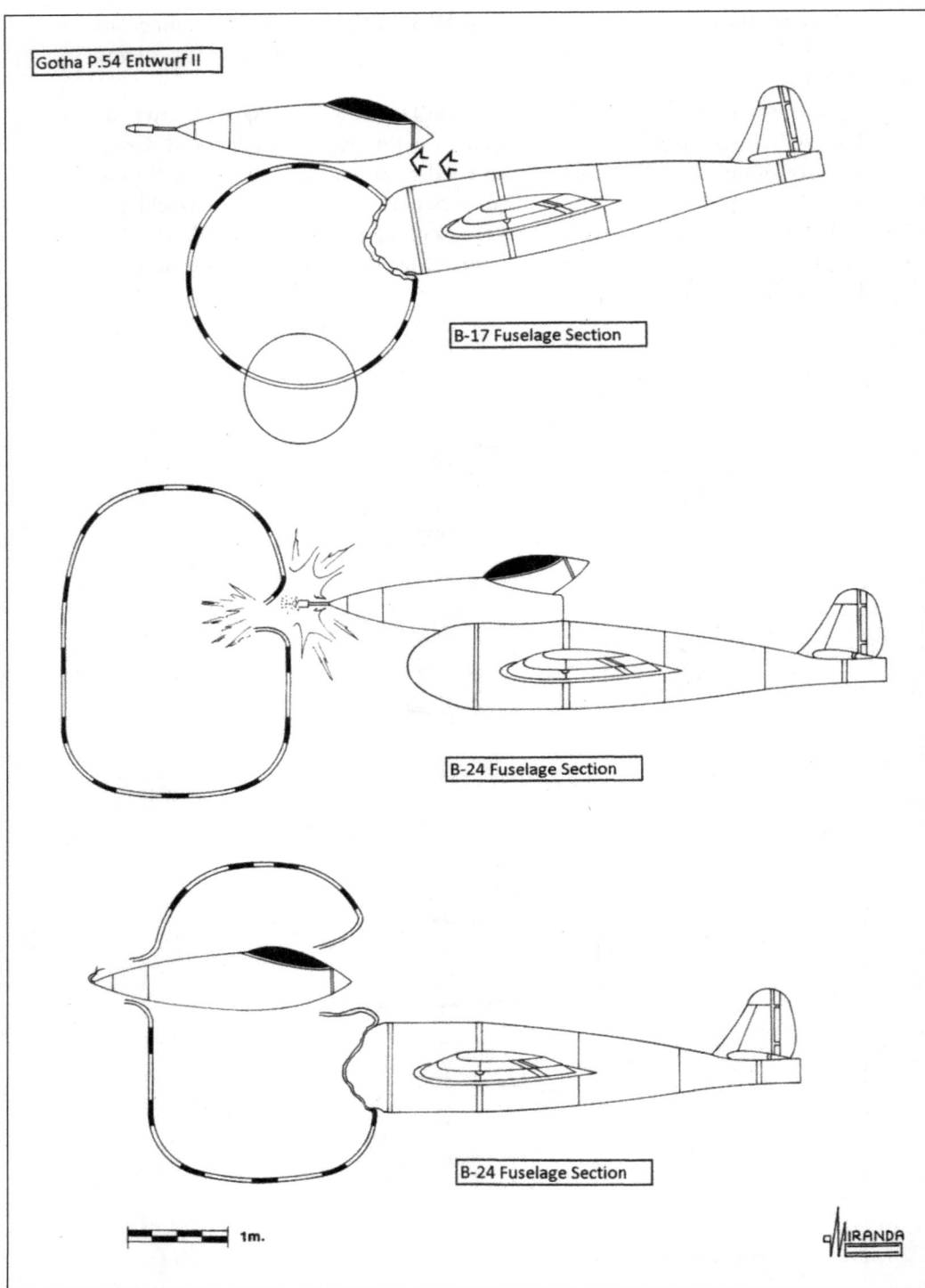

The Stuka flew under a Heinkel He 111 with the engine off while both aircraft stayed joined by a cable in an inverted 'Y', reaching the combat zone without wasting any fuel.

The Hubschlepp system, developed by Gothaer Waggonfabrik AG, was based on the opposite effect. It consisted of a glider designed to fly over a towing aircraft using the same physical principle as a kite. To that purpose, the wingtips of the both aircraft were joined by 10m cables so that the glider was not affected by turbulence generated by the propeller of the mother plane. Initial flight tests, carried out on a Dornier Do 17 and a DFS 230 glider, served to demonstrate the validity of the concept.

Hubschlepp formed the basis for the project P.54.

GOTHA P.54 ENTWURF I TECHNICAL DATA: Wingspan: 5.7m. Length: 6.2m. Height: 1.25m. Wing area: 6sq.m. Estimated maximum speed: 650km/h. Estimated impact speed: 160/200km/h.

GOTHA P.54 ENTWURF II TECHNICAL DATA: Wingspan: 5.7m. Length: 5.8m. Height: 1.6m. Wing area: 6sq.m. Estimated maximum speed: 600km/h. Estimated impact speed: 600km/h.

Me P.1103 Rammjäger (6 July 1944)

Designed by the Oberbayerische Forschungsanstalt Institut to compete in the Rammschussjäger specification, the Messerschmitt Me P.1103 (6 July 1944) was a small glider with 10mm-thick armoured nose and six armoured-vision panels, with the pilot in prone position to minimise frontal area. The wings and tail planes were built from those of a Fieseler Reichenbeg manned missile. It should make the take-off on a detachable twin wheel dolly, towed by a Me 262 jet-fighter in Deichselslepp configuration.

After separating from the mother plane its first attack was made in a shallow dive against the 'bomber stream', firing one W.Gr. 28 or one W.Gr. 21 spin-stabilised rocket projectile, afterwards using its two ventral Rheinmetall-Borsig 109-502 rockets, with 600kg thrust each, gaining altitude for a second attack with its ventral gun MK 108/30 (with 30 rounds only) and ending with the ramming of the tail surfaces of one of the bombers of the 'box'. The P.1103 would descend using a recovery parachute after the pilot abandoned the aircraft using his own parachute.

ME P.1103 (6 JULY 1944) TECHNICAL DATA: Wingspan: 5.3m. Length: 4.7m. Height: 1.58m. Wing surface: 5.8sq.m. Fuselage diameter: 80cm. Maximum speed: 770km/h. Maximum weight: 1,048kg. Ceiling: 12,500m.

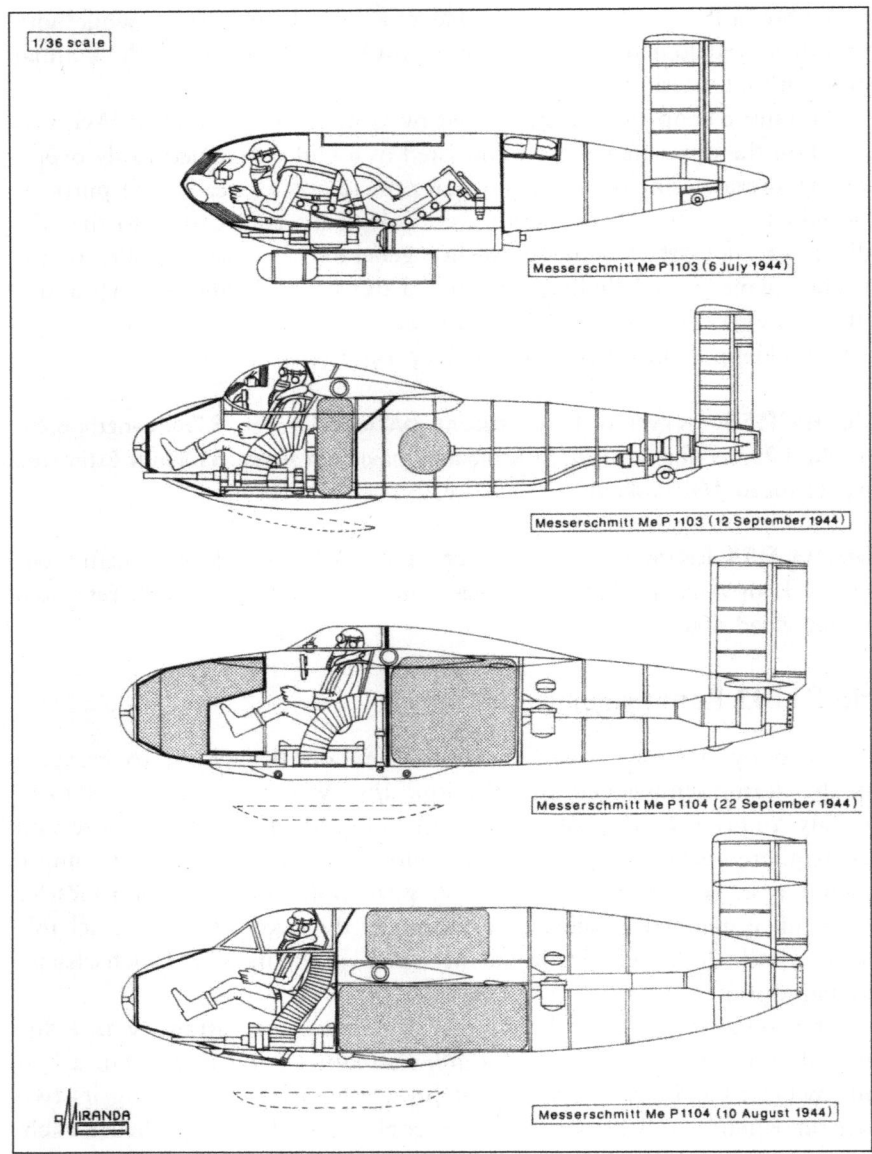

Zeppelin Rammer (Entwurf I, II & III)

At the end of 1944, the firm Luftschiffbau Zeppelin GmbH proposed a rammer that would be fully built in steel. It should be towed to the vicinity of the 'bomber stream' by a Messerschmitt Me 262 using the Starrschlepp pole-tow method. The launch would be at an altitude of around 6,000m, and 2,000m ahead of the bomber stream.

The first attack would be made with a shallow glide, using a very powerful weaponry and high rate of fire, because the reaction time to shoot and avoid the collision at a relative speed of 1,000km/h would be only 1.5 seconds.

The second attack required the use of one rocket engine to gain altitude and speed over the stream bomber and would begin with a 45-degree dive directed against the back of one of the boxes, ending with an impact on the tail surfaces of a bomber. For this type of manoeuvre, the rammer was equipped with a 30mm-thick armoured nose, an IG Farben armoured glass windshield of 90mm thick, and a strengthened wing with four tubular spars and Kuto-Nase devices installed on the leading edge.

The engine would be a Schmidding 109-533 solid-fuel rocket of 1,000kg peak-thrust and 12 seconds of life. The Schmidding would be interchangeable with a Rheinmetall-Borsig 109-515, with 4,000kg thrust peak and 6 seconds of life.

The initial version proposed to the OKL would be armed with a Sondergerät 119 Rohrbatterie consisting of forty-nine barrels of MK 108/30 cannon, with an effective range of 400m and a rate of fire of 12,000 rounds per minute. The SG119 could be replaced by nineteen air-to-air R4M Orkan rockets housed within a cylindrical container located in the extreme nose.

In January 1945 flying trials were conducted with an unpowered glider and the construction of a pre-series sixteen machines began, but a bombing of the Friedrichshafen factory prevented its completion.

The second version would have a smaller front fuselage section, with ogival armoured nose and the pilot seat in a reclined position. The armament was reduced to 14 R4M rockets with an Abgasbleitung system for laterally discharging the gases produced during shooting. The selected engine was a Schmidding 109-553 with 1,750kg peak-thrust and 4 seconds of life.

The third version would have a wing of simplified structure with only three spars to save weight. The flaps had been replaced by a dorsal brake-parachute similar to that used by the Arado E 381. The armament of fourteen R4M fin-stabilised rockets could be replaced by a Bienenwabe B3-7 container with seven spin-stabilised air-to-air Föhn rockets of 73mm which had an effective range of 1,200m.

It was expected that the rammer would survive the collision, landing on a retractable skid with the help of compressed-air operated flaps.

ZEPPELIN RAMMER ENTWURF I TECHNICAL DATA: Wingspan: 4.95m. Length: 5.10m. Height: 1.75m. Wing chord: 1.2m. Wing area: 6sq.m. Maximum speed: 785km/h. Landing speed: 110km/h. Maximum weight: 860kg.

ZEPPELIN RAMMER ENTWURF IR TECHNICAL DATA: Wingspan: 4.83m. Length: 5.10m. Height: 1.32m. Wing chord: 1.15m. Wing area: 5.8sq.m.

ZEPPELIN RAMMER ENTWURF III TECHNICAL DATA: Wingspan: 4.90m. Length: 5.10m. Height: 1.20m. Wing chord: 1.10m. Wing area: 5.72sq.m.

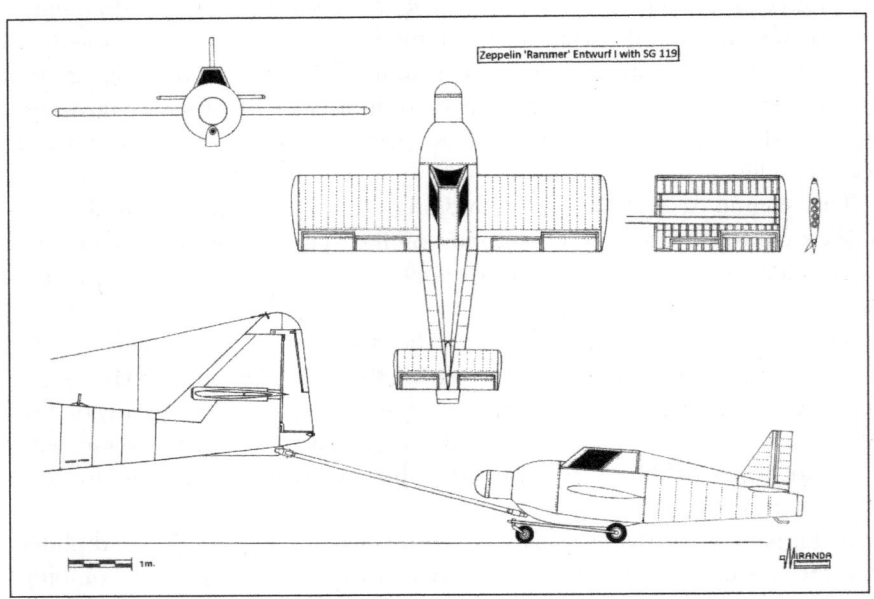

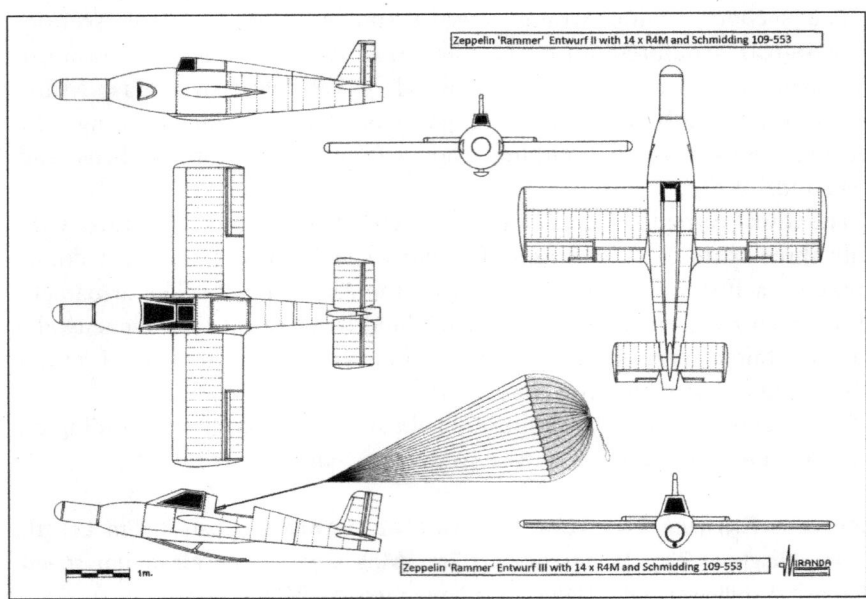

Rammschussjäger Specification

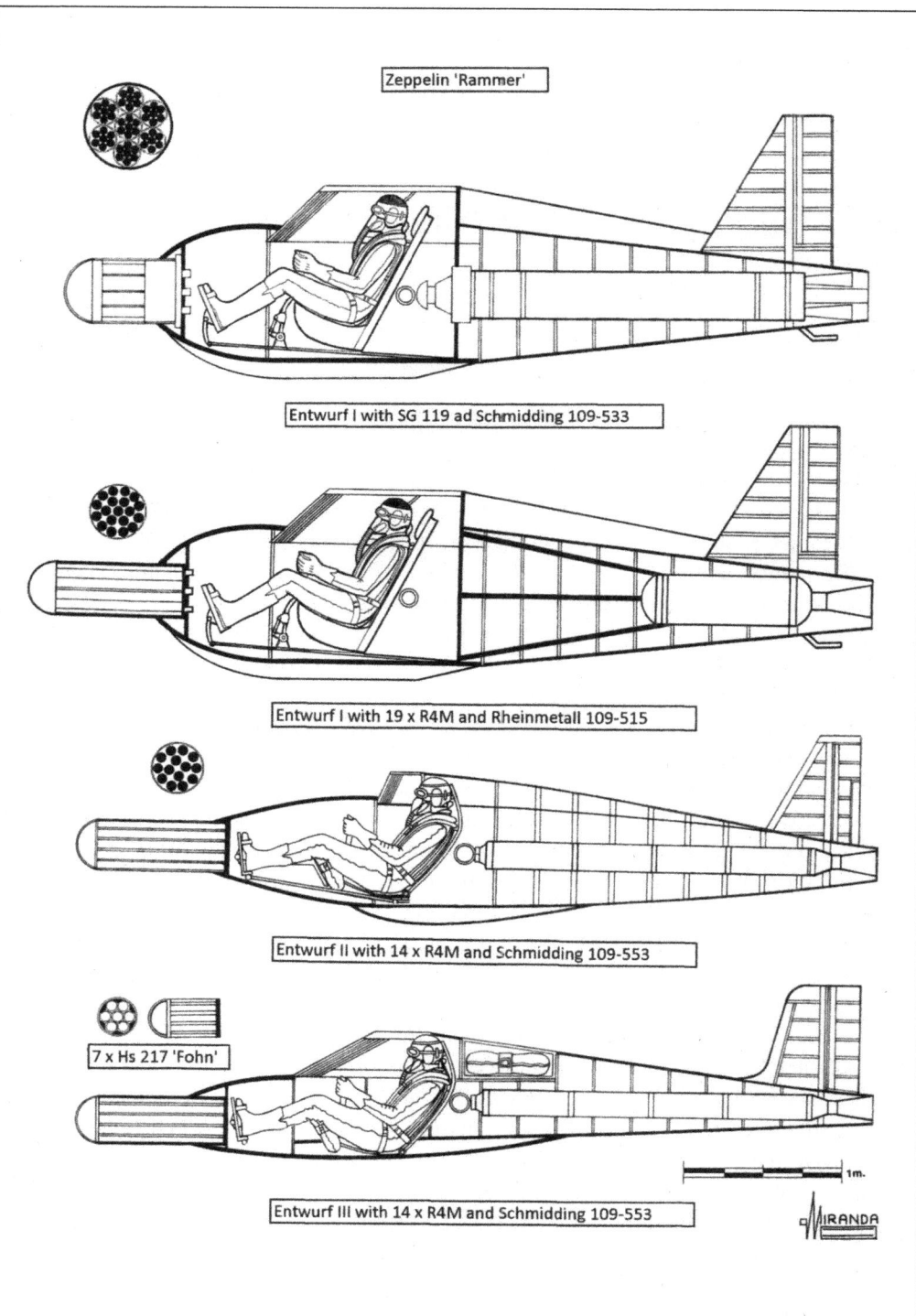

8

Turbojet/Rocket Mixed Power Plant

In 1939, the Heinkel-Rostock team, led by Max A. Mueller was working at the development of the HeS 8 centrifugal turbojet, which was expected to be used in the He 280 fighters. With a planned thrust of 700kg and a diameter 20 per cent shorter than the HeS 3, the development of this new turbojet required a great research effort and an extensive test program. Numerous technical problems had to be solved before starting its mass production and the whole project suffered excessive delays.

In December 1941 the engine only produced 500kg static thrust, at the time the British centrifugal turbojet Rover W2B/2 produced 680kg, and the Metropolitan-Vickers F.2, 997kg.

The root cause was the reduction of the diameter, recommended by the aerodynamicists to minimise the drag produced by the engine nacelles when installed under the wings of the He 280. Trials revealed that the most effective way to increase thrust in this type of turbojet was to also increase the diameter, to improve the performance of the centrifugal compressor. In 1939, the HeS 3B, with 93cm of diameter, produced 450kg.

In June 1943 the British DH Halford IB, with 127cm in diameter, produced 1,114kg thrust. With this power it was possible to build a single-engine jet-fighter, with the centrifugal turbojet installed inside the fuselage.

In 1943, the British chose the Halford to propel their new fighters, Gloster E5/42 and De Havilland E6/41 Vampire. The Americans used the same turbojet to power the Lockheed XP-83 prototype, in early 1944.

In Germany. Max A. Mueller proposed to build the 'ZTL' version of the HeS 8, with a ducted-fan of 1m diameter and a planned thrust of 900kg.

Focke-Wulf engineers also proposed to modify a HeS 8 to be used as a nose-mounted power plant in an Fw 190. The modification would consist of replacing the radial inflow turbine with another of 122cm diameter and the exhaust nozzle by three outlets located underneath and on both sides of the cowling. The outlets were equipped with deflectors to prevent hot gases from damaging the airframe. The new turbojet, called T.1, would have had a thrust of 600kg by the end of 1942.

In the spring of 1943, the OKL decided to cancel all research work with centrifugal turbojets to focus on the development of axial-flow type engines.

In September 1943 the Junkers Jumo 004 B-0 produced only 840kg thrust and the centrifugal British D.H. Goblin I, 1,223kg.

In October the BMW 003 A-0 produced 800kg thrust.

In November the production version Ju 004 B-1 produced 900kg.

During 1944 the prototype Ju 004 C produced 996kg in July, the production version BMW 003 A-1 produced 900kg in October and the prototype Ju 004 D, 1,050kg in November.

Early in 1945 the HeS 011 V6 prototype generated 1,300kg and the Ju 004 B-4 (production version) 900kg in January, the US turbojet General Electric J33 (production version) generated 1,744kg in February, the production version HeS 011 A-0 still produced 1,300kg in April, and the Ju 004 E prototype 1,200kg in July.

By mid-1943 it became clear that it would not be possible to build the high-performance interceptor needed by the Jagdwaffe using available turbojets.

In July, the Messerschmitt AG Projektbüro proposed a modification on the Me 262 fighter with the installation of one Walter 109-509 A-2 rocket booster motor.

The BMW Company reply was the mixed-power BMW 003R (TLR) proposal that was accepted by Technisches Amt in September.

The new engine received the official designation BMW 109-003R and consisted of a BMW 003 A-0 modified to drive the propellant pumps of a BMW 109-718 rocket-motor. The 200hp required to drive the two pumps, were taken from the turbojet via one gearbox, one extension shaft with two universal joints and one electrohydraulic coupling.

During the development of the rocket-motor, BMW experimented with various types of hypergolic (self-igniting) propellants: SV-Stoff, S-Stoff and T-Stoff as oxidants and M-Stoff, Tonka 93, Tonka 250 and Tonka 500 as fuels.

The mixture ratio, by weight, of both types was 1 part of fuel to 3.5 parts of oxidant.

In November 1944, two BMW 003R engines were mounted into the Messerschmitt Me 262 Werk.Nr. 170074 prototype, but during the first ground test one rocket exploded.

ROCKET PROPELLANTS' COMPOSITION:

S-Stoff: Mixture of nitric acid (96%) and ferrous chloride (4%), also called Salbei.
SV-Stoff: Mixture of nitric acid (94%) and nitrogen dioxide (6%), also called Red fuming nitric acid, or 90–98% nitric acid and 2–10% sulfuric acid.

T-Stoff:	Mixture of hydrogen peroxide (80%), oxyquinoline or phosphate (20%) as stabiliser.
M-Stoff:	Methanol, also called methyl alcohol.
Tonka 93:	Mixture, by weight, of xylidine (20%), aniline (20%), ethylaniline (20%), isquexylamine (20%), sulphate benzine (10%) and watery solution of Benzol (10%).
Tonka 250:	Mixture, by weight, of xylidine (50%) and triethylamine (50%).
Tonka 500:	Mixture, by weight, of xylidine (12%), aniline (15%), monomethylaniline (22%), triethylamine (21%), sulphate benzine (16%) and watery solution of Benzol (14%).

Me 262 Interzeptor and Me 262 Heimatschützer Programmes

By mid-1943 the Oberkommando der Luftwaffe (OKL) had to accept that the Messerschmitt Me 262, specifically designed as heavy fighter to destroy bombers, left a lot to be desired when used in a dogfight against the conventional Allied fighters. Below 7,000rpm the throttle had to be increased slowly to avoid the turbojets stopping without warning. A larger problem was the flaming out of the Jumo 004 turbojets and many service pilots lost their lives during high-speed combat dives.

The aircraft service ceiling was insufficient, manufacturing expensive, and maintenance complex.

Besides, the Me 262 had serious problems of compressibility buffeting, an aerodynamic phenomenon unknown until 1941 that caused the nacelles to generate a turbulent transonic flux and tail buffet during combat diving between 9,000 and 5,000m of altitude. At Mach 0.86 the aircraft went out of control in a dive that the pilot could not counter. Near the critical Mach number the elevator could not be used for recovery, only elevator trim worked at these speeds.

The prototype Me 262 V3 (W.Nr. 0003) was tested at Rechling research centre diving from 9,000m. The highest Mach number attained was 0.88, and the rear fuselage of the prototype suffered heavy structural damage caused by tailplane buffeting.

In July 1943, the Dipl.-Ing. Althoff proposed to Technisches Amt the use of a Walter rocket engine to boost the Me 262 during take off and climb, the rocket assisted fighter could reach its combat altitude of 12,000m in 4.5 minutes, only 7 per cent of the time taken by the turbojet version.

Fascinated by the exceptional climb rate of the Me 163 Komet, the OKL authorised the modification of the Me 262 under the code name Interzeptor.

In the Projekbaubeschreibung (Detailed Project Description) published by Messerschmitt on 11 September 1943, three rocket-propelled variants called Interzeptor I, II and III are described.

MESSERSCHMITT ME 262 INTERZEPTOR I (7 JULY 1943) TECHNICAL DATA: Power plant: one fuselage-mounted Walter 109-509 A-2 bi-propellant rocket engine rated at 1,700kg peak-thrust and two wing-mounted Jumo 004 B-1 turbojets rated at 900kg static thrust. Fuel tanks: two with 900 and 250l of J2 jet fuel (diesel oil + K1 kerosene) housed in the forward fuselage. Propergol tanks: one with 900l of T-Stoff and one with 625l of C-Stoff housed in the rear fuselage and one with 395l of T-Stoff mounted beneath the forward fuselage. Armament: six nose-mounted Mk 108/30 cannons. Wingspan: 12.65m. Length: 10.6m. Height: 2.8m. Wing area: 21.7sq.m. Maximum weight: 7,875kg. Maximum speed: 880km/h flying at 12,000m. Climb rate: 2,600 m/minute. Endurance: 42 minutes (5.7 minutes with rocket propulsion). Range: 745km.

On 6 July 1943 was proposed the Me 262 D-1 Series powered by two BMW 003 TLR engines with 2,000kg static thrust each. The new TLR mixed-power plant comprised one standard BMW 003 turbojet to which was added one BMW 109-718 rocket-motor with the propellant pumps driving by the turbojet.

The project was built as Me 262 C-2b Interzeptor II by modification of the Me 262 (V074) W.Nr.170074, but the prototype was partially destroyed by the explosion of one of the rockets.

MESSERSCHMITT ME 262 INTERZEPTOR II (6 JULY 1943) TECHNICAL DATA: Power plant: two wing-mounted BMW 003 TLR mixed-propulsion engines each rated at 800kg static thrust (turbojet) and 1,250kg peak-thrust (rocket). Fuel tanks: two with 900l of S-Stoff and three with 250, 900 and 435l of R-Stoff housed in the fuselage and one with 375l of S-Stoff mounted beneath the forward fuselage. Armament: six nose-mounted Mk 108/30 cannons. Wingspan: 12.65m. Length: 10.6m. Height: 2.8m. Wing area: 21.7sq.m. Maximum weight: 7,092kg. Maximum speed: 740km/h flying at 12,000m. Climb rate: 3,077 m/minute. Endurance: 51 minutes. Range: 845km.

On 21 July 1943 was proposed the Interzeptor III, a target-defence rocket-fighter powered by two wing-mounted HWK 109-509 S-2 rockets, with 3.07 minutes climbing time to 52,500ft (16,000m).

MESSERSCHMITT ME 262 INTERZEPTOR III (21 JULY 1943) TECHNICAL DATA: Power plant: two wing-mounted Walter 109-509 S-2 bi-propellant rocket engines each rated at 2,000kg peak-thrust. Propergol tanks: two with 900 and 200l of C-Stoff and two with 900 and 750l of T-Stoff housed in the fuselage, and one with 220l of C-Stoff mounted beneath the forward fuselage. Armament: six nose-mounted Mk 108/30 cannons. Wingspan: 12.65m. Length: 10.6m. Height: 2.8m. Wing area: 21.7sq.m. Maximum weight: 6,964kg. Maximum speed: 740km/h flying at 12,000m. Climb rate: 5,200 m/minute. Endurance: 7.6 minutes. Range: 313km. Service ceiling: 16,000m.

This project was not developed in favour of the Me 263 rocket-fighter that demonstrated better behaviour during unpowered landings.

By the spring of 1944 the Interzeptor program was renamed as Heimatschützer (Home defender) and the Me 262 A-1a (Werk. Nr. 130186) was modified as the Me 262 C-1a Heimatschützer I prototype with one HWK 109-509 A-2 rocket mounted in the rear fuselage.

The aircraft was flown on 27 February 1945 reaching 26,000ft in 3 minutes. During flight tests it turned out that the excess of power provided by the Walter rocket should be counterbalanced by flying with the nose slightly upwards, thus avoiding that the aircraft reached the critical Mach figure.

HEIMATSCHÜTZER I TECHNICAL DATA: Maximum speed: 590mph (950km/h). Maximum weight: 11,420lb (5,180kg). Range: 463 miles (745km). Endurance: 42 minutes. Power plant: two Jumo 004 B-1 turbojets rated at 897kg static thrust each and one Walter HWK 109-509 A-2 rocket-motor rated at 2,000kg static thrust.

On 26 March 1945 was modified the Me 262 W.Nr. 170078 that was flown, as Heimatschützer II.

HEIMATSCHÜTZER II TECHNICAL DATA: Maximum speed: 547mph (880km/h). Maximum weight: 15,640lb (7,092kg). Range: 525 miles (845km). Endurance: 51 minutes. Power plant: two BMW 003 TLR engines with 2,000kg static thrust each.

Heimatschützer III was cancelled in favour of the Me 263.

The internal mounting of the rocket and its dangerous propellants was problematic. To circumvent the Technisches Amt criticism the Dipl.-Ing. Karl Althoff proposed the Heimatschützer IV on 11 January 1945.

The new project, named Me 262 C-3a, had the rocket engine and the T-Stoff tank mounted in two jettisonable fairings beneath the fuselage.

Three prototypes were to be built but none was completed before the end of the war in Europe.

HEIMATSCHÜTZER IV TECHNICAL DATA: Maximum weight: 18,331lb (8,315kg). Climb to 22,966ft (7,000m): 4.5 minutes. Endurance: 42 minutes. Power plant: two Jumo 004 D turbojets rated at 930kg static thrust each and one Walter HWK 109-509 A-2 rocket engine rated at 2,000kg static thrust.

BMW 109-003 R (TLR) ROCKET/TURBOJET TECHNICAL DATA: Thrust: 800kg static, 775kg at 900km/h and sea level, 565kg at 4,000m. altitude. Maximum

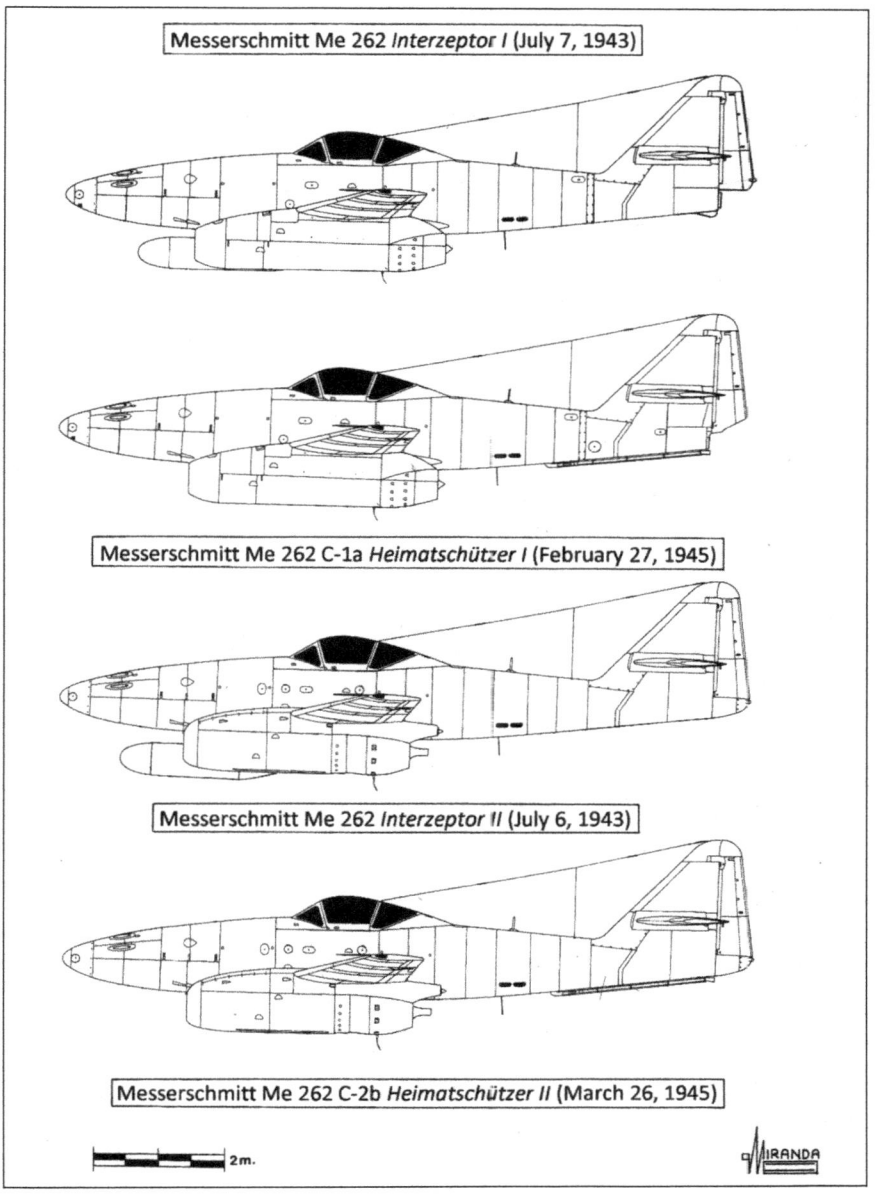

Messerschmitt Me 262 *Interzeptor I* (July 7, 1943)

Messerschmitt Me 262 C-1a *Heimatschützer I* (February 27, 1945)

Messerschmitt Me 262 *Interzeptor II* (July 6, 1943)

Messerschmitt Me 262 C-2b *Heimatschützer II* (March 26, 1945)

speed: 9,500rpm. Specific fuel consumption: 1.33. Compressor efficiency: 80 per cent. Weight: 570kg. Specific weight: 0.711. Diameter: 0.690m. Length: 3.565m (with exhaust bullet extended).

BMW 109-718 ROCKET TECHNICAL DATA: Thrust: 1,250kg. Exhaust velocity: 2,040 m/sec. Weight: 80kg. Propellant consumption rate: 6.5kg/sec. Length: 1.270m. Height: 0.292m.

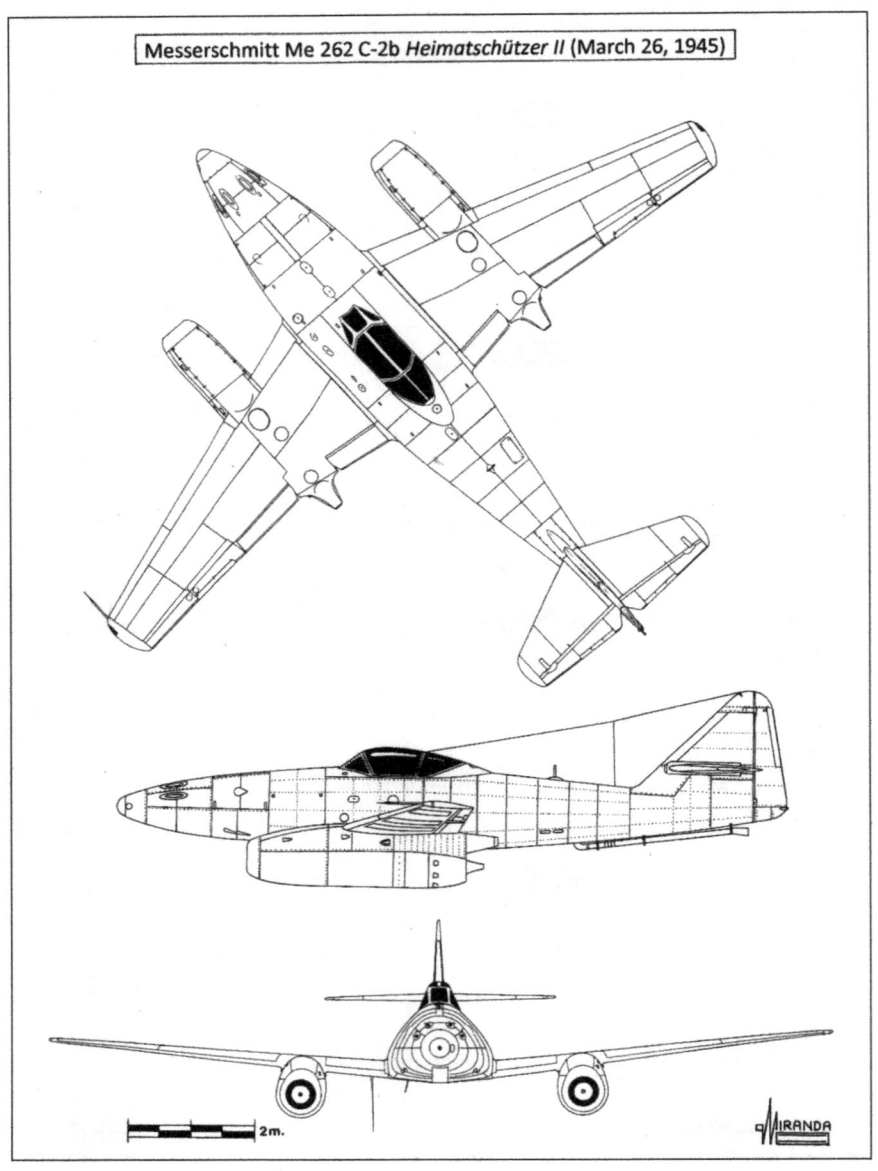

Messerschmitt Me 262 C-2b *Heimatschützer II* (March 26, 1945)

Turbojet/Rocket Mixed Power Plant

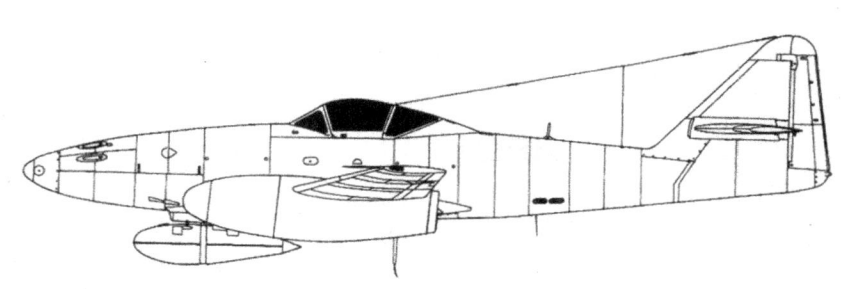

Messerschmitt Me 262 *Interzeptor III* (July 21, 1943)

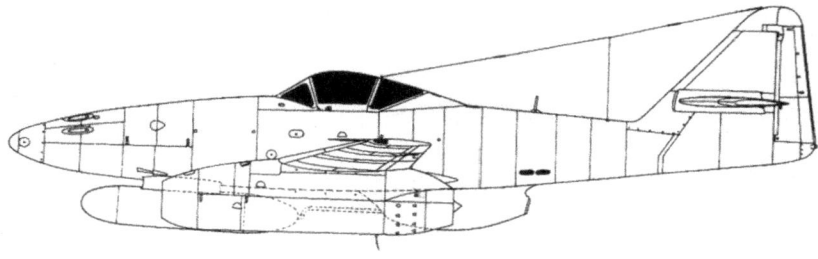

Messerschmitt Me 262 C-3a *Heimatschützer IV* (January 11, 1945)

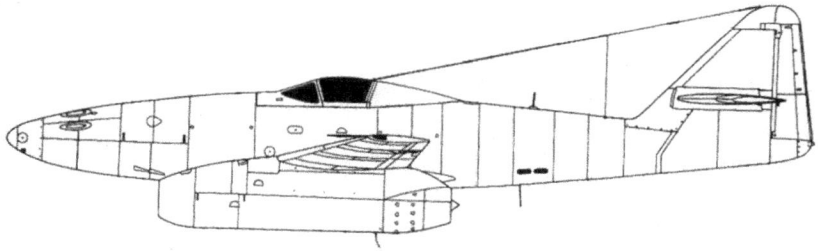

Messerschmitt Me 262 V9 (January 17, 1945)

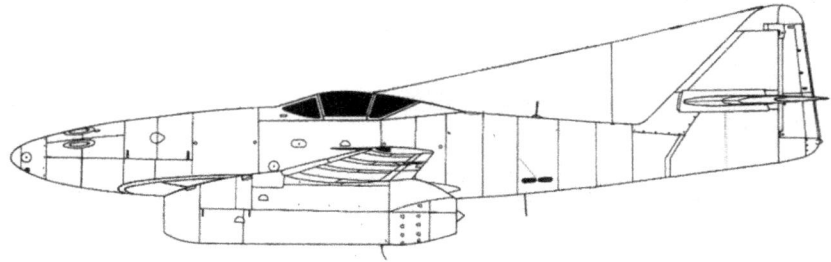

Messerschmitt Me 262 HG I (April 18, 1944)

2m.

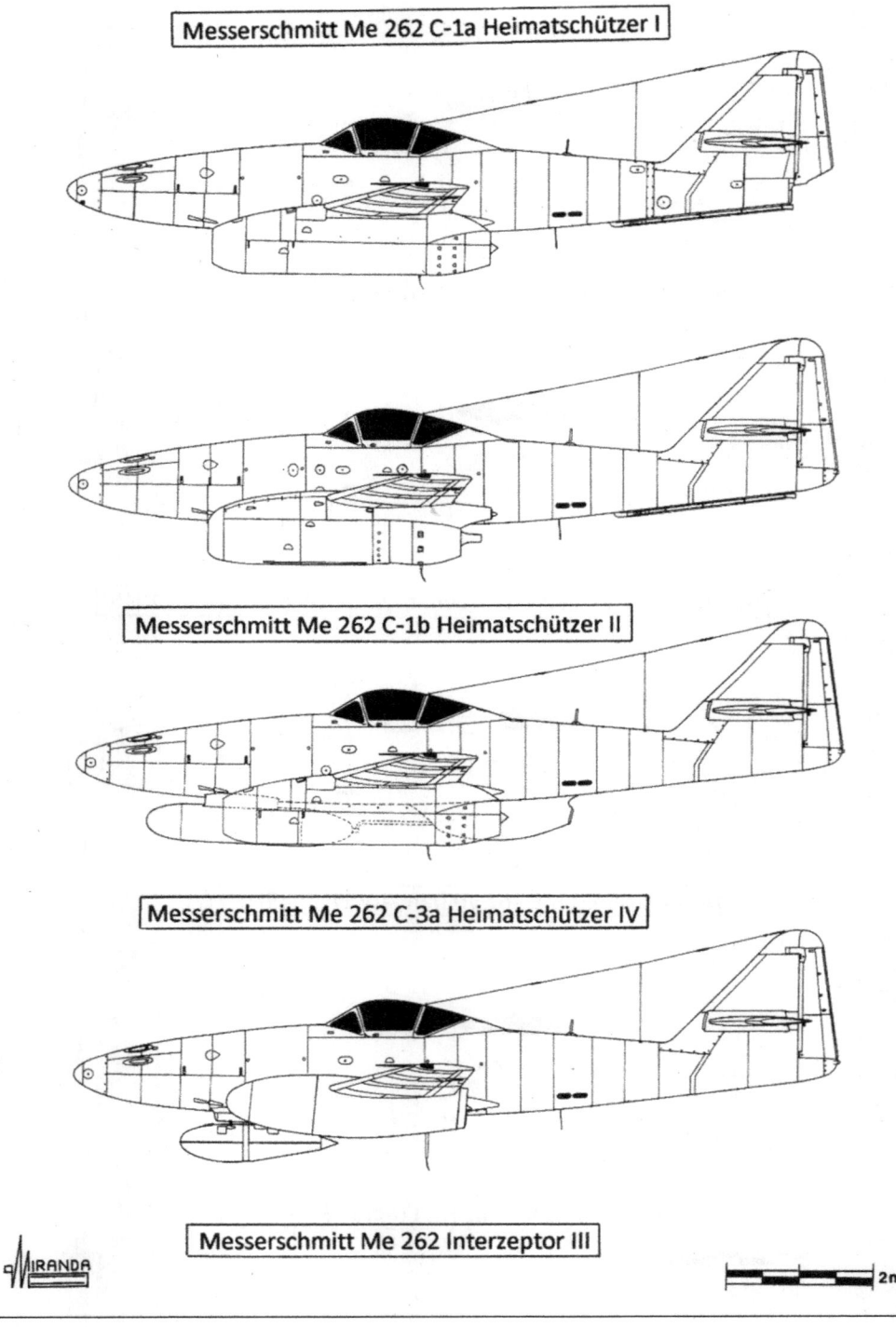

Turbojet/Rocket Mixed Power Plant

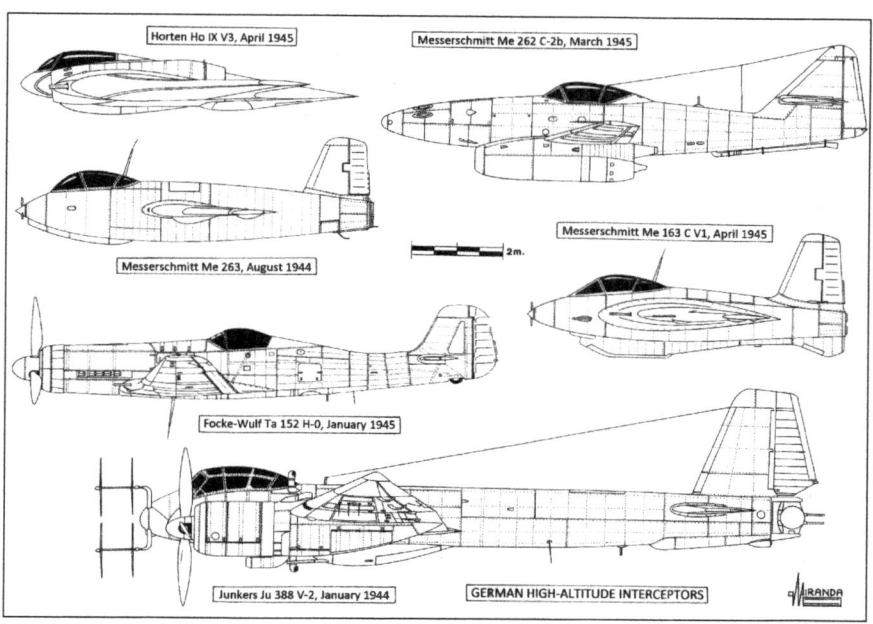

GERMAN HIGH-ALTITUDE INTERCEPTORS

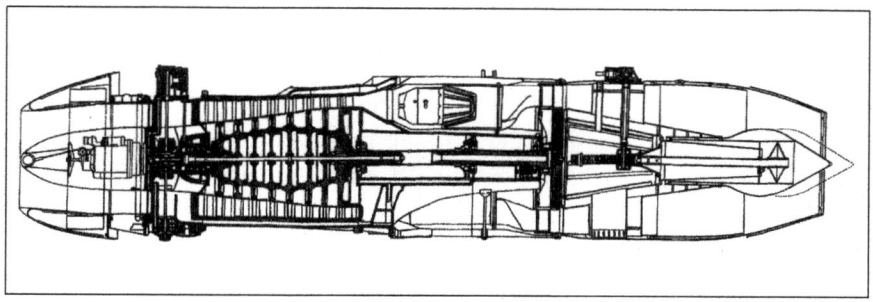

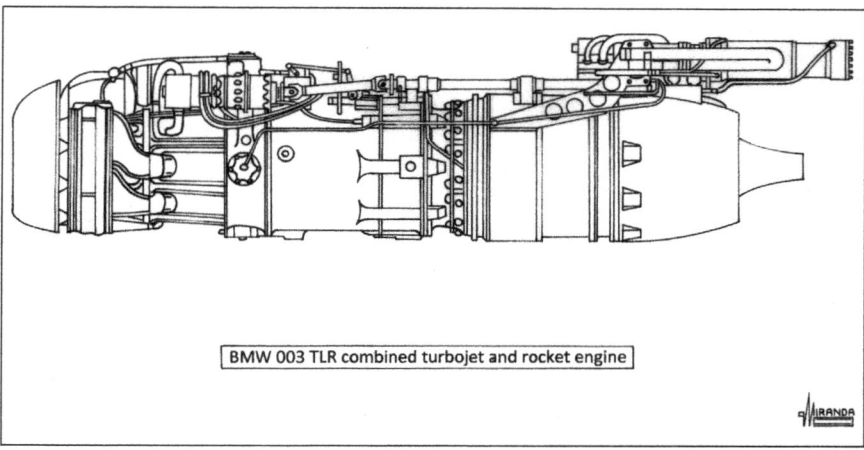

BMW 003 TLR combined turbojet and rocket engine

Arado TEW 16/43-15

Early in 1944 Walter Blume concluded that the performances demanded by the OKL for the future Hochleistungsjäger (air-superiority jet-fighter) could not be reached using neither the Jumo 004C nor the HWK 109-509. The solution seemed to be a compound power plant that combined the endurance of the turbojet with the bi-propellant rocket punch.

Using both types of engines, the new fighter would have great operational flexibility. It could act as a point-defence interceptor, combining the full power of the two engines, to reach the combat ceiling in the shortest time possible; it could also carry out air-patrol missions equipped with droppable fuel tanks for increased endurance, it could use the extra speed of the rocket to reach the interception area very fast, and it could get away from numerically superior enemy by climbing above the operational ceiling of the Allied fighters.

The Arado K-Jäger (Kombinations Jäger) was proposed to the OKL on 18 August 1943 under the denomination TEW 16/43-15 (20 March 1943). The type was a 118 per cent scaled-up version of the R-Jäger powered by one Jumo 004C dorsal turbojet and one Walter HWK 509 A-0 rocket-motor mounted in the tail.

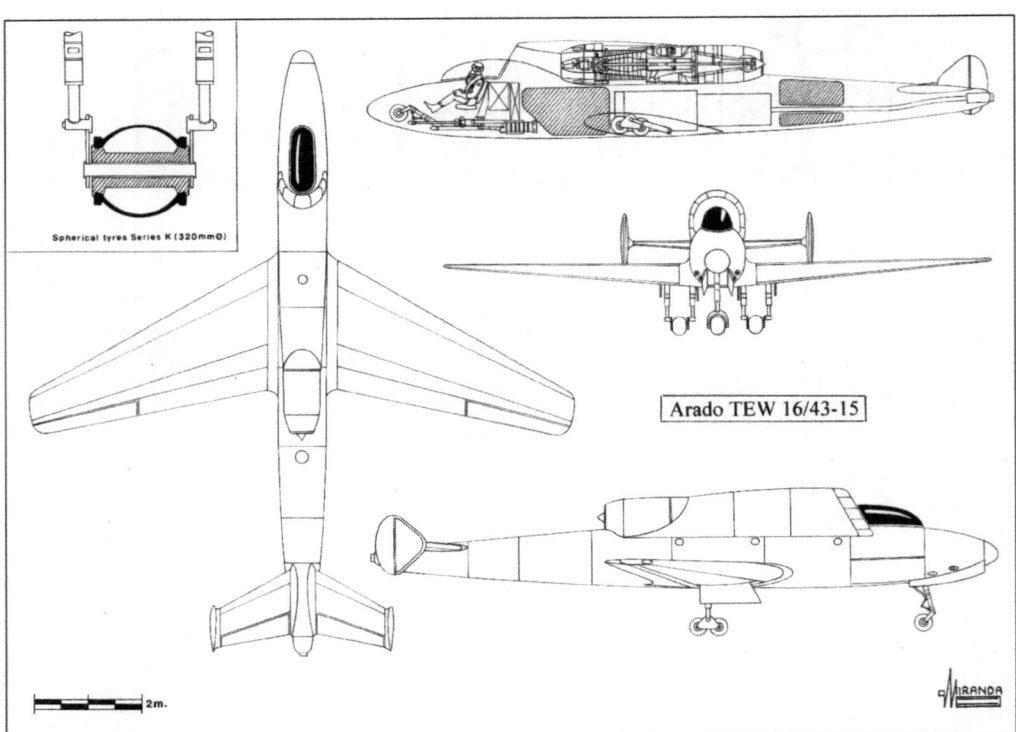

The project was rejected by the OKL due to the position of the air intake mounted in the aerodynamic shadow area generated by the nose and the cockpit hood. It was feared that the turbojet receiving insufficient air flow during the take off rotation, would risk loss of thrust.

ARADO TEW 16/43-15 TECHNICAL DATA: Wings: with a 25-degree sweep at 0.25 chord, 5.6:1 aspect ratio and 10.3m span. Length: 11.75m. Height: 2.8m. Wing area: 19sq.m. Maximum weight: 6,670kg. Maximum speed: 856km/h at 8,000m with the jet engine and 920km/h at 10,000m with the rocket-motor. Service ceiling: 18,800m. Power plant: one Jumo 004C turbojet rated at 1,000kg static thrust and one Walter HWK 509 A-0 rocket-motor rated at 1,500kg peak-thrust. Armament: two MK 108/30 and two MG 151/20 nose-mounted cannons.

Focke-Wulf 1-TLR *Jäger Projekt V*

Early in 1944 Kurt Tank concluded that the performances demanded by the OKL for the future air-superiority jet-fighter could not be reached using neither the Jumo 004C nor the HeS 011A, at a time when British turbojets already generated over 2,000kg. The solution seemed to be a compound power plant that combined the endurance of the turbojet with the bi-propellant rocket punch.

Combining the use of both types of engines, the new fighter would have great operational flexibility. It could act as a point-defence interceptor, using the full power of the two engines, to reach the combat ceiling in the shortest time possible; it could also carry out air-patrol missions equipped with droppable fuel tanks for increased endurance, and using the extra speed of the rocket to very quickly reach the interception area, or it could also get away from numerically superior enemy by climbing above the operational ceiling of the fighters of the Allies.

The twin-boom configuration with short fuselage, to avoid the thrust loss in the turbojet tailpipe, also limited maximum speed due to the drag penalty generated by the tailplane. To solve the problem, Dipl.-Ing. Hans Multhopp proposed the adoption of a T-tailplane, a configuration criticised by the Technisches Amt for being too radical. Its main objection was based on the danger the tailplane posed to a pilot attempting to bail out at high speed. The ejector seat designed in 1942 to equip future versions of the Fw 190 could launch the pilot at a height of 2m above the cockpit floor, with a margin of 43cm over the tailfin. But the T-tailplane, designed to avoid the turbulent airflow generated by the cockpit hood, had to be installed more than 3m high above the level of the cockpit floor to be effective.

The Technisches Amt calculated that during an ejection at a critical Mach number, the T-tailplane would reach the pilot in only 0.018 second. In 1944, the most effective ejector seat in the world was the Heinkel Kartusche propelled by an explosive cartridge with 30 grams of powder, with an ejection speed of 11 m/sec and 12G. It was designed for speeds not exceeding 700km/h. At 1,000km/h and using a T-tailplane, it was necessary to increase the ejection speed to 200G, with equally lethal effects for the pilot.

In January 1944, the firm Focke-Wulf proposed to the OKL a first transonic design called P.011.001, described in the Baubeschreibung Nr.279 dossier as Projekt V. It was a high-altitude interceptor of the Moskitojäger class (De Havilland Mosquito hunters) with light armament and a compound power plant formed by a HeS 011A turbojet, with 1,115kg static thrust, and a bi-propellant rocket-motor Walter HWK 109-509 B-0 with 350kg peak-thrust. This was the firm's first design in which the phenomena of compressibility buffeting, local transonic flux, air viscosity in the boundary layer, and Mach critical number (as defined by the aerodynamicist of the LFA Institut) were taken into account. A frontal air-intake was adopted to delay the appearance of vibrations, and a 37/43-degree double swept wing, with 9 to 13 per cent chord/thickness ratio, served to delay the back displacement of the lift centre of pressure and aileron reversement. To facilitate manoeuvrability at high speeds, the tips of the ailerons were clipped.

To avoid the 38-degree-swept T-tailplane being affected by the fuselage turbulence at critical Mach numbers, it was installed on a long tailfin with a 60-degree rear sweep. This configuration worsened the usual lateral stability on short-fuselage aircraft. During the Korean War, the Soviet MiG-15, which was nearly 2m longer than the P.011.001, suffered directional snaking problems at high speeds that affected weapon precision during combat manoeuvres.

Several attempts made to eradicate this problem included the extension of the tailfin up to 3.5m and the total length of the plane to 8.9m, as well as increasing the dihedral angle of the tailplane up to 11 degrees, which made the ejection problem even worse.

To reduce the height of the tailplane, wind tunnel tests were carried out with a scale model equipped with an inverted-Vee tailplane. But it was verified that the new configuration increased drag because of the vortex generated in the junction between the tailfin and the tailplane.

The P.011.001 should be built in light alloy using the well proven technology of the Fw 190. The wings, spanning 8.7m with an area of 17sq.m and a chord of 306cm at the root, contained 1,400l of K1 heavy kerosene for a 600km endurance using the turbojet. The fuselage, with egg section, housed the landing gear, the pressurised cockpit with ejector

Turbojet/Rocket Mixed Power Plant

seat and Revi 16C gunsight, two MG 17 machine guns, two MG 151/20 rapid-fire cannons, one rocket-propellant tank, containing 1,800l of T-Stoff for 210 seconds of rocket-powered flight, one rocket-propellant tank containing 800l of C-Stoff, the turbojet, the rocket engine and the electronic equipment.

Designed as a Moskitojäger, the P.011.001 was insufficiently armed to combat the four-engine heavy bombers. In 1944 the standard armament of an Fw 190 A-7/R2 Sturmböck (assault rammer) were two MG 17, two MG 151/20 rapid fire and two MK 108/30 heavy cannons. Despite offering an estimated maximum speed of 925km/h and an absolute ceiling of 12,600m, the propulsion system was a victim of the Technisches Amt criticism—following on from bad experiences with the Messerschmitt Me 163 and its dangerous rocket propellants.

FOCKE-WULF P.011.001 TECHNICAL DATA: Wings: built in light alloy and steel with 37/43 degrees variable sweep at the leading edge, 8.7m span, 17sq.m. area, 306cm chord at the root and 9 to 13 per cent chord/thickness ratio, housed six fuel tanks with 1,400l of J2 kerosene, flaps and ailerons. Fuselage: built in light alloy and steel with egg section, housed the landing gear, the pressurised cockpit with ejector seat and Revi 16C gunsight, the armament, one rocket-propellant

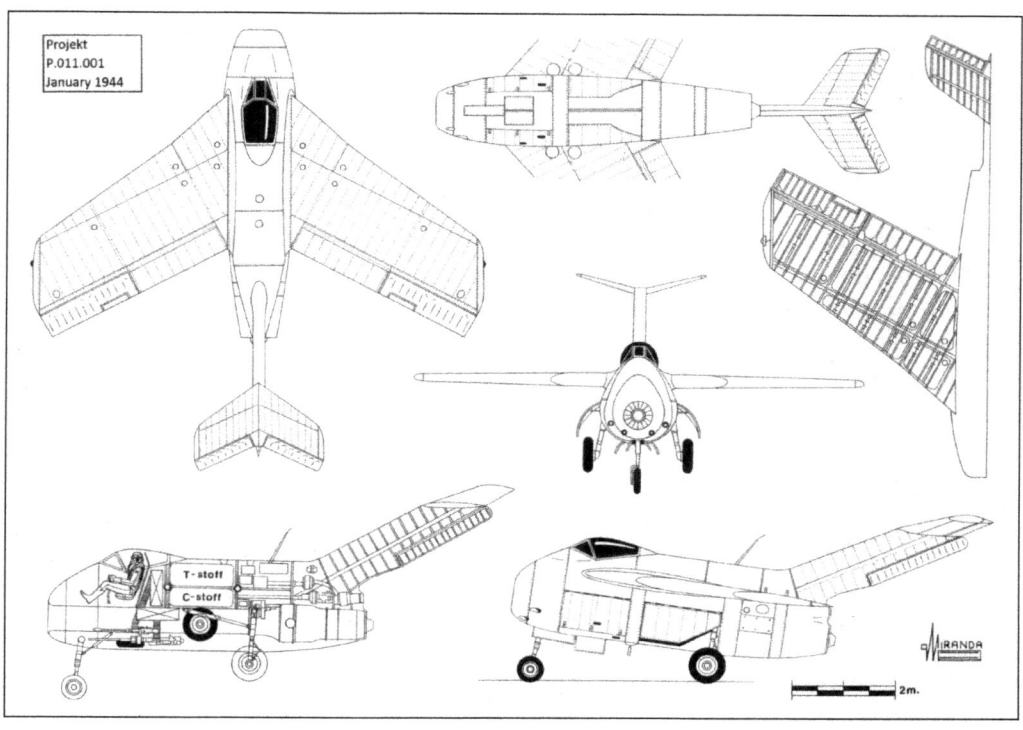

Projekt P.011.001 January 1944

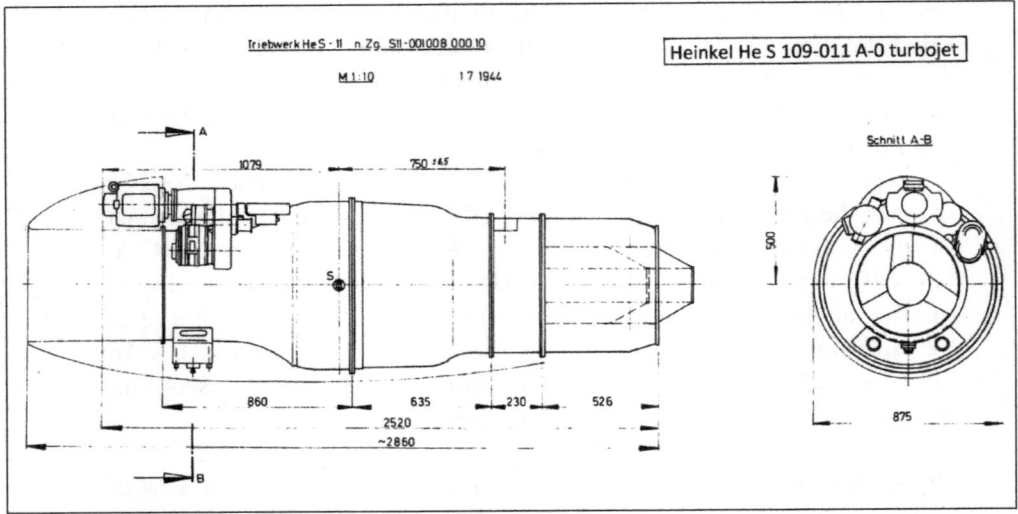

tank, containing 1,800l of T-Stoff for 210 seconds of rocket-powered flight, one rocket-propellant tank containing 800l of C-Stoff, the turbojet, the rocket engine the tail ensemble and the electronic equipment. Length: 9.2m. Height: 3.35m. Armament: two fuselage-mounted MG 151/20 rapid-fire cannons and two fuselage-mounted MK 108/30 heavy cannons. Power plant: one HeS 011 A turbojet rated at 1,115kg static thrust and one HWK 109-509 B-0 rocket-motor with 350kg peak-thrust. Range: 600km.

Focke-Wulf Ta 183 Ra-1

In December 1944 Kurt Tank decided to build four prototypes called Rechnerische Ankündigung (Ra) to test in flight the basic airframe of the Ta 183 powered by different engines. The program was due to start on January 1945 with the construction of the Ta 183 Ra-1, an advanced version of the P.011.001 powered by a HeS 011 A-0 turbojet and a HWK 109-509 B-1 bipropellant rocket engine. For safety reasons, the rocket propellants were stored in two detachable tanks slung under the wings.

The 35ol T-Stoff oxidant tank was positioned asymmetrically to the C-Stoff fuel tank, with only 18ol of capacity and of shorter diameter, to compensate for the drag-braking effect. The K1 heavy kerosene for the turbojet was stored in a rear tank of 29ol and additional 1,300l inside the wings. To improve the longitudinal stability, with respect to P.011.001, the tailfin chord was increased by 10cm and the sweep angle of the tailplane was reduced to 37 degrees. The tailplane span was increased by 36cm. The wingspan was reduced by 6cm and the sweep angle to 40 degrees, but the wing surface remained unchanged. When the nose leg was shortened, the ground incidence was reduced by 2 degrees and the length of the cockpit hood was increased by 68cm to reduce turbulence on the rudder. The weaponry proposed for this version was two MG 151/20 rapid-fire cannons and two MK 108/30 heavy cannons.

FOCKE-WULF TA 183 RA-1 TECHNICAL DATA: Wings: built in wood/plywood with 40 degrees sweep at the leading edge, 8.64m span and 17sq.m. area, housing six fuel tanks with 1,300l of J2 kerosene, flaps and ailerons. Fuselage: built in light alloy and steel housing the undercarriage, the armament, the pressurised cockpit, the engine, one dorsal kerosene tank with 290l of J2 and the tail ensemble. Length: 8.86m. Height: 3.56m. Armament: two fuselage-mounted MG 151/20 rapid-fire cannons and two fuselage-mounted MK 108/30 heavy cannons. Power plant: one HeS 011 A-0 turbojet rated at 1,300kg static thrust and one HWK 109-509 B-1 rocket-motor with 400kg peak-thrust.

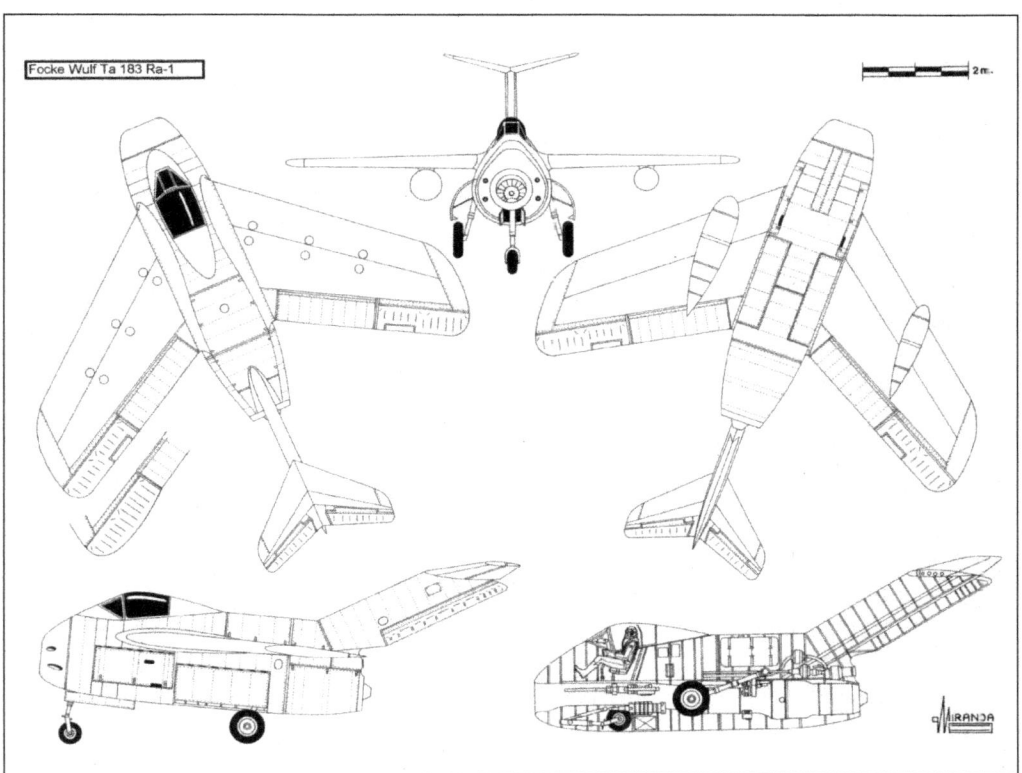

Focke-Wulf I-TL Jäger Projekt VI (Flitzer I)

Anticipating that the Technisches Amt would reject Baubeschreibung Nr.279 (P.011.001) because of its T-tail configuration, Kurt Tank proposed to the RLM the construction of a more conservative, twin-boom design fighter called Flitzer (1 February 1944).

Flitzer was described in the Baubeschreibung Nr.280 dossier as an air-superiority Moskitojäger, with turbojet/rocket mixed power plant, which could be constructed using 52 per cent steel, 45 per cent of light alloy and 3 per cent plastics. Its estimated performances were slightly higher than the T-tail design, with an initial rate of climb of 18.2 m/sec, an absolute ceiling of 13,000m and a maximum speed of 955km/h.

The wingspan was only 8m, the wing area had been reduced to 15.5sq.m and the height to 2.35m. The twin-boom formula required to increase the overall length up to 10.55m to maintain longitudinal stability. The wings, newly designed and with a 3.77: 1 aspect ratio, had 280cm chord at the root, 29 degrees sweep at the leading edge and 4 degrees sweep at the trailing edge. They were fitted with fixed leading-edge slots, split-flaps and double ailerons to optimise roll-rate at different speeds. Each wing panel housed one fuel tank with 210l of K1 heavy kerosene, one landing gear leg with 240 x 210 wheel, one MK 108/30 cannon with 60 rounds and one air-intake/air-duct ensemble.

The fuselage had a design like that of Projekt IV. It housed the nose leg, with 560 x 200 wheel, the pressurised cockpit with standard armour, seat ejector and Revi 16C gunsight, two MK 151/20 rapid-fire cannons with 175 rounds each, two T-Stoff rocket-propellant tanks with 560 and 350l, sufficient for 400 seconds of powered flight, one Heinkel HeS 011A turbojet with 1,115kg static thrust, one Walter 109-509 B-0 bi-propellant rocket with 350kg peak-thrust, one FuG 15Zy RT device and one IFF transponder FuG 25a.

For safety reasons, the C-Stoff rocket propellant was stored in the tail-booms, in two 160l tanks. The estimated range, with 1,071l of rocket propellants and 420l of K1, was 890km, with a maximum take-off weight of 4750kg. The estimated maximum speed was 810km/h, using only the turbojet. The Mauser MG 151/20 were very effective against the Tempest and Thunderbolts, but they lacked the punch needed to destroy a four-engine heavy bomber.

In February 1944, the Fw 190 A-6 of the Sturmstaffel I, armed with four MG 151/20 rapid-fire cannons, were forced to perform risky head-on pass against the B-17 and B-24 trying to achieve some hits in the cockpit or in the unprotected engines, the only places where the low destructive capacity of the 20mm ammunition could achieve results. In April, the new Fw 190 A-7/R2 of the 5/JG1 armed with 30mm cannons Rheinmetall-Borsig MK 108, a weapon capable of destroying a heavy bomber with only five impacts of its powerful ammunition 30 x 90RB of the type Minengeschoss. But the MK 108 had prematurely entered into service, with a low effective range and high dispersion fire factor that forced the Sturmjägern to shoot from less than 100m from the target to obtain results.

There was another 30mm cannon that used a much more powerful 30 x 184B type munition, with a muzzle velocity that doubled to that of the MK 108 and an effective range of 1,000m. It was the Rheinmetall-Borsig MK 103, derived from an antitank cannon, which was very difficult to integrate into the single-engine fighters because of its powerful recoil and its weight, equivalent to three MK 108.

On 20 June 1944, Kurt Tank proposed to the RLM the construction of a *zerstörer* version called Flitzer II. Basically, it was the same airframe armed with two MK 103/30 in the nose. The main modification consisted in reducing the amount of rocket propellant to only 663l, enough for 250 seconds of powered flight, extending the wing area up to 17sq.m and the wing chord at the root up to 307cm, with the trailing edge sweep angle being decreased by 1 degree. The estimated range was reduced to only 570km but was considered sufficient for the defence of important targets.

Each wing panel contained 210l of K1 and a MG 151/20 cannon with 350 rounds. The two MK 103/30s were installed under the cockpit floor, with 80 rounds per gun. The Revi 16C gunsight was replaced by a Zeiss ZFR 4a Zielfernrohr (telescopic gunsight). The fuselage housed a tank with 560l of T-Stoff and another with 330l of K1. The C-Stoff was reduced to 100l stored in the twin-booms.

The new turbojet proposed for this version was a HeS 011 A-0 with 1,300kg static thrust and the rocket engine a HWK 109-509 B-1 with 400kg peak-thrust. The take-off weight was increased by 100kg and the absolute ceiling up to 13,800m due to the increase in power and the modification of the wings. The maximum speed, with turbojet only, was estimated of 830km7h and with both engines of 965km/h.

FOCKE-WULF FLITZER I (1 FEBRUARY 1944) TECHNICAL DATA: Wingspan: 8m. Length: 10.55m. Height: 2.35m. Wing area: 15.5sq.m. Maximum weight: 4,750kg. Maximum speed: 955km/h, flying at 6,000m altitude. Range: 890km. Endurance: 46 minutes. Rate of climb: 18.2 m/sec. Service ceiling: 13,000m. Armament: two fuselage-mounted MG 151/20 rapid-fire cannons with 175 rounds per gun and two wing-mounted MK 108/30 heavy cannons with 60 rounds per gun.

In July 1944 both projects were cancelled in favour of the Ta 183 Jägernotprogramm.

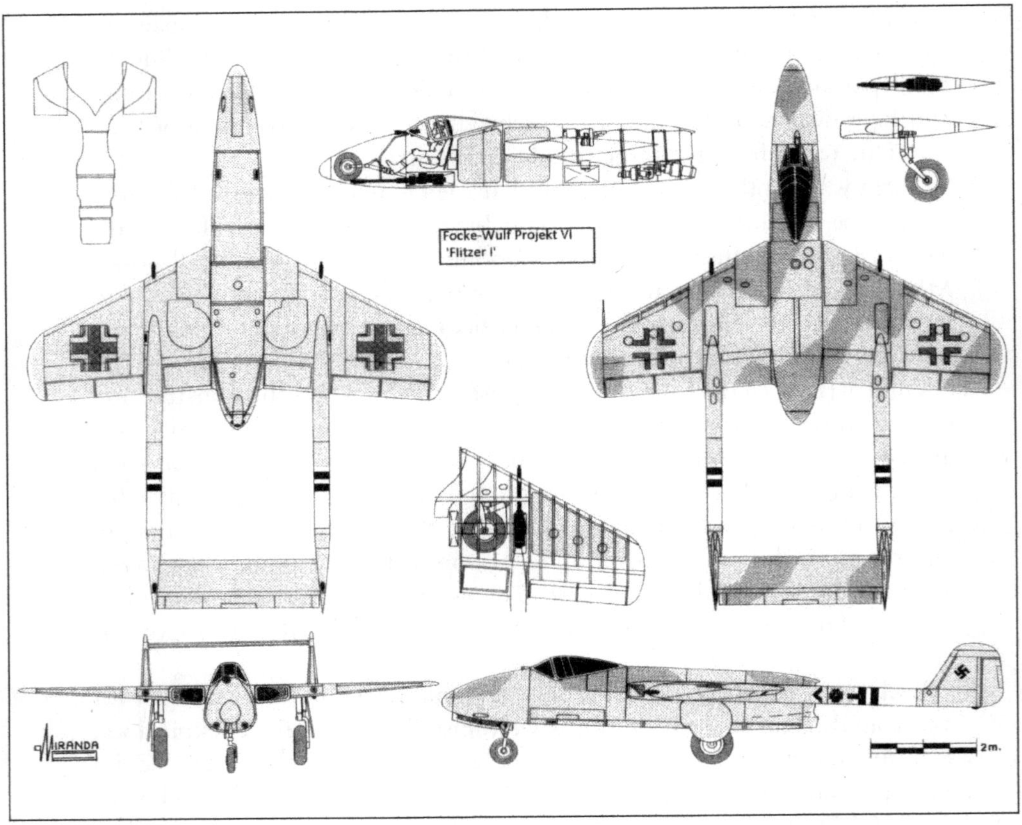

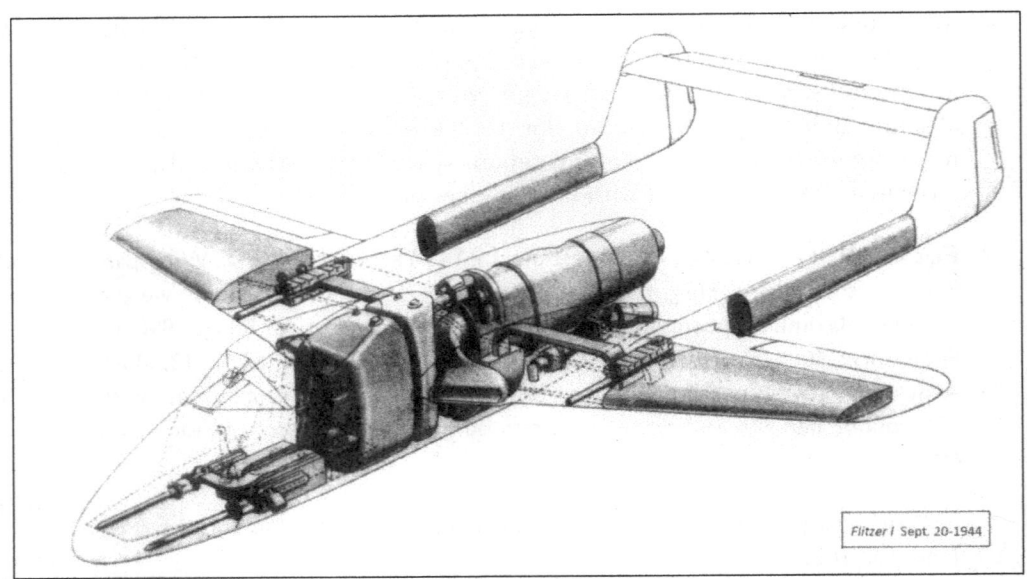

Focke-Wulf Projekt VI
'Flitzer I'
MIRANDA
2m.

Flitzer I Sept. 20-1944

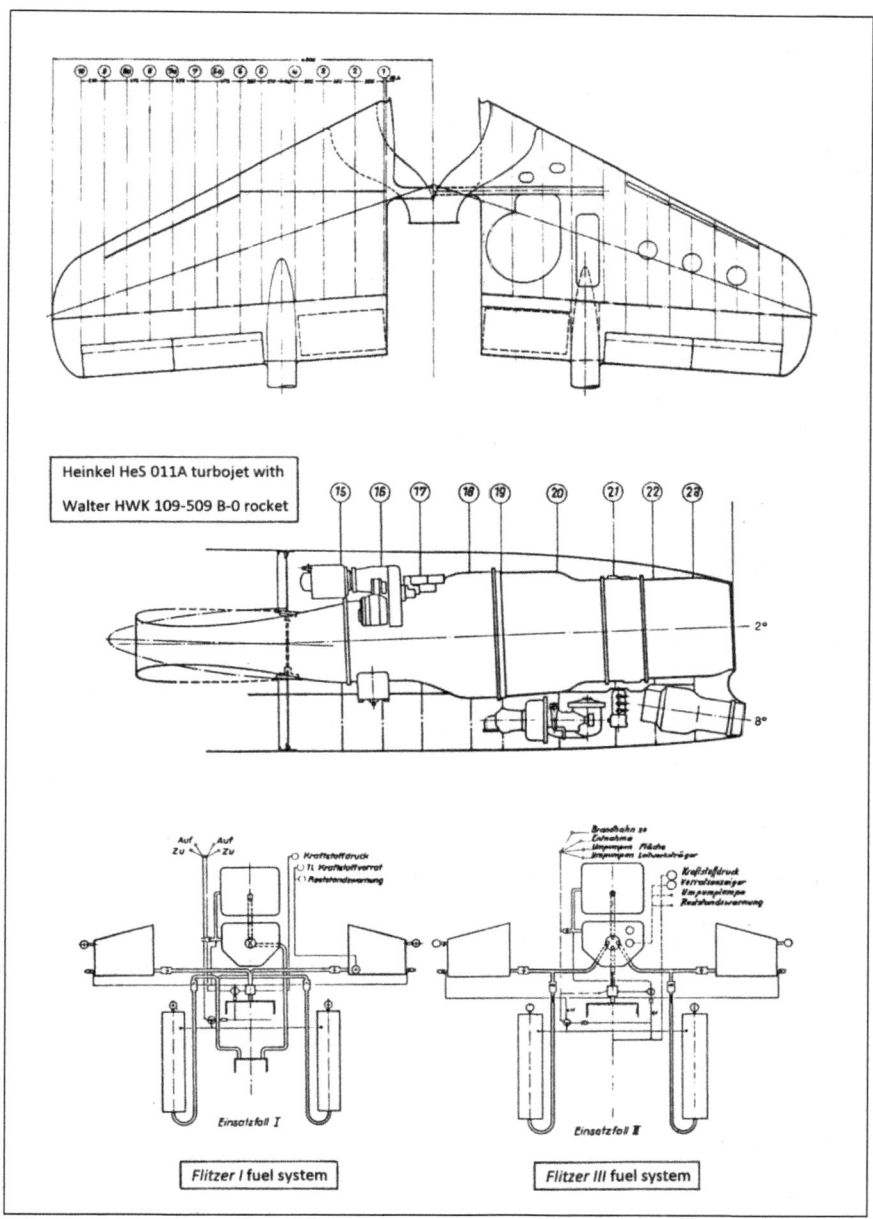

Heinkel He 162.01-42 (12 March 1945)

When details of the new BMW 003R engine were released, Heinkel decided to build a fast target-defence fighter with mixed power plant (TLR Jäger), modifying a He 162 A airframe as He 162 E type.

The rocket propellant increased the take-off weight and the undercarriage had to be strengthened, the fuselage was also lengthened by 15cm to increase the volume of the main tank of S-Stoff. To compensate the extra weight the wing would have to be moved rearwards by 20cm.

In its original configuration, the rocket was installed over the turbojet exhaust nozzle by means of two mounting brackets. BMW chose this structural solution to be able to use a shaft extension as short as possible and avoid the loss of power in the transmission.

This was not a problem for installation in a Messerschmitt Me 262, but the Heinkel designers realised that a similar installation in the He 162 would not be possible, because the rocket combustion chamber would be located 1.33m from the longitudinal axis of the fuselage. This configuration was considered unacceptable because it significantly affected the longitudinal stability of the aircraft.

On 9 February 1945 the Heinkel design team proposed to locate the rocket on the underside of the rear fuselage, an area that had been structurally reinforced for the future installation of a Schmidding RATO booster.

To make this modification it was necessary to design a complex power-transmission system between the turbojet and the rocket pumps gearbox.

The BMW was provided with two gearboxes, one to drive the fuel pumps and the other to drive the electricity generator.

During the design of the He 162.01-42 (12 March 1945) it was decided to connect the rocket to the port gearbox; in order to avoid increasing the complexity of the system it was necessary to install the rocket offset to fuselage port.

Heinkel hoped to start the mass production of the operational version He 162 A-9 in the early summer of 1945, but the project was abandoned on 27 March 1945 over concerns about the volatility of mixed fuel. One prototype would be completed and flight-tested, experimenting problems with electric wiring, pressurised cockpit and the DUCO sealing of the propellant tanks.

HEINKEL HE 162.01-42 TECHNICAL DATA: Wingspan: 7.2m. Length: 9.2m. Height: 2.6m. Wing area: 11.2sq.m. Maximum weight: 3,828kg. Maximum speed: 1,010km/h (Mach 0.82) at sea level and 985km/h flying at 5,000m. Service ceiling: 15,500m. Climb rate: 98 m/sec. Range: 550km. Endurance: 44 minutes flying at 10,000m. Armament: two fuselage-mounted Mk 108/30 cannons. Power plant: one BMW 003 TLR mixed-power engine rated at 800kg static thrust (turbojet) and 1,250kg peak-thrust (rocket). Fuel tanks: two, with 470l of J2 each housed in the wing panels. Propergol tanks: one with 540l of S-Stoff mounted under the turbojet, one with 280l of T-Stoff housed in the central section of the wing and one with 100l of T-Stoff mounted over the rocket. Electronics: FuG ZY and FuG 25a.

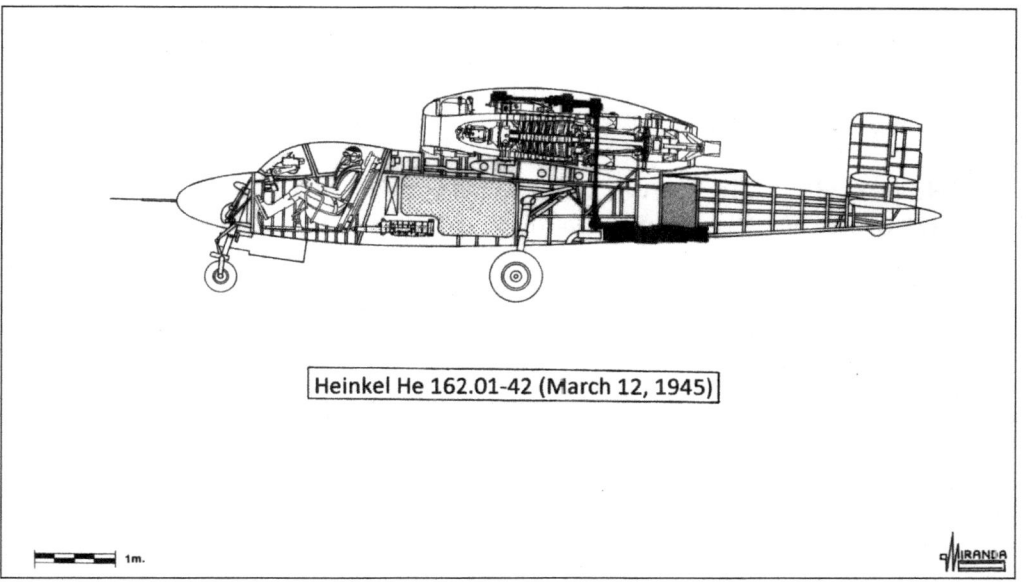

Heinkel He 162.01-42 (March 12, 1945)

Horten Ho XIIIb Überschalljäger

It was designed early in 1945 to cure the main defects of the first generation of German jet-fighters. The Horten could fly 3,500m higher than the Me 262 A without suffering any compressibility problems during combat. It also was 240km/h faster and could use its rocket engine during 5 minutes more than the Me 163 B.

When the propellants were exhausted, the Horten was not rendered defenceless against the enemy fighters like the Komet. It could continue the combat using the turbojet. Its manoeuvrability at high altitude was excellent thanks to its wide wing area, and its performance at low altitude was as good as that of the Komet.

The wing had increased capacity for carrying propellants, which allowed several rocket ignitions during flight providing greater operational flexibility. As target-defence interceptor, it would have been able to hunt the British Mosquito using both engines from take off and climb.

In CAP missions its range was 950km wider than the Me 262 A and could use the high speed of the rocket to reach any enemy aircraft found by ground control. The location of the engines, ahead of the centre of gravity gave stability during supersonic flight, reducing the pilot effort to action the flight controls.

The main disadvantage of the Ho XIIIb was the bad visibility during combat and landing, caused by the cockpit design within the tailfin. It was also very difficult to install the standard frontal armour against the US 12.7mm ammunition.

To face the new B-29 heavy bombers, the MG 213/20 cannons could be easily replaced by the MG 213/30 ones. The structure of the wing leading edge also allowed the installation of R4M rockets within, without diminishing its aerodynamic qualities.

HORTEN HO XIIIB TECHNICAL DATA: Wings: type delta with a 60-degree leading edge and 7 per cent profile thickness. Wood structure and Formholz cladding. Fuselage: welded steel tube framework, metallic cladding. Landing gear: tricycle type, hydraulically retractable. Power plant: one Heinkel HeS 011 R turbojet rated at 1,300kg static thrust coupled with an HWK 109-718 rocket

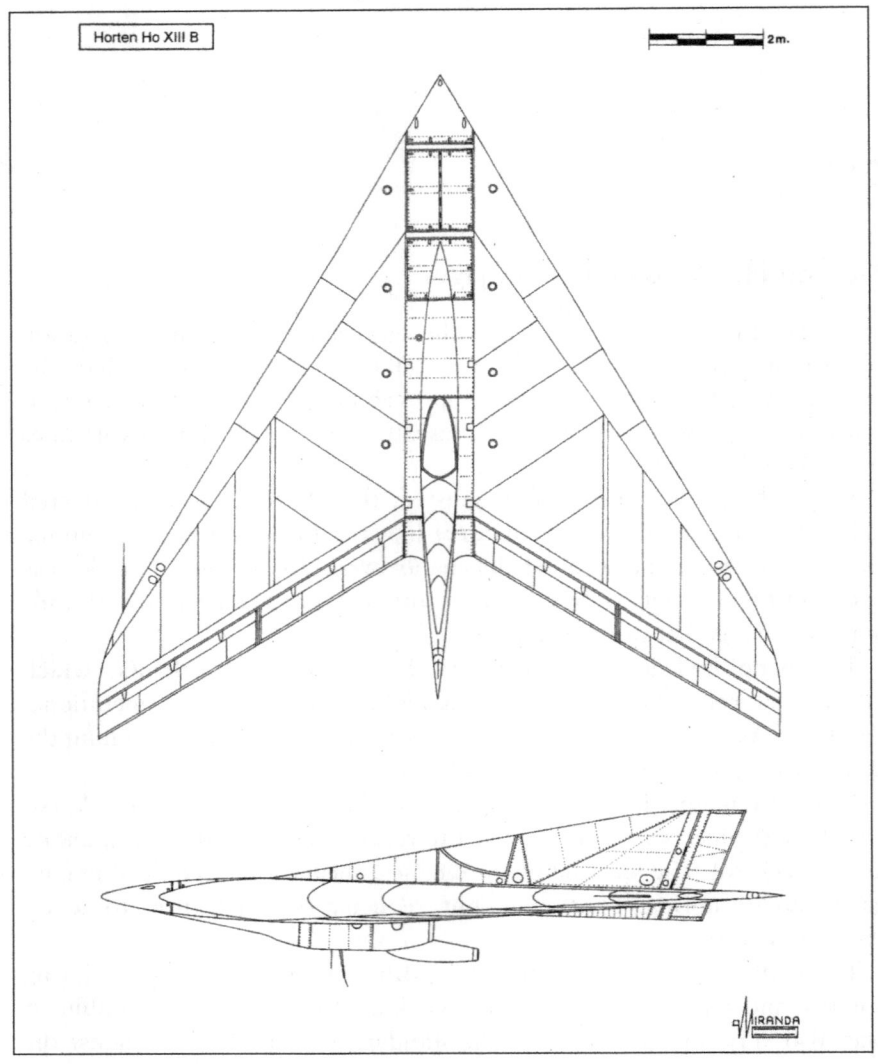

with 1,000kg peak-thrust. Propellant tanks: two 570l tanks of R-Stoff and two 530l tanks of SV-Stoff, mounted in the wing roots. Fuel tanks: two of J2 kerosene with 400l each housed in the wing roots, and two more of 120l in the leading edge. Armament: one MK 108/30 and two MG 213/20 cannons mounted in the nose. Equipment: pressurised cockpit, Heinkel-Kartusche ejector seat, EZ 42 gyroscopic gunsight, FuG 25a Erstling IFF, FuG 24 SE VHF R/T device, FuG 125a Hermine radio-beacon receiver. Wingspan: 12m. Length: 12m. Height: 4.2m. Wing area 53sq.m. Maximum weight: 9,000kg. Maximum speed: 1,200km/h (Mach 1.07) at 6,000m. Service ceiling: 15,000m. Range: 2,000km. Rocket endurance: 13 min.

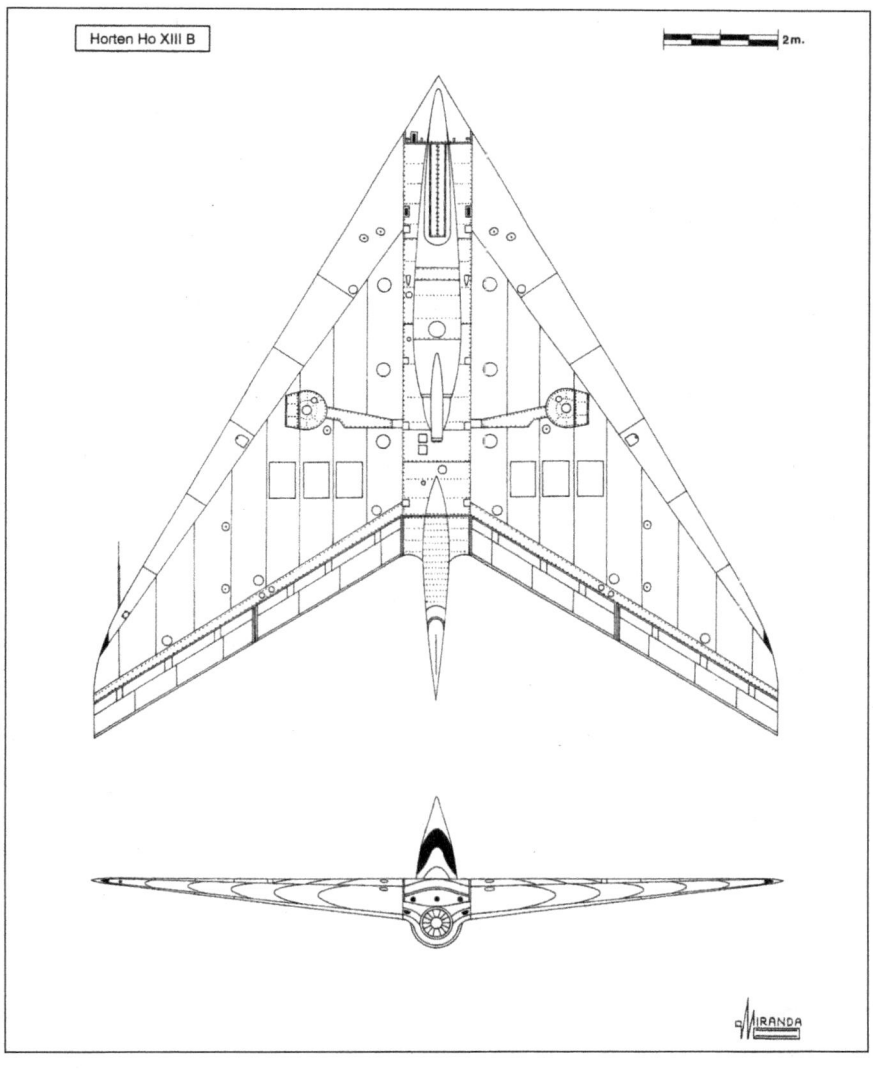

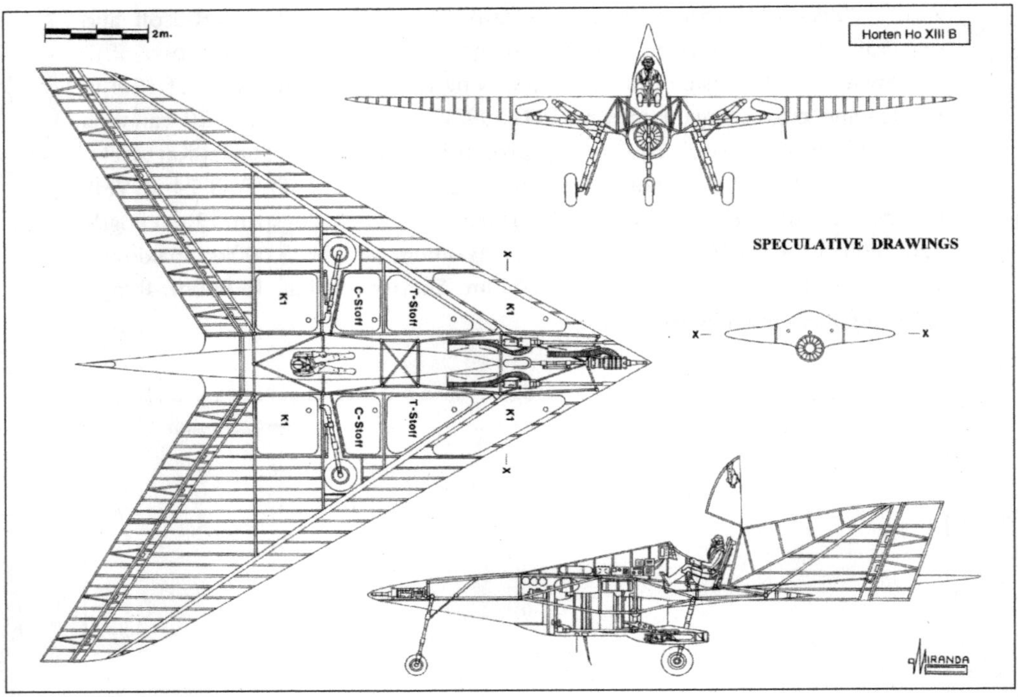

86 Rocket Interceptors: 1941–1947

Horten Ho XIII B

SPECULATIVE DRAWINGS

Horten Ho XIII B

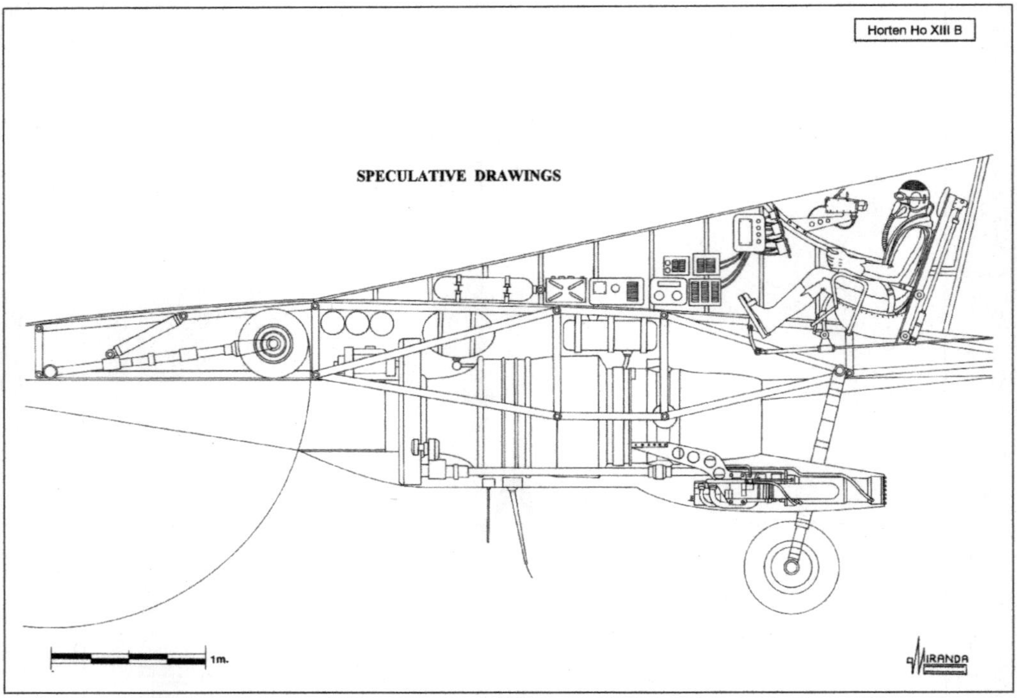

SPECULATIVE DRAWINGS

Gotha P.60 A

On their quest for aerodynamic perfection, the Horten brothers designed the Ho IX interceptor with the mentality of a racer plane. Margins of longitudinal stability and available inner space were sacrificed to achieve a faster plane with a minimum frontal section. However, such a tight design would seriously hamper its potential for further development as a combat aircraft when facing the realities of the industrial production.

This happened when the RLM ordered the Gothaer Waggonfabrik AG the manufacturing of 40 units (under the designation Ho 8-229) in May 1945. When examining the scale drawings of the project the engineers of the company found a series of deficiencies that hindered the development of future more powerful versions of the aircraft.

The Ho 8-229 lacked the required inner space to install new equipment or widen the number of crew members to convert to training or night fighter versions.

The only way to achieve that without creating any protuberances on the wing surface consisted of enlarging the nose. This solution affected the longitudinal stability and overloaded the nose oleo-leg, already in the frontier of its structural resistance. The air intakes operation was also disturbed by the turbulence generated by the new frontal configuration. The Ho 229 V6 found insurmountable difficulties to integrate the new parabolic antennae radars Berlin N-3 and Bremen O.

There was also the structural problem of the central section of the wing. This had been designed to house two BMW 003 A-1 engines with a diameter of 69cm. When it was decided to install the new Jumo 004 B engines with 80cm. of diameter, the limit of the design was reached. It could not be modified again to house the future HeS 011 of 108-cm. For that purpose it would have been necessary to redesign the central section of the wing and perform a new series of aerodynamic tests; there was no time for either.

In January 1945, the design team of the Gothaer Waggonfabrik AG, led by Dr Ing. Hünerjäger proposed the construction of the P.60 to the RLM. It was a project for a high-altitude interceptor that used the same manufacturing methods than the Ho 8-229 but without some of its structural and aerodynamic limitations. The new model could use any type of German turbojet either in service or in project. It was therefore decided to install them in the outer part of the wing in dorsal and ventral position, along the centreline, thus leaving room inside for fuel and equipment.

The pilot canopy was removed to counterbalance the increase of drag produced by the engines. The two members of the crew (in prone position) were located in a pressurised and armoured container in the forward area of the wing central section. It was considered at the time that the prone position allowed the pilot to stand high G values during the combat manoeuvres. A symmetrical profile wing with an increased sweep compared to the one in the Ho 8-229 (58/50 degrees at the leading edge) was also adopted.

To cure stall at landing the leading edge was fitted with hydraulically activated slats. It also had conventional flaps in the ventral side of the wing central section. They were installed with a 15-degree forward sweep and could also act as airbrakes.

There were three types of control surfaces:

Elevators—located in the inner trailing edge and provided with auxiliary trim tabs

Ailerons—located in the outer trailing edge with internally balanced control flaps.

Drag rudders—designed to avoid an excessive physical effort from the pilot during the manoeuvring at high speed. They were installed by pairs in the inner wingtips with an 18-degree slope in relation to the centreline.

They twisted vertically over an axis, like the blades in a pair of scissors, sticking out from above and under the wing surface. The resulting drag delayed a wingtip in relation to the other (remaining in smooth configuration) thus achieving very accurate directional control.

For small corrections of path (for example to aim the guns) only the tips, with a 20-degree slope, jutted out. The 45-degree slope was used for bigger adjustments (for example to neutralise the cross-wing effect when landing) and the 90-degree slope only during the combat manoeuvres. The system defaulted to zero degrees/zero drag when the pilot pressure over the controls stopped. The new distribution of weights made the oleo-leg stands just a 15 per cent out of the total (against the 45 per cent in the Ho 8-229) allowing an asymmetrical position.

The armament was to be of four MK 108 guns for the Höhenjäger (high-altitude interceptor) version, two MK 103 for the Zerstörer (destroyer) version and two MK 108 and two RB 50/18 cameras for the Aufklärer (reconnaissance) version. It has also been planned to increase the ceiling and climb rate of the Höhenjäger with the installation of a bi-fuel HWK 509 B rocket in the space located between the engines. This version would have been denominated Gotha P.60 A/R.

There were many critics during the life of the project for the difficulties of the crew to abandon the machine through the ventral hatch without being sucked in by the air intake of the lower engine. The same problem also existed in case of landing with the undercarriage in a folded position.

The pressurisation of the cockpit made the installation of another hatch in dorsal position difficult and it did not eliminate the risk during bail-out. A solution (also adopted in the Arado E-583) consisted of installing both engines in ventral position and the access hatch in dorsal position. This version was denominated Gotha P.60 A-2. The configuration did not remain because it diminished the rate of roll in combat and further versions were to have ejector seats installed.

GOTHA P.60 A TECHNICAL DATA: Type: two-seat heavy fighter. Phase: project. Wings: wood structure, plywood and Formholz cladding, containing a fuel tank of 1,200l each. Fuselage: formed by the wing central section, welded steel tube framework, plywood and Formholz cladding, including crew, frontal armour

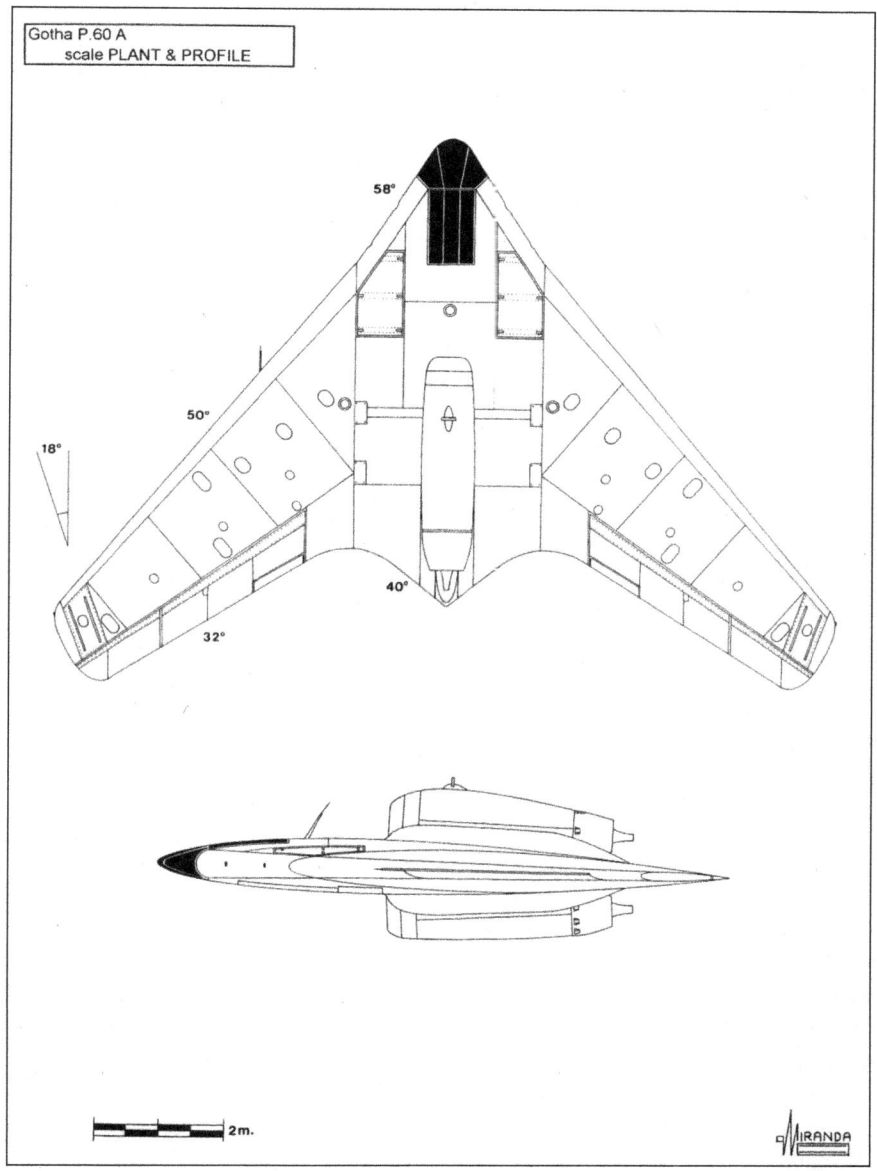

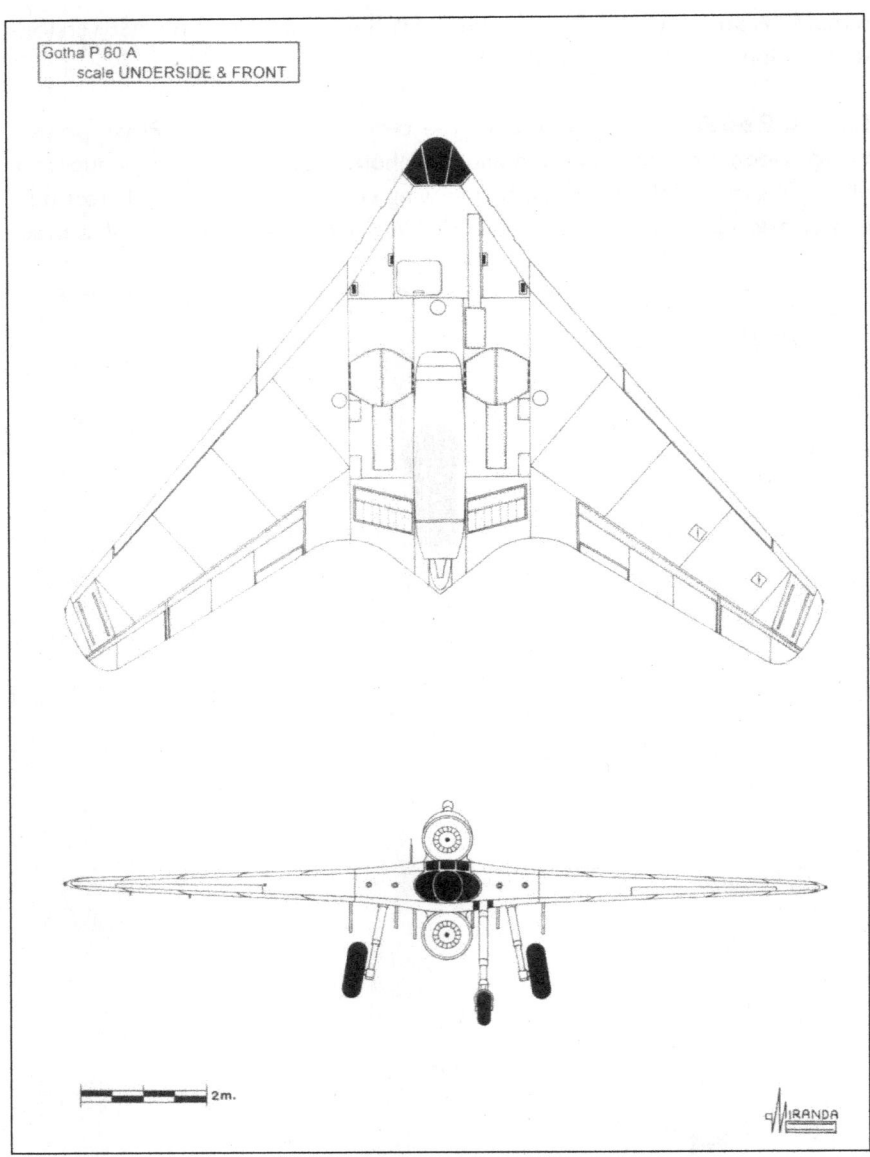

against 12.7mm rounds and rear against 20mm rounds, pressurisation system, electronic equipment, landing gear, a fuel tank of 1,200lt, four cannons and 650 cartridges. Landing gear: the main wheels are stowed flat, with 90 degrees of rotation, in the mid-portion of the centre section. The asymmetric nose oleo-leg was rearwards retractable and housed port of the cockpit. Engines: two BMW 003 A-1 turbojets each rated at 800kg static thrust were mounted to the rear of the centre-section, one above and one below. Fuel tanks: two in the outer wings and one in the centre-section with a total capacity of 3,600l. The

Turbojet/Rocket Mixed Power Plant

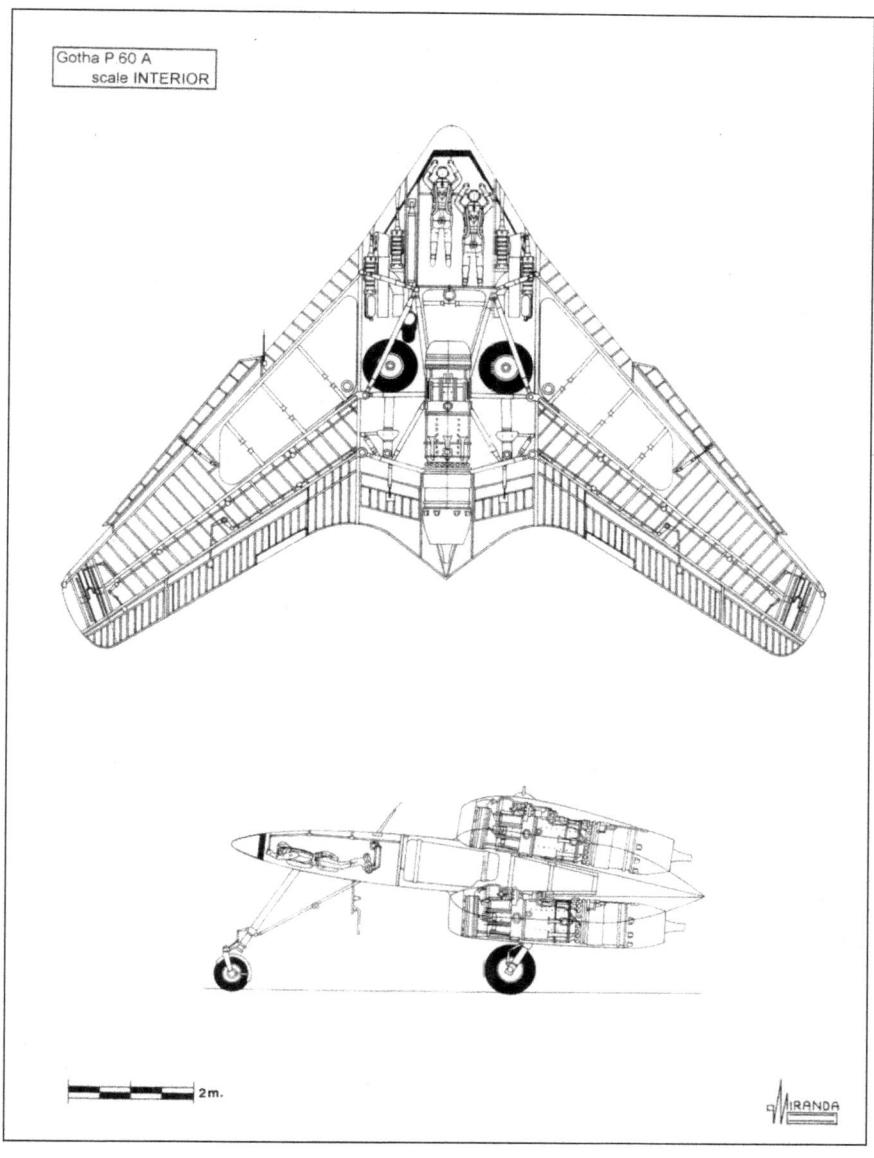

P.60 A/R carried a 620l tank of T-Stoff and a 330l tank of C-Stoff in the central section, enough for 6 minutes of flight. Armament: four Rheinmetall-Borsig MK 108/30 cannons in the wing roots, with 150 rounds per gun (outer) and 175 rounds per gun (inner). The Zerstörer version used two Rheinmetall-Borsig MK 103/30 cannons with 175 rounds per gun. Wingspan: 12.2m. Overall length: 8.82m. Fuselage length: 7.63m. Height: 3.4m. Wing area: 46.8sq.m. Overall area: 110sq.m. Maximum weight: 7,450kg. Maximum speed: 915km/h. Ceiling: 12,500m. nRange: 1,600km.

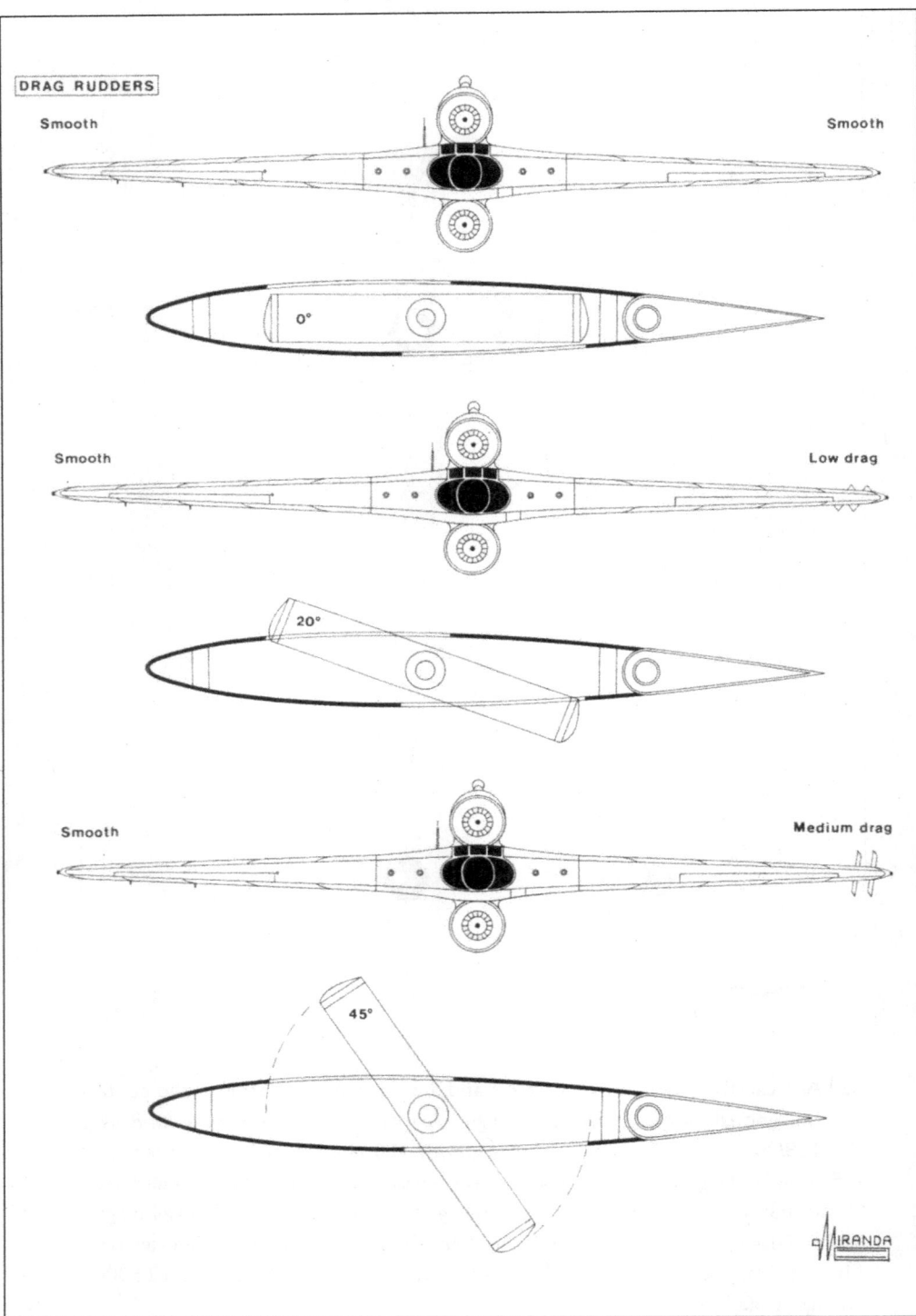

Turbojet/Rocket Mixed Power Plant

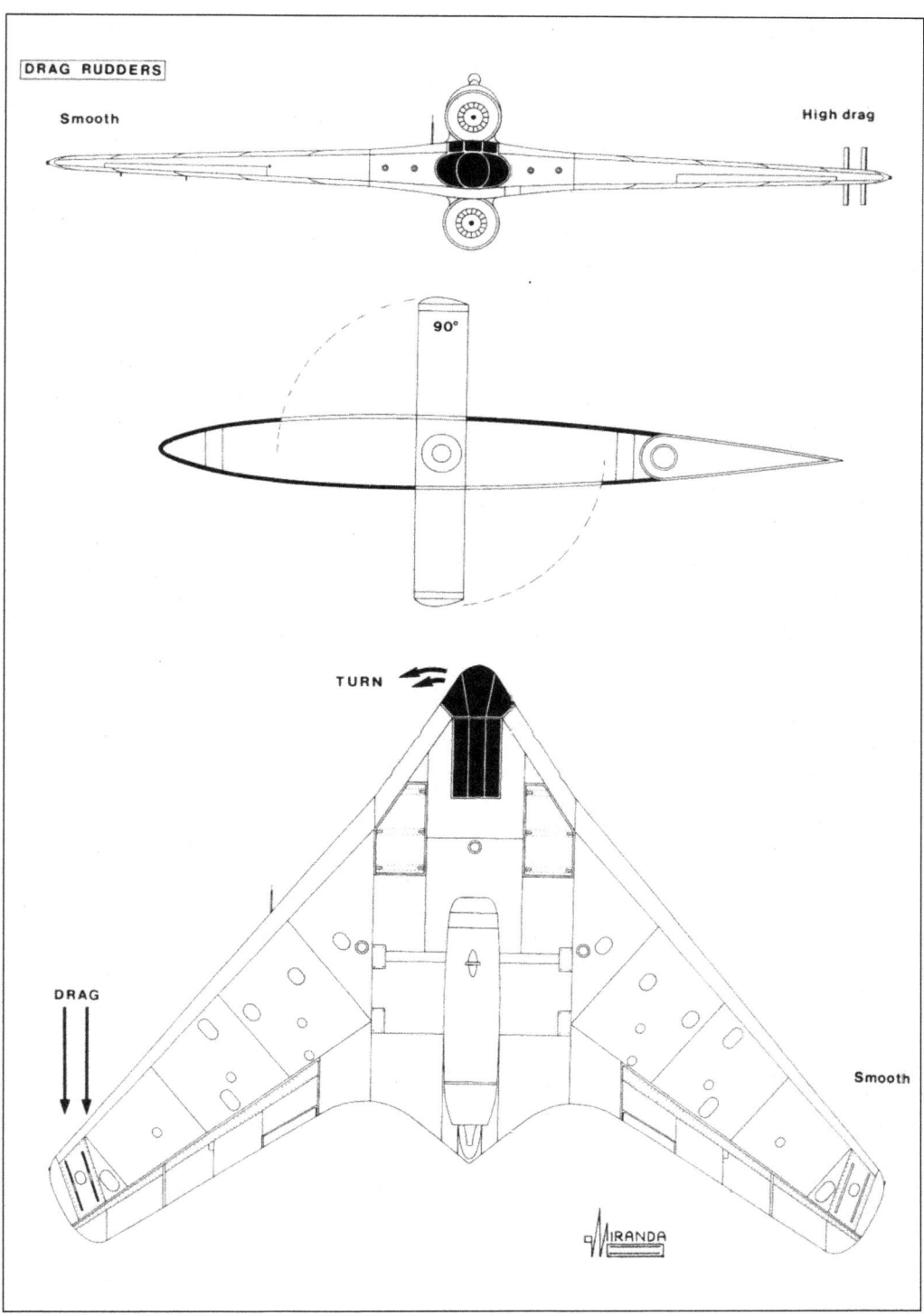

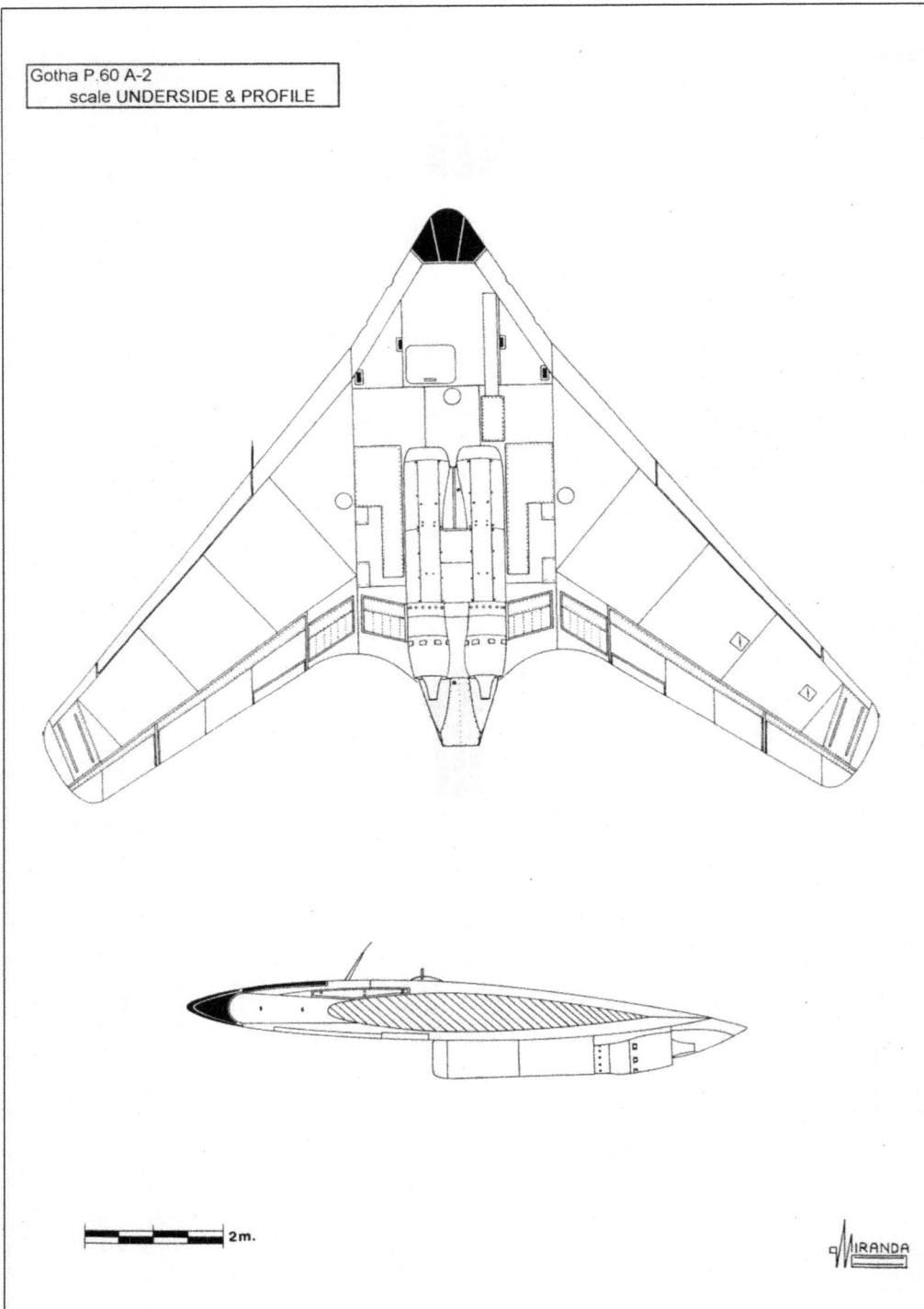

Turbojet/Rocket Mixed Power Plant

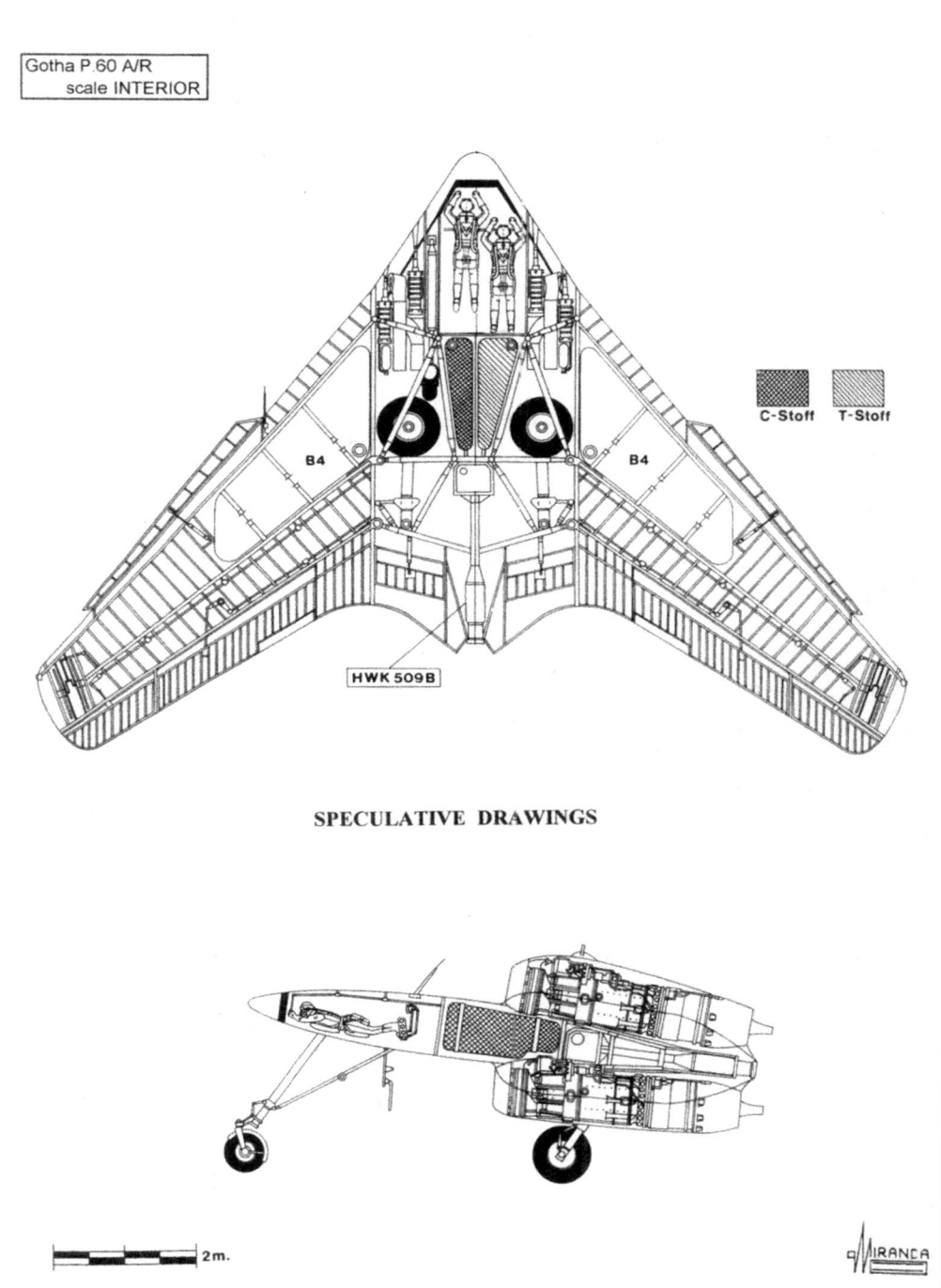

SPECULATIVE DRAWINGS

9
Combat Rocket-Planes

Messerschmitt Me 163 Komet

For many years Alexander Lippisch was one of the most audacious aeronautical designers of the world. Always ahead of his time and seldom understood for his technological innovation, he obtained some official support thanks only to the exceptional circumstances created during the Second World War.

During the 1920s and '30s he methodically followed his dream of building a tailless aircraft that would be stable and safe enough for civil use. His working method consisted of testing the new ideas, first as a flying balsa model, then as a manned glider and finally as a powered aircraft. The results achieved with his sport designs Ente, *Storch* and *Delta* were not very good. They were machines difficult to fly that required seasoned pilots.

Lippisch then began experimenting with a new type of wings in several prototypes of the Delta IV series.

Actually, the Delta IV *c* developed in 1936, with the support of the Deutsche Forschungsanstalt für Segelflug (DFS), was the first Lippisch design to obtain a full certificate of airworthiness as DFS 39.

The prototype was used to demonstrate that tailless planes could fly at higher speeds using low-powered engines.

Dr Lorenz of the Technisches Amt (Research Department of the Air Ministry of the Reich) which was sponsoring the Walter rockets developments, was convinced that the conventional aircrafts were not suitable for the installation of the new power system.

In his opinion, the tailless/swept wing design would be right to reach high speeds.

Being Lippisch the German designer with most experience in this field, Dr Lorenz contacted him to propose the development of a DFS 39 version (able to fly at 500km/h) as technological demonstrator of the Walter HWK RI-203 rocket that promised enormous power for its weight.

The engine used compressed air to force a weak concentration of monopropellant hydrogen peroxide into a reaction chamber, lined with a paste catalyst, which instantly changes it into water and oxygen. The reaction is so violent that the water emerges as superheated steam, able to provide power after accelerating in the *venturi* nozzle.

By the beginning of 1937, the RLM signed a contract with the DFS for the construction of the aircraft, classified as Projekt X under great security measures. Lippisch was only informed on the size, weight and engine thrust, but he was not provided with blueprints. The first tests performed with wind tunnel models, in the AVA Göttingen facilities, proved that the DFS 39 airframe was not fitted either to support the rocket thrust or the flight at high altitude.

To that purpose a completely new aircraft known as Delta IV d was designed. Two different variants were considered: Ausführung I with anhedral wingtips and reduced tailfin and Ausführung II with straight wingtips and a higher tailfin. On 7 July 1938 it was decided to proceed with the development of the Ausführung II as it was more stable at high speed.

To test its performance at low speed, they considered building the DFS 194, a wooden prototype powered by a conventional piston engine with pusher airscrew, as technological demonstrator for the future Messerschmitt Me 163 rocket-fighter.

A wind tunnel model driven by an electric motor was successfully tested at Göttingen facilities in December 1938.

The prototype DFS 40 (Lippisch Delta V), a tailless research aircraft conceived to provide a comparison between the combination of mid-mounted blended-wing and the well-streamlined fuselage used by the DFS 194, flew in 1939.

The prototype crashed in the summer due to a miscalculation in the CG.

DFS 39 TECHNICAL DATA: Wingspan: 10.2m (33.5ft). Length: 5.6m (18.4ft). Height: 2.35m (7.7ft). Wing surface: 13.4sq.m. (144sq.ft). Maximum weight: 600kg. (1,322lb). Maximum speed: 220km/h (137mph). Service ceiling: 6,300m. (20,660ft). Power plant: one Pobjoy R. seven cylinder, air-cooled, radial engine, rated at 75hp.

DFS 40 TECHNICAL DATA: Wingspan: 12m (39.4ft). Length: 5.1m (16.7ft). Height: 2.8m (9.2ft). Power plant: one Argus As 8, four cylinder, air-cooled engine, rated at 100hp.

DFS 194 (FIRST CONFIGURATION) TECHNICAL DATA: Wingspan: 10.4m (34.2ft). Length: 5.8m (19ft). Height: 2.8m (9.2ft).

DELTA IVD (FIRST CONFIGURATION) TECHNICAL DATA: Wingspan: 9.45m (31ft). Length: 5.2m (17ft). Height: 1.54m (5ft).

DELTA IVD (SECOND CONFIGURATION) TECHNICAL DATA: Wingspan: 8.85m (29ft). Length: 5.25m (17.2ft). Height: 2m (6.6ft).

The DFS lacked the technical means to build a metallic fuselage and contacted Heinkel for that, given its experience with the RI-203, but the OKL (worried by the research made by the Soviets on this same field) vetoed any contact between DFS and Heinkel, to avoid potential leaks.

This was to be a problem because Lippisch had just discovered that the highly volatile rocket fuel could react with wood causing fires.

On 1 January 1939, the whole Projekt X team was moved to the Messerschmitt-Augsburg plant where it was integrated as Abteilung L (Lippisch) design team. The DFS 194 fuselage with steel tube and Electron (magnesium) sheet skinning was built there and Projekt X was then renamed Messerschmitt Me 163.

Using the facilities offered by Messerschmitt, it was possible to mount a Walter RI-203 cold rocket engine, with 400kg thrust, in the metallic fuselage. But the power plant assemblies were integrated with the aircraft airframe, only the fuel and compressed air lines being removable. As a result, all static tests had to be carried out in the airframe, and to avoid corrosion, the wooden wings were not installed.

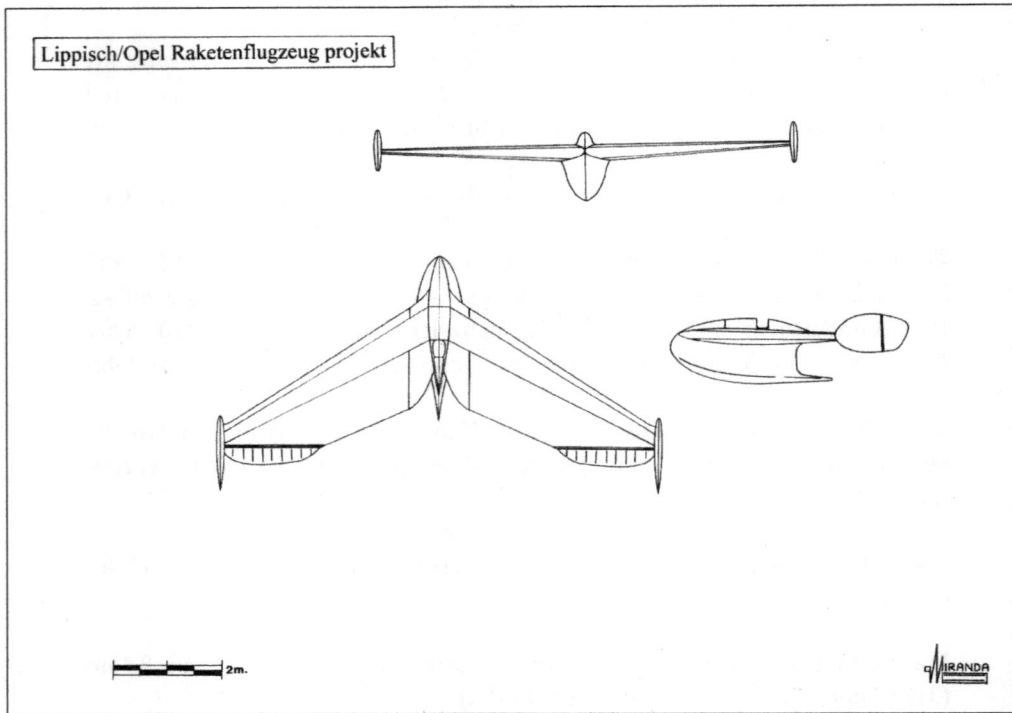

Lippisch/Opel Raketenflugzeug projekt

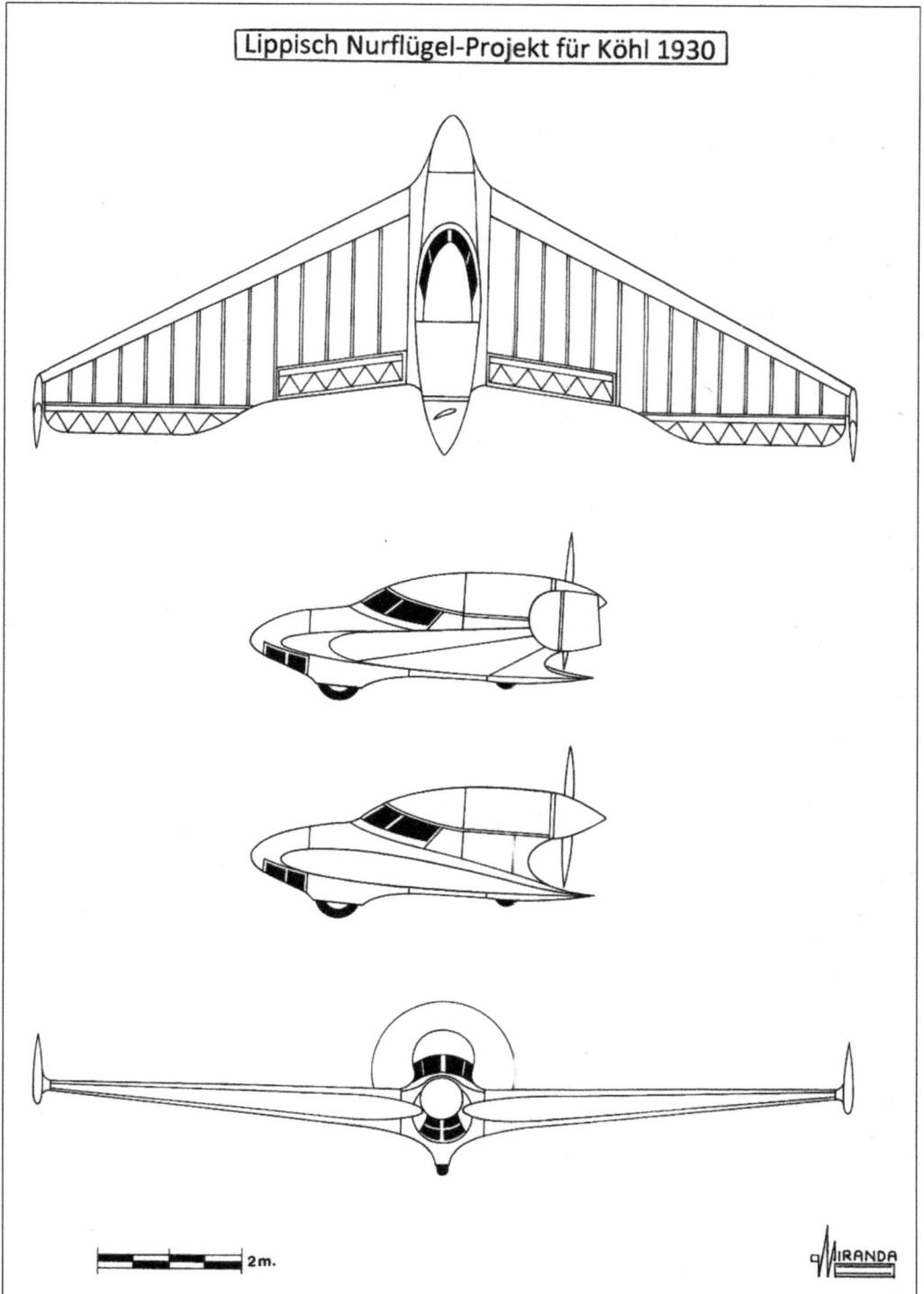

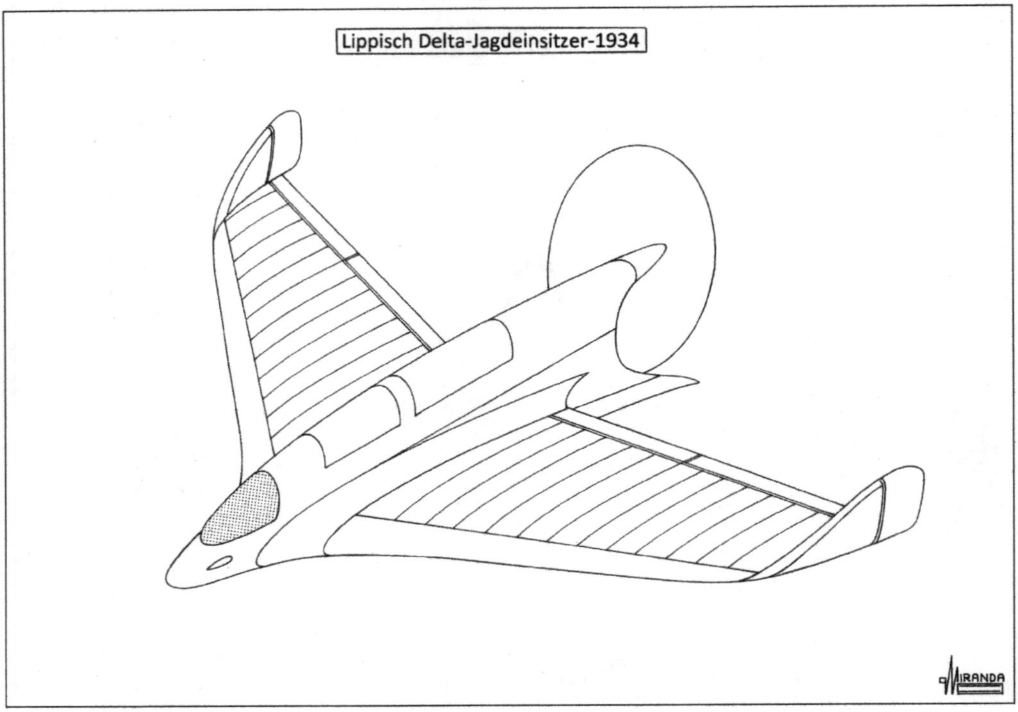
Lippisch Delta-Jagdeinsitzer-1934
MIRANDA

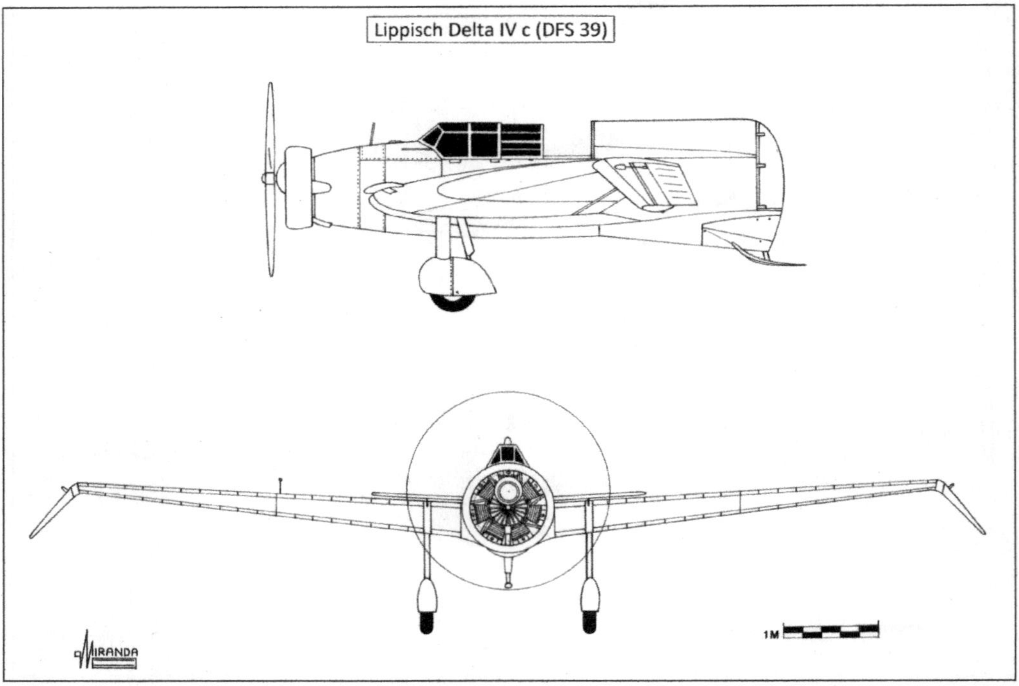
Lippisch Delta IV c (DFS 39)
1M
MIRANDA

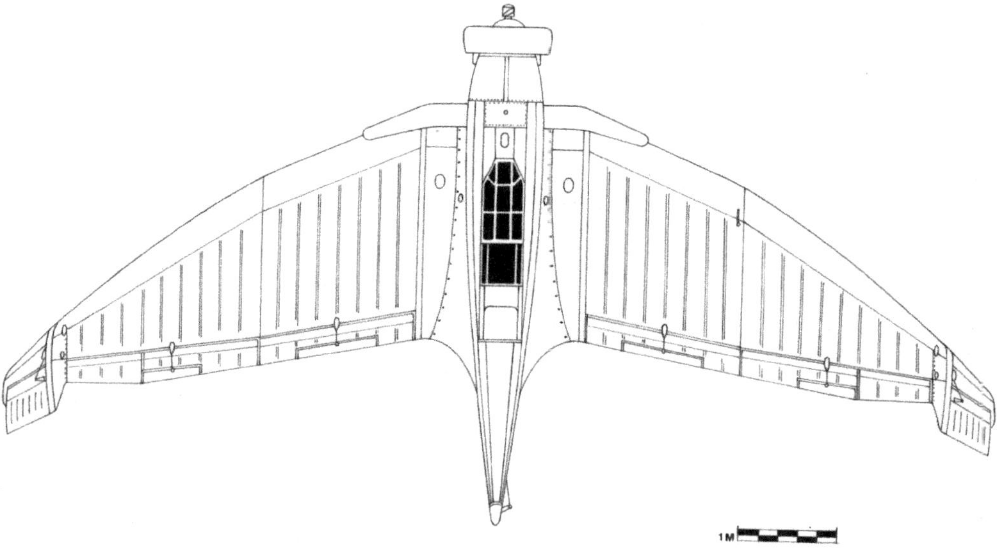

Lippisch Delta IV c (DFS 39)

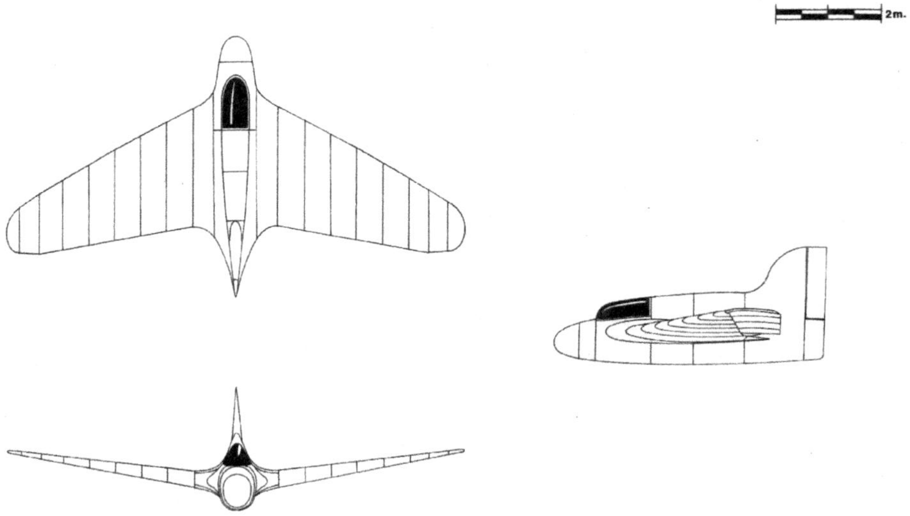

Lippisch Delta IVd - Projekt X (July 7, 1938)

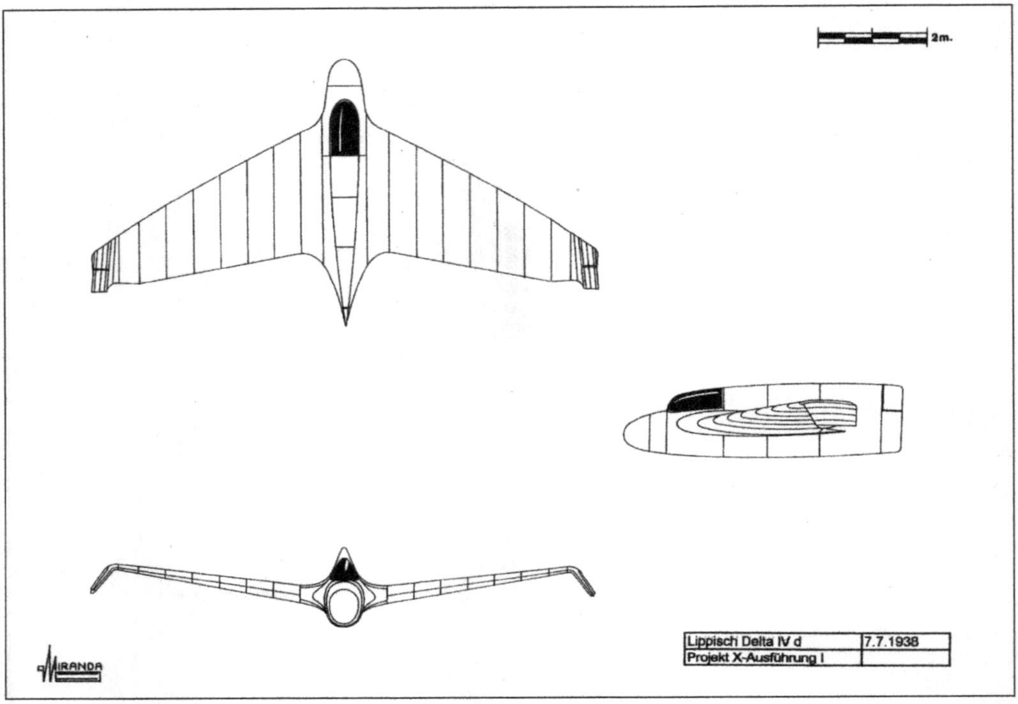
2m.
MIRANDA
Lippisch Delta IV d
7.7.1938
Projekt X-Ausführung I

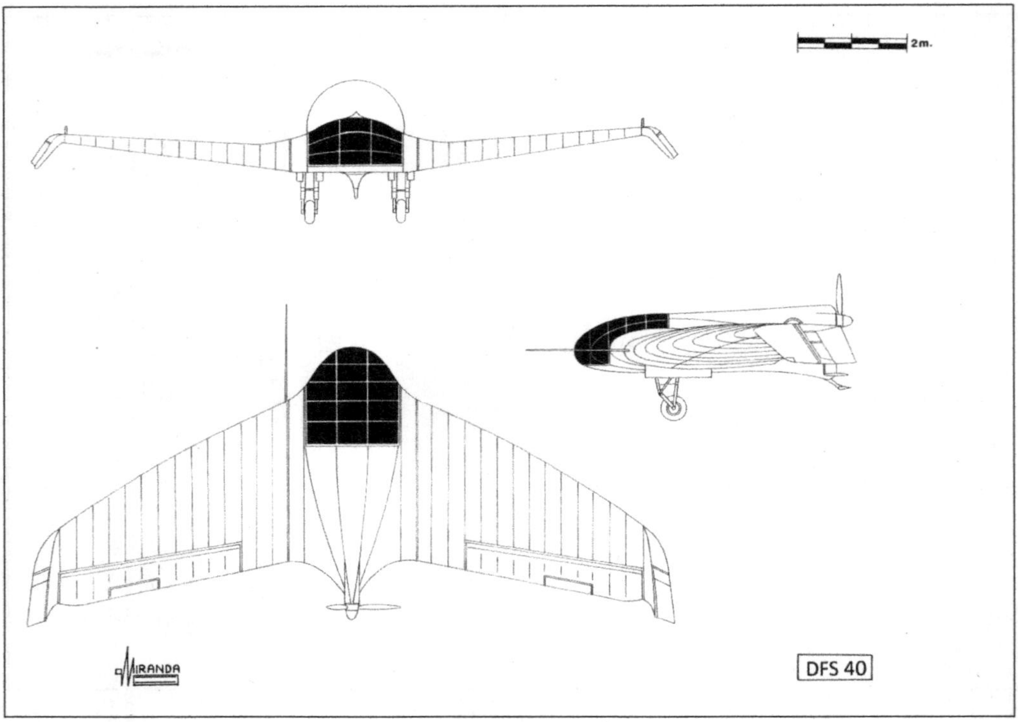
2m.
MIRANDA
DFS 40

Lippisch-DFS 194 technical data: Type: single-seat research rocket-aircraft. Wings: wooden structure, plywood cladding, 20/29 degrees sweep at the leading edge and 7 degrees at the trailing edge. Fuselage: steel tube and magnesium cladding. Undercarriage: detachable twin wheels trolley and landing skid. Power plant: one Walter RI 203 cold rocket engine rated at 400kg static thrust, propellant tanks: in the fuselage, behind the pilot. Wingspan: 34ft (10.40m). Length: 20.9ft (6.40m). Height: 7ft (2.13m). Wing area 200sq.ft (18sq.m). Maximum weight: 4,600lb (2,100kg). Maximum speed: 342 miles (550km/h). Rate of climb: 5,297ft/min. (1,615 m/min).

In August 1940, the DFS 194 made several test flights in Peenemünde-West research centre, reaching 550km/h top speed. After the good results achieved, the construction of the Me 163 A prototype received the highest priority.

Problems of accessibility and low serviceability advised to design the Me 163 A in a way that the rocket was easily removable.

It was conceived as a transitional experimental model, to obtain information applicable to a future fighter version. The Me 163 A had a wooden wing that was 78cm shorter than the one in the DFS 194 and the trailing edge swept increased from 7 to 10 degrees, to improve the pitch

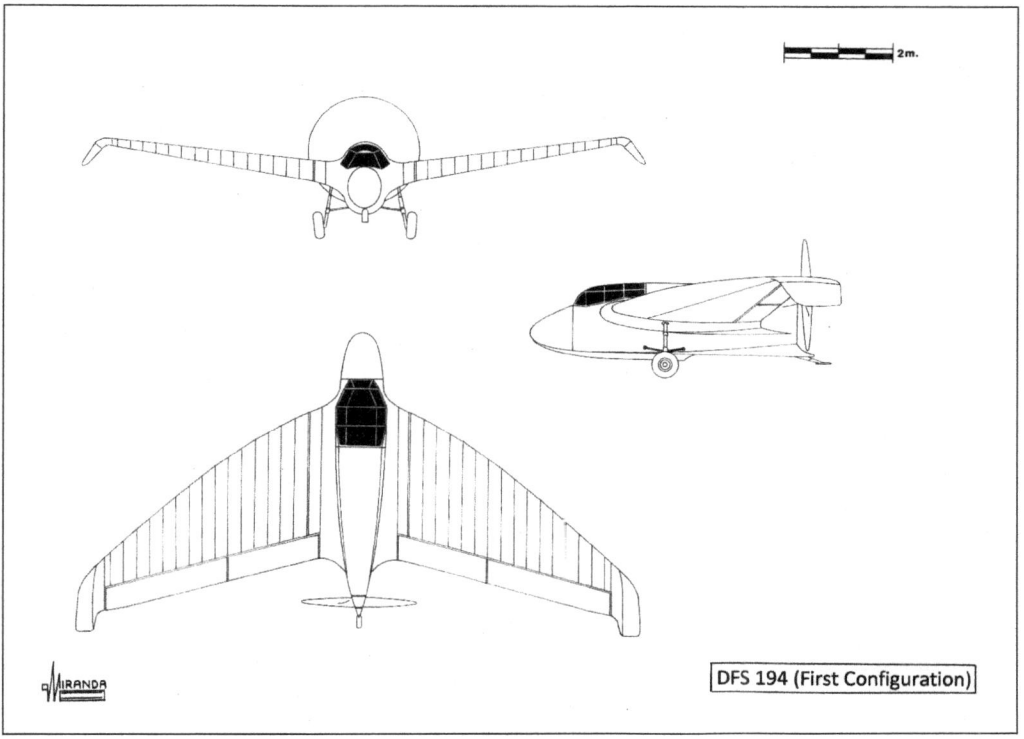

DFS 194 (First Configuration)

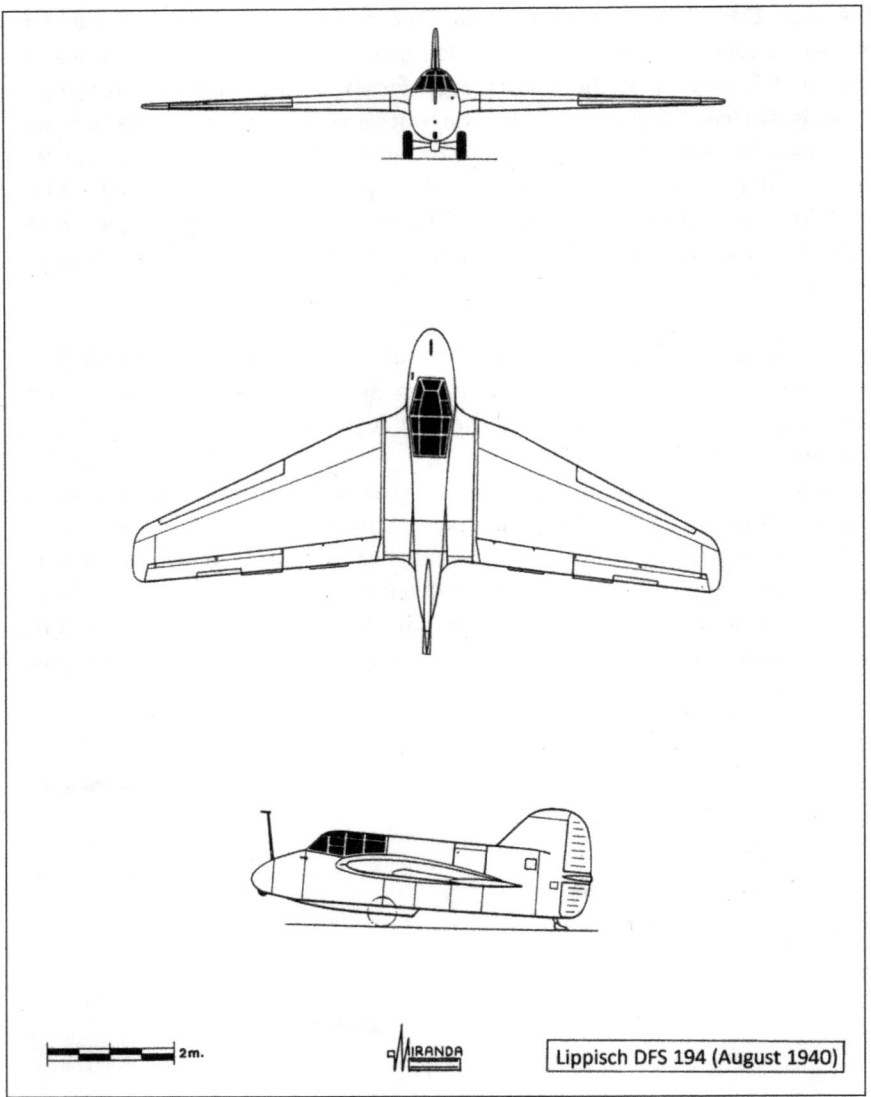

Lippisch DFS 194 (August 1940)

moment of the elevons at 0.8 Mach critical number. Aerodynamically, the aircraft was exceptionally clean; it had a tendency to float in ground effect, which caused some accidents during the first flights.

To improve the landing stalling characteristics two Type C leading-edge slots, designed by J. Hubert, were installed in the 40 per cent span.

The fuselage was modified to facilitate access to the engine, a cold HWK RII-203 with 750kg pneumatic controllable thrust and operational temperature of 500° C. The canopy improved its aerodynamics and the tailfin increased its height by 22cm.

Five prototypes (Werk. Nr. 163000001 to 163000005) were manufactured by Messerschmitt at Augsburg-Haunstetten plant, between January 1941 and June 1942.

The Me 163 A V4 (KE+SW) W.Nr.16300000001 made its first unpowered flight on 13 February 1941, reaching a speed of 850km/h in a dive. On 13 August the V4 flew for the first time powered by a variable-thrust Walter R II-203 b. In a subsequent test (performed in Peenemünde-West airfield at the Usedom Island) it reached 902km/h in level flight.

The aircraft could not accelerate more because the fuel was exhausted.

On 2 October 1941, to find out the limits, the Me 163 A V4 with full load of fuel was towed up to 13,000ft by one Messerschmitt Bf 110 C. After the rocket ignition, the aircraft reached Mach 0.84 before suffering the compressibility effects.

The shock wave caused the air flow over the outer wing to separate suddenly and the aircraft pitched nose down at 11G, plunging into an uncontrollable dive. Shutting the engine, the pilot recovered control, landing normally. It was afterwards ascertained that it had flown at 1,004.5km/h. The record was kept in secret for security reasons and the construction of five additional prototypes Me 163 A-0 fitted with redesigned wing was ordered to serve as trainers of the Me 163 B fighter version.

Drag landing flaps were mounted under the inboard half of the wings. They have the hinge line well forward of the trailing edge, so that the pitching moment was not affected.

MESSERSCHMITT ME 163 A TECHNICAL DATA: Type: single-seat research rocket-aircraft. Wings: wooden structure, plywood cladding, 29/34 degrees sweep at the leading edge and 10 degrees at the trailing edge. Type C slots in the 40 per cent span, landing flaps and elevons (Lippisch patent No. 55811). Fuselage: light alloy structure and cladding. Undercarriage: detachable twin wheels trolley and landing skid. Power plant: one Walter HWK RII 203 b cold rocket engine with pneumatic-controllable thrust, rated at 750kg. Propellant tanks: one of 530l in the fuselage, behind the pilot. Wingspan: 29ft (8.85m). Length: 17.2ft (5.25m). Height: 7ft (2.16m). Aspect ratio: 1:4.4. Wing area: 194sq.ft (17.50sq.m). Maximum weight: 5,198lb (2,400kg). Maximum speed: Mach 0.85. Landing speed: 180km/h. Gliding ratio: 1:20. Powered endurance: 4.5 minutes.

Komet's future pilots had to learn how to perform unpowered precision landings, the training began with 100 flights in Grunau Baby sailplanes of 13.5m wingspan at the Lastensegles Schulen in Rangsdorf-Brandenburg and ended at the Gelnhausen-Frankfurt Segelschule with DFS 108 F53 Habicht (a high aerobatic sailplane with 8m. span) and DFS 108 G53 Stummel Habicht (6m. span) gliders towed by Henschel Hs 126 tugs.

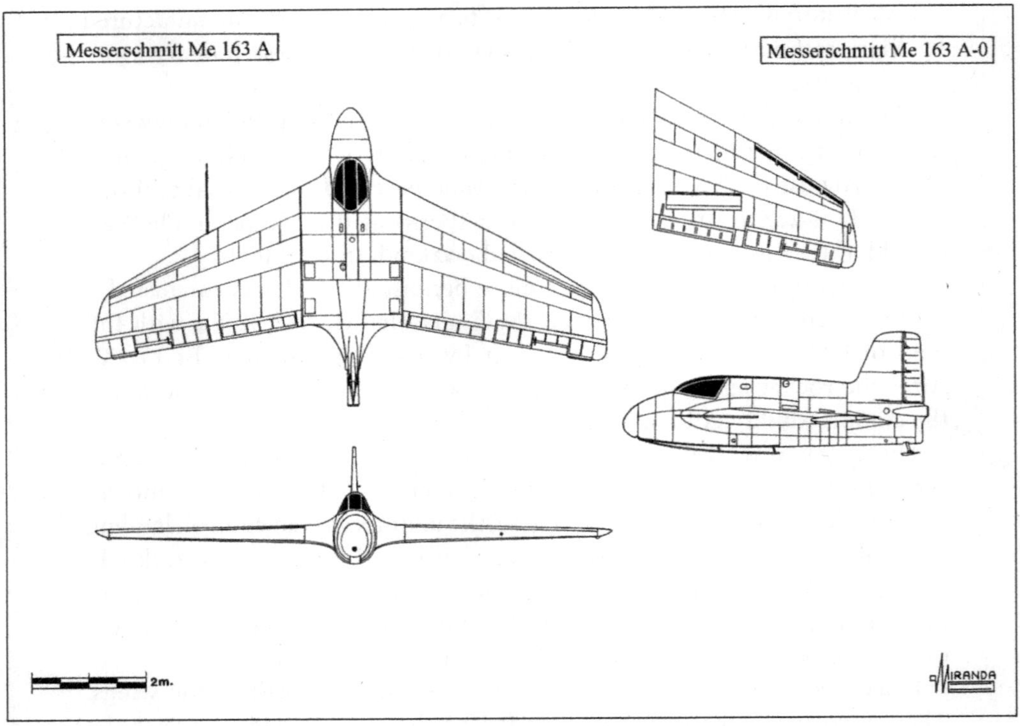
Messerschmitt Me 163 A
Messerschmitt Me 163 A-0
2m.
MIRANDA

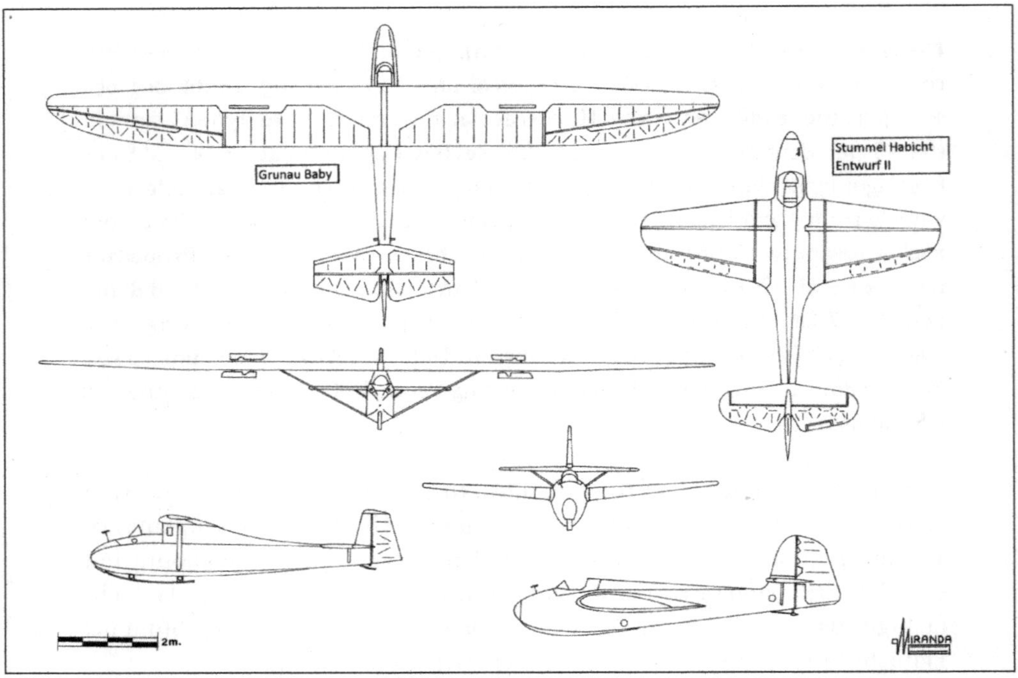
Grunau Baby
Stummel Habicht
Entwurf II
2m.
MIRANDA

The training programme included a number of gliding flights with unpowered Me 163 A-0 and Me 163 B-0 trainers.

Pilots soon grew accustomed to the high gliding ratio and the higher landing speed of the Me 163 A-0 (180km/h) and Me 163 B-0 (230km/h).

They, too, had to be trained in decompression techniques to withstand a change in altitude of 10km in 3 minutes, climbing at an angle of 50 degrees, in an unpressurised cockpit.

For this purpose they trained in a high-altitude chamber under the supervision of Dr Duncker. They also had to undergo a four-week acclimatisation course at the facilities of the Institut für Luftfahrmedicin-München located at an altitude of 3,000m on the Zugspitzplatt, and were fed a special diet.

Training with the Me 163 B-0 Kraftei began with three towed flights (behind a Messerschmitt Bf 110 C-2 tug) in an empty plane. There were then two flights with water ballast, landing at 230km/h.

After completing the full program, a pilot could ascend to 13,500m without pressurisation and descend alive.

Training with Me 163 gliders was carried out at the Erprobungskommando (EK) 16, an experimental unit formed in the Erprobungsstelle Peenemünde West test centre.

EK 16 had the additional task of evaluating several models of jet aircrafts (Messerschmitt Me 163, 262 and 328, Heinkel He 162 and 280) for fighter operations and developing combat tactics for these aircraft.

While testing the Me 163A, the EK 16 reported many shortcomings and malfunction problems that were later solved in the production series of Me 163 B.

The Erprobungskommando also took part in test flying of every Komet delivered from production lines.

Aircraft that were considered combat-ready were towed by Messerschmitt Bf 110 E-2 tugs to interceptor bases.

The five Me 163 A-0 prototypes built by Wolf Hirth at Segelflugzeugbau-Göttingen differed from the Me 163 A in three aspects: in the new shock-absorber devices in the landing skid, and in the improved landing split-flaps and wing-mounted airbrakes in the pilot seat.

The fuselage of the A-0 was 35cm longer and the maximum take-off weight was 2,500kg. The type was used for test purposes and training. Training on the Me 163 A-0 started in the summer of 1943

Following the bombing of Peenemünde during the night of 17–18 August 1943, EK 16 was moved to a new base at Bad Zwischenahn.

An experimental communications detachment was also formed at Bad Zwischenahn with experts in the Würzburg Riese radar to provide course corrections to Komet's pilots, but the detection of the small fighters was difficult because of their stealth characteristics, which were discovered by Oberleutnant Gustav Korff.

To make them easier to locate, the Me 163 B-1 aircraft of the latest production series were equipped with the Y-Verfaren navigation system.

By March 1944, thirty-three pilots were ready for the first powered flight, they were instructed in the use of the acid-resistant and fire-proof Asbestos-Mipolamfibre suit to provide protection from the T-Stoff, the high-speed special parachute and the portable oxygen equip for parachuting from high-altitudes.

The recommended bail out speed was below 450km/h, at a higher speed the air pressure prevented the cockpit hood from opening.

In April 1944 training began with the Me 163 B-0 armed with two MG 151/20 rapid fire cannons. The training comprised three towed take-offs with empty tanks, three more with water ballast, two powered take-offs with half and full-endurance fuel.

On 30 May and 15 August, the Bad Zwischenahn base was bombed, the strength of aircraft was reduced to six and the EK 16 was moved to Brandis to weapon tests.

Between September 1941 and March 1942, Messerschmitt built eleven Me 163 B-0 prototypes at Augsburg-Haunstetten plant, six of them (Werk. Nr. 310045 to 310050) were delivered to EK 16, armed with MG 151/20 guns, between February and April of 1944.

During the summer of 1943 eighteen Me 163 B-0/R1 airframes were manufactured (Werk. Nr. 16310022 to 16310045), these aircrafts were delivered to the EK 16 armed with MK 108/30 heavy cannons.

Seventy Me 163 B-0/R2 airframes were built in Regensburg between September and December 1943.

Late in 1943 production of B-1 and B-2 series was transferred to Klemm Technick Leichtflugzeugbau plant at Stuttgart-Böblingen.

Klemm manufactured 230 airframes of Me 163 B-1s in 1944 and 37 in 1945.

The B-0 series aircraft were powered by a rocket engine HWK 109-509 A-0 rated at 1,500kg static thrust, those of the B-1 series used an HWK 109-509 A-1 with 1,600kg, and those of the B-2 series an HWK 109-509 B-1 with two combustion chambers.

The Komets manufactured by Klemm were equipped with the Y-Verfaren navigation system.

The HWK 109-509 A-0 motor was used only as stop gap measure.

Fourteen Me 163 B-0/R1, twenty-nine Me 163 B-0/R2 and thirty-two Me 163 B-1 machines were delivered to the combat unit JG 400 via EK 16.

The Me 163 B-1 was produced in two versions: Me 163 B-1/R1 and Me 163 B-1/R2. The R2 had wooden wings with modified wingtips manufactured by Junkers.

The Me 163 B-2 was never built due to lack of engines.

In January 1945, the Komet production was stopped in favour of the Bachem Natter.

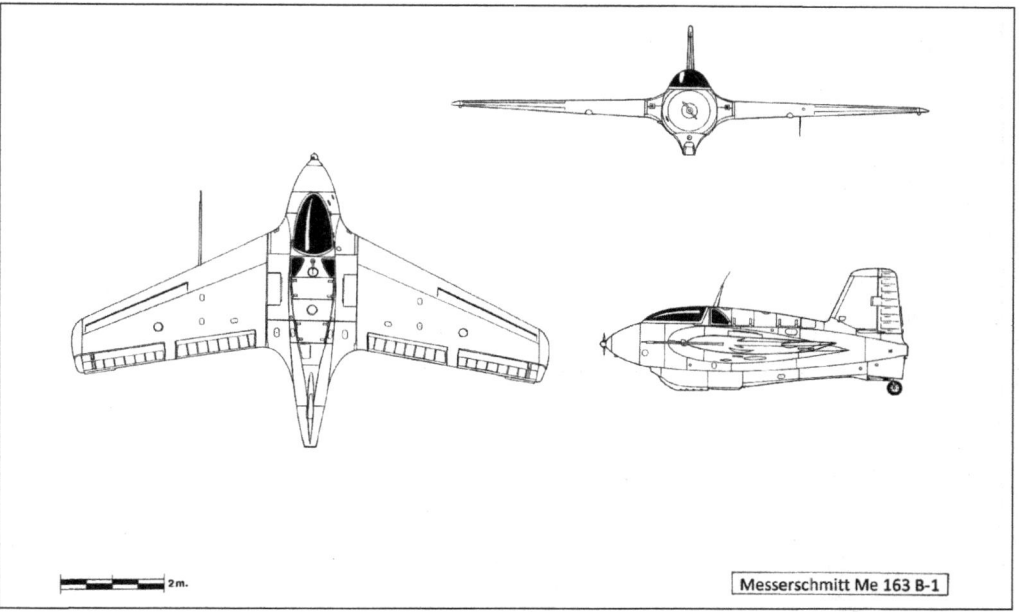

Messerschmitt Me 163 B-1

Compared to the Me 163 A-0, the B-0 series aircraft had a wingspan extended by 45cm and a length extended by 32cm, a new metal skid, tailwheel and a new pilot's seat equipped with a torsion spring Latscher capable of withstanding impacts at 8G.

The optical quality of the cockpit hood had also been improved by reducing the thickness of the Plexiglas from 8 to 6mm and engine problems had been considerably reduced.

The pilot's protection consisted of a 15mm-thick armoured nose cap, a 90mm-thick plate of bullet-proof Plexiglas mounted behind the windshield and 13mm armour plates against 20mm shelling mounted in the cockpit sides and pilot seat.

ME 163 B-0 TECHNICAL DATA: Wings: built in wood/plywood with a 23.3-degree swept angle at quarter-chord and reduced trailing edge, fixed slots, elevons, split flaps and airbrakes, housing four C-Stoff tanks and two guns. Fuselage: built in light alloy and steel housing armoured nose cap, wind generator, cockpit, two ammunition cases, three T-Stoff tanks, the rocket engine and the landing gear. Wingspan: 9.3m. Length: 5.92m. Height: 2.5m. Wing area: 19.6sq.m. Maximum weight: 3,950kg. Maximum weight (B-0/R1): 4,300kg. Maximum speed: 900km/h. Landing speed: 160km/h. Climb rate: 3.45 min to 12,000m. Service ceiling: 15,100m. Power plant: one HWK 109-509A rocket-motor rated at 1,500kg static thrust, throttleable from 150 to 1,700kg maximum. Propellant tanks: one with 463kg of C-Stoff

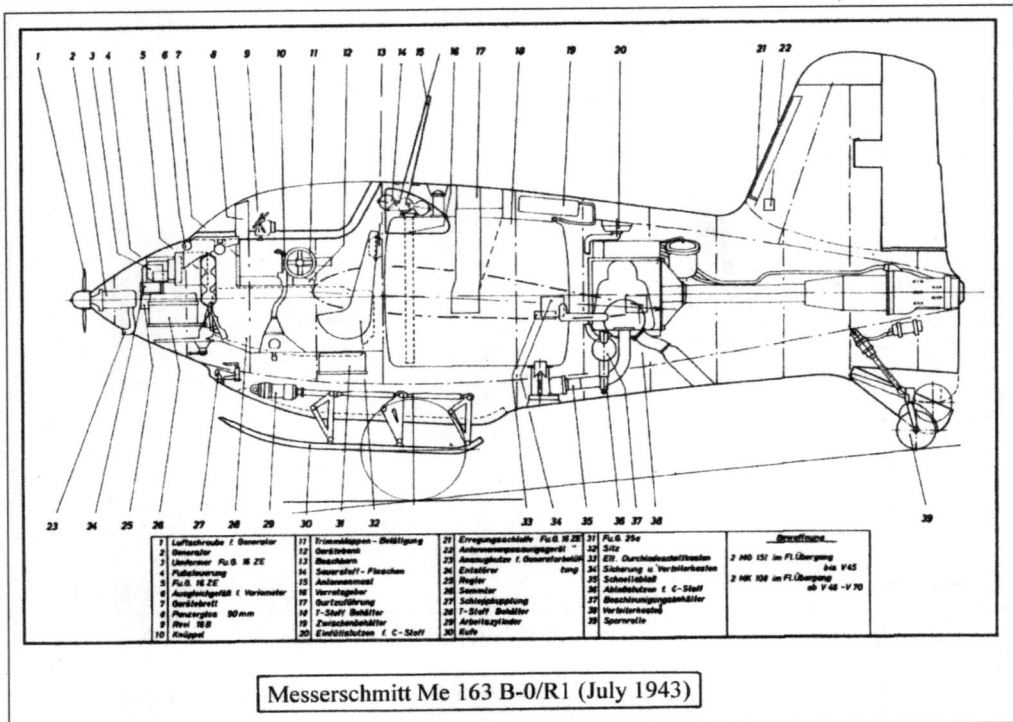

Messerschmitt Me 163 B-0/R1 (July 1943)

and one with 1,550kg of T-Stoff. Armament: two MG 151/20 rapid fire cannons mounted in the wing roots. Armament (B-0/R1): two MK 108/30 heavy cannons mounted in the wing roots with 60 rpg. Electronics: FuG 16 ZE, FuG 25.

Take-off was by means of a two-wheel detachable dolly, landing on retractable wooden skid.

EK 16 used some Me 163 B-0s received in February 1944 to make the first interception attempts.

ME 163 B-1/R1 TECHNICAL DATA: Wings: built in wood/plywood with a 23.3-degree swept angle at quarter-chord and reduced trailing edge, fixed slots, elevons, split flaps and airbrakes, housing four C-Stoff tanks and two guns. Fuselage: built in light alloy and steel, housing an armoured nose cap, wind generator, cockpit, two ammunition cases, three T-Stoff tanks, the rocket engine and the landing gear. Wingspan: 9.3m. Length: 5.92m. Height: 2.76m. Wing area: 19.6sq.m. Maximum weight: 3,600kg. Maximum speed: 900km/h. Landing speed: 160km/h. Climb rate: 3.45 min to 12,000m. Service ceiling: 15,500m. Power plant: One HWK 109-509A-1 rocket-motor rated at 1,600kg static thrust, throttleable from 150 to 1,600kg maximum. Propellant tanks:

one with 500kg of C-Stoff and one with 1,160kg of T-Stoff. Armament: two MK 108/30 heavy cannons mounted in the wing roots with 60 rpg. Electronics: FuG 16 ZY, FuG 25.

ME 163 B-1/R2 TECHNICAL DATA: Wings: built in wood/plywood with a 23.3-degree swept angle at quarter-chord and reduced trailing edge, fixed slots, elevons, split flaps and airbrakes, housing four C-Stoff tanks and two guns. Fuselage: built in light alloy and steel housing armoured nose cap, wind generator, cockpit, two ammunition cases, three T-Stoff tanks, the rocket engine and the landing gear. Wingspan: 9.3m. Length: 5.7m. Height: 2.5m. Wing area: 19.6sq.m. Maximum weight: 3,850kg. Maximum speed: 900km/h. Landing speed: 160km/h. Climb rate: 3.45 min to 12,000m. Service ceiling: 15,500m. Power plant: One HWK 109-509A-1 rocket-motor rated at 1,600kg static thrust, throttleable from 150 to 1,600kg maximum. Propellant tanks: one with 560kg of C-Stoff and one with 1,550kg of T-Stoff. Armament: two MK 108/30 heavy cannons mounted in the wing roots with 60 rpg. Electronics: FuG 16 ZY, FuG 25.

On 23 September 1944, in order to increase the powered endurance of the Me 163 B, testing began with two detachable fuel tanks of 600l each and two RI 503 solid-fuel rockets mounted under the wings, so that they could take off from the smaller airfields without any problems. The behaviour of the machine in the event of a unilateral failure of a starter was investigated. As it turned out, the propellant was unable to compensate for the lateral deflection that occurred. For this reason, the suspension of the RATO rockets was tilted to 21 degrees. However, there was a downside: the flaps could only be adjusted up to 45 degrees.

Using two 1,000kg thrust RATO rockets, the aircraft was able to take off in just 14 seconds and at a distance of 495m. Without the system, the Komet needed almost 900m of runway and almost 20 seconds of taxiing time to take off from the concrete runway.

This modification would have required the redesign of part of the fuel system and, as a result of simpler production, the RATO rockets planned for series production were eventually omitted.

On 13 May 1944 the pre-production machine Werk. Nr. 310050 armed with two MG 151/20 cannons, flew the first combat mission performed by the Komet.

The aircraft took off to intercept a pair of P-47 Thunderbolt fighters that had been detected by the Würzburg Riese of Bad Zwischenahn.

The Komet climbed normally, but its engine flamed out to an altitude 1,000m below the flight altitude of the Americans. Several subsequent attempts also failed.

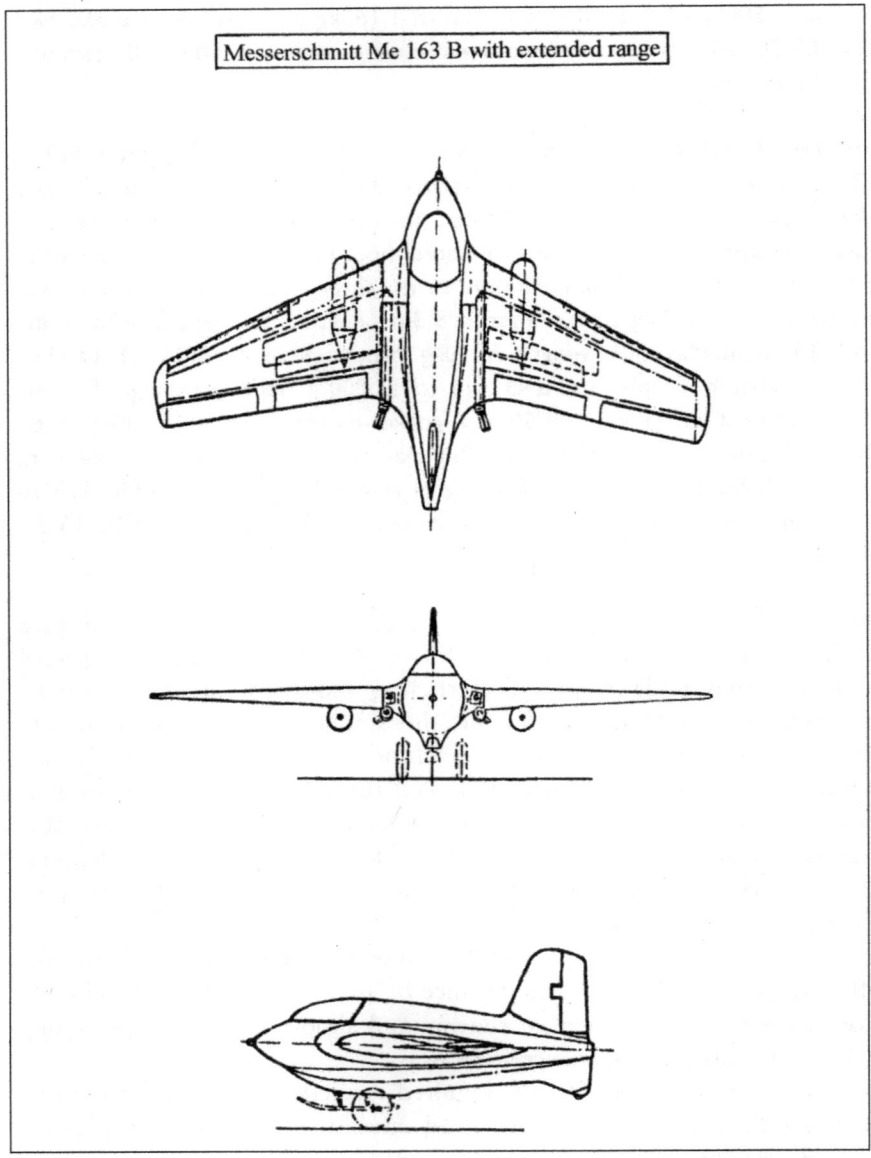

Messerschmitt Me 163 B with extended range

The problem of engine failures was solved by the EK 16 working closely with Walter engineers when it was discovered that the flame out was caused by the negative-G forces that the Komet experienced when resuming horizontal flight after an ascent at an angle of 50 degrees.

The propellants did not behave normally in these conditions causing the fuel control unit to shut down the engine to prevent an explosion.

Other combats failed because of the troublesome armament.

The heavy cannon Rheinmetall-Borsig MK 108/30 Kurzgerät was a weapon capable of destroying a B-17 bomber with only five impacts of 30mm ammunition (360 grams of H.E.).

However, the gun had prematurely entered into service, with a low effective range and high dispersion fire factor.

In a classic 900km/h astern attack, the Komet should start shooting from 450m range of a bomber (flying at 360km/h) reaching up to 200m range before breaking contact to avoid ramming the target.

During the time it took the fighter to cover that distance, it was only possible to fire 34 rounds of Minengeschoss 30x90 RB ammunition.

According to Luftwaffe statistics, it would take 52 rounds to achieve five lethal hits.

In straight flight the Kurzgerät remained jam-free but in combat its 30-round ammunition belts would break under the G-forces.

The Mauser MG 151/20 rapid fire cannon doubled the effective range of the Mk 108 and had a 130 per cent higher rate of fire, but lacked the punch needed to destroy a Viermot, due to the low destructive capacity of its 20mm ammunition.

Further analysis of the films made with gun cameras determined that the optimal firing range with the Kurzgerät was 200m, when the four engines of the bomber appeared to be in the target circle of the Revi 16 gunsight.

The only sure way to destroy a Viermot with the Me 163 was to make a near-suicide pass shooting from less than 100m.

There was a project in 1945 for the MK 108/30A, with a rate of fire of 900rpm but its mass production was left aside in favour of the Mauser MK 213/30 cannon.

Experienced Komet pilots could fly and attack at 800km/h in 45-degree climb.

Using that tactic it was more likely to get a few hits by firing into the bellies of the bombers before breaking through their formation.

This manoeuvre allowed the fighter to make a second attack from above against the last bombers in the 'box'.

Despite all the difficulties, Komet's pilots managed to destroy sixteen enemy aircraft, but the continuity of the project required a solution to the armament problem.

The EK 16 considered two possibilities: use airbrakes to slow the attack speed to that of a Focke-Wulf Fw 190 or develop a new type of weapon.

The Komet's armour was not designed to do the job of a Sturmböck, a single 12.7mm bullet hitting the fuel system would cause the fighter to explode.

The OKL suggested using the new Ruhrstahl-Kramer X4 air-to-air missile, but during flight tests conducted in November 1944, using an

Fw 190 A-8, the cable guidance system was found to be very problematic. The pilot had to keep his eyes on both the target and the missile using two joysticks while controlling the fighter.

The X4 project was cancelled after the raid against the Stargard plant where the BMW 109-584 rocket engines were manufactured.

In October 1944 the Me 163 A Werk. Nr. 163000007 (CD + IO) was fitted with twenty-four R4M Orkan rockets mounted under the wings in two Abschussrosten rail launchers. The ballistic properties of this fin-stabilised air-to-air 55mm rocket were similar to those of the MK 108/30 cannon and could be fired with the help of a standard Revi 16 b gunsight. Results of the tests performed at Udetfeld-Silesia with the III./JG400 were satisfactory, but the R4M early production was awarded to the Me 262 A-1a jet-fighters of the Jagdverband 44.

The success achieved with some heavy night fighters equipped with angled guns in Schräge Musik configuration, favoured the design of new Vertikalbordwaffen weapons capable of being used by single-engine fighters.

The Hasag Sondergerät SG 500 Jagdfaust of 50mm developed by Dr Langweiler to produce a recoil-free weapon by firing a counterweight from the back of the gun.

In the Jagdfaust, the counterweight was the cartridge case, which was also extended upwards to act as the barrel and was held in place by a pair of frangible pins.

Barrel was rifled, for greater stability in flight of the 50mm Minengranate shell that weighted 1kg, out of which 513-grams were H.E. The muzzle velocity was of 400 m/sec, the range of 100m.

Its release was photo-electric by means of either the Zossen selenium cell manufactured by AEG or the Selenzelle manufactured by Auge.

Tests were carried out between August and October of 1944 using the Fw 190 piloted by Lt Gustav Hachtel at the Brandis-Waldpohlenz airfield and in Tarnewitz test centre by the EK 25 Gruppe.

The Fw 190 was fitted with five SG 500s and a sensor in each wing. Barrage balloons were used for testing, achieving 7 hits.

It was planned its installation in the Me 163 B-1 (five on each wing) in the Me 262 (twelve in the nose) and in the Me P.1101 project (eight in the nose).

The SG 500 measured 648mm of length and weighed 8kg ready to fire.

The Jagdeschwader (JG) 400 was the only combat unit to use the Me 163. It consisted of four JagdStaffeln: 1./JG 400 (May 1944), 2./JG 400 (July 1944), 3./JG 400 (August 1944) and 1./JG 400 (October 1944), one replacement Ergänzungsstafel/JG 400 and one towing Staffel with several Messerschmitt Bf 110 E-2 tugs.

The JG 400 was disbanded on 19 April 1945.

In January 1944 the OKL ordered the construction of a ring of fifteen Komet bases in the west, north-west and north of Germany, lying across

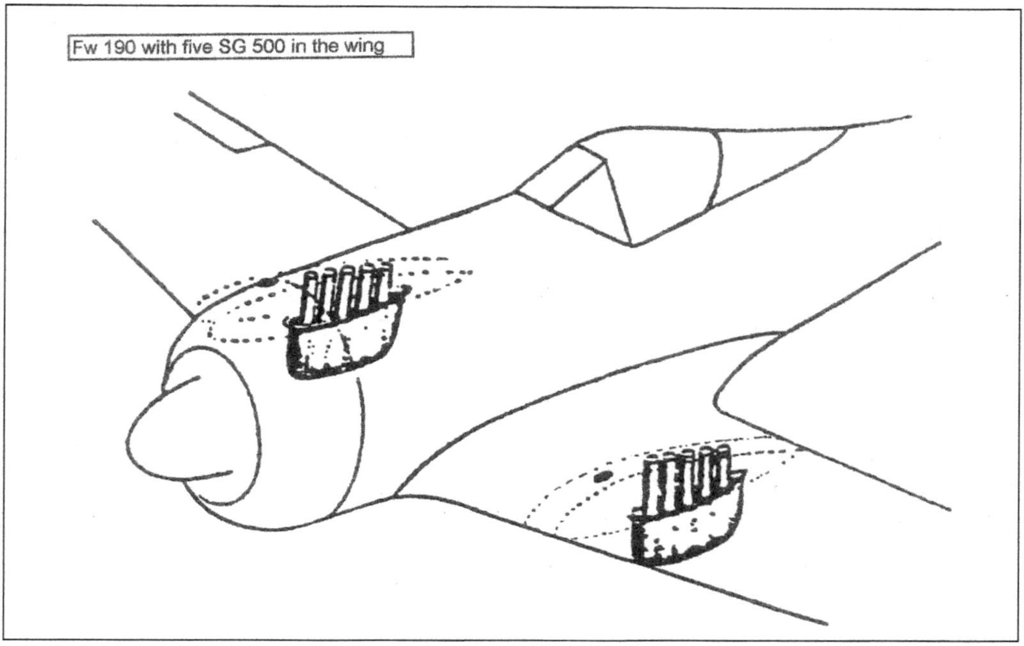

Fw 190 with five SG 500 in the wing

W. K. W
M 12 -4
Aluminium - Führungsrohr
M Geschoß
Zündmittel
Scherstifte
Zündkabel
S G 500

SG 500 Einbau
in Flügel mit Behältern

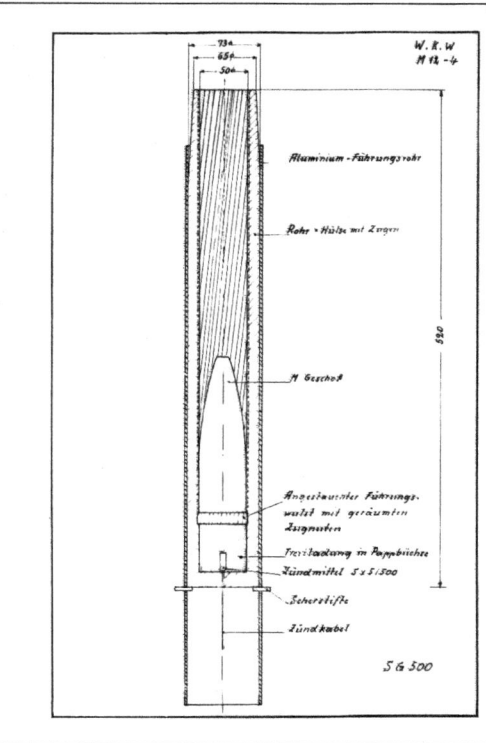

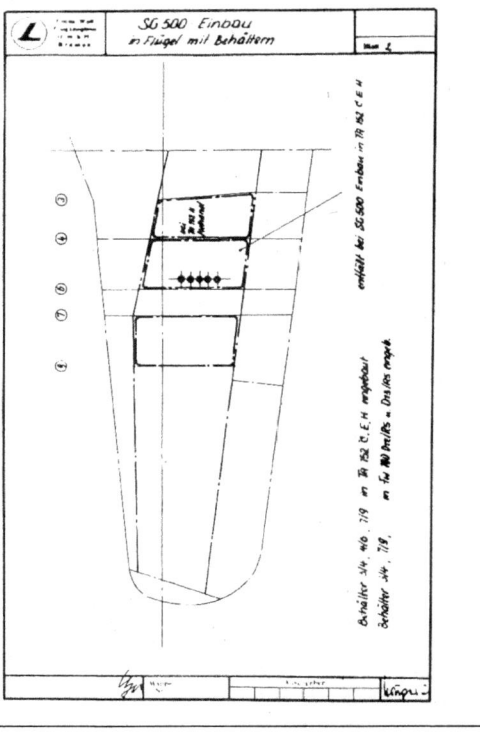

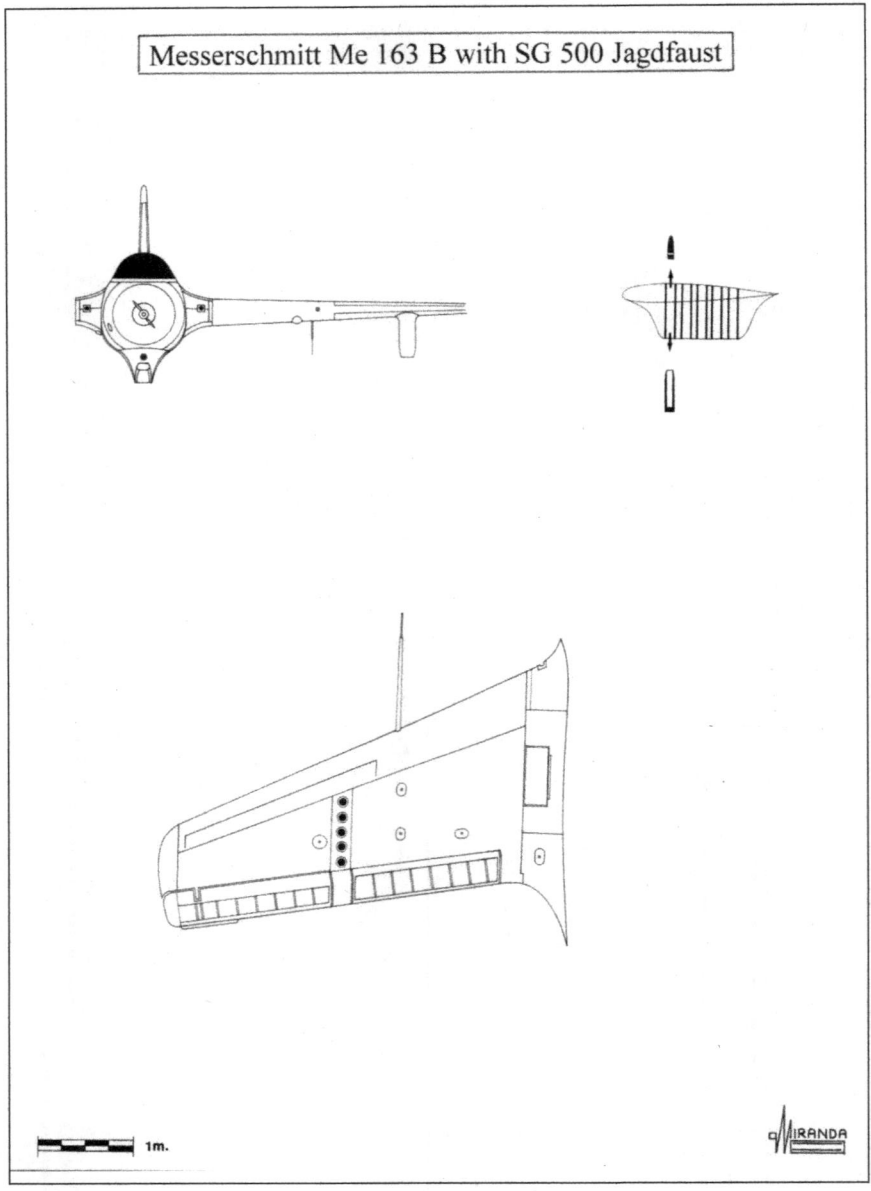

Messerschmitt Me 163 B with SG 500 Jagdfaust

the main Allied bomber routes to the east: Achmer, Bad Zwischenahn, Brandenburg-Briest, Brandis, Deelen, Husum, Kaltenkirchen, Lechfeld, Nordholz, Oranienburg, Parchim, Rechlin, Stargard, Twente and Venlo.

These airfields would be within the Komet gliding range of one another.

Each of these bases was equipped with Würzburg Riese radars, Seeburg control interception centres and other equipment necessary for the rocket-fighters operations: underground propellant-tanks, retrieving vehicles, maintenance hangars and bomb-proof shelters.

In July 1944 two Staffeln of JG 400 were moved to Brandis-Leipzig for the defence of the synthetic fuel plant at Leuna, and two others were based on Stargard-Stetting for the defence of the Pölitz refinery.

The plan was for the new Komet units to be used in the defence of Berlin, the Ruhr and the German Bight.

In April 1944 the US fighter pilots were ordered to pursuit the German interceptors to their bases and attack them while refuelling.

The Fw 190 Sturmböck was a sure prey in dogfight for the Mustangs or Thunderbolts and had to be escorted by high-altitude Messerschmitt Bf 109 G conventional fighters.

But the hit-and-run tactics used by the Komet gave neither the US fighters nor the Bf 109s time to intervene.

Allied pilots preferred to attack the rocket-fighters as they glided out of fuel back to their bases.

The Komet was extremely manoeuvreable in gliding, but due to poor rearward visibility could be surprised by a stern-attack.

At the end of 1944, all the JG400 air bases were within reach of the long-range Mustangs and were regularly strafed after the Kometen were landed.

The Me 163 lacked the capability to taxi after landing and required specialised recovery vehicles Scheuch-Schlepper equipped with hydraulic arms which raised the landed aircraft for towing.

Very few of the 39,807 German aircraft manufactured in 1944 had the opportunity to fight. Paralysed on land for lack of fuel, they were destroyed by air strikes. By 1945 the few survivors were forced to operate from the Autobahnen.

After the Bodenplatte Operation, only 1,300 German aircrafts continued fighting. They were turbojet-propelled machines Arado Ar 234, Messerschmitt Me 262 and Heinkel He 162 and a hundred Messerschmitt Me 163 rocket-fighters that used *sonderkraftstoff* (experimental propellants).

As German fuel reserves declined, the OKL cancelled a large number of aircraft projects; first the heavy bombers, then the piston fighters and finally the turbojet-powered aircraft that required long runways. They also eliminated the rocket-fighters with landing skids when the experience gained with the Messerschmitt Me 163 proved that their low mobility on the ground made them extremely vulnerable to strafing attacks.

10

Chasing the Mach One—German Supersonic Projects

Aircraft of that era were subsonic, despite the excess power available with rocket engines.

After suffering twenty deathly accidents following dives between April and May 1942, the Messerschmitt Bf 109 G-2 fighter dive speed was fixed at 850km/h, before the appearance of the first compressibility shockwaves. At Mach 0.86 the Messerschmitt Me 262 went out of control in a dive that the pilot could not offset. During flight tests of the Me 262 C-1a Heimatschützer I, it turned out that the excess of power provided by the Walter rocket should be counterbalanced by flying with the nose slightly upwards, thus avoiding the aircraft reaching the critical Mach figure.

The compressibility was an odd aerodynamic phenomenon, usually referred to as 'compressibility buffeting'. Affecting different types of aircraft diving between 25,000ft and 18,000ft at different speeds, it manifested itself in different ways—sometimes causing catastrophic structural failures.

The cause of all this was the physical phenomenon known by aerodynamicists as 'Coanda effect', which states that any fluid running above a curved surface tends to adhere to it and increase its speed proportionally to its curvature.

The theoretical studies about compressibility were completed in Germany by 1941 and there were five different rocket programs of supersonic aircrafts running by the end of the war.

On 3 October 1942 one V-2 German rocket achieved a maximum speed of 2,998mph, proving that it was not just bullets that could withstand the pressure of supersonic flight; however, when the A4b prototype disintegrated at 2,684mph on 24 January 1945, some scientists doubted that winged aircraft could exceed the speed of sound.

Messerschmitt P.1106 R

The P.1106 project aimed to find aerodynamic solutions that would delay the appearance of compressibility shock waves in the P.1101 airframe.

The experiments conducted with the Me 262 Werk. Nr.130015 in November 1944 showed that the internal drag in air ducts reduced the turbojet thrust by 45 kg for each metre in length. In the P.1106 the turbojet was put forward more than 2m and the '8' shaped fuselage section was changed by an elliptical one. The new wing had a reduced wingspan with the chord increased until an aspect ratio of 1/3.5 against the 1/5 of the P.1101 was achieved.

The first shockwave was avoided using a new cockpit installed within the tailfin (2, 12 and 14 December 1944 configurations) but this original cockpit hood was not useful for a combat fighter, given that it created optical distortions and did not leave any space to install either the EZ 42 gunsight or the armoured windshield.

To solve the problem of the second shockwave it was proposed the adoption of a 'T-tail' plane that prevented their interaction with the turbulence generated by the wing but the wind tunnel tests proved that the 'T-tail' plane produced too much drag, this led to a design with a 50-degree-widening 'V-tail' unit.

In January 1945 the Messerschmitt design team proposed replacing the HeS 011 A-0 turbojet of the P.1106 project fighter with a Walter 109-509 S2 rocket with 1,993 kg static thrust, to investigate the behaviour of the airframe to Mach 1, but the P.1106 R project was dismissed because of the excessive cost of the modification.

The 'V-tail' configuration reduced the maximum speed by 100 km/h, as there appeared to be no improvement over the P.1101 performance, the P.1106 was abandoned in February 1945.

MESSERSCHMITT P.1106 (14 DECEMBER 1944) TECHNICAL DATA: Power plant: one Heinkel HeS 011 A turbojet with 1,115 kg static thrust. Wingspan: 24.3ft (7.37m). Length: 28.3ft (8.65m). Height: 10.3ft (3.15m). Wing area: 145sq.ft (13sq.m). Estimated maximum speed: Mach 0.968 at 7,000m, 677mph (1,090km/h). Maximum weight: 8,740lb (3,958kg). Estimated ceiling: 45,920ft (14,000m).

MESSERSCHMITT P.1106 (12 JANUARY 1945) TECHNICAL DATA: Power plant: one Heinkel HeS 011 A-0 turbojet with 1,300kg static thrust. Wingspan: 21.8 f.t (6.65m). Length: 30ft (9.19m). Height: 11ft (3.37m). Wing area: 146sq.ft (13.17sq.m). Estimated maximum speed: Mach 0.882 at 7,000m, 617mph (993km/h). Maximum weight: 8,830lb (4,000kg). Estimated ceiling: 43,624ft (13,300m).

MESSERSCHMITT P.1106 R TECHNICAL DATA: Wingspan: 6.74m. Length: 8.42m. Height: 3.05m. Wing area: 13sq.m. Maximum take-off weight: 4,000kg. Estimated maximum speed: Mach 1.

MIRANDA
Messerschmitt P 1106 (January 12, 1945)
2m.

MIRANDA
2m.
Messerschmitt P 1106 (December 14, 1944)

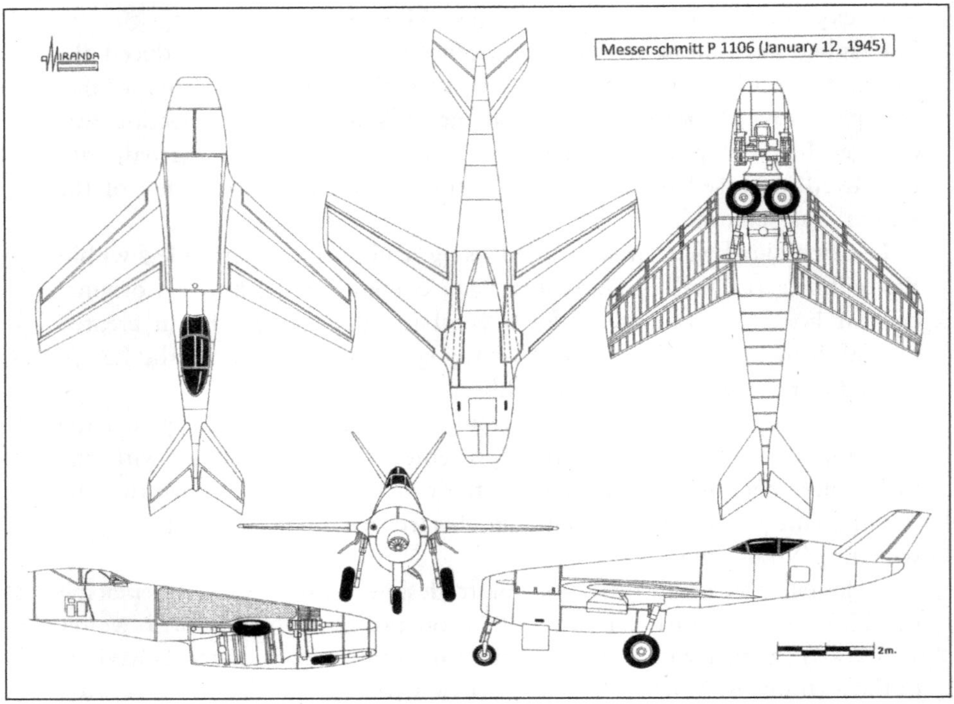

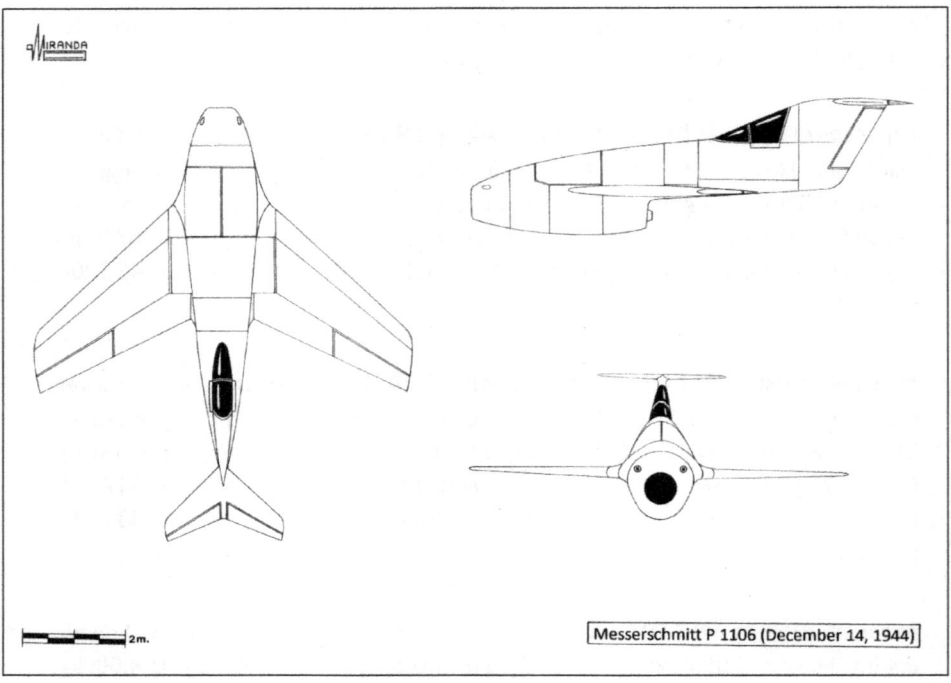

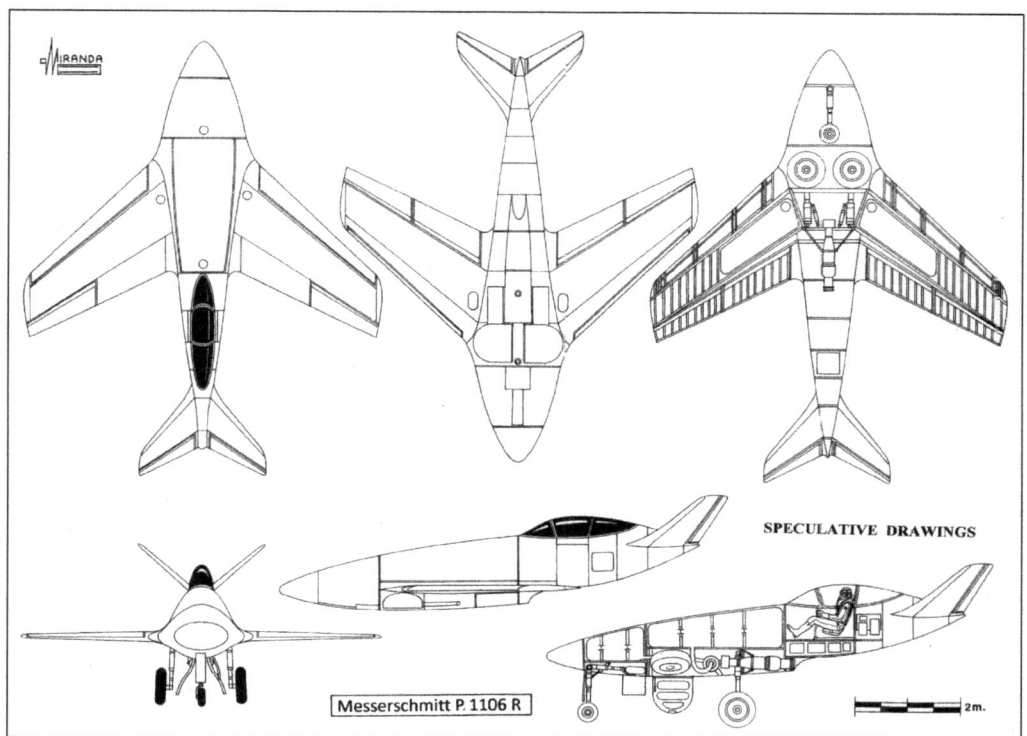

SPECULATIVE DRAWINGS

Messerschmitt P. 1106 R

Alexander Lippisch Deltas

The spindle is the perfect aerodynamic shape but, at speeds below Mach 5, this type of body does not produce enough lift to keep on flying. Any attempt to add a wing during supersonic flight encounters a problem known as 'area rule', consisting of a proportional increase of drag.

In 1942 the team of aerodynamics of the Aerodynamische Versuchs Anstalt (AVA) research centre, led by Dr Ing. Alexander Lippisch, built a heart-shaped model of a delta wing, with a 60-degree sweep, that proved to be an ideal supersonic body. Tests performed in the Göttingen wind tunnel showed that the body offered the minimum drag at over Mach 1, using less power than any of the other tested configurations. Known as Überschall Delta, this shape was unstable during flight, given the technology available at the time, and therefore it could not be used as a base to build a supersonic aircraft.

Most of the research work done by Lippisch during the rest of the war had the objective to create a *transsonischen deltaflügel* (transonic delta wing) apt for stable and long-range supersonic flight. This meant that they should reach and surpass Mach 1 in horizontal flight using very powerful engines and should have a great sweep.

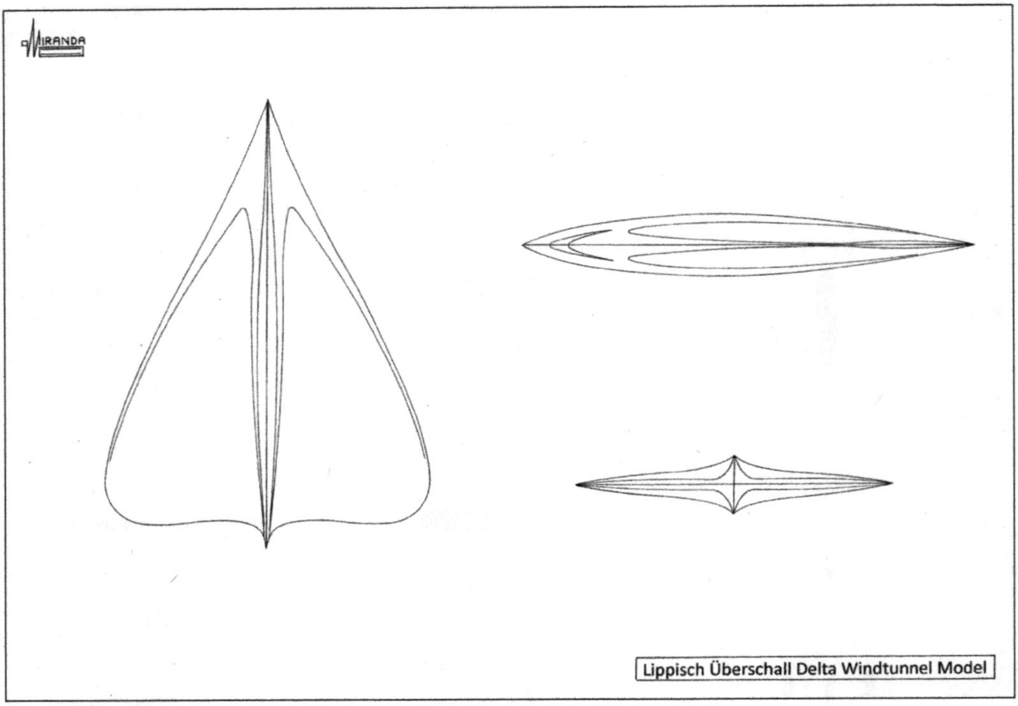

Lippisch Überschall Delta Windtunnel Model

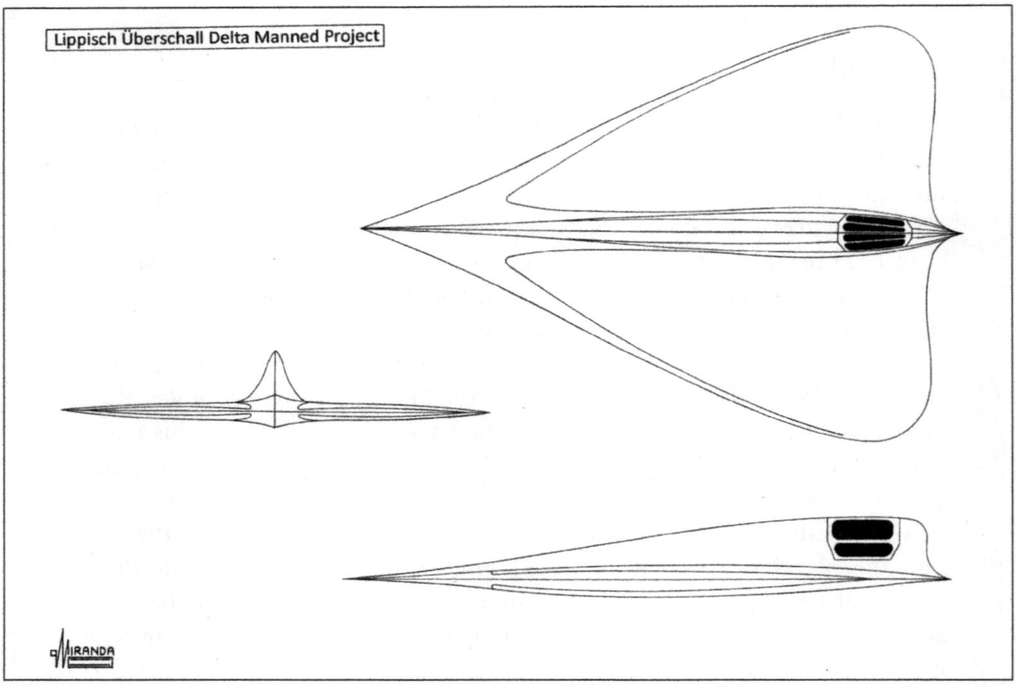

Lippisch Überschall Delta Manned Project

At the time, the aerodynamicists were afraid that the behaviour of this type of wing would be dangerous during landing at high speed. In order to prove the concept, one wooden test glider named DM-1 was built in 1945 with the cooperation of the FFG Darmstadt and the FFG München.

It had a delta wing with a 60-degree sweep on the leading edge and -15 degrees on the trailing edge, and the cockpit was built within the tailfin. It should be carried in Mistel (piggyback) configuration over a Siebel Si 204A and taken to an altitude of 8,000m (26,240ft). The plan was to reach 497mph (800km/h) powered by two Rheinmetall-Borsig 109-502 rockets with 771kg peak-thrust each and 348mph (560km/h) in unpowered flight. The landing speed was to be of 72km/h at 35 degrees of AOA.

After the war, the DM-1 was moved to the USA where its development was pursued by the Scientific Advisory Group of the USAF under the direction of Professor Theodore Von Kármán in the NACA and in the Langley wind tunnel. The static tests tried different configurations of cockpit and tailfin and several types of new leading edges. They were trying to find out why the 'Reynolds coefficient' (that measured the relative viscosity of the air flow at high speed) was too high. The final version was named NACA #8. It had a new leading edge with sharp edges and 64.2 degrees, a bubble cockpit and a triangular tailfin with 15 per cent thickness and a 35-degree sweep. It was declared stable at supersonic speed but, due to its small size, it would not have been able to carry enough fuel if a rocket engine would have been installed or would it have reached Mach 1.

The real transonic project was the DM-2. It was 150 per cent bigger than the DM-1 and doubled the fuel capacity of the Komet. The design of February 1945 included a HWK 509 A-1 rocket able to work for 17 minutes with a static thrust of 1,600kg. It was expected that this should be enough to study its behaviour during flight, in the range between Mach 0.8 and 1.2. When fully loaded, the aircraft was too heavy to take off using the frail landing gear that appears in the designs. It possibly was carried up to 8,000m (26,240ft) by an aircraft of the Junkers Ju 390 or Heinkel He 274 type and launched from there to save rocket propellant.

LIPPISCH DM-2 TECHNICAL DATA: Type: transonic rocket-plane. Wings: 64.2-degree sweep at the leading edge and -3 degrees at the trailing edge, 12 per cent thickness at root, delta planform with elevons, metallic structure and cladding. Tailfin: 36 degrees sweep, 12 per cent thickness, metallic structure and cladding. Fuselage: housing the pressurised cockpit, with the pilot in a prone position, the forward landing gear and the rocket-engine, metallic structure and cladding. Landing gear: tricycle type, similar to the DM-1 one, engine: one Walter HWK 509 A.1 with 1,600kg static thrust, fuel tanks: two with 765l of T-Stoff (80% hydrogen peroxide and 20% oxyquinoline phosphate) and another two with 430l in the wings, behind the main spar. Two with 435l of

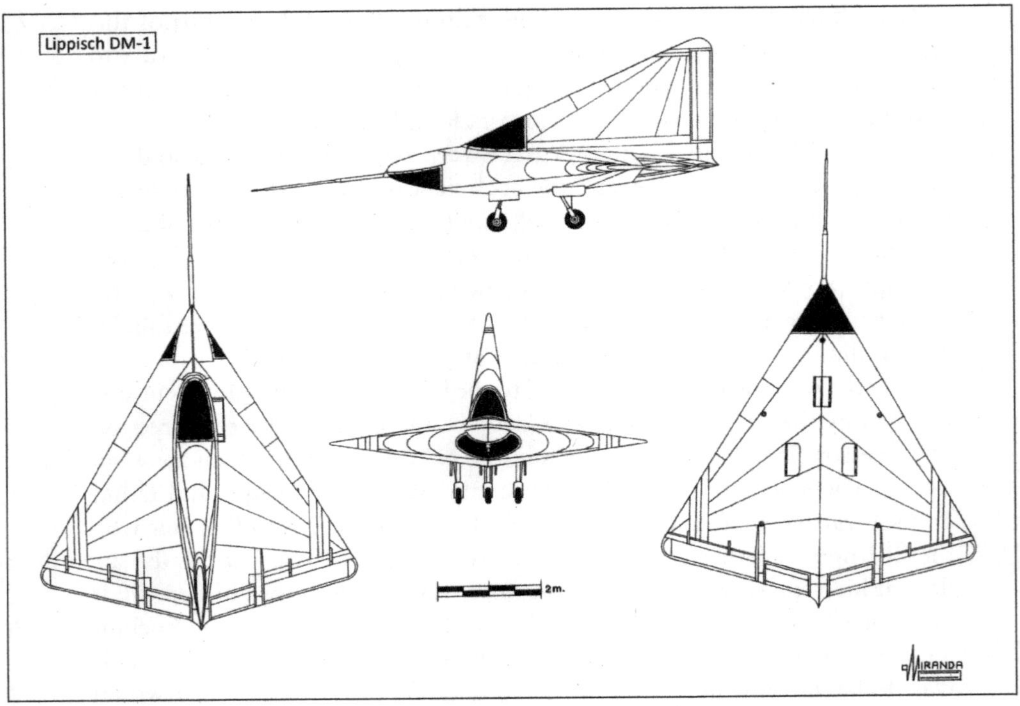

Rocket Interceptors: 1941–1947

Lippisch DM-1

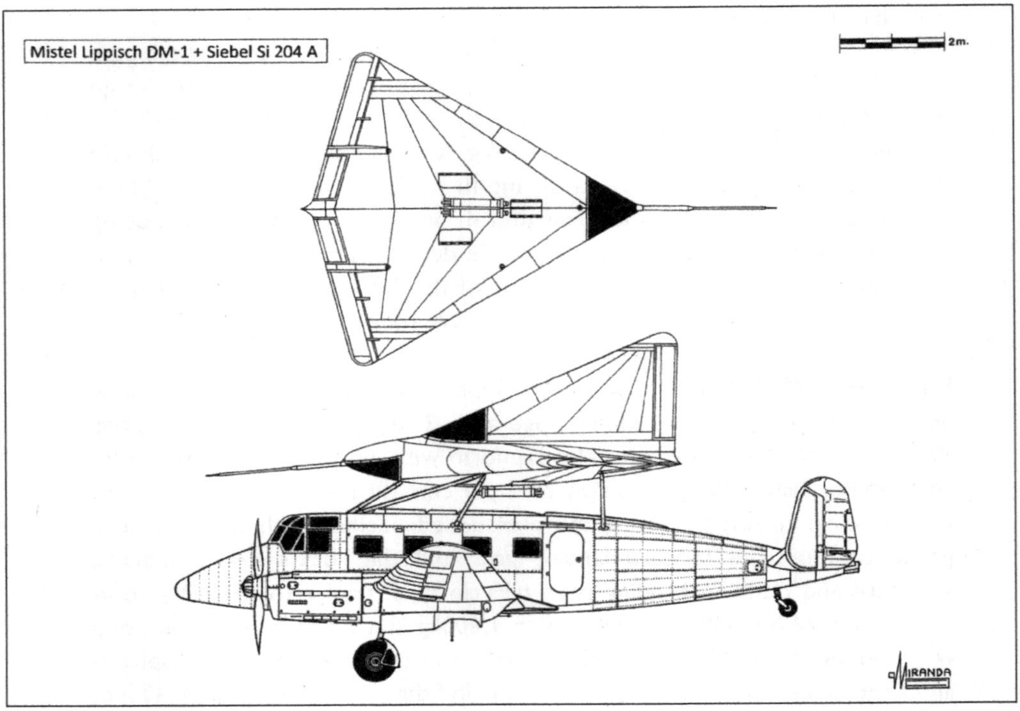

Mistel Lippisch DM-1 + Siebel Si 204 A

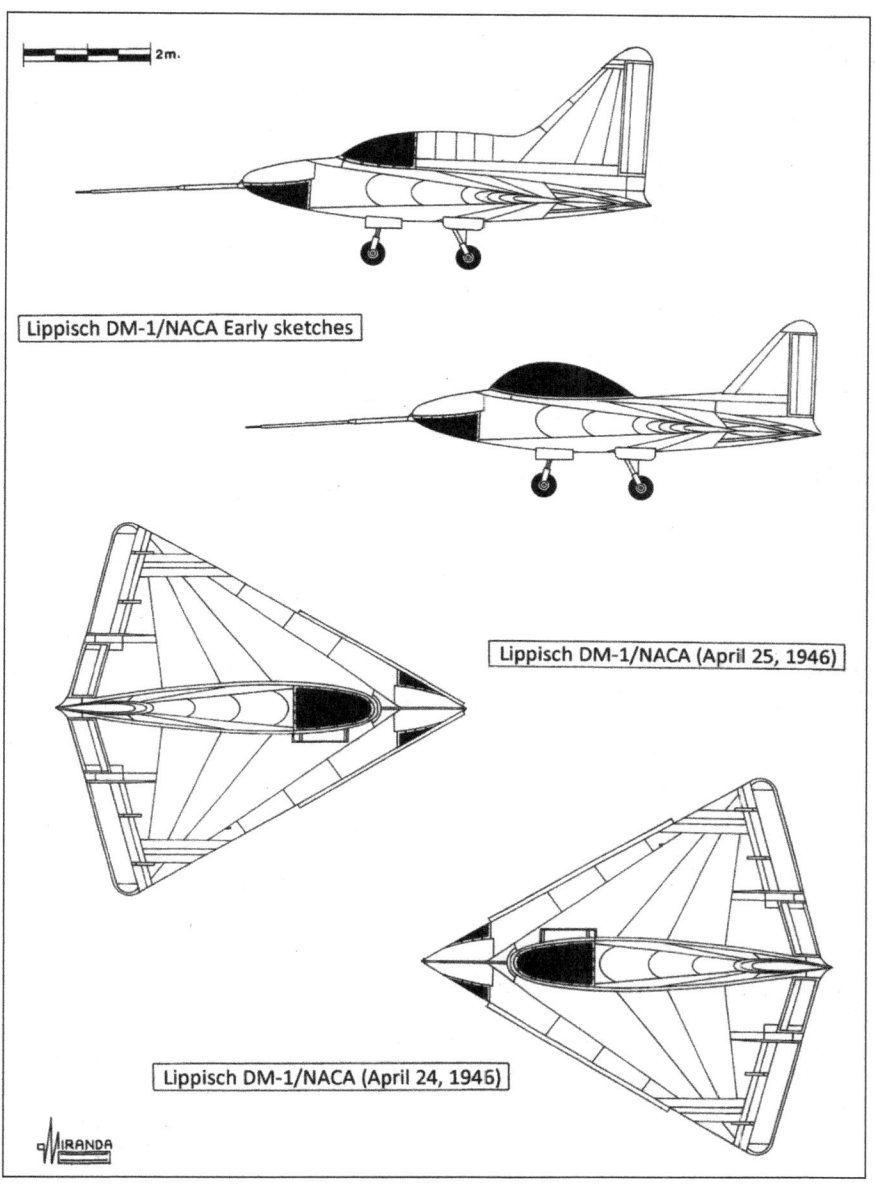

C-Stoff (Mixture of 57% Methanol, 30% Hydrazine Hydrate and 13% Potasium Cuprocyanide) and another two with 200l in the wings ahead of the main spar. Armament: none. Wingspan: 8.25m (27ft). Length: 8.94m (29.3ft). Height: 4.12m (13.5ft). Wing area: 38sq.m (422sq.ft), empty weight: 3,700kg (8,168lb). Take-off weight: 11,500kg (25,386lb). Estimated maximum speed: Mach 1.2. Service ceiling: 12,000m (39,360ft). Range (maximum powered endurance): 17 min.

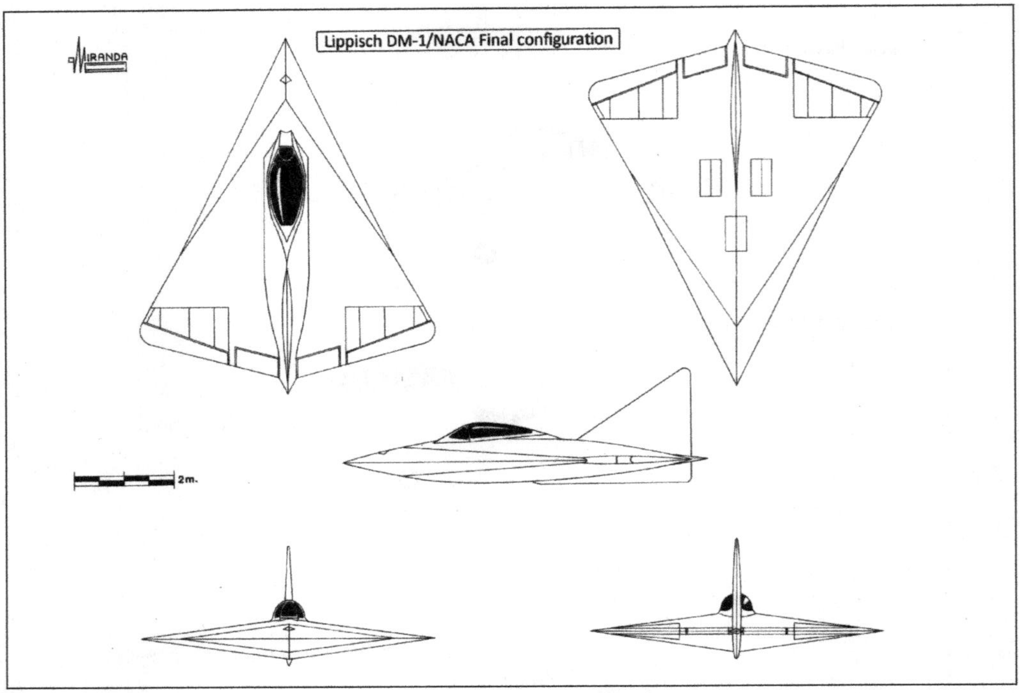

126 Rocket Interceptors: 1941–1947

Lippisch DM-1/NACA Final configuration

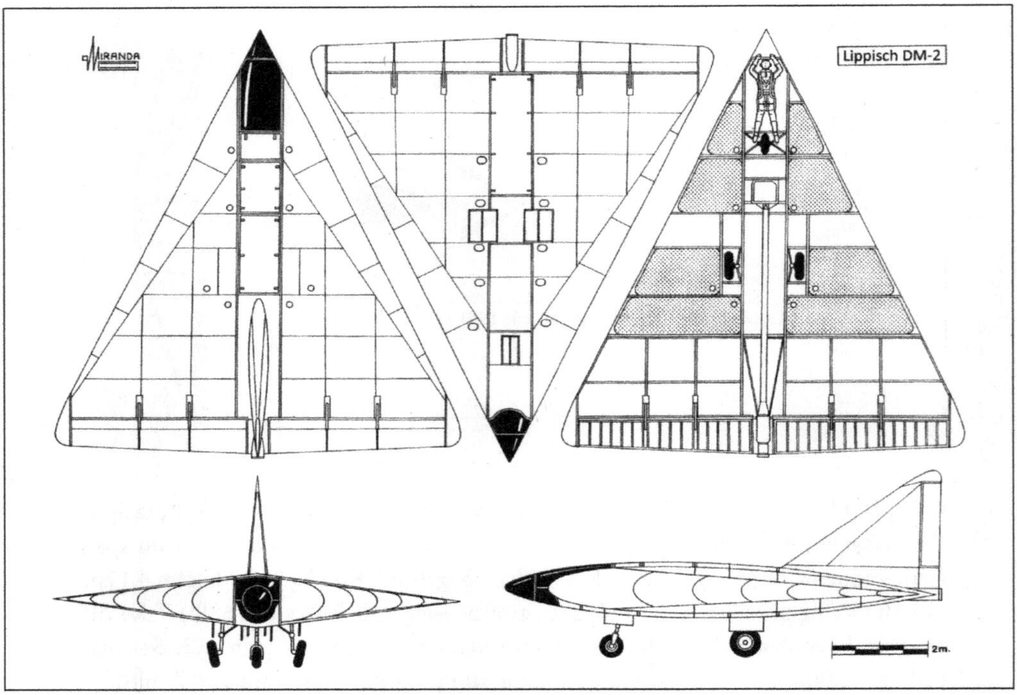

Lippisch DM-2

The Lippisch DM-3 project was the supersonic version of the DM-2 powered by two rocket engines.

LIPPISCH DM-3 TECHNICAL DATA: Type: supersonic research rocket-plane, wings: 64.2 degrees sweep at the leading edge and -3 degrees at the trailing edge, 12 per cent thickness at root, delta planform with elevons, metallic structure and cladding. Tailfin: 36 degrees sweep, 12 per cent thickness, metallic structure and cladding. Fuselage: housing the pressurised cockpit, with the pilot in a prone position, the forward landing gear and the rocket-engine, metallic structure and cladding. Landing gear: tricycle type, similar to the DM-1 one, engine: two Walter HWK 509 A.1 rockets with 1,600kg static thrust each, fuel tanks: two with 765l of T-Stoff (80% hydrogen peroxide and 20% oxyquinoline phosphate) and another two with 430l in the wings, behind the main spar. Two with 435l of C-Stoff (mixture of 57% methanol, 30% hydrazine hydrate and 13% potassium cuprocyanide) and another two with 200l in the wings ahead of the main spar. Armament: none. Wingspan: 8.25m (27ft). Length: 8.94m (29.3ft). Height: 4.12m (13.5ft). Wing area: 38sq.m (422sq.ft). Estimated maximum speed: Mach 2. Range (maximum powered endurance): 8.5 min.

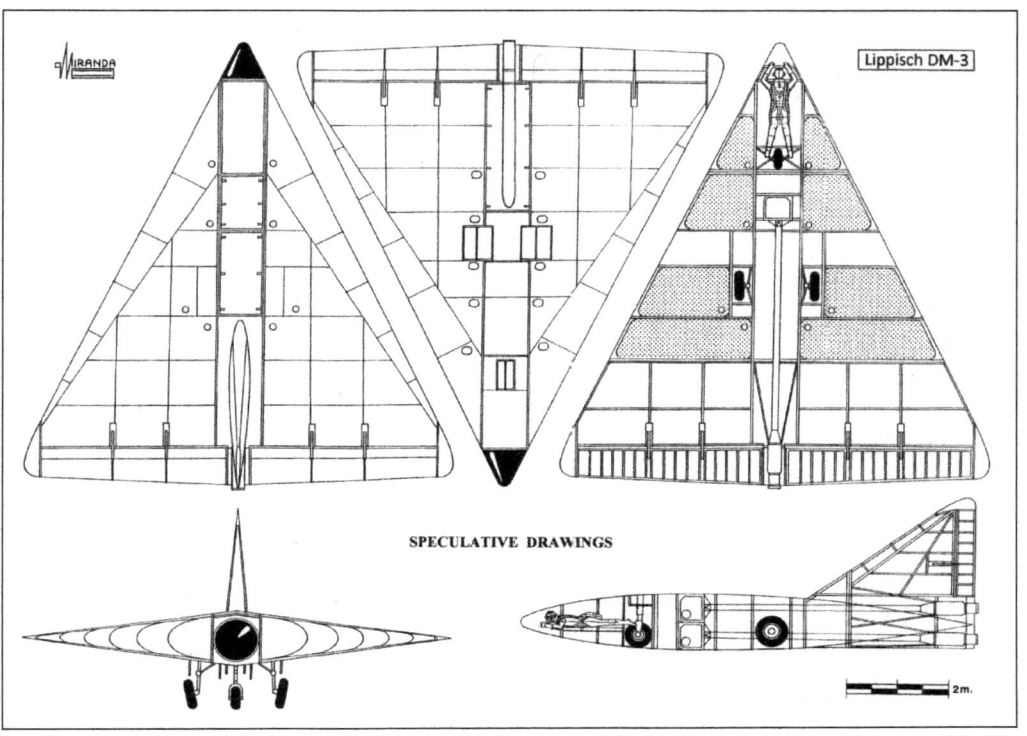

SPECULATIVE DRAWINGS

Siebel/DFS 346

In 1942 the Deutschen Forschungsinstitut für Segelflug (DFS) initiated a series of design studies for high-altitude and high-speed research aircraft.

In 1943 the DFS-Ainring design team, under the leadership of Dr Alexander Lippisch and the Dipl.-Ing. Felix Kracht, started the DFS 346 Mach-Projekt research program for supersonic speeds above 932mph (1,500km/h).

Wind tunnel tests began in August 1944 and the design work being finished on 30 November. Early in 1945 started the construction of three prototypes at Siebel-Halle Flugzeugwerke.

The basic DFS 346 configuration had cigar-shaped fuselage, with pressurised cabin, prone pilot and landing skid, mid-wing with a 45-degree sweep, 9.2/7.5 per cent thickness and T-tail plane.

The DFS 346 (V1) was a glider with water ballast, the DFS 346 (V2) was to be powered by one HWK 109-509 C-1 dual chamber rocket-motor with 2,000kg + 400kg thrust, the DFS 346 (V3) was powered by two throttleable HWK 109-509 B-1 superimposed rocket-motors with 2,000kg peak-thrust each.

The V2 was designed to reach 1,250mph (Mach 1.9) at 66,000ft (20,120m) and the V3 was designed to reach 1,718mph (Mach 2.65) at 114,830ft (35,000m).

To save propellant, the DFS 346 (V2) was carried aloft atop a Dornier Do 217 or one Heinkel He 274 modified bombers, prior to launch at 32,800ft (10,000m).

SIEBEL/DFS 346 (V2) TECHNICAL DATA: Type: transonic research rocket-aircraft. Wingspan: 29.2ft (8.9m). Length (without nose probe): 38.9ft (11.85m). Height: 11.86ft (3.53m). Wing area: 221sq.ft (19.86sq.m). Maximum launch weight (V1): 4,812lb (2,180kg). Maximum launch weight (V2): 11,611lb (5,260kg). Range: 31 miles (50km).

SIEBEL/DFS 346 (V3) TECHNICAL DATA: Type: supersonic research rocket-aircraft. Wingspan: 29.5ft (9m). Length (without nose probe): 44ft (13.45m). Height: 9.7ft (2.97m). Wing area: 222sq.ft (20sq.m). Maximum launch weight: 15,232lb (6,900kg).

When US troops seized the Siebel-Halle facilities in April 1945 they found the Mach-Projekt DFS 346 V1 prototype under construction.

It was built throughout of Duralumin alloy with 45-degree swept-back wings, T-tail plane and ejection nose cockpit.

In July 1945 the Siebel factory was transferred to Soviet control and moved entirely by train to the USSR, along with technical crews, to complete the DFS 346 development.

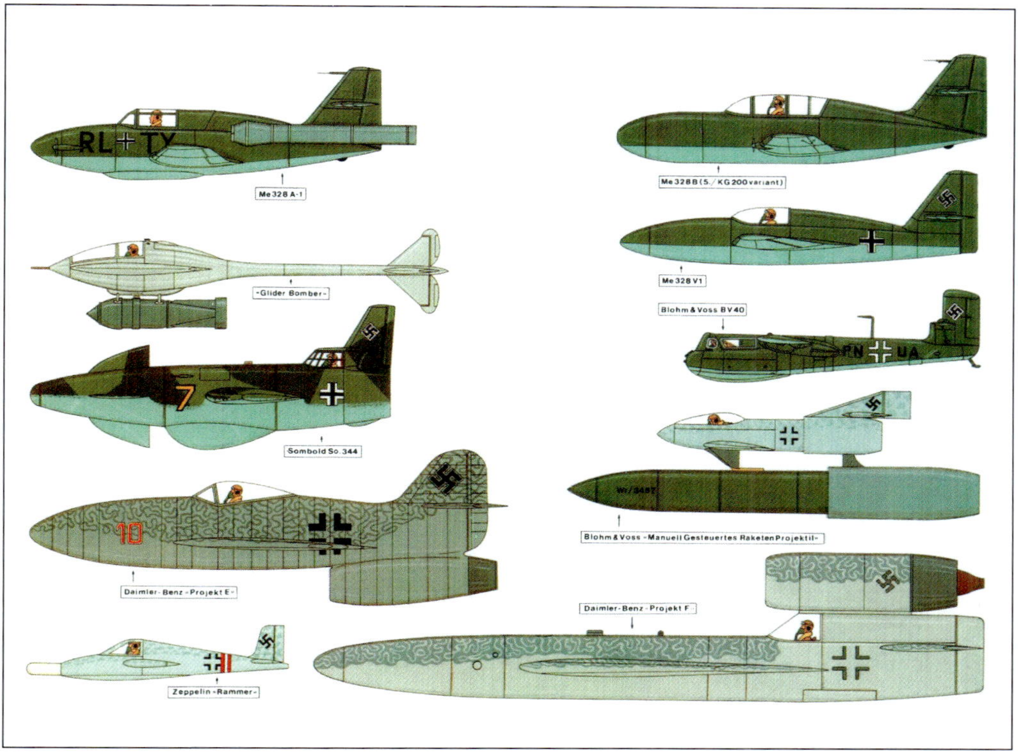

Messerschmitt Me 328 A-1 (December 15, 1942, project), DFS/Lippisch *Bombensegler* (1944 project), Sombold So 344 *Rammschussjäger* (January 22, 1944, project), Daimler-Benz *Projekt* E (January 10, 1945, project), Zeppelin *Rammer Entwurf* III (1944 project), Messerschmitt Me 328B S.O. (1944 project), Messerschmitt Me 328 V1(mock-up July 23, 1941), Blohm und Voss BV 40 (prototype December 13, 1943), Blohm und Voss *Manuell Gesteuertes Raketen Projektil* (1944 project), Daimler-Benz *Projekt* F (May 1944, project).

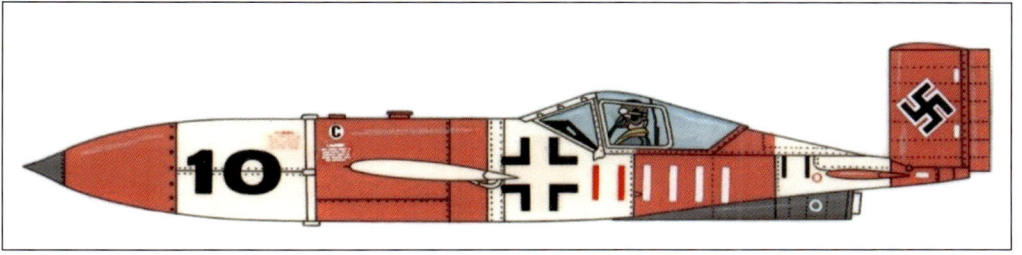

Focke-Wulf 1-R *Rammjäger* (September 1944 project).

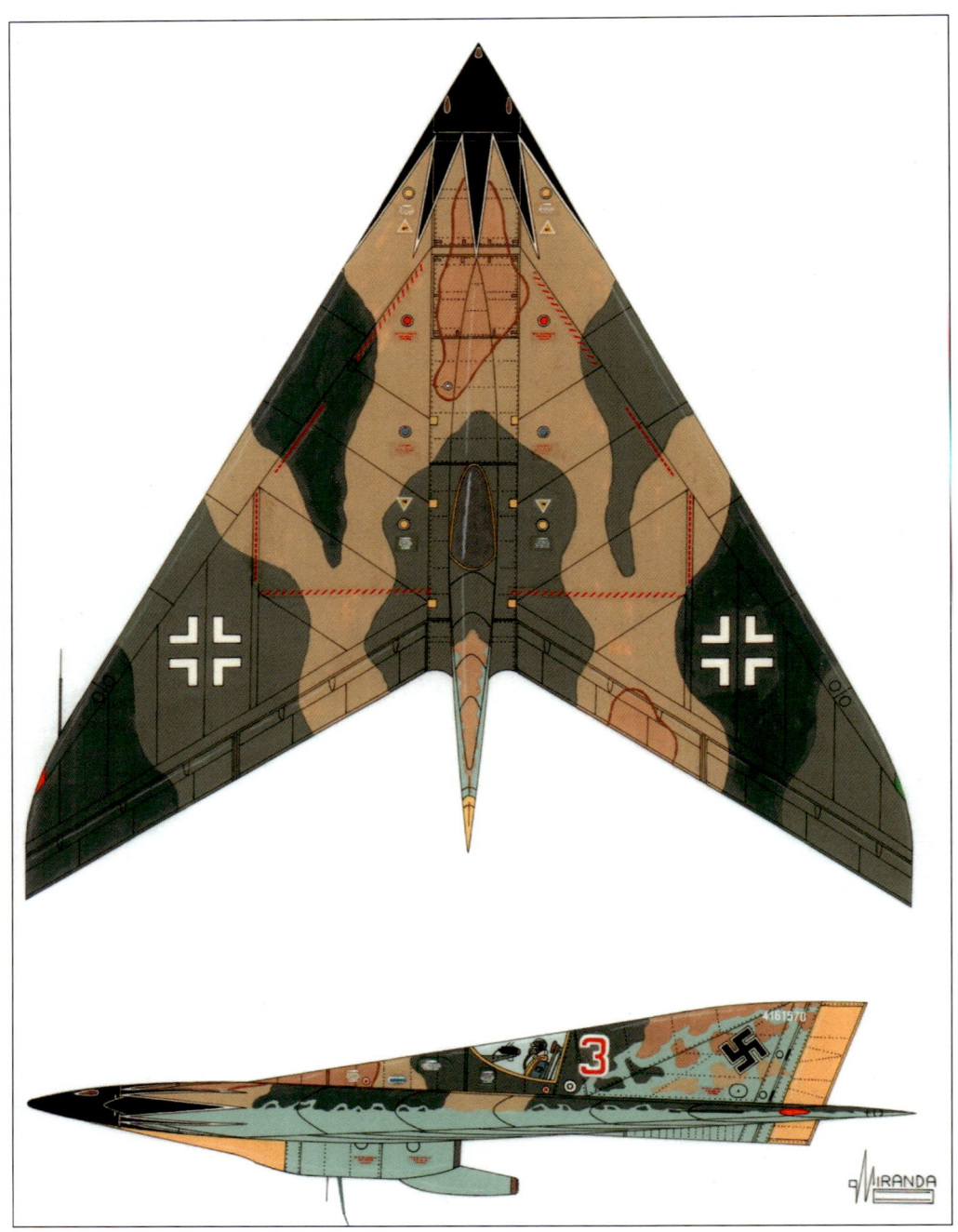

Horten Ho XIIIB operational version (1945 project).

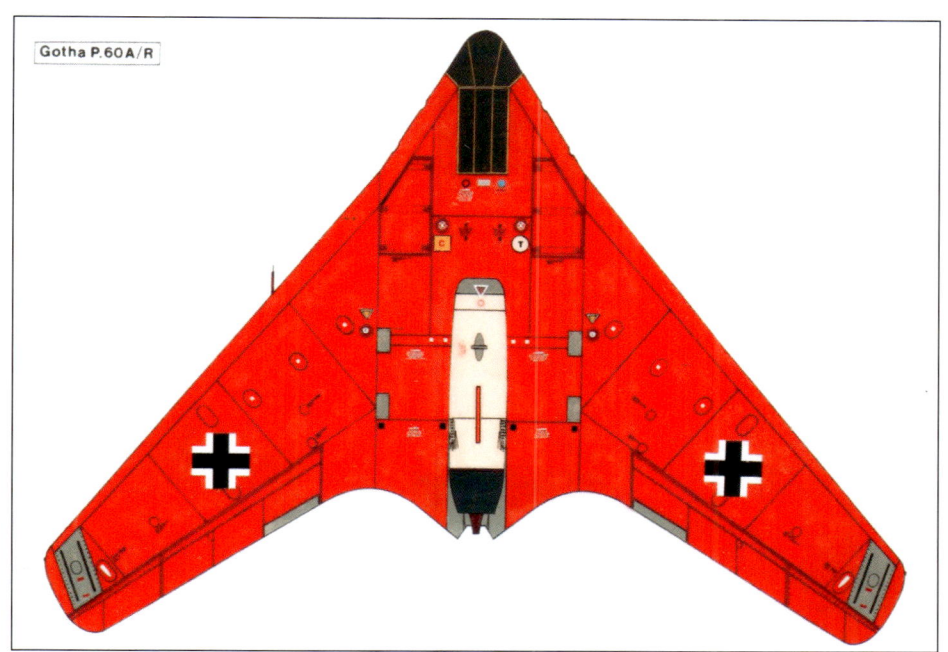

Horten Ho XIIIB prototype (1945 project).

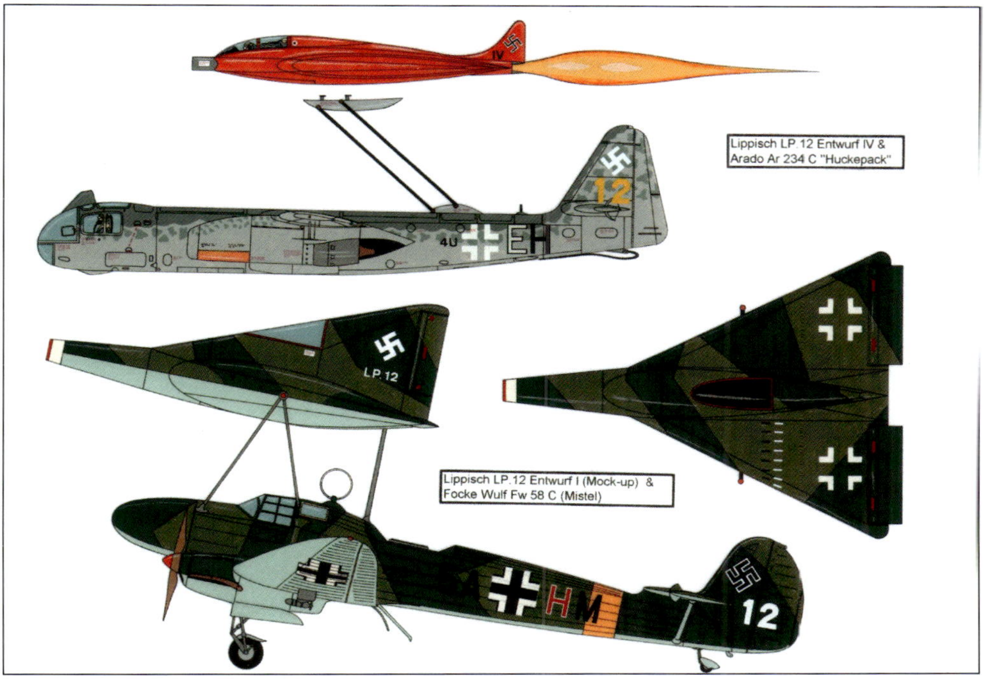

Arado Ar 234 C-5 *Huckepack* + Lippisch LP. 12 *Entwurf* IV (Mistel project).

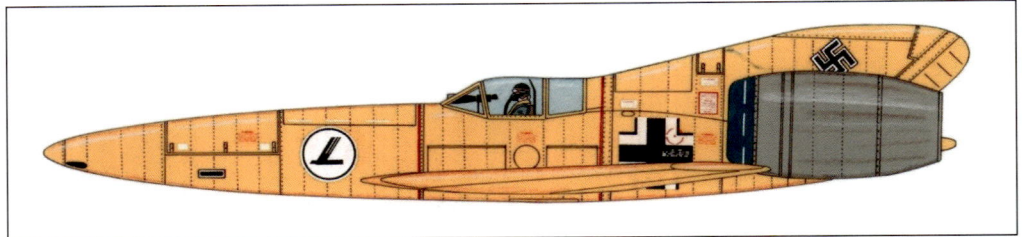

Focke-Wulf Ta 283 *Strahlrohrjäger* (August 4, 1944, project).

Focke-Wulf 1-R *Volksjäger* (1944 project).

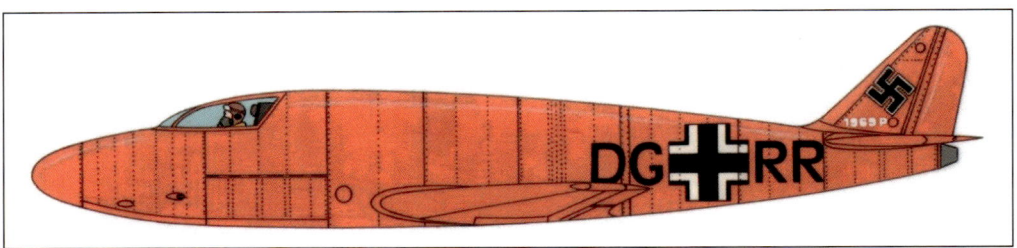

Arado TEW 16/43 (August 18, 1943, project).

Opposite above: Bachem M-1 (November 22, 1944, prototype), Bachem M-17 (February 1945 prototype), Bachem M-22 (February 1945 prototype), Bachem M-23 (March 1945 prototype).

Opposite below: Bachem M-23 (March 1945 prototype), Bachem Ba 349 A (April 1945 prototype), Bachem BP-20 M52 (March 1945 prototype), Bachem Ba 349 A-1 (1944 project), Bachem Ba 349 B (1944 project).

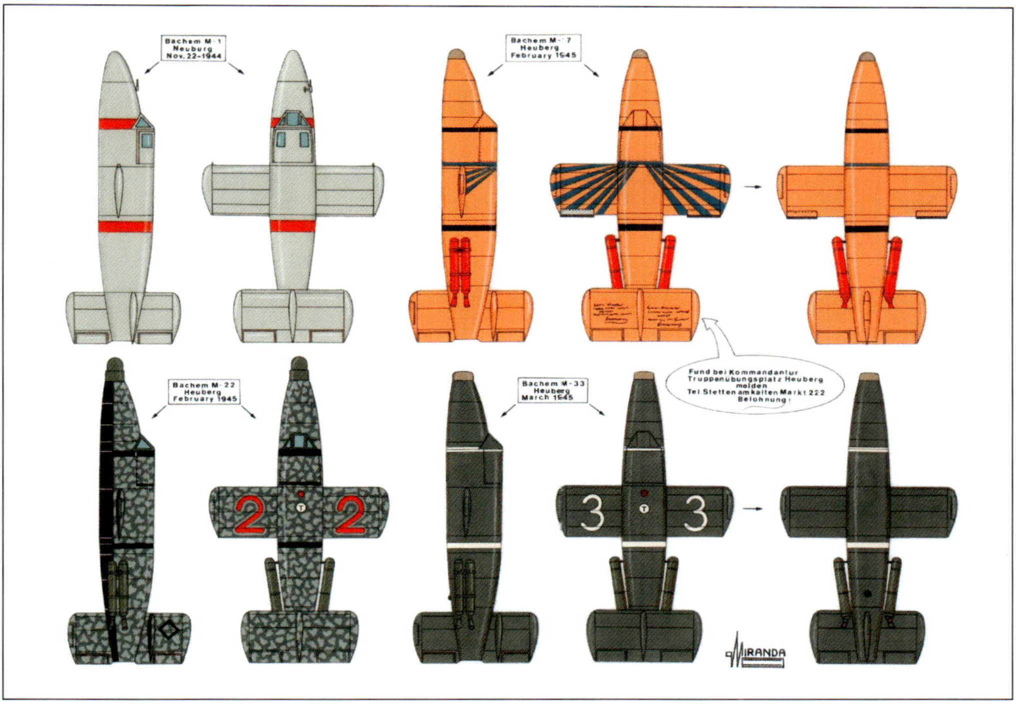
Bachem M-1
Neuburg
Nov. 22-1944
Bachem M-7
Heuberg
February 1945
Bachem M-22
Heuberg
February 1945
Bachem M-33
Heuberg
March 1945
Fund bei Kommandantur
Truppenübungsplatz Heuberg
melden
Tel Stetten am kalten Markt 222
Belohnung!
MIRANDA

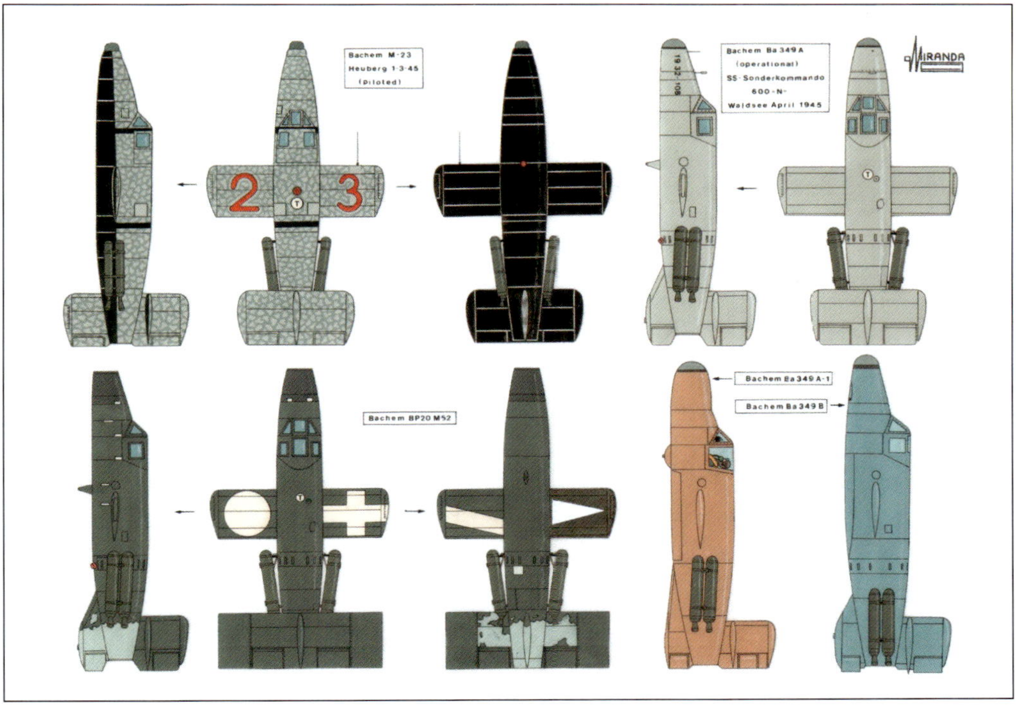
Bachem M-23
Heuberg 1-3-45
(piloted)
Bachem Ba 349 A
(operational)
SS-Sonderkommando
600-N-
Waldsee April 1945
MIRANDA
Bachem BP20 M52
Bachem Ba 349 A-1
Bachem Ba 349 B

Bachem Ba 349 escape system.

Bachem Ba 349 launch pad.

Heinkel He 112 V3 *Rückstossjäger* Werk Nr. 1292 (March 1937 prototype).

HVA *Stratosphärenjäger* I (July 6, 1939, project).

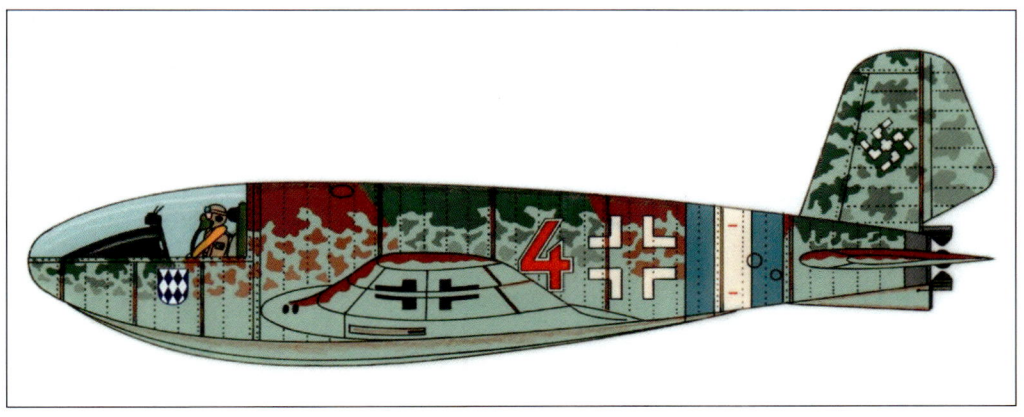

HVA *Stratosphärenjäger* II (March 27, 1941, project).

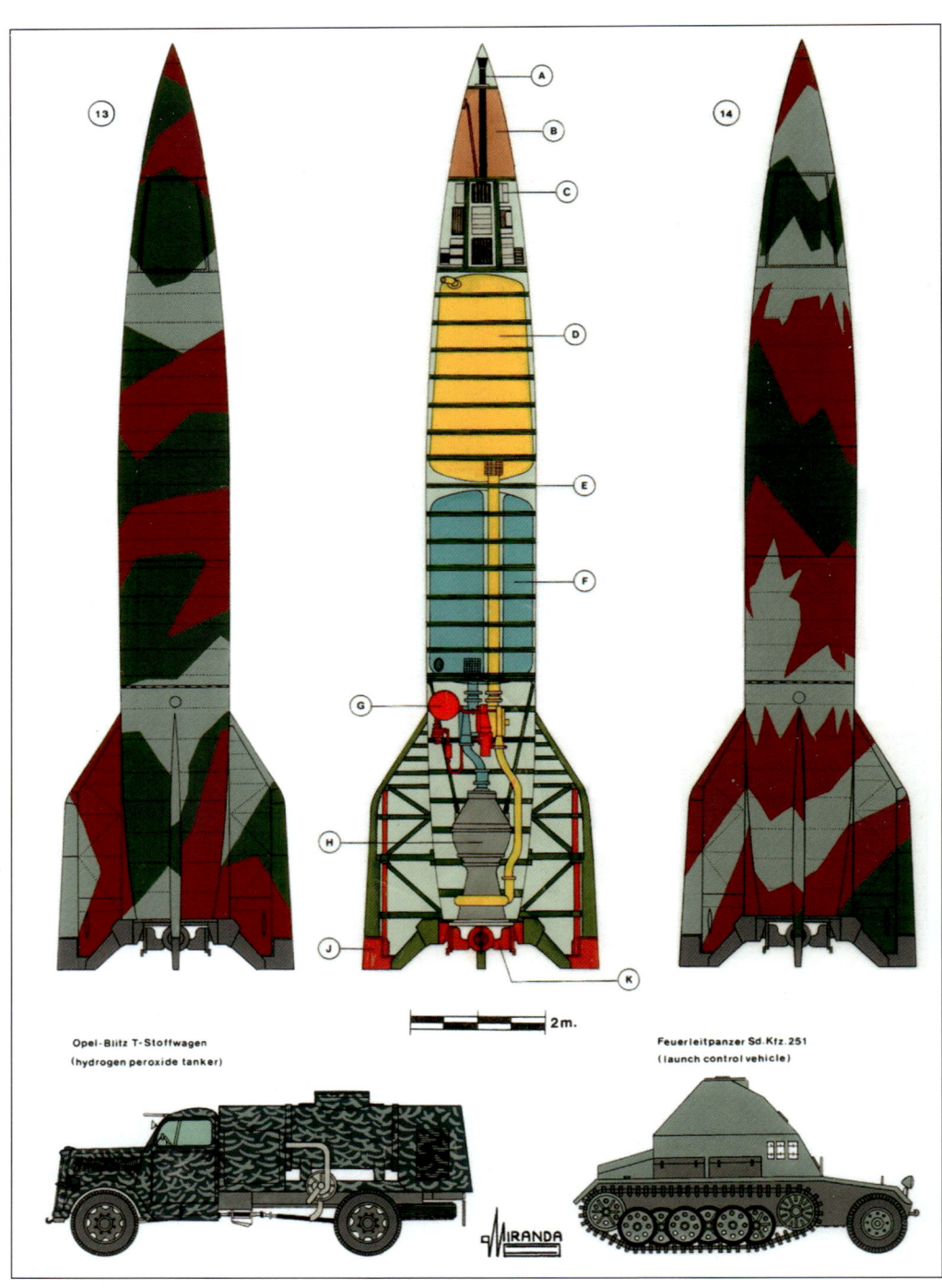

EMW V2 operational, EMW V2 cut away, EMW V2 operational, Opel Blitz hydrogen peroxide tanker, Sd.Kfz. 251 launch control armored vehicle.

EMW V2 operational, EMW V2 operational, EMW V2 operational, Sd.Kfz. 7/3 launch control armored vehicle, liquid oxygen container.

EMW A6 second configuration (1944 project).

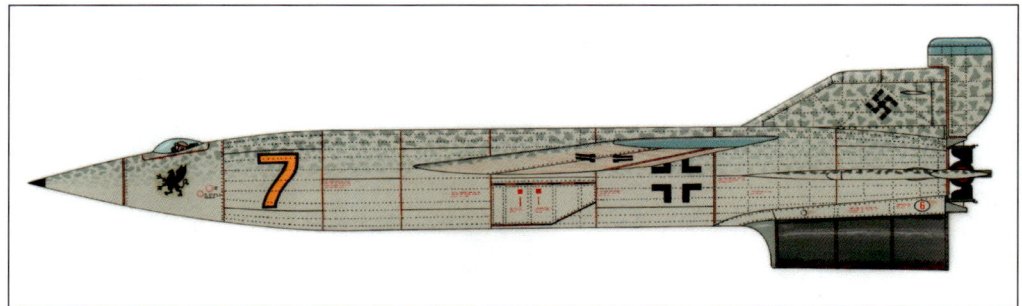

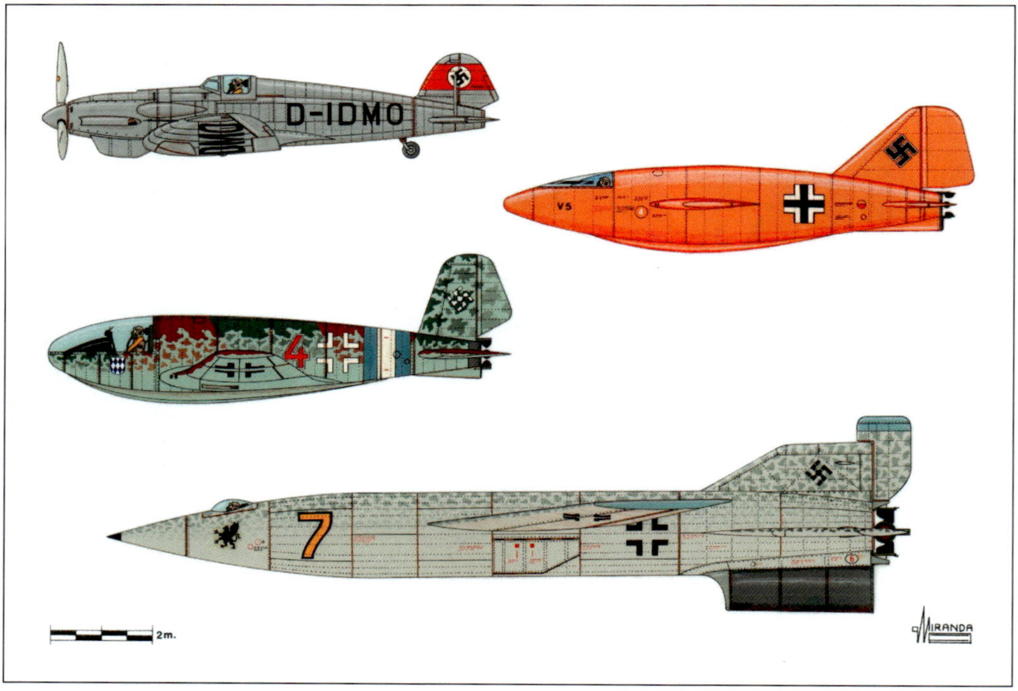

Heinkel He 112 V3 prototype, HVA *Stratosphärenjäger* I project, *Stratosphärenjäger* II project, EMW A6 second configuration project.

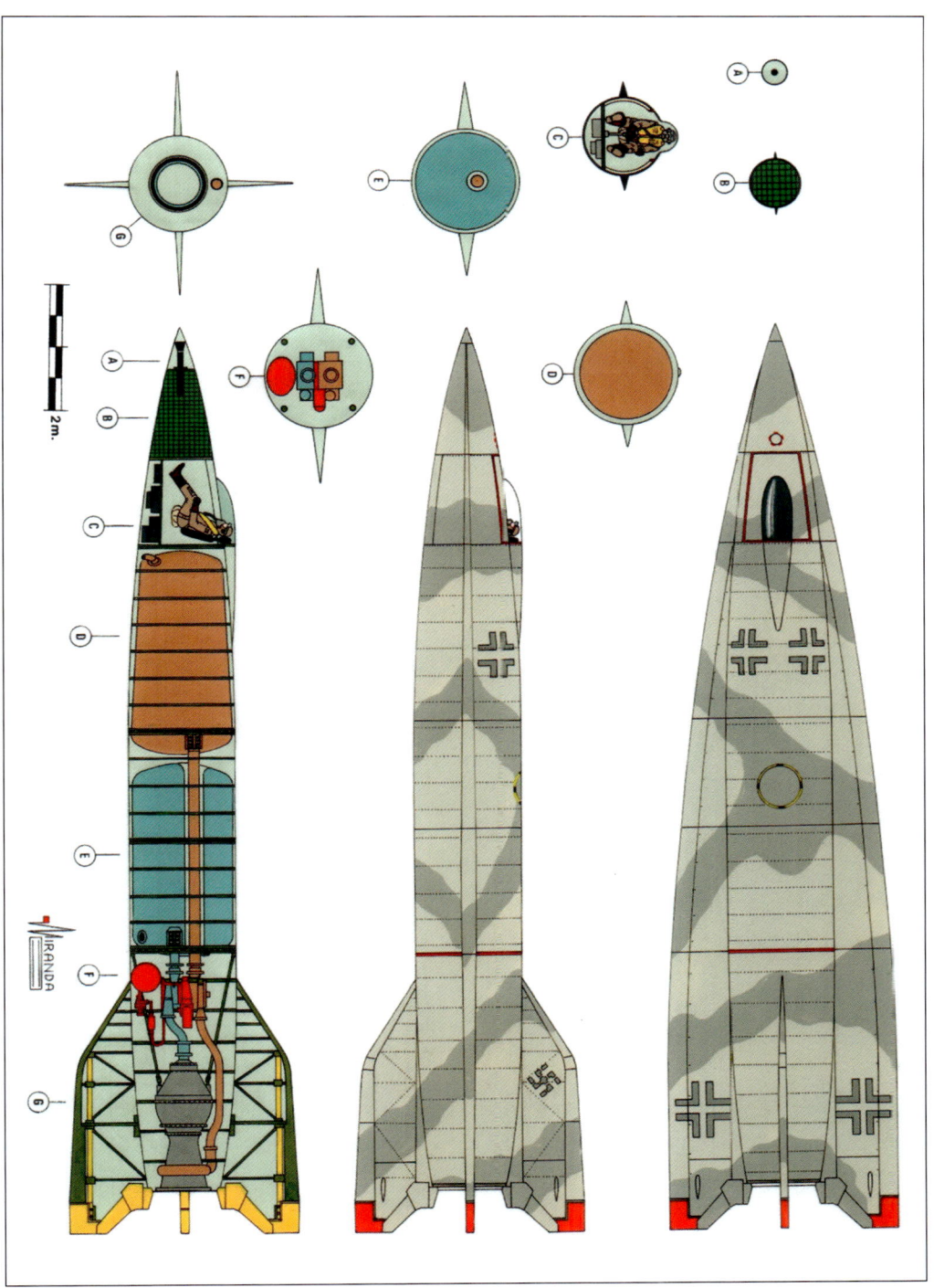

EMW A9 third configuration (1945 project).

EMW A9/A10 second configuration (1944 project).

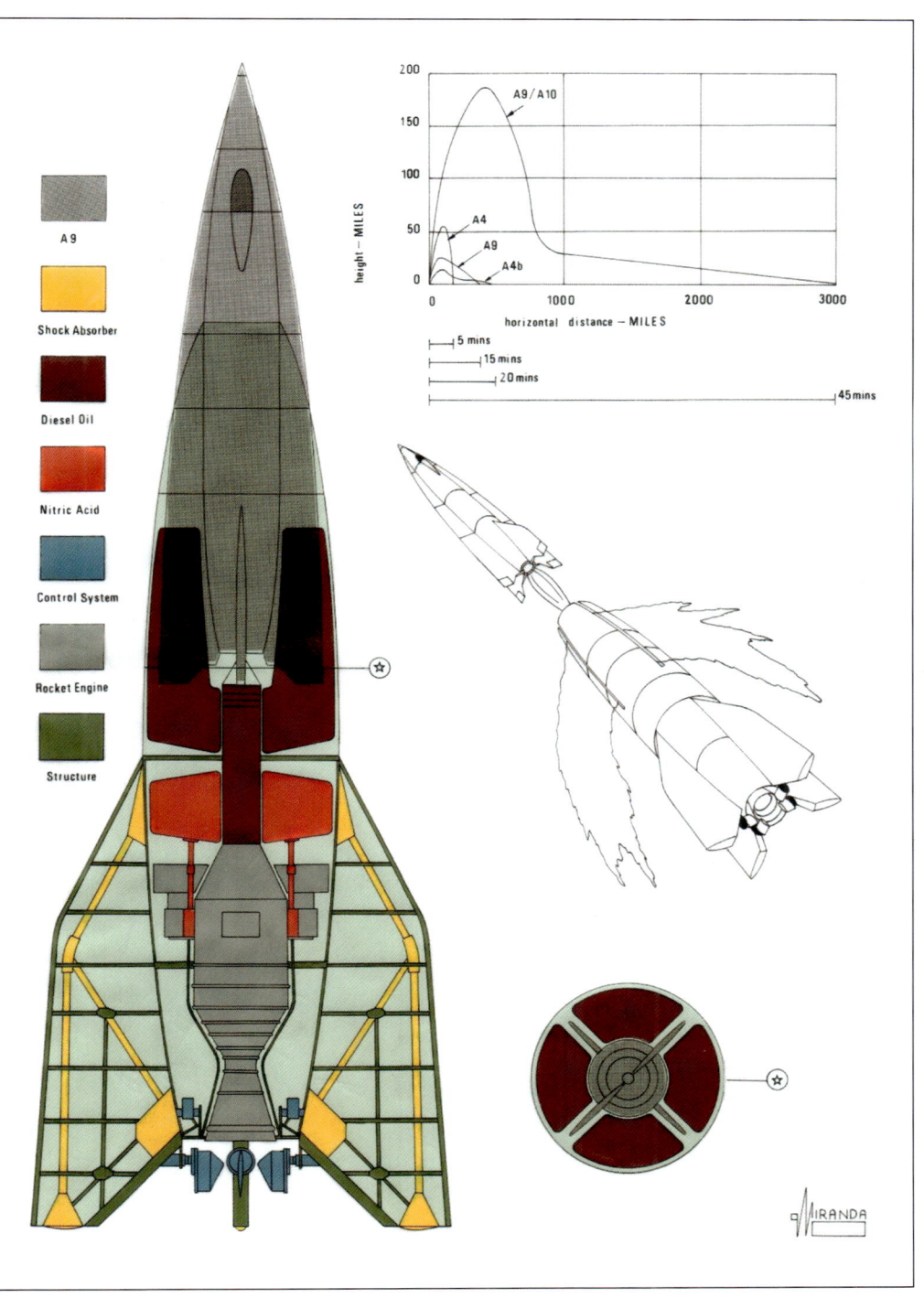

EMW A9/A10 third configuration (1945 project).

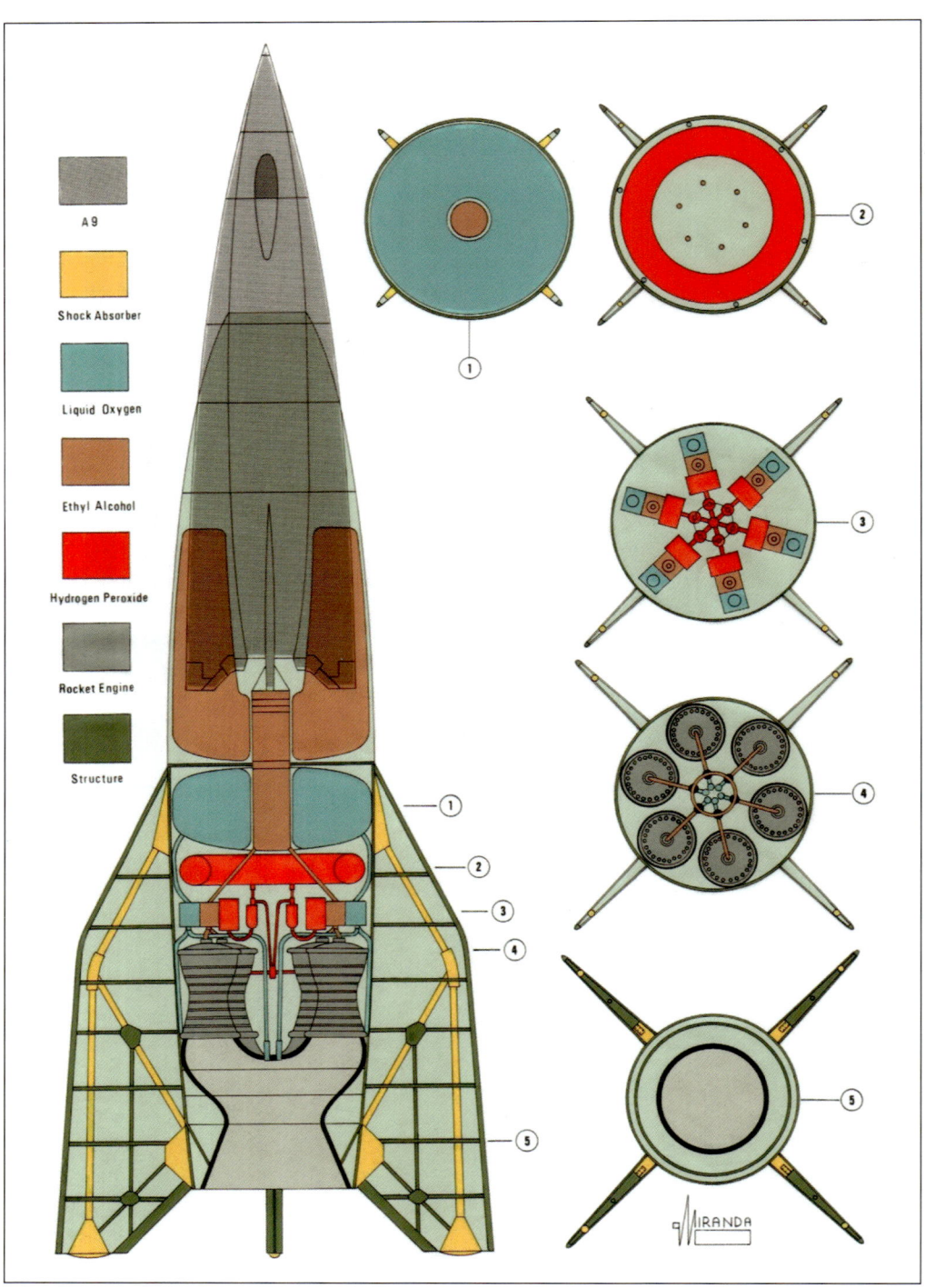

EMW A9/A10 second configuration (1944 project).

Golovin IVS (1941 project).

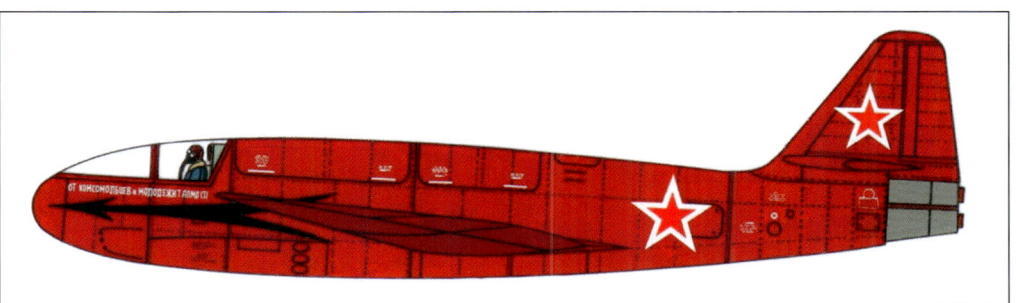
Lavochkin I-162-1 (1947 project).

Northrop XP-79 (mock-up September 1944).

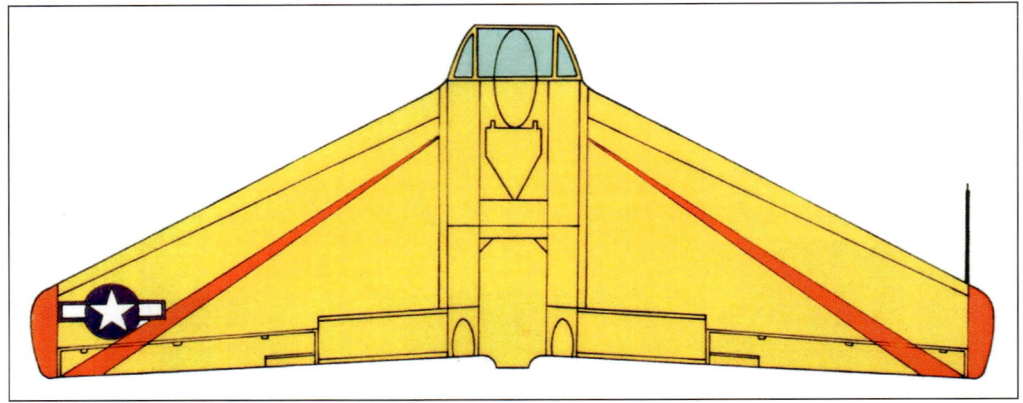

Northrop MX-334-II (prototype July 5, 1944).

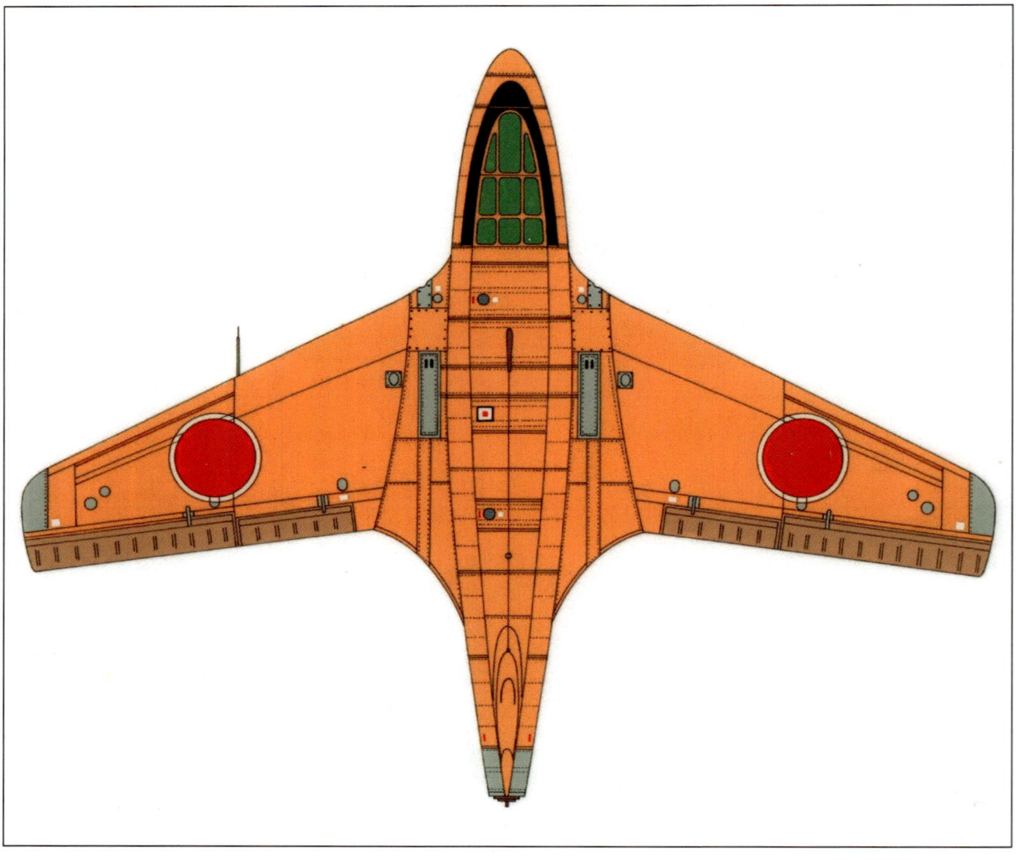

Rikugun Ki.202 (1945 project).

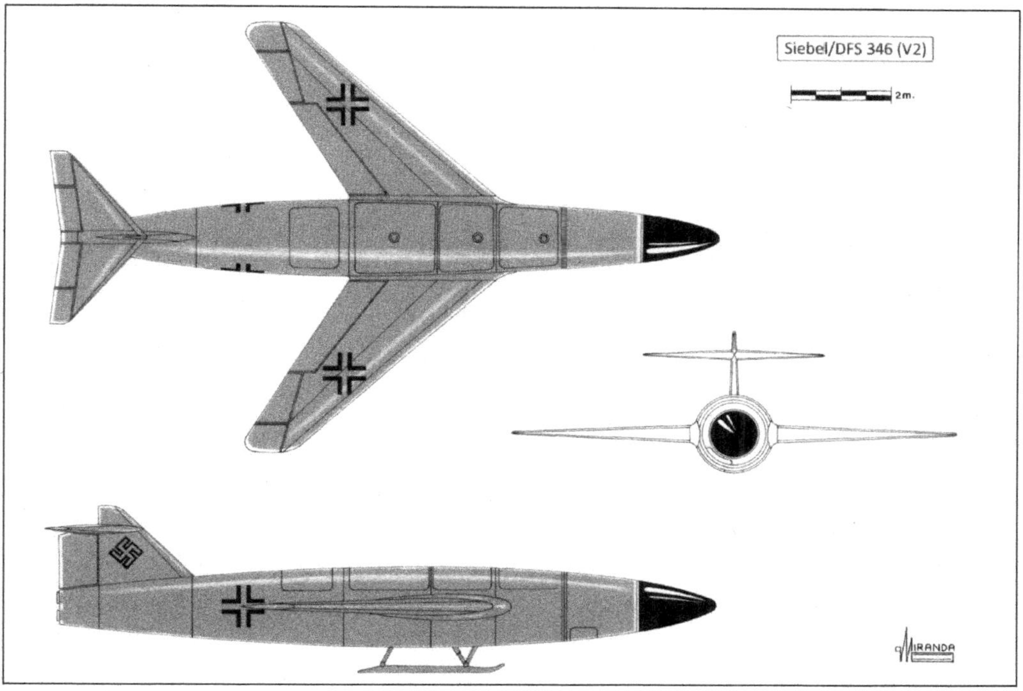
Siebel/DFS 346 (V2)
2m.
MIRANDA

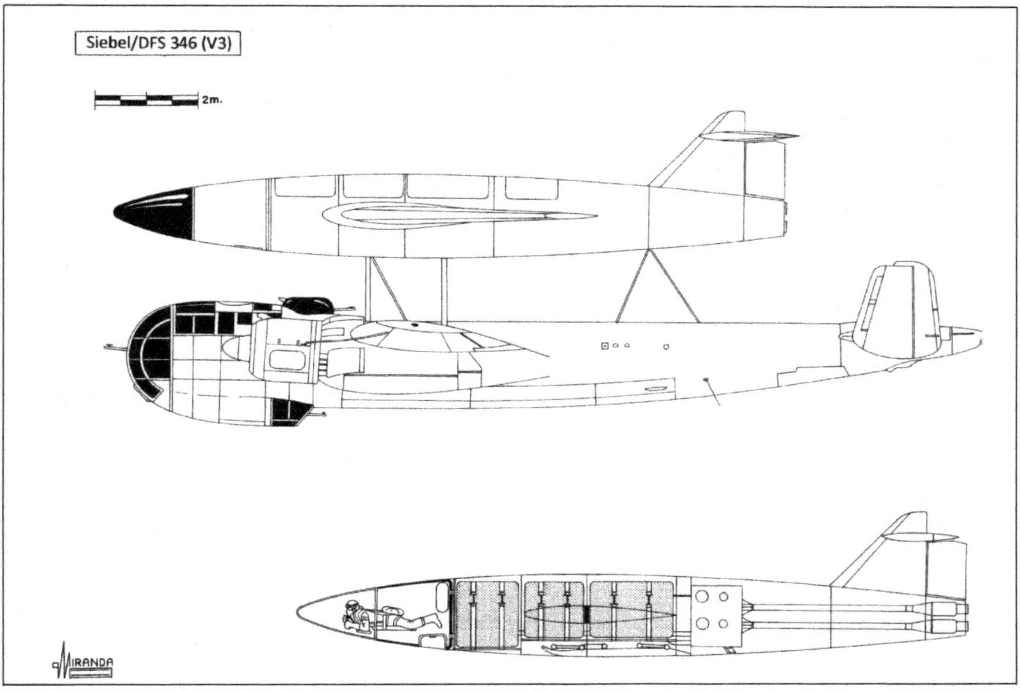
Siebel/DFS 346 (V3)
2m.
MIRANDA

11
The Strahlrohrjäger Concept

Despite their appearances, the short range of the rocket-planes seriously hindered its military use. The logical alternative was to favour the development of the turbojet to achieve more reliable and powerful engines. Unfortunately, the German industry was not able to produce the required metallic alloys, especially resistant to heat and stress. They lacked metals like chromium and molybdenum that were essential to harden the steel.

Chemists produced silicones, to replace the rubber, and synthetic oil of low quality from coal. But the advanced materials for the compressor blades of the turbojets would not be ready on time and everyone was aware of it. The pulse-jet of the V-1 cruise missile did not have power enough and, though different variants of the He 162, Me 262 and Me 328 were designed (powered by two, four and even six pulse jets) it was soon made evident that they were a deadend because the vibrations they generated were destructive to the aircraft structure.

The situation demanded a new type of power plant capable of running on any fuel and easy to build with cheap metals, so the German aircraft industry was forced to consider the use of ramjets.

The theory elaborated by René Lorin in 1913 established that this type of engine produced the maximum thrust at Mach 2, but the theoretical work carried out by Dr Eugen Sänger in 1940 showed that a ramjet built with length/diameter ratio of 5 to 1 could work in the high subsonic speed range, with lower specific fuel consumption than a rocket and higher thrust than a turbojet.

In the forward conical portion of the engine, the air flow would be decelerated, with a simultaneous pressure increase to approximately one-sixth of the flight speed. In the cylindrical combustion chamber the fuel is injected according to the throttling, and mixed with the flowing air. At a speed above 200km/h the air inlet pressure is sufficient to start ignition using a ring of spark plugs, with the gases ejected from the jet pipe at a superior speed than that of flying. The first tests carried out in 1941 in the

LFA-Volkenrode produced very long flames which discouraged wind tunnel test with ramjets. Ground test began in autumn 1941 with a prototype mounted above the Opel-Blitz truck.

In March 1942, a Sänger ramjet with 500mm diameter was tested in flight, mounted above a Dornier Do 17 Z bomber, provided by the DFS-Ainring Institut. In December, a second test was carried out with a ramjet of 1,500mm mounted above a Dornier Do 217 E-2. In the summer of 1944 the same aircraft was used to test the final version of 1,000mm. The ramjet worked correctly every time, although with low thrust due to the low speed of the bomber. In theory, the Sänger 1000 had a nominal output of 17,400hp, the Sänger 1,500 of 22,000hp and the Sänger 2000 of 61,000hp. But this could only be demonstrated by installing them on an aircraft capable of flying at a speed of Mach 0.8 and an altitude of 15,000m.

In January of 1945, the DFS Institut issued a report that suggested mounting two Sänger 1000 above the wings of a Me 262 A-1. This was expected to give an increase of 200km/h in maximum speed, an increase of 4,000m absolute ceiling and the reduction of the climbing time to 10,000m from 26 to 6 minutes. The plan was thereby frustrated by the shortage of J2 fuel available for flying tests.

On 30 November 1944, the RLM requested the design of a ramjet propelled fighter. In December, the Oberammergau project bureau started working on a version of the Messerschmitt P.1101 powered by a Sänger 1000 in anticipation that the HeS 011 turbojet would not be ready on time. The modifications involved increasing the diameter of the fuselage, installing three fuel tanks of 1,500, 500 and 120l and designing a new landing gear whose main wheels would retract in tandem under the engine. The take-off was effected with the help of eight detachable RATO rockets of the Schmidding type 109-533, with 1,000kg peak-thrust each, which accelerated the aircraft to 120 m/sec. The new version was called Messerschmitt P.1101 L (Lorinantrieb).

In December 1944, Professor Sänger designed the Überschall-Staustrahljäger (supersonic ramjet-fighter), a high-altitude interceptor of 7 tons propelled by a ramjet of 60,000hp, but the DFS Institut lacked the facilities for its construction. In February 1945, the firm Skoda-Kauba Flugzeugbau-Cakowitz, who had carried out some discouraging experiments with coal-propelled foam ramjets, issued an order to the RLM for the design of an interceptor with ramjet propulsion based on the theoretical work of Sänger.

On 25 February 1945, the company produced the SK P14-01 design, a Mach 0.815 fighter powered by a Sänger 1500 with 22,000hp nominal thrust, 1,000l of fuel, pilot in prone position, one MK 103/30 heavy cannon, landing skid and 10,000m estimated absolute ceiling. The definitive design

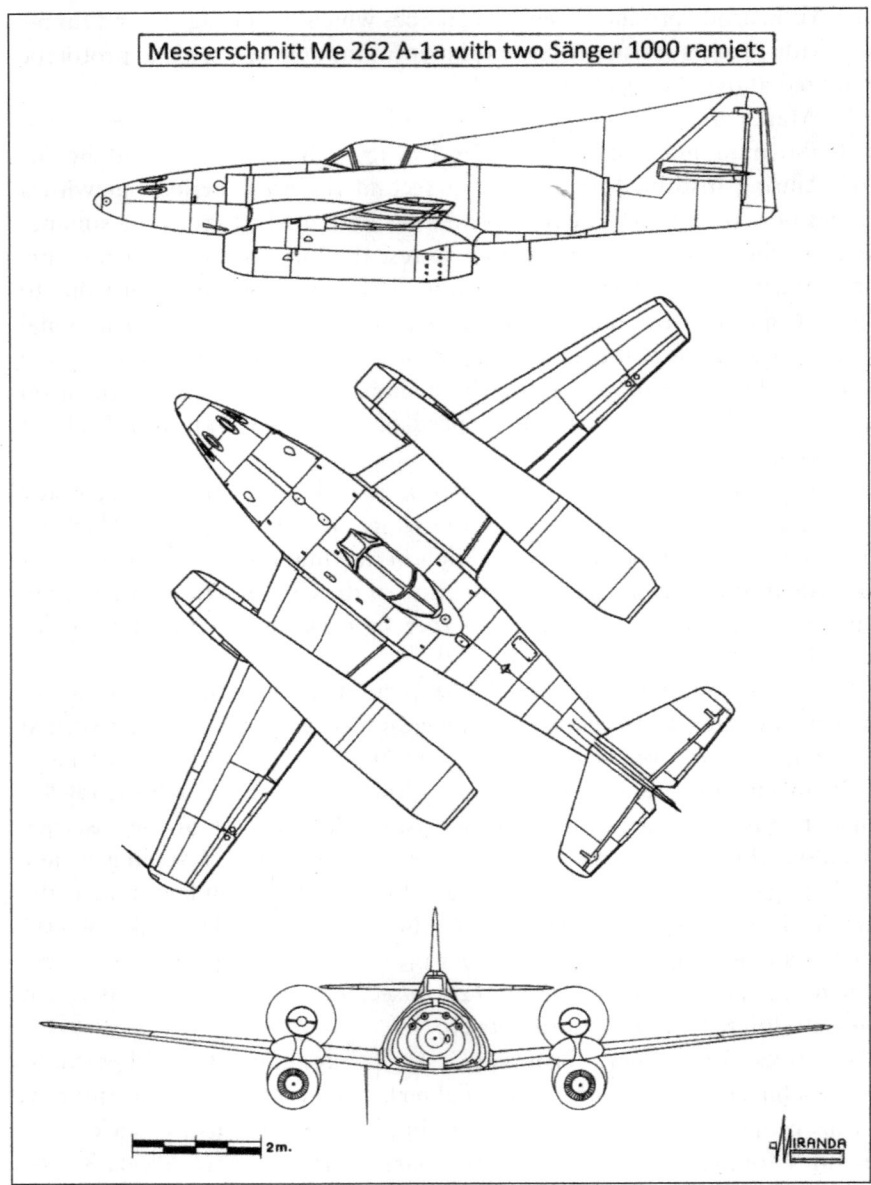

Messerschmitt Me 262 A-1a with two Sänger 1000 ramjets

dated in April was the 7-tone SK P12-02, powered by a Sänger 2500 with 60,000hp nominal thrust, 1,400l of fuel and 850km/h maximum speed. Take-off acceleration was provided by four Schmidding 109-533, mounted above a detachable tricycle trolley.

In March 1945, a Heinkel design team under the leadership of the Dipl.-Ing. Siegfried Günter, designed a high-altitude tailless interceptor named He P.1080, with a 15,100hp Sänger 900 mounted in each wing root,

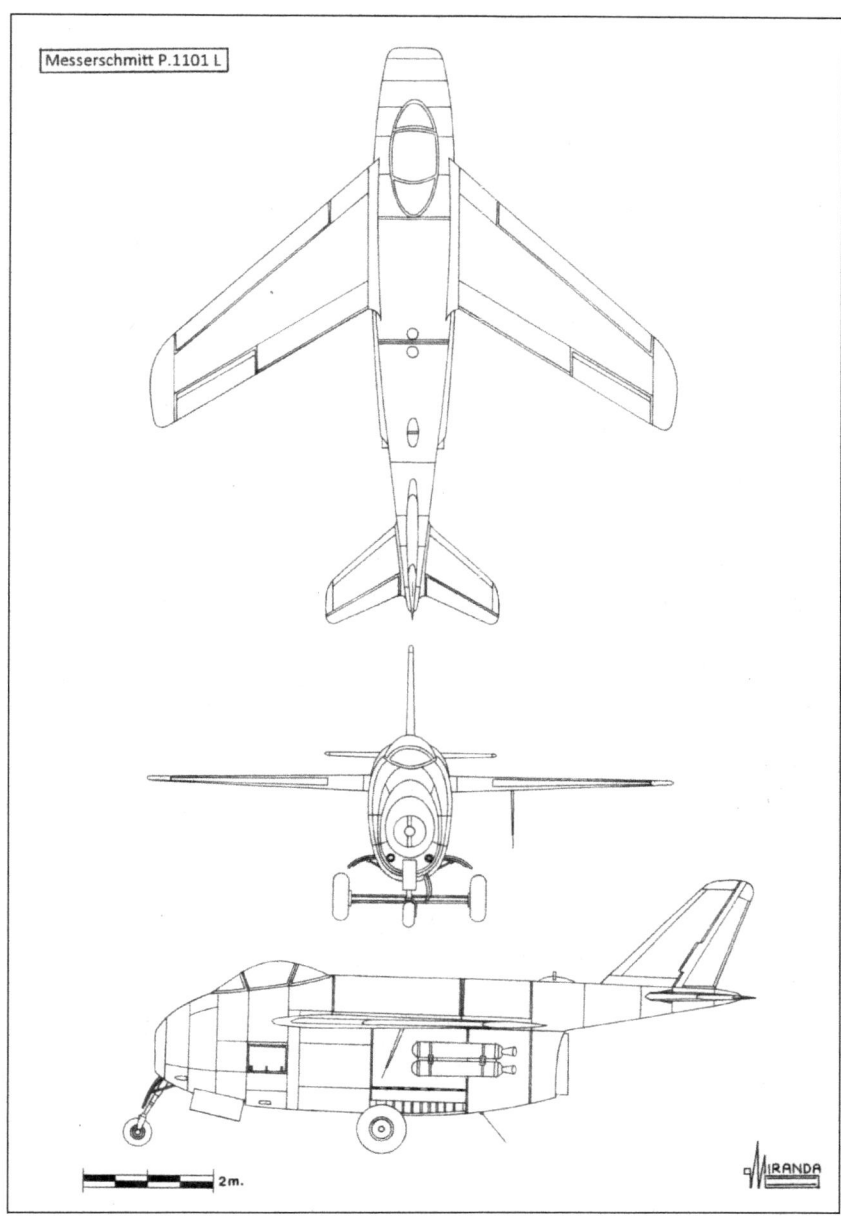

Messerschmitt P.1101 L

an armament of two MK 108/30 cannons and a maximum take-off weight of 3.325kg. The P.1080 could fly for 90 minutes, with 1,100kg of fuel, at an estimated maximum speed of 980km/h. The take-off was carried out from a detachable trolley propelled by four Schmidding 109-533 solid-fuel rockets. The P.1080 was the last project developed by the firm during the second world war.

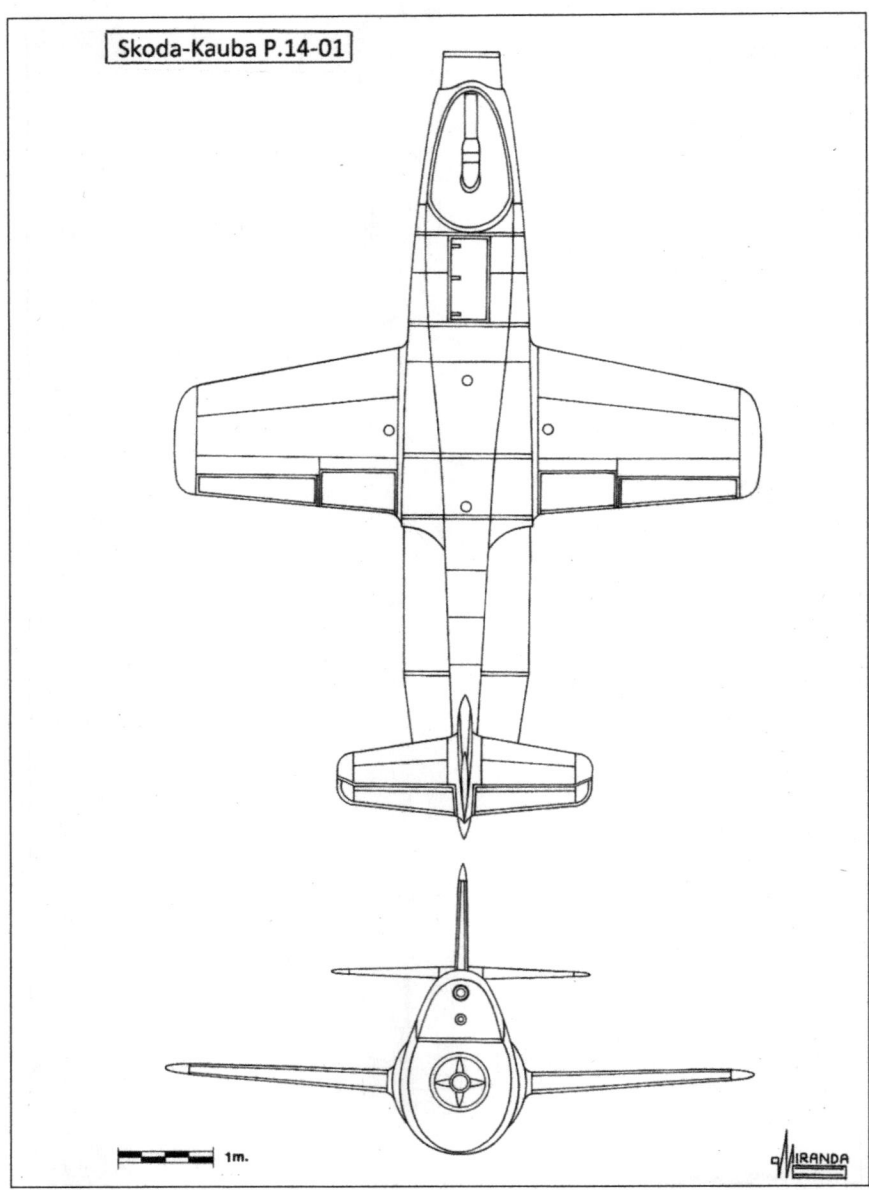

In October 1941, it was evident that the rocket engines planned for the Me 163 B would take months or even years to be ready and Alexander Lippisch started to consider the possibilities of the new Junkers T1 turbojets (early version of the Jumo 004) but they were too long for a Komet airframe. They would have to be installed in a larger aircraft, a heavy fighter of six tons, equivalent to the Me 262 that, with the Me 163 aerodynamics, would have a better ceiling, climb rate and maximum speed.

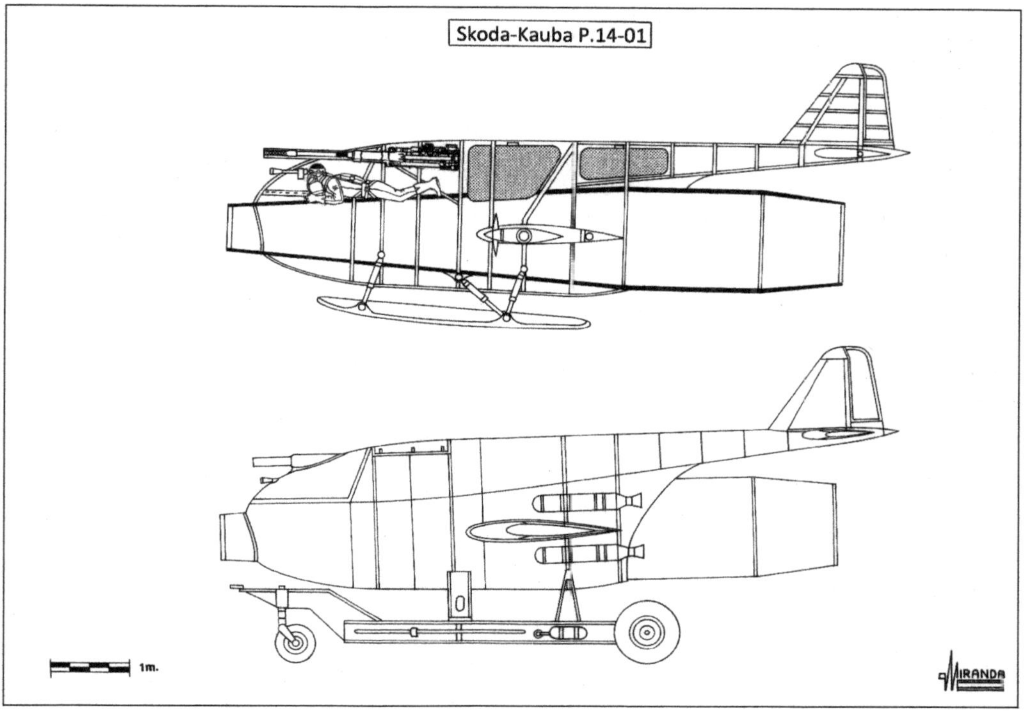

The Strahlrohrjäger Concept

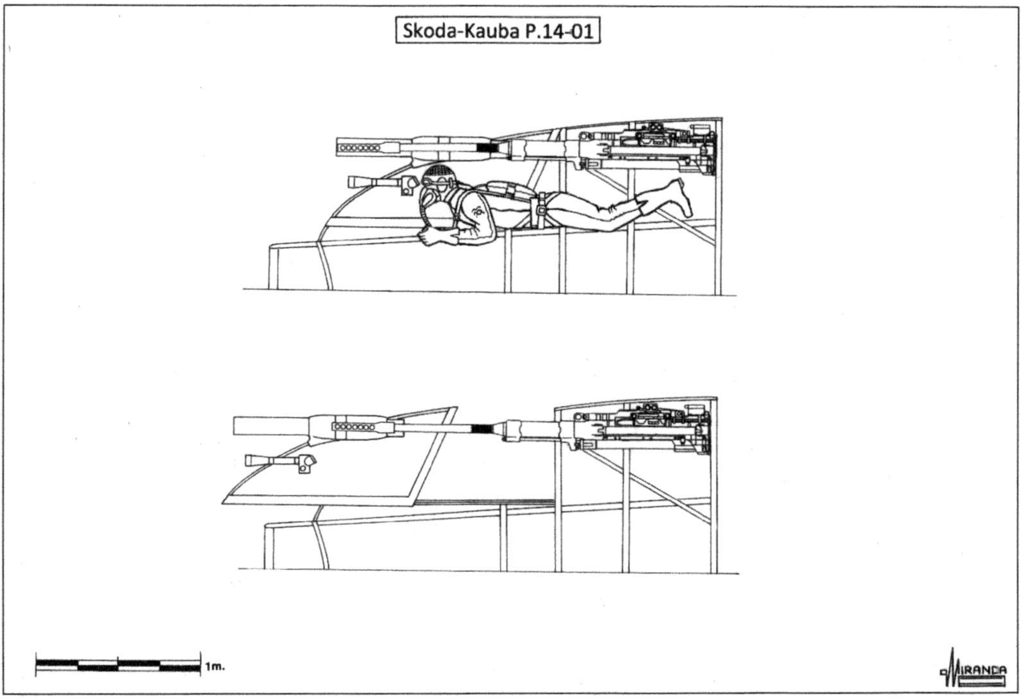

135

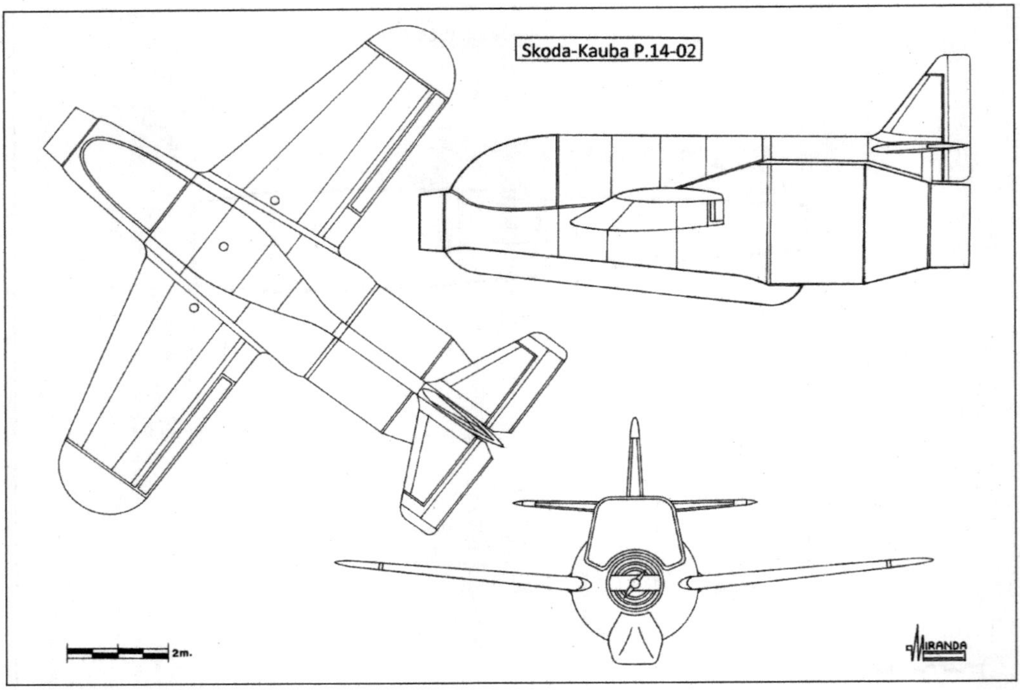
Skoda-Kauba P.14-02
2m.
MIRANDA

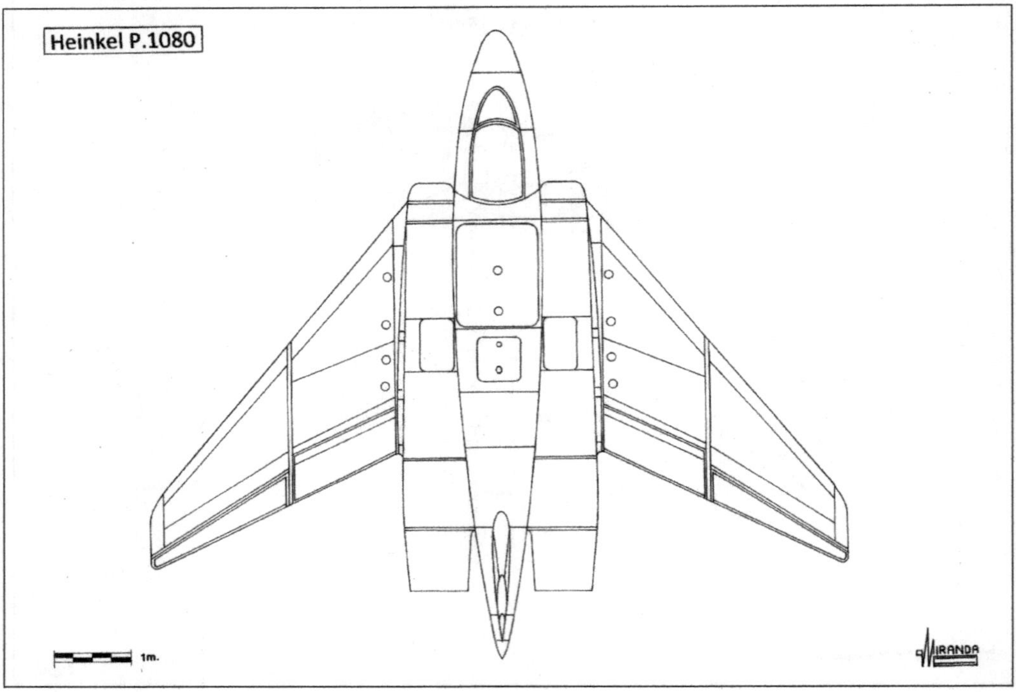
Heinkel P.1080
1m.
MIRANDA

The Strahlrohrjäger Concept

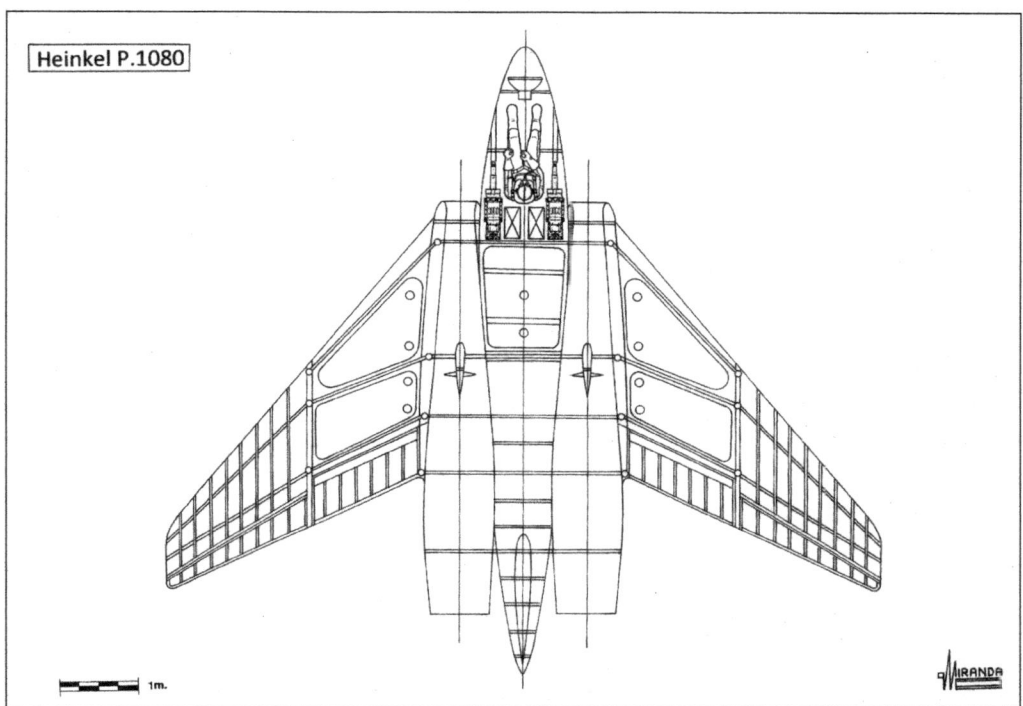

Heinkel P.1080

The project Lippisch P.11-92 (13/09/42) was presented to the OKL as the response to the specification published by the RLM's Technical Department on 20 October 1942. It required a twin-engine jet bomber with 1,000kg payload, 700km/h maximum speed and 1,046km penetration depth.

Abteilung L was disbanded within Messerschmitt in April and the Lippisch design team moved to Vienna, to form the Aeronautical Research Institute Luftfahrtforschungsanstalt Wien. The works on the P.11 continued there.

The original single tailfin was replaced by a double one in the *zerstörer* version (named Delta VI projekt) based on the P.11-121 formula.

The whole production of turbojets was absorbed by the assembly lines of the Me 262 and Ar 234. The Jumo 004 and BMW 003 were unreliable and difficult to manufacture in great quantities, given that the additives to harden the special steel of the blades, the spare parts and the fuel were scarce. The new HeS 011 was just an unfinished prototype.

Lippisch turned his attention to the third type of jet engines, the Lorin Ramjets, to power his future designs. His first try, on 12 April 1944, projected the integration of a Delta VI airframe with a 20,000hp Lorin Stahlrohr of oval section, with liquid fuel carbon disulphide self-igniting at the compression temperature of the air, at the end of the multiple-shock diffusers of the Oswatitsch-type.

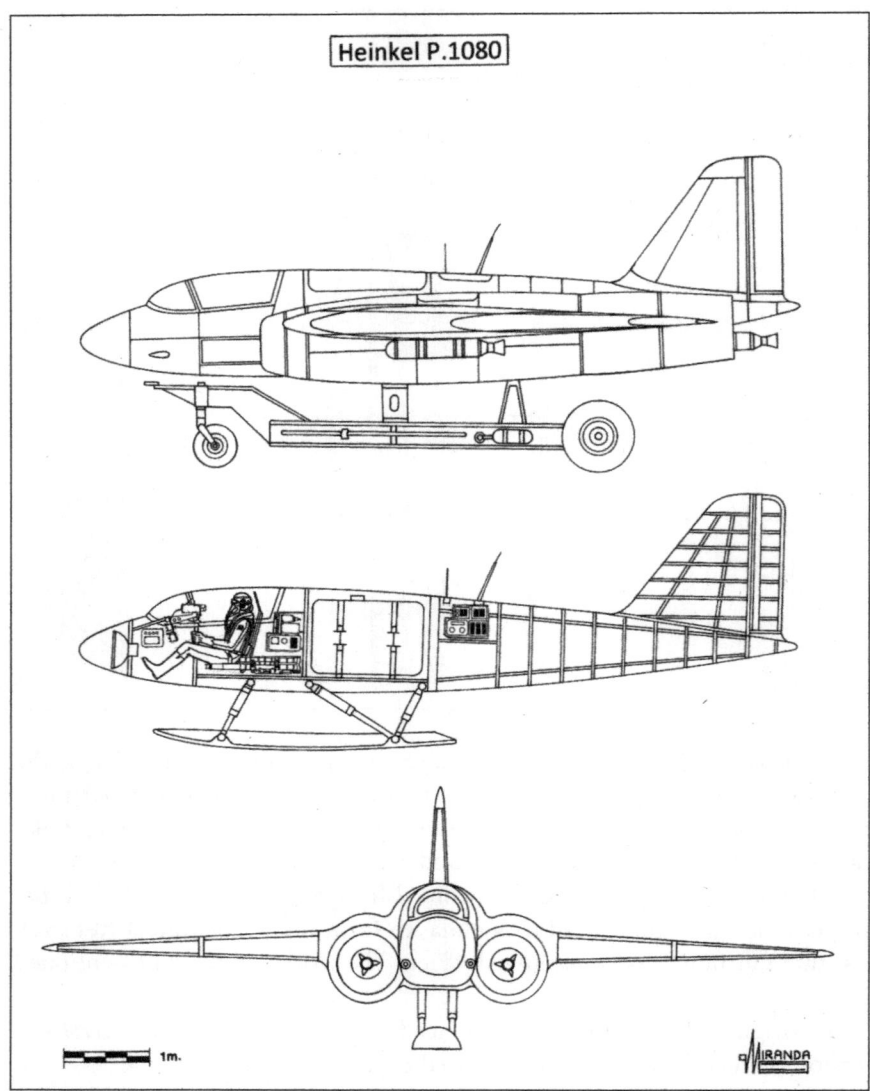

The research continued with the P.12 and P.13 that already included ramjets designed by him.

The new design, named LP12 Entwurf I, consisted of a set of triangular wing and tailfin fitted to the ramjet tube that acted as fuselage. The pilot occupied the tailfin and the fuel tanks were housed in the wing. The ramjet needed to move at a minimum speed of 200km/h before being started. To achieve this, in August 1944 it was proposed to carry the LP12 up to 4,000m over a Focke-Wulf Fw 58, in Mistel configuration, and launch it from there.

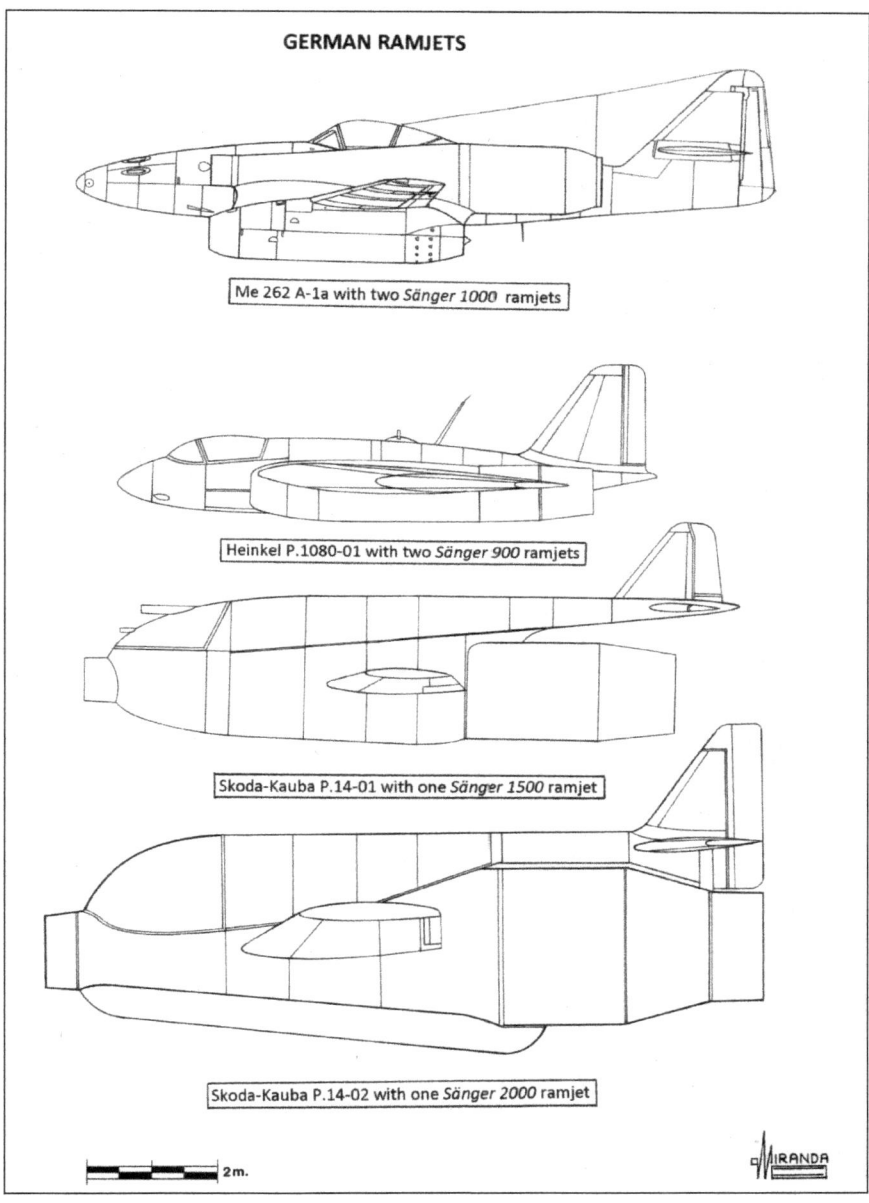

GERMAN RAMJETS

Me 262 A-1a with two *Sänger 1000* ramjets

Heinkel P.1080-01 with two *Sänger 900* ramjets

Skoda-Kauba P.14-01 with one *Sänger 1500* ramjet

Skoda-Kauba P.14-02 with one *Sänger 2000* ramjet

However, tests performed in April 1944 on the use of a ramjet for the project P.11 Delta VI, proved that they could generate more power by increasing the number of sprinklers in the grid of the fuel injection system and the volume of the combustion chamber.

The new airframe Entwurf II was designed around a bigger ramjet, to adapt the new power plant to the LP 12. Entwurf II kept the circular intake.

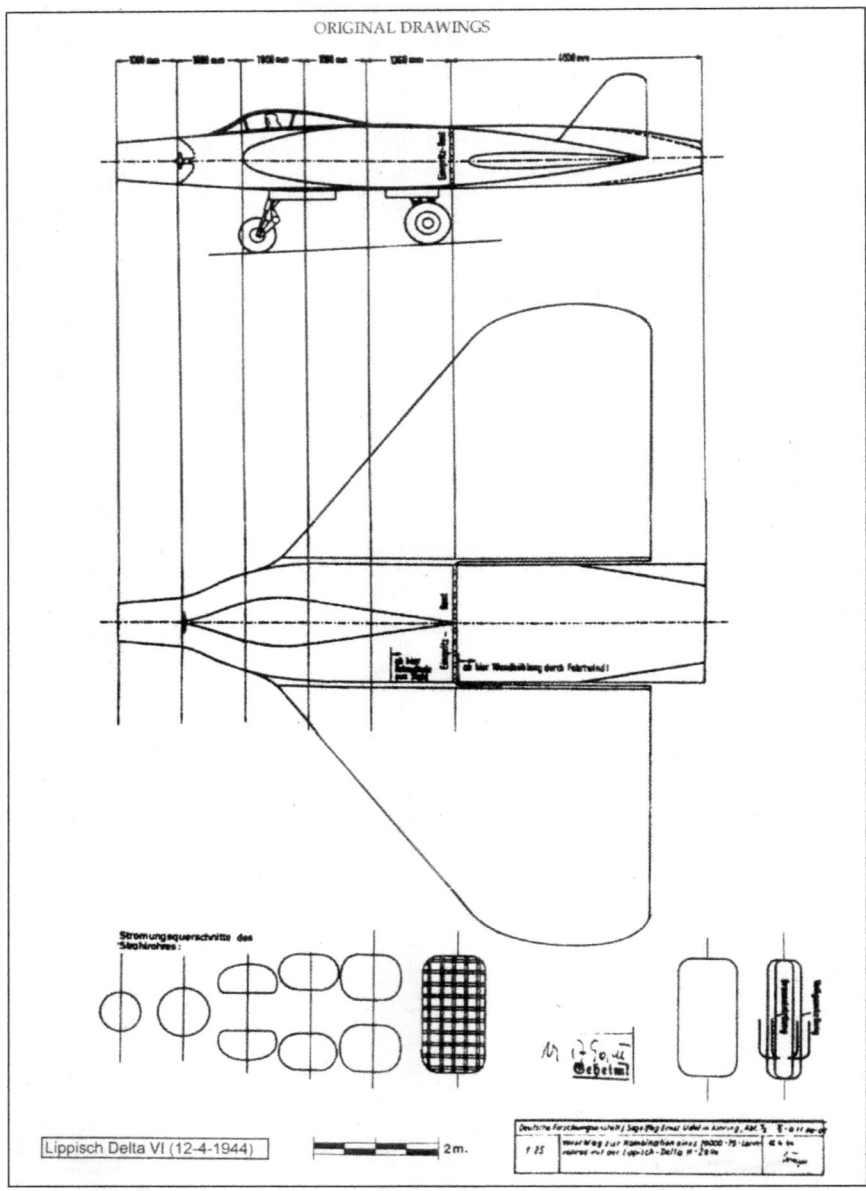

A dividing wall within this intake split the air in two D-shaped ducts to both sides of the pilot cockpit. The fuel mixed in those ducts, after passing through the two sprinkling grids separated 25cm from each other. Both ducts joined again in a combustion chamber of hexagonal section, located behind the cockpit that stretched towards the exhaust nozzle. The wind tunnel tests proved that the model had too much drag.

Entwurf III added internal aerodynamic refinements, like the adoption of an elliptical section along the whole ramjet. As for the outer parts, the wing and tail surfaces were redesigned and the landing gear consisted of a unique retractable wheel. Even so, the model still generated a great degree of drag due to the complex system of inner ducts, and had no transonic capacity.

Entwurf IV simplified the air intake by removing the bifurcation. To that purpose, the pilot should be in prone position, lying over the air intake, within an aerodynamic clear canopy. The air intake had an elliptical section, but with a flatter axis relation of 2.8:1, ending in an elliptical sprinkler grid that led to a hexagonal combustion chamber. The nozzle, equipped with four hydraulically operated flaps, had a variable geometry rectangular section.

During the last year of the war, the scarcity of oil suffered by Germany induced scientists and engineers to experiment with alternative fuels. The most refined types of gasoline were used for conventional piston engines. The BMW 003 turbojets worked with B.4 (87-octane petrol). The J2 and K1, burnt by the Jumo 004 and Heinkel He S 011 turbojets, were heavy kerosene. The Argus pulsejet of the V-1 worked with crude petrol. The Peenemünde engineers designed a V-2 that worked with diesel oil and S-Stoff (mixture of nitric acid (96%) and ferrous chloride (4%), also called Salbei). Dr Pabst, from the Gas Dynamics section of the Focke-Wulf Company, suggested that the ramjets of the future Triebflügel fighter burned even less volatile fuels as pitch oil or lignite tar. To that purpose, they had to design a compact evaporating plant that could be installed onboard.

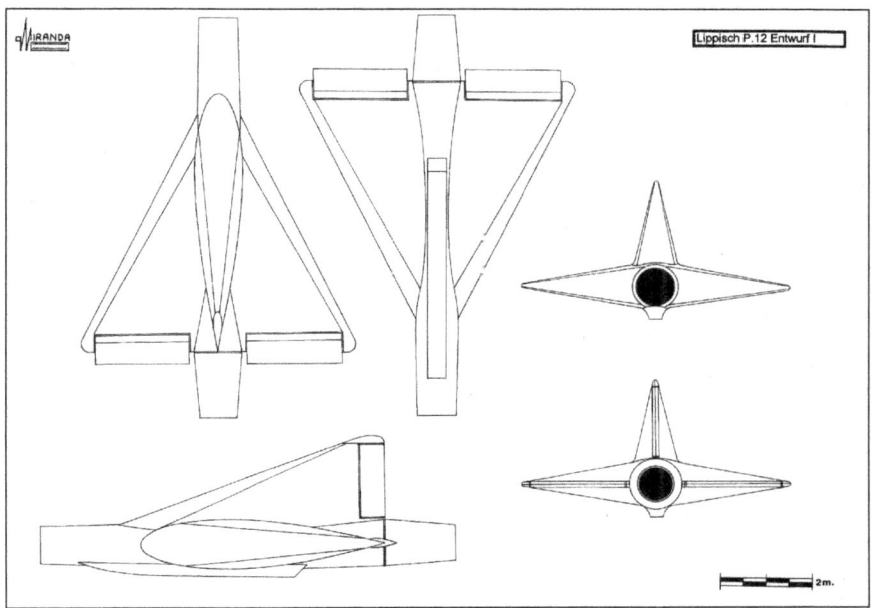

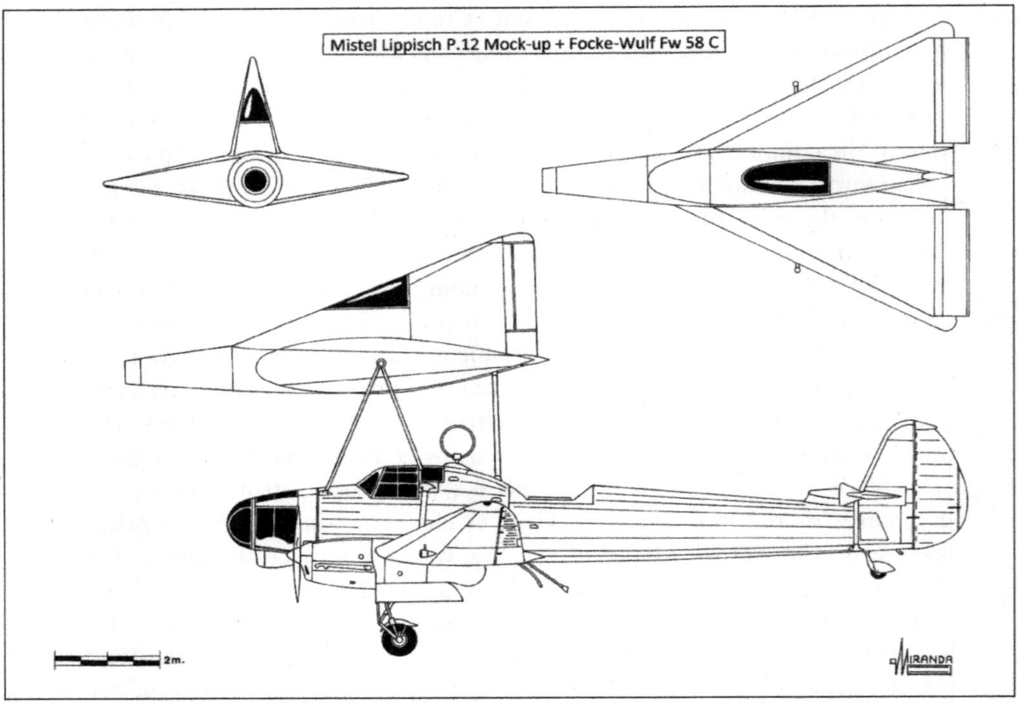
Mistel Lippisch P.12 Mock-up + Focke-Wulf Fw 58 C
2m.
MIRANDA

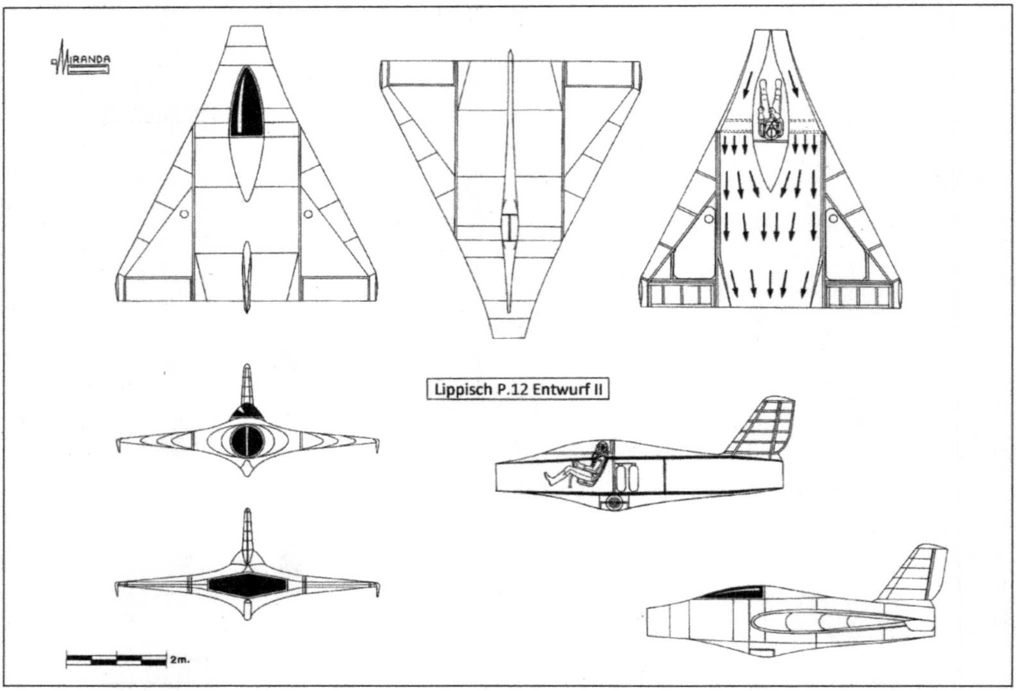
MIRANDA
Lippisch P.12 Entwurf II
2m.

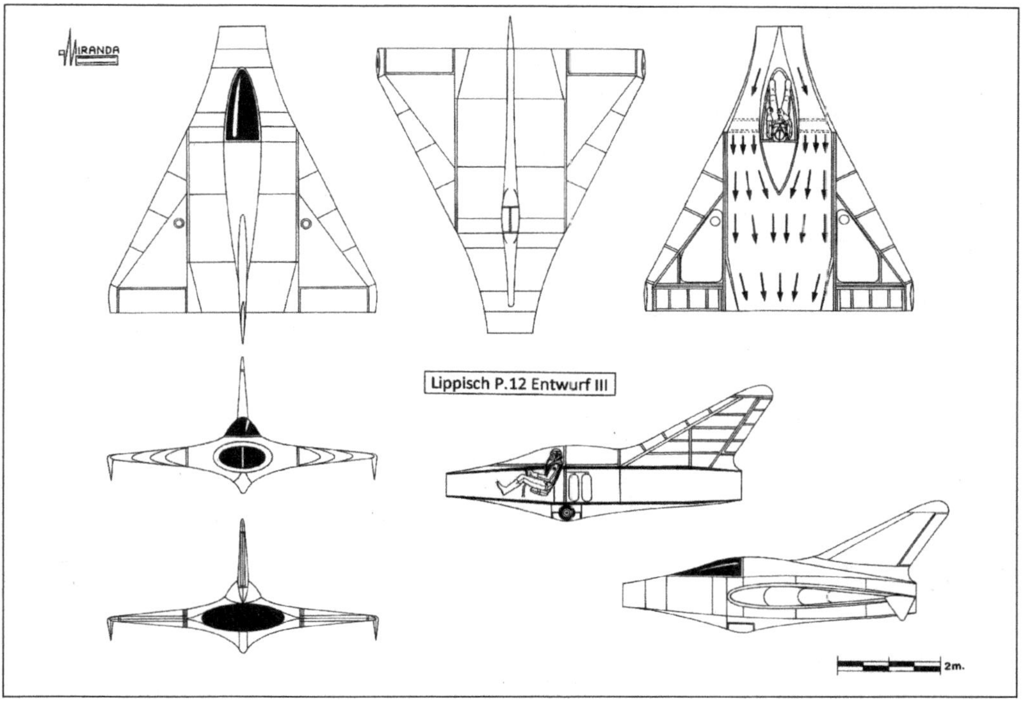

The Strahlrohrjäger Concept

143

Lippisch P.12 Entwurf III

2m.

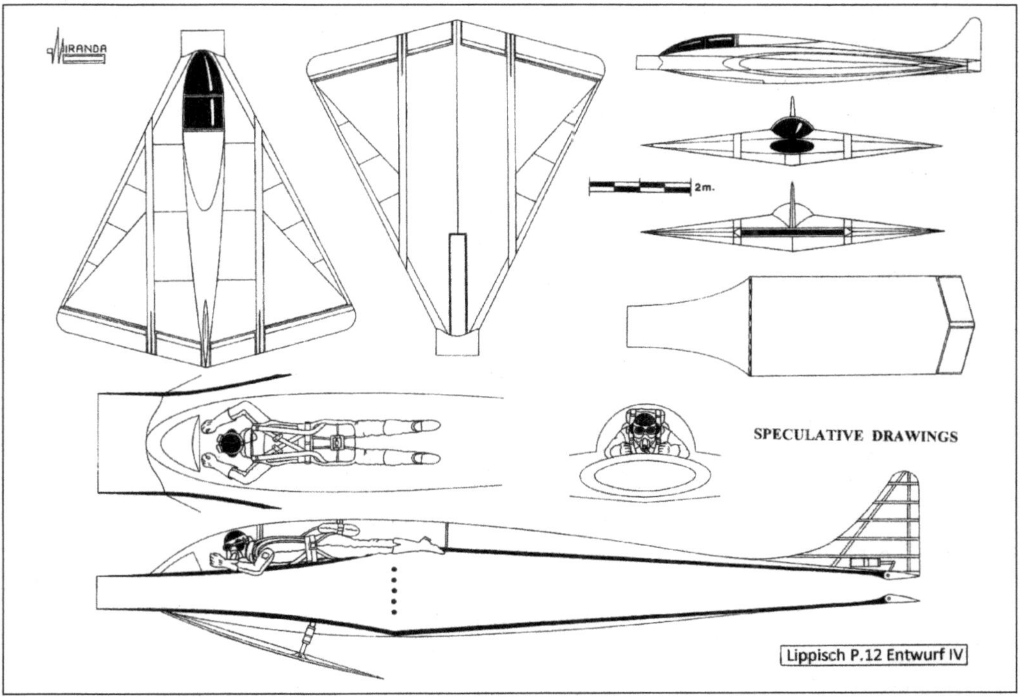

Lippisch P.12 Entwurf IV

SPECULATIVE DRAWINGS

2m.

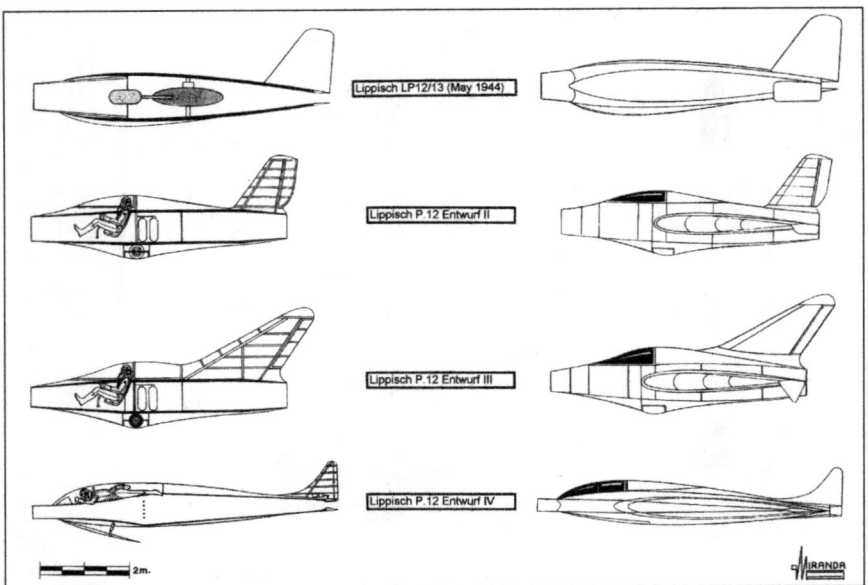

And what about coal? An aircraft is certainly not a locomotive and neither can it carry the weight of a steam boiler. But it is common knowledge among coal miners that air saturated with coal dust is a powerful explosive. Dr Zippermeyer, at the Speer Ministry research establishment near Lofer, built the vortex gun Wirbelkanone and the atmospheric whirlwind gun Luftwirbelkannone, both based on this type of combustion.

Dr K. Wahl, of the Kirchheim Technische Institut, made a Lorin ramjet that worked with coal dust fuel. They built a burner prototype of rectangular section, to that effect, that burnt a brown coal tablet in the middle of a strong wind flow. The tablet was made of suspended coal dust in pressurised inflammable oil foam and was carried to the air stream in a wire mesh container, set in the duct at a small angle of 6 degrees. It was 265 x 200 x 15cm and weighted 670kg.

The idea was adopted by Lippisch, to power his P.13 project.

The first configuration of the P.13 was named P.13a Entwurf I. The air came into the combustion chamber through two oblique air intakes fitted with deflector vanes. It was then guided by a hydraulically operated flap towards the upper part of the carbon tablet, already burning thanks to a gas burner. The air was forced to run through the whole surface of the tablet, spreading the combustion, thus increasing its volume and temperature and converting it into carbon dioxide. Afterwards, it went to an expansion chamber and was expelled through a rectangular nozzle fitted with hydraulically operated flaps. The burning speed (320km/h) was achieved by means of a Walter rocket located at the base of the tailfin.

As it happened, with the LP 12 the wind tunnel tests proved that the deflectors and the flap located within the air duct produced too much drag.

This conclusion led to the P.13a Enwurf II version, equipped with an air intake based on that of the Entwurf I, rounded wingtips and tailfin tips, and a cockpit with improved visibility. A reduced-scale air model named LP 12/13 was also built to test the new ramjet in flight.

It was discovered that the slope of the tablet generated too much drag and that the combustion geometry was not right. To obviate those defects, the P. 13a Entwurf II was equipped with a new type of burner (that would hopefully be the production version) and renamed P. 13a Entwurf III.

This modification consisted of changing the tablet to an oval axial-section block of 800kg, housed in a wire mesh circular basket of the same section, within the duct and positively rotated around its vertical axis at some 60rpm by means of an electric engine.

The combustion was initiated by a gas burner and could use liquid fuel to facilitate starting up. The coal now used took the shape of small granules and not irregular lumps as previously, since granules produced a more controlled and even burning.

The system was tested in the LFW in Vienna before the end of the war and worked fine.

It was expected that the new engine had a power superior to the 60,000hp reached by the Sänger ramjets, which ran on liquid fuel and had a range of 45 minutes' powered flight.

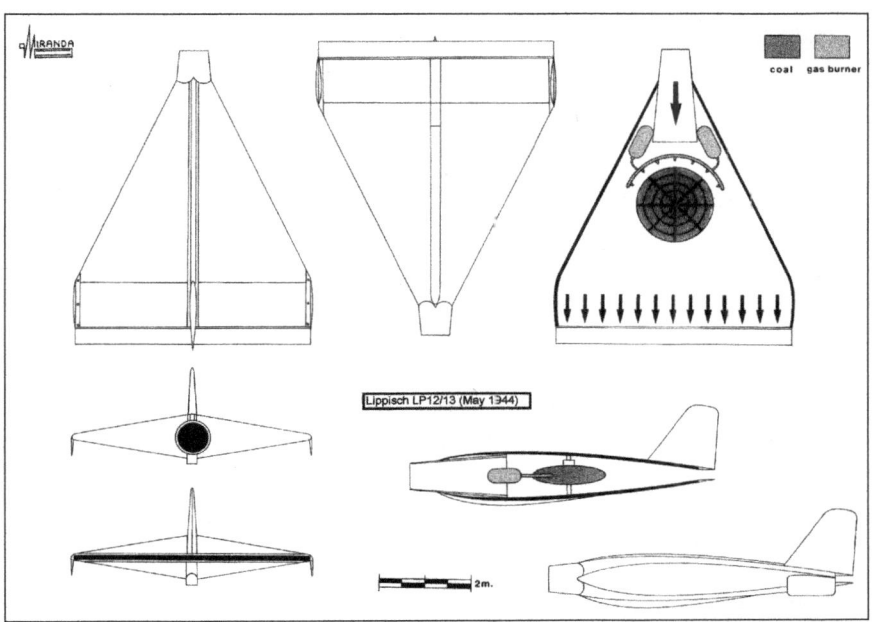

Lippisch LP12/13 (May 1944)

Although the power of the engine could be regulated by opening or closing the nozzle flaps, this could not be stopped at will by the pilot.

At the end of 1944 tests were carried out with several ramjet engines of the type called RL (Raketen-Lorin) in the BMW wind tunnel at Oberweisenfeld. They consisted of a 'cold' Walter rocket embedded into the air-intake of a Lorin ramjet, to induce the necessary airflow for operation while stationary. The rocket would be deactivated when ignition velocity was reached. Research with RL ramjets was sponsored by the Junkers company with the objective of increasing the range of the Me/Ju 263 fighter by adapting two RL of 84cm diameter under the wing roots.

By mid-1944 Dipl-Ing. Heinz Stöckel designed a ramjet bomber called Manuell Gesteuertes Raketenprojektil for the Blohm und Voss firm. It was 11m long and 1.8m in diameter and could carry a warhead of 4,500kg at 300km with an accuracy far superior to that of the V-2 rockets, because it was a piloted missile. The bomber was guided from a parasite ramjet aircraft docked on its back in Mistelschlepp configuration. Its pilot could change the trajectory of the whole set by operating the airbrakes located on the sides of the bomber.

During the terminal dive, at 800m per second, the guidance plane detached, performing a high-G manoeuvre and using the speed to ignite its own ramjet engine that would allow it to return to base landing like a glider. To better support the separation manoeuvre, the pilot adopted a prone position. In August, the Blohm und Voss firm proposed a reduced version,

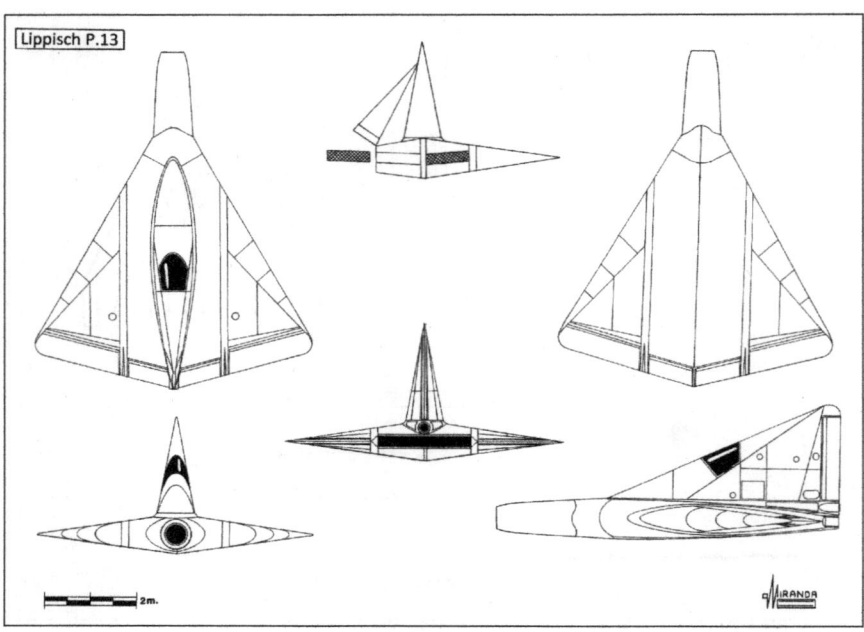

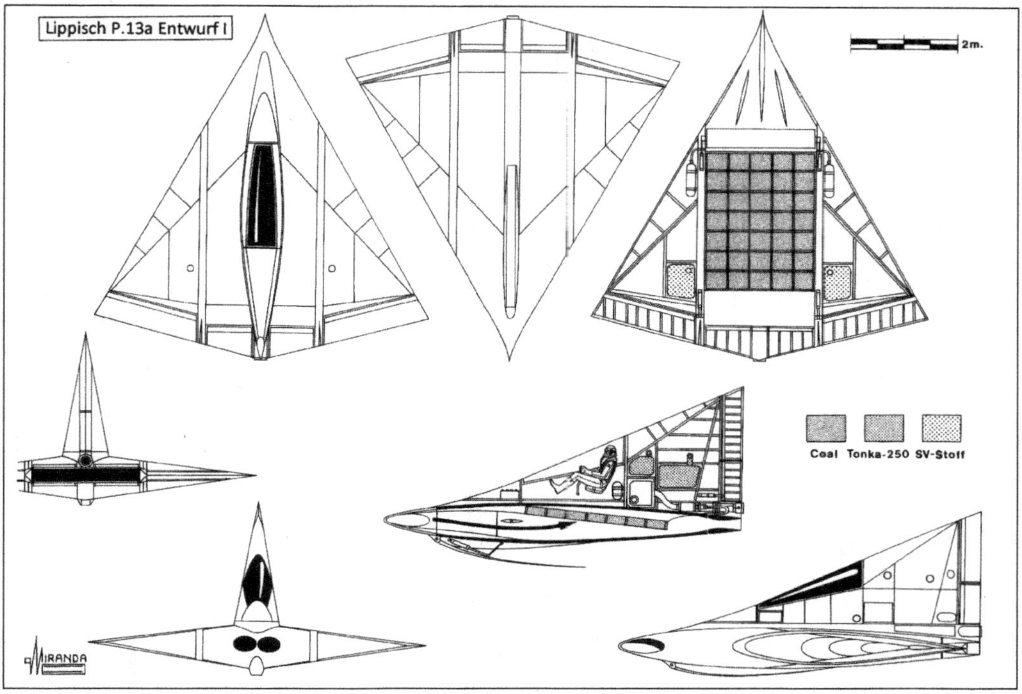

The Strahlrohrjäger Concept

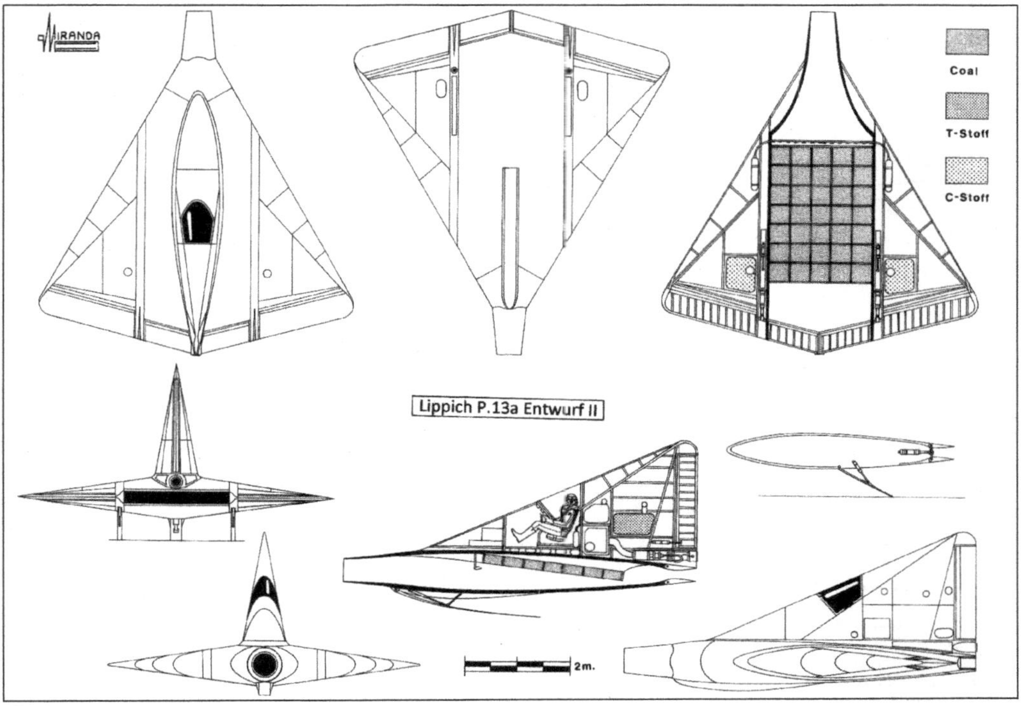

147

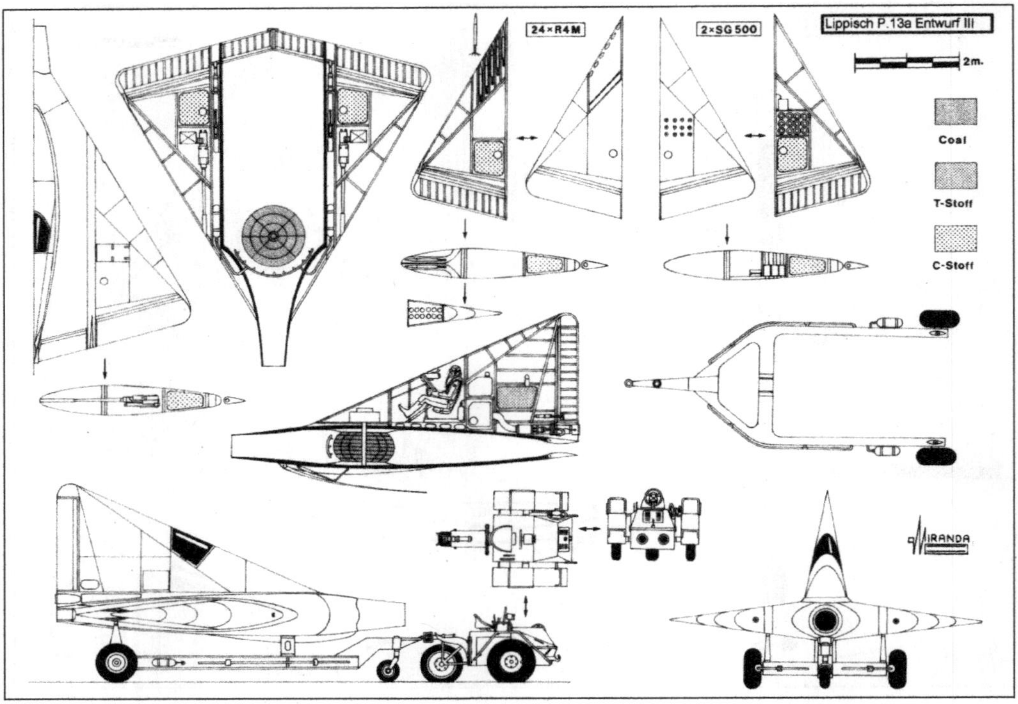

148　　　　　　　*Rocket Interceptors: 1941–1947*

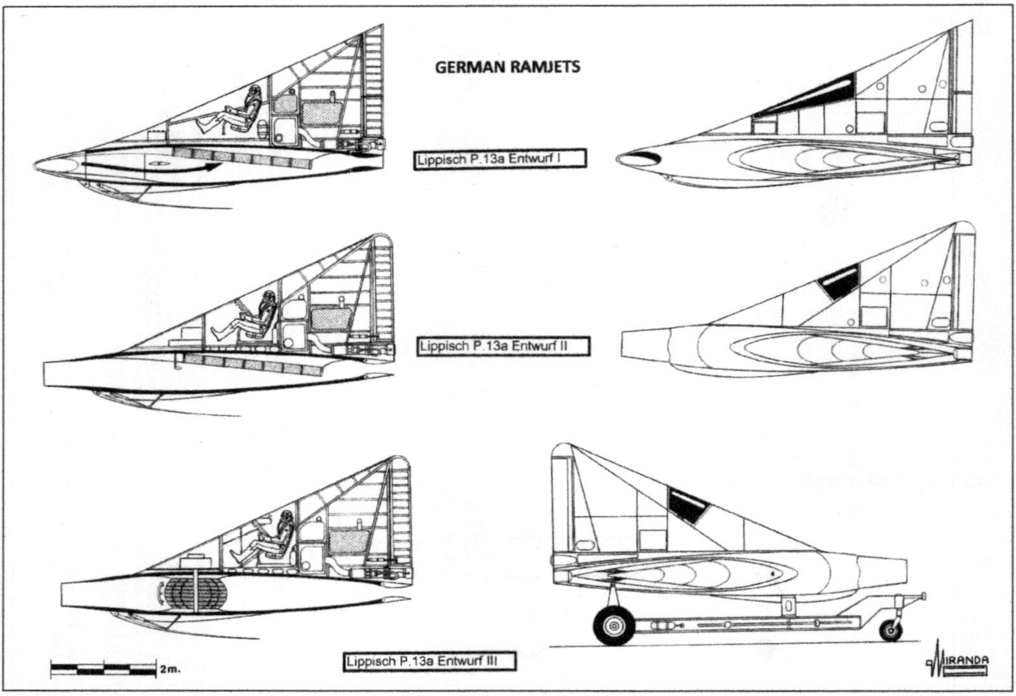

called P.214, which could be used either as anti-ship or Pulkzerstörer. The lower element of 8m long and 1m diameter could carry a warhead of 2,300kg over 1,000km. It would be powered by a ramjet which should activate after its launch from a Dornier Do 217 Mistelschlepp.

In late August, Heinz Stöckel proposed the construction of a rammer based on the guidance aircraft of the P.124, with an armoured nose cone of 150kg, provided with eight radial blades and a pilot seated conventionally. The engine, which was called Rammrakete and was based on the Walter RL, consisted of a monopropellant 'cold' rocket with 1,500kg of thrust. With this power, the rammer could be launched vertically from a ramp of three rails, like a Natter. By increasing the height and speed, the air coming through the annular air-intake mixed with the hot gases of the engine in a post-combustion chamber, acting as the oxidiser component of a bi-fuel rocket.

The ramjet ignition speed was set at 720km/h with a thrust augmentation of 10,000kg. The project was presented to the RLM as Rammschussjäger Entwurf I, a dispensable VTO rammer.

After the impact, the heavy armoured cockpit detached from the airframe falling to a safe altitude before the pilot could complete the descent using his own parachute. The system was used by the Douglas D-558-1 in 1947.

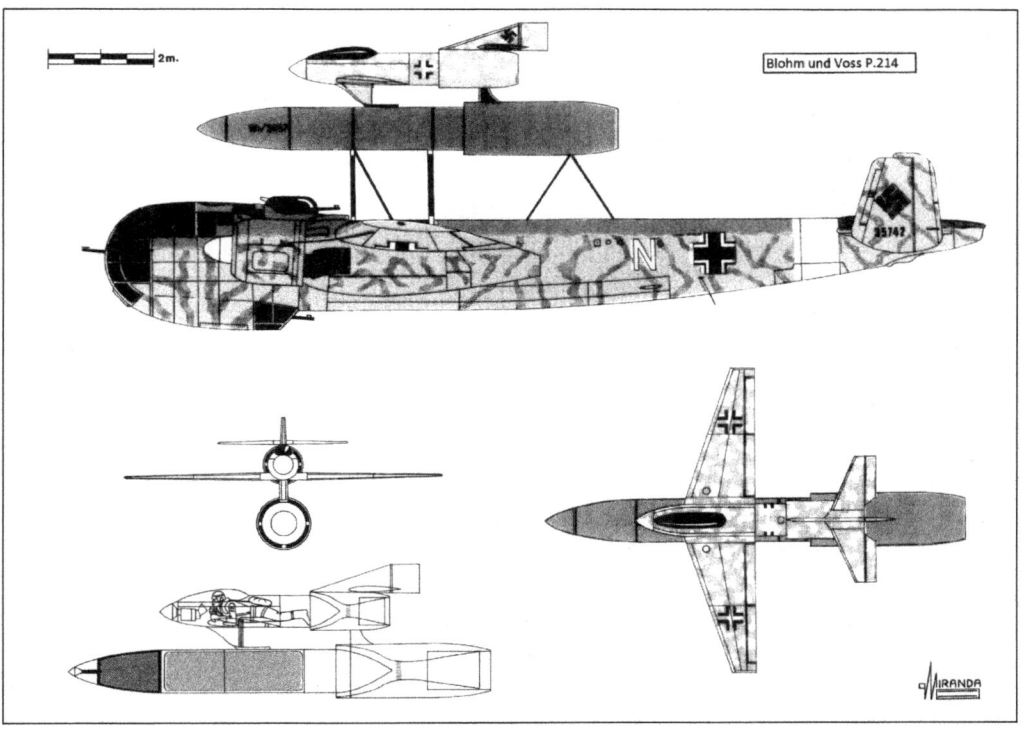

RAMMSCHUSSJÄGER ENTWURF I TECHNICAL DATA: Wingspan: 4m. Length: 5.2m. Height: 1.65m, ramjet diameter: 0.9m. Wing area: 3sq.m. Maximum weight: 1,000kg. Estimated maximum speed: 900km/h. Ceiling: 19,000m. Range: 200km. Endurance (with 450kg of mono-propellant T-Stoff): 11.5 minutes.

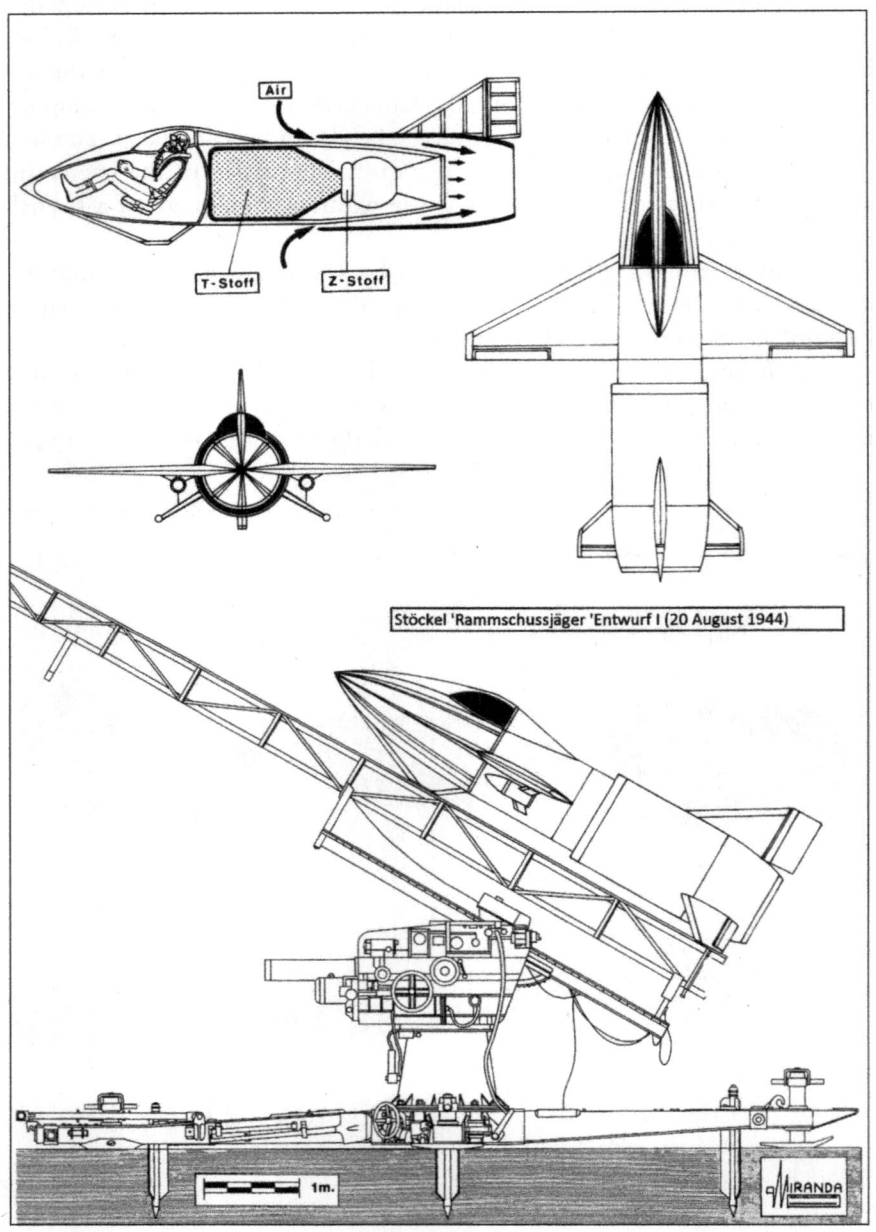

Stöckel 'Rammschussjäger' Entwurf I (20 August 1944)

The Strahlrohrjäger Concept

The RLM considered the vertical launch too radical as this type of engine did not allow to adjust the thrust and it was feared that a full power take-off could cause unconsciousness to the pilot, as it happened during the flying test of the Bachem BP 20 M23 in March 1945. Stöckel modified the project as Rammschüssjäger Entwurf II, a Pulkzerstörer/Rammer carried under the belly of a Dornier Do 217. In losing its VTO status, the aircraft could be bigger and transport 1,500kg of T-Stoff extending its range to 600km.

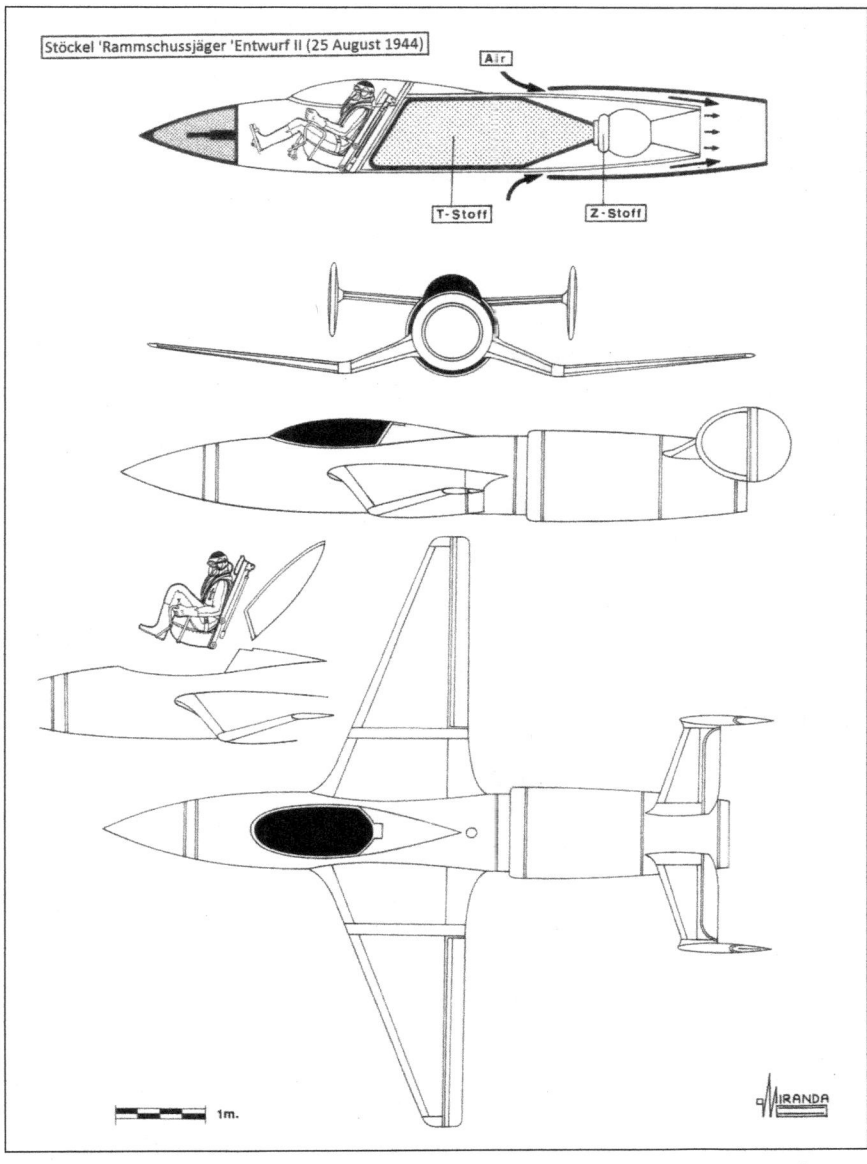

The rocket was activated after launch to take the plane up to an altitude of 10,000m, where the ramjet was ignited, raising the speed to 1,000km/h.

The Entwurf III version was presented at the same time. Slightly larger and powered by a more powerful engine, it was based on the principle of the Walter EinStoff -RL but using two types of propellant and one catalyst. In this model, the combustion chamber had been replaced by four smaller ones located inside the air annular duct. In these cameras, the T-Stoff reacted with the Z-Stoff catalyst producing steam at 550° C which then mixed with

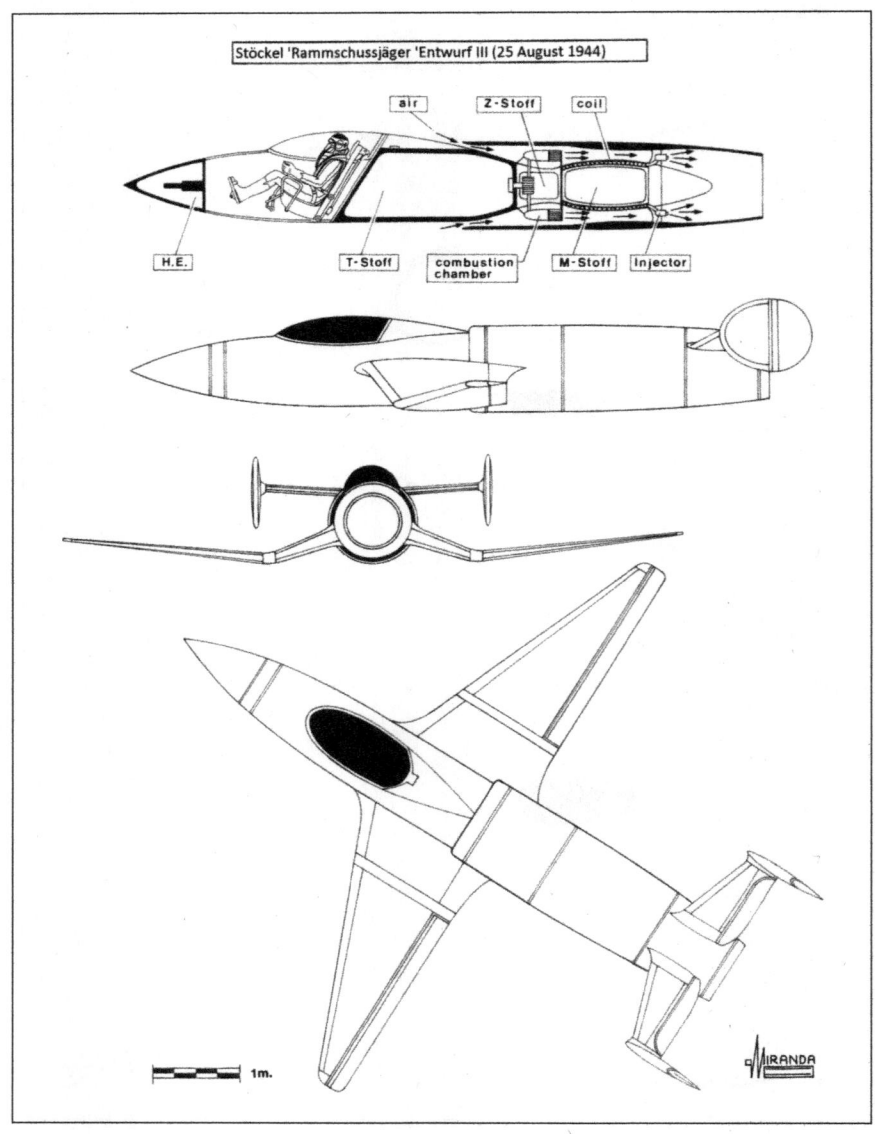

air from the outside in a ratio of 1 to 7. The steam increased its speed and temperature after crossing an annular *venturi*. It then went through a ring of sprinkling injectors where it was mixed with M-Stoff (methyl alcohol) that had been superheated to 700° C in a pressurised coil. The ignition was spontaneous and the thrust superior to that of the Entwurf II.

Based on data published at the end of 1943 on the tests carried out at the Deutsches Forschungsinstitut für Segelflug (DFS) with the Sänger ramjets, Kurt Tank decided to construct a *strahlrohr* of his own design. The programme was led by the Dr-Ing. Otto E. Pabst in the Focke-Wulf gas dynamic department at Kirkhorsten. The first designs of the new engine, dated in the spring of 1944, represent a type of ramjet much shorter than the Sänger, with a length/diameter ratio of 2 to 1. The first prototype, described in Report No. 09045 in mid-August, was 237mm diameter and had 59 injectors of the Fang-Diffuseur type. It was tested in the Luftfahrt Forschungs Anstalt (LFA) Brunswick using hydrogen as fuel.

Starting September, hydrogen was replaced by propane in some tests, but the bombardment of the Leuna-Werks factories advised to replace the propane with vaporised petrol in the operational versions. For this, it was necessary to design a compact heat exchanger to vaporize and superheat the fuel. The thrust produced by this type of ramjet depended on an absolute aerodynamic perfection of both the external surface and the

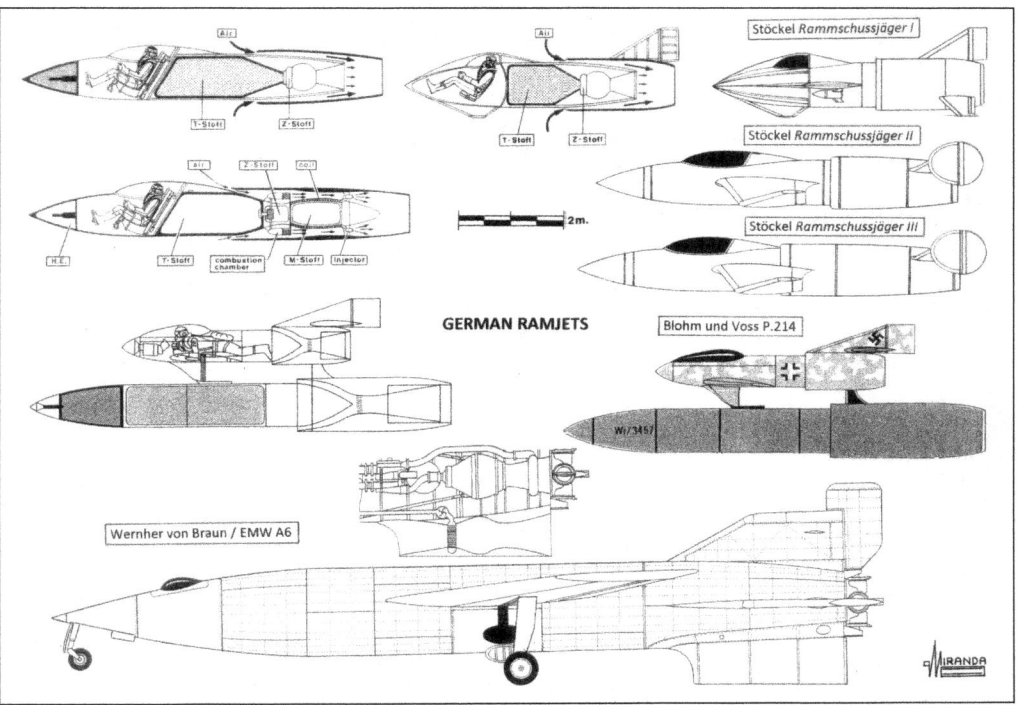

internal air duct, in the design of which intervened Dr-Ing. Theodor Zobel of the LFA Volkenrode and Dr-Ing. Küchemann of the Aerodynamische Versuchs Anstalt (AVA) Göttingen.

The construction of the first two prototypes of 960mm turned out to be more difficult than expected, due to the high internal pressures and the deformation of the outer surface caused by the heat. At the end of the war in Europe, no units had yet been finished. Flight tests were expected to be performed using a Fw 190 A-10 (23 April 1944 project) with a

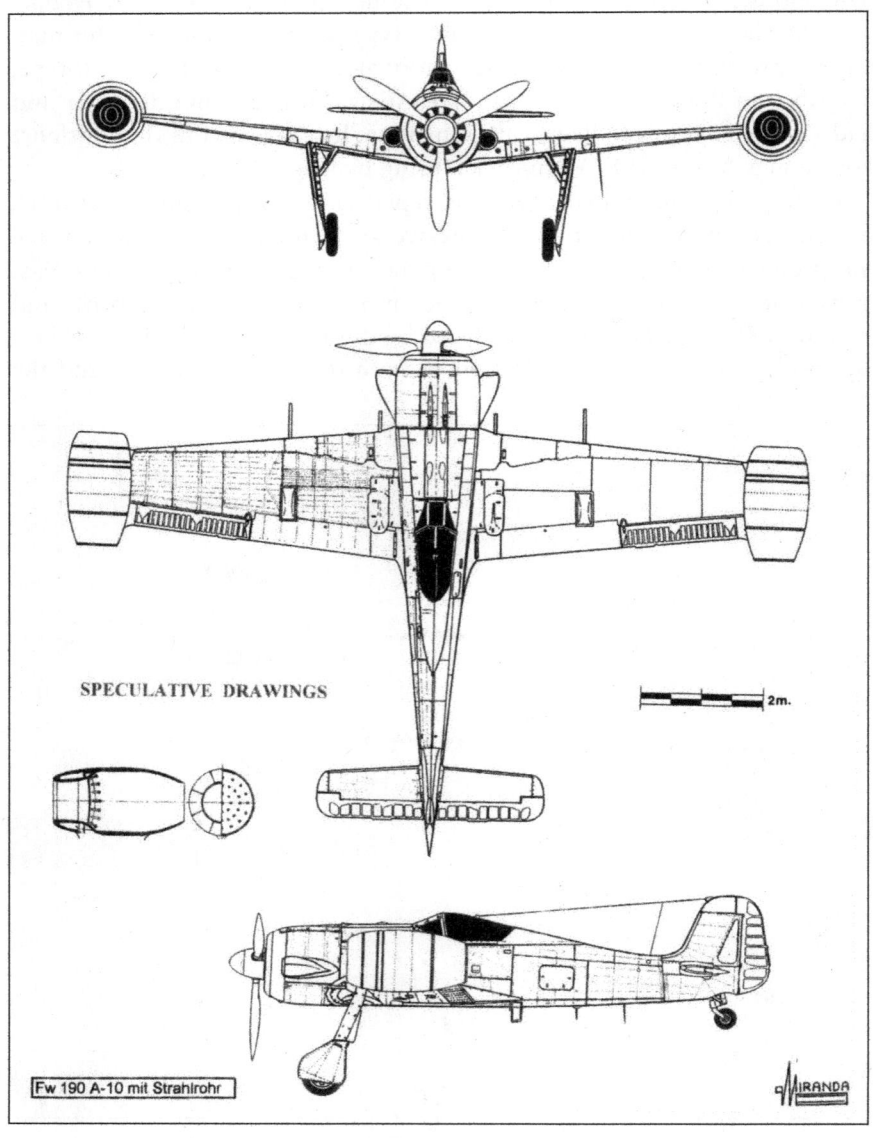

SPECULATIVE DRAWINGS

Fw 190 A-10 mit Strahlrohr

BMW 801 F-1 piston engine and two Pabst ramjets (with 50 injectors, 960mm diameter, 1,920mm length and 1,150kg estimated thrust), installed on the wingtips.

Focke-Wulf Ta 283

The combat version, described in dossier Baubeschreibung Nr.283, was presented to the OKL on 4 August 1944. Commonly referred to in the literature as Focke-Wulf Ta 283, it was a Mach 1.05 high-altitude interceptor faster and better armed than the projects proposed by Messerschmitt, Heinkel and Skoda. It could take off and land using an internal bipropellant rocket engine and reach combat altitude in less than 3 minutes. It also had good ground mobility after landing, thanks to its retractable undercarriage.

The long fuselage of triangular section, built in light alloy, housed the landing gear, the two fuel tanks, with 1,400 and 406l of K1 heavy kerosene, one rocket-propellant tank with 960l of T-Stoff (sufficient for a 420 seconds autonomy, that would allow it to fly another circuit after a missed landing approach) one rocket-propellant tank with 163l of C-Stoff, the pressurised cockpit with ejector seat, the integral tailfin and one Walter rocket engine. The wings, set low on the fuselage with sharply 50 degrees sweep-back angle, were made of wood/plywood/steel using the same technology than those in the Ta 183. They housed six fuel tanks with 1,000l of K1 kerosene, as well as the ailerons and flaps.

The tail planes, with 60 degrees swept-back angle, were entirely constructed in steel to withstand the vibrations and temperatures of 1,000° C generated by the ramjets that were mounted at the tips to avoid detrimental disturbance of the airflow. The nose leg, with a wheel of 479 x 173mm retracted backwards and the narrow track main undercarriage wheels of 740 x 210mm retracted vertically with rocking levers. The armour consisted of three steel plates of 20mm, to protect the cockpit and main fuel tank, another of 10mm to protect the instrument panel and an armoured glass wind screen of 50mm.

The armament proposed initially consisted of two Mk 103/30 heavy cannons, with ZFR 4a telescopic gunsight. Later, considering the short duration of attack, density of fire was preferred and two other possible configurations were proposed to the OKL with four MK 108/30 heavy cannons or four MG 213/20 rapid-fire cannons, with EZ 42 Adler gyroscopic gunsight. Take-off acceleration was provided during 33 seconds by the Walter HWK 109-509 A-1 rocket-motor, with 1,700kg peak-thrust. This was sufficient to reach 240km/h, the ignition velocity of the Pabst ramjets of 135cm in diameter and 270cm in length, each providing 10,850kg thrust at sea level and 2,270kg at 11,000m. Limited controllability of their

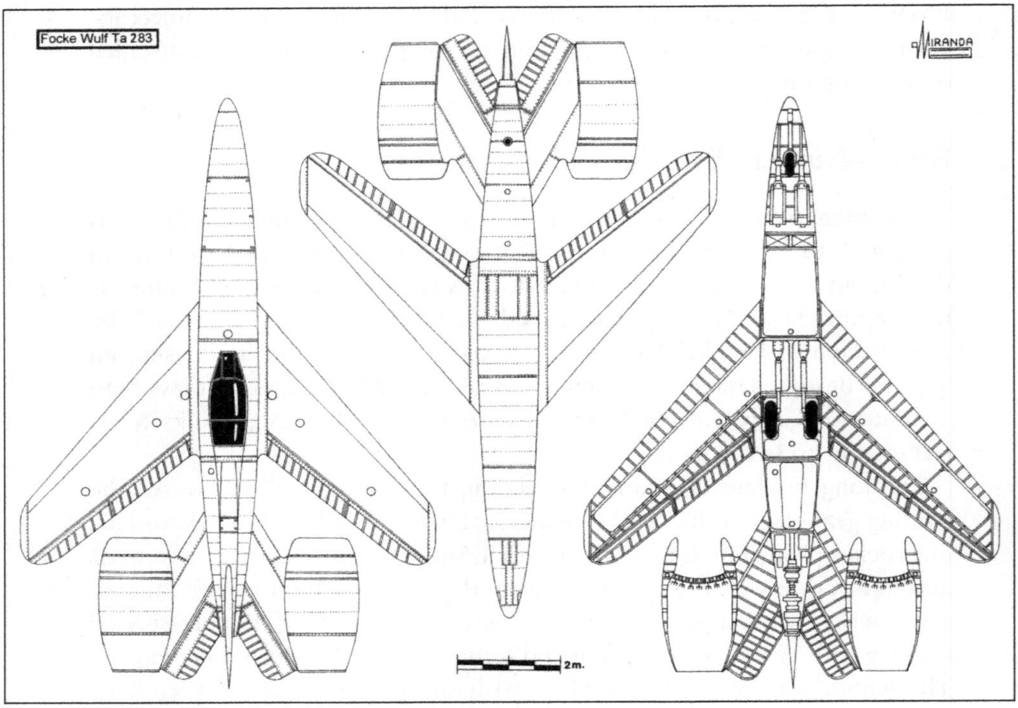

156 Rocket Interceptors: 1941–1947

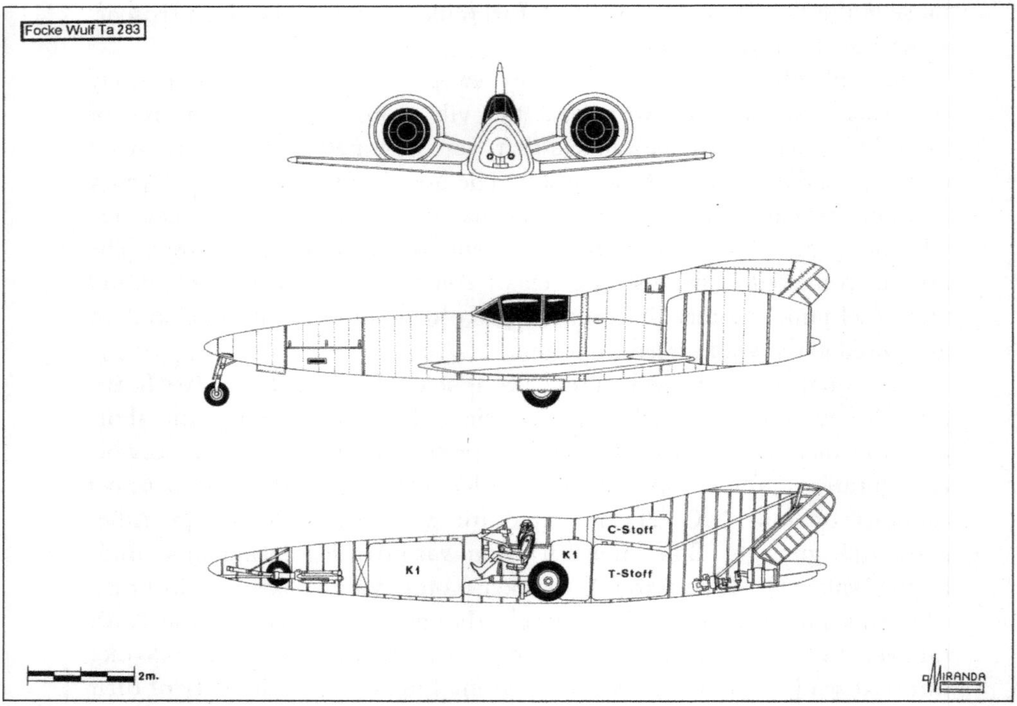

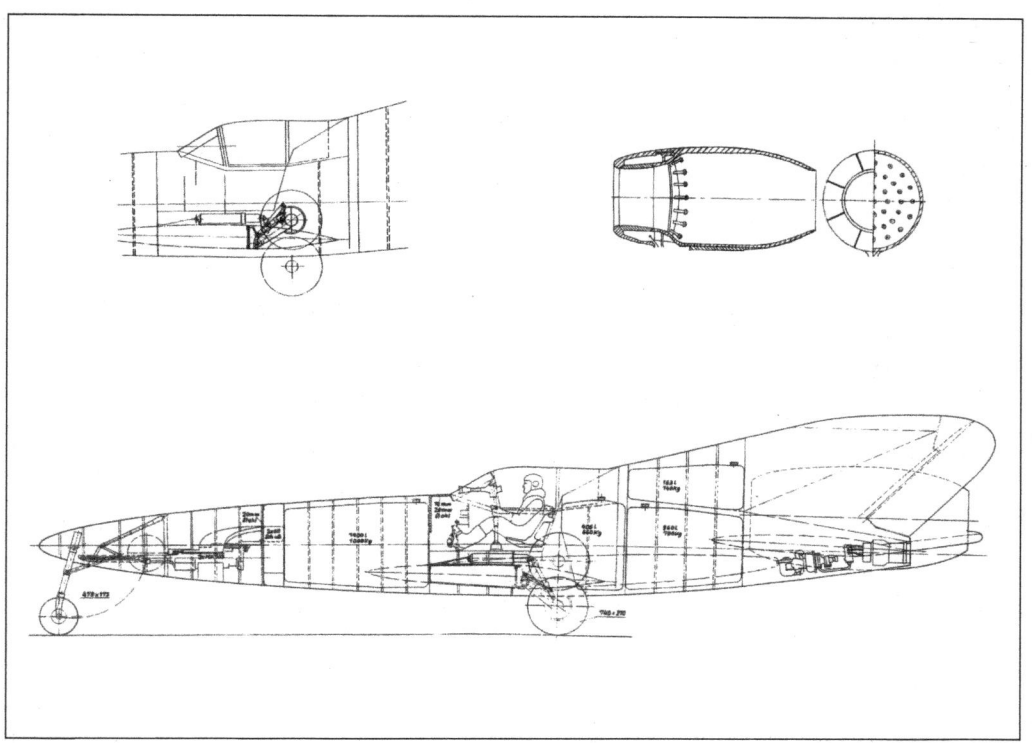

engines was caused by the difficulty in synchronising the throttling using the two electric driven pumps. A wooden mock-up may have been finished, but the project was cancelled by the OKL in the autumn of 1944 due to an excessive landing speed.

FOCKE-WULF TA 283 TECHNICAL DATA: Estimated maximum speed: 1,125km/h at 10,000m. Take-off weight: 5,388kg. Estimated ceiling: 11,000m. Initial climb rate: 160 m/sec. Take-off run: 500m. Range: 690km. Endurance: 43 minutes. Wingspan: 8m. Length: 11.88m. Height: 2.9m. Wing area: 19sq.m.

Focke-Wulf Jäger mit 2 Lorin-Triebwerken und 1 TL

To solve the problem of the excessive landing speed of the Ta 283, the project team led by the Dipl.-Ing. von Halem sent to the OKL the dossier Baubeschreibung Nr.246 describing a short-span STOL variant of the Super TL with an auxiliary turbojet providing vertical lift, one bi-propellant rocket and two ramjets. This project has been commonly described in the literature as Focke-Wulf Super Lorin.

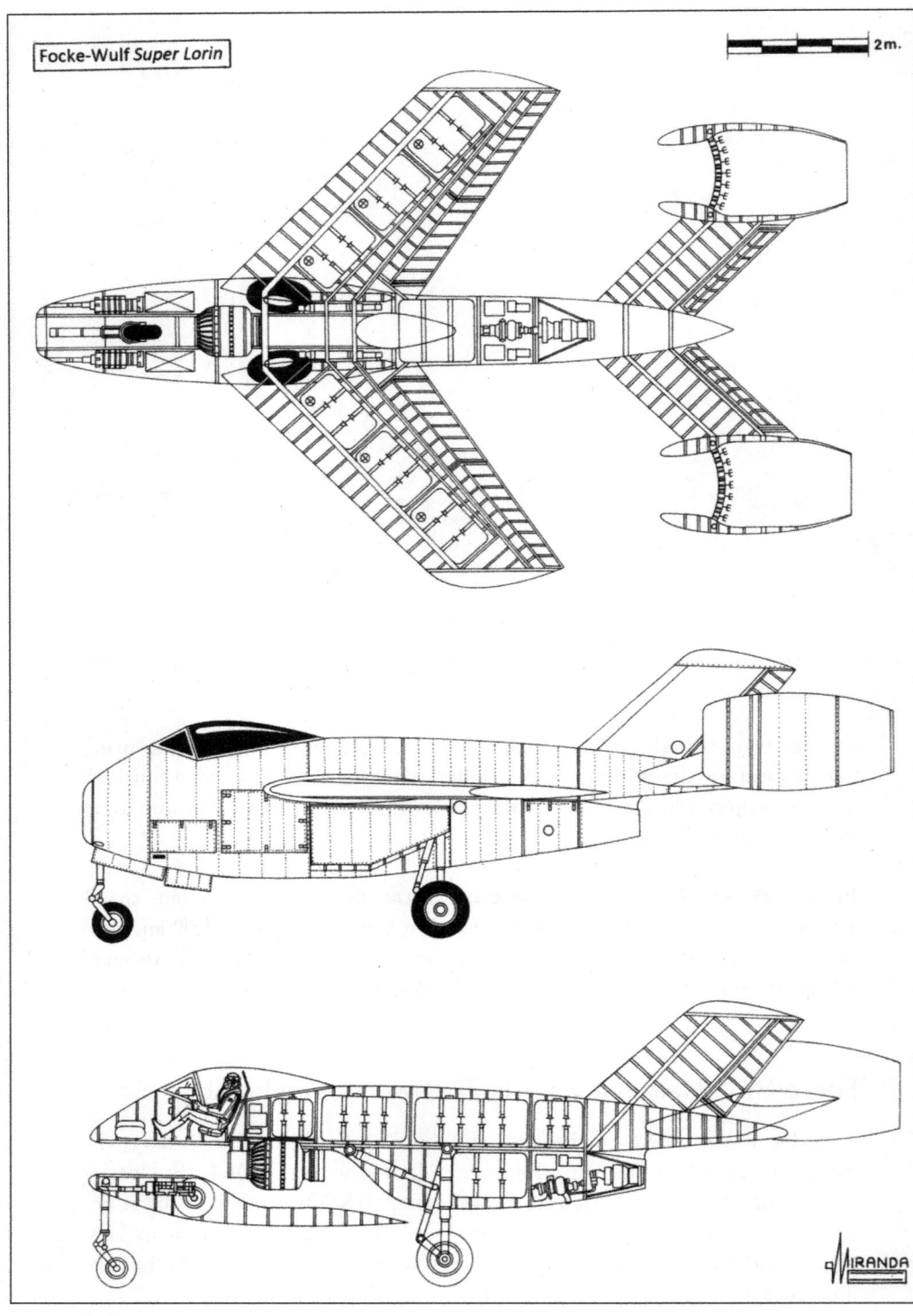

The Strahlrohrjäger Concept

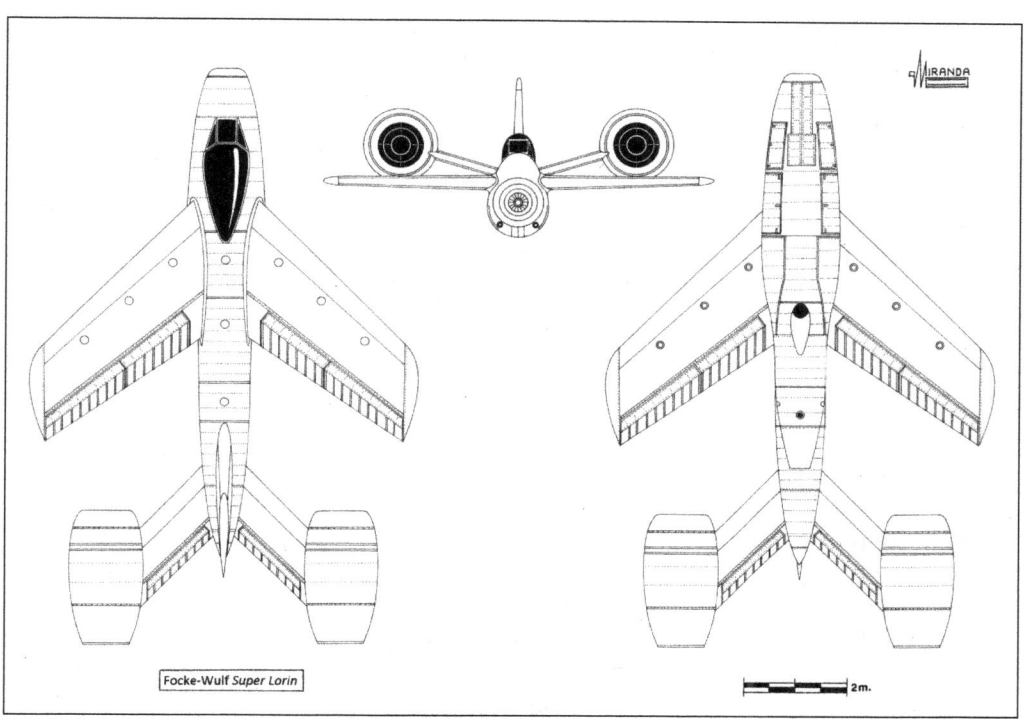

Focke-Wulf Super Lorin

Built in light alloy, the fuselage housed the pressurised cockpit with ejector seat, two MK 108/30 heavy cannons, the landing gear, one 270l tank containing the B.4 petrol for the turbojet, two K1 heavy kerosene fuel tanks of 650 and 845l for the ramjets, one C-Stoff rocket-propellant tank of 345l, one T-Stoff rocket-propellant tank of 575l, one HeS 8 turbojet with 720kg static thrust, and one bi-propellant rocket Walter 109-509 A-1 rocket with 1,700kg peak-thrust. The wings, spanning 7.6m and with a 15sq.m area, were built in wood/plywood/steel and housed six K1 fuel tanks with 150l each.

The tail planes were built of steel and served as support for two Pabst ramjets of 10,850kg thrust each. The landing gear was of the same type than that developed for the Super TL. The exhaust nozzle of the turbojet was located on the fuselage belly to the purpose of generating lift thrust during take off and landing. High-altitude performances could also be improved, although a shorter wingspan might make the aircraft very fast at lower altitude, where the ramjets could produce the maximum thrust.

12
Objektschutzjäger Programme

In June 1944, the Technisches Amt issued the Verschleissjäger requirement for a small and inexpensive point-defence interceptor of the type Objektschutzjäger for the protection of important targets, to be powered by one 109-509 A/B or by one 109-509 A-1 rocket engines. The new rocket-fighter should be manufactured in two versions: A light one, to be towed or launched with the help of RATO rockets from a mobile launch ramp with 40 degrees slope and an acceleration that would not exceed 2.06G.

The second version (heavy), with greater propellant capacity, should carry out the take-off in only 350m using a three-wheel jettisonable dolly and four Rheinmetall 109-502 RATO rockets. It was expected that the heavy version could replace the 109-509 A/B, with 1,700 peak-thrust, by the most advanced HWK 109-509 C with 2,000kg.

The Verschleissjäger contest received eleven proposals during the summer of 1944.

Bachem proposed the ramp-launched VTOL fighter BP-20-04 (13 August 1944) and Bachem Ba 349 C (November 1944).

Heinkel proposed the P.1068 (16 August 1944), the P.1077 Julia I (16 August 1944) with the pilot in prone position, the P.1077 Julia II with the pilot in conventional position.

Junkers submitted the EF127/I Walli (16 December 1944) with mobile launch ramp.

Focke-Wulf participated with its Volksjäger design (December 1944) that could use both launch systems with the help of two or four Rheinmetall 109-502 rocket boosters of 770kg peak-thrust each.

Messerschmitt proposed the Me P.1103 (11 September 1944), Me P.1103 b (6 July 1944), the Me 163 C-1 (6 July 1944), the Me 163 D (11 October 1944), the Me P.1104 in both versions: ramp-launched (10 August 1944) and trolley launched (22 September 1944).

The acceptance of projects continued during the first months of 1945 with the Junkers EF 127/II Elli (February 1945) and the Henschel P.136.

By early April 1944 the US fighter pilots were ordered to pursuit the German interceptors to their bases with groups of more than fifty Mustangs and attack them while refuelling.

This situation especially affected the Messerschmitt Me 163 B-1 rocket-fighters from the JG 400, these aircraft were immobilised on the ground after landing, away from the *Flak* protection, until they were rescued by a special vehicle that transported them to their base. Many Komets were destroyed on ground by staffing. After this bad experience the Luftwaffe did not want more aircraft equipped with landing skids and the OKL rejected all Objektschutzjägern projects in favour of the expendable Natter and the Messerschmitt Me 263 which was equipped with a conventional landing gear.

This allowed it to be recycled to other previously rejected designs such as the Henschel P.136, the Messerschmitt Me 163D and the Arado TEW 16/43-13.

13
Towed Projects

Messerschmitt P.1103 (12 September 1944)

Bordjäger designed by the Oberbayerische Forschungsanstalt Institut to compete for the HWK 109-509 B-1 engine. While improving the performances of the parasite fighter, its rocket propellants were too sensitive to shocks and designers decided to do without the rammer option.

The new version was configured as a conventional rocket-fighter, with the pilot in sitting position and frontal and rear armour against 12.7mm shells.

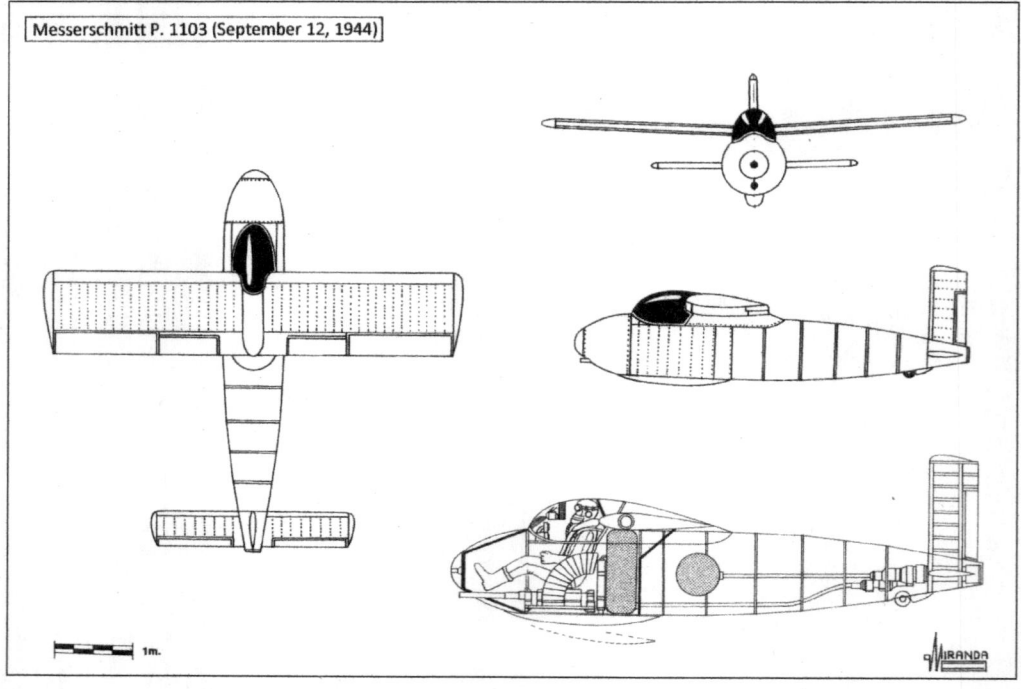

The wings and tail planes were built from those of a Fieseler Reichenberg manned missile.

It should make the take-off on a detachable twin wheel dolly, towed by a Me 262 jet-fighter in Deichselslepp configuration, and landing with the help of flaps, a retractable skid and a tailwheel.

Me P.1103 (12 September 1944) technical data: Wingspan: 5.3m. Length: 5m. Height: 1.58m. Wing Area: 5.8sq.m. Fuselage diameter: 80cm. Maximum weight: 1,100kg. Maximum speed: 930km/h. Power plant: one Walter HWK 109-509 B-1 rocket engine with 300kg peak-thrust. Propellant tanks: one with 167l of C-Stoff mounted behind the cockpit and one with 40l of T-Stoff in the central section of the fuselage. Armament: one nose-mounted MK 108/30 heavy cannon with 100 rounds.

Messerschmitt P.1104

Improved version of the P.1103 powered by one bi-fuel rocket HWK 109-509 A-2 with 1,700kg thrust. 150kg of T-Stoff and 54kg of C-Stoff.

The small rocket-plane could perform the take off and climb towed aloft behind a Messerschmitt Bf 109 G and land with the help of flaps and skid/tailwheel devices.

The RLM believed that the low capacity of propellants, sufficient only for 3 minutes of powered flight, would only allow for one attack, with time to shoot up to six times its unique Mk 108/30, without any real chance of achieving the destruction of a *Viermot* (four-engine bomber). The project was cancelled in September 1944.

Me P.1104 *Entwurf* XVIII-118 (22 September 1944)

Variant of the P.1103 with expanded propellant capacity: up to 900kg of T-Stoff and 300kg of C-Stoff. The increased uptime of use of the rocket would allow to reach a ceiling of 13,000m with a climb rate of 3,600 m/min. The range was 90km.

The new version retained the armament, the take-off and landing systems and the shoulder wing of the P.1103. It was cancelled in November 1944, in favour of the Me 263 that could make the take-off by itself.

Me P.1104 (22 September 1944) technical data: Wingspan: 6.37m. Length: 5.48m. Height: 2.15m. Wing area: 6.5sq.m. Maximum speed: 800km/h. Maximum weight: 2,570kg. Service ceiling: 13,000m. Range: 90km. Take-off run: 155m.

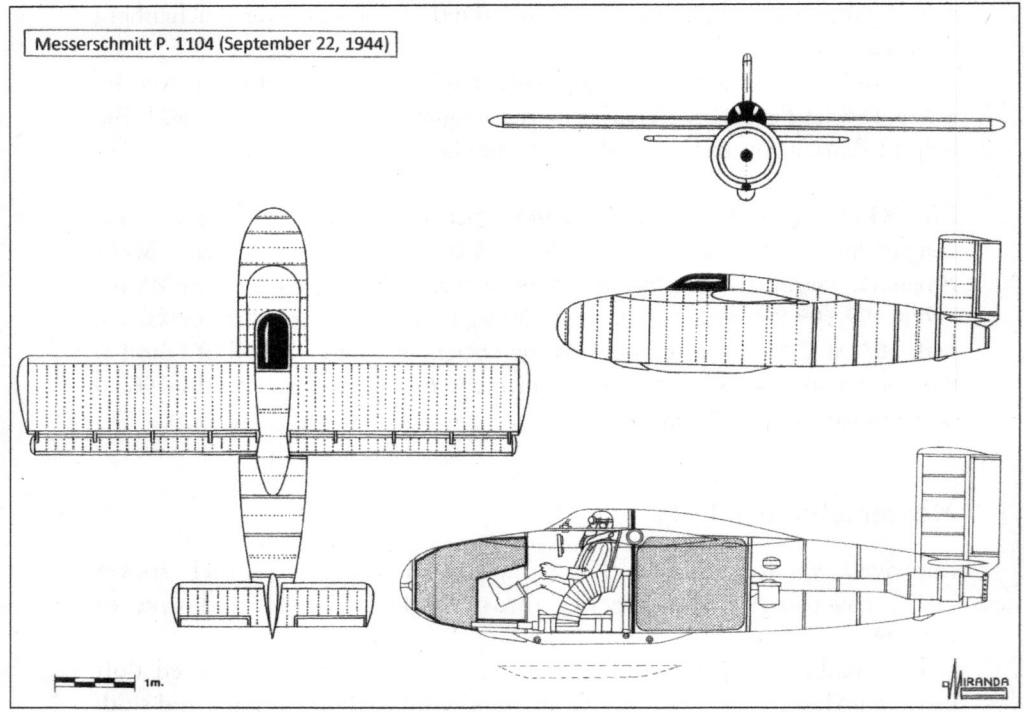

Messerschmitt P. 1104 (September 22, 1944)

Sombold/Bley So.344 Rammsuchssjäger

It was a Pulkzerstörer rocket-fighter that could carry a specially designed detachable warhead filled with 400kg of H.E. capable of destroying a bomber box.

The So.344 project (22 January 1944) was to be towed by a Me 262 jet-fighter to the vicinity of the bomber stream and released between 1,000 and 1,500m over the flight level of the enemy planes.

The pilot was to steer the fighter inward of a 'box' and activate the rocket-warhead ejection mechanism consisting of four Schmidding 109-543 solid-fuel rockets with 150kg peak-thrust each.

The warhead could be detonated by a radio signal from the mother plane by means of a Marder radio-fuse developed by the Orlich Institut for the air-to-air guided bomb Henschel Hs 293H. The explosion at a defined altitude could also be programmed by a barometric fuse type Baro-1 or an acoustic trigger Stimmgabel that was activated when the sound of the engines of the bombers reached certain intensity.

After ridding itself of the extra weight of the warhead, the So.344 could be piloted like a fighter and was armed with two heavy machine guns and frontal and rear armour against 12.7mm shells, to fend off the American escort fighters, then could use its own rocket-motor to move away from the bomber stream and land with the help of flaps and retractable ventral skid devices.

The project was cancelled in favour of other models equipped with conventional landing gear.

SOMBOLD/BLEY SO.344 TECHNICAL DATA: Wingspan: 5.7. Length: 7m. Height: 2.18m. Wing Surface. 6sq.m. Maximum Speed: 770km/h. Maximum Weight: 1,350kg. Ceiling: 6,000m. Power plant: one bi-fuel rocket HWK 109-509 A-2 with 1700kg thrust. 150kg of T-Stoff and 54kg of C-Stoff. Endurance: 25 minutes.

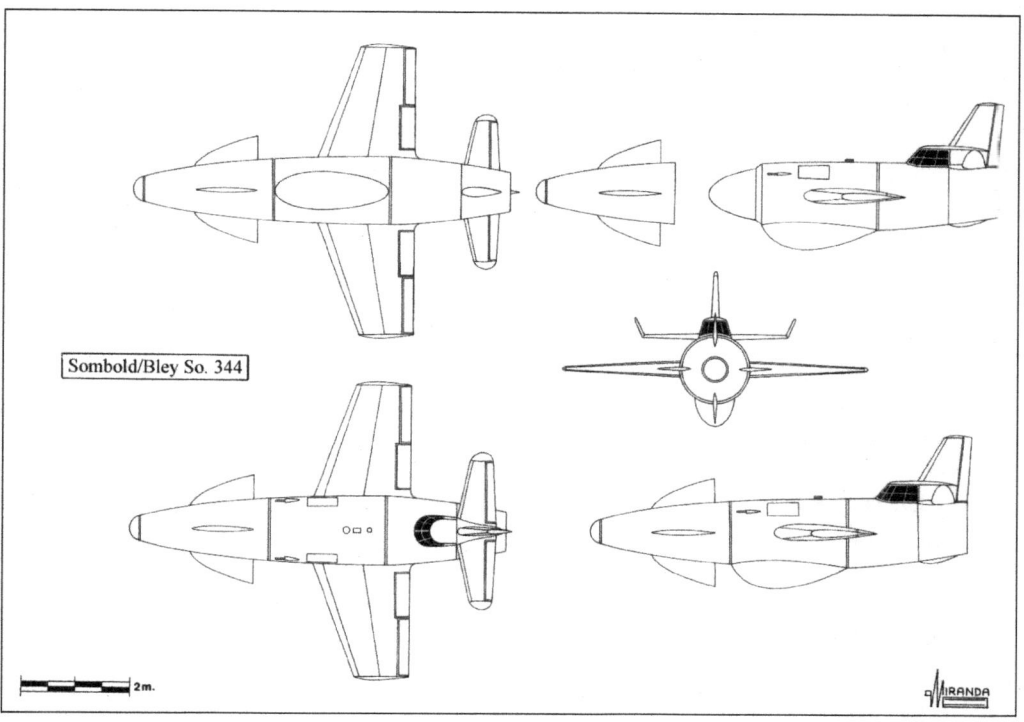

14

Trolley-Launched Projects

Junkers EF.127.02

This project was a target-defence interceptor, with 10 to 12 per cent thickness straight wings, powered by one HWK 109-509 C rocket engine with 2,000kg peak-thrust at the main combustion chamber and 400kg peak-thrust at the cruising chamber. The EF. 127.02 was proposed to the OKL in February 1945 but was cancelled in favour of the Me 263 because of its landing system.

One nose-mounted wind generator with 2,000 watts produced enough electricity to run the instruments and the FuG 16 Zy R/T device.

The take-off was reached in 270m by means of a detachable trolley and two Schmidding 533 RATO rockets. Landing was via an extended fuselage skid, mechanically operated by the pilot.

JUNKERS EF 127.02 (FEBRUARY 1945) TECHNICAL DATA: Wingspan: 8.09m. Length: 10.5m. Height: 2.9m. Wing area: 11sq.m. Maximum weight: 2,960kg. Maximum speed: 900km/h. Power plant: one HWK 109-509 C rocket engine with 2,000kg peak-thrust at the main combustion chamber, 400kg peak-thrust at the cruising chamber. Armament: two wing-mounted SG118 batteries.

The Reinmetall-Borsig Sondergerät SG118 Rohrblocktrommel was an automatic revolving installation housing three SG117 Rohrblock weapons and twenty-one MK 108/30 low-velocity barrels, each loaded with a single Minengranate, mounted around the common axis.

Most of the weapon was installed inside the wing so that only one of the SG117s remained on the outside. When it had been fired, the axis scrolled bringing the next block to the line of fire.

In order to absorb the projected recoil of 2,000kg, a strong pre-loaded spring was to be fitted on the shaft.

In a further development the recoil could be neutralised by a nozzle action and sleeveless cartridges.

SG118 TECHNICAL DATA: Length of *trommel* section: 545mm. Overall length: 1,175mm. *Trommel* diameter: 310mm. Loaded weight: 165kg. Rate of fire: 20,000 rounds per minute.

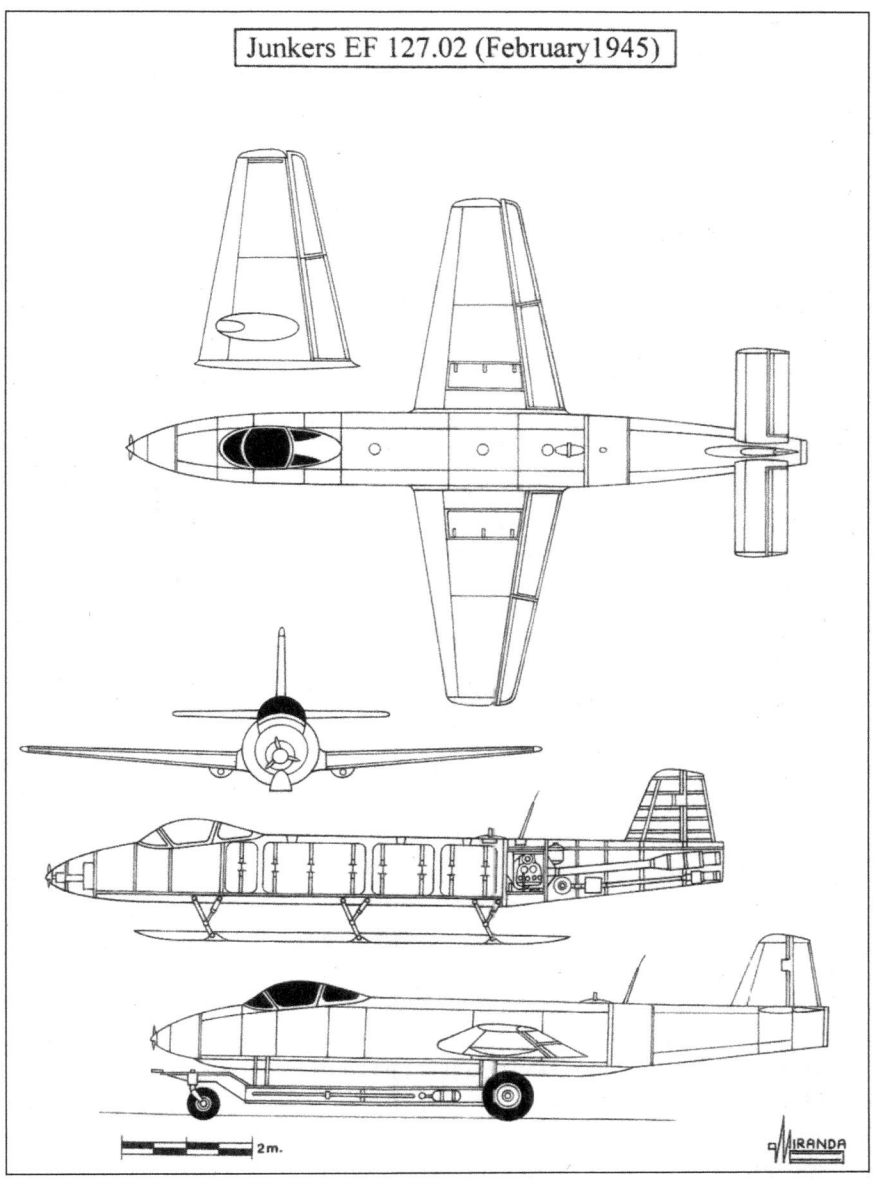

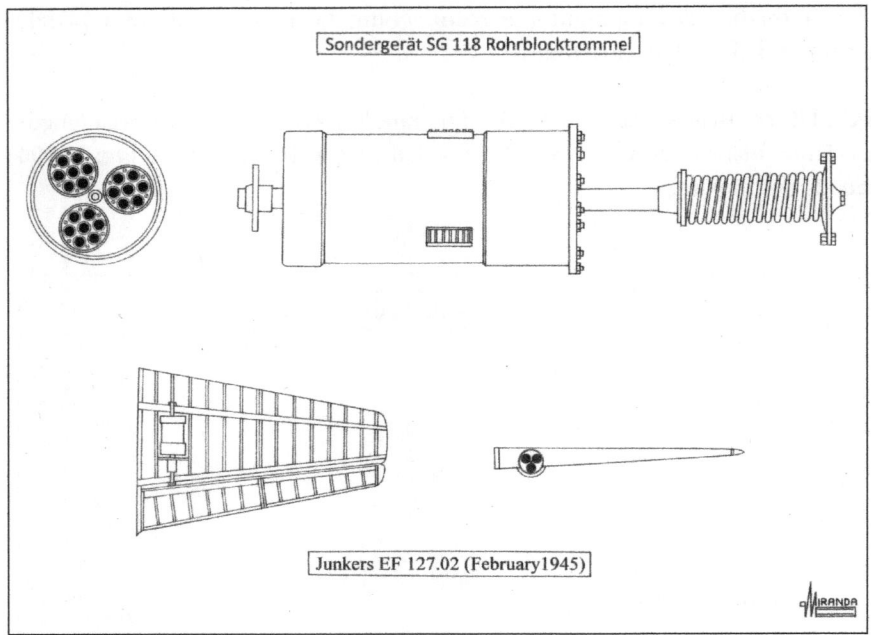

Focke-Wulf Volksjäger

The airframe of this minimal rocket-fighter consisted of a 67-per-cent homothetic reduction of the Ta 183.

The construction of the fuselage would be in light alloy, with a steel-armoured nose cone and plates mounted behind the pilot. It housed one wind generator, the pressurised cockpit, two MK 108/30 cannons, the T-Stoff and C-Stoff rocket propellant tanks, one Walter HWK 109-509 A-1 rocket engine with 1,600kg peak-thrust and one compressed-air-operated landing skid.

Each wing panel, with steel structure and plywood cladding, 40-degree rear-swept and 7.4 per cent thickness, housed five C-Stoff tanks and compressed-air operated flaps. The tail surfaces, with wooden structure and cladding, consisted of a 60 degrees swept tailfin and one 45 degrees swept 'T-tailplane'.

The wheeled trolley had a take off run of 260m.

The electronic equipment proposed would be one R/T device FuG 16 Zy, one IFF discriminator FuG 25a and one direction finder device FuG 16 Zvg.

FOCKE-WULF VOLKSJÄGER (DECEMBER 1944) TECHNICAL DATA: Wingspan: 6.77m. Length: 6.77m. Height: 2.2m. Wing area: 10sq.m. Maximum weight: 2,133kg. Maximum speed: 1,000km/h. Service ceiling: 15,000m. Armament: two fuselage-mounted MK 108/30 heavy cannons with 60 rounds per gun.

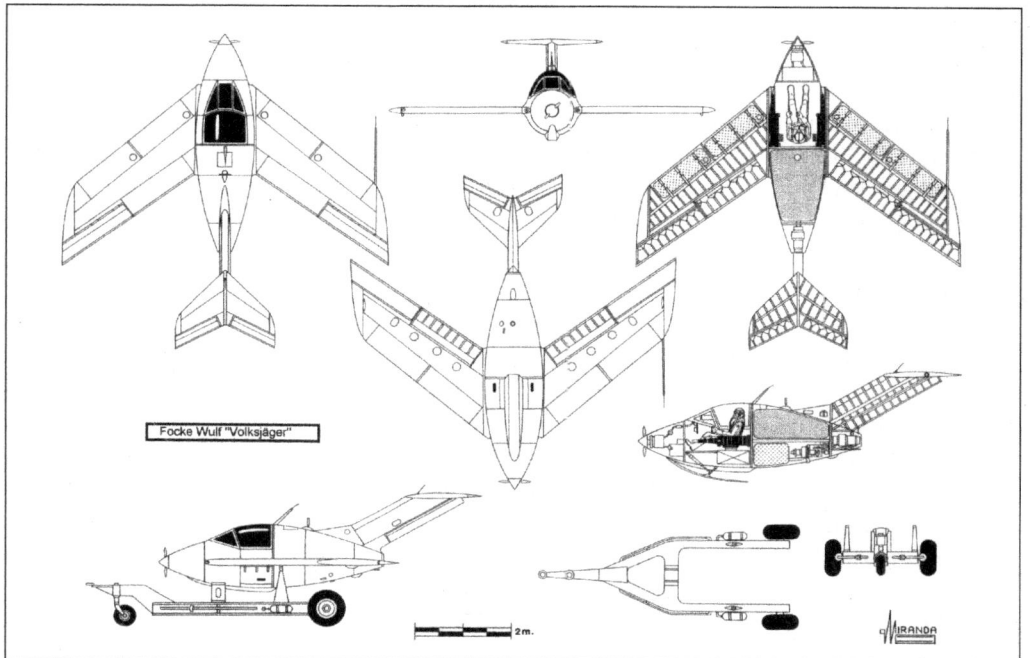

Messerschmitt Me 163 C

The propellant endurance of the Me 163 B-1 rocket-fighter was only 7.5 minutes and its normal radius of action was 25 miles (40km).

To improve these performances, the dual-chambered rocket-motor HWK 109-509B was developed. Its main combustion chamber Hauptofen, with 1,500kg peak-thrust, would be used for take-off only and the auxiliary chamber Marschofen, with only 300kg thrust, was intended for powered cruise flight.

In this way, a better thrust/fuel consumption ratio was possible, the new engine would improve the powered flight endurance from about 12 minutes.

To prove the concept, two prototypes (Me 163 V6 and Me 163 V18) were experimentally fitted with 509 B engines.

On 6 July 1944, the V18 (VA+SP) started a flight test, with a very steep angle of climb at over 4,500 m/min and exceeded the 0.81 critical Mach number using both combustion chambers. Suddenly the aircraft plunged into strong buffeting and a violent nose down pitch at Mach 0.84.

Upon landing back at Peenemünde the ground inspection showed that, during its compressibility event, the V18 had lost the rudder and several of the wing-root fairings had been almost pulled free from their attachments.

It was later determined that the prototype had reached a speed of 1,130km/h but is unclear if the V18 achieved sufficient altitude for its speed to be considered supersonic.

The combat version Messerschmitt Me 163 C was fitted with pressurised cockpit, extended wingspan, increased propellant tankage and one HWK 109-509 C rocket engine, with auxiliary combustion chamber, which provided great operational flexibility. The fighter could use both chambers for take-off, climb and combat and save propellant cruising with the auxiliary chamber.

Late in 1944 three prototypes were completed but, because of their increased weight, its flight time was only one minute more than that of the Me 163 B-1. The OKL decided that the small increase in propellant capacity of the Me 163 C-0 did not justify its construction.

The series production of the Me 163 C-1 was dropped in favour of the Me 163 D, a new rocket-fighter developed to rectify the Komet shortcomings: inadequate flight endurance, difficulties on ground-handling and poor rearward visibility.

MESSERSCHMITT ME 163 C-1 TECHNICAL DATA: Power plant: one HWK 109-509 C rocket-motor with two combustion chambers, Hauptofen, with 1,500kg peak-thrust, for take-off only and the auxiliary chamber Marschofen, with

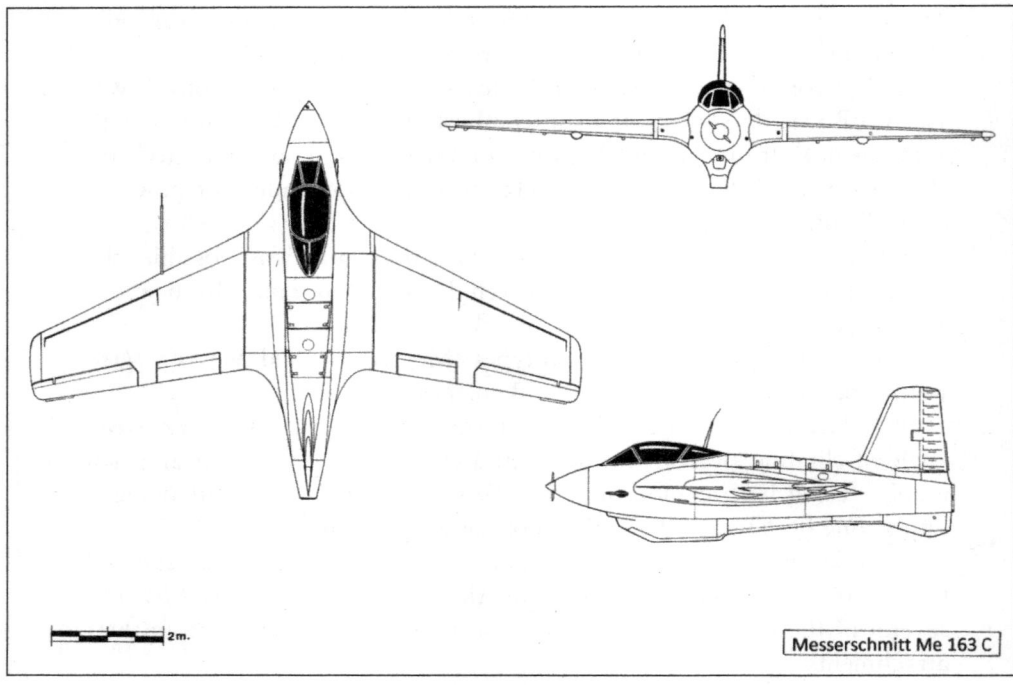

Messerschmitt Me 163 C

only 300kg thrust, was intended for powered cruise flight. Both chambers could be operated together in an emergency. Wingspan: 9.8m. Length: 7.04m. Height: 2.89m. Wing area: 20.5sq.m.. Take-off weight: 5,110kg. Estimated maximum speed: 958km/h. Estimated ceiling: 16,000m. Armament: two nose-mounted Mk 108/30 and two wing roots-mounted MK 108/30 or MK 103/30 heavy cannons.

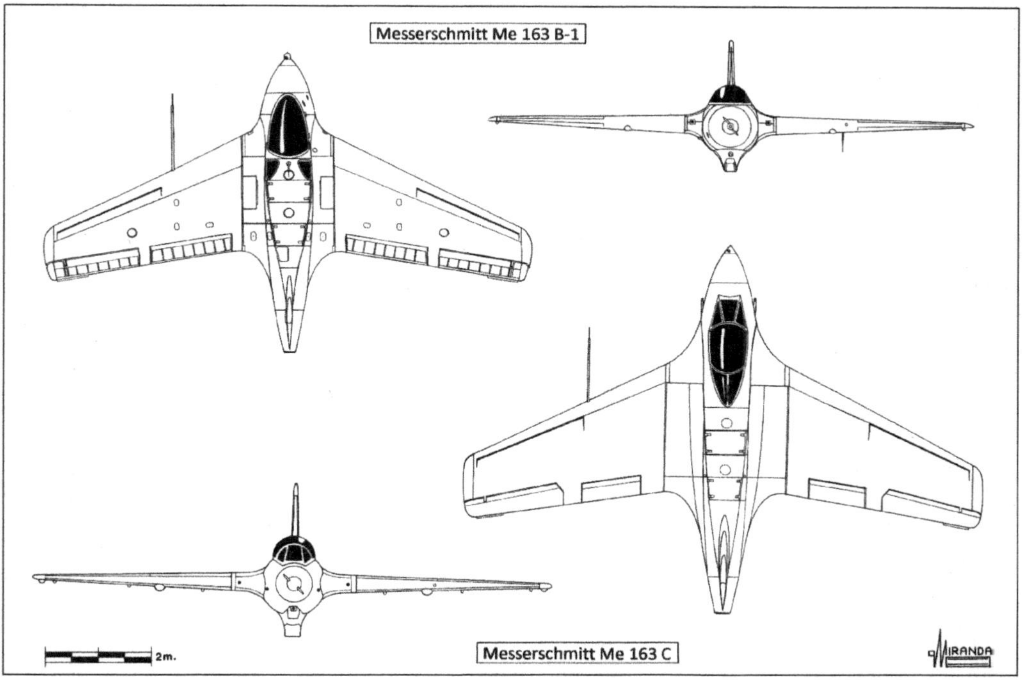

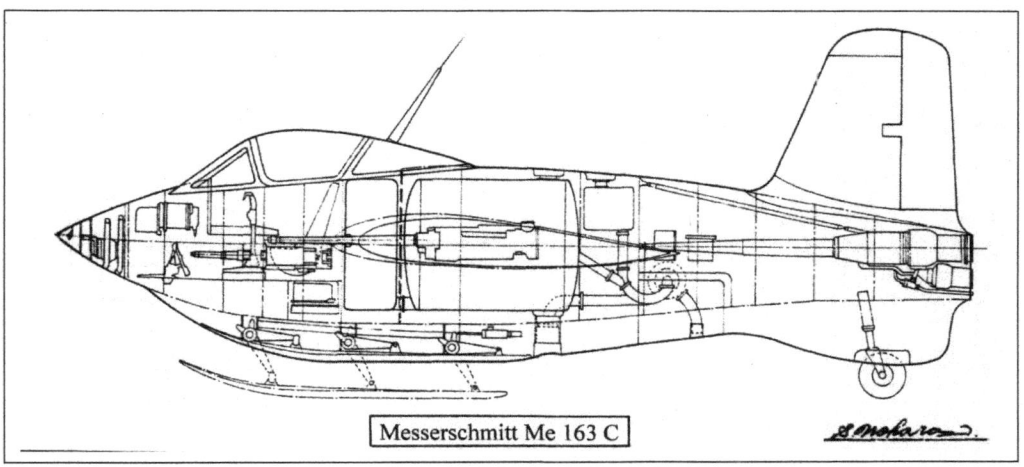

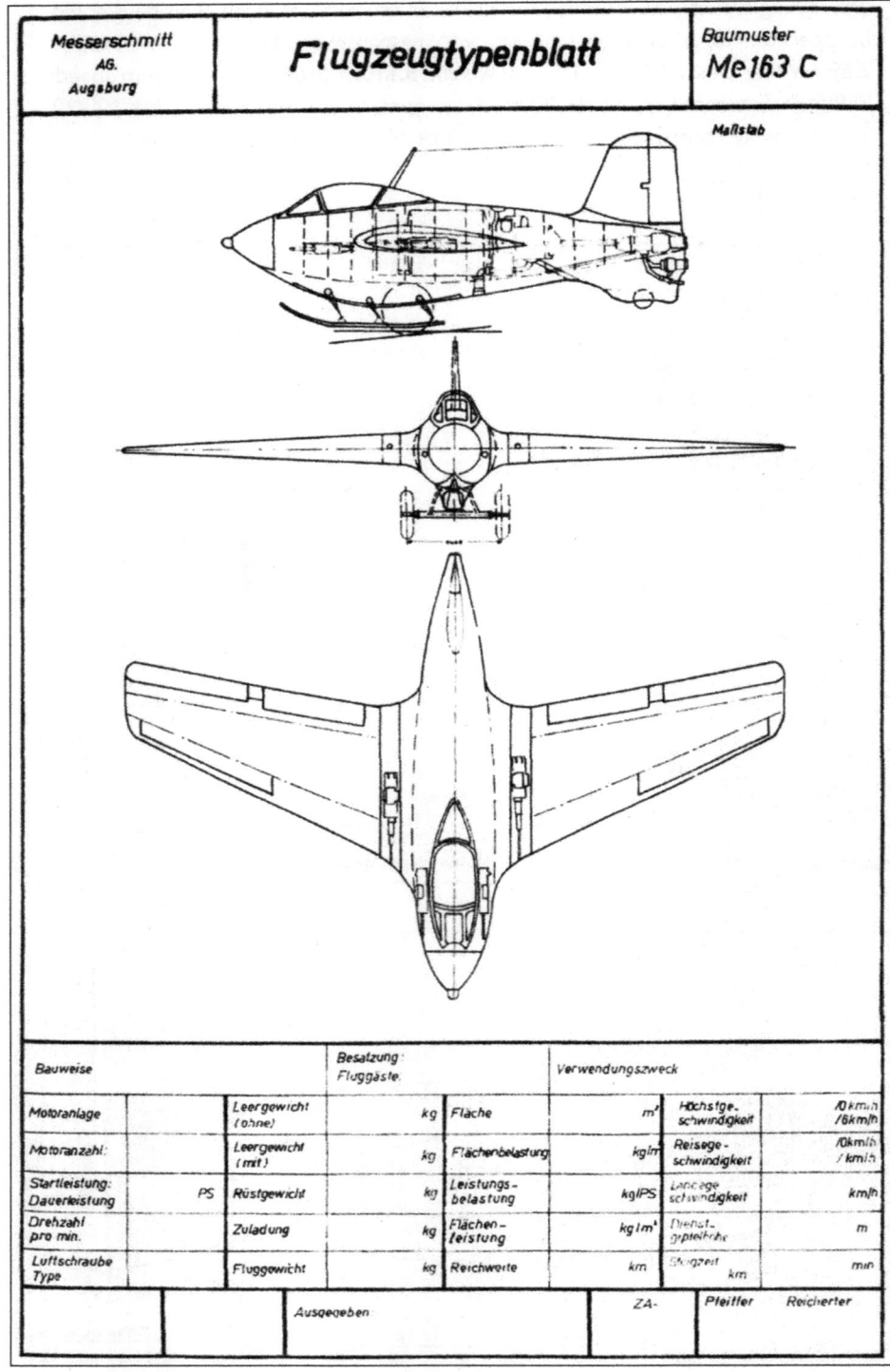

15
Ramp-Launched Projects

Junkers EF 127.01

In this light version the zero-length take-off was reached by means of a mobile launch ramp with a 40-degree slope and four Schmidding 109-533 RATO rockets each rated at 1,200kg peak-thrust.

Landing on extended fuselage skid, mechanically operated by the pilot.

JUNKERS EF 127.01 WALLI (16 DECEMBER 1944) TECHNICAL DATA: Wingspan: 6.55m. Length: 8m. Height: 2.35m. Wing area: 8.9sq.m. Maximum weight: 1,930kg. Maximum speed: 1,000km/h. Endurance: 9.6 minutes. Power plant: one HWK 109-509 C rocket engine with 2,000kg peak-thrust at the main combustion chamber, 400kg peak-thrust at the cruising chamber and four SG 34 Schmidding 109-533 RATO rockets with 1,200kg peak-thrust each. Range: 120km. Climb rate: 133 m/sec. Fuel propellants: 500kg of C-Stoff in the wings and 1,088kg of T-Stoff in the fuselage. Armament: two fuselage-mounted MK 108/30 cannons and twelve R4M air-to-air rockets carried under the wings.

Me P.1104-S53 Entwurf XVIII-125 (10 August 1944)

Modification of the Entwurf XVIII-118 with mid-wing and propellant tanks located in the central section of the fuselage. The result was very similar to the Natter and looked like an attempt to compete against Bachem for the scarce HWK engines available. The VTO capacity of the Natter resulted decisive and the S53 project was cancelled on 26 December 1944.

ME P.1104-S53 (10 AUGUST 1944) TECHNICAL DATA: Wingspan: 6.37m. Length: 5.47m. Height: 2.9m. Wing area: 13sq.m. Maximum weight: 1,100kg. Maximum speed: 840km/h. Range: 87km. Power plant: one

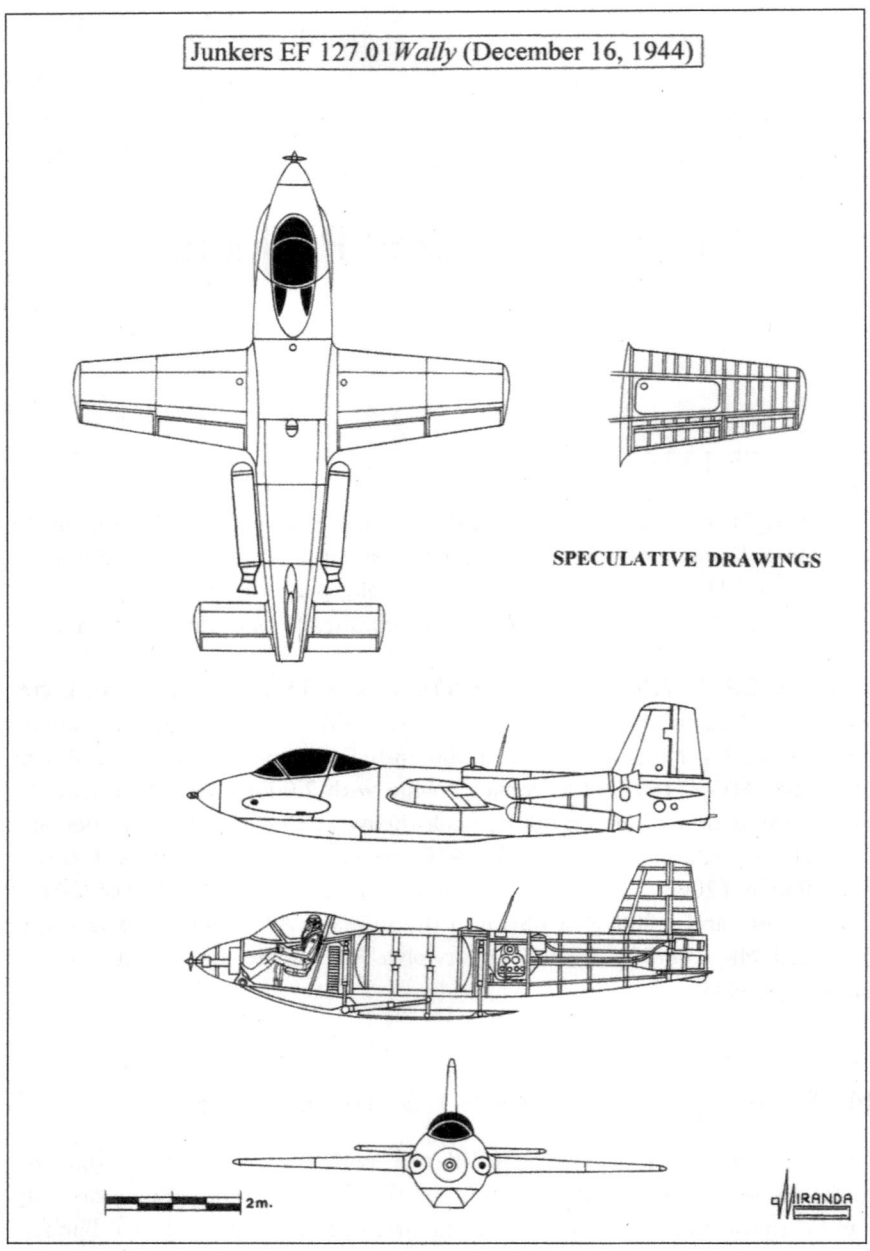

Junkers EF 127.01 *Wally* (December 16, 1944)

SPECULATIVE DRAWINGS

HWK 109-509 A-2 rocket engine with 1,700kg peak-thrust and four SG 34 Schmidding 109-533 RATO rockets with 1,200kg peak-thrust each. Armament: one MK 108/30 cannon, with 100 rounds, mounted under the pilot seat.

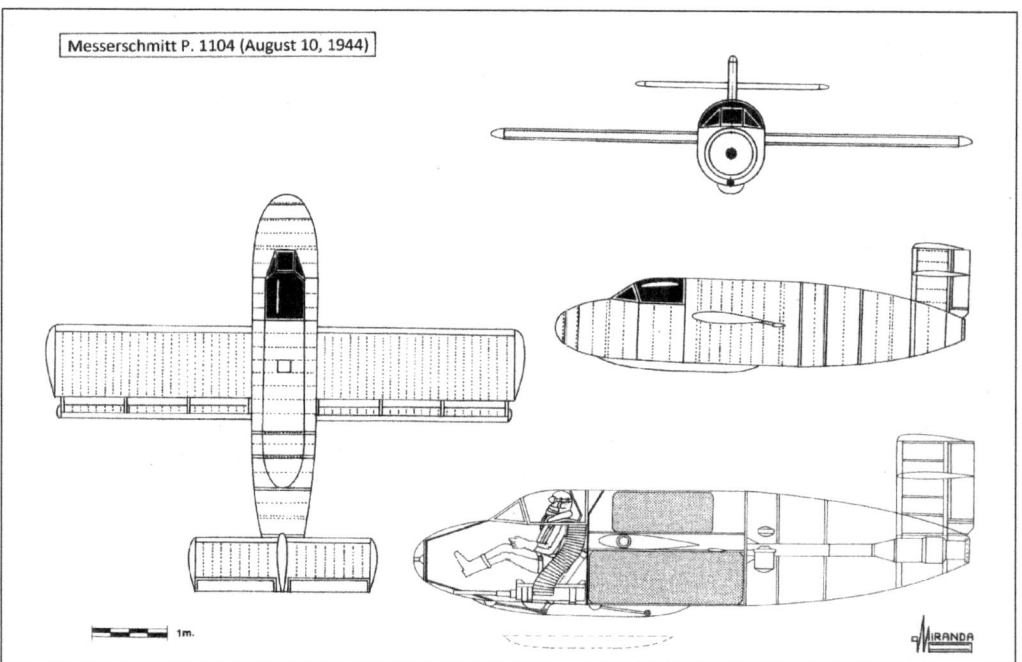

Messerschmitt P. 1104 (August 10, 1944)

Lippisch Rammer

On 9 September 1944, Dr Paul Karlson published the study Ramm-Raketen nach Dr Alexander Lippisch describing a VTO rocket rammer designed to take off vertically from a short ramp powered by a liquid-propellant Walter rocket of the 109-501 type, a 'power egg' of 1,500kg thrust originally designed to assist the Arado Ar-234 C jet-bombers to take off. During the first 6 seconds of flight, the rammer used the auxiliary power of three solid-fuel rockets Rheinmetall-Borsig 109-515, with 1,000kg peak-thrust each, originally developed to assist in the take-off to the missile Feuerlilie F-55.

The Rammer was expected to reach the flying altitude of the bomber stream in 40 seconds, with an impact momentum of 125,000 newton. This force would allow the rammer to slice through the bomber airframe without suffering excessive loss of speed after the impact. The rocket engine still retained propellants for another 20 seconds of flight, which would allow the pilot to make a second diving attack if the first attempt would fail.

The aircraft was equipped with a brake dorsal-parachute to slow the rate of fall allowing the pilot to abandon the armoured cockpit at a safe altitude and complete the descent using his own parachute.

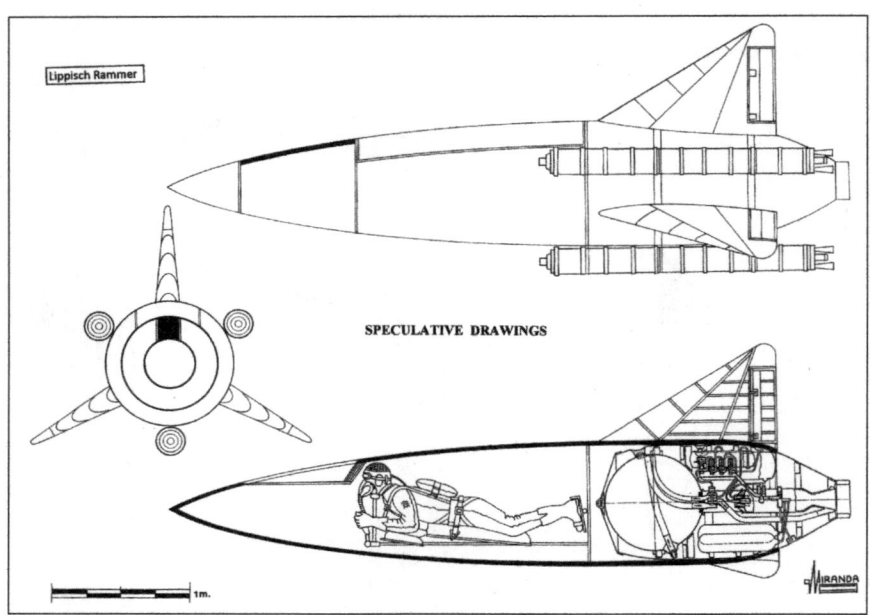

The author has outlined some speculative drawings based on data published in 2006 by researcher Dr Brett Gooden in his book 'Projekt Natter, Last of the Wonder Weapons'

LIPPISCH RAMMER TECHNICAL DATA: Wingspan: 2m. Length: 5m. Take-off weight: 1,000kg. Impact weight: 500kg. Maximum speed: 1,080km/h. Ceiling: 10,000–12,000m.

Heinkel P.1068 and P.1077 *Julia* I & II

In 1944 the Heinkel Company decided to use the prone pilot concept in its He P.1068 and He 355A Lerche VTO interceptors, but LFM subsequent investigations showed that the tolerance of the human body to VTO acceleration in prone position was quite limited and the second-generation VTOs P. 1077 Julia II and Heinkel He 355 B Wespe were designed with seated pilots and ejection seats.

The P.1068 point-defence interceptor armed with two MG 151/15/20 cannons was proposed to the OKL on 10 August 1944.

On 8 September 1944, the RLM declared the Heinkel P.1068 as winner of the Verschleissjäger contest, ordering the construction of 20 prototypes and a mass production of 300 aircraft per month, but it was cancelled in October because its armament, specially designed to combat the DH Mosquito bombers, was deemed insufficient against the four-engine American bombers.

A new design called He P.1077 was proposed to the OKL on 14 November 1944. It differed externally from the P.1068 by two tandem skids mounted on the fuselage centreline and two blisters located on either side of the forward fuselage containing the MK 108/30 cannons with 70 rounds per gun.

The increase in weight due to the addition of armament and ammunition required the installation of a new power plant. The HWK 109-509 A-1 bi-propellant rocket engine was replaced with an HWK 109-509 A-2, which had an additional cruise chamber. Four solid-fuel booster rockets and a three-axis autopilot, ground-controlled by radio link, meant that an almost vertical take-off could be achieved.

Early in 1945 the OKL approved the construction of three prototypes, four mock-ups and twenty pre-production aircraft.

By this time, the armament of 2 MK 108/30 cannons that had been originally planned was not considered effective (because of the experience gained by the Messerschmitt Me 163 Komet) since, given the speed attack of a rocket-fighter, the MK 108 could only make three shots at effective range. Then, Heinkel proposed to use the Sondergerät SG119, an experimental multiple-shot battery composed of forty-nine barrels of MK 108, with a rate of fire of 9,900rpm that could dismantle a B-17 in 1/5 sec. The SG119 was installed to the back of the plane in an aerodynamic pod called Rohrbatterie.

The aerodynamic faired cover could be jettisoned by igniting combustible bands just before opening fire.

The P.1077 was proposed in two versions: Julia I with prone pilot and Julia II with seated pilot. In the latter the capacity of the C-Stoff tank had been expanded to 214kg and the SG119 had been replaced by two RA 55 containers, with nineteen R4M rockets each, suspended under the wings by means of two ETC 250 bomb racks.

Flying in gliding mode, after consuming the rocket propellant, Julia could fly at 360km/h only in gliding mode, being an easy prey for the Mustang fighters. Therefore, on 22 December 1944, the OKL decided that the Julia held insufficient endurance and was cancelled in favour of the Bachem Ba 349 Natter, a new model that did not require the use of landing strips.

HEINKEL P.1068 (16 AUGUST 1944) TECHNICAL DATA: Wingspan: 4.6m. Length: 6.9m. Height: 2.0m. Wing area: 6.9sq.m. Maximum weight: 2,169kg. Maximum speed: 980km/h. Service ceiling: 12,000m. Range: 50km. Power plant: one Walter HWK 109-509 A-1 bi-propellant rocket engine with 1,700kg peak-thrust and four fuselage-mounted SR 34 solid-fuel RATO rockets with 1,000kg peak-thrust each. Armament: two MG 151/15/20 cannons mounted in blisters under the wings, with 5 degrees slope, reflector gunsight, prone pilot.

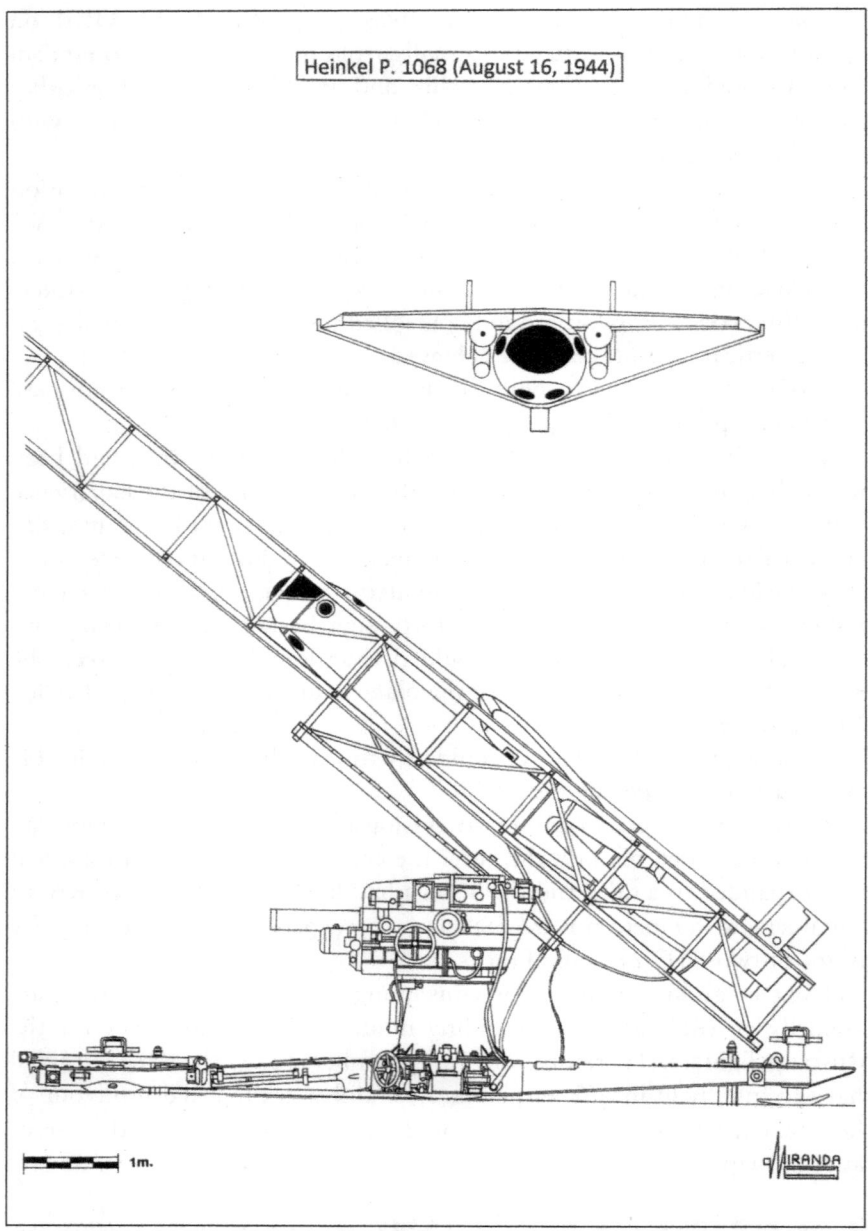

Heinkel P. 1068 (August 16, 1944)

HEINKEL P.1077 JULIA I (14 NOVEMBER 1944) TECHNICAL DATA: Wingspan: 4.6m. Length: 7.09m. Height: 1.35m. Wing area: 6.9sq.m. Maximum weight: 2,275kg. Maximum speed. 980km/h. Service ceiling: 15,000m. Range: 65km. Endurance: 5 minutes. Climb rate: 200 m/sec. Power plant: one Walter HWK 109-509 A-2 bi-propellant rocket engine with 1,700kg peak-thrust main chamber, 300kg cruising

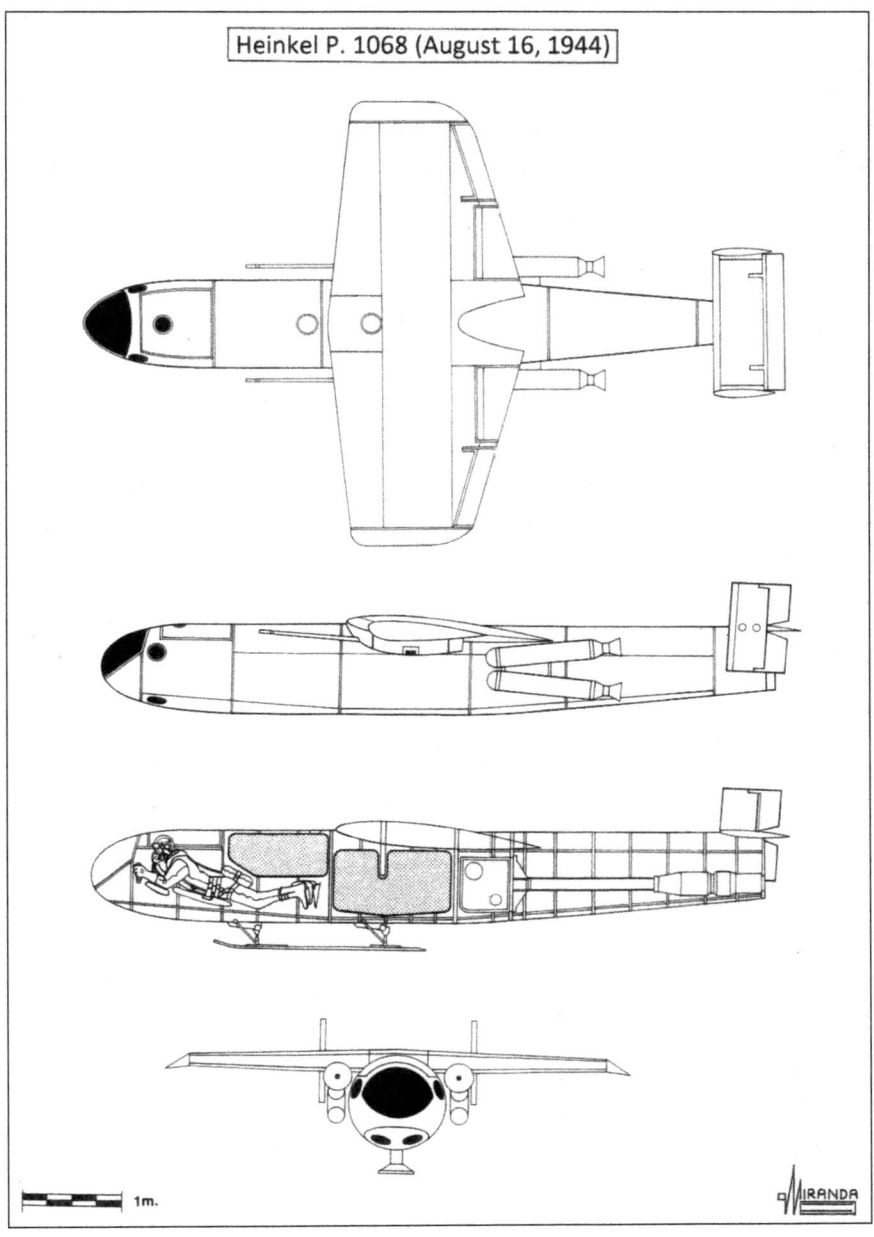

chamber and four fuselage-mounted SR 34 solid-fuel RATO rockets with 1,000kg peak-thrust each. Armament: two MK 108/30 cannons mounted in blisters (to fire at an upward angle of 3.5 degrees to the horizontal) on each side of the fuselage and one dorsal SG119 recoilless weapon with 49 barrels reflector gunsight, prone pilot.

Heinkel P.1077 Julia II (15 November 1944) technical data:

Wingspan: 4.6m. Length: 7.03m. Height: 1.52m. Wing area: 6.9sq.m. Maximum weight: 2,735kg. Maximum speed. 900km/h. Service ceiling: 15,000m. Range: 73km. Endurance: 5 minutes. Climb rate: 200 m/sec. Power plant: one Walter HWK 109-509 C-1 bi-propellant rocket engine with 2,000kg peak-thrust main chamber, 400kg cruising chamber and four fuselage-mounted SG 34

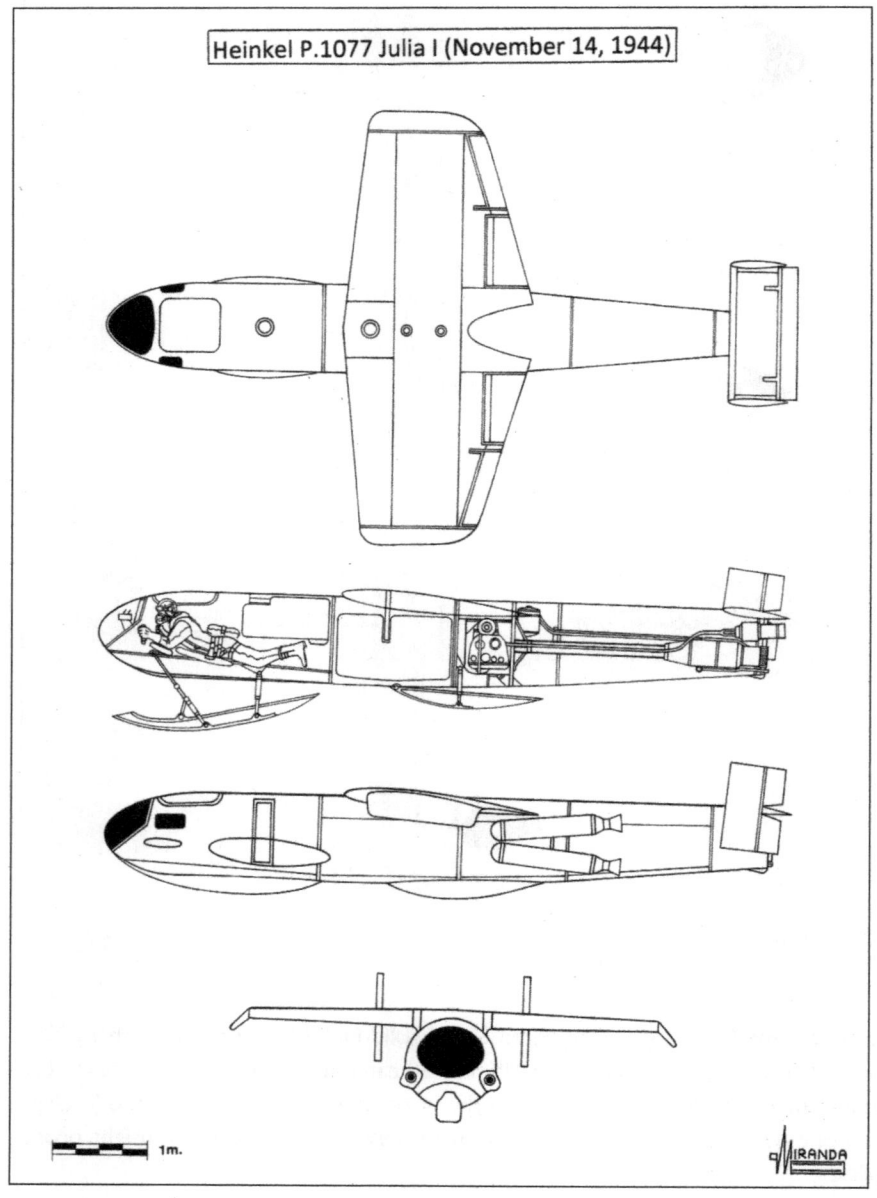

Heinkel P.1077 Julia I (November 14, 1944)

solid-fuel RATO rockets with 1,200kg peak-thrust each. Armament: two MK 108/30 cannons with 40 rounds per gun mounted in blisters (to fire at an upward angle of 3.5 degrees to the horizontal) on each side of the fuselage and by two RA 55 containers, with nineteen R4M rockets each, suspended under the wings, reflector gunsight, seated pilot and Heinkel Kartusche ejector seat.

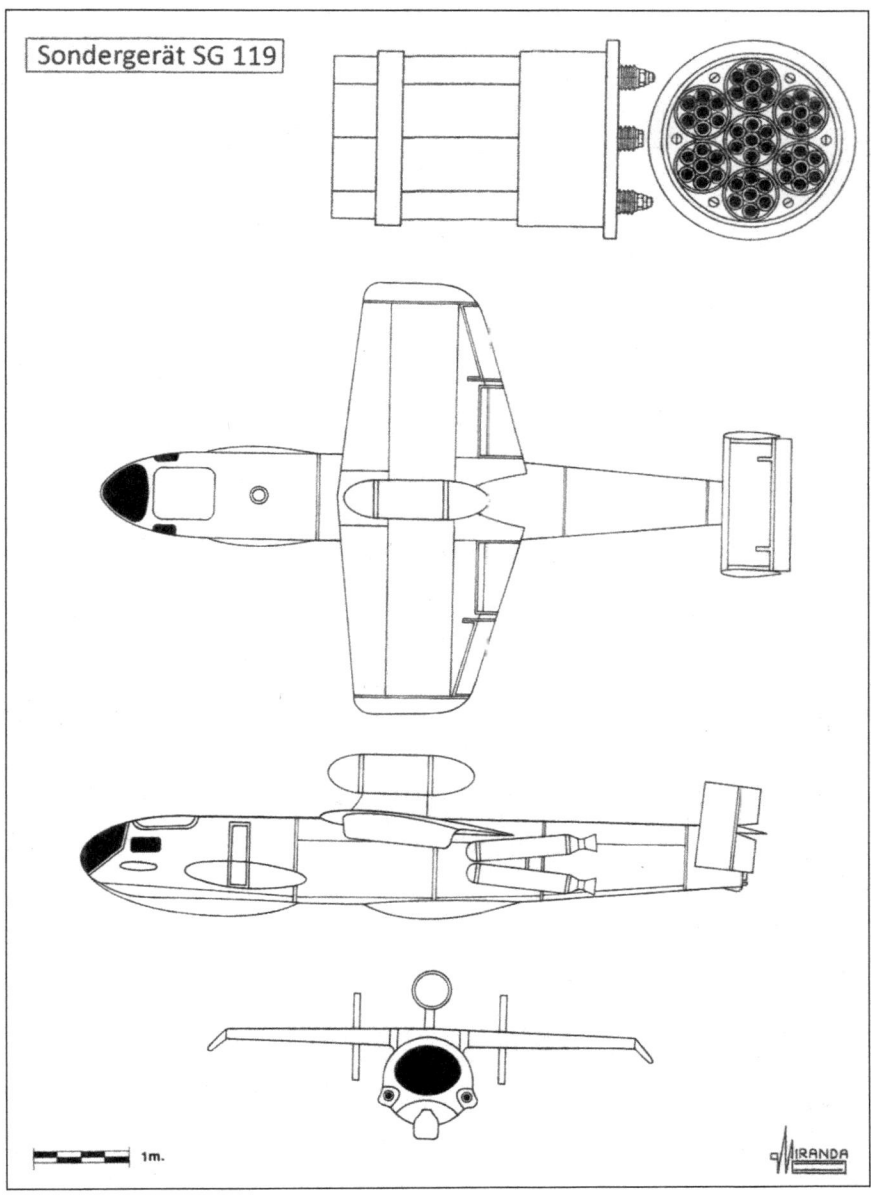

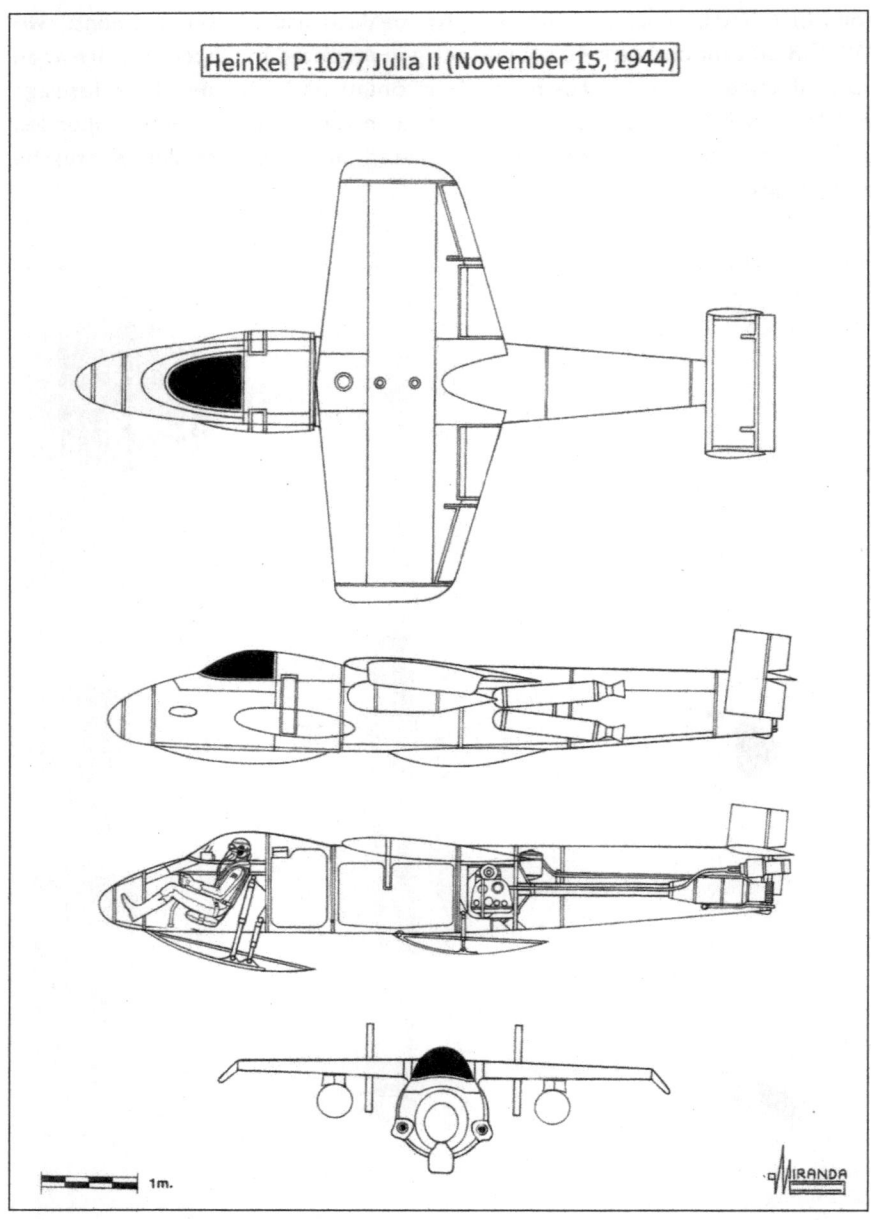

16
Conventional Landing Gear

Henschel P.135

The interest of the Henschel firm in tailless aircrafts initiated at the end of 1943, during their cooperation with Dr Alexander Lippisch on the design of the Delta VI.

In autumn of 1944 the team led by Dipl. Ing. Friedrich Nicolaus designed the Henschel P.130, a tailless fighter powered by a Daimler Benz DB 603 piston engine with pusher airscrew and double cranked wing. The special design of the wing was expected to solve the problem of compressibility buffeting, keeping the good features at low speed flight.

The Henschel P.135 was the Jägernotprogramm version powered by a HeS 011 turbojet.

HENSCHEL P.135 (DECEMBER 1944) TECHNICAL DATA: Wings: built of wood, with a double cranked leading edge and (42/-38/-15) degrees compound sweep. It had leading-edge slats to improve stall characteristics and flaps ahead of the rudders. The inner rudders acted as ailerons and the outboard rudders as elevons. Thickness of 12 per cent at the root and 10 per cent outboard. Fuselage: light alloy structure, housing the armament, undercarriage, fuel tanks and engine. Cockpit: pressurised, control heating, frontal armour against 12.7mm shelling and from the rear against 20mm. Heinkel Kartusche ejector seat. Tailfin: light alloy structure and cladding. Undercarriage: tricycle type, nose wheel would have retracted to the rear, rotating 90 degrees to lie flat in the wheel bay. The main wheels retracted forward into the fuselage. Engine: one Heinkel-Hirth HeS 011 turbojet rated at 1,300kg static thrust. Fuel tanks: two, located in front and behind the cockpit, with a total capacity of 1,920l. Armament: Two MK 108/30 cannons under the cockpit and two MK 108/30 in the wing roots. Electronics: EZ 42 gyro gunsight, FuG 16 ZY VHF transmitter/receiver, FuG 25a IFF radio set. Wingspan: 9.20m. Length: 7.80m. Height: 4.10m. Wing area: 20.50sq.m. Maximum Weight: 5.500kg.

Henschel P.136

The Focke-Wulf Ta 183/I, which manufacturing of 5,000 units by month would use the whole production capability of the HeS 011 turbojet. Therefore there was a proposal to modify the Henschel P.135 Jägernotprogramm project so that it could use a bi-fuel rocket engine Walter HWK 509 C, with double combustion chamber.

The new version was named Henschel P.136.

HENSCHEL P.136 TECHNICAL DATA: Wings: built of wood, with a double cranked leading edge and (42/-38/-15) degrees compound sweep. It had leading-edge slats to improve stall characteristics and split flaps ahead of the rudders. The inner rudders acted as ailerons and the outboard rudders as elevons. Thickness of 12 per cent at the root and 10 per cent outboard. Fuselage: tricycle type, nose wheel would have retracted to the rear, rotating 90 degrees to lie flat in the wheel bay. The main wheels retracted forward into the fuselage. Engine: one Walter HWK 509 C bi-fuel rocket engine with two combustion chambers. Propellant tanks: one with T-Stoff in front of the cockpit and one with C-Stoff behind. Armament: two MK 108/30 cannons under the cockpit and two MK 108/30 in the wing roots. Electronics: EZ 42 gyro gunsight, FuG 16 ZY VHF transmitter/receiver, FuG 25a IFF radio set. Wingspan: 9.20m. Length: 8.40m. Height: 4.10m. Wing area 20.5sq.m. Aspect ratio 4.13:1.

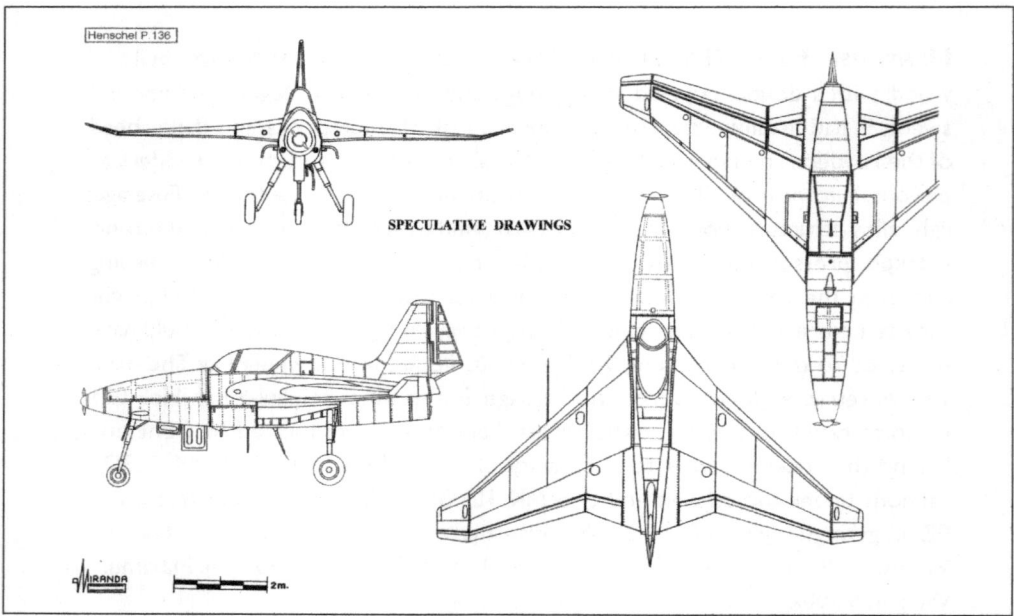

SPECULATIVE DRAWINGS

SPECULATIVE DRAWINGS

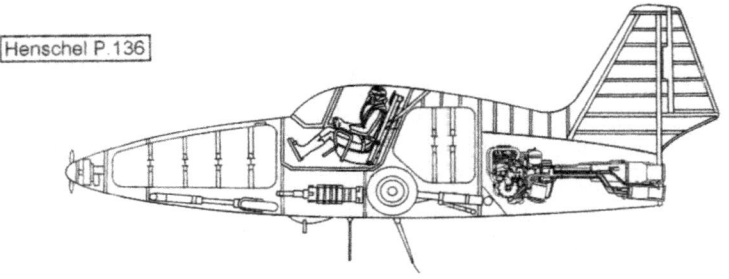

Henschel P.136

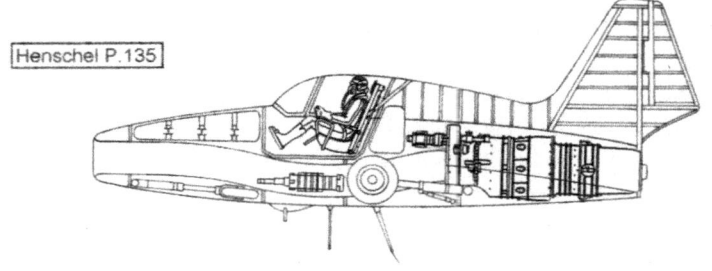

Henschel P.135

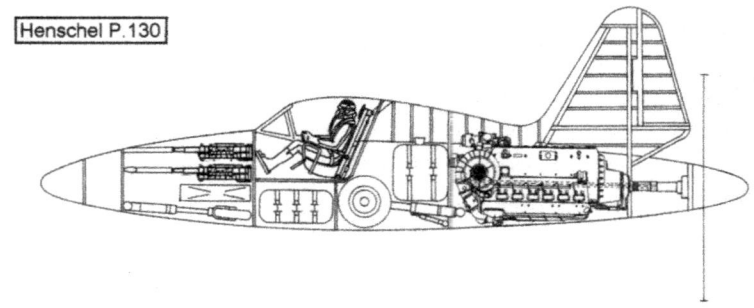

Henschel P.130

2m.

Messerschmitt Me 163 D

The Luftwaffe estimated that a rocket-fighter should have at least 15 minutes of powered endurance to be effective and instructed Messerschmitt to redesign the Me 163 with enlarged fuselage, increased propellant tankage and retractable tricycle undercarriage.

The Me 163 B V18 (VA+SP) prototype was completed in late spring of 1944, it had fixed tricycle landing gear, increased propellant tankage and was powered by one HWK 109-509 C-1 dual-chambered rocket-motor.

On 6 July 1944, the prototype attained 702mph (1,130km/h) top speed.

On 11 October 1944 the V 18 prototype was modified as Me 163 D V1 by extending the fuselage up to 6.82m with a central section that increased the capacity of propellants. The new aircraft was built to test the feasibility of a fixed tricycle landing gear, it was flown unpowered in late spring 1944, towed by one Messerschmitt Bf 110, showing overall better handling as the Me 163 B.

The Me 163 D V1prototype was redesigned by one Junkers team under the leadership of Professor Heinrich Hertel.

The 19-degree swept wings were fitted with automatic leading-edge slots and landing flaps with increased area.

By September 1944 the HWK 109-509 C-3 rocket-motor was installed and the aircraft performed its (unpowered) first flight at Brandis, towed by one Junkers Ju 188 bomber.

The Ju 248 (V1) prototype Werk.Nr. 381001 (DV+PA) was completed at Dessau in August 1944. The new aircraft had pressurised cockpit, partially retractable landing gear, tear drop canopy and cut down aft fuselage decking for high rear visibility.

On 21 October 1944, the RLM ordered that the combat version would be produced by Junkers, under the designation Ju 248, to ease the Messerschmitt team's workload.

On 22 January 1945, the prototype was transferred to Messerschmitt to plan his mass production under the denomination Me 263 A-1, with fully retractable landing gear and external detachable T-Stoff tanks, but the production was stopped because the rocket-fighters were not part of the high-priority Jägernotprogramm.

By April 1945, 18 airframes were under construction in Junkers-Husum facilities.

MESSERSCHMITT ME 263 A-1/JUNKERS JU 248 TECHNICAL DATA: Power plant: one HWK 109-509 C-3 twin chambered rocket-motor with 2,400kg thrust main combustion chamber and 400kg thrust auxiliary chamber. Wingspan: 9.54m. Length: 7.88m. Height: 3.17m. Wings area: 17.8sq.m. Take-off weight: 5,300kg. Estimated maximum speed: 998km/h. Estimated rate of climb: 4,200 m/min. Estimated ceiling: 16,000m. Endurance: 15 minutes. Range: 165km.

The RLM proposed that the Walter motor should eventually be supplanted by one BMW 708 throttleable rocket engine, with 2,496kg peak-thrust and diesel fuel/fuming nitric acid propellants.

To install the new engine it would be necessary to increase the length of the fuselage up to 9.1m.

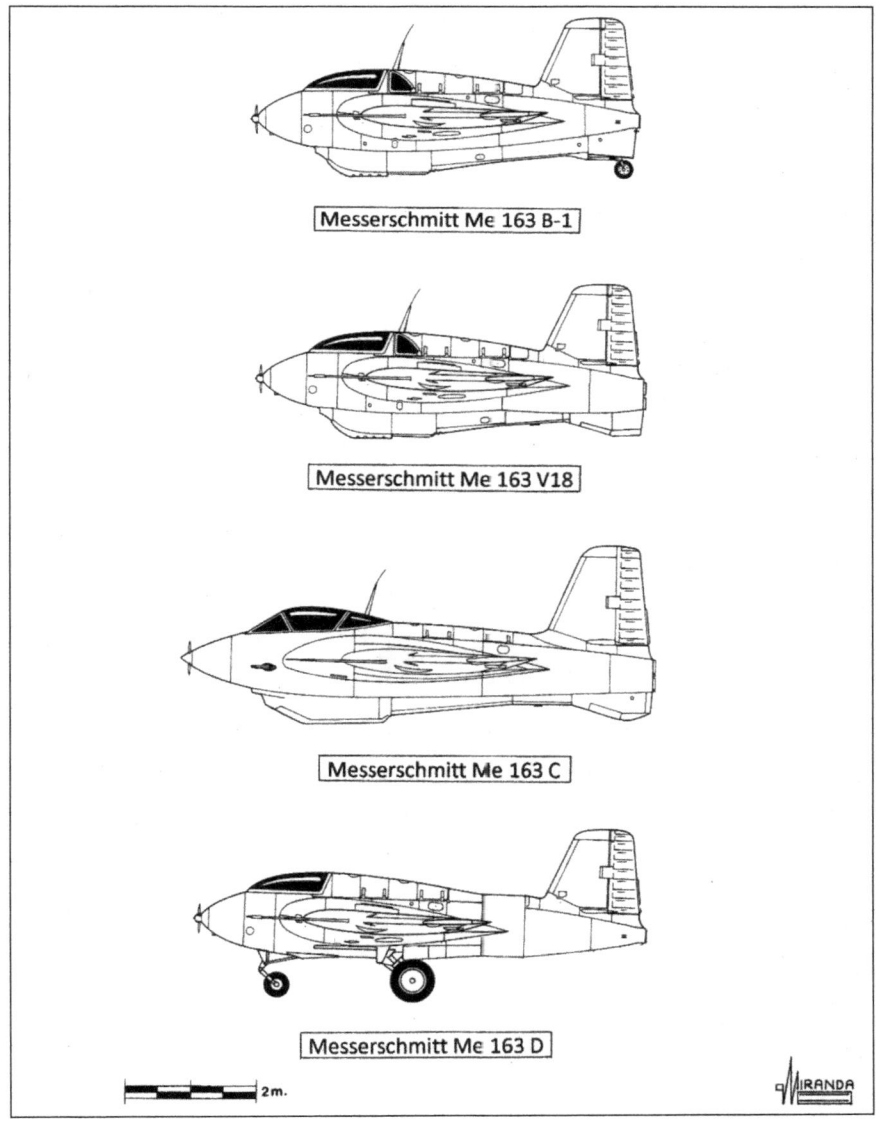

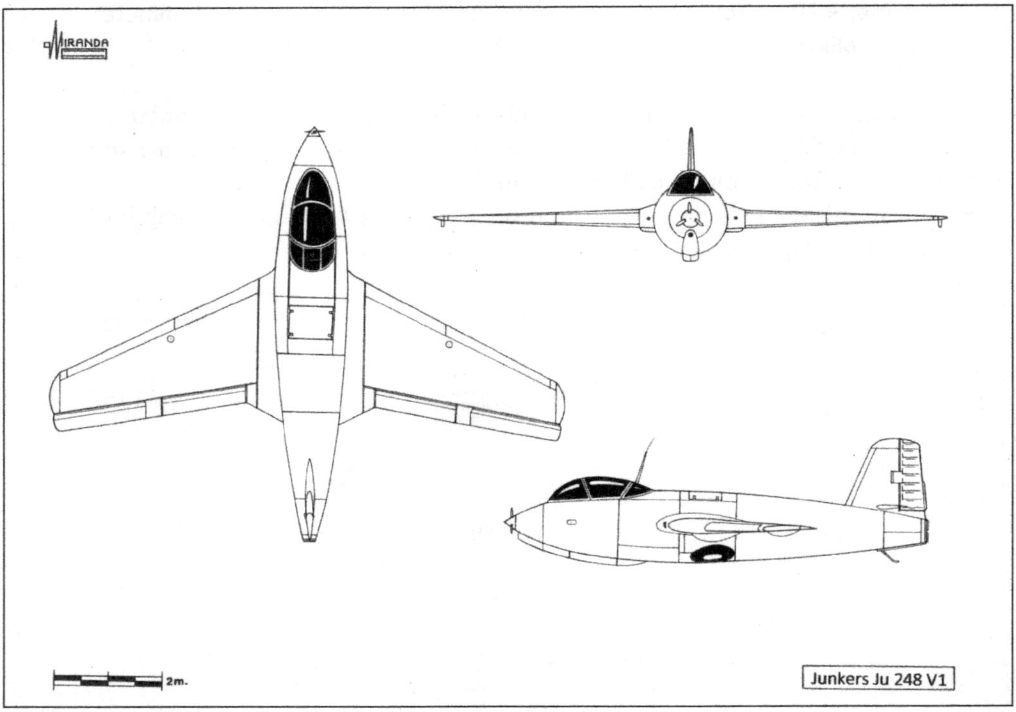

Junkers Ju 248 V1

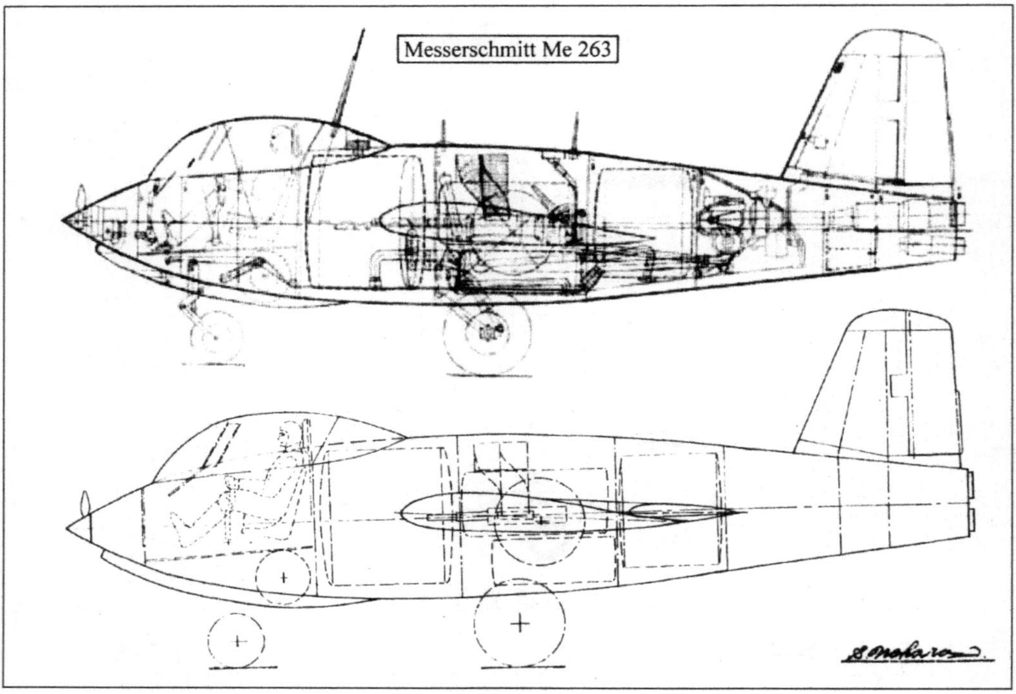

Messerschmitt Me 263

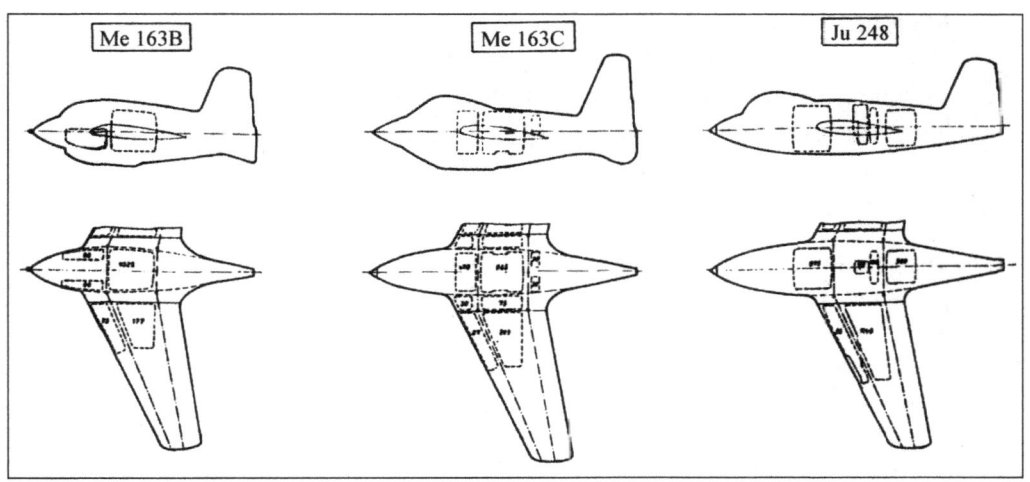

Messerschmitt Me P.1103 B

Because of the bad experiences suffered by the Komet in August 1944, the Luftwaffe did not want more aircraft equipped with landing skids.

The P. 1103 B was developed to rectify the shortcomings of 12 September version.

The new design would have a partially retractable landing gear, best rearward visibility and flaperons, the pilot was seated in a reclined position and the C-Stoff tank was moved to the armoured nose.

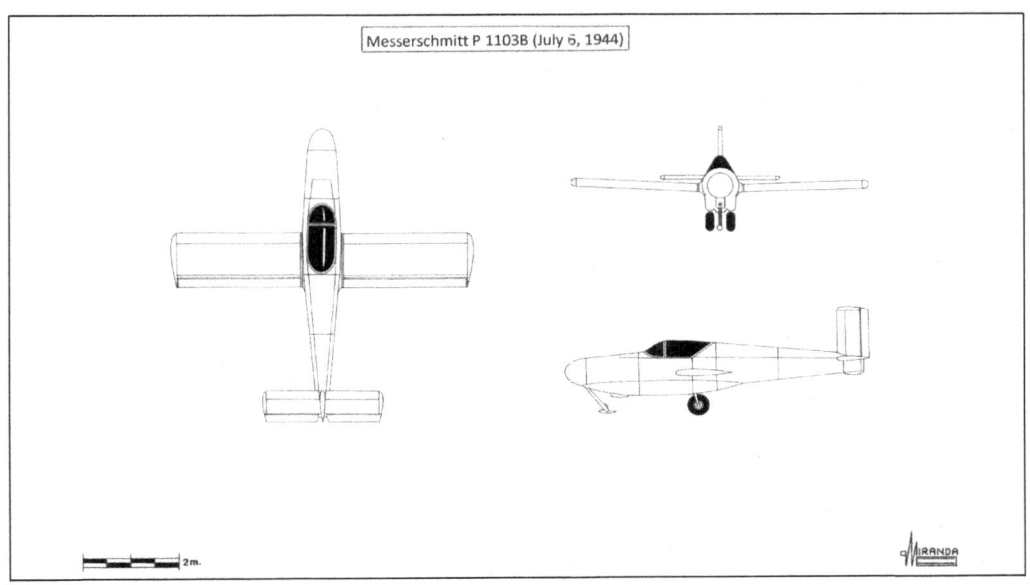

ME P.1103 B (6 JULY 1944) TECHNICAL DATA: Wingspan: 6.3m. Length: 6.37m. Height: 2.03m. Wing Area: 7sq.m. Power plant: one Walter HWK 109-509 B-1 rocket engine with 300kg peak-thrust. Armament: one belly-mounted MK 108/30 heavy cannon with 100 rounds.

Arado TEW 16/43-13

The Arado R Jäger was a swept-wing rocket-fighter interceptor project proposed to the OKL on 18 August 1943 under the denomination TEW 16/43-13 (15 March 1943). The type was designed to rectify the Me 163 Komet shortcomings: inadequate flight endurance and difficulties on ground-handling.

Its retractable landing gear was fitted with specially developed DVL spherical tyres to save space and weight.

There were two propellant tanks containing 1,700l of T-Stoff and 70l of C-Stoff located within the fuselage.

ARADO TEW 16/43-13 TECHNICAL DATA: Wings: with 25 degrees swept at 0.25 chord, 5.6:1 aspect ratio and 8.85m span. Length: 9.70m. Height: 2.0m. Wing area: 14.0sq.m. Maximum weight: 4,620kg. Maximum speed: 850km/h. Service ceiling: 17,700m. Power plant: one Walter HWK 509 A-0 rocket-motor rated at 1,500kg peak-thrust. Armament: two MK 108/30 and two MG 151/20 nose-mounted cannons.

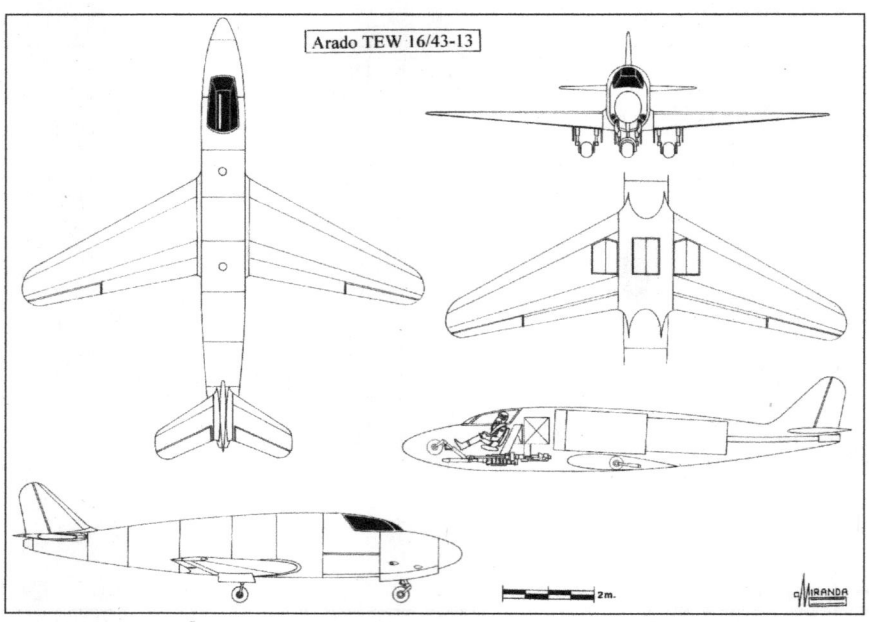

17
Ejector Seats

On 19 April 1945, a flight of Hawker Tempest fighters of the 222nd RAF Squadron, on a patrol mission over the German aerodrome of Husum, saw a new type of previously unknown aircraft. It was one of the Heinkel 162 jet-fighters of the I./JG1 coming back to its Schleswig-Holstein base. Its pilot, Lieutenant Schmitt, worried by the low level of fuel, didn't know who had shot him, he just found himself suddenly trapped in his cockpit while the small fighter twisted in a crazy spin after losing one wing. Like many other pilots shot down during that terrible winter, Schmitt started to count the seconds until his death... but this time something different happened: his left hand pulled a lever and, with a low explosion, the seat was launched far from the fireball that was now his aircraft.

From 1939 the Luftwaffe Aviation Medicine Branch (LFM) were actively experimenting with ejection systems. The physiological tests performed showed that a sitting human body could stand a vertical acceleration of +20G during 0.1 second without major damage. During the war the company Heinkel developed three different ejector seats and from the end of 1942, all the experimental aircrafts tested by the Luftwaffe were equipped with any of them. The first tests took place in 1939 and 1940 using sandbags and anthropomorphic dummies in a ground rig at Heinkel's plant in Rechlin.

The first launch with human pilot was at the end of 1941 in Erprobungsstelle-Rechlin, when the trained parachutist Wilhelm Buss ejected from the back seat of a Junkers Ju 87B using a catapult device with spring mechanism. This type of seat was very heavy and maintenance was difficult, so it was not considered appropriate for it to be used in combat. It was used in flight tests with the new prototypes of aircrafts like the Messerschmitt Me 262 V2 and the Me 163B V1.

The second system, developed by Heinkel used bottles of compressed air at very high pressure (1,700psi) and was able to launch a seat of 120kg, with a pilot of 80kg, at a 6m. distance above the fuselage of the aircraft. The ejection speed was of 17 m/s at 27G.

The auxiliary equipment was very heavy and presented considerable maintenance problems to be successfully operational. It was tested during the flight tests of the He 280 and was used for the first time in an emergency by test pilot Schenk during a flight with the He 280 V1 (DL+AS) on 13 January 1943.

Three test-launches were performed with this seat in 1944 from the back seat of the He 219 (DV+DI) prototype, before installing it on the production version of the new night fighter.

After the successful testing, it was designed as a double seat for the pilot and the radar operator, sitting back to back. It was used in combat units until the end of the war, working successfully in at least four different occasions:

- When the He 219 of the NJG 1, crewed by the Uffz. Herter and the Gefr. Perbix on 11/04/1944, suffered a mechanical failure.
- When the He 219 (G9+GK) of the NJG 1, crewed by Lt Otto Fries and Fw. Alfred Staffa, was shot down by a British Mosquito night fighter on 19 May 1944.
- When the He 219 (G9+EK) of the NJG1, with same crew than previous one, was shot down by a Mosquito night fighter on 16 January 1945.
- When the He 219 (G9+HH) of the NJG1, crewed by Hptm. Wilhelm Modrow and the Fw Alfred Staffa, was shot down by a Mosquito night fighter on 1 February 1945.

The third system, Schleudersitz Heinkel-Kartusche, was developed in cooperation with Dornier. It used an explosive cartridge with 30 grams of powder and a catapult tube fixed to the upper-end of the seat and to the lower-end of the aircraft frame.

The ejection speed was only 11m/s at 12G, but the system was light, easy to maintain, could be installed in small aircraft and used at speeds of up to 700km/h. It was installed on Dornier Do 335 and Heinkel He 162 of operational series and in some Messerschmitt Me 262, Gotha Go 229 and Arado Ar 234B.

A He 162 from I/JG1, crewed by Lt Rudolf Schmidt used it during combat on 20 April 1945.

The seat was fitted with a Sutton-type harness and the seat-type parachute pack included emergency oxygen equipment in the seat cavity.

The Focke-Wulf Company developed two types of explosive ejector seats.

The first one was very similar to the Heinkel design, and it was tested in a Fw190 A-0/U4 in Rechlin Roggenthin at the end of 1941, using an anthropomorphic dummy. Its installation was planned in the last series of the Fw 190 D and in the Ta 154 C night fighter.

The Fw190 A-0/U4 of Rechlin was also used to test an explosive system to eject the cockpit canopy at speeds above 250mph at which it is not possible to make it manually due to the air pressure. It consisted of two standard 20mm cartridges located to both sides of the armoured windshield in a similar disposition to those used by the Lockheed F-104 in the 60s.

The second type was a downward-operating ejector seat designed for the suicidal variant *pulk-zerstörer* of the Ta 154 A-1 from which at least six copies were built. By the end of the war, 60 aircrew had used ejection seats in combat.

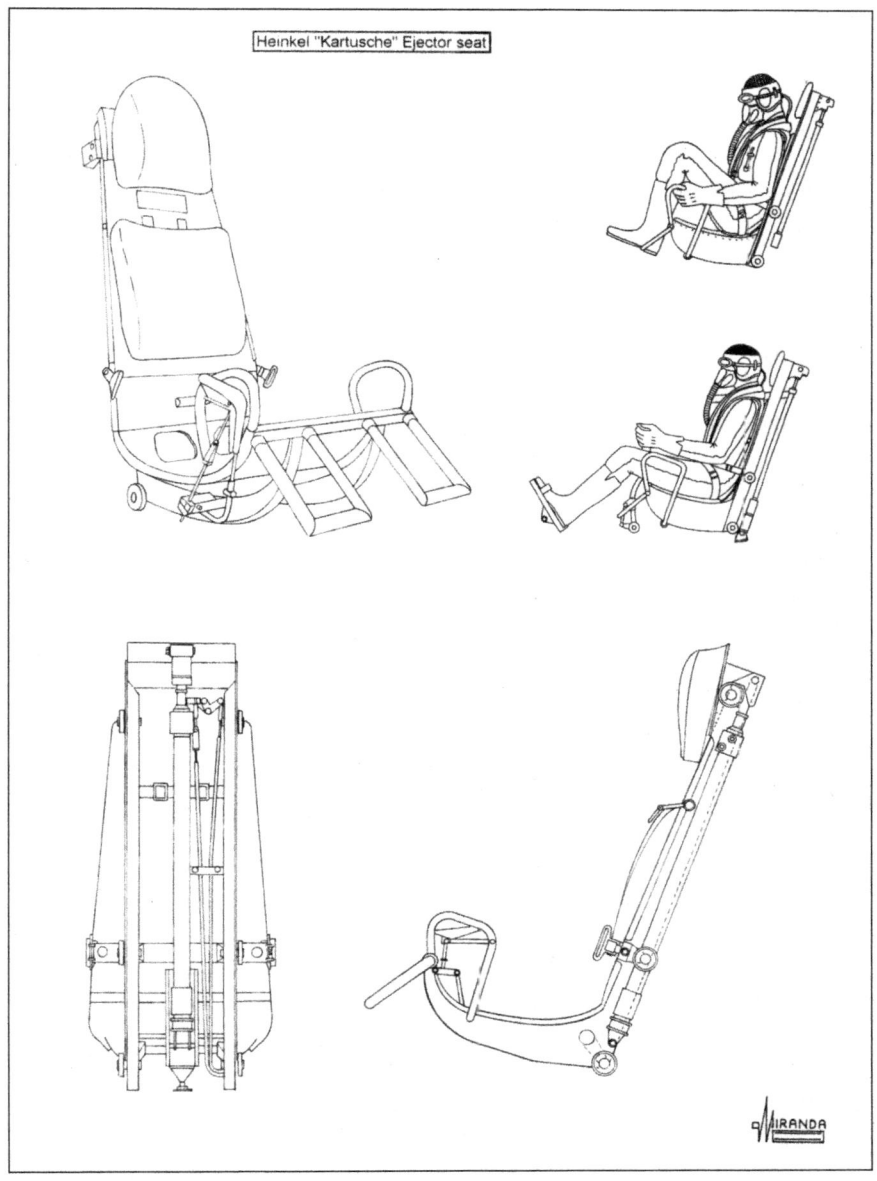

18
Bi-Propellant Rocket Engines

- Walter RI-203 (June 1939), T-Stoff + M-Stoff, 400kg thrust, used in the Heinkel He 176 experimental aircraft and in the Messerschmitt Enzian E-1 anti-aircraft missile.
- Walter RII-203 (October 1941), T-Stoff + Z-Stoff, 750kg thrust, used in the Messerschmitt Me 163 V4 prototype.
- Walter HWK 109-500 (summer 1937), T-Stoff + Z-Stoff, 500kg thrust, used in DFS 194 prototype.
- Walter HWK 109-501, T-Stoff + Z-Stoff, 1,000kg thrust, used in Junkers 287 prototype.
- Walter HWK 109-502, T-Stoff + Z-Stoff, 1,500kg thrust, used in the Messerschmitt Enzian E-2 nad E-3 anti-aircraft missiles.
- Walter HWK 109-507, T-Stoff + Z-Stoff, 590kg thrust, used in the Henschel 293 V3-V5 gliding bomb.
- Walter HWK 109-509 A-0, (May 1943), T-Stoff + Z-Stoff, 1,500kg thrust, used in the Messerschmitt Me 163 B-0.
- Walter HWK 109-509 A-1, (August 1944), T-Stoff + Z-Stoff, 1,600kg thrust, used in the Messerschmitt Me 163 B-1.
- Walter HWK 109-509 A-2, T-Stoff + Z-Stoff, two combustion chambers with 1,700 and 200kg thrust, used in the Messerschmitt Me 163 B-1a, Messerschmitt Me 262 C-1a, Messerschmitt P. 1104, Junkers EF 127 and Heinkel P. 1077 Julia.
- Walter HWK 109-509 B-1, (March 1944), T-Stoff + C-Stoff, two combustion chambers with 2,000 and 300kg thrust, used in the Messerschmitt Me 163 V18 and Bachem Ba 349 B Natter.
- Walter HWK 109-509 C-1, (August 1944), T-Stoff + C-Stoff, two combustion chambers with 2,000 and 400kg thrust, used in the Messerschmitt Me 163 C and Messerschmitt Me 263.
- Walter HWK 109-509 C-3, (August 1944), T-Stoff + C-Stoff, two combustion chambers with 2,000 and 400kg thrust, used in the Junkers 248.

- Walter HWK 109-509 D-1, (January 1945), T-Stoff + C-Stoff, 1,700kg thrust, used in the DFS 346.
- Walter HWK 109-509 E, (January 1945), T-Stoff + C-Stoff, 1,700kg thrust, used in the Ba 349 C Natter.
- Walter HWK 109-509 S-1, (January 1945), T-Stoff + C-Stoff, 1,700kg thrust, used in the Messerschmitt Me 262 C-1.
- Walter HWK 109-509 S-2, (January 1945), T-Stoff + C-Stoff, 1,993kg thrust, used in the Messerschmitt Me 262 C-3 and Messerschmitt P. 1106 R.
- Walter HWK 109-509 S-3, (January 1945), T-Stoff + C-Stoff, 1,993kg thrust, used in the DFS 229.
- Walter HWK 109-559, (August 1944), T-Stoff + C-Stoff, two combustion chambers with 1,700 and 150kg thrust, used in the Ba 349 A Natter.
- Walter HWK 109-739, 1,500kg thrust, SV-Stoff + Ergin-Bencene, used in the Messerschmitt Enzian E-3 anti-aircraft missile.
- BMW 109-510 A, M-Stoff + SV-Stoff, 1,500kg thrust used in the Messerschmitt Me 163 B-0.
- BMW 109-510 B, M-Stoff + SV-Stoff, 1,500kg thrust used in the Messerschmitt Me 163 B-1.
- BMW 109-510 C, M-Stoff + SV-Stoff, 1,500kg thrust used in the Messerschmitt Me 163 C.
- BMW 109-511, M-Stoff + SV-Stoff, 600kg thrust used in the Henschel Hs 298 air-to-air missile.
- BMW 109-548, R-Stoff + SV-Stoff, 140kg thrust used in the Ruhrstahl-Kramer X-4 air-to-air missile.
- BMW 109-558, R-Stoff + SV-Stoff, 380kg thrust used in the Henschel Hs 117 Schmetterling anti-aircraft missile.
- BMW 109-708, (November 1944), R-Stoff + SV-Stoff, 2,500kg thrust used in the Messerschmitt Me 163 C.
- BMW 109-718, (1943), R-Stoff + SV-Stoff, 1,800kg thrust mounted in the mixed power plant BMW 003 R, used in the Messerschmitt Me 262 Heimatschützer II, the Heinkel He 162.01-42 and the Horten Ho XIIIb.
- DVK Konrad VfK Zg.613-A01, (February 1945), SV-Stoff + Visol, 1,000 to 2,000kg thrust, used in the Messerschmitt Enzian E-4 anti-aircraft missile.
- DVK Konrad VfK Zg.613-A02, (February 1945), SV-Stoff + Visol, 1,800 to 2,180kg thrust, used in the Rheinmetall-Borsig Rheintochter III (R-3f) anti-aircraft missile.
- DVK Konrad VfK Zg.613-A03, (February 1945), Br-Stoff + SV-Stoff, 1,500 to 2,500kg thrust, used in the Messerschmitt Enzian E-5 anti-aircraft missile.

19

Projekt Natter

A little-known designer named Erich Bachem proposed to the RLM the draft of a Verschleissflugzeug (expendable aircraft) that could be built entirely with non-strategic materials and launched vertically from any location, using minimum ground equipment.

The first sketches, dated 16 June 1944, represent a very simple plane partially built in concrete, a technology that the firm Blohm und Voss had been developing to build the wings of the anti-ship missile BV246 Hagelkorn.

Nose and cockpit were made of one piece of concrete, designed for ramming. To make it lighter, the cockpit height was reduced by placing the pilot in semi-prone position. Forward viewing was provided by a channel in the nose, and an armoured windshield was fitted into the rear end of that channel. The wings, rear fuselage and tail surfaces were made of steel, using the technology developed for the V-1 missiles by the firm Fieseler. The engine would be a solid-fuel rocket of unspecified type and the armament one air-to-air rocket RZ 15/8 of 158mm.

The project evolved into two more sophisticated versions—a rammer and a semi-expendable rocket-fighter—and was proposed to the OKL in August. The first version from 9 August 1944, was named BP-20 Berak-I (*bemannte rakete projekt*), being powered by a ring of eight solid-fuel rockets of the Schmidding 109-563 or 109-553 types, installed around a central rocket of the Schmidding 109-533 type. The concrete nose cone contained four automatic rocket launchers Trommelgerät of 73mm with capacity for up to 32 air-to-air spin-stabilised RZ 65 rockets.

The fighter would take off vertically, firing a salvo of RZ 65 against the belly of the enemy bombers. Afterwards, it would continue its ascent until exhausting the power of its thrusters at 12,000m. During the fall, it could reach a maximum speed of 800km/h and ram another bomber. Before the impact, the pilot could leave the plane through a hatch back. Berak-I would have a wingspan of 2.6m, a length of 6.5m and a fuselage diameter of 0.6m and weighed 1,230kg at take-off.

The second version, called BP-20-04 (13 August 1944) would be powered by a Walter bi-fuel liquid rocket and armed with a honeycomb rocket-launch cluster designed to hold twenty-four Föhn air-to-air spin-stabilised rockets. The sophistication of the bi-propellant Walter engine prevented its use as rammer.

This project was subsequently known as Bachem Ba 8-349 Natter, when it was declared the winner of the Objektschutzjäger contest in replacement of the Heinkel Julia II.

In the middle of September 1944, 150 machines were ordered by the Waffen-SS Sonderkommando Waldsee and fifty by the Luftwaffe's Komet units.

The Natter was originally designed for taking-off from a completely vertical launch ramp, but not for landing. The pilot was expected to leave the plane using his personal parachute, but when the Bachem firm was authorised to use the valuable Walter rocket engines that had been manufactured to propel the Heinkel Julia, it was necessary to modify the project.

Instead of falling freely to the ground and being destroyed by the impact, the abandoned plane descended, braked by a high-speed *bänder fallschirm* parachute that would be later recovered, rebuilt and installed on a launch pad by ground crews from SS Sonderkommando-N.

In August 1944 the pilot's prone position was changed to the kneeling semi-prone 'praying mantis' position, already adopted in the Horten Ho IV sailplane, which allowed better visibility in combat.

The Luftwaffe Aviation Medicine Branch (LFM) subsequent investigations showed that the tolerance of the pilot to VTO acceleration in these positions was quite limited.

In the BP 20-09 (7 October 1944) tests were carried out with a swivel seat positioned forward, for vertical flight, and normal seated pilot position, for horizontal flight.

During the planned experimental flight program, fifty prototypes were to be built to investigate gliding characteristics (M1 to M10), VTO characteristics (M11 to M20). Parachute recovery systems (M21 to M30), vertical launch with automatic pilot (M31 to M40) and pre-production operational-test aircrafts (M41 to M50).

The M51 was expected to be the first K-Aktion (Krokus) operational fighter of a production series.

The Bachem BP 20 M1 test glider was flown on 3 November 1944, at Neuburg-Donau airfield, towed in Tragschlepp mode by the Heinkel He 111 H-6 bomber (DG+RN). The prototype was mounted for taking-off on a detachable tricycle trolley.

After checking the proper functioning of all control surfaces, with 53 ol of water ballast, the pilot left the plane using his personal parachute to descend without incident, but the M1 was destroyed when the Heinkel attempted to land with the prototype still attached to the 60m. tow rope.

The BP 20 M3 was fitted with fixed tricycle undercarriage and airbrakes mounted on both fuselage sides. The prototype was flown on 14 December 1944, towed at an altitude by one He 111 modified bomber.

At 900m. altitude and 170km/h, the pilot jumped, and the bomber managed to land towing the prototype that was only slightly damaged. This flight confirmed the results of the M1.

The BP 20 M8 was launched in free flight from 5,500m altitude and its manoeuvrability was tested at 520km/h. The pilot jumped at 1,200m. and 300km/h.

On 22 December 1944, the unmanned M6 was successfully launched from a vertical ramp accelerated by four SR 34 RATO rockets.

The first manned vertical take-off was performed by the M23 on 1 March 1945. Unfortunately, one SR 34 rocket failed to jettison, and the prototype crashed killing the pilot.

There is no evidence of other manned launches, the M25, M34, and M52 prototypes were launched with pilot dummies.

The M52, fitted with auxiliary launch tailfins, was used to test the Zündstangen-Lafette wooden pole launcher.

On 16 March, the LGW 3-axis guidance autopilot was flight-tested in the M14 unmanned prototype.

Production of the operational version Ba 349 A-1 Natter (Operation Krokus) started on 7 March 1945, at Bachem-Werk Waldsee, Nabern and Gräfenroda. But this aircraft type didn't get into combat before the war ended in Europe.

Four completed machines were captured by the US. Troops in St Leonhard (Austrian Alps) and another was captured by the Red Army in Bad Wörishofen.

It was planned that the A-1 would be launched vertically from a Zündstangen-Lafette, fixed to a concrete base. The RATO rockets were detached at 1,500m. altitude and the pilot regained manual control to carry out the interception.

The Natter armament consisted of twenty-four gyro-stabilised 73mm rockets Hs 217 Föhn that were to be fired in a single salvo at 600m. range from the target.

The rockets were stored in a cylindrical honeycomb container mounted on the nose, with a system for discharging the propulsion gases, called Abgasableitung openings, located on either side of the forward fuselage.

The primitive pin and ring sight device was pre-calculated to fire from 600m. and should also serve to align the Revi gunsight when some units were available.

After carrying out the attack, the pilot descended to 3,000m altitude, disconnected the control stick, all mechanical and electrical connections between the cockpit and the rest of the aircraft, and activated the ejection mechanism of the high-speed parachute, housed in the starboard side of the fuselage.

The sudden deceleration detached the nose cone, the windscreen, the front armour, and the control pedals. The pilot was also ejected out of the cockpit and descended using his personal parachute.

The Ba 349 B was designed to increase the powered flight endurance using one HWK 109-509 B-1 rocket engine, with an additional low-thrust cruising combustion chamber for economic cruise, and increased propellant tankage. This led to a 10 per cent speed decrease, but the Type B could maintain combat altitude for 8 minutes and could destroy several bombers, multiplying its effectiveness.

It was necessary to modify its armament by installing two MK 108/30 guns under the pilot's seat and replacing the honeycomb container with a cylinder containing thirty-two fin-stabilised 55mm rockets of the type R4M Orkan.

This air-to-air unguided rocket had a range of 1,800m and it was estimated that, from such distance, a salvo of twenty-four units had a field of fire of 30 x 14m, approximately the size of a B-17 US bomber. The salvo was electrically fired by means of one automatic sequencer Schaltwalze at fifty millisecond intervals.

A single R4M should be enough to destroy a heavy bomber and the Schaltwalze could be programmed to fire only four or five rockets at a time.

The Ba 349 C was a pressurised version with 'T' tailplane, powered by one HWK 109-509 D-1 dual chamber rocket engine.

BACHEM ROCKET-FIGHTER (16.7.44) TECHNICAL DATA: Prone pilot. Wingspan: 3.24m. Length: 8.1m. Height: 2.8m. Power plant: one solid-propellant rocket-motor. Armament: one spin-stabilised 158mm rocket RZ 15/8. Airframe: steel and concrete.

BACHEM BP 20 BERAK I TECHNICAL DATA: Prone pilot. Wingspan: 3.8m. Length: 9.7m. Height: 1.8m. Power plant: nine solid-propellant rocket-motors. Armament: four Trommelgerät automatic rocket launchers with 32 spin-stabilised 73mm rockets RZ 65. Airframe: wood/plywood and concrete.

BACHEM BP 20-04 (13.8.44) TECHNICAL DATA: Prone pilot. Wingspan: 2.49m. Length: 6.77m. Height: 1.26m. Wing chord: 1.0m. Maximum weight: 1,230kg. Maximum speed: 1,000km/h. Service ceiling: 12,000m. Range: 16km. Endurance: 2 min. Power plant: one Walter HWK 109-509 A-1 bi-propellant rocket engine with 1,700kp peak-thrust and one belly-mounted SR 34 solid-fuel RATO rocket with 1,000kp peak-thrust. Propellants: a 75l C-Stoff tank mounted above the pilot's legs and a 350l T-Stoff tank in the mid-fuselage section. Armament: four Trommelgerät automatic rocket launchers with 32 spin-stabilised 73mm rockets RZ 65. Airframe: wood/plywood and steel, launch device one Holzmast (wooden pole).

BACHEM BP 20-09 (10.7.44) TECHNICAL DATA: Prone pilot. Wingspan: 3.2m. Length: 5.72m. Height: 2.0m. Wing chord: 1.0m. Maximum weight: 1,710kg.

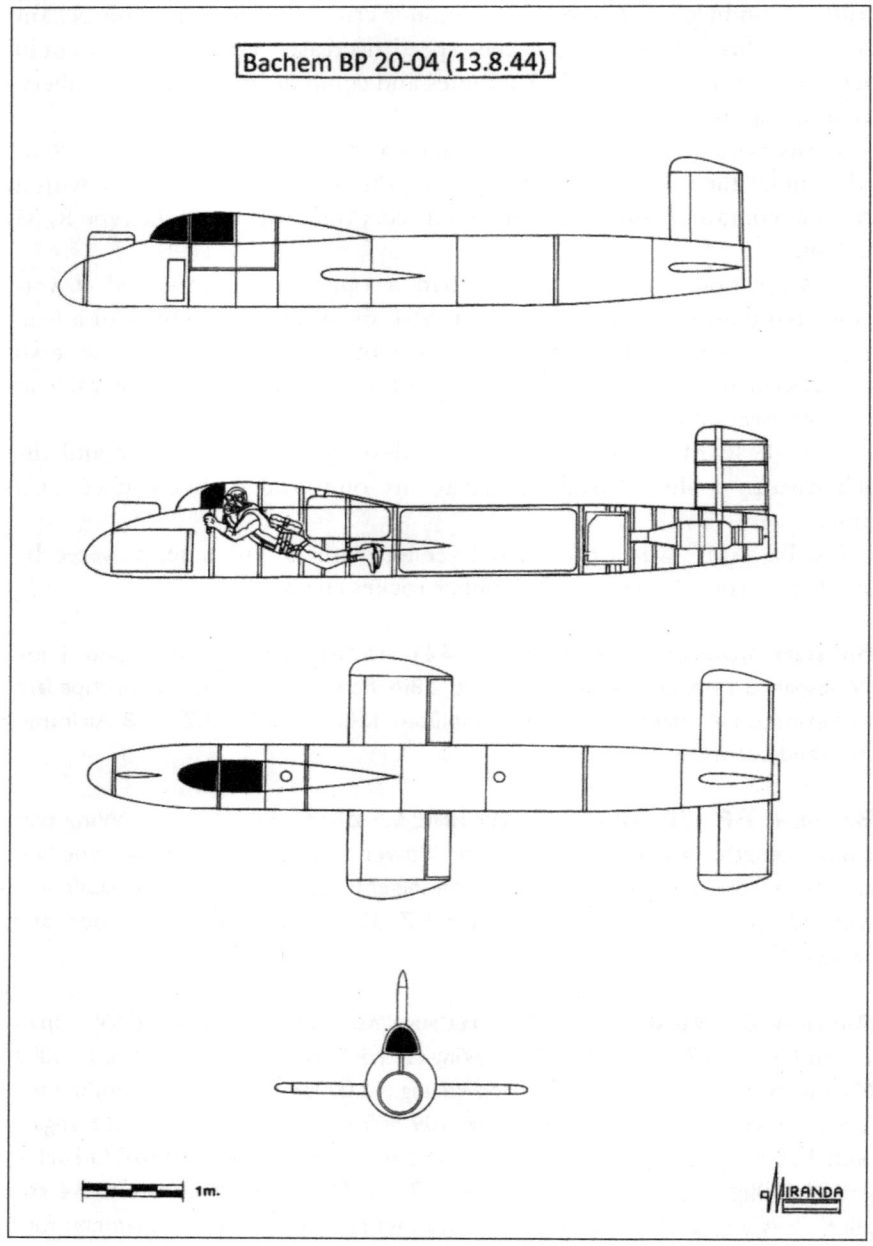

Maximum speed: 1,000km/h. Service ceiling: 12,000m. Range: 12km. Power plant: one Walter HWK 109-509 A-1 bi-propellant rocket engine with 1,700kp peak-thrust and two fuselage-mounted SR 34 solid-fuel RATO rockets with 1,000kp peak-thrust each. Airframe: wood/plywood and steel.

BACHEM BP M1 GLIDER (11.3.44) TECHNICAL DATA: Seated pilot. Wingspan: 3.6m. Length: 6.12m. Height: 2.59m. Wing chord: 1.08m. Maximum speed: 520km/h. Airframe: wood/plywood and steel.

BACHEM BA 349 A-1 (OPERATION KROKUS) TECHNICAL DATA: Seated pilot. Wingspan: 3.6m. Length: 6.06m. Height: 2.2m. Wing area: 3.6sq.m. Wing chord: 1.0m. Maximum weight: 2,200kg. Maximum speed: 880km/h. Climb rate: 194 m/sec. Service ceiling: 12,000m. Range: 64km. Power plant: one Walter HWK 109-509 A-1 bi-propellant rocket engine with 1,700kp peak-thrust and four fuselage-mounted SR 34 solid-fuel RATO rockets with 1,000kp peak-thrust each. Propellants: a 165l tank of C-Stoff mounted above the wing and a 365l tank of T-Stoff mounted below the wing. Airframe: wood/plywood and steel. Armament: one nose-mounted battery of 24 spin-stabilised 73mm rockets Hs 217 Föhn or one Grosse Rhorbatterie 108.

BACHEM BA 349 B (11.27.44) TECHNICAL DATA: Seated pilot. Wingspan: 4m. Length: 6.02m. Height: 2.22m. Wing area: 4.7sq.m. Wing chord: 1.2m. Maximum weight: 2,270kg. Maximum speed: 790km/h. Climb rate: 176 m/sec. Service ceiling: 19,000m. Range: 97km. Power plant: one Walter HWK 109-509 B-1 bi-propellant rocket engine with two combustion chambers with 300 and 2,000kp peak-thrust and four fuselage-mounted SR 34 solid-fuel RATO rockets with 1,000kp peak-thrust each. Propellants: a 190l C-Stoff tank mounted above

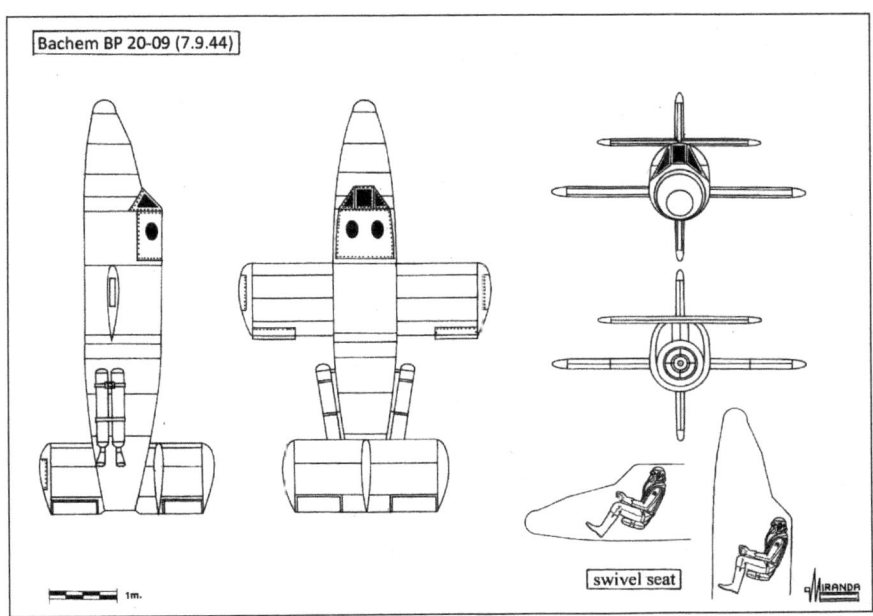

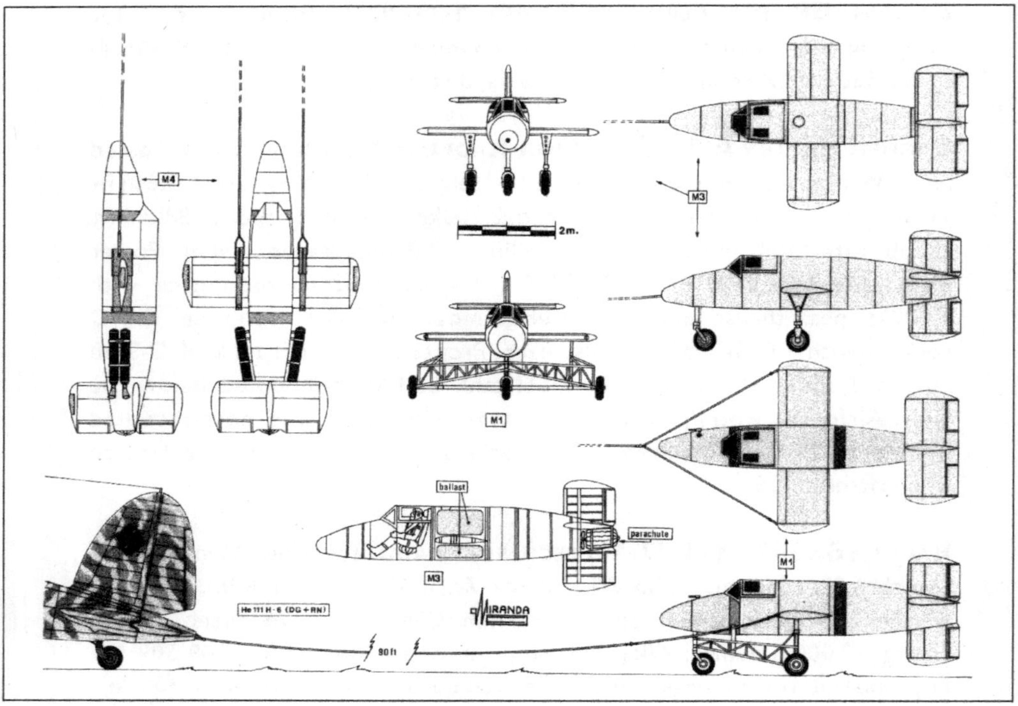
M4
M3
2m.
M1
ballast
parachute
M3
M1
He 111 H-6 (DG+RN)
MIRANDA
90 ft

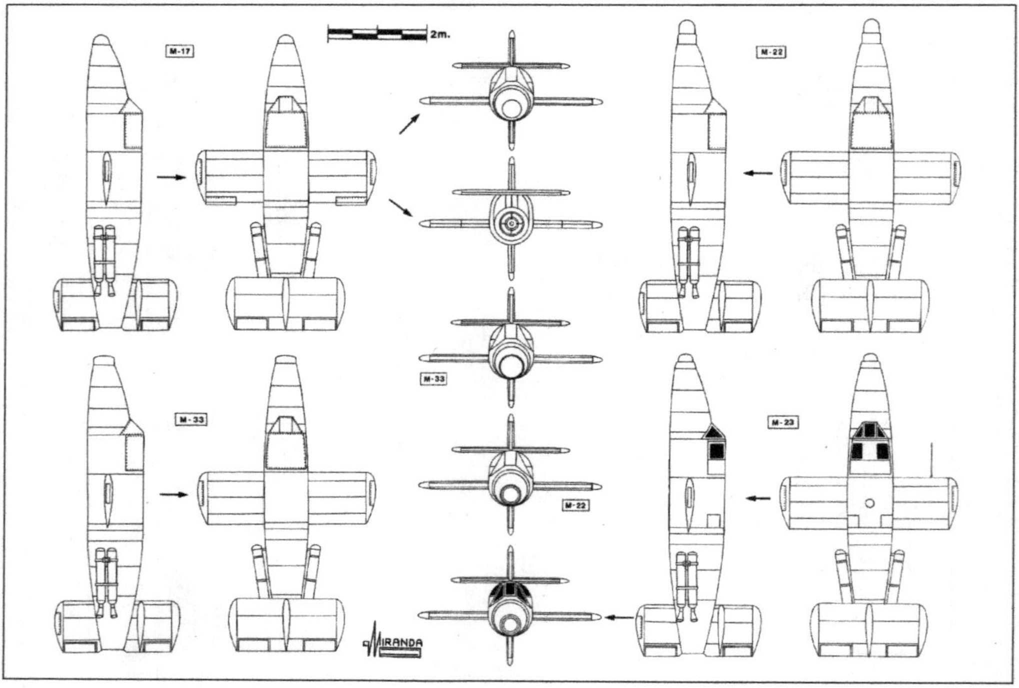
2m.
M-17
M-22
M-33
M-33
M-22
M-23
MIRANDA

the wing and a 400l T-Stoff tank below the wing. Airframe: wood/plywood and steel. Armament: one nose-mounted battery of thirty-two fin-stabilised 55mm rockets R4M Orkan and two fuselage-mounted Mk 108/30 cannons Revi 16b gunsight.

BACHEM BA 349 C (NOVEMBER 1944) TECHNICAL DATA: Seated pilot, pressurised cockpit. Wingspan: 4m. Length: 6m. Height: 2.2m. Wing area: 4.7sq.m.

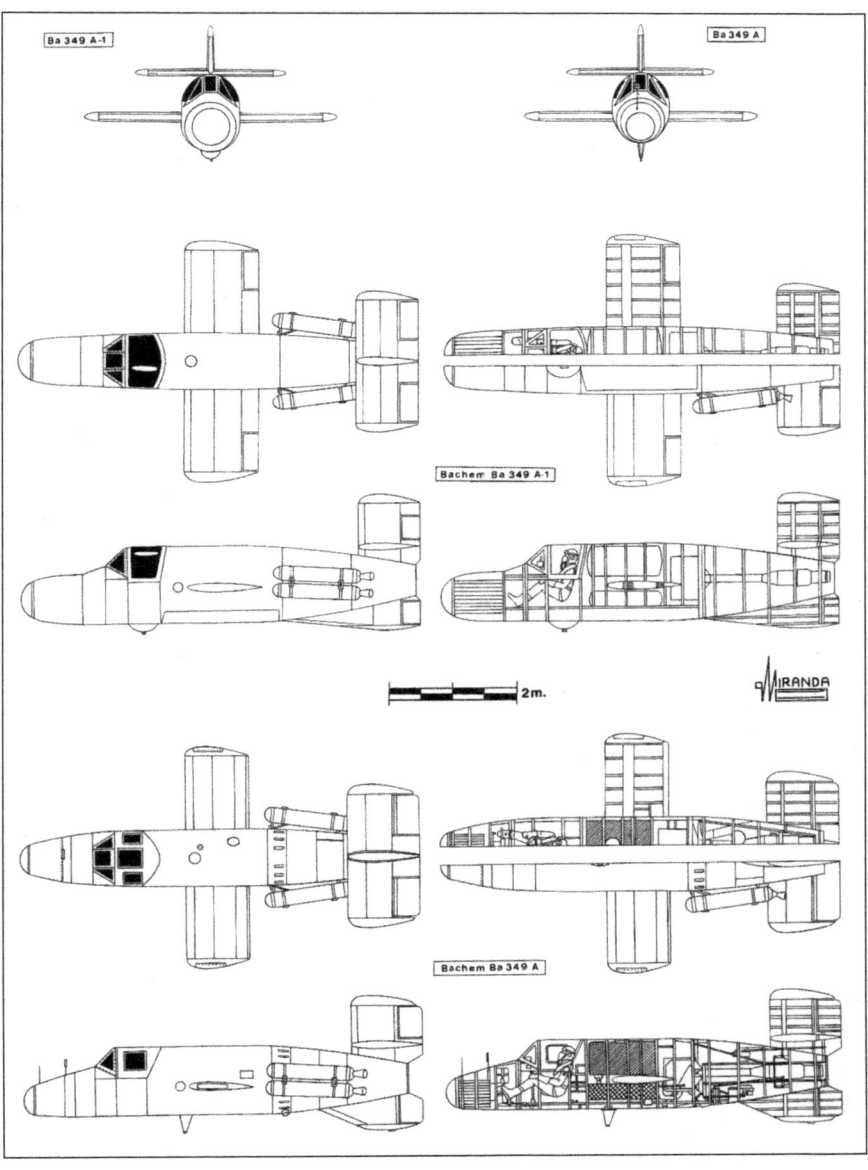

Bachem Ba 349 C
1m.
SPECULATIVE DRAWINGS
MIRANDA

Fahr-Lafette
2000
Schnitt C-D
Schnitt A-B
A
800
B
C
12000
D
Maßst. 1:100
Tk
4.1.45
BSK 032-126a

MIRANDA

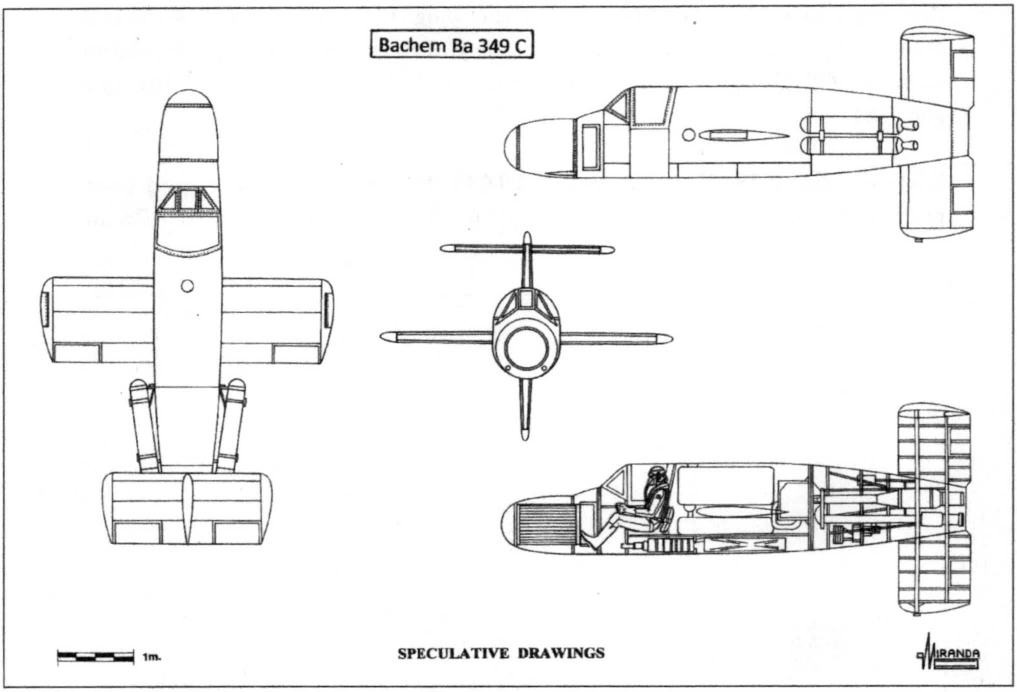

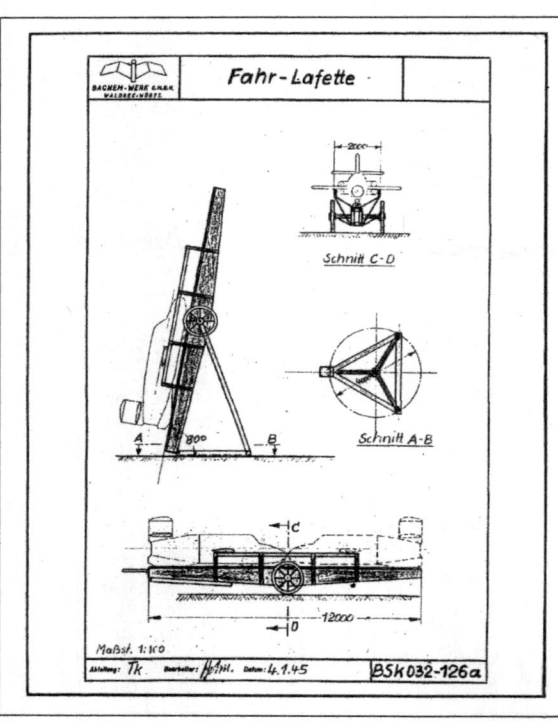

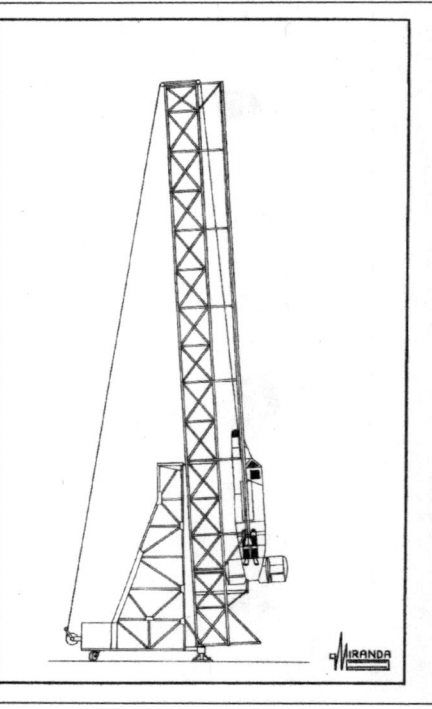

AIRBORNE GUNS

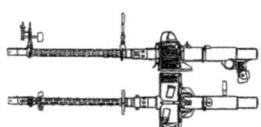

Rheinmetall-Borsig MG 15 / 7.92 mm

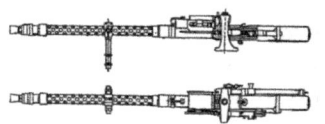

Rheinmetall-Borsig MG 17 / 7.92 mm

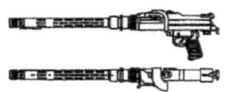

Waffenfabrik Mauser MG 81 / 7.92 mm

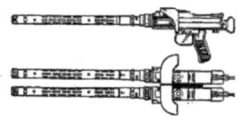

Waffenfabrik Mauser MG 81Z / 7.92 mm

Rheinmetall-Borsig MG 131 / 13 mm

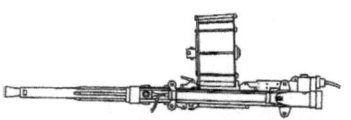

Ikaria Werke Berlin MG FF / 20 mm.

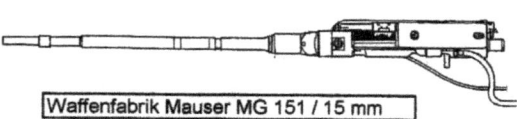

Waffenfabrik Mauser MG 151 / 15 mm

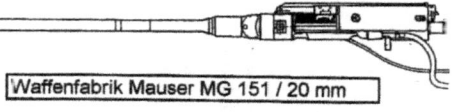

Waffenfabrik Mauser MG 151 / 20 mm

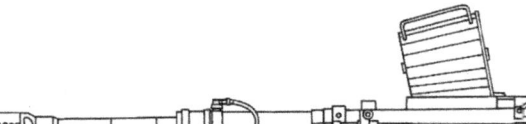

Waffenfabrik Mauser MK 213 C / 20 mm

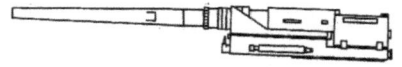

Waffenfabrik Mauser MK 213 C / 30 mm

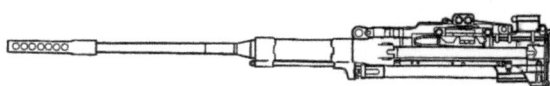

Rheinmetall-Borsig MK 101 / 30 mm

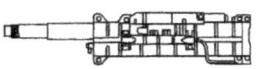

Rheinmetall-Borsig MK 108 / 30 mm

Rheinmetall-Borsig MK 103 / 30 mm

Wing chord: 1.2m. Maximum weight: 2,050kg. Maximum speed: 790km/h. Climb rate: 143 m/sec. Service ceiling: 12,000m. Range: 73km. Power plant: one Walter HWK 109-509 D-1 bi-propellant rocket engine with two combustion chambers with 400 and 2,000kp peak-thrust and four fuselage-mounted SG 34 solid-fuel RATO rockets with 1,200kp peak-thrust each. Propellants: a 250l C-Stoff tank mounted above the wing and a 450l T-Stoff tank below the wing. Airframe: wood/plywood and steel. Armament: one nose-mounted battery of thirty-two fin-stabilised 55mm rockets R4M Orkan and two fuselage-mounted Mk 108/30 cannons Revi 16b gunsight.

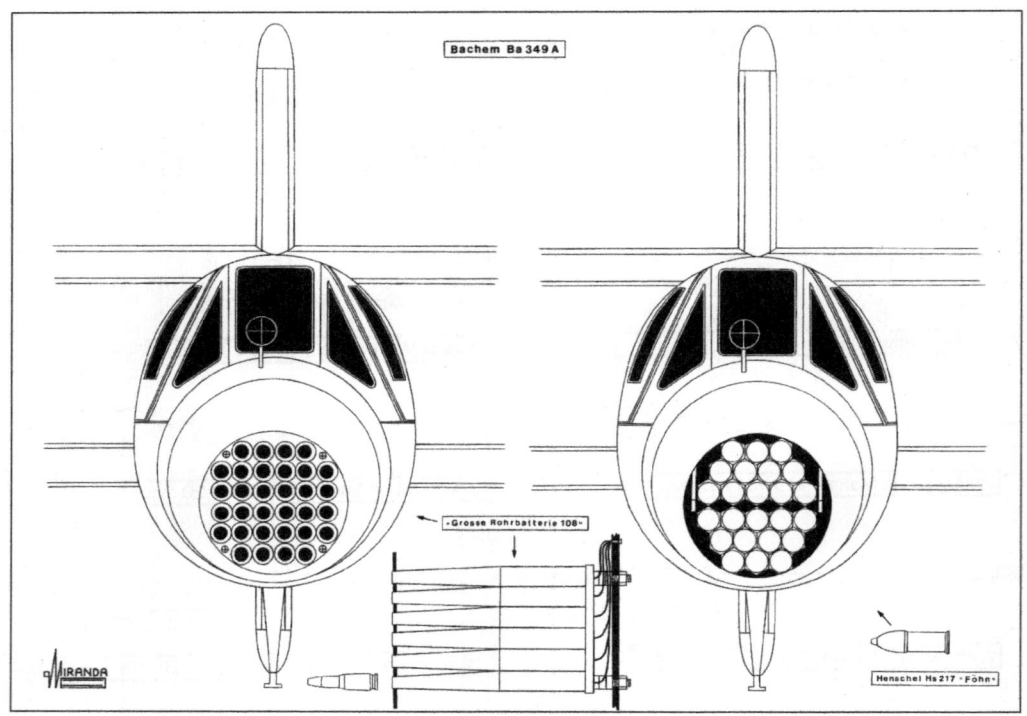

20
Air-to-Air Spin-Stabilised Rockets

In 1936 research started to provide the Luftwaffe with a Bordrakete unguided rocket capable of being launched from any aircraft. After the testing performed at the research centre of Tarnewitz in 1937 it was decided to manufacture the RZ 65 (Rauch Zylinder) model presented by the Rheinmetall-Borsig company.

It was a spin-stabilised rocket of 73mm calibre fitted with a Ra Z_{51} (Raketenaufschlag zünder) nose percussion-fuse and a powerful explosive charge of 280g of RDX/TNT able, in theory, to shoot down a heavy bomber with just one hit.

The rotation was achieved with six inclined exhaust venturis located at the base of the cylinder following the Baron von Unge system, improved by Krupp in 1909. It was a practical design, easy to store, that could be shot from a tube (Einzelschussrohr) by means of an electrically activated percussion mechanism. The launcher had a slightly higher calibre (75mm) and the rocket was kept at the centre of the tube thanks to the three longitudinal fins fixed to its inner walls to allow the gases to be expelled with the minimum friction.

On the other hand, its use from aircrafts proved to be a failure for different reasons:

- The process of the venturis drilling at the rocket base was a costly operation that did not suit the German tactics of mass production. The result was not very accurate, affecting the rocket flying path until making it unpredictable. During further tests performed in November 1941, it was proved that after 544 launches only 15 per cent had hit a target with the size of a bomber. In comparison, the MG/FF guns of 20mm, considered an average 'transition' design in 1940, had a 26 per cent rate of good shots.
- The low quality of the DEGN powder as propellant provided the RZ 65 a practical range of just 250m. This meant that the launching

aircraft had to fly well into the 100 yards area covered by the artillery of the B-17.

The Luftwaffe did many tests in 1941 trying to adapt the RZ 65 to the design of the aircrafts in service at the time. Multiple launchers of four tubes were installed under the wings of a Messerschmitt Bf 109 F-2 and a F-4/R, and of six tubes on a Focke-Wulf Fw 190 A-3/U2 works no. 135386, reaching the conclusion that a salvo of eight to twelve rockets had no possibility to hit a bomber at more than 100m. The installation of twelve tubes grouped together under the fuselage of the Bf 110 V19 and of sixteen tubes under the wings of a Junkers Ju 88 P-4 did not achieve better results.

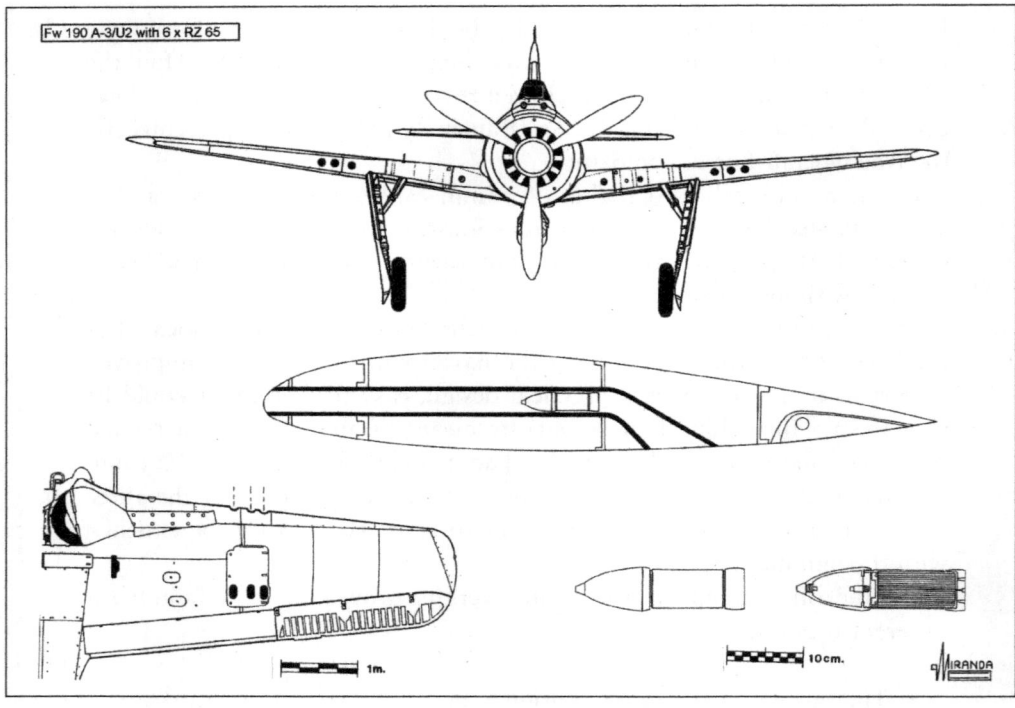

21
Air-to-Air Fin-Stabilised Rockets

After the low success obtained in air combat by the spin-stabilised rockets, Dr Fritz Heber (Kurt Heber-Osterrode) received the order to design the smallest rocket with pop-open fins which could be launched in salvos with the help of a Revi 16 B gunsight.

To achieve that, it used a Diglykol engine, able to accelerate it up to 550 m/sec, thus having the same ballistic characteristics than the 30mm shells of the Mk 108 gun.

The original specification required that a single rocket should be enough to destroy a heavy bomber.

Extensive study of battle casualties indicated that 400g of Hexogen which would penetrate any part of the B-17 bomber would result in their destruction.

Foreseeing that the Allies would enter into combat with heavier aircrafts of the B-29 type, it was decided to increase the explosive load up to 500g.

The final result was a rocket with a diameter of 5.4cm and 71cm of length with eight spring-out fins and an A zRz2 impact fuse.

It was named R4M Orkan (Rakete, 4Kg, Minenkopf/Minengeschoss) rocket of 4kg with a high-explosive, thin-walled warhead.

The R4M had a range of 1800m, and it was estimated that, from such a distance, a salvo of twenty-four rockets had a field of fire of 30 x 14m, approximately the size of a B-17.

From the 20,000 units ordered to the DMW-Lübeck, Siemens LGW-Görlitz, LGW Hakenfelde, Schneider KG and Kratzau Werke-Sudetenland at the end of 1944, around 12,000 rockets were finished before the end of the war in Europe. Circa 10,000 units were used in combat achieving the destruction of around 500 enemy planes.

The flight-testing was done with a Messerschmitt Me163 A-0 rocket-plane. Under its wings, two launchers of twelve rails each known as Abschussrosten were installed. The R4M were electrically fired by means of the automatic Schaltwalze sequencer at fifty millisecond intervals.

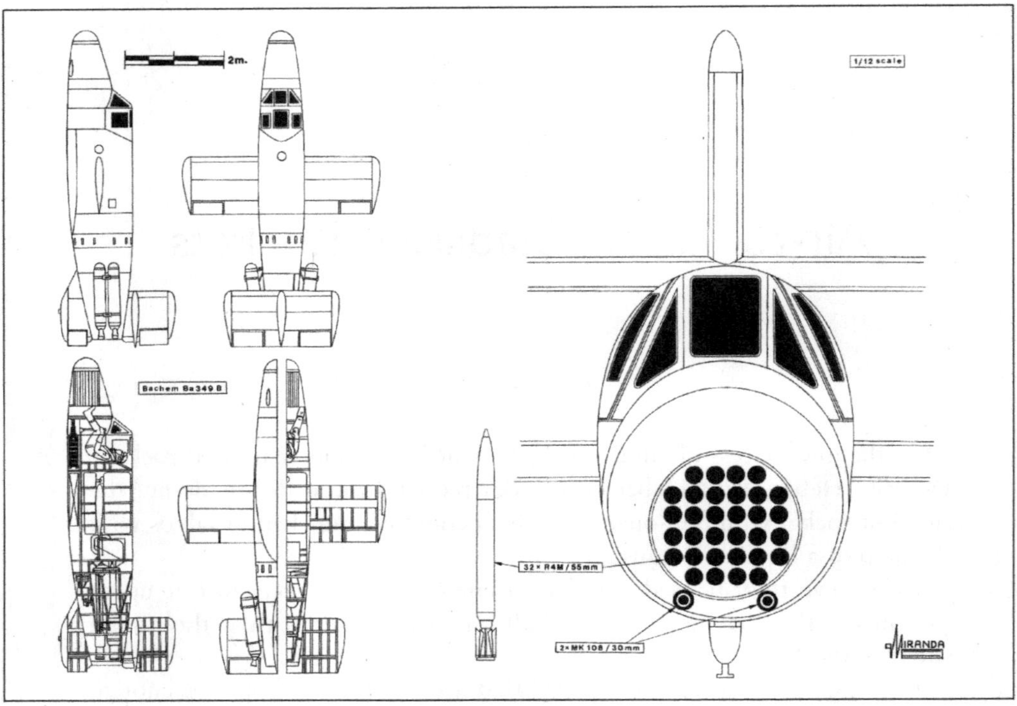

Rocket Interceptors: 1941–1947

Bachem Ba 349 B

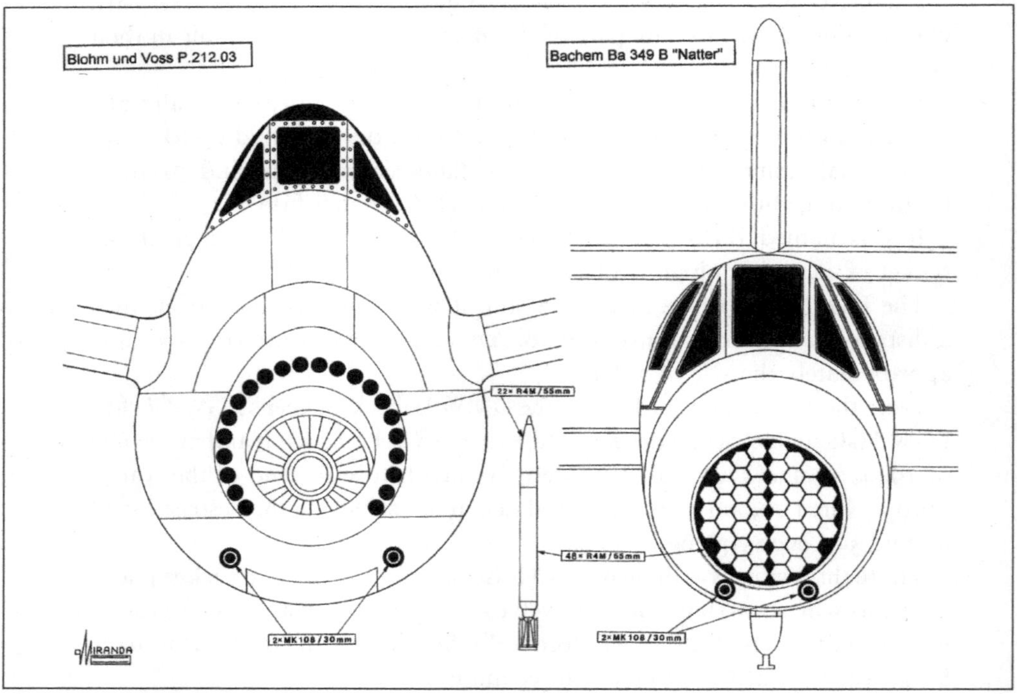

Blohm und Voss P.212.03

Bachem Ba 349 B "Natter"

The Me 262 A-1a of the Jagdverband 44 were equipped with Abschussrosten in March 1945.

Some testing was done in February with launchers of seventeen and twenty-four rails using six Me 262 A-1b in the Messerschmitt experimental plant at Oberammergau. These aircrafts were also tested in combat with great success.

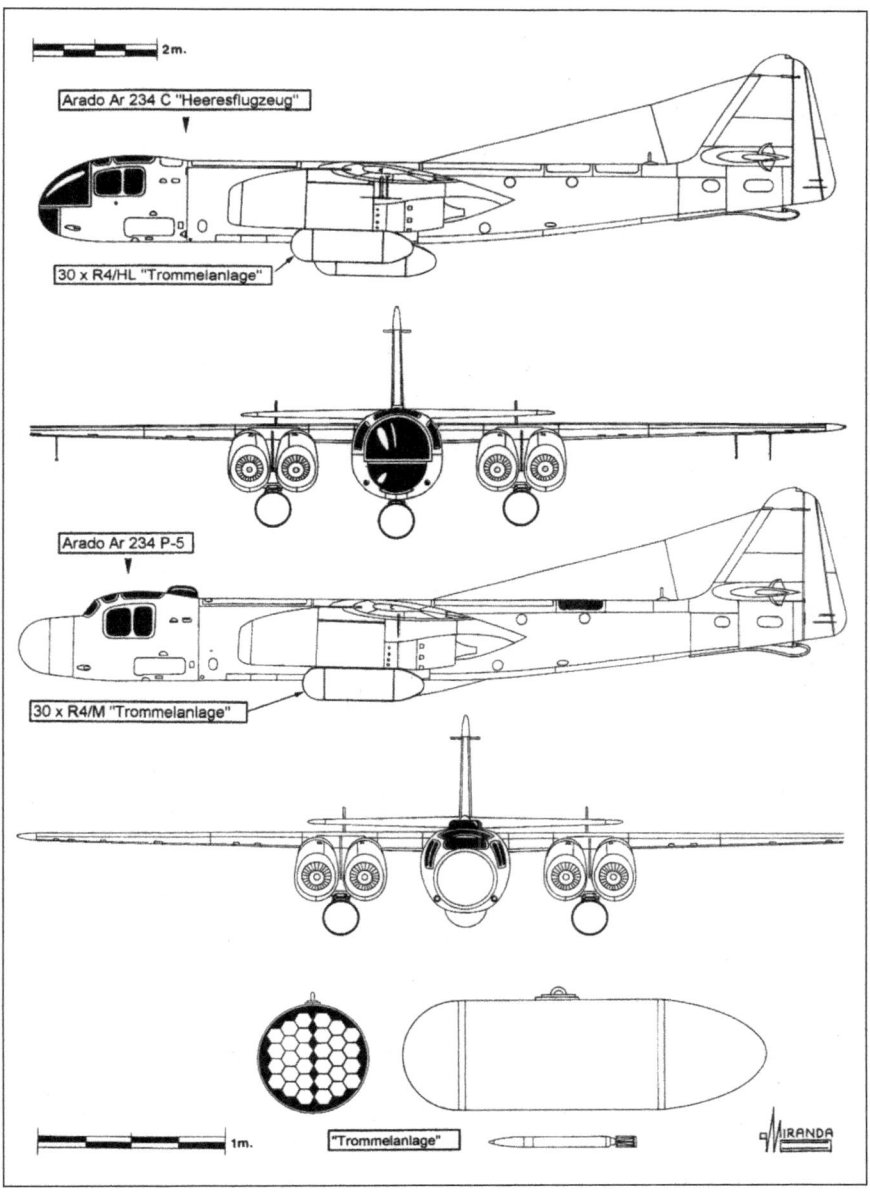

The installation of the Abschussrosten had also been foreseen under the wings of the Focke-Wulf Fw 190 D-9 interceptors of the I./JG 301 and of the new Ta 152 C-1/R31 and Ta 152 H-1/R11.

The hollow-charge principle was applied to the air-to-air rockets foreseeing that they would be necessary to fight against the great B-29 bombers that would soon enter into service.

In addition to the work at TAL and Waffen F, some research was done at the high-explosive research Institute at Kempten and at DWM-Lübeck.

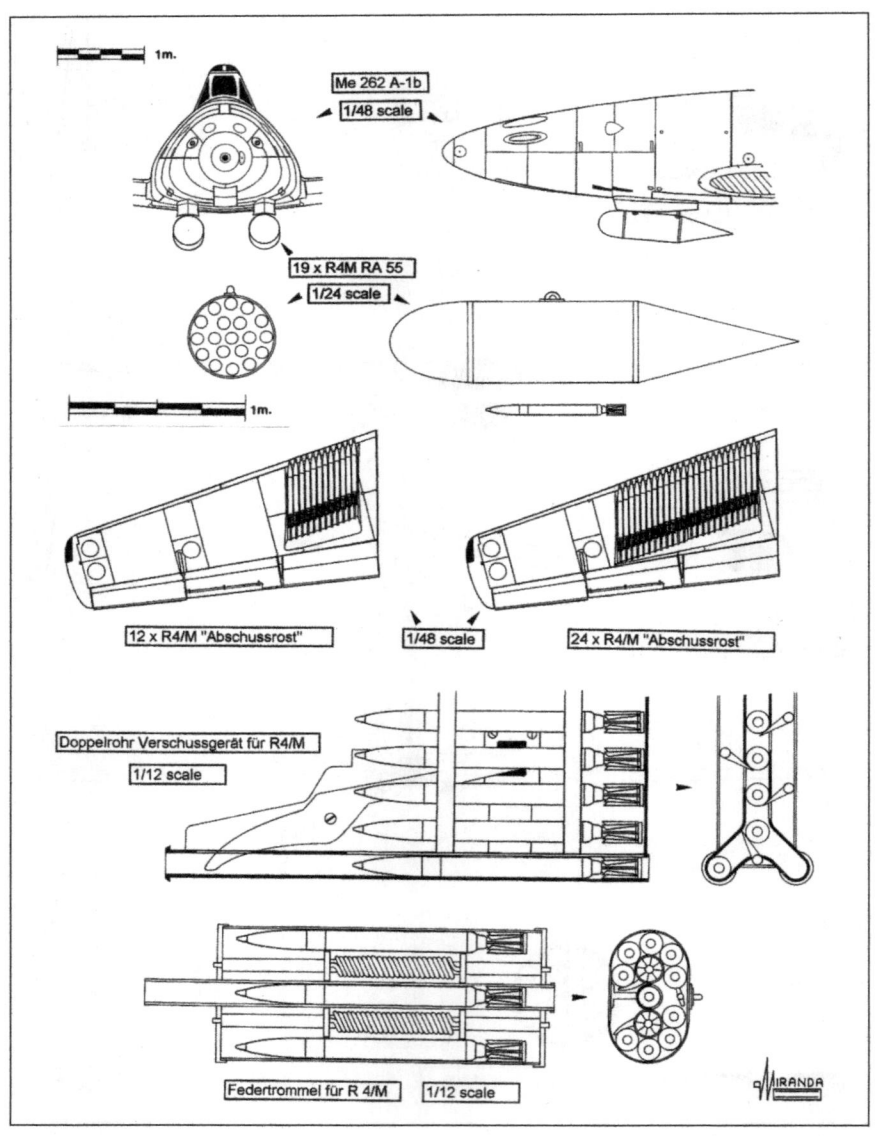

DWM designed a hollow charge of 55mm using an aluminised explosive filler and copper conical liner.

The R4HL (Rakete 4Kg Hollandungskopf) was obtained by adapting the new warhead to the body of an R4M. This was also known as Jägerfaust. The plan was to use it together with the R4M in multiple launches, but it was never mass produced.

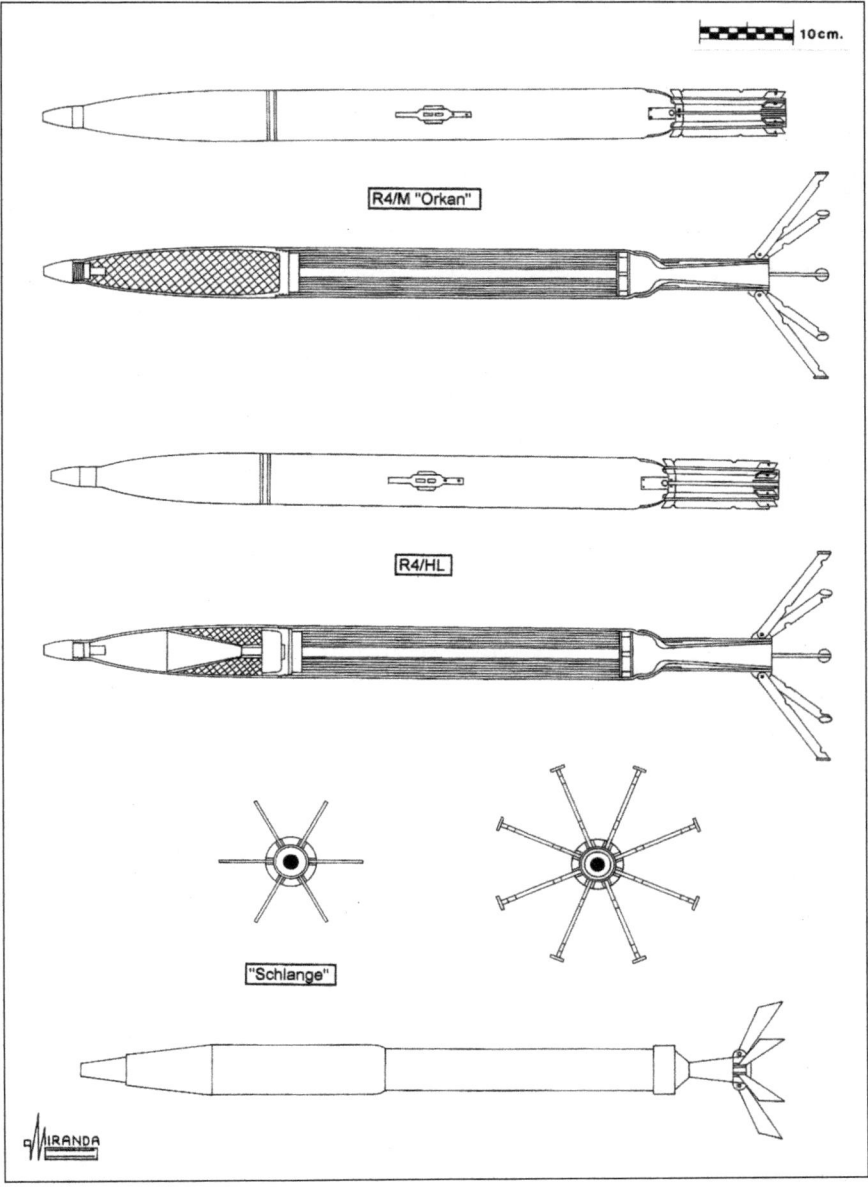

TECHNICAL DATA: R4M (R4HL) (SCHLANGE): Length 812mm (790mm). Diameter 55mm (55mm) ((55mm)). Wingspan 215mm (215mm) Total weight 3.85kg (-) ((3.5kg)). Maximum speed 525 m/sec (525 m/sec) ((450 m/sec)). Range 1,500m (1,500m).

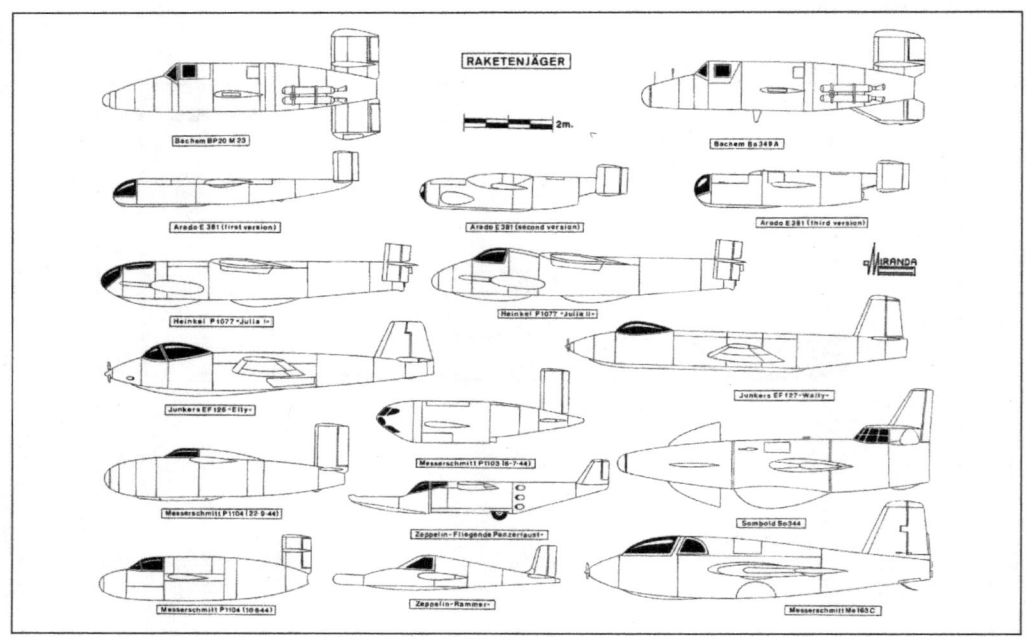

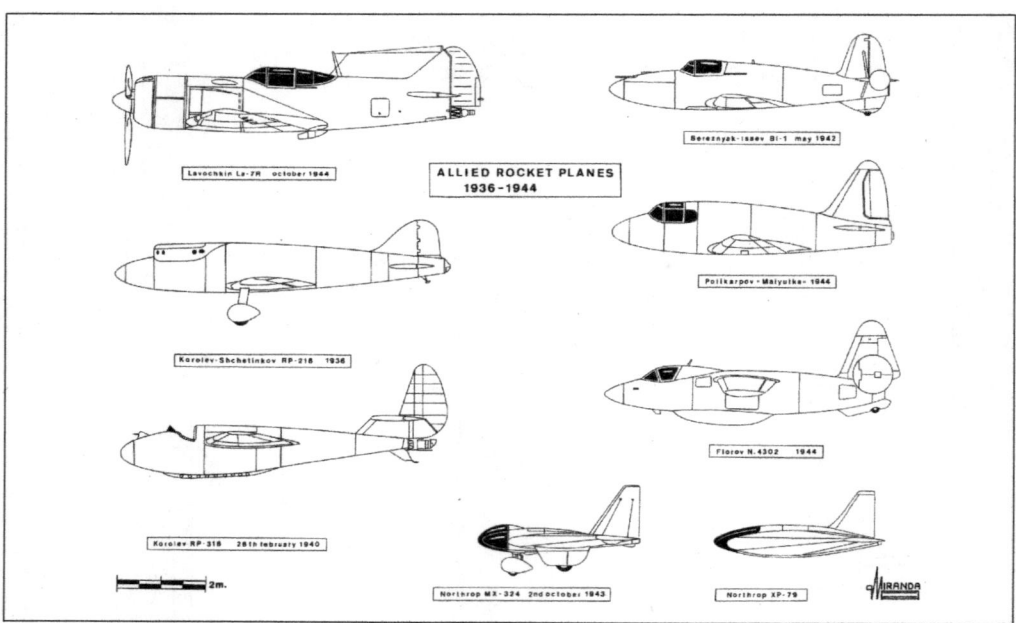

22
Wernher von Braun Rockets

Early in 1936 three prototypes of the Heinkel He 112 piston fighter were fitted with one HVA bi-propellant rocket engine designed by Wernher von Braun.

Between March and August these rocket-planes were tested at E-Stelle Rechlin, Neuhardenberg, Peenemünde and Marienehe.

Both prototypes He 112 V5 Werk. Nr. 1933 (D-IIZO) and He 112 V3 Werk. Nr. 1292 (D-IDMO) were destroyed by the explosion of the rocket engine, but the He 112 V8/U (D-IRXO) managed to fly successfully demonstrating the viability of the power plant.

On 6 July 1939, von Braun proposed to the RLM the project Stratosphärenjäger I, a high-altitude VTO rocket interceptor powered by one HVA rocket engine that used liquid oxygen and methanol as propellants.

This plane would reach an 8,000m altitude in 53 seconds under the control of an SG-52 Kreiselgerät autopilot, and four graphite vanes mounted in the rocket nozzle.

After reaching the maximum altitude the pilot could regain manual control for interception. After the attack the fighter would glide back to the base, landing on a retractable ventral skid.

The RLM showed little interest in the project because the complexity of the exotic propellants and the automatic guidance system.

STRATOSPHÄRENJÄGER I TECHNICAL DATA: Wingspan: 8.5m. Length: 9.3m. Height: 3.2m. Maximum weight: 5,000kg. Maximum speed: 700km/h. Service ceiling: 8,000m. Endurance: 15 min. Power plant: one HVA rocket engine with 10,600 peak-thrust. Propellants: liquid oxygen and methanol. Armament: four wing-mounted machine guns, electronics: R/T device and AI radar of unspecified type.

On 27 May 1941, von Braun proposed the Stratosphärenjäger II, a more fully developed VTO fighter powered by one HVA rocket engine that used

Visol and SV-Stoff hypergolic propellants, instead of the very hard to store liquid oxygen and hydrogen peroxide.

Visol was a mixture of vinyl ethers (isobutyl-vinyl compounds) that could be replaced by Schweröl (diesel oil).

SV-Stoff was a mixture of 90–98 per cent nitric acid and 2–10 per cent sulfuric acid that could be replaced by S-Stoff/Salbei, a mixture of 96 per cent nitric acid and 4 per cent ferrous chloride.

Instead of using vulnerable stationary launch sites, the Type II could be launched from mobile ramps carried on trucks.

In the autumn of 1941, the project was rejected by the RLM. By this time von Braun was fully involved in the development of the V2 missile.

STRATOSPHÄRENJÄGER II TECHNICAL DATA: Wingspan: 8.6m. Length: 9.3m. Height: 3.2m. Maximum weight: 5,080kg. Maximum speed: 690km/h. Service ceiling: 8,000m. Endurance: 15 min. Power plant: one HVA rocket engine. Propellants: Visol and SV-Stoff. Armament: four wing-mounted machine guns, electronics: R/T device and IR seeker of unspecified type.

The Stratosphärenjäger II was developed further by the Heeresversuchsanstalt Peenemünde (HVP) and the Advanced Projects Office of Gerhard Fieseler Werke GmbH, under the leadership of Dipl.-Ing. Erich Bachem.

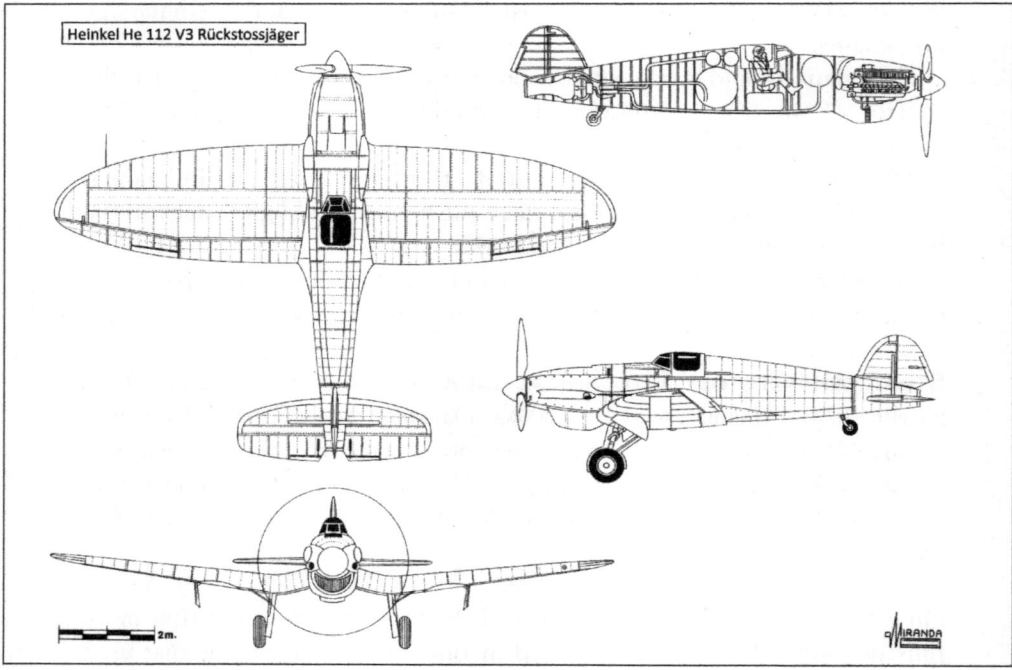

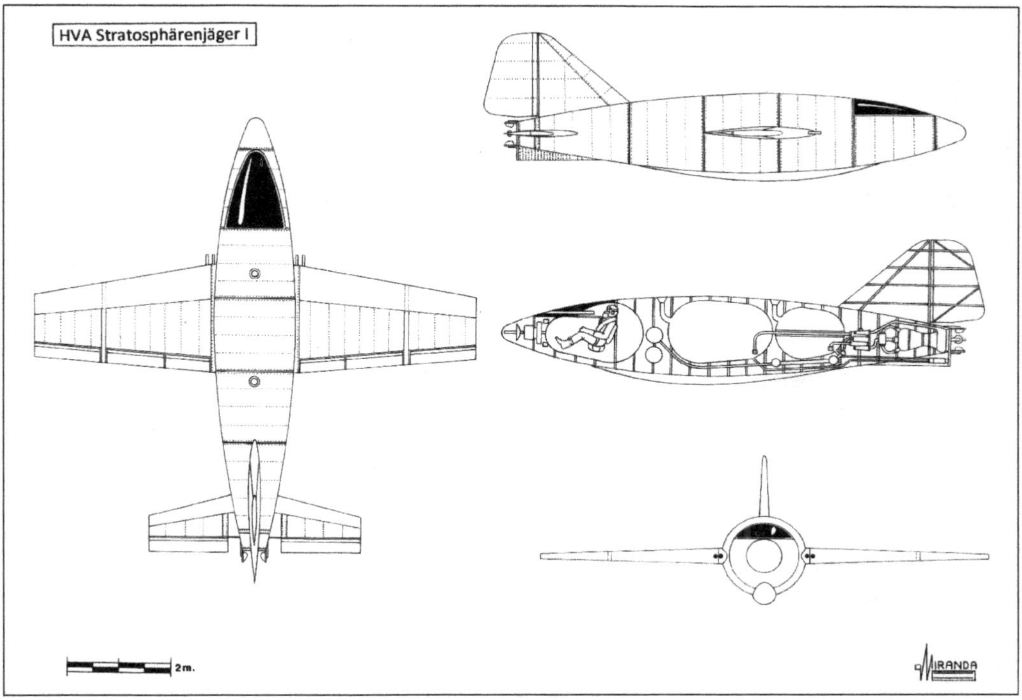
HVA Stratosphärenjäger I
2m.
MIRANDA

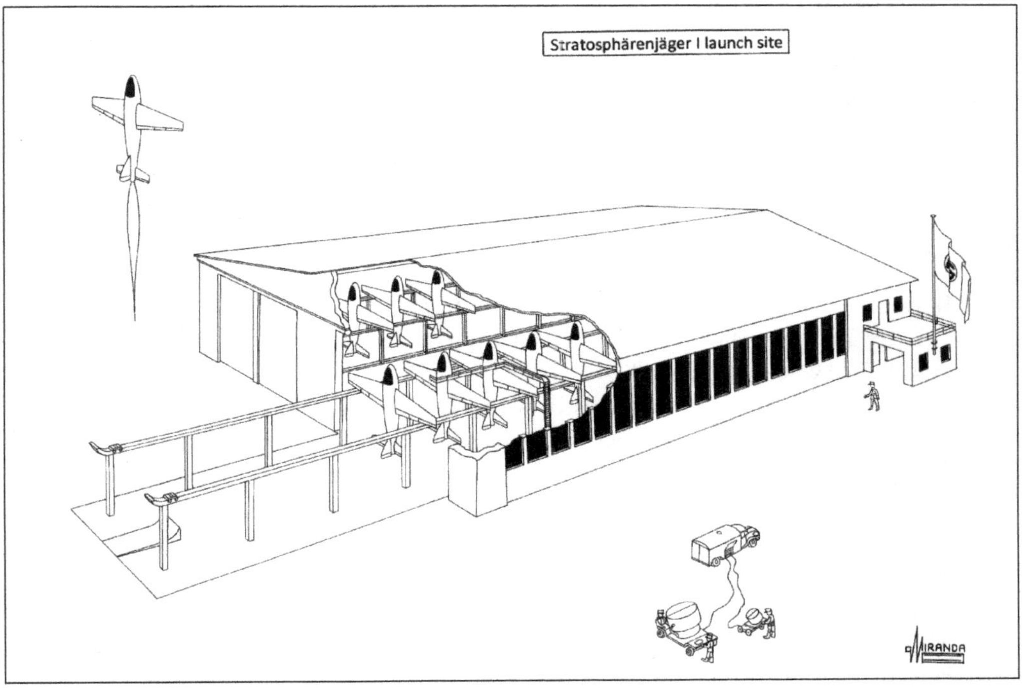
Stratosphärenjäger I launch site
MIRANDA

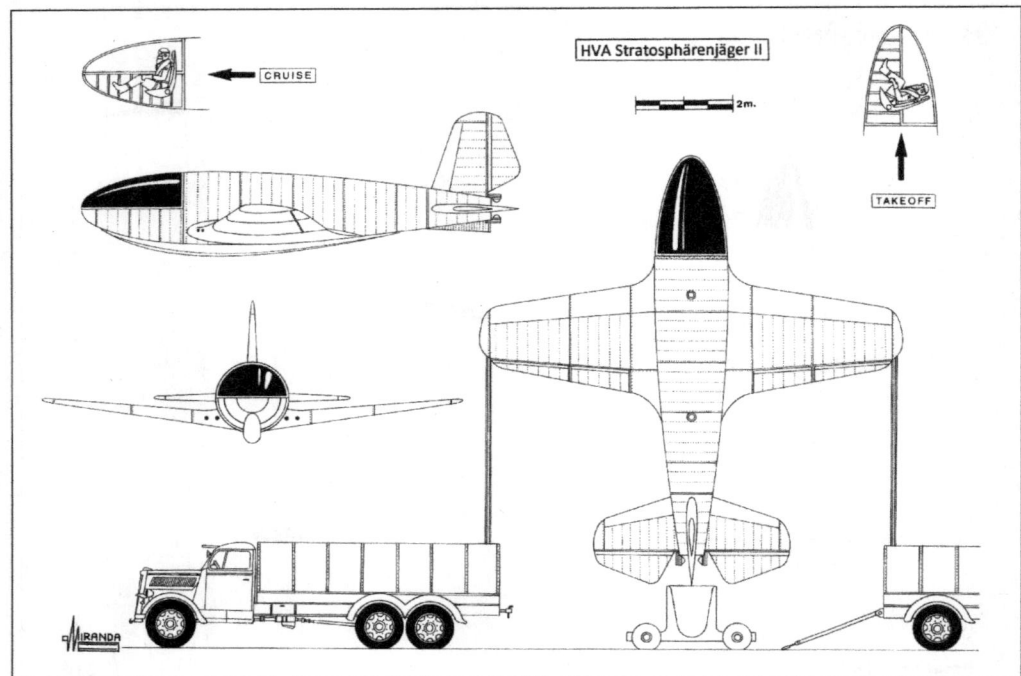

At the end of 1941 Fieseler proposed to the RLM the VTO fighter Fi 166 in two versions:

- Höhenjäger I was a two-seat, point-defence, rocket interceptor.
- Höhenjäger II was a single-seat, long-range, turbojet-fighter the size of a Messerschmitt Bf 110 that could take off vertically by means of a powerful rocket booster, attached to the underside of the fuselage, which was to be jettisoned at 8,000m altitude.

Both types were fitted with retractable ventral skids.

Early in 1942 the Fi 166 was cancelled in favour of the anti-aircraft missile EMW C2 Wasserfall.

The Germans were not successful with the use of hypergolic propellants, the Wasserfall never reached the operational phase and the cost of developing the 'Super V2' EMW A8, 700 million of Reichsmark, was seen unaffordable by the HVP.

FIESELER FI 166 HÖHENJÄGER I TYP R-R-FI TECHNICAL DATA: Wingspan: 16m. Length: 16.56m. Height: 4.7m. Maximum weight: 5,620kg. Maximum speed: 810km/h. Service ceiling: 12,000m. Climb rate: 151 m/sec. Endurance: 5 min. Power plant: one EMW rocket engine with 15,000kg peak-thrust. Propellants:

Visol and Salbei, electronics: R/T device and AI radar of unspecified type. Pressurised cockpit.

Fieseler Fi 166 Höhenjäger II typ TL-R-RuR technical data:
Wingspan: 16m, aircraft length: 13m, overall length: 15m. Height: 4.9m. Maximum weight: 5,930kg. Maximum speed: 830km/h. Service ceiling: 12,000m. Endurance: 45 min. Power plant: two BMW P.3302 turbojets each rated at 550kg thrust and one EMW rocket booster with 20,000kg peak-thrust. Propellants: Visol and Salbei, electronics: R/T device and IR seeker of unspecified type. Pressurised cockpit.

The EMW V2 missile reached a speed of 3,500mph (5,632km/h-Mach 5.3) flying at 317,000ft By the time the rocket was plunging back through the stratosphere, the denser air began to slow down the rocket until it reached 2,237mph (3,600km/h) velocity of impact.

The very high kinetic energy with which the rocket came to earth could be transformed into aerodynamic drive by adding wings and larger air rudders. It was intended to glide after re-entry into dense atmosphere, trading speed for distance. On 30 January 1941, it was expected to reach an extended range of 885–1,207 miles (550–750km). By the time some wind tunnel tests were conducted with winged models of the V2 at the Zeppelin-Friedrichshafen research centre. Seven scale models were used, with four different types of wings, under the denomination Gleiter (Glider).

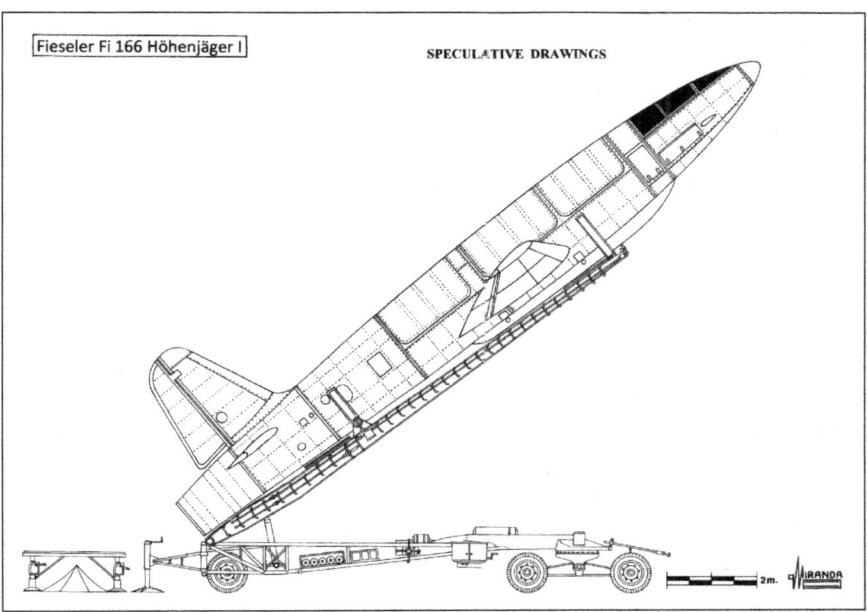

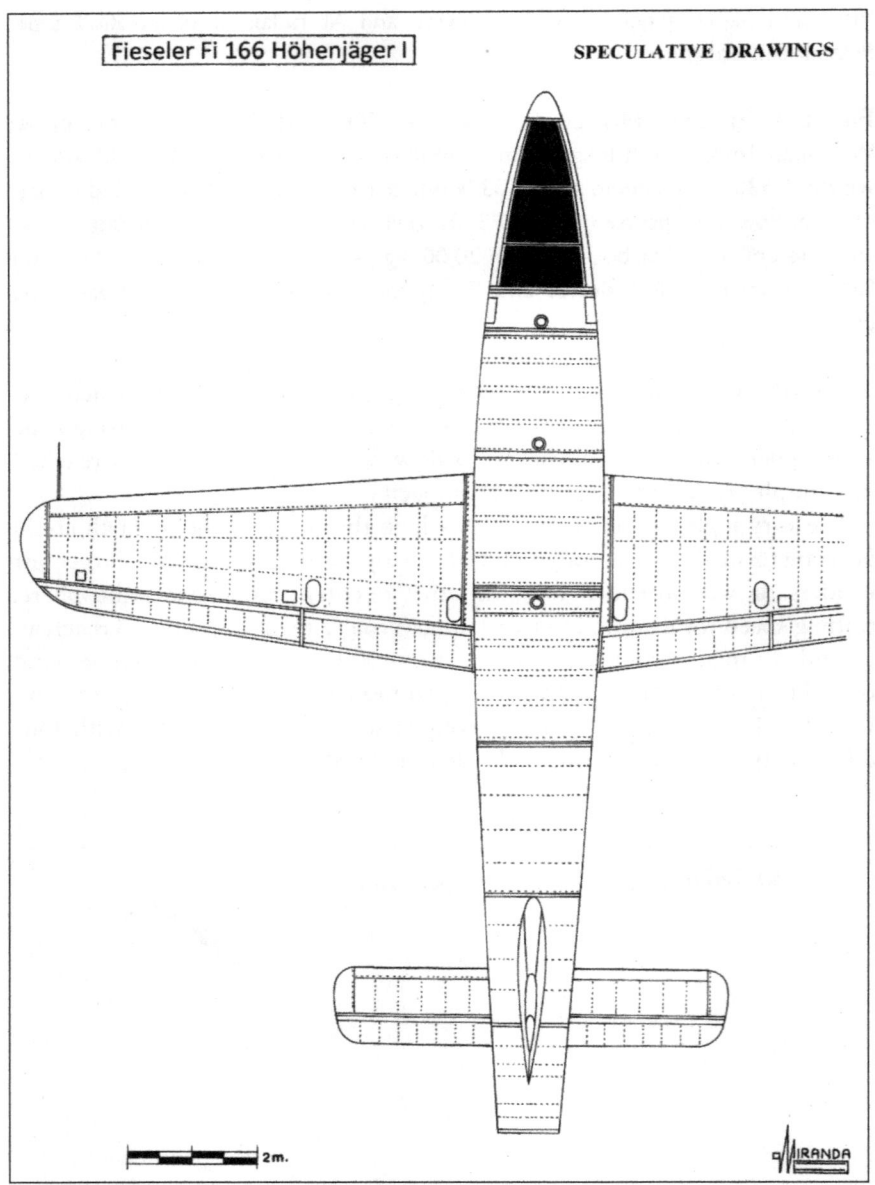

The V13e, V14e and V14f (17-1-41) models were tested with Flossengeschoss (ogival delta) wings, the V12c (21-1-41) with 45-degree swept wings, the V12f with scalloped triple delta wings and the V12a (21-1-41) with Trapezflügel (trapezoidal) wings.

Gleiter A5/V12c was selected as the V-2 aerodynamic successor and Gleiter A4/V13e as the second stage of the A10 intercontinental rocket system.

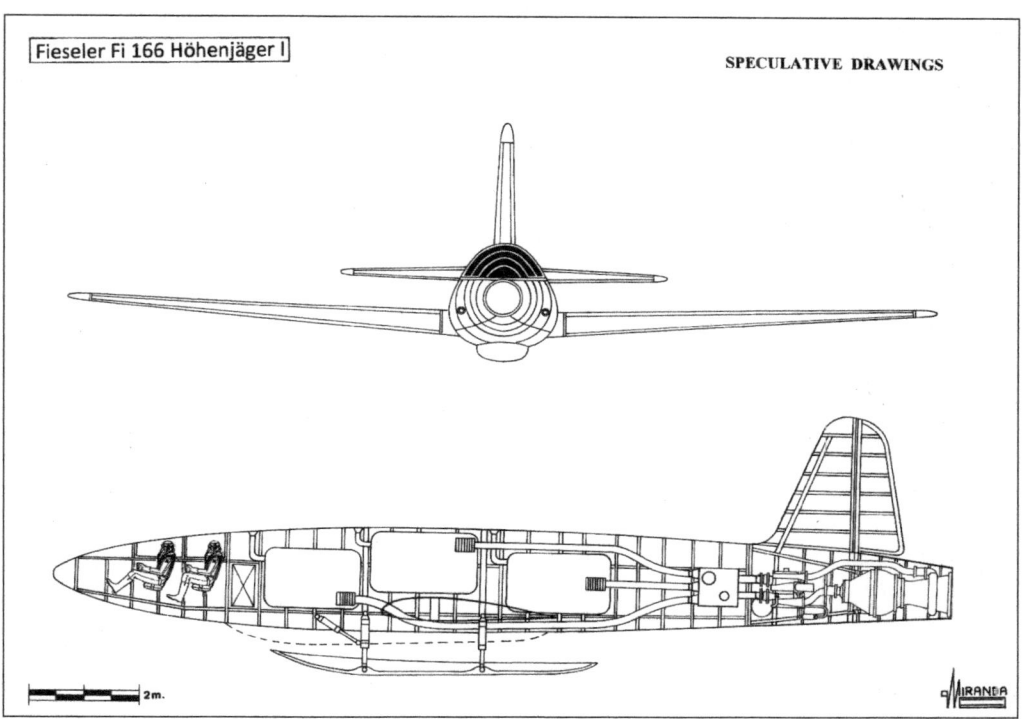

Aerodynamic tests conducted with both configurations showed that the swept wings became unstable around Mach 0.85 but the ogival delta provided better lift and solved the centre of pressure displacing problem at supersonic speeds.

In February 1941, to prove the behaviour of the swept wings at subsonic speeds, three A5 rockets were modified by Elektromechanische Werke GmbH (EMW) as Gleiter A5/V12c tests gliders.

On 25 October 1942, the V12c was carried to an altitude of 19,700ft by the Heinkel He 111 H-4 (NF + AB) modified bomber and released in ballistic flight, without propulsion unit, in order to test flight stability of the new steering control device. The V12c flew in straight glide and recovered by parachute.

In 1942 the project was renamed A7, but further development of winged rockets was halted between October 1942 and June 1944 in order to concentrate on war production of the V2. When the Allies advanced towards German border following the Normandy invasion, all the V2 launch sites in France, Belgium and Holland were lost and the extended-range rocket project was reactivated under the code name EMW A4b.

On 10 October 1944, modification began on sixteen V2 airframes into A4b winged rockets. The first prototype A4b G1, fitted with 45-degree swept wings and standard tail surfaces, was launched from Peenemünde

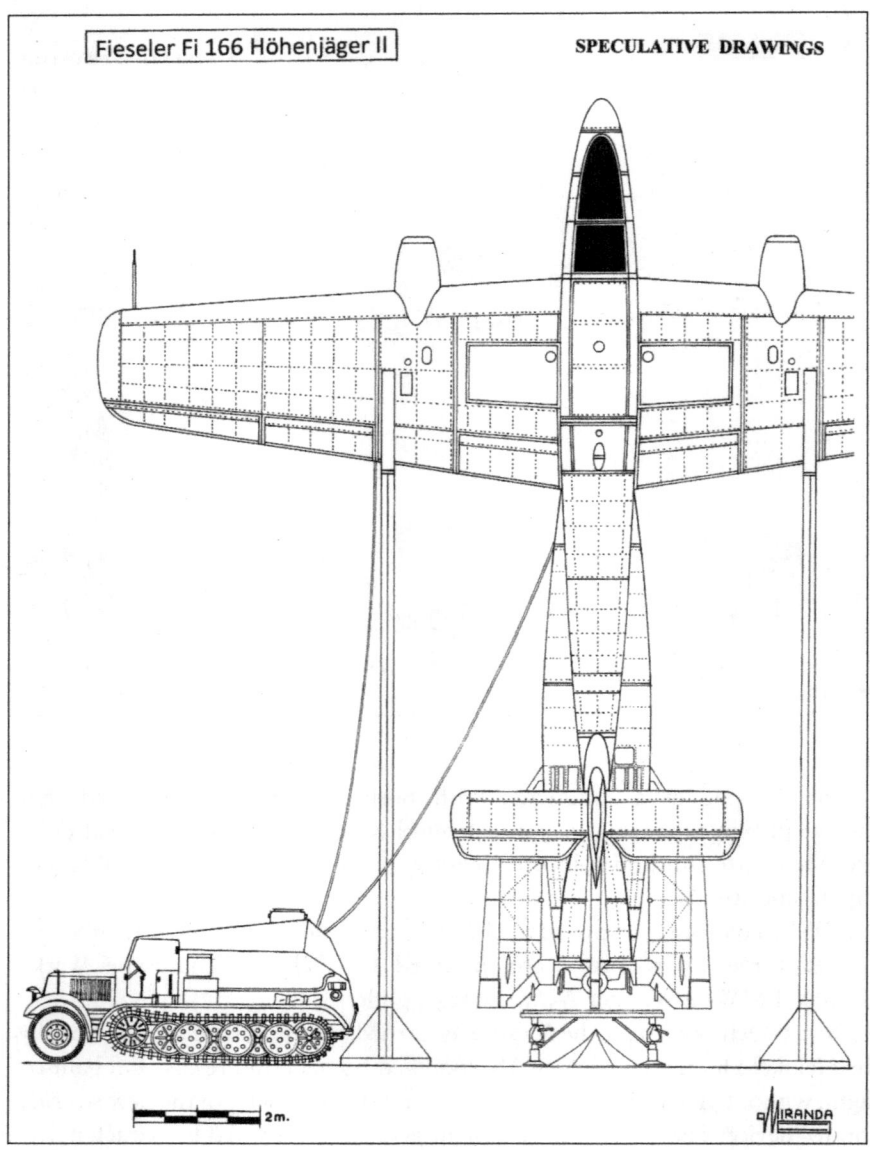

Test Stand X on 1 December 1944, but it was destroyed as a result of failures in the control system.

The second prototype (W.Nr.17543), with modified tail surfaces, was successfully launched on 24 January 1945. It attained a maximum speed of 2,700mph (4,345km/h-Mach 4.1) flying at 253,000ft but following re-entry into the stratosphere one of its wings could not withstand deceleration and the rocket was destroyed.

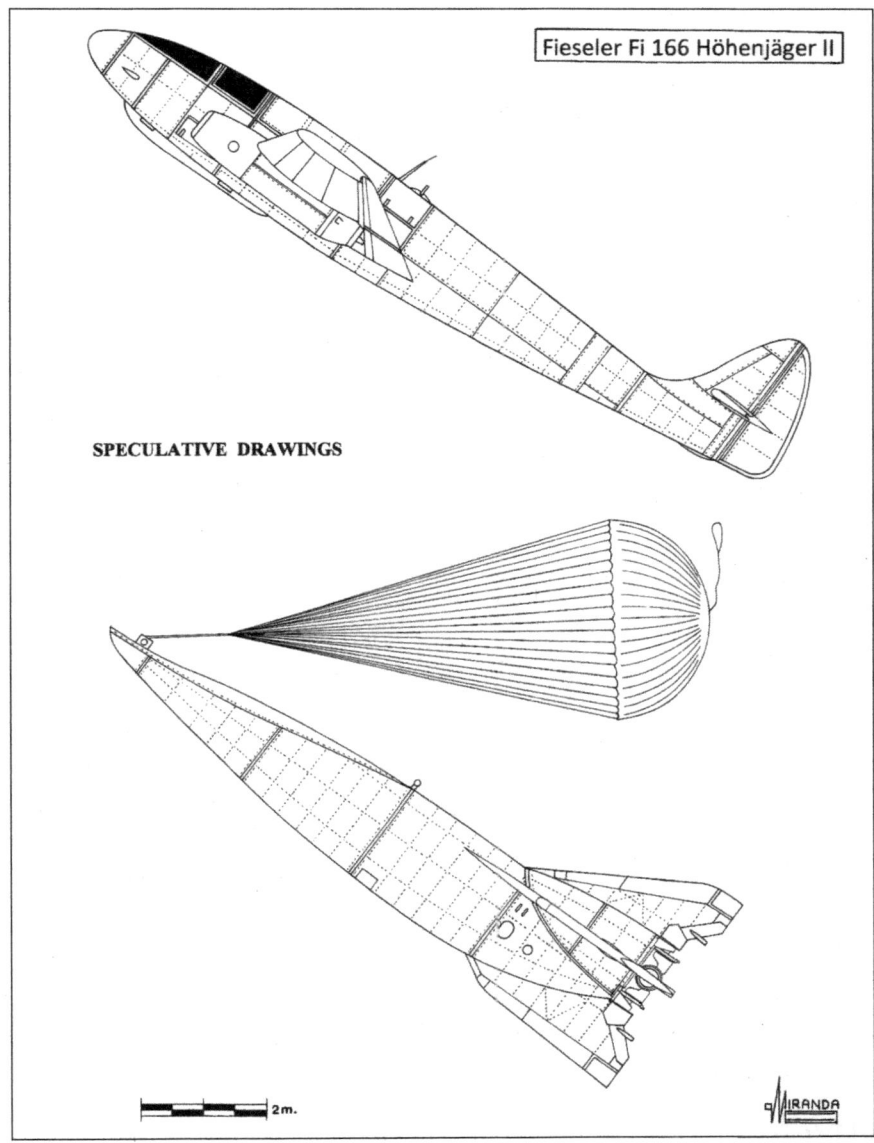

Fieseler Fi 166 Höhenjäger II

SPECULATIVE DRAWINGS

The A4b project was cancelled in favour of an entirely new weapon code named A9.

EMW A5 TECHNICAL DATA: Type: aerodynamic tests rocket for the V2 development program. Stabiliser span: 4.8ft (1.46m). Length: 19ft (5.83m). Maximum diameter: 2.8ft (0.86m). Estimated maximum speed: 1,243mph (2,000km/h). Estimated ceiling: 39,360ft (12,000m). Estimated

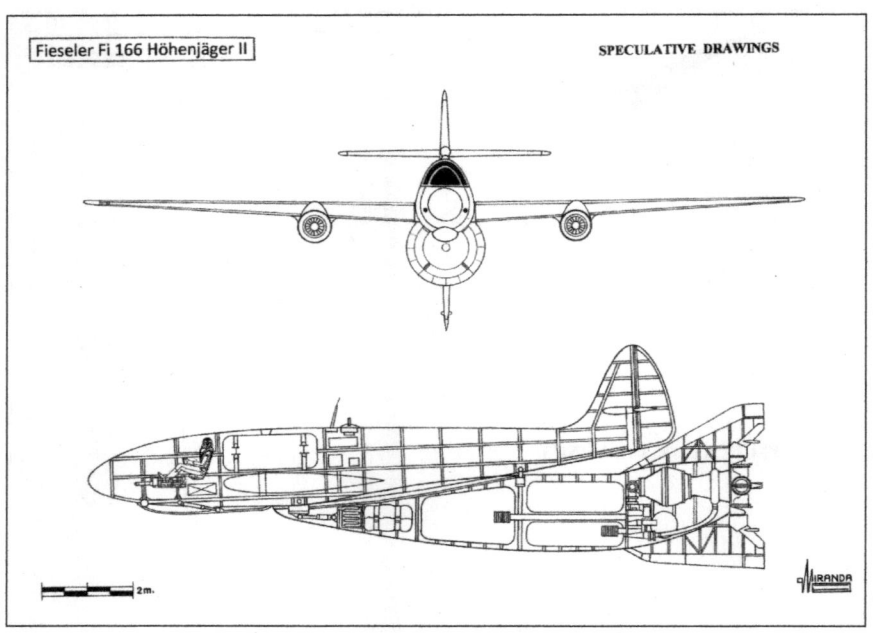

Fieseler Fi 166 Höhenjäger II

SPECULATIVE DRAWINGS

range: 11 miles (18km). Take-off weight: 1,987lb (900kg). Power plant: one Kummersdorf A-2 bi-propellant rocket with 1,500 peak-thrust. Propellants: A-Stoff (liquid oxygen at -183°C) and M-Stoff (Methyl alcohol). Pressuriser: nitrogen.

EMW A7 TECHNICAL DATA: Type: aerodynamic tests rocket for the A4b development program. Wingspan: 8.59ft (2.62m). Stabiliser span: 5.7ft (1.75m). Length: 19.4ft (5.91m). Maximum diameter: 2.8ft (0.86m). Take-off weight: 2,207lb (1,000kg). Power plant: one Kummersdorf A-2 bi-propellant rocket-motor with 1,500kg peak-thrust. Propellants: A-Stoff (liquid oxygen at -183°C) and M-Stoff (Methyl alcohol). Pressuriser: nitrogen.

EMW A4B TECHNICAL DATA: Type: intermediate range boost-glide missile. Airframe: steel structure with riveted steel plates cladding. Power plant: one EMW bi-propellant rocket-motor with 60,500lb (27,500kg) peak-thrust. Propellants: 5,533kg of A-Stoff and 4,173kg of M-Stoff. Pressurisers: 172kg of T-Stoff (80% hydrogen peroxide, 20% oxiquinoline) and Z-Stoff (watery solution of sodium or calcium). Wingspan: 20.3ft (6.2m). Stabiliser span: 13ft (3.99m). Length: 46ft (14.03m). Maximum diameter: 5.5ft (1.8m). Take-off weight: 28,600lb (13,000kg). Estimated maximum speed: 2,700mph (4,344km/h-Mach 4.1). Estimated ceiling: 311,600ft (95,000m). Estimated range: 373 miles (600km).

The ballistic accuracy of the V2 depended on the range. During operations against London the average deviation was some 11 miles. To increase accuracy the rocket was controlled in the initial phase of its flight by two land-based ultra-short-wave transmitters HV-Gerät, intended to prevent the missile from diverging from its predetermined path.

Using radio guidance, it was expected to hit a target of 2.5 x 2.5 miles, but when the range exceeded the available beam horizon, a new steering system was needed.

Engineers believed that a manned A4b would have solved the guidance problem, because no suitable guidance method existed at the time.

The V2 rocket was conceived as a long-range artillery weapon to circumvent the Treaty of Versailles limitations. The entire rocket development and manufacturing program had been funded by the Oberkommando des Heeres (German Army High Command) but the existence of a piloted version would require part of the program to depend on the Luftwaffe.

A piloted A4b had the precision of Reichenberg IV and greater destructive power but, unlike this one, could not be intercepted. Controlling this new weapons system, Göring acquired the ability to eliminate generals, kings, and politburo members and thus the opportunity to negotiate an honourable peace like in 1918.

In the autumn of 1943, Dr Bodo Lafferentz proposed a plan to attack New York and Washington using V2 rockets launched 186 miles from the United States coast.

The Prüfstand XII project involved towing a V2 in a watertight container behind a U-boat Type IX D-2 and ten set up vertically in the water, by means of ballast tanks, prior to the missile launch.

Admiral Doenitz approved the idea; however, the plan was delayed by technical concerns until late 1944 at which time work began, at Vulkanwerft-Stettin facilities, on three large containers 105ft long, displacing 500 tons each.

It was expected that the new Type XXI submarines could tow up to three containers. Once on station, the U-boat crews would enter the container and fuel the V2, set the I-Gerät gyroscopic guidance system and open the launch hatch. The missile would be triggered from the submarine by remote control.

Deploying one V2 launch battery needed hundreds of troops, technical crews and about 275 specialised support vehicles with sophisticated ancillary devices.

The missile was not suitable for naval use. Before launch, it was necessary to perform a countdown of 90 minutes and a U-boat could not remain surfaced for so long near the US coast.

In addition, the rocket was very vulnerable to corrosion, since testing determined that excessive storage time resulted in more failures.

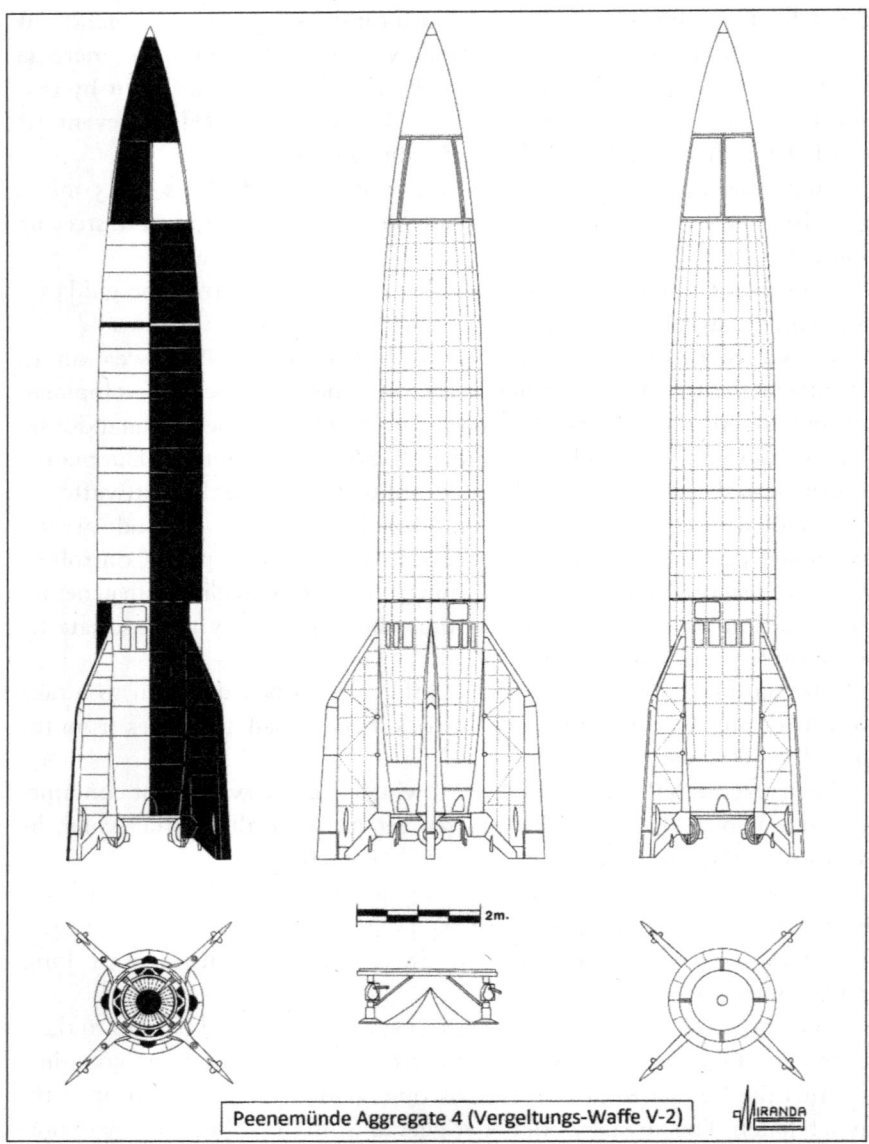

Peenemünde Aggregate 4 (Vergeltungs-Waffe V-2)

There was also the problem of evaporation losses during storage of the T-Stoff and the super-cool liquid oxygen. It was realised that the decomposition rate of hydrogen peroxide would not last the thirty days of voyage to New York and the liquid oxygen would also be lost by evaporation as it couldn't be kept in hermetic tanks.

The T-Stoff required to spin the V2 turbo-pumps was an extremely dangerous chemical to handle because of its extreme oxidising potential;

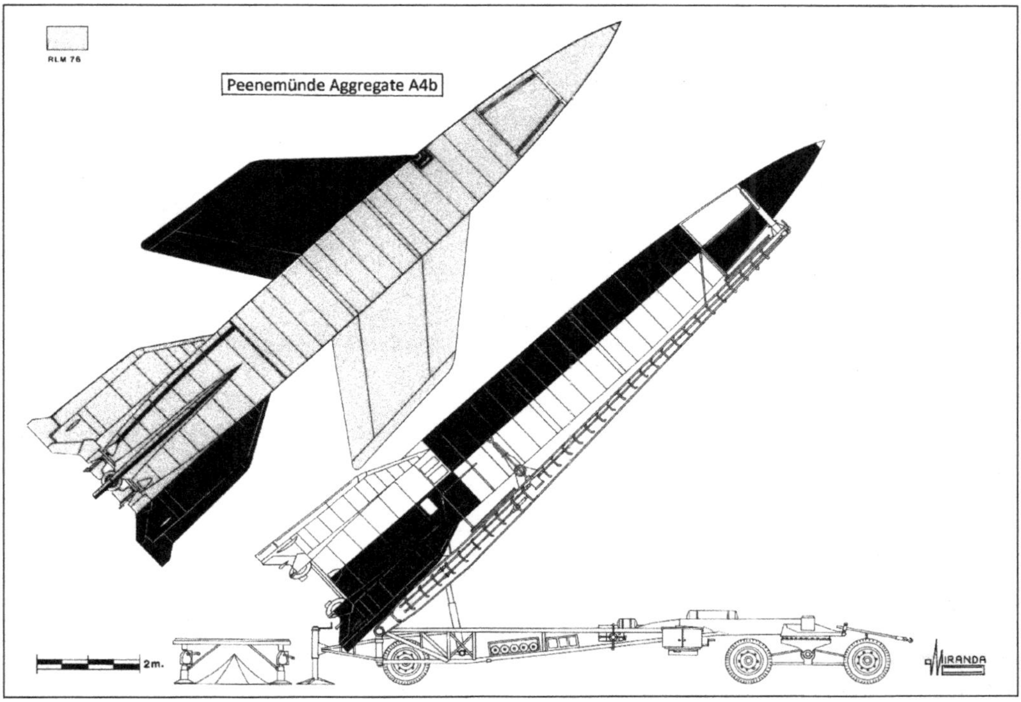
RLM 76
Peenemünde Aggregate A4b
2m.
MIRANDA

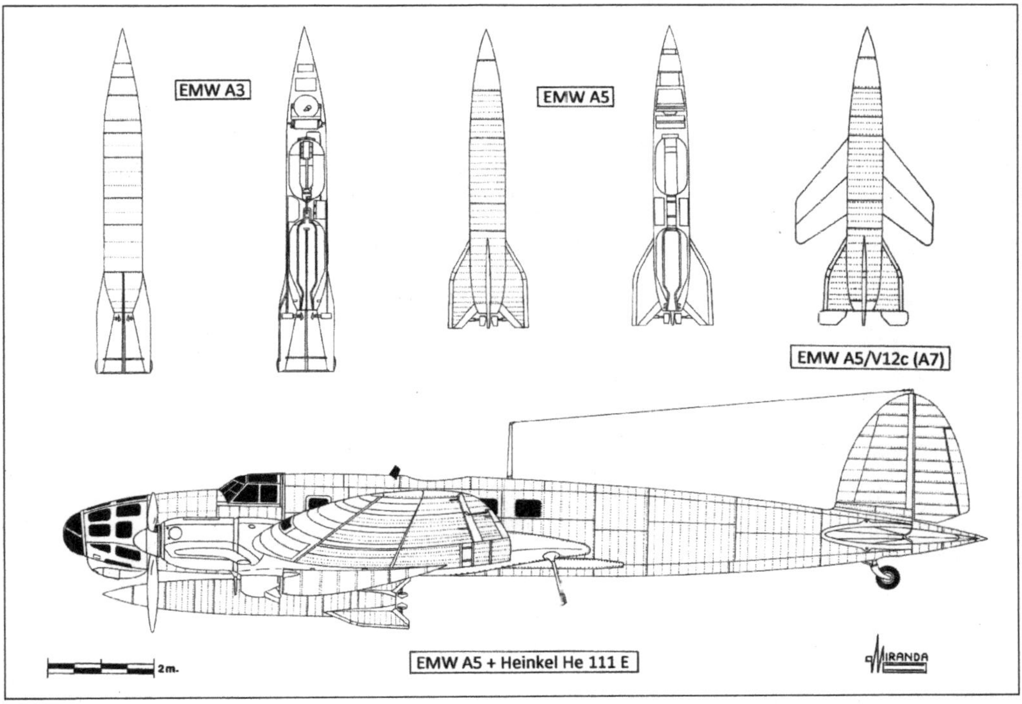
EMW A3
EMW A5
EMW A5/V12c (A7)
EMW A5 + Heinkel He 111 E
2m.
MIRANDA

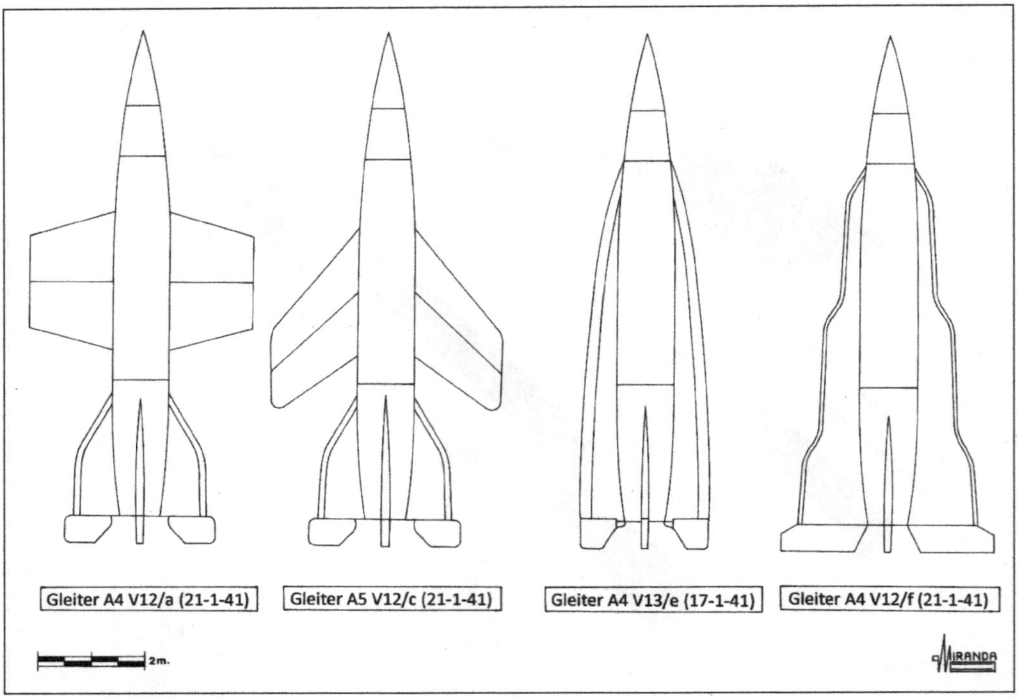
Gleiter A4 V12/a (21-1-41)
Gleiter A5 V12/c (21-1-41)
Gleiter A4 V13/e (17-1-41)
Gleiter A4 V12/f (21-1-41)
2m.
MIRANDA

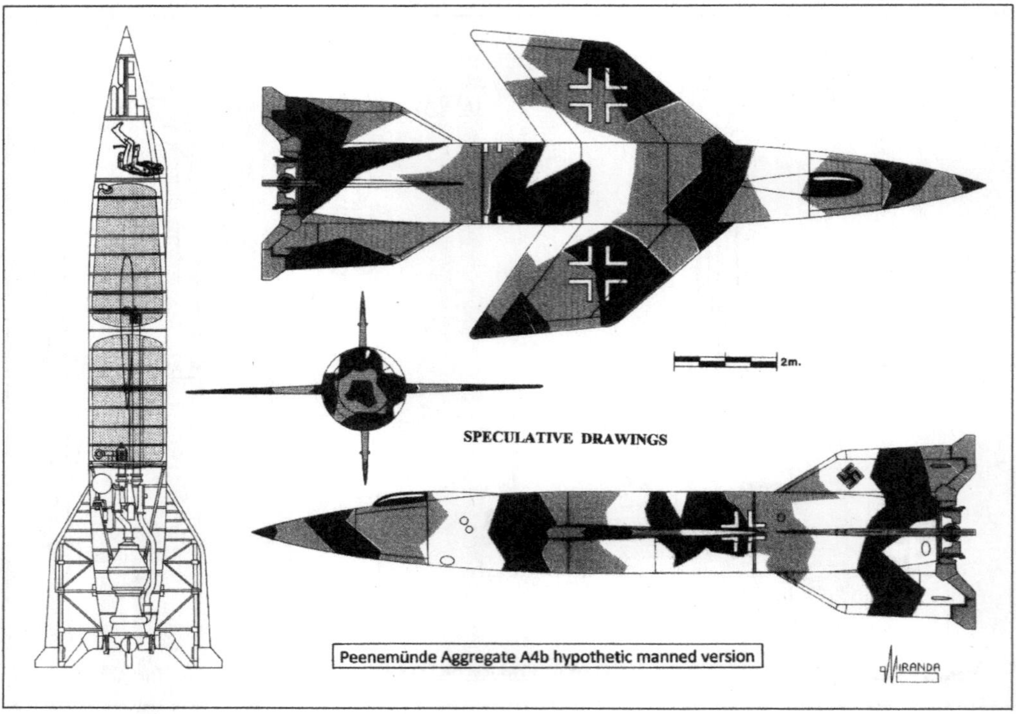
2m.
SPECULATIVE DRAWINGS
Peenemünde Aggregate A4b hypothetic manned version
MIRANDA

it would react with any organic material it came into contact with, producing spontaneous combustion. hydrogen peroxide is highly volatile, and the vapour can ignite or detonate depending on temperature and pressure.

During the development of the Type XVIII U-boat propulsion system, the Kriegsmarine had already encountered numerous problems with high-test peroxide (HTP) and did not want to repeat the experience.

To solve the V2 shortcomings, the new missile EMW A8 was designed to use nitric acid and diesel oil propellants pressurised with nitrogen.

The A8 did not require the use of turbo-pumps and ignition system because the hypergolic propellants spontaneously ignited when they came into contact which each other. Both liquids can be stored at room temperature.

The A8 was to have been derived from the V2, using an extended central section to contain a great number of propellants and with a new control surfaces configuration.

The work on this development as well as other guided missiles was stopped early in 1945 in favour of concentration on the V2, because of the critical condition of manpower and materials caused by the successful bombing raids of the Allies.

EMW A8 TECHNICAL DATA: Type: intermediate range ballistic missile. Airframe: steel structure with riveted steel plates cladding. Power plant: one EMW bi-propellant rocket-motor with 75,700lb (34,337kg) peak-thrust and 90 seconds burning time. Propellants: SV-Stoff (94% of nitric acid, 6% nitrogen dioxide) and Schweröl (diesel oil). Stabiliser span: 13ft (3.99m). Length: 54ft (16.46m). Maximum diameter: 5.5ft (1.8m). Take-off weight: 49,240lb (22,344kg). Estimated ballistic range: 300 miles (482km).

In 1943 one winged version of the A8 was proposed to the RLM as high-altitude reconnaissance aircraft.

The new rocket-plane, named EMW A6, was fitted with 61-degree swept wings, pressurised cockpit, and ventral ramjet for extended range.

The radical wing was object of criticism by the Technisches Amt. Its main objection was based in the excessive landing speed of 280mph estimated in the original project.

New wings with an extended span, a 45-degree sweep, and one drag-parachute for landing on a conventional airfield were adopted, but the project was rejected.

The A6 would be launched vertically, and their powerful rocket-motor would accelerate the aircraft to supersonic speed. After re-entry into the stratosphere and beginning the supersonic glide phase, the ramjet was ignited providing 20 minutes of cruise flight.

EMW A6 TECHNICAL DATA: Type: high-altitude reconnaissance aircraft. Airframe: steel structure with riveted steel plates cladding. Power plant: one EMW bi-propellant rocket-motor with 75,700lb (34,337kg) peak-thrust and 90 seconds burning time and one Lorin Strahlrohr ramjet of the Ta 183 class burning KI heavy kerosene or liquid carbon disulphide. Propellants: SV-Stoff and Schweröl. Wingspan: 33.3ft (10.15m). Length: 51.7ft (15.75m). Maximum diameter: 5.7ft (1.73m), estimated maximum speed: 1,802mph (2,900km/h). Estimated ceiling: 311,600ft (95,000m). Estimated range: 400 miles (644km).

The A9 was designed in January 1941 as a V2 with ogival delta wings, 373 miles (600km) extended range and 17 minutes flight time.

With this new weapon, the Wehrmacht would have the ability to attack Liverpool's industrial region from launch sites placed in northern France, but the A9 lacked enough range to reach Moscow by launching it from eastern Poland.

In October 1942 a proposal was made to launch it from a rocket catapult to increase the range by 1,000–1,300km.

The Rheinmetall-Borsig catapult was made up of a launch ramp with 262ft (80m) length and one rocket-sledge with 66,150lb (30,000kg) peak-thrust and was designed to launch a Fi 103 (V-1) flying bomb at 222.7mph (360km/h). But the Peenemünde engineers argued that the 15G-acceleration could damage the gyroscopic guidance system or disrupt the turbo-pump operation.

In March 1941, it was proposed to develop a two-rocket assembly with the A9 slotted into the top of a V2 boost stage, but the project was stopped in October 1942.

In late 1944 the development of two-rocket combination was resumed, under the code name Projekt Amerika, with 5,000km extended range.

To meet the specification the V-2 was replaced by a new rocket, the A10, with six V2 engines and 165 tons thrust.

The A9's rocket-motor was based on the A8's technology and used Visol (mixture of vinyl-isobutyl ether with aniline) and S-Stoff-Salbei (96% nitric acid, 4% ferrous chloride) as propellants, with estimated peak-thrust between 55,130–70,140lb (24,974–31,770kg) and 68–115 seconds burn time, depending on the version and power of the turbo-pump.

Early in 1945 the A10 project was modified with a new rocket-motor, with 441,500lb (200,000kg) peak-thrust, that used as SV-Stoff (94% nitric acid, 6% nitrogen dioxide) and Visol as propellants.

The Projekt Amerika called for the construction of two launch sites, the first located in Brest, France, should be used to attack New York, and the second, in Cape Roca, Portugal, to attack Pittsburg and Washington DC.

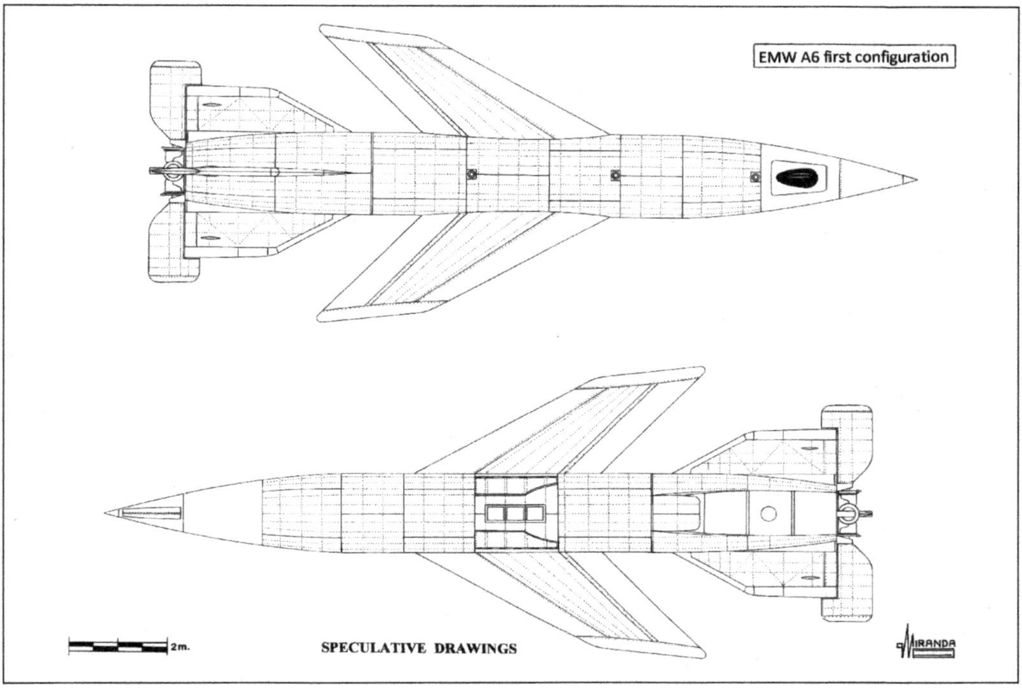
EMW A6 first configuration
2m.
SPECULATIVE DRAWINGS
MIRANDA

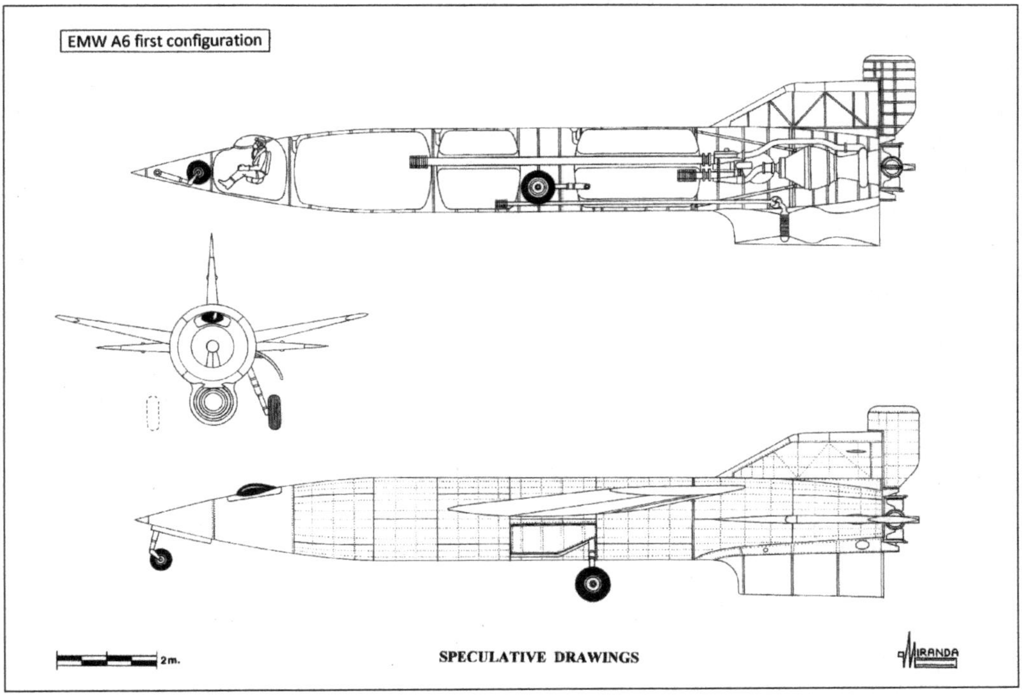
EMW A6 first configuration
2m.
SPECULATIVE DRAWINGS
MIRANDA

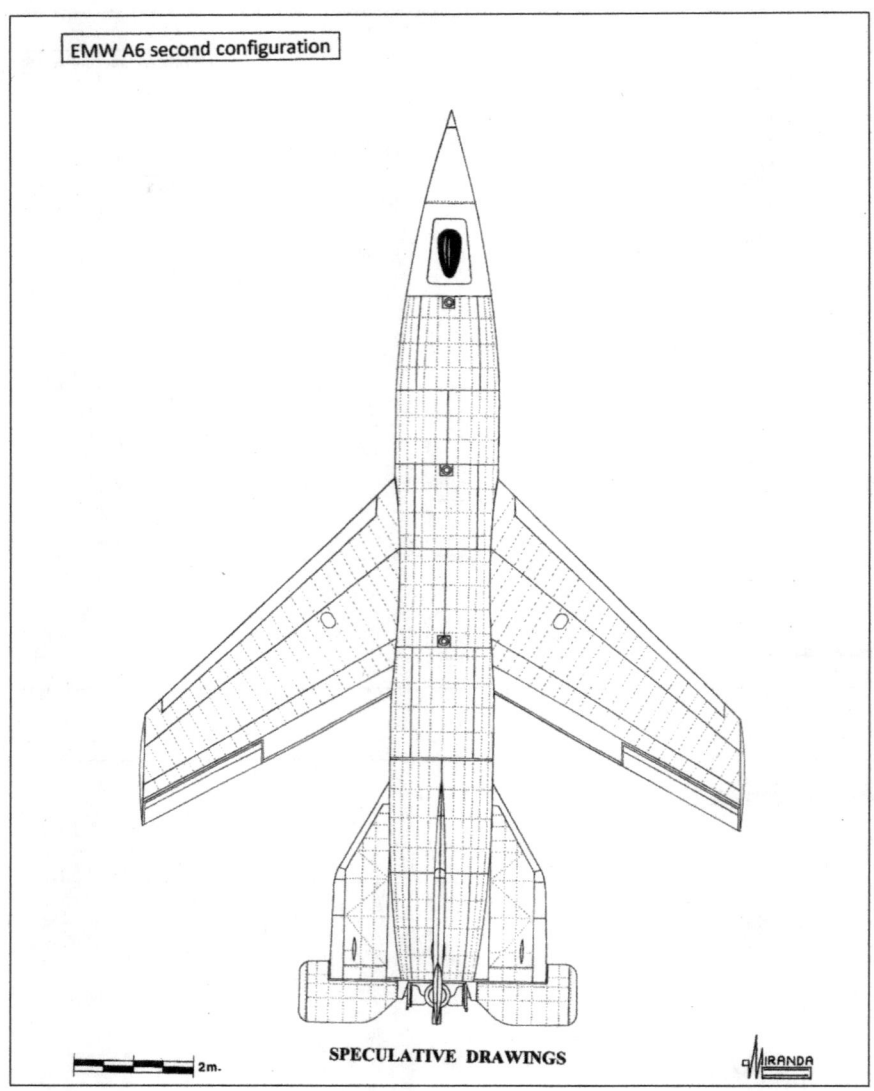

SPECULATIVE DRAWINGS

The A10 boost stage would burn for 55–60 seconds taking the A9 to 80,000ft altitude and was recovered by parachute. The upper stage would separate and burn its engine, accelerating up to 6,165mph and climbing to 100 miles suborbital apogee, followed by a long powerless supersonic glide into the atmosphere.

When the missile descended to 246,000ft it would arc back up to 328,000ft using the kinetic energy accumulated during the supersonic glide.

A 3,108 miles range was attained by means of repeated 'skips' into and out of the atmosphere and one terminal shallow glide towards its target.

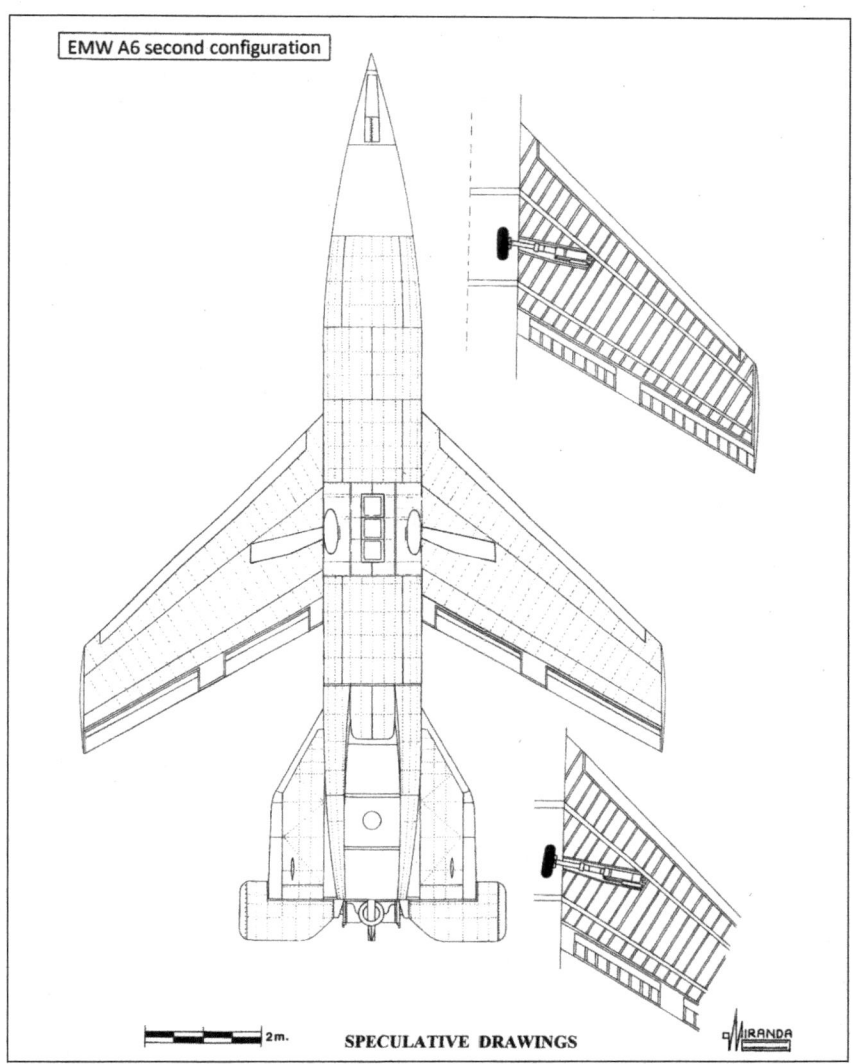

EMW A6 second configuration

SPECULATIVE DRAWINGS

The 'skips' were at the expense of the missile kinetic energy, each 'skip' being slower than the previous one.

It was expected that the A9 would be guided using the four stages of the Rheinland control method.

In the first stage the two-rocket assembly was to be steered, to the A9 separation, by Elsass radio control, with the aid of optical two-axis tracking device and one Rheingold radar set.

The second stage began after the A9 engine cut-off at 390km altitude and 7,600mph top speed. It used radar tracking, and the missile was still steered by means of the Kehlheim radio link system.

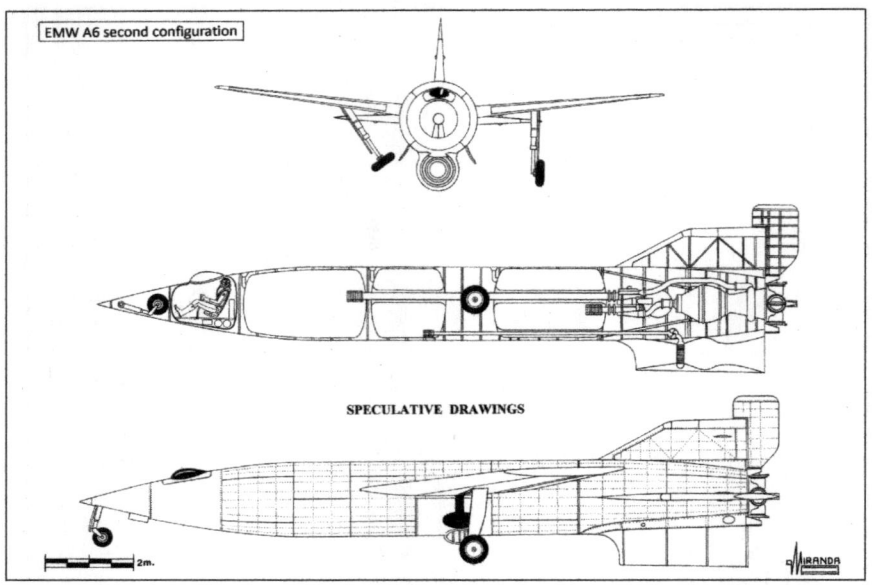

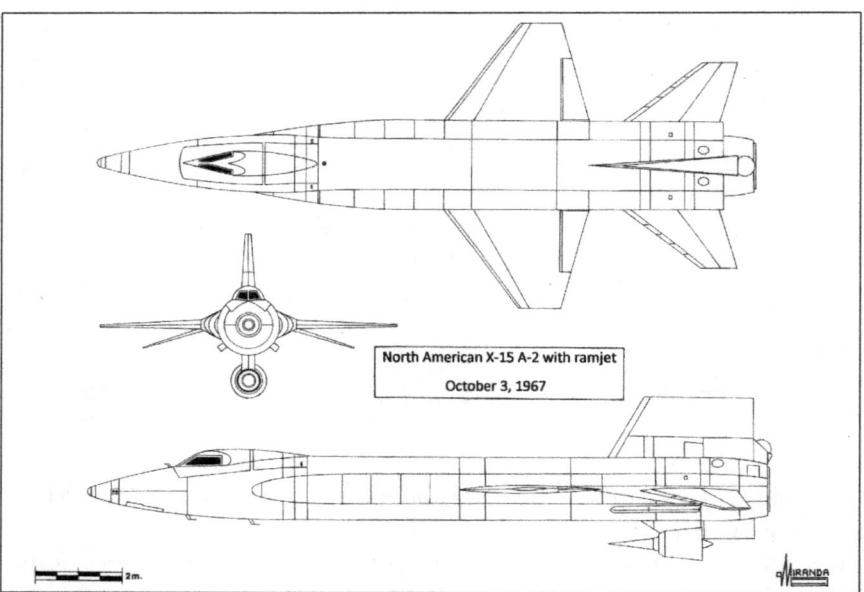

The third stage started when the A9 reached its maximum ceiling at 300 miles of the launch pad. The inertial navigation computer of the missile was coupled with one FuG 102 pulse modulated radio altimeter to perform scheduled skips on the flight plan. The A9 would ride up the radar beam of one Fu SE 75 Mannheim Riese radar set.

During the fourth stage, the missile would use the Elektra-Sonne long-range navigation system and the FuG 126 Baldur automatic-guidance system to make the necessary heading corrections, following a string of radio-beacons deployed by surfaced U-boats across of the Atlantic.

The terminal glide towards the target was to be steered by one rotating reticle infrared homing device developed by Wernher von Braun.

The intercontinental missile concept emerged far ahead of its time. Early in 1945 it was considered that existing guidance systems would not be accurate enough over a distance of 3,100 miles.

Engineers believed that a manned missile would have solved the problem of the added inaccuracies introduced by a long glide path, and could hit small targets with the accuracy of the Reichenberg IV.

There were plans to develop a piloted A9 with pressurised cockpit, FuG 123 Truhe cartographic radar and Butterblüme infra-red ground-mapping device.

EMW A9 FIRST CONFIGURATION (1941) TECHNICAL DATA: Type: long-range boost-glide missile. Airframe: steel structure with riveted steel plates cladding. Power plant: one EMW bi-propellant rocket-motor with 60,500lb (27,500kg) peak-thrust. Propellants: 5,533kg of A-Stoff and 4,173kg of M-Stoff. Pressurisers: 172kg of T-Stoff (80% hydrogen peroxide, 20% oxiquinoline) and Z-Stoff (watery solution of sodium or calcium) actuating a turbo-pump of 730hp. Wingspan: 11.6ft (3.58m). Length: 46ft (14.06m). Maximum diameter: 5.5ft (1.8m). Wing surface: 150sq.ft (13.5sq.m.). Take-off weight: 29,800lb (13,500kg). Estimated maximum speed: 1,740mph (2,800km/h). Estimated ceiling: 316,818ft (96,000m). Estimated range: 373 miles (600km). Warhead: 2,150lb (975kg) with 907kg of Amatol 60/40.

EMW A9 SECOND CONFIGURATION (1944) TECHNICAL DATA: Type: long-range boost-glide missile. Airframe: steel structure with riveted steel plates cladding. Power plant: one EMW bi-propellant rocket-motor with 55,130lb (24,974kg) peak-thrust. Propellants: Visol and S-Stoff. Pressurisers: T-Stoff and Z-Stoff. Wingspan: 11.6ft (3.58m). Length: 46ft (14.06m). Maximum diameter: 5.5ft (1.8m). Wing surface: 150sq.ft (13.5sq.m.). Take-off weight: 35,850lb (16,260kg). Estimated maximum speed (with A10 booster): 6,165mph (9,920km/h- Mach 9.4). Estimated ceiling: 524,800ft (160,000m). Estimated range: 3,180 miles (5,000km). Warhead: 2,150lb (975kg) with 907kg of Amatol 60/40.

EMW A9 THIRD CONFIGURATION (1945) TECHNICAL DATA: Type: long-range boost-glide missile. Airframe: steel structure with riveted steel plates cladding. Power plant: one EMW bi-propellant rocket-motor with 70,170lb (31,787kg) peak-thrust. Propellants: Visol and SV-Stoff. Pressurisers:

T-Stoff and Z-Stoff. Wingspan: 11.6ft (3.58m). Length: 46ft (14.06m). Maximum diameter: 5.5ft (1.8m). Wing surface: 150sq.ft (13.5sq.m.). Take-off weight: 35,850lb (16,260kg). Estimated maximum speed (with A10 booster): 6,835mph (11,000km/h). Estimated ceiling: 574,000ft (175,000m). Estimated range: 3,418 miles (5,500km). Warhead: 2,150lb (975kg) with 907kg of Amatol 60/40.

EMW A10 FIRST CONFIGURATION (1941) TECHNICAL DATA: Type: boost-stage for the A9 missile. Airframe: steel structure with riveted steel plates cladding. Power plant: one EMW bi-propellant rocket-motor with 60,500lb (27,500kg) peak-thrust. Propellants: 5,533kg of A-Stoff and 4,173kg of M-Stoff. Pressurisers: 172kg of T-Stoff (80% hydrogen peroxide, 20% oxyquinoline) and Z-Stoff (watery solution of sodium or calcium). Wingspan: 20.3ft (6.2m). Stabiliser span: 18ft (5.5m). Length: 46.2ft (14.1m). Maximum diameter: 9.3ft (2.72m).

EMW A9/A10 FIRST CONFIGURATION (1941) TECHNICAL DATA: Length: 78.7ft (24m). Take-off weight: 56,000lb (25,370kg).

EMW A10 SECOND CONFIGURATION (1944) TECHNICAL DATA: Type: boost-stage for the A9 missile. Airframe: steel structure with riveted steel plates cladding. Power plant: six V2 combustion chambers with a total thrust of 363,000lb (164,439kg) used as pre-burners of an additional low pressure

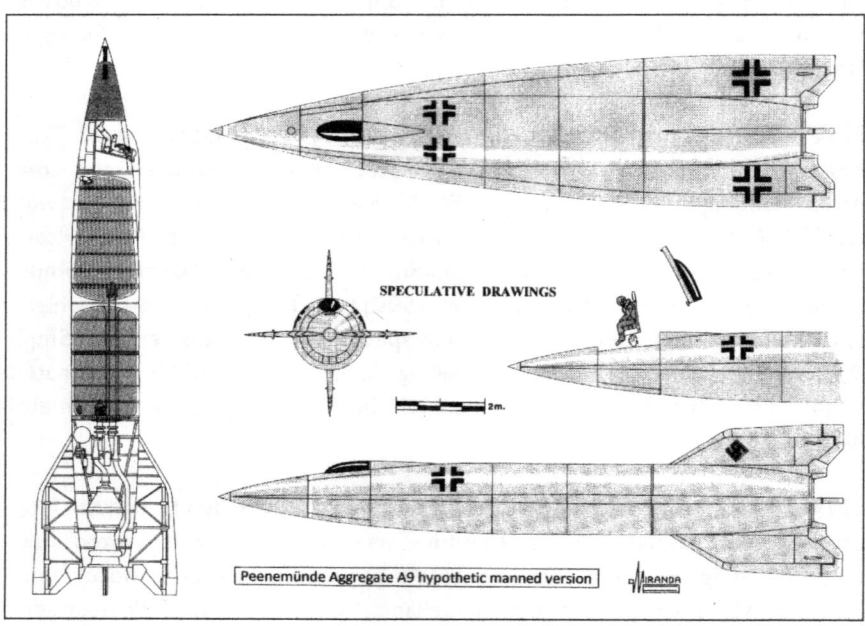

Peenemünde Aggregate A9 hypothetic manned version

combustion chamber formed by the main nozzle that form an aerospike with 440,920lb (199,737kg) peak-thrust. Propellants: 111,470lb (50,560kg) of A-Stoff and M-Stoff. Pressurisers: 410lb (186kg) of T-Stoff and Z-Stoff. Tailfins span: 29.5ft (9m). Length: 65.6ft (20m). Maximum diameter: 13.8ft (4.2m). Take-off weight: 152,240lb (69,060kg). Estimated maximum speed: 2,685mph (4,320km/h). Estimated ceiling: 80,000ft (24,000m). Parachute recovery of 2,990 square yards.

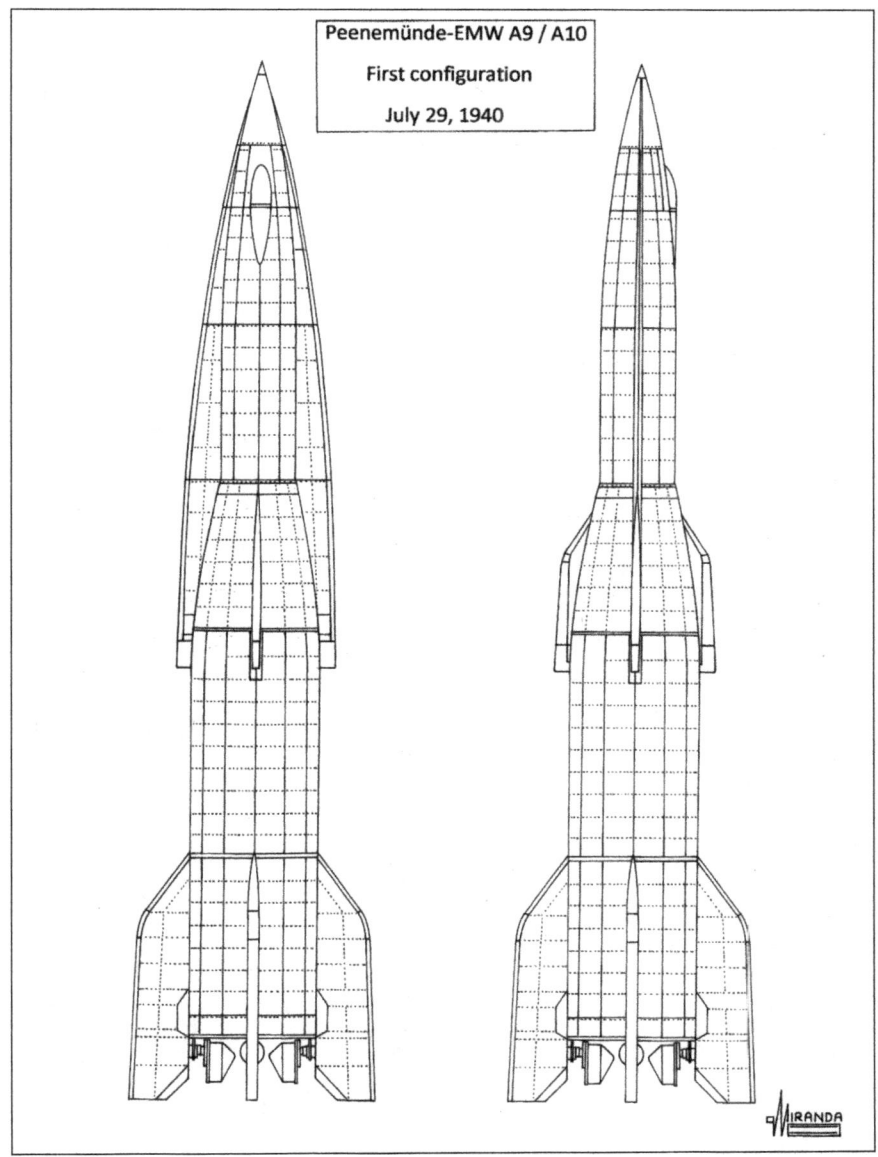

EMW A9/A10 SECOND CONFIGURATION (1944) TECHNICAL DATA: Maximum weight: 191,835lb (87,000kg). Length: 84.3ft (25.7m).

EMW A10 THIRD CONFIGURATION (1945) TECHNICAL DATA: Type: boost-stage for the A9 missile. Airframe: steel structure with riveted steel plates cladding, power plant: one EMW rocket-motor with 449,600–518,611lb (203,670–234,926kg) peak-thrust. Propellants: 136,700lb (61,490kg) of Visol and

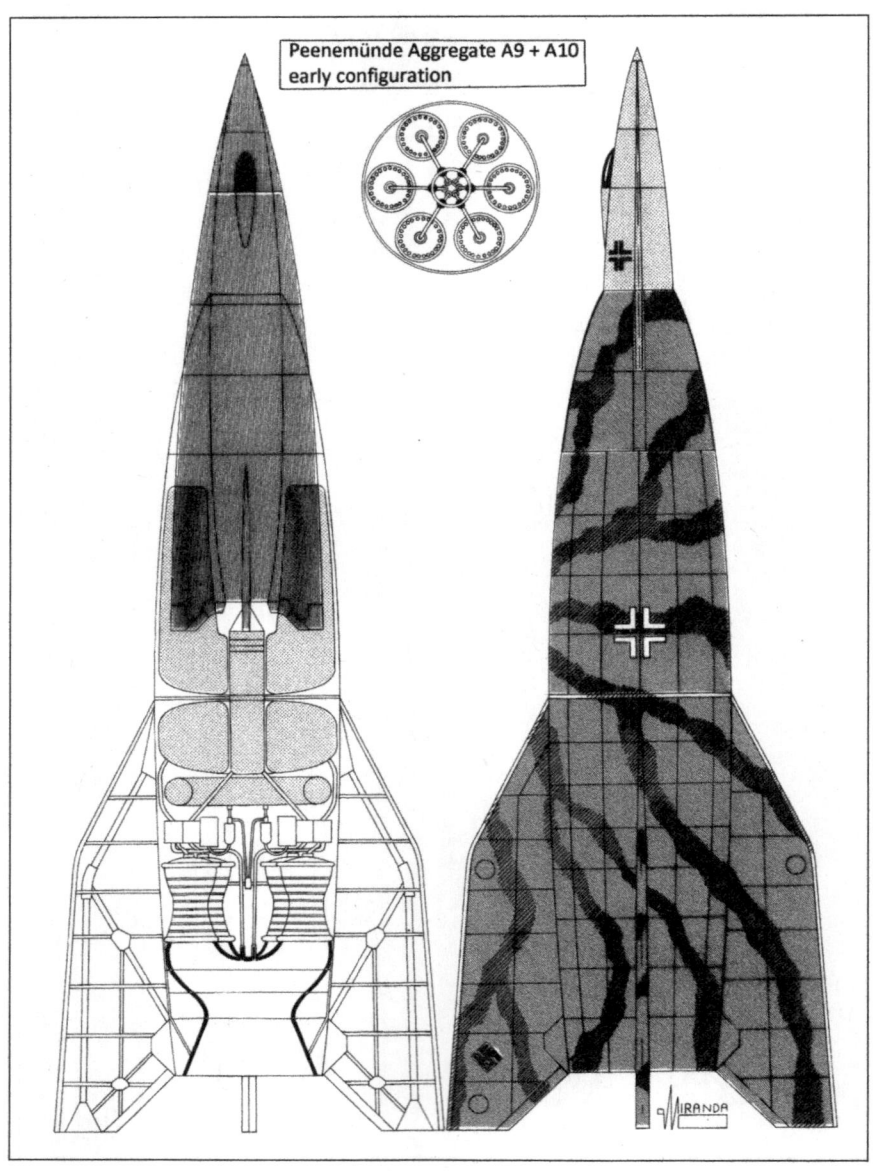

SV-Stoff. Pressurisers: 410lb (186kg) of T-Stoff and Z-Stoff. Tailfins span: 29.5ft (9m). Length: 65.6ft (20m). Maximum diameter: 13.8ft (4.2m). Take-off weight: 188,000–191,800lb (85,300–86,960kg). Parachute recovery of 2,990 square yards.

EMW A9/A10 THIRD CONFIGURATION (1945) TECHNICAL DATA: Maximum weight: 223,746-220,460lb (101,580–99,960kg). Length: 84.3ft (25.7m).

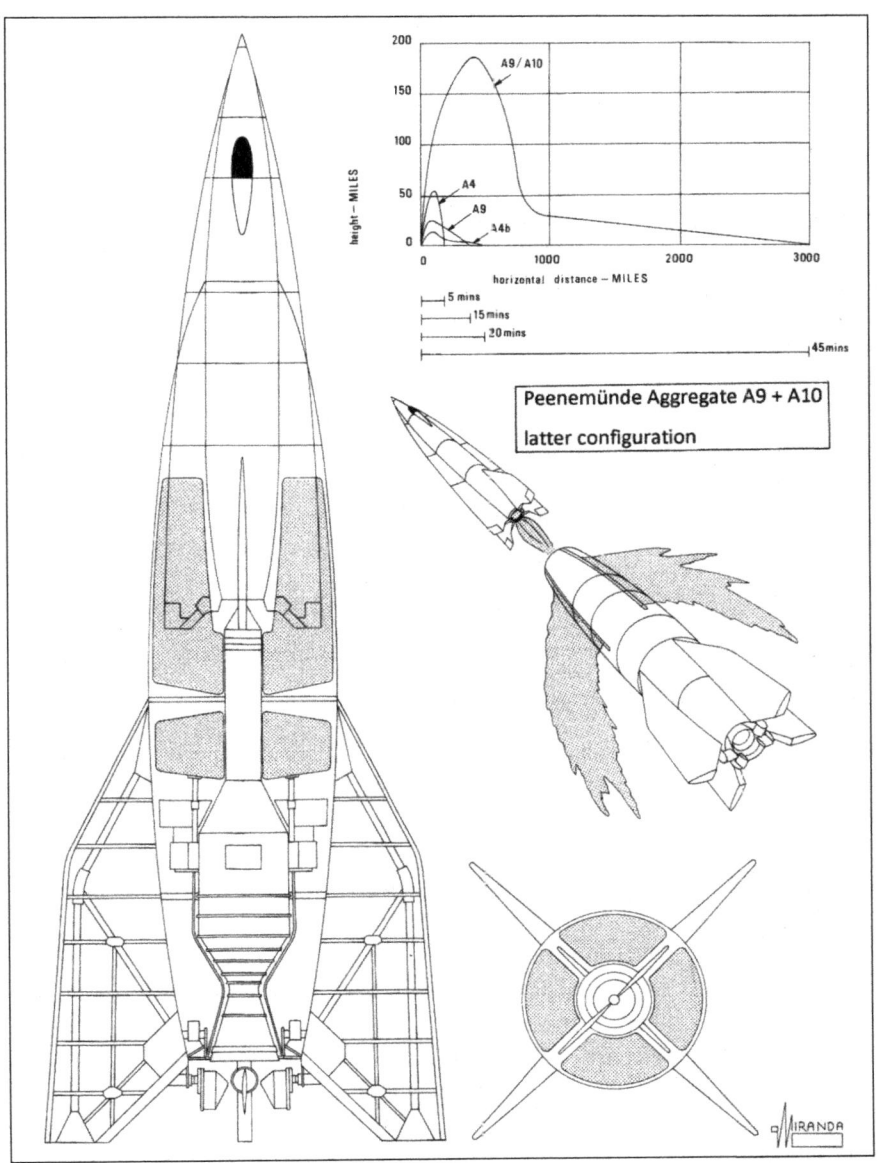

23
Russian Rocket-Planes

In 1929 Russian engineer Valentin Glushko of the Gas Dynamic Laboratory (GDL) developed the ORM-1, a bi-propellant rocket engine that generated 100kg peak-thrust by burning methanol and nitric acid.

In 1931 the Study Group on Gas Propulsion (GIRD) was formed in Leningrad and in 1933 Fridrikh Tsander developed the OR-2 rocket engine, capable of producing 65kg thrust by burning a mixture of gasoline and liquid oxygen (LOX).

After Tsander's death on 28 March 1933, the rocket-glider project RP-1 (Rakentny Planer-1), developed jointly with the flying wings builder Boris Cheranovsky, was cancelled.

Instead of using Tsander's proposed OR-2 rocket engine, the Cheranovsky flying wing prototype BICh-11 flew powered by a 22hp ABC Scorpion piston engine.

BICH-11 TECHNICAL DATA: Wingspan: 12.10m. Length: 3.81m. Height: 2.0m. Wing surface: 27sq.m.

On 21 September 1933, Marshall Tukhachevsky created the RNII (Reactive Scientific Research Institute), unifying the GDL and the GIRD to guide research towards the creation of air-to-ground solid-fuel rockets of 82 and 132mm.

In August 1939, RS-82 rockets were used over Khalkin Gol by Soviet fighters I-16 Type 17 in air-to-air combat against Japanese fighters Nakajima Ki. 27.

In 1935 the RNII had developed the bi-propellant rocket engine ORM-12a, rated at 400kg peak-thrust, to use as take-off booster for the Tupolev TB-1 bomber.

The development of rocket aircraft in the Soviet Union suffered constant setbacks with few results due to political interference.

Despite the successes achieved by the RNII, Tukhachevsky was executed for political reasons, along with the director of the RNII Ivan Kleimenof

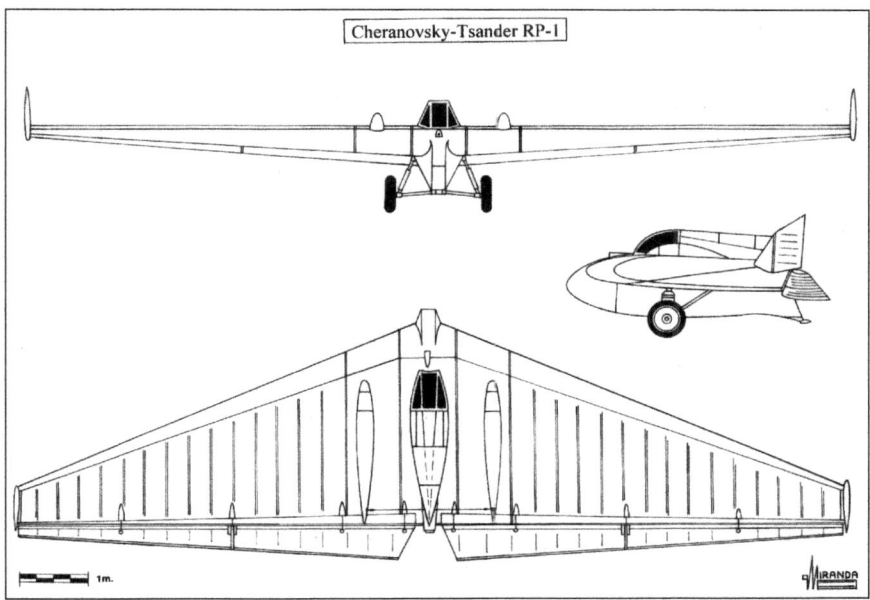

and the chief engineer Georgi Langemak. In 1936 the RNII was renamed NII-3.

In 1937 Valentin Glushko proposed installing an ORM-65 rocket engine, with 175kg thrust (using a mixture of methanol and nitric acid), in an SK-9 glider designed by the Chief Design of NII-3, BICh-11 Sergei Korolev. The new rocket-plane was designated RP-318-1.

The ORM-65 was developed as a missile booster and was considered unsafe for use in manned flight. Korolev decided to replace it with one of the throttleable rocket engines developed by NII-3 engineers Leonid Dushkin and Alexis Isaef.

The RDA-1-150, rated at 100kg peak-thrust, used a mixture of methanol and nitric acid, the RDK-1-150, rated at 100kg peak-thrust, used a mixture of methanol and LOX.

The NII-3 lacked experience in handling cryogenic liquids and it was eventually decided to install an RDA on the RP-318-1.

On 28 February 1940, the rocket-glider was towed to 2,900m altitude by one Polikarpov R-5 tug.

The rocket then fired and ran for 110 seconds, accelerating to 140 m/sec, until the 75kg of propellants were exhausted.

KOROLEV RP-318-1 TECHNICAL DATA: Wingspan: 17m. Length: 7.44m. Height: 1.8m. Wing surface: 22sq.m. Maximum weight: 700kg. Maximum speed: 160km/h. Gliding ratio: 19:1.

The RP-318-1 flew nine times before the German invasion ended the project.

Following the technological failure of Soviet aviation in Spain, China, Khalkin Gol and Finland, there was renewed interest in rocket-powered aircraft.

During the last months of 1940, the Luftwaffe's special long-range reconnaissance unit Aufklärungsgruppe Ob.d.L. was operating a mixture of Dornier Do 215 B-4, Dornier Do 217 A-0, Junkers Ju 86 P-2 and Junkers Ju 86 R-1 spy planes.

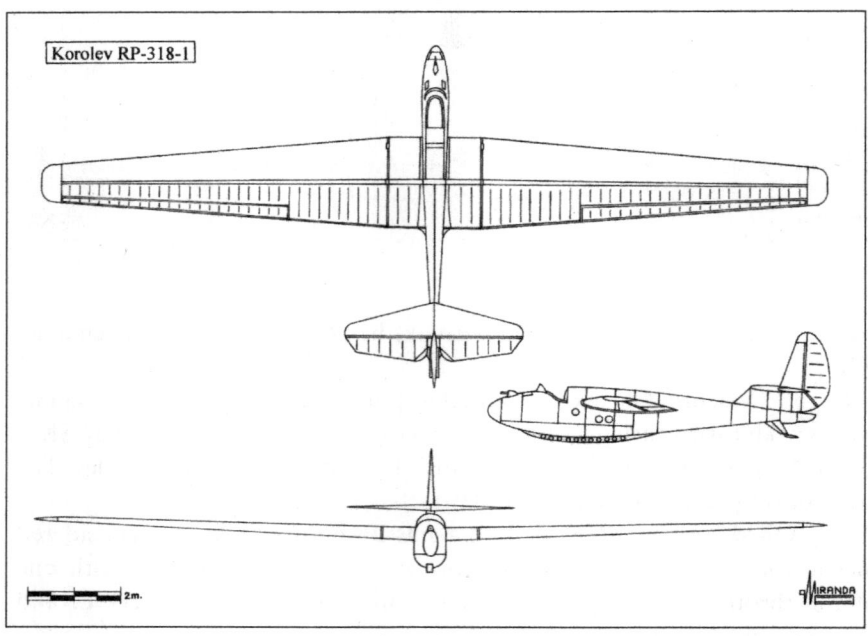

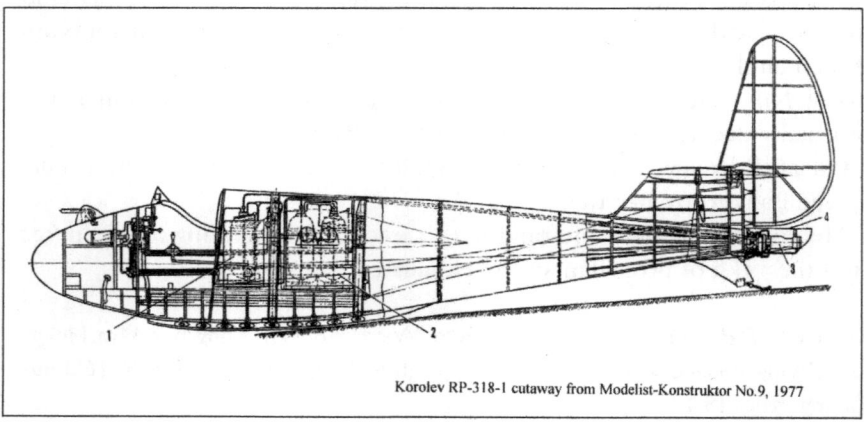

Korolev RP-318-1 cutaway from Modelist-Konstruktor No.9, 1977

The Gruppe began its operational life performing clandestine reconnaissance sorties in civil disguise, deep into the Soviet airspace, in preparation for Operation Barbarossa.

They took photographs of the Soviet defences which were to play an important role when the Germans invaded Russia in June 1941.

The Do 215 B-4 could fly at 29,520ft (9,000m) altitude and 292mph (470km/h) top speed, the Do 217 A-0 at 24,928ft (7,600m) and 298mph (480km/h), the Ju 86 P-2 at 41,000ft (12,500m) and 224mph (360km/h), and the Ju 86 R-1 at 47,232ft (14,400m) and 261mph (420km/h).

By mid-1941 some Henschel Hs 130 A-0 preproduction aircrafts started its operational evaluation with the Aufklärungsgruppe Ob.d.L reaching 43,300ft (13,200m) absolute ceiling and 292mph (470km/h) top speed, but the OKL dismissed its serial production because of the weak opposition made by Soviet fighters.

After learning about the performances of the high-altitude Junkers Ju 86 P-2 reconnaissance aircraft, the GKO authorised the use of rocket engine propulsion system for high-performance fighters.

The I-200 high-altitude interceptor was designed in 1939 by the Polikarpov Design Bureau, inheriting all the deficiencies of its lineage and thus proving the correctness of the Latin sentence, *Errare humanum est, sed perseverare, diabolicum*. (To err is human, but to persist is diabolical).

The extremely short fuselage had originally been designed for the I-185 fighter (powered by one radial engine) and was totally inadequate to compensate for the long and heavy AM-35A V-12 engine, with 1,350hp.

During the flight tests performed on 29 August 1940, the prototype showed longitudinal instability, heavy control and a dangerous tendency to flat spin.

It was difficult to fly and deadly in combat for an inexperienced pilot. Its instability at high speeds could make aerial gunnery difficult, requiring constant pilot intervention to remain on target.

A feature common to all Polikarpov fighters was the 'snaking effect' that affected weapon accuracy during combat manoeuvres.

The triangular wing planform, with leading and trailing edge sweep and larger roots that tapered to the tips, were the cheapest compromise between performance, strength and drag. It was strong at the root, light at the tips and easy to build, and could be lethal, because the strongly tapered wings had a dangerous tendency to low-speed stall.

In combat, the I-200 was prone to spinning out of a steep banking turn. Despite the seriousness of the shortcomings displayed by the prototype, it was ordered into immediate mass production, as OKO MiG-1, in September 1940.

Some aircraft from GAZ-1 were delivered to the VVS-RKKA (Soviet Air Force) and PVO (Soviet Air Defence Force) in April 1941, but little is known of their performance in combat because more than half of all Soviet fighters were destroyed on the ground or in the air within forty-eight hours of the Luftwaffe assault.

Meanwhile, the Mikoyan-Gurevich Design Bureau (OKO-Kiev) worked feverishly to correct the MiG-1 deficiencies.

The MiG-3 was ordered into production in December 1940, but the improvements added nearly 500lb to the take-off weight and exacerbated its instability at high speeds. Its poor climb performance was caused by the excessive weight (1,830lb) of the AM-35A engine (Soviet version of Fiat A.20 V.12 with single-stage gear-driven supercharger) and the steel wing spar.

The aircraft was originally designed as a high-altitude interceptor with 37,700ft (11,500m) service ceiling, but in practice few MiG-3 managed to reach that altitude due to the poor design of the fuel and oil pumps and the M-100's supercharger malfunction, as the impeller alloy AK-1 was prone to material fatigue.

In real combat conditions some planes entered irrecoverable spins flying at 30,000ft (9,150m).

The MiG-3 had a take-off weight of 7,395lb (3,350kg) at a time when the Yak-1 weighed 6,309lb (2,858kg) and the Messerschmitt Bf 109 F-1 4,943lb (2,239kg).

Designers were forced to reduce the armament to just three machine guns so as not to further degrade its climb performance.

The aircrafts used by the PVO in Moscow's defence failed to reach the high-flying Ju 86 P-2s during the day and, at night, their inaccurate PAK-1 gunsights, the low optical quality of the Plexiglas windscreen and the poor firepower, proved inadequate to destroy the Heinkel He-111 H bombers fitted with 270kg armour.

Production of the MiG-3 was stopped in December 1941 and six fighter regiments in charge of the defence of Moscow were equipped with Lend-Lease Hawker Hurricanes Mk. II A and Mk. IIB.

In October 1941, the NII-3 was evacuated to the Ural region.

After the German attack, several designs for potential rocket interceptors eventually came to be created in the Soviet Union.

Undoubtedly the smallest fighter in the history, similar to the German Bachem Natter, a project was conceived by the military engineer Lev Golovin in 1941, based in the aerodynamic and rocket propulsion principles of Konstantin E. Tsiolkowski. It was designed in two versions:

1. The 'IVS' (Istrebitel Voyskovogo Soprovozhdeniya) version for the Soviet Air Force was designed for the target defence of factories, communication nodes, refineries and headquarters. The 'IVS' was launched from a 40-degree truck ramp with 8m length, helped by two

solid-fuel rockets. The launching team was formed by the pilot, the mechanic, and the truck driver.
2. The 'ISF' (Istrebitel Soprovozhdeniya Flota), the naval version, was designed for the target defence of the naval bases and warships.

The mass production of the Golovin fighter was rejected in favour of the conventional antiaircraft artillery.

GOLOVIN IVS/ISF TECHNICAL DATA: Type: VTO rocket interceptor. Structure and cladding: light alloy. Landing gear: retractable skid and brake-parachute with 9.39m of diameter, engine: one Dushkin/Glushko RD-1 bi-propellant rocket with 300kg thrust and two RATO solid-fuel rockets with 1,000kg peak-thrust each, propellant tanks were mounted to both sides of the pilot containing nitric acid and kerosene in a ratio of two to one (probably 70l of acid and 30l of kerosene). Pressuriser: nitrogen. Armament: one 20mm ShVAK cannon. Wingspan: 5.74ft (1.75m). Length: 9.48ft (3m). Height: 3.4ft (1.05m). Wing surface: 11sq.ft (1sq.m). Maximum weight: 662lb. (300kg). Estimated maximum speed: 659mph (1,060km/h). Estimated climb rate: 820ft/second. Estimated ceiling: 24,600ft (7,500m).

During ground tests conducted in the spring of 1941, the Dushkin-Isayev D-1A-1100 nitric acid/kerosene rocket-motor produced 1,100kg peak-thrust.

To achieve that power, the engine used fuel pumps that suffered serious corrosion problems due to acid, which could not be solved. It was necessary to reuse the old pressurisation system of compressed air, thus reducing the powered endurance to just 15 minutes.

In June 1941 it was decided to use the D-1A-1100 for the propulsion of a small point-defence interceptor designed by the engineers A.Ya Bereznyak and A.A. Isayev.

The prototype BI-1 was flown, in glider configuration, on 10 September 1941.

The rocket engine exploded during ground test on 20 February 1942, due to the fragility of the combustion chamber, and the first powered flight was conducted by the second prototype BI-2 on 15 May 1942. During this first flight the engine worked for just under a minute.

The BI airframe was not properly designed for high-speed flight. On 27 March 1943, the BI-3 prototype suffered compressibility buffeting and was destroyed because of an uncontrollable nose-down pitch at 497mph (800km/h).

All the work on the fifty pre-production machines was abandoned but some flight-testing was continued with the BI-6 and BI-7 prototypes until 1945.

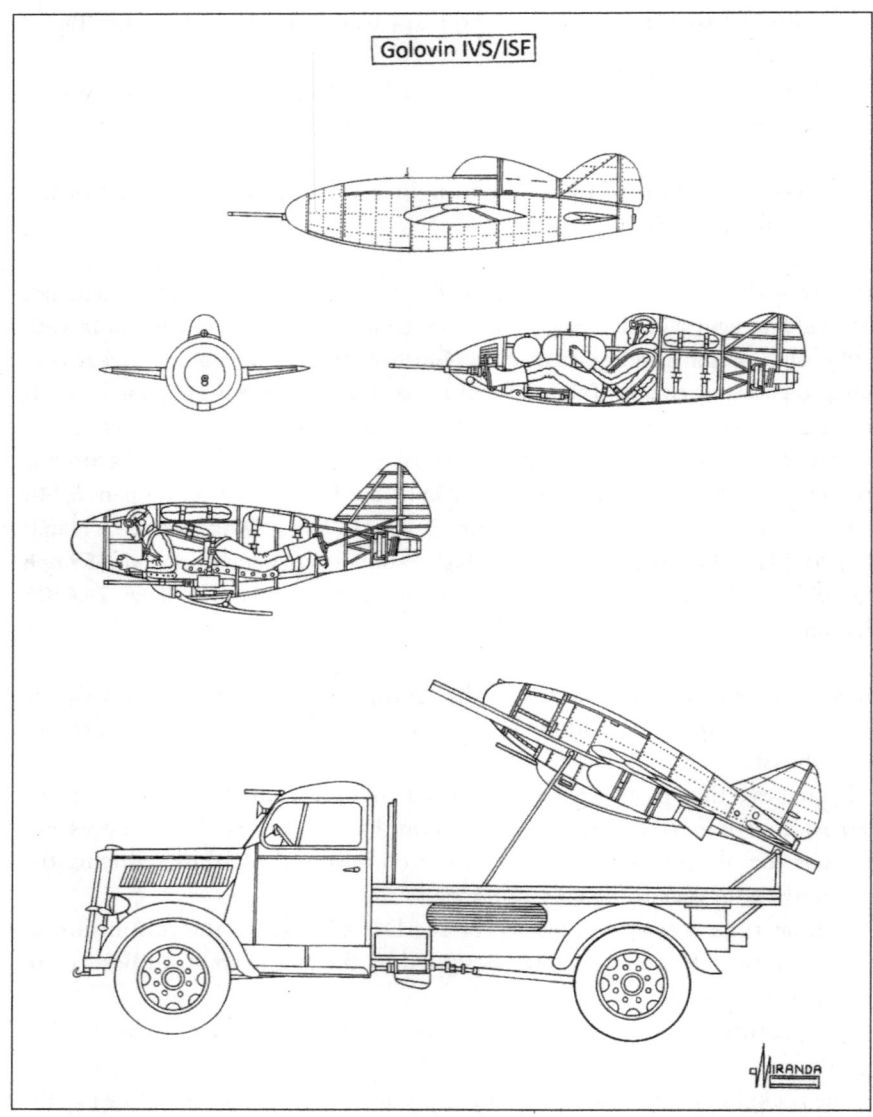

BEREZNYAK-ISAYEV BI TECHNICAL DATA: Wingspan: 21.2ft (6.48m). Length: 21ft (6.4m). Height: 6.8ft (2.06m). Wing surface: 75.35sq.ft (7sq.m). Take-off weight: 3,710lb (1,683kg). Estimated maximum speed: 559mph (900km/h).

In the Yak-7R modification, proposed in 1942, the M-105 piston engine was replaced by the pilot cockpit and the nose armament. One D-1A rocket-motor was mounted in the rear fuselage and two

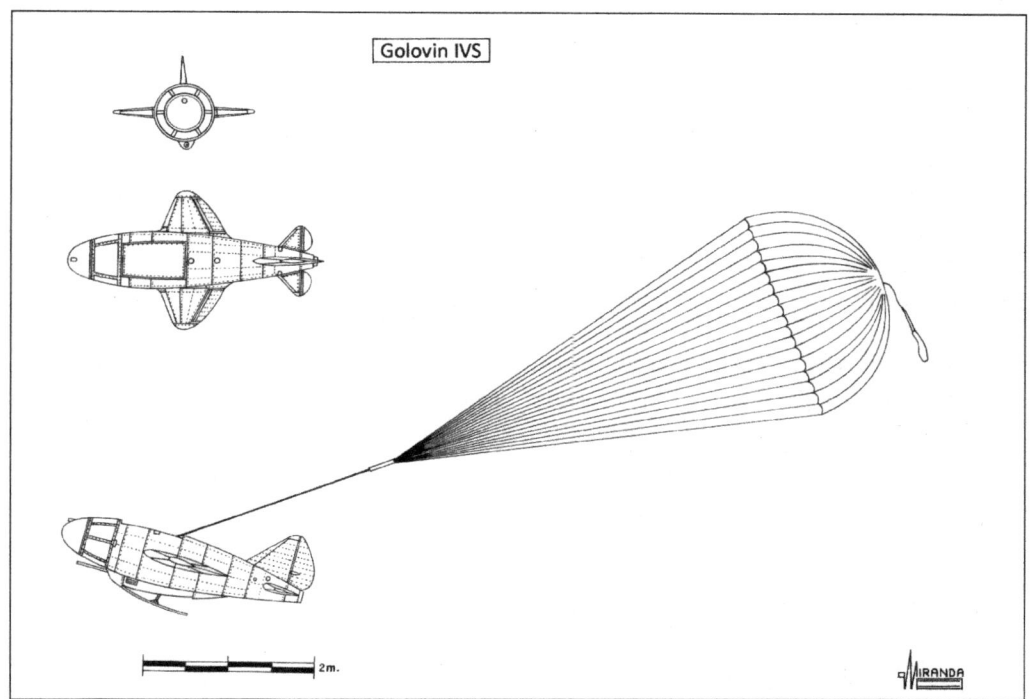

Merkulov DM-4C ramjets were fitted under the wings, but the GKO did not authorise the project and the airframe conversion was never completed.

YAK-7R TECHNICAL DATA: Wingspan: 32.8ft (10m). Length: 31.4ft (9.58m). Height: 7.4ft (2.26m). Wing surface: 190.5sq.ft (17.15sq.m).

The loss of official interest in rocket interceptors also affected development of the Tikhonravov I-302, Florov 4302 and Polikarpov Malyutka projects.

The I-302 was flight-tested as a glider from August 1943, but the project was cancelled in March 1944 before the rocket engine was installed in the prototype. The Dushkin/Shtokolov RD-2-M-3V rocket (kerosene + LOX) had a main combustion chamber rated at 1,100kg thrust and a cruise chamber rated at 450kg thrust.

Two DM-4C ramjets fitted under the wings of the second prototype I-302 P had been planned.

TIKHONRAVOV I-302 TECHNICAL DATA: Wingspan: 37ft (11.4m). Length: 26.2ft (8m). Height: 7.7ft (2.36m). Wing surface: 198sq.ft (17.8sq.m). Take-off weight: 19,205lb (8,700kg). Estimated maximum speed: 559mph (900km/h).

In 1943 a design team of the Air Force Research Institute (NIIVS) under the leadership of Ilya Florov, was tasked with developing an aerodynamic research rocket-plane for testing high-speed wings and control systems.

In 1946, the first prototype, known as Aircraft 4302, was flight-tested in glider configuration.

In August 1947, the second prototype was flown at 323mph (520km/h) powered by one RD-2M-3 rocket-motor with two combustion chambers rated at 1,450 and 400kg thrust.

The project was cancelled in favour of the MiG I-270.

FLOROV 4302-02 TECHNICAL DATA: Wingspan: 22.7ft (6.93m). Length: 23.3ft (7.12m). Height: 7ft (2.12m). Take-off weight: 5,243lb (2,398kg). Estimated maximum speed: 323mph (520km/h).

The Malyutka project had not yet reached the prototype stage when it was cancelled on 30 July 1944.

POLIKARPOV MALYUTKA TECHNICAL DATA: Wingspan: 21ft (6.4m). Length: 20.7ft (6.3m). Height: 8.8ft (2.69m). Wing surface: 108sq.ft (10sq.m). Take-off weight: 5,622lb (2,550kg). Estimated maximum speed: 544mph (875km/h).

Sergei Korolev proposed a rocket-boosted version of the Lavochkin La-5 standard under the La-5 VI (Visotnyi Istrebitel) code name.

The modification consisted on three Glushko RD-1 Khz bipropellant rocket-motors, with electric ignition system, mounted under the wings and in the rear fuselage.

A top speed of 590mph (950km/h) and a ceiling of 55,760ft (17,000m) was expected, but the Lavochkin design bureau theorised that the rocket fuel could react with wood and cause fires, so decided to use an La-7, with metallic structure.

The prototype La-7R was flight-tested in October 1944, reaching 461mph (742km/h) powered by one M-82 reciprocating engine and one acid/kerosene rocket-motor RD-1 KhZ with 300kg peak-thrust.

The second prototype attained 494mph (795km/h) and 42,640ft (13,000m) ceiling powered by one ZhRD-1 rocket with hypergolic chemical ignition.

On 12 May 1945, the engine exploded during a ground test, destroying the prototype. Operation with the ZhRD-1 was found to be extremely hazardous, with explosions a common occurrence.

Flight-testing continued until February 1945.

LAVOCHKIN LA-7R TECHNICAL DATA: Wingspan: 32ft (9.8m). Length: 28.4ft (8.67m). Height: 2.54ft (2.7m). Wing surface: 189.3sq.ft (17.59sq.m). Take-off weight: 7,704lb (3,490 Kg).

A third prototype, named La-120 R and powered by one RD-1 CH2-X3 rocket, was flown in January 1945, reaching 500mph (805km/h).

The Yak-3 RD prototype was flight-tested on 22 December 1944, powered by one VK-105 PF2 piston engine and one RD-1 KhZ.

The rocket engine proved to be unreliable and was replaced by a ZhRD-1. The Yak-3R attained 486mph (782km/h) flying at 25,590ft (7,800m).

Rocket malfunction continued. On 14 May 1945, there was an explosion during the ground tests.

On 16 August 1945, during a 510mph (820km/h) run at 8,200ft (2,500m), the prototype suddenly entered a steep dive and crashed.

YAKOVLEV YAK-3 RD TECHNICAL DATA: Wingspan: 30ft (9.2m). Length: 29.6ft (9.02m). Height: 7.9ft (2.42m). Wing surface: 159.6sq.ft (14.83sq.m). Take-off weight: 7,616lb (3,450 Kg).

On 17 April 1945, the Luftwaffe airbase at Leipzig-Brandis was captured by the US Army's 9th Armoured Division.

This airfield had become the centre of operations of Messerschmitt Me 262 A-1 jet-fighters from JG7 and the Me 163 B rocket-fighters from JG400.

The retreating Germans had sabotaged many of the planes, including two prototypes of the Junkers Ju 287 jet bomber and the Sack AS6 experimental flying saucer, but many fighters rested under camouflage netting in the surrounding woods.

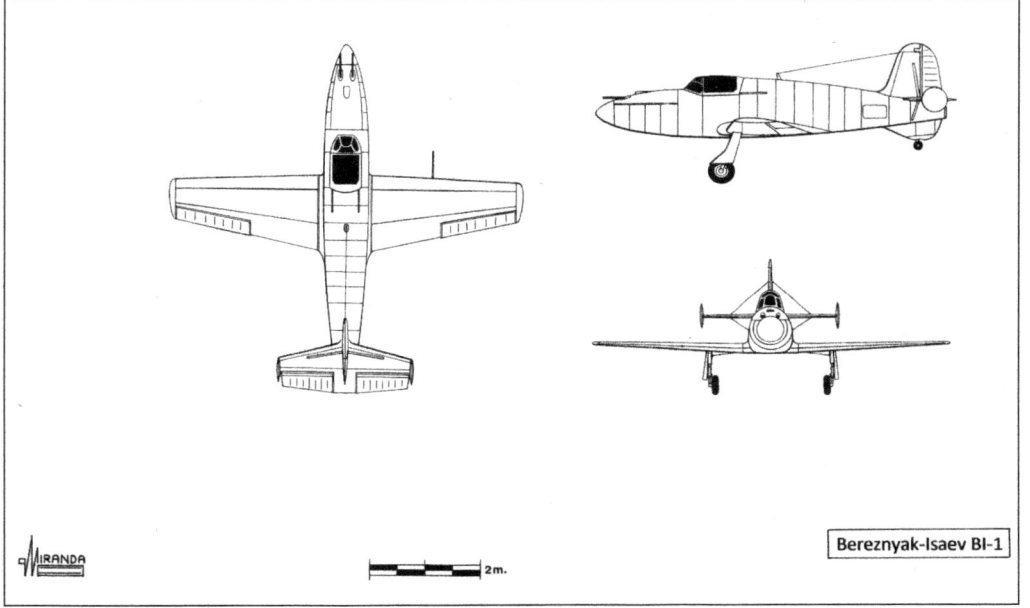

Bereznyak-Isaev BI-1

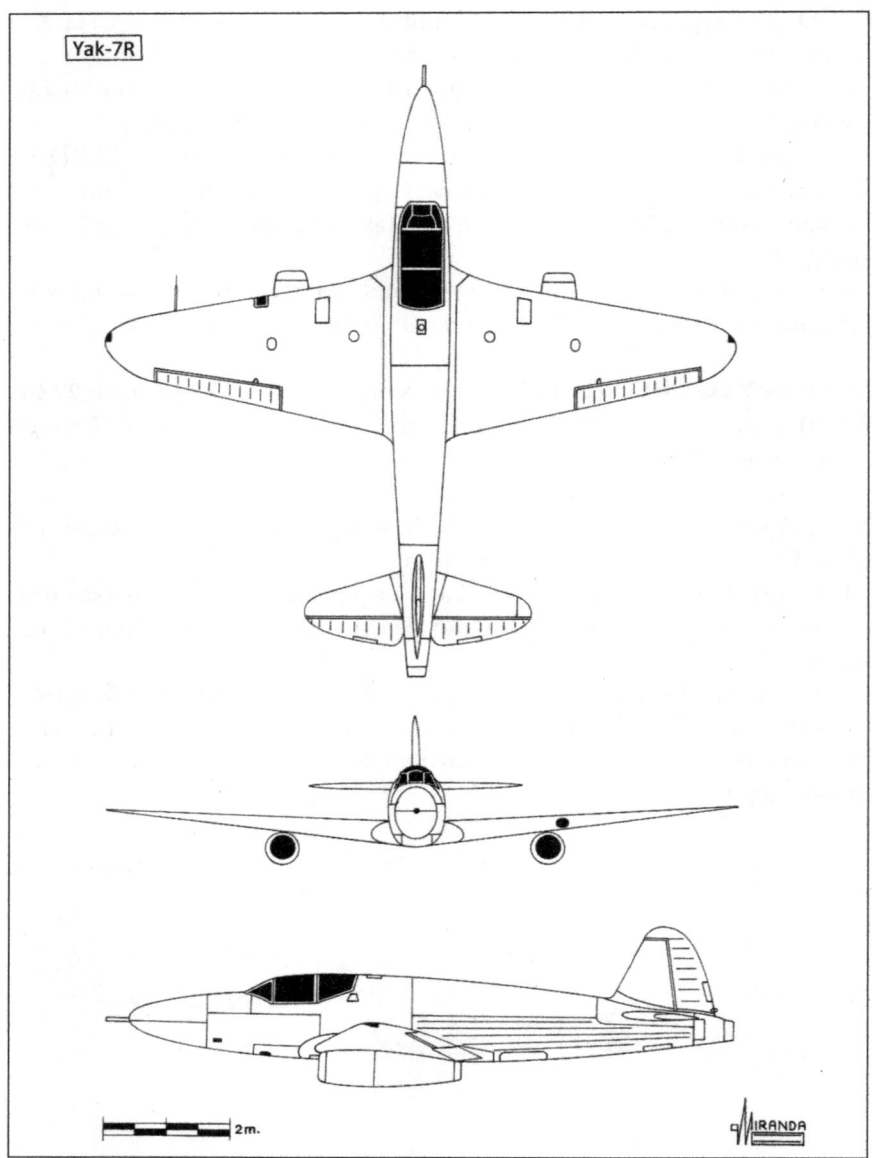

When the giant base was inspected by Allied intelligence, the following was discovered: five Me 163 B fighters, three Me 163 S two-seat trainers, the Horten Ho 9 V1 flying wing, many tanks of rocket propellants, Walter HWK 109-509A engines, several Jumo 004 turbojets and technical documentation on Junkers Ju 248 flight tests.

On 2 July 1945, the airbase was handed over to the Soviets allowing them access to the German secret technology.

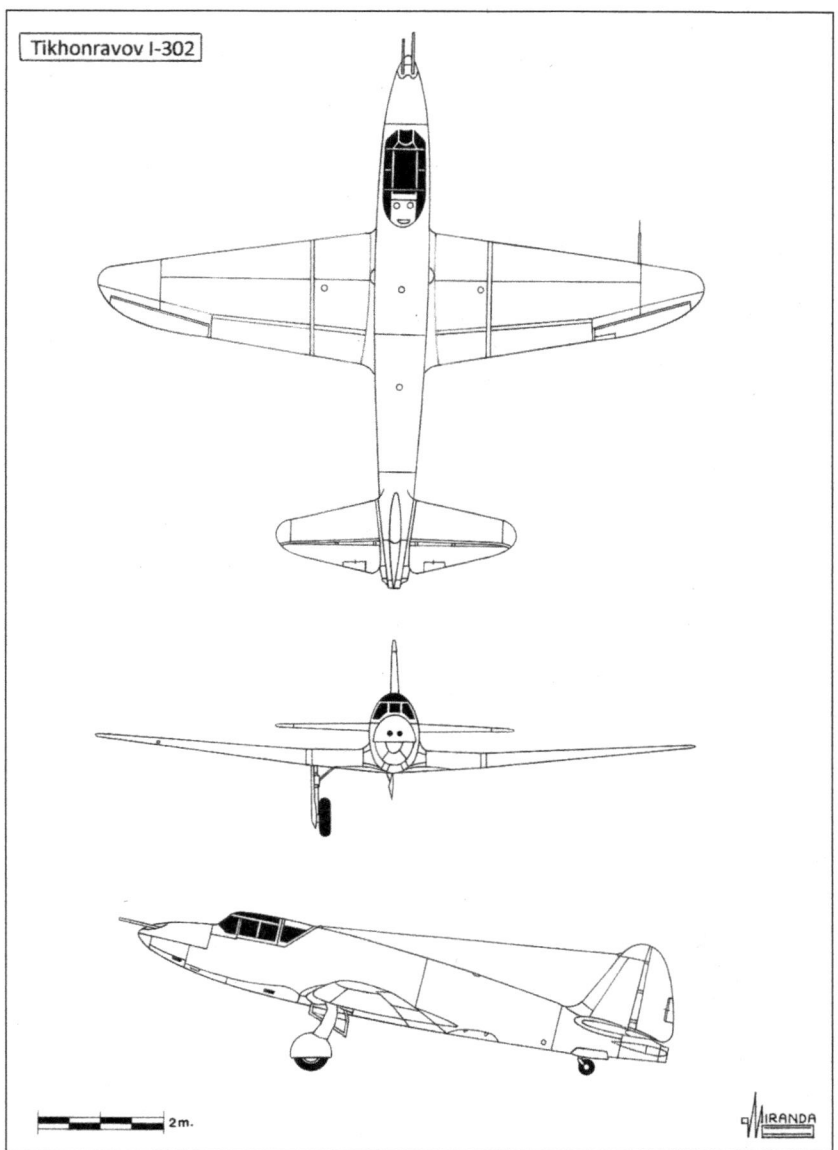

In Brandis, the Soviets managed to capture two Me 163 B and one Me 163 S that was used for aerodynamic testing at the Aviation Research Institute TsAGI wind tunnel in 1946. Late in 1945, the Me 163 B fighters were flight-tested at NII-VVS, in glider configuration, towed by one Tupolev Tu-2 bomber.

No powered flights were made, the small number of rocket propellants captured in Brandis was used in bench testing with the Walter rocket.

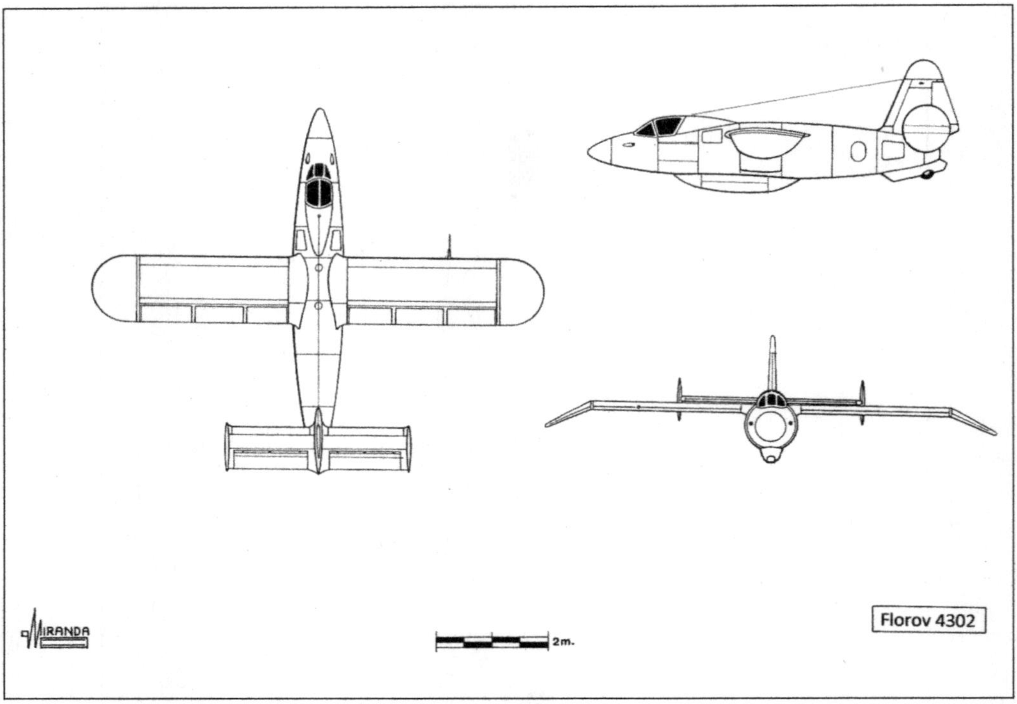
MIRANDA
2m.
Florov 4302

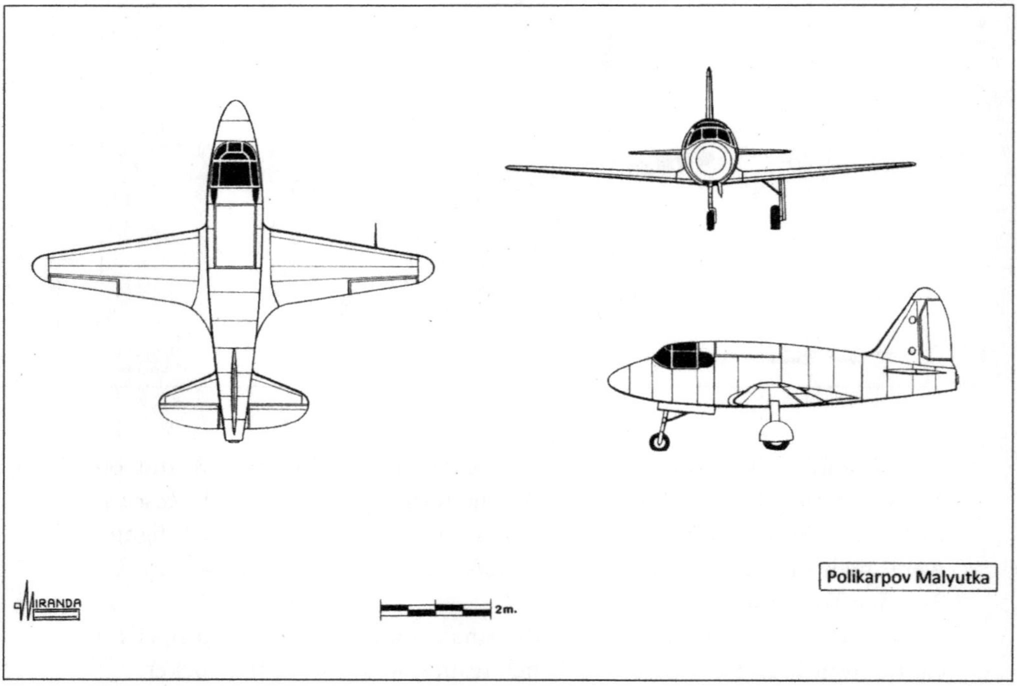
MIRANDA
2m.
Polikarpov Malyutka

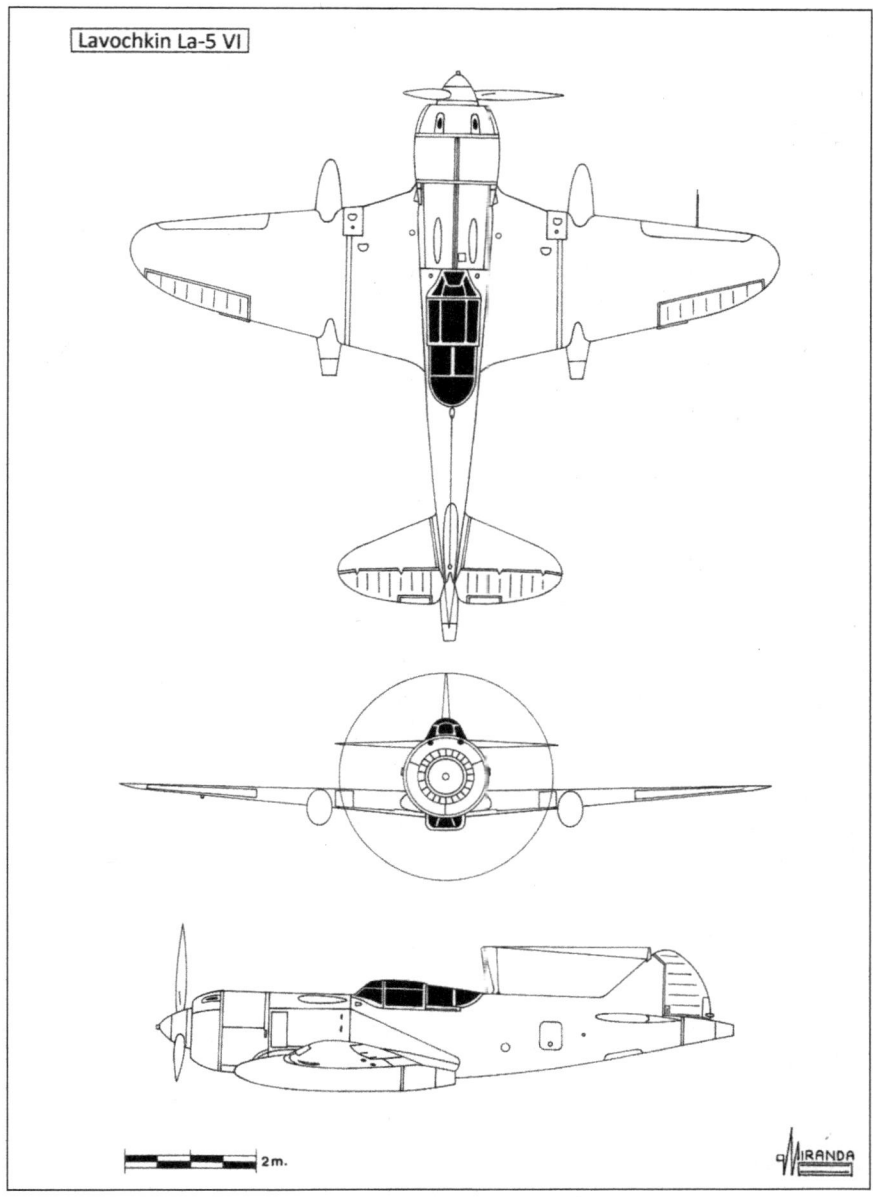

The Komet was a very dangerous aircraft to land and the Soviets decided that the tailless configuration was not suitable for high-performance rocket aircrafts.

The production facilities at Junkers Flugzeugwerke-Dessau were totally destroyed by six air raids, then it was occupied by the First US Army in April 1945.

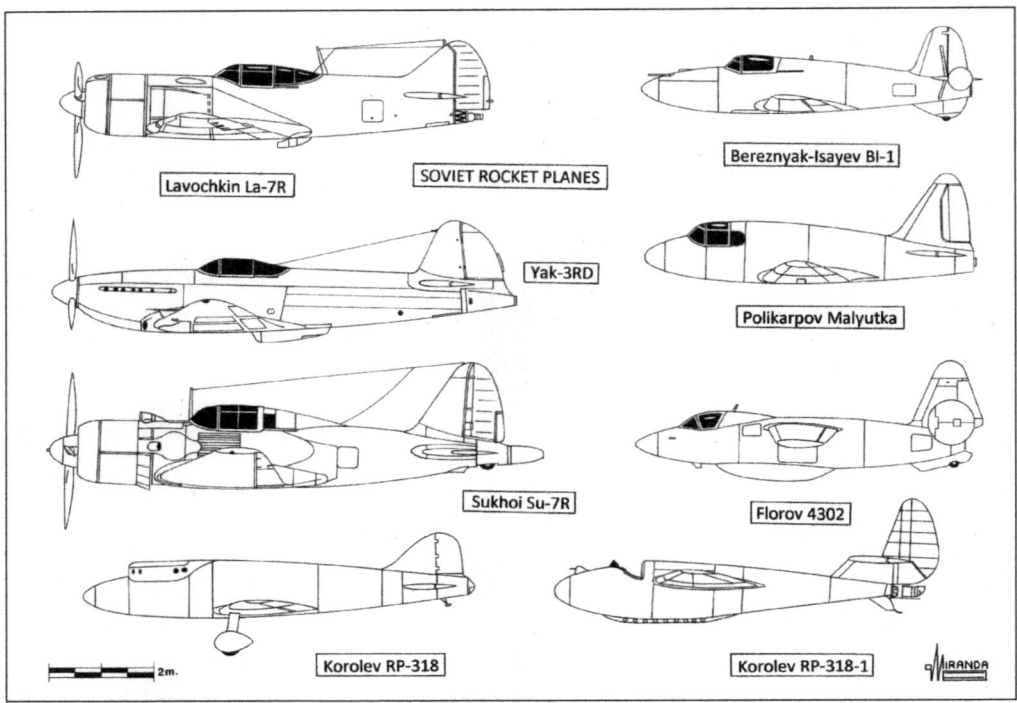

SOVIET ROCKET PLANES

Lavochkin La-7R • Bereznyak-Isayev BI-1 • Yak-3RD • Polikarpov Malyutka • Sukhoi Su-7R • Florov 4302 • Korolev RP-318 • Korolev RP-318-1

On 1 July 1945, when the Dessau plant was handed over to Soviet occupation troops, in accordance with the Yalta agreements, most of the documentation, patents, licences and films had been transferred to the Junkers-Gernrode documentation branch and the rest were taken over by Allied intelligence.

The Soviets obtained the fuselage of the damaged prototype Ju 248 V2 rocket-fighter, captured by US troops at Kassel-Bettenhausen, technical documentation on Junkers Ju 248 flight tests captured in Brandis and one Walter HWK 109-509 C engine at the Siebel-Halle plant.

On 22 October 1946, all the captured German engineers, material and tools were transferred to the USSR.

The Soviets attempted to continue the development of the Junkers EF 126, EF 127 and Ju 248 projects. Specialists in fuselage construction were sent to Podberezhye, near Moscow, and the rocket engine team was transferred to Uprawlentscheski Gorodok, but the Ju 248 wooden wings were built by the unknown Puklitsch German firm and the Soviets couldn't get the manufacturing plans.

Following the atomic bombs dropped on Hiroshima and Nagasaki, the Soviet government urgently needed a reliable, fast-climbing point-defence interceptor to counter the potential threat of nuclear-armed B-29 bombers in a future war.

On 26 February 1946, Josef Stalin ordered the development of two rocket interceptors using technology captured from the Germans, but the Soviet industry proved unable to build reverse-engineered copies of the double-walled combustion chamber or turbine-driven fuel pump of the German Walter HWK 109-509 A-1 rocket-motor, and only managed to produce small amounts of T-Stoff and C-Stoff, sufficient for ten partial rocket starts and five full-powered take-offs.

The designers were forced to continue using the RD-2-M-3V domestic rocket engine.

The MiG bureau was assigned to design a mass-production daylight interceptor and the Lavochkin bureau was tasked to design a limited-production all-weather/night-fighter fitted with AI radar.

The project, named I-270, developed by the MiG design team was based on information retrieved on the Junkers Ju 248 V2. The TsAGI recommended lengthening the fuselage to contain more propellants, but the German chemicals were abandoned. Instead, the plane used RFNA (96% nitric acid) and kerosene.

In the preliminary configuration of March 1946, the I-270 was designed with 20-degree (25% chord) swept wings based on those of the MiG-8, but the insufficiency of data about the Ju 248 28-degree swept wings, and the bad experiences suffered during landings with the Me 163, forced the design team to use the straight wing of the Junkers EF 127 project, with 9 per cent thickness.

Following the TsAGI calculations, work was stopped on April and the project was revised with a 12 per cent wing.

On 30 May 1946, a 30-degree swept T-tail plane was adopted to compensate for the extremely small longitudinal stability margin of the tailless designs.

To prevent the turbulence generated by the wings at Mach 0.9 affecting the tailplane, the OKB calculated that it should be installed at a height above the wings equivalent to 1.2 times the average value of the chord (1,772mm).

Final configuration was approved on 8 August 1946, with one RD-2 MZV two-chamber rocket engine that used a turbo-pump unit driven by hydrogen peroxide.

On 3 February 1947, the prototype I-270 F2 was flown, in glider configuration, towed by one Tupolev Tu-2 bomber. On 16 July, the cruise combustion chamber exploded during ground tests, damaging the aft fuselage.

The I-270 F2 made its first powered flight on 2 September 1947, but it was damaged beyond repair during landing.

The prototype I-270 F1 was flown on 4 October, reaching 382mph (615km/h) only, far from the expected 1,000km/h.

The engine failures caused by acid corrosion and explosions continued and, by March 1948, the top speed of the I-270 was only 39km/h faster than a Lockheed P-80C standard.

MiG was instructed not to fly and preserve the aircraft.

MiG I-270 TECHNICAL DATA: Wingspan: 25.4ft (7.75m). Length: 29.3ft (8.92m). Height: 9.2ft (2.8m). Wing surface: 130sq.ft (12sq.m). Take-off weight: 9,085lb (4,121kg). Estimated maximum speed: 544mph (875km/h), real attained speed: 382mph (615km/h). Estimated service ceiling: 56,000ft (17,000m), real attained ceiling: (14,596ft (4,450m). Equipment: pressurised cockpit and Heinkel Kartusche ejector seat.

The all-weather specification called for a rocket-fighter with one Slepushkin NII-17 Toriy (AI) radar, 684mph (1,100km/h) top speed, 59,055ft (18,000m) ceiling and 6 minutes powered flight endurance.

By the end of 1946 the Lavochkin I-162 preliminary design was proposed, inspired in the Junkers EF 127, with a jettisonable two-wheel take-off trolley and retractable landing skid, but the project was rejected by the TsAGI who had had numerous problems with the Messerschmitt Me 163 landing system.

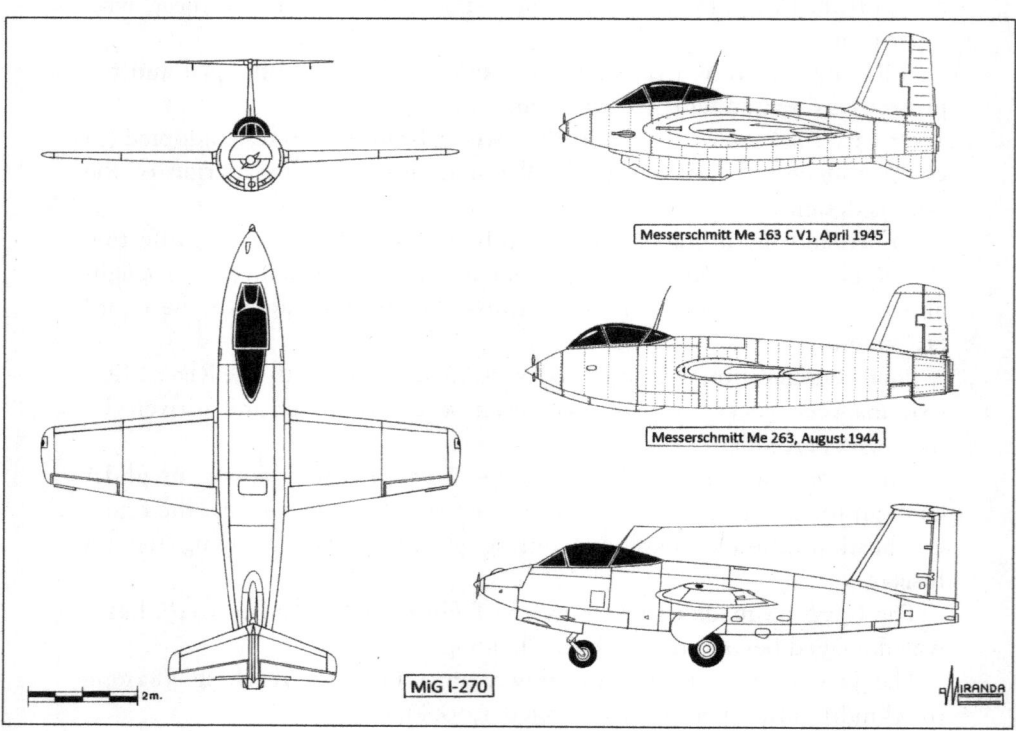

The project was reformed as I-162-I, with retractable tricycle landing gear and forward-swept wings, a new design based on the Heinkel He 162 B prototype, captured by the Allies at the Heinkel-Schwechat plant.

The I-162-I would be powered by an RD-2 MZV rocket engine, but it was soon found that the turbo-pump-drive electric generator was to be too weak to provide sufficient electrical power for the AI radar.

Early in 1947, the low reliability and heavy maintenance of the engine led the Lavochkin OKB to halt work on the I-162-I in favour of the MiG I-320 all-weather jet-fighter.

LAVOCHKIN I-162 TECHNICAL DATA: Wingspan: 29.3ft (8.96m). Length: 37.2ft (11.35m). Height: 11.9ft (3.62m). Wing surface: 314.4sq.ft (28.3sq.m). Take-off weight: 12,119lb (5,490kg).

LAVOCHKIN I-162-I TECHNICAL DATA: Wingspan: 30ft (9.14m). Length: 29.5ft (8.98m). Height: 11.7ft (3.56m).

As a result of the Junkers' technical interrogations in Dessau—particularly the vibration tests carried out on the wing of a Ju 287 in July 1944 and the monitoring of the flight behaviour of the prototype Ju 287 V1—the RLM ordered the cancellation of two projects with forward-swept wings. These were the Blohm und Voss P. 209-02 and Heinkel He 162 B. They also cancelled the construction of the prototypes Ju 287 V3 and Ju 287 V4 as they did not possess adequate technology to resolve the wing rigidity problem. The Soviets knew this and cancelled their own German projects that were reliant on the same unavailable technology.

In 1946 several wing planforms were wind-tunnel tested at TsAGI, as a result of which the OKB-256, under the leadership of Pavel Tsybin, developed three research aircrafts with different wings with the same surface area.

The first LL-1 prototype was built by the Beresnev OKB with straight wings and of wood/plywood construction.

It was flown in glider configuration by mid-1947, being towed to a launch altitude by a Tu-2.

The LL-1 made thirty high-speed diving trials powered by one Kartukov PRD-1500 solid-propellant rocket with 3,311lb (1,500kg) peak-thrust.

The glider wings were attached to the fuselage on a dynamic suspension, which allowed them to moderate the pressure on the wing and tail at the approach to the critical Mach number.

A typical dive would start between 16,400–23,000ft and 45–60 degrees until, at full speed, it was levelled out and the rocket fired.

The aircraft reached 656mph (1,050km/h-Mach 0.87) maximum speed.

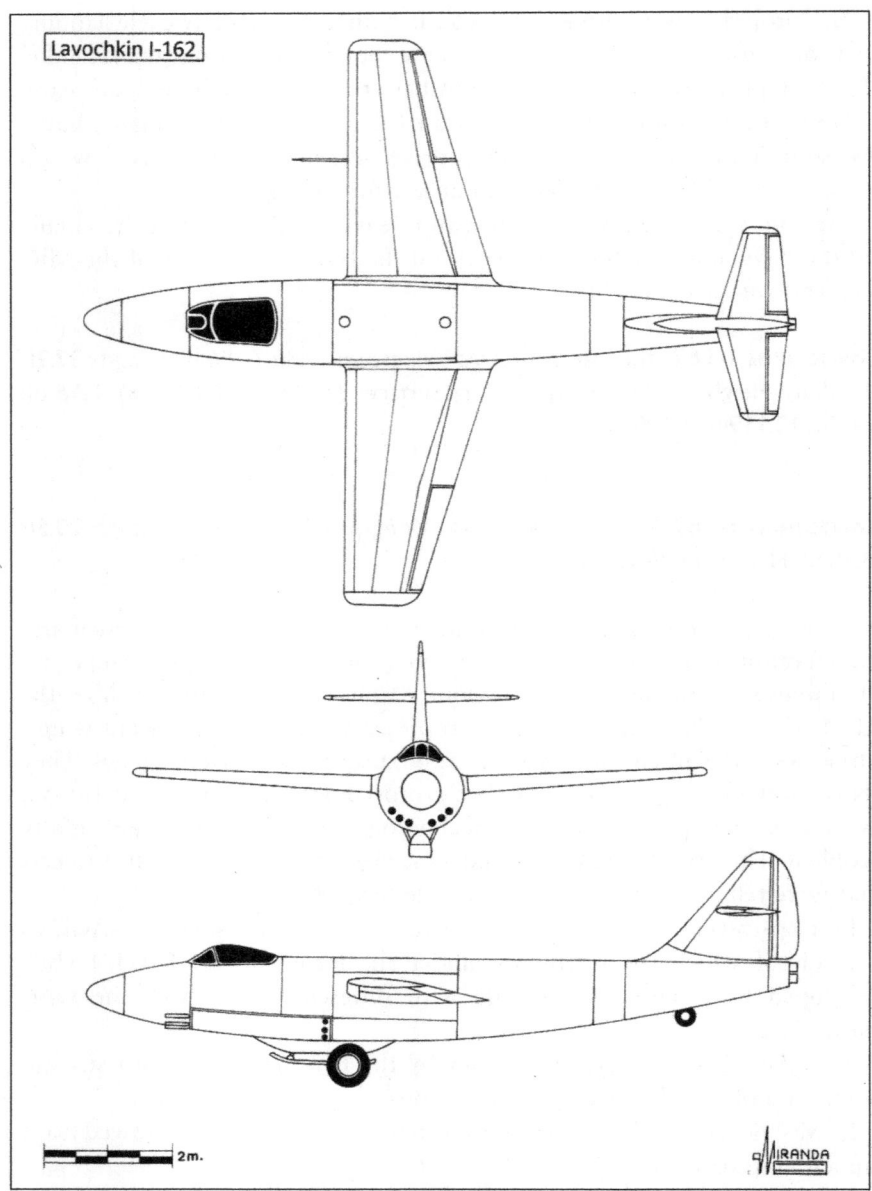

At the end of the year the prototype was refitted with 30-degree forward-swept wings to become the LL-3.

According to some authors, the prototype made more than a hundred flights reaching 746mph (1,200km/h-Mach 0.97).

Effects of aero-elastic divergence of the Duralumin wings was not noticed, but the TsAGI recommended the use of swept-back wings in

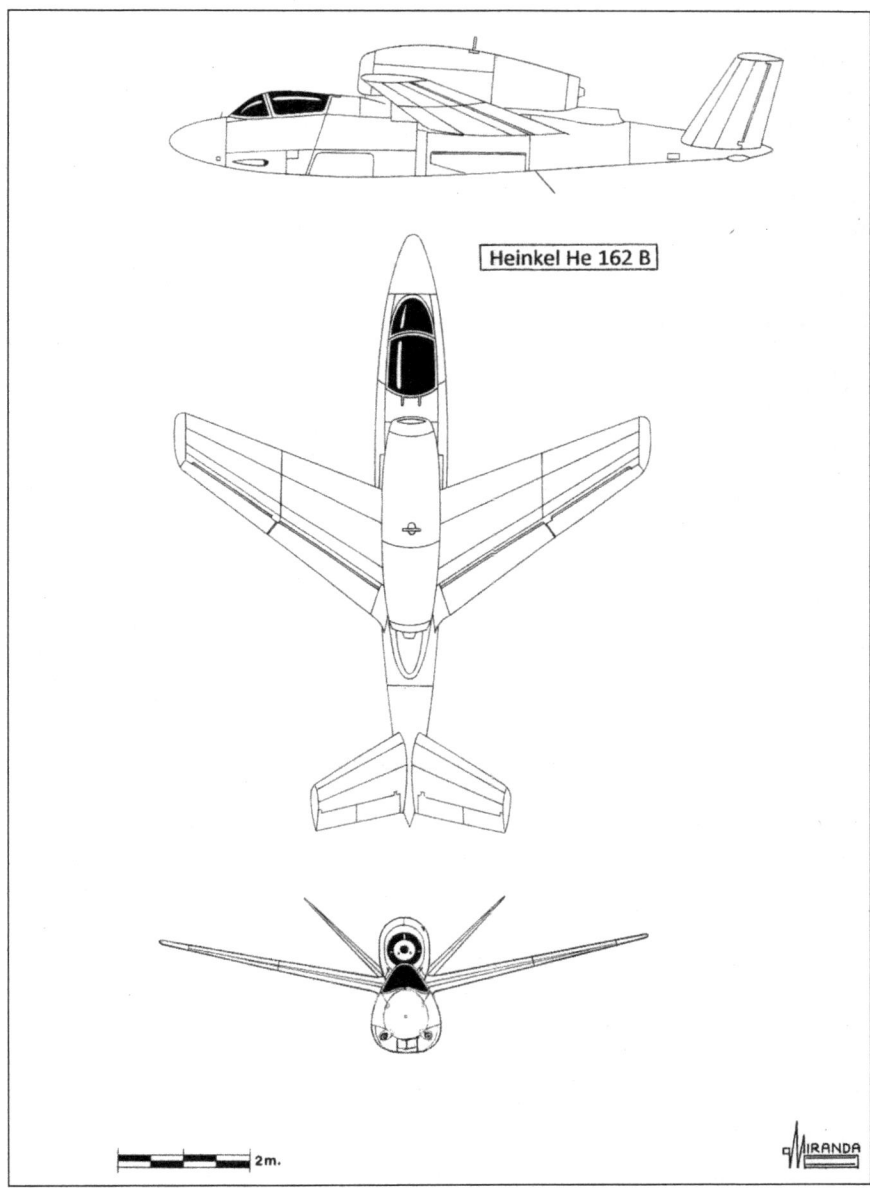

Heinkel He 162 B

the future Alekseyev 150 bomber, and also that the Junkers EF 131 V1 prototype did not exceed Mach 0.75 during flight tests.

On 31 July 1947, this aircraft experienced several problems with vibration during the second flight and could not be flown in the Tushino air display planned for 18 August. The project was cancelled on 21 June 1948.

A third Tsybin research plane, named LL-2, was planned to be built with 30 degrees swept-back wings, but the project was dropped in favour of the German DFS 346 transonic research rocket-plane, designed to reach 1,250mph (Mach 1.9).

TSYBIN LL-1 TECHNICAL DATA: Wingspan: 23.3ft (7.1m). Length: 29.4ft (8.98m). Height: 8ft (2.45m). Wing surface: 113.3sq.ft (10.2sq.m). Launch weight: 4,501lb (2,039kg).

TSYBIN LL-3 TECHNICAL DATA: Wingspan: 23.7ft (7.22m). Length: 29.4ft (8.98m). Height: 8ft (2.45m). Wing surface: 113.3sq.ft (10.2sq.m). Launch weight: 4,415lb (2,000kg).

When US troops seized the Siebel-Halle facilities in April 1945 they found the Mach-Projekt DFS 346 V1 prototype under construction.

It was built throughout of Duralumin alloy with 45-degree swept-back wings, T-tail plane and ejection-nose-cockpit.

In July 1945 the Siebel factory was transferred to Soviet control and moved in its entirety by train to the USSR, along with technical crews, to complete the DFS 346 development.

On 22 October 1946, the project was moved at Podberezhye, under the OKB-2 code name, and the prototype was completed. In autumn 1946 it was transferred to the TsAGI and used for wind tunnel tests.

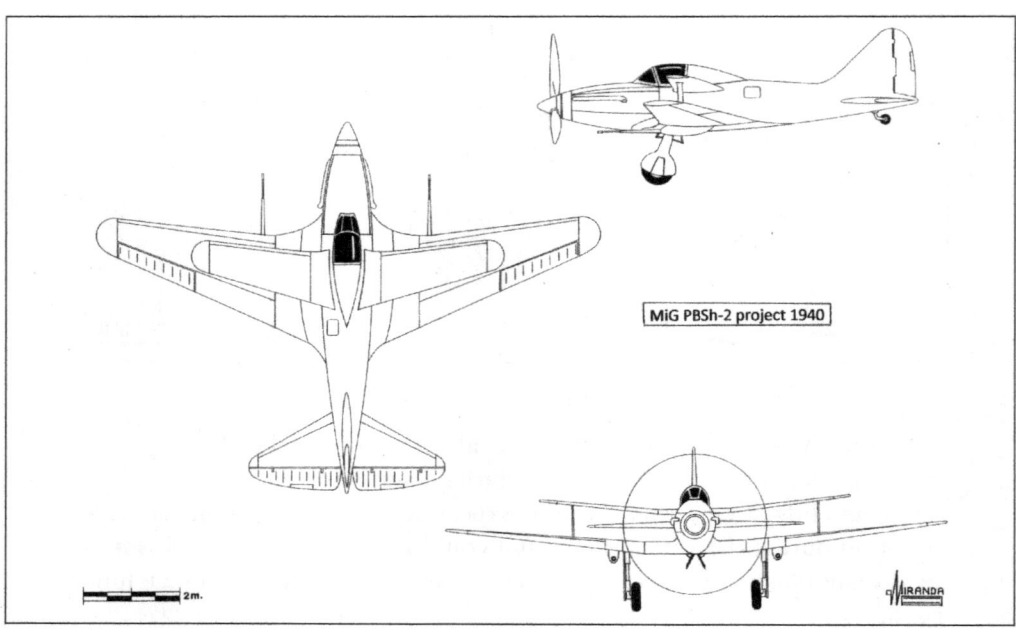

MiG PBSh-2 project 1940

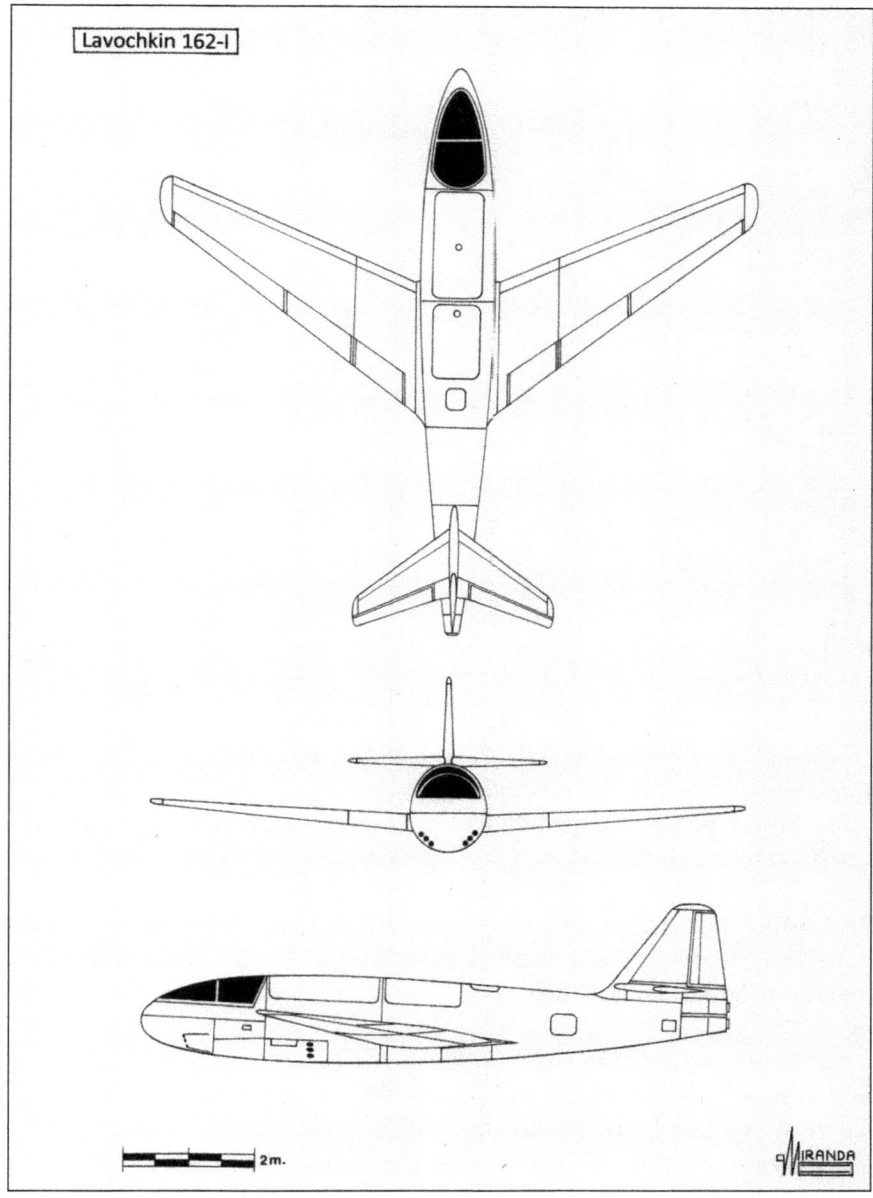

One glider prototype named DFS 346 P (Planer) was completed in 1947 incorporating several modifications suggested by the TsAGI. The fuselage was lengthened by 1.6m, the moving top of the tailfin was removed, the wingtips were modified, and wing fences were installed to delay the rearward migration of the centre of pressure during the transonic acceleration.

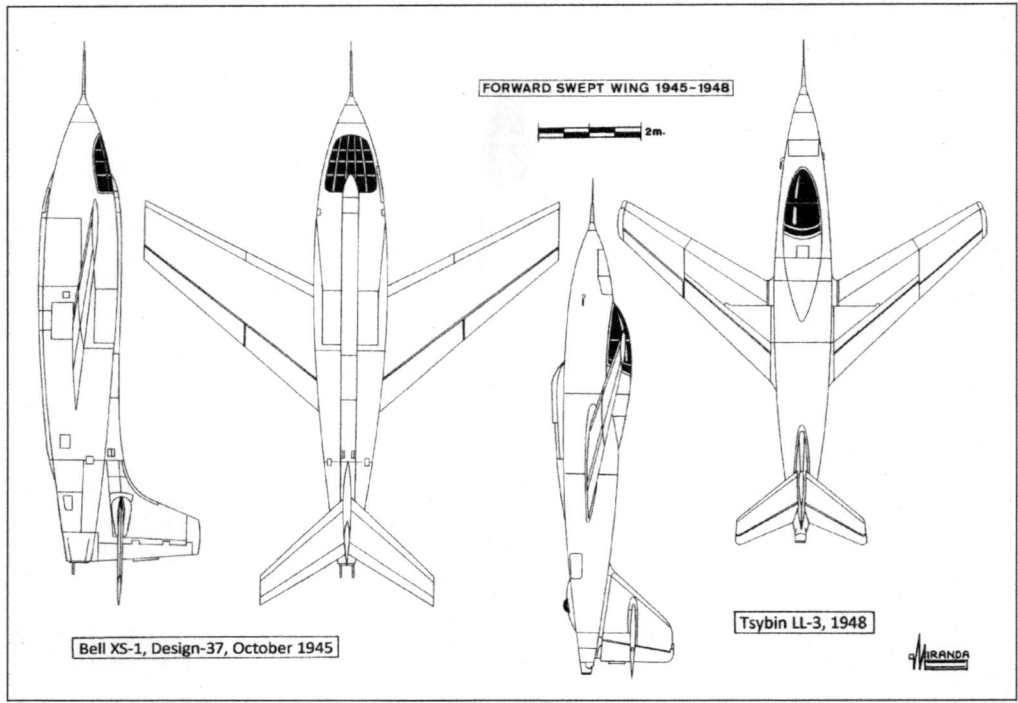

Although not outfitted with the rocket-motor, water ballast was added to simulate the weight of the propellants.

The prototype was successfully flown in several slow-speed gliding tests which led to the construction of three rocket-powered research aircrafts.

DFS 346 P TECHNICAL DATA: Wingspan: 29.52ft (9m). Length (without nose probe): 44ft (13.45m). Height: 11.6ft (3.54m). Wing surface: 211sq.ft (19.86sq.m). Launch weight: 4,812lb (2,179kg).

In the spring of 1947, the DFS 346 P was released at 30,500ft from under the starboard wing of the Boeing B-29-5-BW (42-6256) Ramp Tramp that had been captured by the Soviets near Vladivostok on 29 July 1944.

During the war, the VVS only used ninety-three Petlyakov Pe-8 heavy bombers, but Stalin understood that in a future confrontation with the United States it would be necessary to use long-range strategic bombers and made a formal request for Lend-Lease B-29s—without success.

The Tupolev OKB was tasked with developing its own comparable Tu-10, under the code name 'Project64', but in 1944 three Boeing B-29 bombers from 462 and 468 BG, based around Chengtu in China, were damaged by flak over Anshan, Omura and Kyushu. Their crews decided to divert to Vladivostok and the aircrafts were interned by the Soviets. Early in

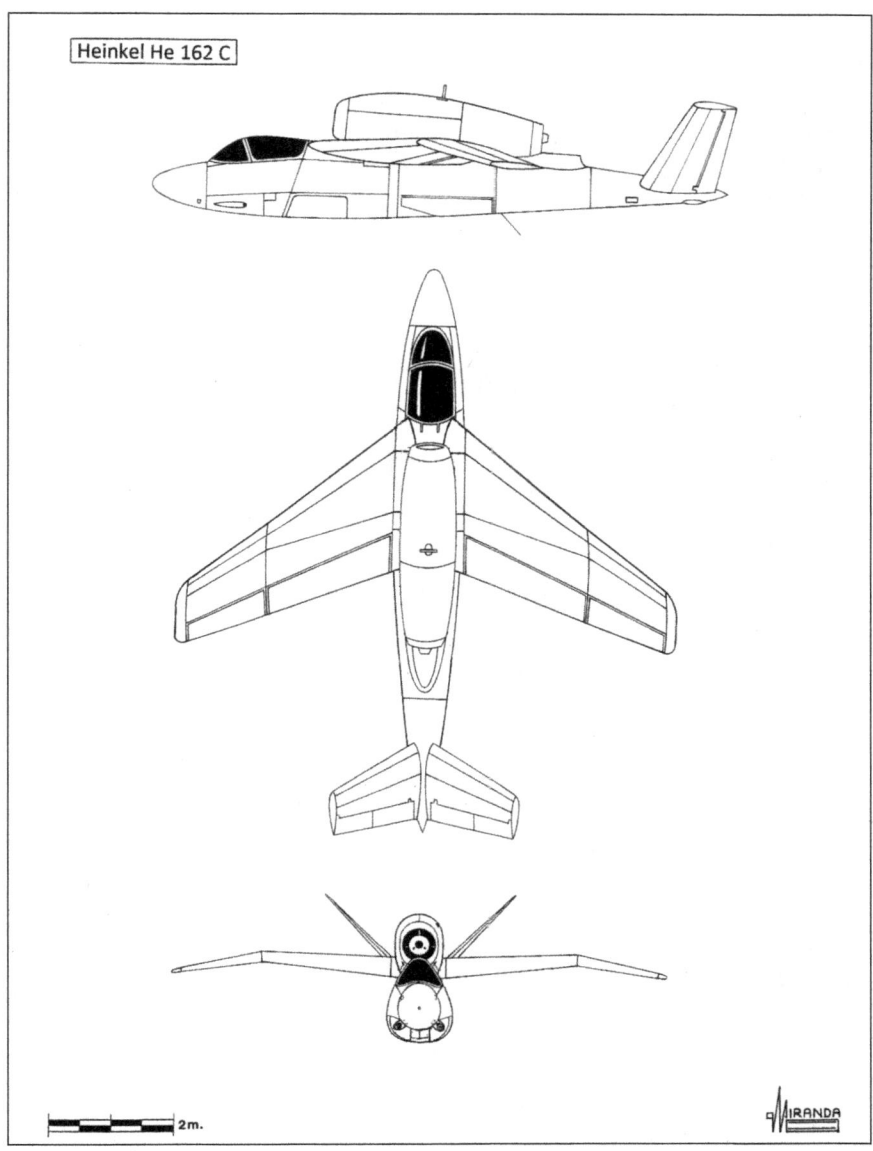

1945 a full-scale reverse-engineering program was started to produce B-29 copies powered by Soviet Shvetsov Ash-73 engines.

The first Tupolev Tu-4 strategic bomber was flown on 19 May 1947, and its existence was discovered that same year when an RB-29 spy plane on a reconnaissance mission overflew a Soviet airfield.

By 1952, 847 Soviet copies had been built. Engine and propeller failures were encountered throughout the bomber service life.

On 5 May 1949 the DFS 346-1 prototype was completed, with a dummy engine installed.

It was flown on 30 September, launched from 32,000ft in glider configuration and was damaged when landing at 193mph (310km/h).

The DFS 346-3 rocket-powered research plane was completed by mid-1951.

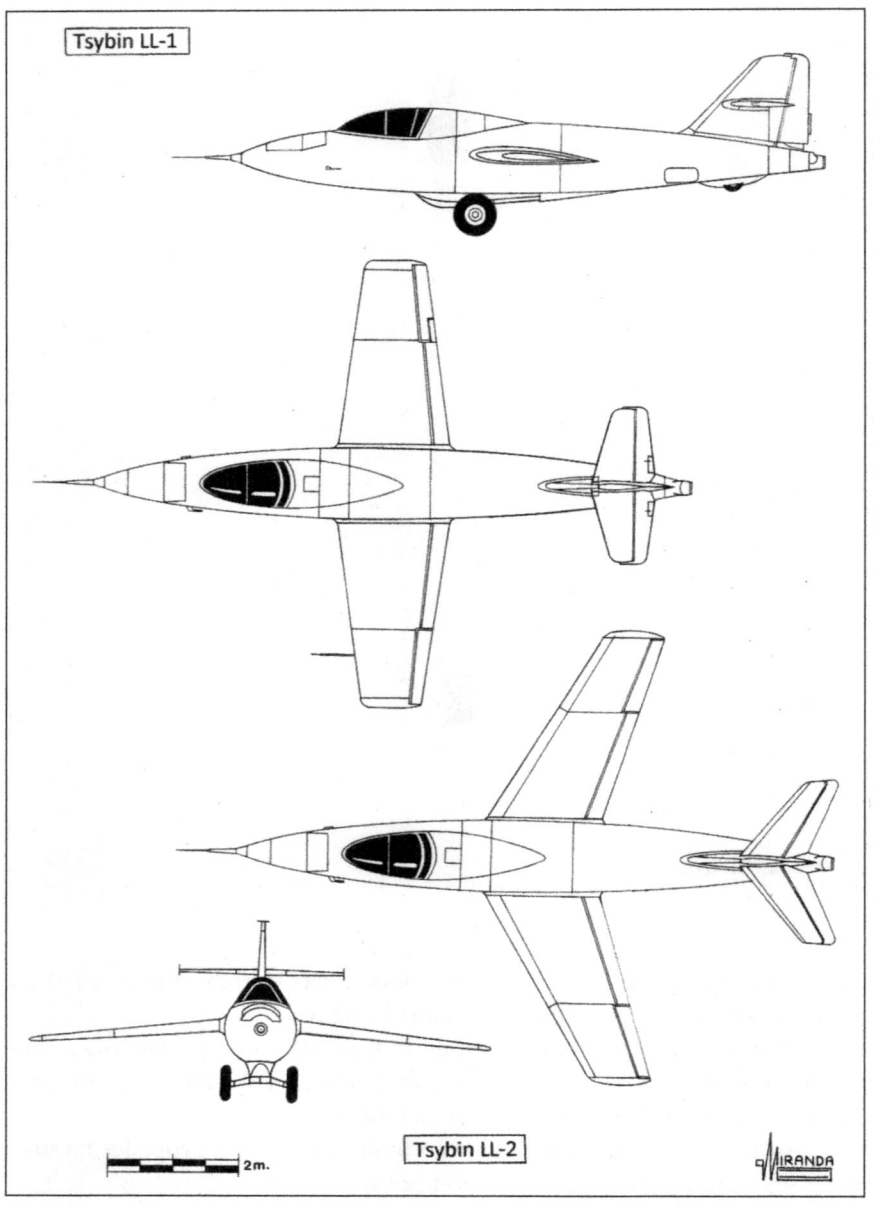

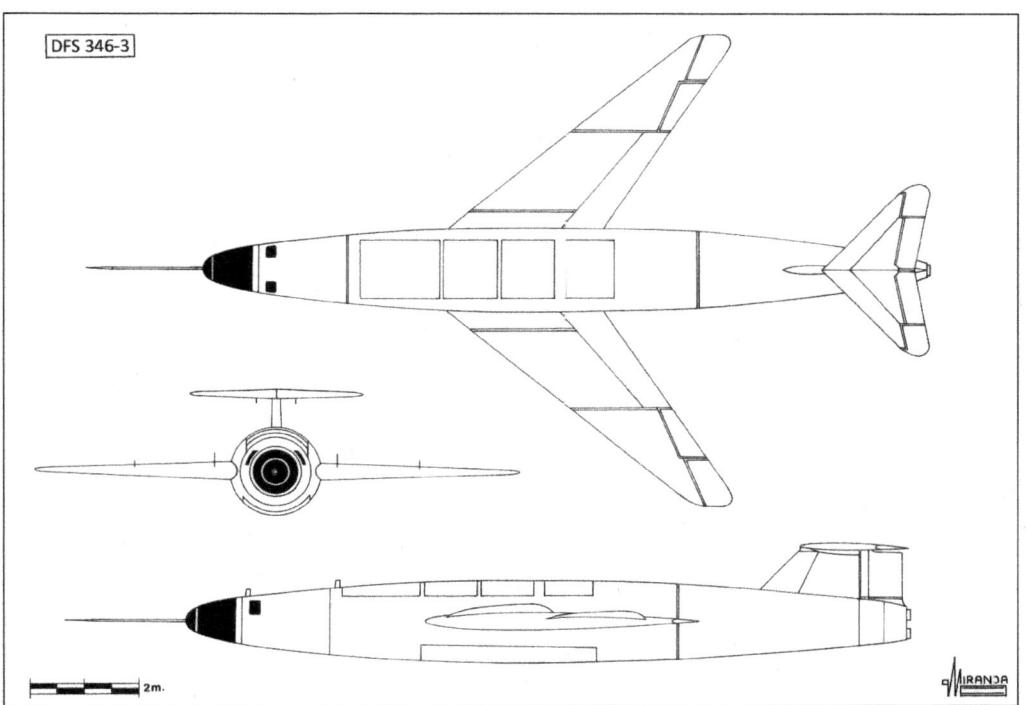

Meanwhile, the Junkers crews, who had worked on the OKB-1 at Uprawlentscheski Gorodok, had begun reconstructing one Walter HWK 109-509 C (called ZhRD-109-510 in the USSR) out of salvaged components.

On 13 August 1951, the DFS 346-3 performed the first powered flight launched from 30,500ft over Lukovici airfield.

The two combustion chambers worked as expected and the prototype quickly accelerated, reaching Mach 0.93.

During the second flight, performed on 14 September, flying at 590mph and 39,360ft, the aircraft did not respond to the controls and the pilot ejected at 21,000ft

After spending 55 million roubles, the crash of the prototype put an end to the program.

DFS 346-3 TECHNICAL DATA: Wingspan: 29.52ft (9m). Length (without nose probe): 44ft (13.45m). Height: 11.6ft (3.54m). Wing surface: 211sq.ft (19.86sq.m). Launch weight: 11,611lb (5,260kg).

In late 1946 TsAGI theorists concluded that, with the Jumo 004 turbojets available at the time, it would be necessary to use wings with a 45-degree

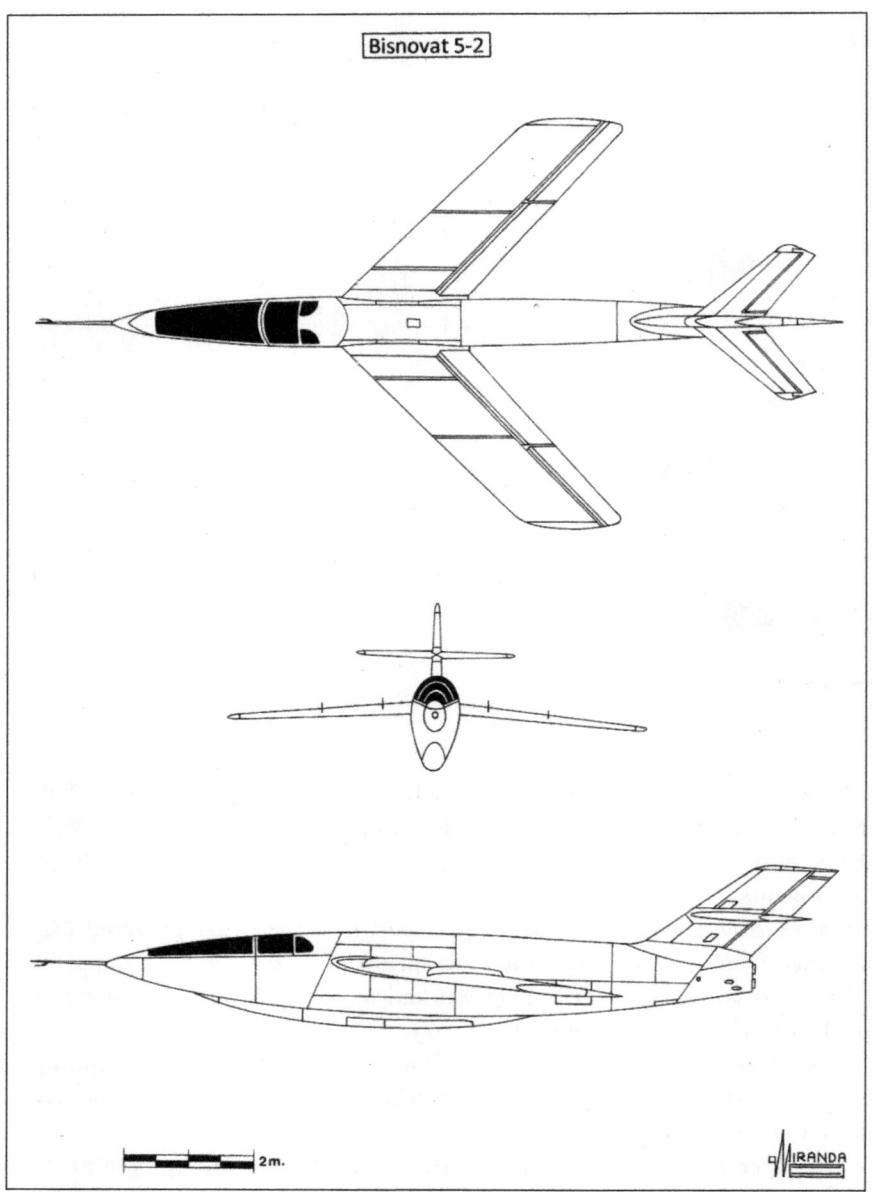

sweep to reach Mach 1, but the T-106 wind tunnel only allowed to test the new designs up to Mach 0.9.

It was necessary to create a new OKB under the leadership of M. R. Bisnovat, assigned to design a supersonic research aircraft, with constant chord, 45-degree swept-back wings and tailplane (based on those of Lavochkin la-160 project) and powered by one Dushkin RD-2 MZVF rocket-motor. The project was approved on 11 March 1947, under the 'Aircraft 5' code name.

On 14 July 1948, the prototype '5-1' was released (in glider configuration) from under the starboard wing of one Petlyakov Pe-8 LL heavy bomber.

The launch system was poorly designed, and the plane was damaged when it collided with the mothership at 23,000ft, and during the subsequent emergency landing.

During the second flight performed on 3 September 1948, the '5-1' proved to have poor longitudinal stability and was destroyed while landing at excessive speed on a primitive ventral skid.

In January 1949, the '5-2' prototype was tested in glider configuration. The rocket engine was mounted without the aircraft making a single powered flight.

The project was cancelled in June 1949.

BISNOVAT '5-2' TECHNICAL DATA: Wingspan: 21ft (6.4m). Length: 32.5ft (9.92m). Wing surface: 121.8sq.ft (11.3sq.m). Launch weight: 7,020lb (3,148kg). Estimated maximum speed: 750mph (1,200km/h), real attained speed: Mach 0.775.

24
Cold War

In 1952 the British RAF began using North American RB-45 reconnaissance planes on night missions over the USSR and Eastern Europe under the code name Operation Jiu-Jitsu.

The objective of these deep-penetration sorties of 1,600km, flying at 35,000ft and Mach 0.72, was to obtain SIGINT radar pictures of thirty potential targets for the Bomber Command.

During the night of 21/22 March, an RB-45 flew over Berlin and East Germany to test the Soviet defences.

On 17/18 April three RB-45 spy planes based at RAF Sculthorpe entered Soviet airspace, exploring three routes of penetration and taking radar pictures of airfields and anti-aircraft defences.

The Northern route overflew Kaliningrad and Tallinn, the Central route Warsaw and Belorussia, the Southern route Prague, Krakow, Kiev and Kharkov.

On 18/19 December four RB-45s repeated the mission. They were tracked by Soviet radars and some night fighters tried to intercept them without success.

On 15 October 1952, one USAF bomber Boeing B-47B, based at Eielson AFB, Alaska, was fitted with K-17 and K-38 cameras and overflying the airfields of Ambarchik, Anadyr and Providenya in Northeast Siberia and Chukotskii Peninsula to determine the operational status of Soviet bases.

In 1953 a British bomber Canberra B2 (WH726) was modified with the installation of a K-30 Perkin-Elmer camera in the bomb bay.

In August, as part of Operation ROBIN, the plane took off from Giebelstadt, West Germany, overflying Kiev, Kharkov and Stalingrad at 46,000–48,000ft. It was unsuccessfully attacked by fifteen MiG-17 fighters.

At that time the MiG-17 F could reach 46,000ft in 6.3 minutes, but at that altitude the Canberra was faster, and the MiG could not achieve interception.

After the Canberra managed to photograph the missile test facility at Kapustin Yar, flying at 48,500ft, it was again attacked and damaged by Soviet fighters, although it managed to land safely in Iran.

The MiG-17 F could reach 54,500ft (16,600m) if it had enough time, being able to intercept the Canberra over Kapustin Yar. But at that altitude the Soviet fighter could only manoeuvre to make a single attack.

On 19 March 1954, to counter the threat, the Council of Ministers ordered the development of a new Mach 2 clear-weather interceptor, with 65,600ft (20,000m) ceiling.

The MiG bureau proposed two basic configurations: swept-wing and delta-wing, powered by one Tumansky turbojet type AM-9B or AM-11.

The delta-wing prototype, named Ye-4 (Yedinitsa-single unit), was flown on 16 June 1955, and its development continued with the Ye-5 and Ye-6 until reaching production phase as MiG-21.

The swept-wing prototype Ye-2 flew on 14 February 1955, reaching 1,920km/h and 62,300ft (19,000m) ceiling, powered by one AM-9B turbojet rated at 3,250kg thrust with afterburner.

But these performances were considered insufficient, and the project was modified as a mixed-power, short-range point-defence interceptor, under the code name MiG Ye-50.

To prove the concept, three prototypes were built, powered by one Tumansky AM-9 turbojet rated at 3,800kg with afterburner and one Dushkin S-155 bi-propellant rocket-motor with 1,300kg peak-thrust at sea level and 1,600kg at high altitude.

The Ye-50/1 flew on 9 January 1956, but it was damaged beyond repair in a rough landing on 14 July 1956.

The Ye-50/2 attained Mach 2.33 and 84,000ft (25,600m) ceiling on 17 June 1957, and the construction of a pre-production batch of twenty aircraft was ordered, under the code name Ye-50A.

The new fighter was expected to reach 89,216ft (27,200m) ceiling powered by one AM-11 turbojet and one R11E-300 rocket-motor, but the project was cancelled following the destruction of the Ye-50/3 caused by the rocket explosion on 8 August 1957.

In March 1955 the MiG-19 P (Farmer B) entered service as a standard all-weather interceptor for the Soviet Air Defence Command (PVO), the Soviet Air Force (VVS) and the Soviet Naval Air Arm (AV-MF).

Due to the high fuel consumption of their afterburners the MiG-19 P had to use two 540l drop tanks on its underwing pylons.

With lower performances than the MiG-19 S (1,370km/h top speed and 17,600m ceiling) and unreliable short-ranged RP-1 Izumrud-1 (Scan Odd) radar, the MiG-19 P proved unable to defend Soviet air space when the first Lockheed U-2 overflew the Soviet Baltic coast, Leningrad, Balbasovo and Warsaw at 70,000ft (21,340m).

Between 4 July 1956 and 1 May 1960, the U-2 spy planes carried out twenty-six overflights, photographing about 15 per cent of the Soviet Union, resulting in 5,500 intelligence reports.

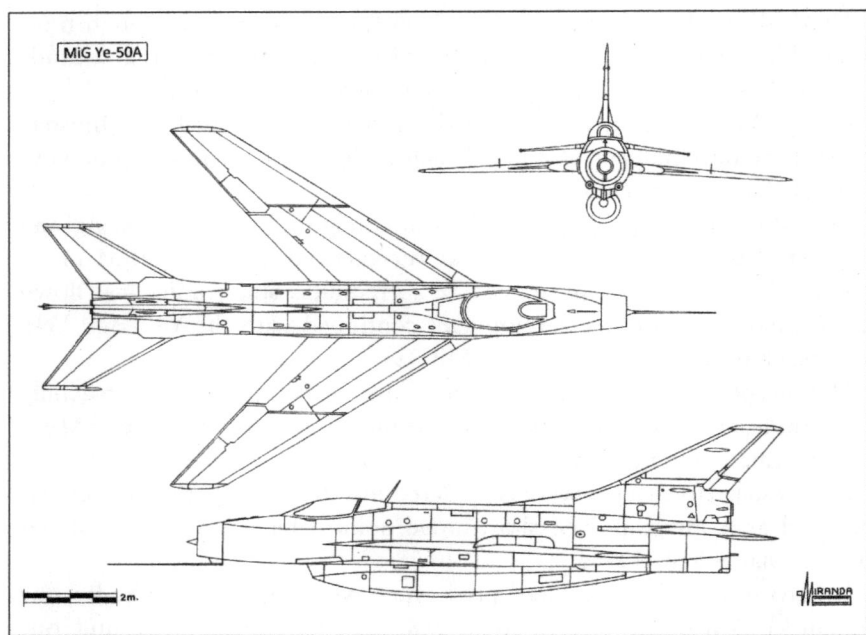

During this time the U-2s gained valuable information about the Soviet submarine production on Leningrad shipyards, the number of Mya-4 Bison strategic bombers that were operational, the SA-1 anti-aircraft missile sites around Moscow, the Fili Airframe Plant where the Bison bombers were built, the Kaliningrad missile plant, the Khimki rocket-engine plant, the Soviet naval facilities in Kerch, Simferopol, Severomorsk, Olenegorsk, Grozny, Monchegorsk and Odessa, the Ramenskoye bomber arsenal and nine bomber bases in the Western USSR, the Kapustin Yar missile test range, the atomic facilities in Tomsk and Krasnoyarsk, the Semipalatinsk nuclear test site, the aircraft factories in Omsk and Novosibirsk, the industrial facilities in Stalinsk and Kuznetsk, the uranium concentration plants in Alma Ata, Kadzhi-Say and Bystrovka, the tracking radar station at Sary Shagan and the Tyuratam ICBM test site.

The MiG-19 pilots performed snap-up attacks applying full throttle to the afterburners, trading speed for altitude in the hope of getting some hits on the U-2.

In this manoeuvre, ground-based radar operators would direct the fighter along the same flight path as the U-2, flying more than 10,000ft above him.

At 70,000ft altitude the MiG was completely out of control, its small wings and control surfaces provided insufficient lift to maintain the aircraft stability. The fighter reached the apex of the zoom climb and then fell away toward the earth.

These attempts demonstrated the Soviet's ability to track the U-2, along with their inability to intercept it.

In an attempt to improve the behaviour at high altitudes of the MiG-19S, to counter the U-2 overflights, one aircraft was modified, increasing its wing surface by 2sq.m. To reduce weight, they also removed some equipment: RV-2 radio altimeter, wing-mounted cannons, wing pylons, brake parachute, pilot armour, signal flare launcher, radar-warning receiver and fire extinguisher.

The prototype, named MiG-19 SV, was powered by two RD-9BF-2 experimental uprated turbojets, with 3,296kg thrust each and turbine temperature increased to 730°C.

Their afterburners were also modified, causing critical heating in the rear fuselage structure, and reducing engine reliability.

These modifications increased the ceiling by 700m but pushed the engines to their limit.

On 6 December 1956, the prototype reached 20,740m and 1,572km/h but it could not manoeuvre at such altitudes.

In an effort to increase the manoeuvrability at 18,000–20,000m, the prototype wingspan and area were enlarged by fitting an extended leading edge outboard of the boundary layer fence. In 1955 an aerodynamic solution inspired by the dogtooth wings of the Swedish fighter SAAB J29 E was built.

The aircraft, redesignated MiG-19 SVK, was flown on 29 April 1957, reaching only 19,100m ceiling (rather than the anticipated 21,740m) due to the excessive weight of the modified wing.

The basic MiG-19 airframe had reached its limit and the only option of the MiG OKB was to return to the times of mixed propulsion.

But after the bad experience suffered with the rocket explosion of the Ye-50/3 it became necessary to use a jettisonable ventral pod, housing a liquid-fuel rocket booster.

The prototype was one MiG-19 S, renamed MiG-19 SU (SM-50) that flew at the end of December 1957 powered by two RD-9BM turbojets with 3,200kg thrust each and one U-19/SZ-20M rocket rated at 3,000kg thrust.

Early in 1958 the SM-50 reached 24,500m ceiling and 1,800km/h top speed, its rate of climb was 120m per second, but only when the fuel cells Nos. 3 and 4 were removed. The flight time was reduced to just 11 minutes.

The hardest part of the U-2 interception was to maintain the correct trajectory since the booster required a g-load to operate.

Accurate ground guidance was necessary and the new Kaskad command guidance relay was developed to indicate to the pilot the interception trajectory and the most appropriate time for rocket ignition.

But the Kaskad system never functioned properly and only five MiG-19 SU fighters were manufactured before the cancellation of the SM-50 project.

Also in December 1957, two production MiG-19P fighters were modified as MiG-19 PU (SM-51).

This prototype was powered by two RD-9BF turbojets and one U-19D/RU-013 booster.

The new rocket engine had the same maximum thrust as the U-19 but could vary between 1,300 and 3,000kg and was designed for use in five missions.

The SM-51 prototype was flown early in 1958, reaching 24,000m ceiling and 1,930km/h top speed but, like the SM-50, it could stay at high-altitudes only briefly and the semi-active radar homing AA-1 missiles needed to track the target for a considerable time.

The second prototype, SM-52P, was fitted with Uragan-1 radar, SRD-5A Baza-6 rangefinder and Svod LORAN equipment that automatically determined the range and azimuth with respect to a ground beacon.

At the end of 1958 one production MiG-19S fighter was modified as an all-weather, high-altitude mixed-power interceptor, under the code name MiG SM-12 PMU.

The prototype was powered by two Sorokin R3M-26 turbojets rated at 3,800kg thrust each and one U-19D rocket pack.

In January 1959 the SM-12 reached 24,000m ceiling and Mach 1.69 top speed carrying two beam-riding AA-1 missiles, TSD-30 radar, Vozdookh-1 ground guidance system and Lazoor command link system.

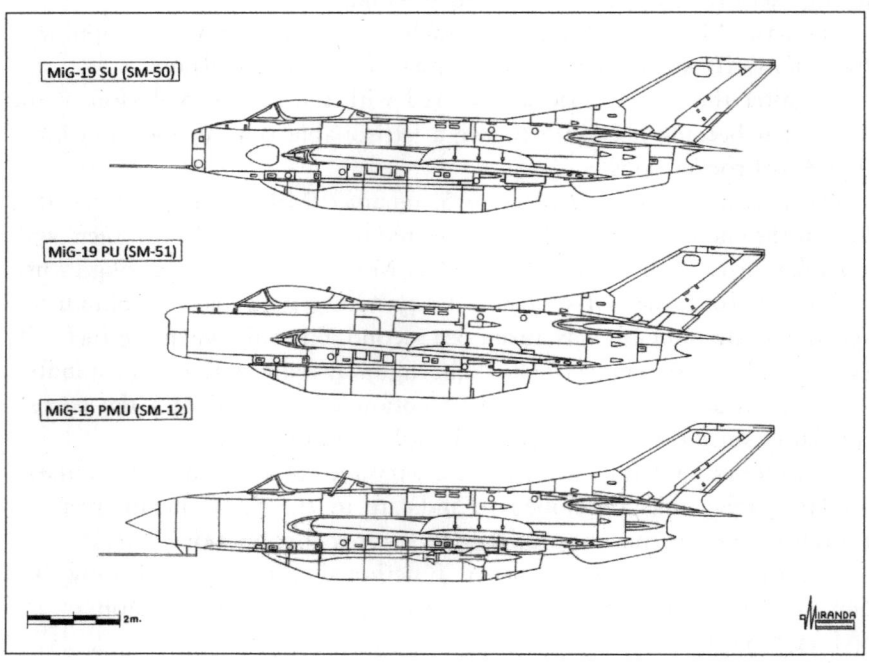

25

American Rocket-Fighters

In July 1944 RAF Fighter Command launched a desperate attack against the new German cruise missiles V-1, to face the 'robot offensive' with their high performance interceptors P-51 Mustang Mk. III.

The aerodynamic drag of the V-1 airframe was higher than anticipated due to low standards of manufacturing, decreasing from projected 900km/h (559mph) to the real 640km/h (398mph). Fortunately for the Allies this made the new missile susceptible to being intercepted by conventional fighters, but the game was dangerous.

It was necessary to modify the fighters to make them fast enough to intercept the V-1, the British Mustangs used the new aviation fuel '150 grade trimethylpentane' produced in the USA and changed their engine exhaust by those of the Spitfires that generated less drag. Rearview mirrors and armour plates were also stripped. Even the camouflage paint was removed to reduce drag and gain speed on some aircraft.

The appearance in combat over the Reich of the German swept-wing fighters Messerschmitt Me 163 and Me 262 took the American escort fighters by surprise.

The Germans used an unknown technique to avoid the undesirable wingtip stall phenomena experienced in November 1943 during flight tests of the Curtiss XP-55. The Allies did not know that the solution was to use a new type of automatic leading-edge slat, until technicians were able to examine the first Messerschmitt Me 262 captured in 1945.

The only way for a Mustang to compete with the 870km/h (541mph) of a Me 262 A-1 or the 960km/h (597mph) of a Me 163 B-1 was by adopting a mixed power plant.

In the summer of 1944, several wrecked German V-1 missiles were flown from Great Britain to the United States. The first parts arrived at Wright Field where the scientist 'reverse engineered' the Argus As 109-014 pulsejet and rebuilt it as Ford PJ-31 F-1.

The American version, producing 405kg (891lb) of thrust, was used to propel the JB-2 cruise missile based in the V-1 airframe.

In late 1945, one P-51 D-NA was fitted with two Ford pulsejets below the wings.

The flying tests revealed the same problems that forced the Germans to cancel the Messerschmitt Me 328 project: the pulsejets losing power very quickly above 2,744m (9,000ft) with high fuel consumption, and the operation of two pulsejets could not be synchronised in flight as the pilot lacked effective control over the pressurised fuel system. The vibrations

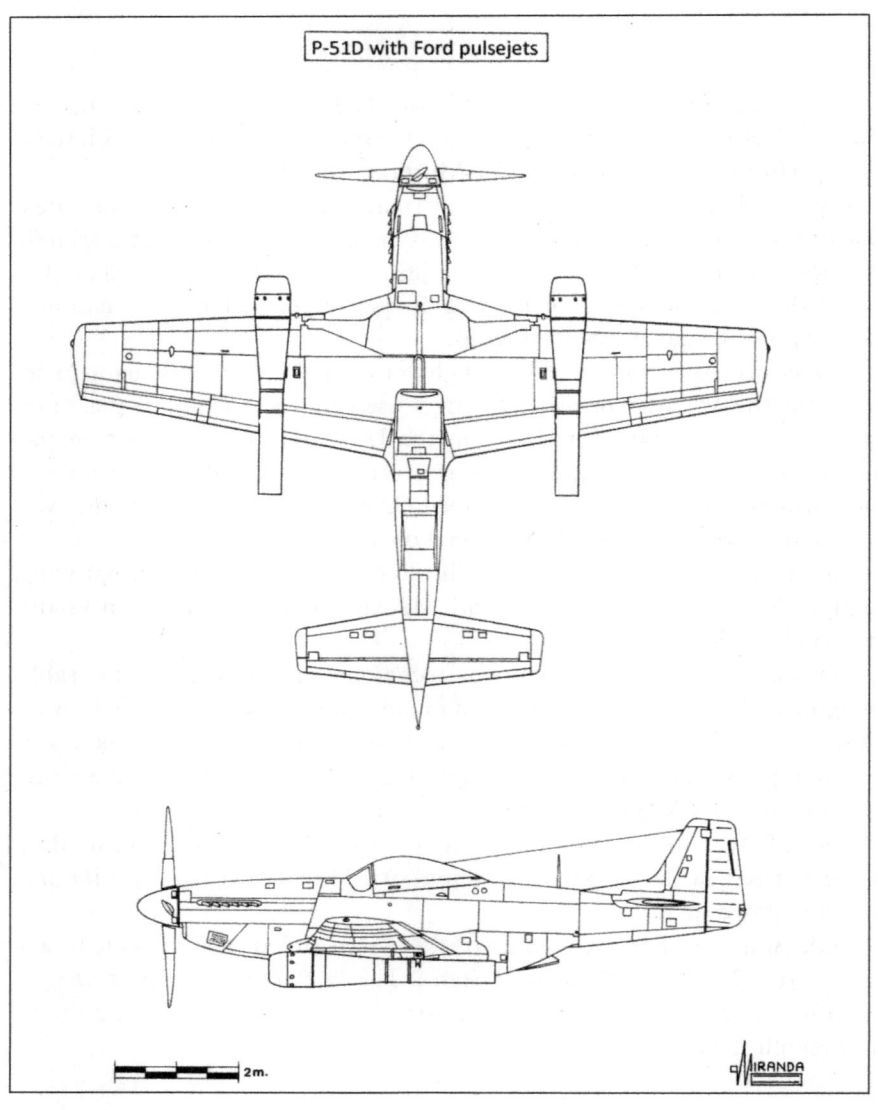

they generated damaged the aircraft structure and it soon became evident that they were a dead end.

Because of these limitations the idea was dropped in 1946.

To improve the performance of the Mustang, America was forced to consider the use of ramjets.

In early 1946, two Marquardt XRJ-30-MA ramjets, with 50.8cm (20-in) of diameter, were installed on the wingtips of the F-51D c/n 44-63528.

During the flying tests the aircraft reached 772km/h (480mph), experiencing synchronisation problems and dangerous directional instability.

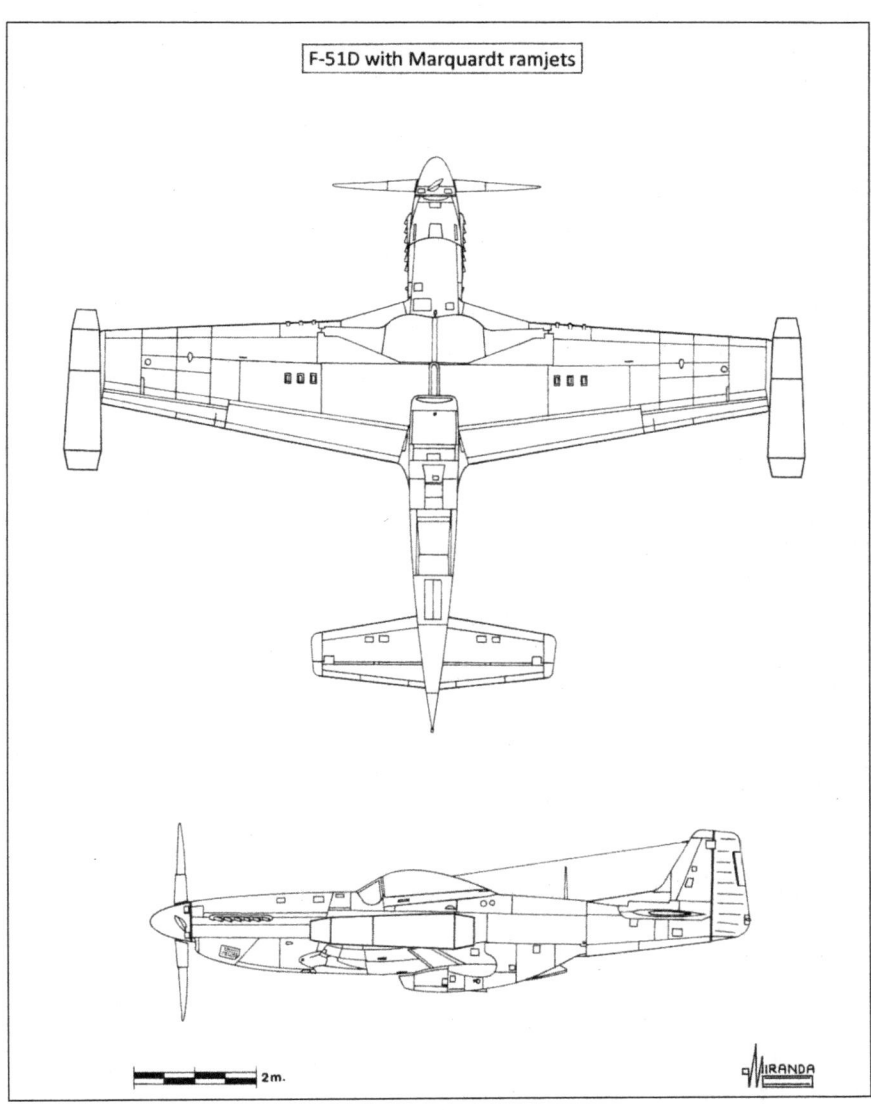

F-51D with Marquardt ramjets

On 19 August 1948, one of the ramjets exploded, lateral control with asymmetric thrust was nearly impossible and the pilot successfully bailed out.

Anticipating the emergence of a second generation of faster German V-1 missiles, propelled by the new Argus As 109-044 pulsejet, North American considered using auxiliary rockets to provide 'flash performance' to the P-51 fighters then in service.

In the spring of 1945, one Aerojet 1.3K 'super-performance' non-throttleable rocket boost was installed in the P-51 D-25-NA c/n 44-73099.

The rocket engine, rated at 589kg (1,300lb) peak-thrust, used as fuel a mixture of 65 per cent monomethylamine and 35 per cent furfuryl alcohol, the oxidant was RFNA nitric acid. Both propellants were carried in two non-jettisonable underwing tanks of 285l each, the system was pressurised by means of nitrogen bottles compressed at 2,000psi.

The Aerojet rocket was mounted at the aft end of the radiator exit duct, but the weight of the installation had a very undesirable effect on the stability and handling characteristics of the aircraft.

On 23 April 1945 lack of experience with the new technology almost caused an accident during the first flight; an oxidant leak in the outlet line produced extremely toxic and corrosive vapours in the cockpit and the pilot nearly became unconscious.

In the next test, a malfunction of the propellant valves caused the accidental auto-ignition of the rocket during the preflight pressure checks. The exhaust was deflected into the fuselage through the tail-wheel housing, causing heavy damage to the airframe.

The panic caused by kamikaze attacks and the possibility of the Japanese starting to use suicide versions of the V-1 German missile prevented the cancellation of the 'flash performance' project and the USAAF Proof Division decided to continue rocket-powered flight tests with a new aircraft.

In June 1945 one Aerojet rocket engine, rated at 690lb (312kg) was installed in the P-51 D-25 c/n 44-74050.

The aircraft performed four flights at 1,524m (5,000ft), 3,048m (10,000ft) and 6,097m (20,000ft) reaching a maximum speed of 733km/h (456mph), but the USAAF determined that the danger inherent in the handling of nitric acid was excessive and acid-aniline rockets were not operationally suitable in any aircraft operation.

The test programme was terminated on 1 March 1946.

The Northrop N-1M was a technology demonstrator aircraft built in the early 1940s to prove that a 'flying wing' would fly.

The prototype was a 45 per cent scaled-down version of the Northrop N-1 medium bomber project. It was built in wood/plywood and powered by two 65hp Lycoming 0-146 engines.

American Rocket-Fighters

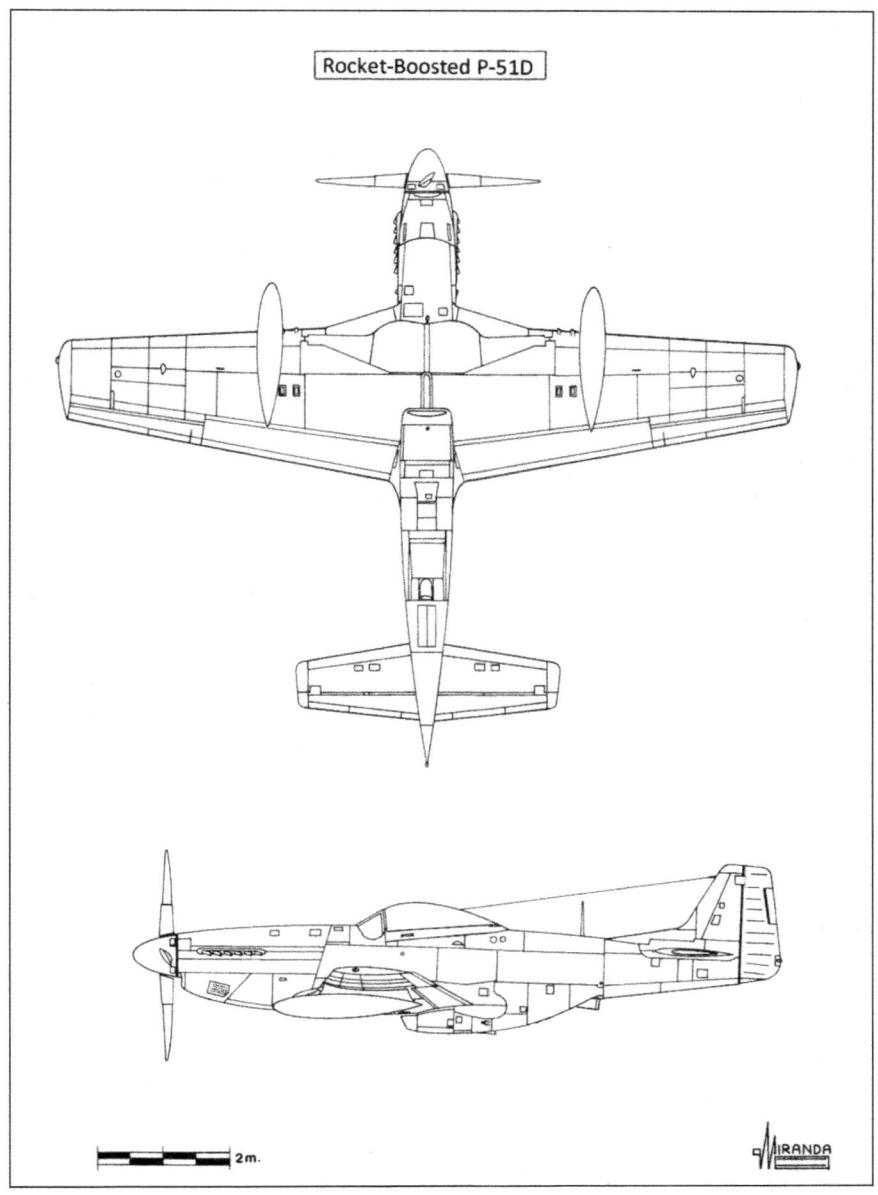

Rocket-Boosted P-51D

The N-1M had drooped wingtips to improve directional stability, and elevons which combined the functions of elevators and ailerons.

The wing sweep could be varied (on the ground) from 6 to 12 degrees, and the wingtips anhedral angle from 0 to 30 degrees.

Between July 1940 and December 1941 the prototype conducted 200 flying tests that showed that in a gentle dive, the Northrop flying wing would accelerate at a much faster rate than any other contemporary aircraft.

During testing it was determined that the wings with a 30-degree sweep, and the wingtips with 0 degrees anhedral, were the most effective aerodynamic configuration.

Northrop N-1M technical data: Wingspan: 11.80m (38.7ft). Length: 5.47m (18ft). Height: 1.50m (4.9ft). Wing area: 20.10sq.m (223sq.ft). Maximum weight: 1,769kg (3,905lb). Maximum speed: 232km/h (373mph). Ceiling: 1,200m (3,936ft). Range: 480km (772 miles).

In September 1942 John Northrop proposed to the US Army Air Force the construction of the MX-322, a rocket-powered point-defence interceptor with flying-wing configuration and prone pilot, with glass 'bubble' nose. The aircraft would be powered by an Aerojet XCAL R-2000 A-1 bi-propellant rocket-engine, with 906kg (2,000lb) peak-thrust, and was theoretically capable of reaching an altitude of 12,000m (39,360ft) and a maximum speed of 865km/h (538mph).

The prone position would permit greater manoeuvring with G-forces than a conventionally seated pilot and save the drag generated by a conventional windshield/canopy ensemble.

The proposed armament was four wing-mounted 0.50 cal. Browning M-2 heavy machine guns, with 250 rounds per gun.

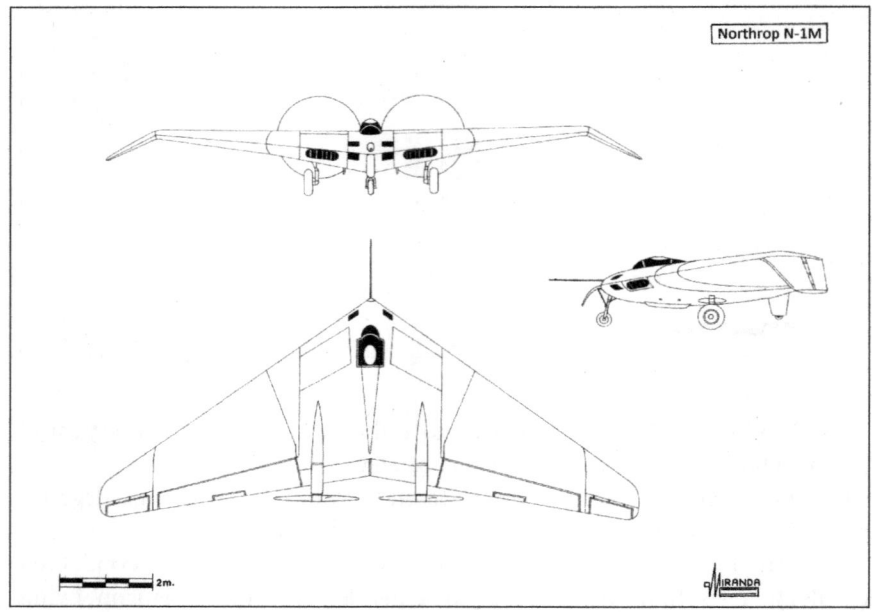
Northrop N-1M

The airframe would be built in welded magnesium alloy and included 20mm-thick plates angled at 45 degrees to provide armoured protection for the propellant tanks.

In many published reports the armoured leading edge was misinterpreted as a collision-tactics ramming device and the XP-79 was erroneously called 'Flying Ram'.

The mock-up was initially equipped with a fixed skid and the original blueprints include a modified landing gear with two retractable skids, but at a later stage of design (MX-365) it was again replaced by four retractable legs with wheels in July 1943.

The XP-79 should use two GALCIT Jet Assisted Take Off solid-fuel rockets, with 453kg (1,000lb) peak-thrust each.

The Aerojet engine employed two primary combustion chambers, with 339kg (748lb) peak-thrust each, and two auxiliary chambers with 113kg (250lb) each.

The whole ensemble, called 'Rotojet', rotated to generate propellant pumping action through centrifugal force, but the excessive complexity of the mechanism caused considerable delays in availability of the engine and the XP-79 was cancelled in September 1944.

XP-79 TECHNICAL DATA: Wingspan: 10.90m (35.7ft). Length: 3.65m (12ft). Height: 1.05m (3.44ft). Wing area: 25.82sq.m (287sq.ft). Maximum weight: 3,115kg (6,876lb). Estimated maximum speed: 865km/h (538 miles). Ceiling: 12,200m (40,000ft).

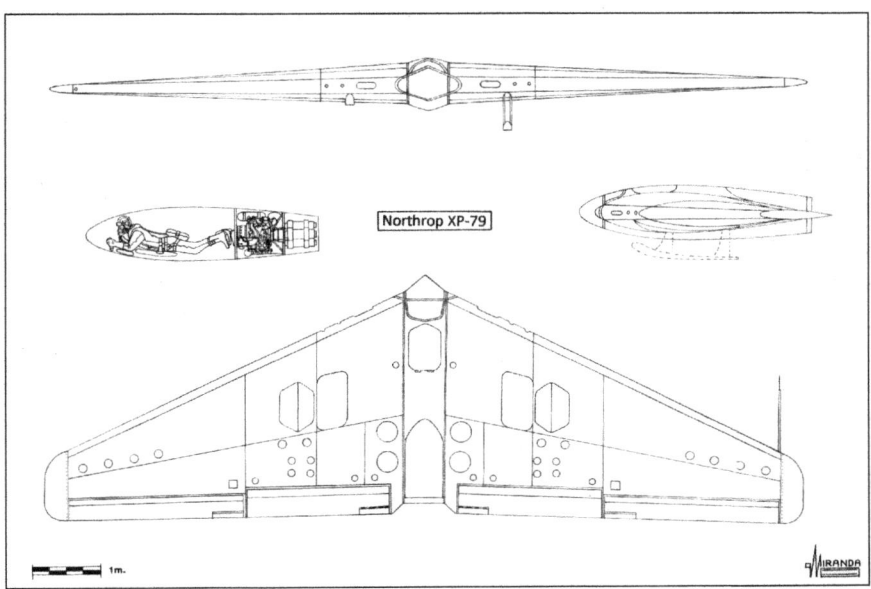

On 12 January 1943 Northrop-Maywood was authorised to build three prototypes, but in March the USAAF decided to modify the third airframe (43-52437) as XP-79B powered by two Westinghouse 19 B turbojets.

The wingspan of the new model was reduced by 61cm (24in) and the overall length is increased by 23cm (9in).

The wing trailing edge had elevators, flaperons and split decelerons, the foot pedals were connected to air valves located in ducts on the wingtips that opened the split surfaces to provide a braking effect, causing the aircraft to turn.

Following the accident suffered by demonstrator N-9M-1 on 19 May 1943, the USAAF ordered the installation of a pair of large vertical stabilisers to prevent flat spin.

The XP-79B was destroyed during its first flying test on 12 September 1945 and the project was cancelled in January 1946.

XP-79B TECHNICAL DATA: Wingspan: 11.58m (38ft). Length: 4.26m (14ft). Height: 2.13m (7ft). Wing area: 25.83sq.m (287sq.ft). Maximum weight: 3,933kg (8,682lb). Estimated maximum speed: 880km/h (547mph). Ceiling: 12,000m (39,360ft). Range: 480km (298 miles). Power plant: two Westinghouse 19 B (XJ 30) turbojets with 618kg (1,364lb) thrust each.

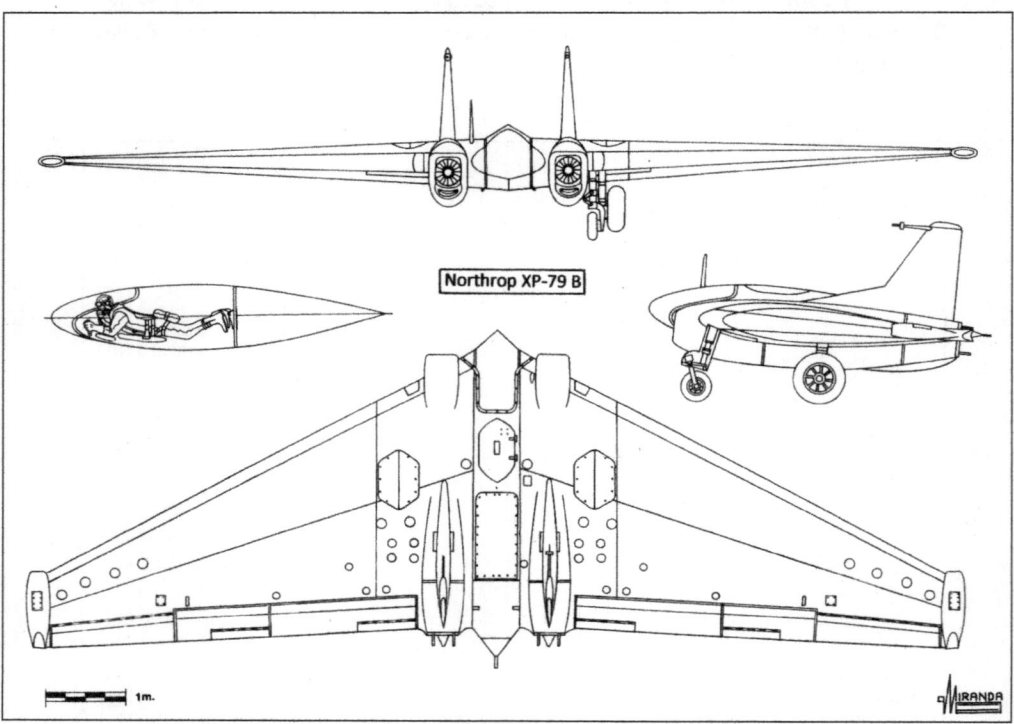
Northrop XP-79 B

In January 1943, the Air Material Command ordered the construction of three gliders to test the XP-79 concept.

The MX-334/I was used in aerodynamic tests in the NACA-Langley wind tunnel.

The MX-334/II was provided with skids and made its first flight in 4 September 1943, towed by one Cadillac, but the take-off was quite bumpy and it was decided to install a detachable trolley. The next flight took place in 2 October, towed by one P-38 Lightning.

In June 1944 an Aerojet XCAL R-200 rocket engine, with 90kg peak-thrust was installed. On 5 July, the MX-334/II was towed to 2,500m (8,200ft) and successfully made its first powered flight, becoming America's first rocket-plane.

The MX-334/III was destroyed at take-off on 10 November 1943. After the N-9M-1 accident, the other two prototypes were provided with vertical surfaces stabilising, with support wires.

The MX-334/II changed the designation to MX-324 and received a new (fixed) tricycle landing gear, the main wheels having trousers and the asymmetric nose wheel a spat.

The engine installation weighted 194kg (428lb), this included a tank of monomethylamine fuel, a tank of nitric acid oxidant, four pressurised gas bottles, the combustion chamber and the electric control system.

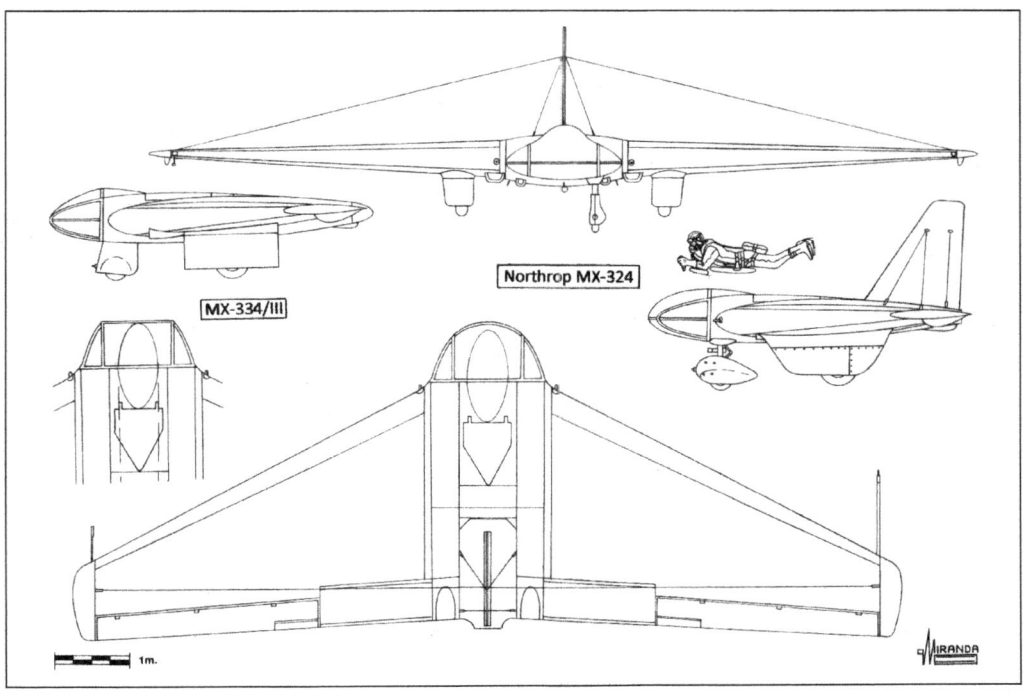

Rocket Interceptors: 1941-1947

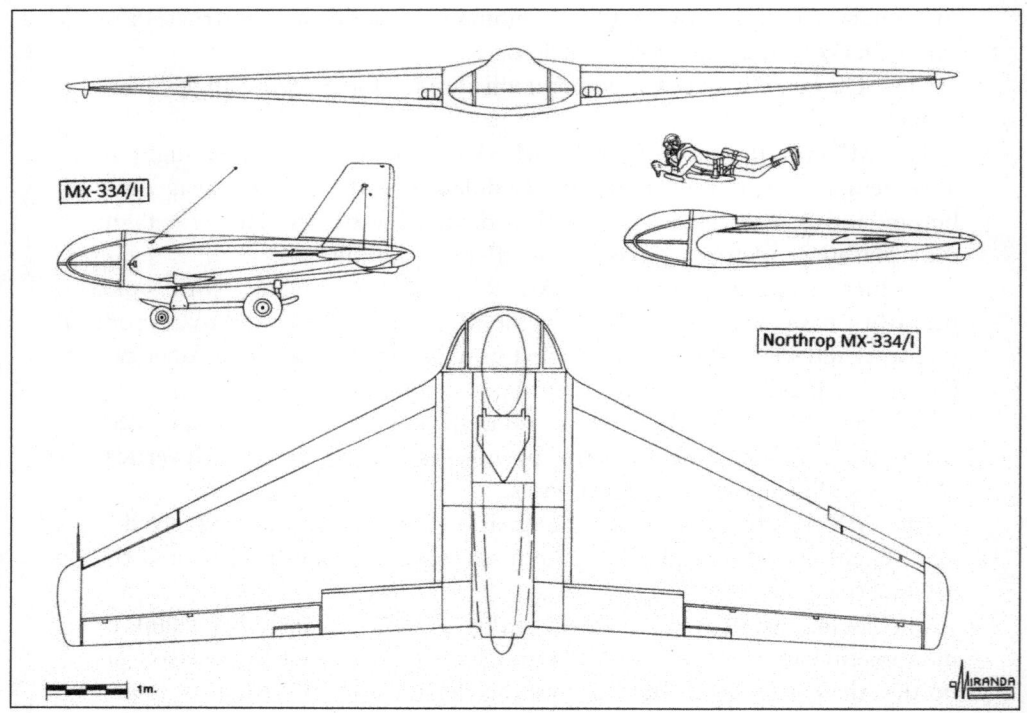

MX-324 TECHNICAL DATA: Wingspan: 10.90m (35.7ft). Length: 4.34m (14.2ft). Height: 2.13m (7ft). Wing area: 23.41sq.m (260sq.ft). Maximum weight: 1,656kg (3,656lb). Estimated maximum speed: 480km/h (298mph). Ceiling: 5,200m (17,056ft). Range: 480km (298 miles). Airframe: wood/plywood/steel tubing.

26

Japanese Rocket-Fighters

During the 1930s, the Western powers that constrained the Japanese territorial expansion were developing four-engine heavy bombers. The Tupolev TB.3, capable of reaching Tokyo taking off from Soviet territory, flew for the first time in 1930. In 1932 the French Farman 222 also performed its first flight; although ugly, as all its kind, it was very effective to control navigation in the area to the south of Formosa, operating from Saigon. The Boeing B-17 prototype was in the air in 1935 and the British Short Sunderland and Short Stirling prototypes, capable of transatlantic flights, followed in 1938 and 1939. Even the Dutch worked on a four-engine version of the Fokker T-IX, named T-VI /115.

The B-17 had a 2,000 miles range, turbocharged engines and a powerful armament that allowed this aircraft autonomous defence. When the Imperial Japanese Army (IJA) was aware of these excellent performances, they realised that the American bomber was above the interception capabilities of the standard fighter Ki.27 and possibly exceeded its successor Ki.43 that had not yet entered service.

Given the potential threat that the B-17s based in the Philippines could represent, the IJA Koku Hombu (Imperial Japanese Army's Air Headquarters) requested Nakajima to design the Ki.44, a point defence interceptor with high climb rate and twice the armament of the Ki.43. Realities of war showed that this effort would not be enough though, since the US industry was able to design, test and mass-produce a new aircraft in a third of the time than the Japanese.

In February 1942, the US government placed an order for 1,600 Boeing B-29 Superfortresses, able to fly at 595km/h and 9,700m of altitude.

The IJA intelligence services awaited the first B-29 attack in April 1944, but this was delayed by lack of supplies at the Chinese airfields of Kweiling and Liuchow. The first contact with the B-29 occurred on 26 April, when six Ki.43 fighters of the IJA 204th Sentai had a worrying experience with a B-29 of the 444th BG, which was flying supplies from India to China.

The giant plane, heavily loaded and with its tail gun malfunctioning, was shot twelve times without apparent results. It just ascended until the Japanese fighters were forced to abandon the pursuit through lack of oxygen.

On 1 November 1944, the first American bomber flew over Tokyo; it was not the expected B-17 but a giant B-29 F-13 42-93852, of the 3rd Photo Recon Sqn, ironically named 'Tokyo Rose'. When the Ki.44-II-Otsu of the 47th Sentai tried to intercept it, they discovered that the Superfortress flew so high and fast that they could not reach it. It turned out that the Japanese plane used for the intended interception, equivalent to the Lockheed Starfighter of the time and with an astonishing climb rate of 5,000m in 4 minutes, was not good enough to do the work for which it had been designed.

The psychological impact caused by this realisation on the Koku Hombu had important consequences. The IJA needed interceptors equipped with turbo superchargers, but the Japanese industry was unable to build them or even replicate those of the enemy bombers that had been shot down.

The Japanese tried to increase the power of their engines with methanol, water and oxygen injection power boost devices, but these systems only worked below 10,000m. Mitsubishi engineers tried to develop an exhaust-driven turbo-supercharger based on the study of North American P-43 and B-17 aircraft captured in China and Philippines.

By mid-1944 turbo-superchargers were indispensable to fight the B-29 bombers at altitudes over 10,000m, but the Japanese industry was unable to duplicate the captured aircrafts.

The General Electric turbo-supercharger was a product that required enormous technical and manufacturing resources that were not available in Japan. The high temperatures reached by exhaust gas and the high rotation speeds of turbines (26,000rpm) required the use of austenitic stainless-steel chrome-molybdenum alloys and the development of work-hardening techniques that enabled the turbo-supercharger to withstand stresses caused by centrifugal forces. The precision machining of turbines and impellers could only be made possible by sophisticated machine tools and surplus of raw materials.

In August 1944 the Mitsubishi J2M4 Raiden 34 flew with one Ru-303 exhaust-driven turbo-supercharger mounted in the starboard side of the fuselage, just behind the Kasei 23c engine. The new supercharger did not work properly either, provoking fires during the tests, and never became operational.

The exhaust-driven turbo-superchargers were larger, involved extra piping and increasing an aircraft size, weight, complexity and cost. It is not possible to install them in a conventional single-engine fighter and its use requires aircrafts specially designed, with enough room for installation of the turbo, the intercooler and the heavy tubing system.

Grabbing the opportunity of having the new solid-propellant rocket engines developed for the suicide bomber Kugisho MXY7 Ohka, early in 1945 the engineers of the glider builder Mizuno K.K. decided to develop their own rocket-glider Shinryu II.

It had an unusual canard configuration to facilitate the short take-off and it was built of wood, plywood and iron plate, with four Type 2 rocket engines at the rear of the fuselage.

Three different versions would have been manufactured: suicide, antitank and interceptor.

The suicide version had no undercarriage, using the same rails and rocket cart system as the Ohka 43-Otsu for take-off. It would have been able to carry a bomb of 250kg in the fuselage, behind the pilot.

Like the suicide bombers D4Y4 Suisei and the Type 5 Shinyo motorboats, the Shinryu II would have possibly been equipped with two or four barrage ISR rockets of 12cm that would have made more difficult for the enemy gunners to reach the target during the terminal dive.

The anti-tank version took-off by its own means over a primitive landing gear of skids, helped by a Type 1 ventral rocket that was detachable. It is assumed that it had the four rocket engines in the fuselage to maintain its flight altitude during the attack. It used eight anti-armour hollow charge ROTSU rockets of 8cm, housed in iron tubes welded to the undercarriage, with a minus 7-degree pitch so that they could be fired without any loss of altitude or speed. The aircraft had spoilers, allowing it to survive, to be able to land and refuel for the next attack.

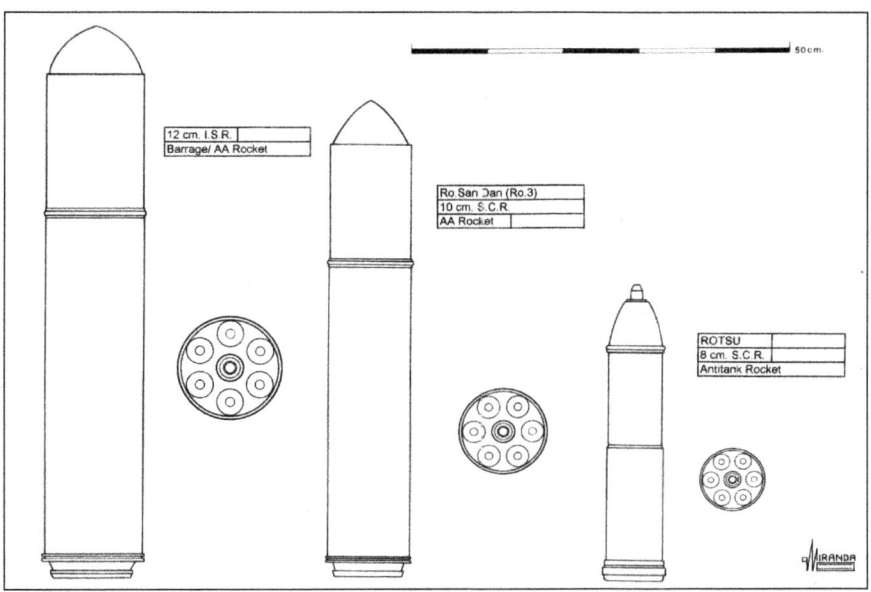

Although this version has been described as anti-tank, as it used that type of armament, it seems more realistic to assume that it would have been used to attack the LCA. The interior of the island would have had thousands of suicide commands waiting for the Sherman tanks with magnetic demolition charges of 10kg of the 'lung mine' type.

The interceptor was equipped with oxygen, pressurised cockpit and reflex gunsight. It was towed by a conventional piston-engine fighter that took it above 8,000m, releasing it over the stream of bombers. It was armed with eight Ro.3 rockets that exploded by means of a time fuse at a predetermined distance, releasing shrapnel and incendiary pellets in a conic pattern.

Like its German counterpart W.Gr 21, the Ro.3 was not very accurate and lost altitude very fast. For that reason, the launching tubes were fixed at a plus 7-degree pitch, calculated so that the parabolic path of the rocket would be compatible with the performance of the reflector gunsight.

All versions of the Shinryu II had machine guns with ammunition tracer to help the correction of the attack trajectories. These would also be of use to the interceptor to defend from the escort fighters, evade them thanks to its manoeuvrability and return to base on a gliding flight. The four rocket engines, started sequentially, would serve to regain altitude after an attack over the formation of B-29s or to distance away from the escort fighters.

SHINRYU II TECHNICAL DATA: Airframe: wood, fabric and iron plate; Wingspan: 10m; Length 7.80m in the interceptor version; Height: 2.70m; Wing area: 19sq.m; Maximum speed: 500km/h in the kamikaze version; Ceiling: over 8,000m in

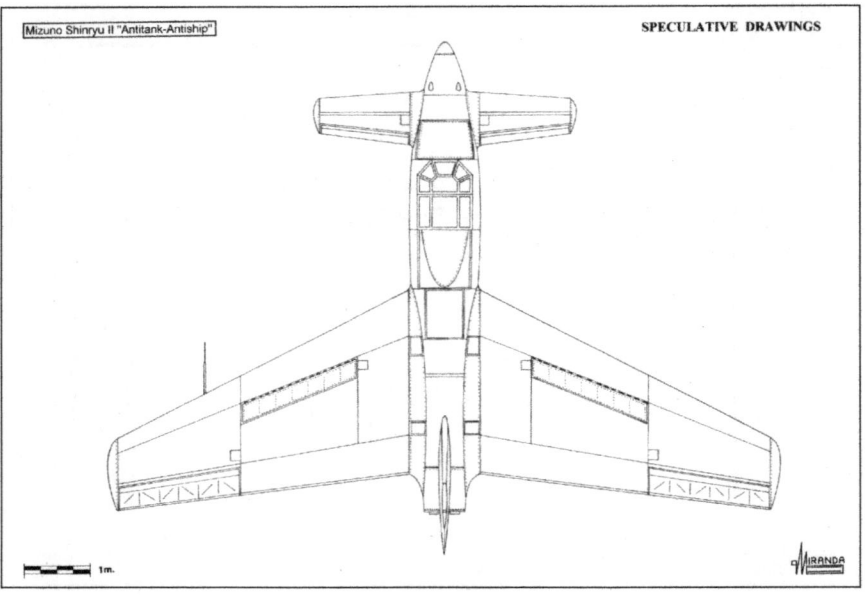

the interceptor version; Range: 15km in the kamikaze version; Engines: four Toku-Ro.1 Type 2 with 600kg peak-thrust during 30 sec. In the anti-tank and kamikaze version another Toku-Ro.1 Type 1 was used with 300kg peak-thrust during 10 sec, in ventral position, to provide additional boost during take-off. Armament: four Type 89 7.7mm guns that were reduced to two in the kamikaze version. Eight Ro.San Dan (Ro.3) 10cm SCR AA rockets in the interceptor version, eight ROTSU 8cm SCR hollow charge rockets in the ant ship/antitank version, two or four RAK 12cm ISR barrage rockets and one 248,7kg Type 99 Number 25 Model 1 bomb in the kamikaze version.

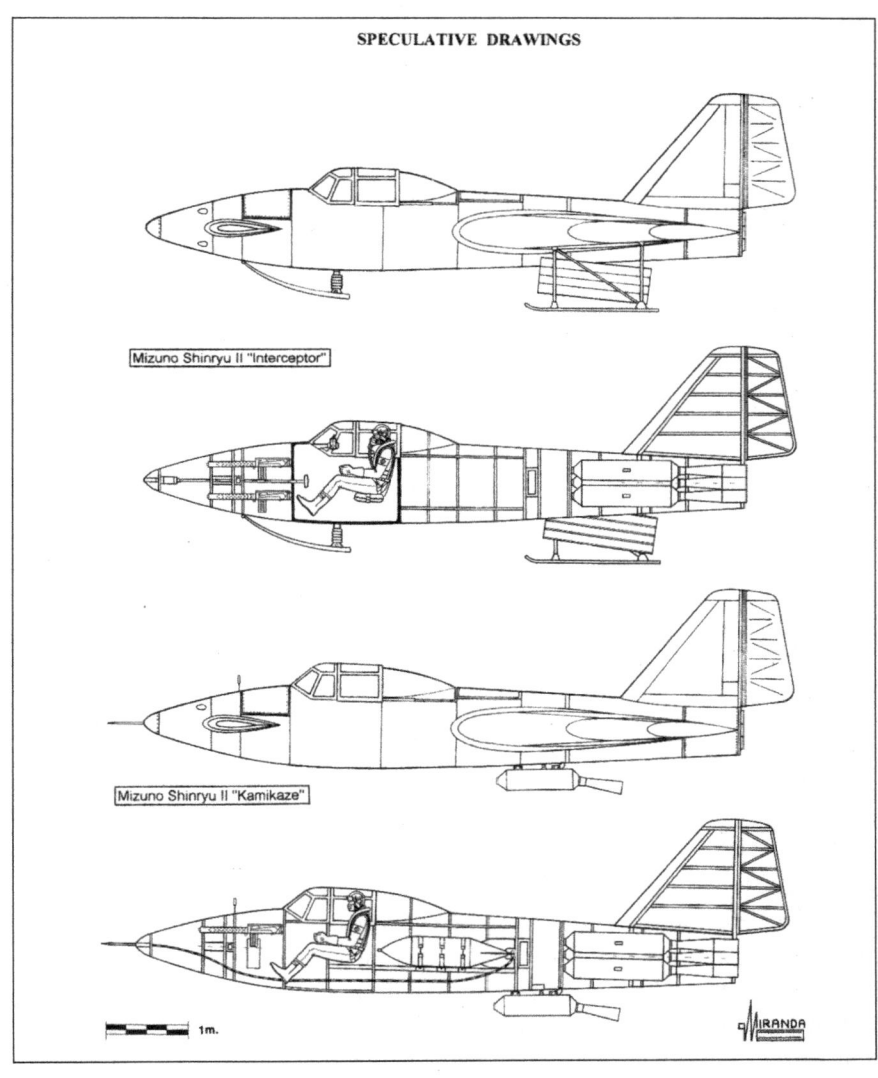

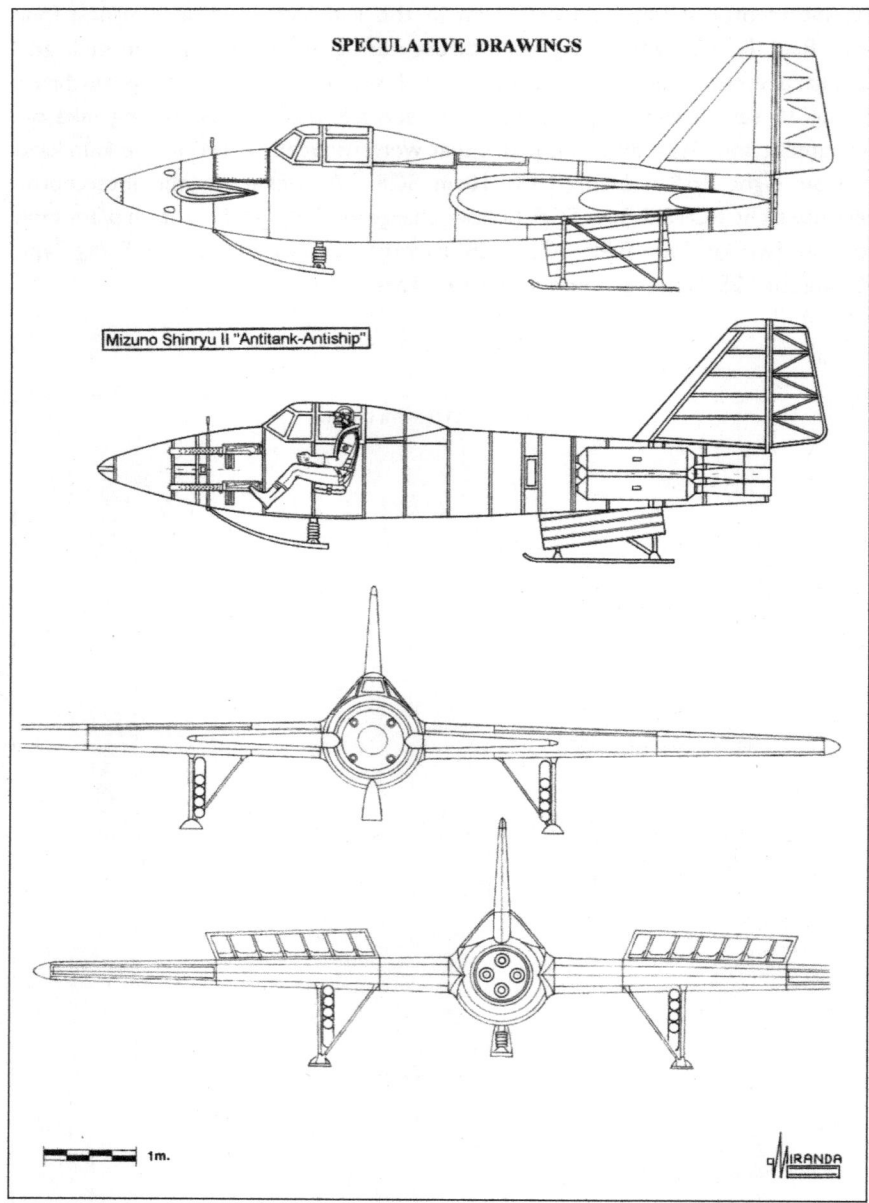

The Kakukyoku rammer was project of radio-guided antiaircraft, vertically launched, ramming missile designed by Yujiro Murakami in March 1945, following a requirement of the IJN. It was exclusively propelled by solid-fuel rockets and should reach 9,000m of altitude in 100 seconds.

The absence of explosive warhead required a degree of accuracy impossible to achieve with the primitive guidance systems of the time.

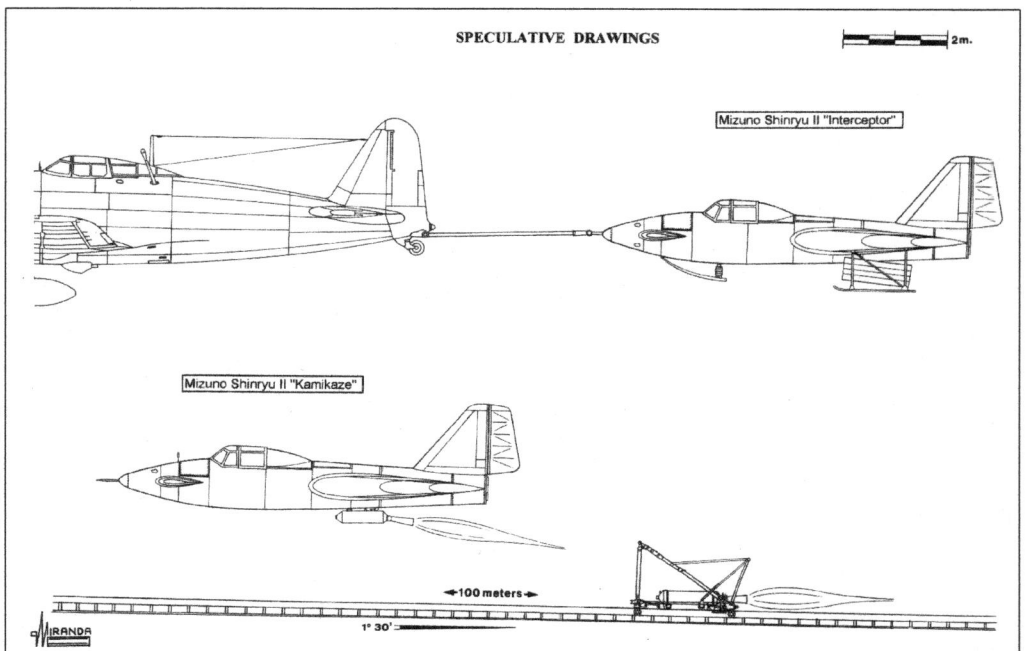

Therefore, the missile was reconverted into a piloted rammer, a project shared between the Imperial Japanese Navy (IJN) and the IJA to be handed over to the Kawasaki Company.

The vertical take-off was discarded as the G-forces would have been too excessive for the pilot to remain conscious. The rammer would be towed by a high-altitude interceptor up to 10,000m and released near the bomber stream. The pilot would then fire the four rockets until reaching Mach 0.91 in 6 seconds and fly in a collision path towards the American heavy bomber, without any possibility of surviving.

KAKUKYOKU RAMMER TECHNICAL DATA: Airframe steel and wood. Cockpit pressurised, with oxygen system and telephonic link with the towing plane. It had no control panel, just the controls of a glider plus a handle to detach the trolley after take-off and another to get detached from the towing plane. Engines: four solid-fuel rockets Toku-Ro.1 Type 1 with 300kg thrust each for 10 seconds. Wingspan 4.44m. Length 3.45m. Height 1.80m. Wing area 5sq.m. Maximum weight 800kg. Maximum speed Mach 0.91. Ceiling 10,000m. Climb rate 312m/s.

By mid-1943, the effective blockade by the US Navy Submarine Force began to strangle the Japanese economy, and the aeronautical industry was particularly affected by increasing shortages of high aviation fuel and

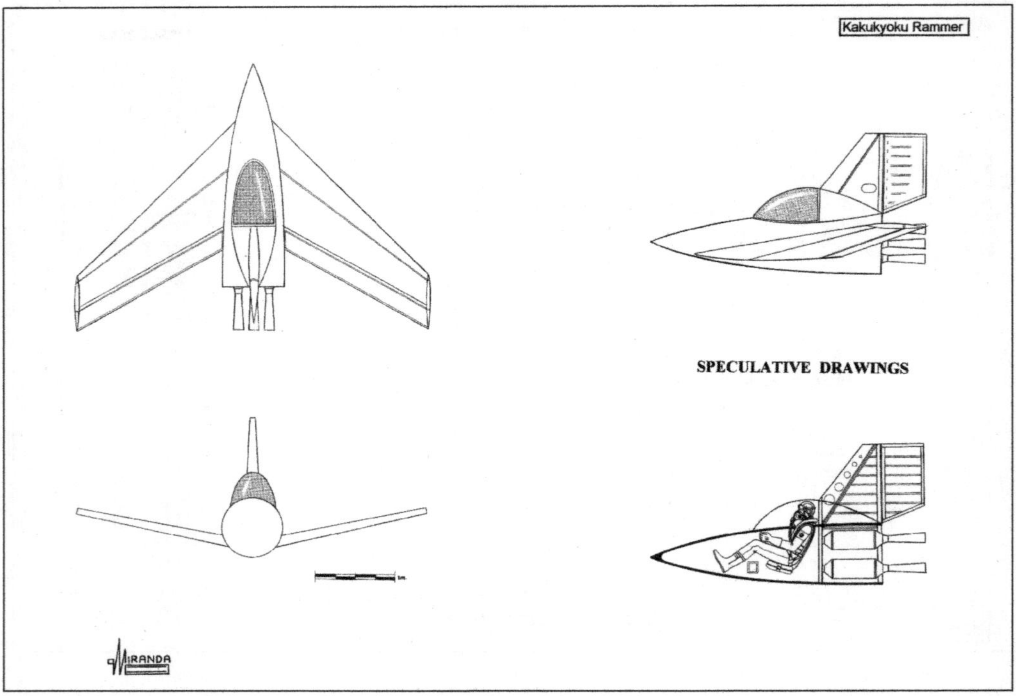
Kakukyoku Rammer
SPECULATIVE DRAWINGS
MIRANDA

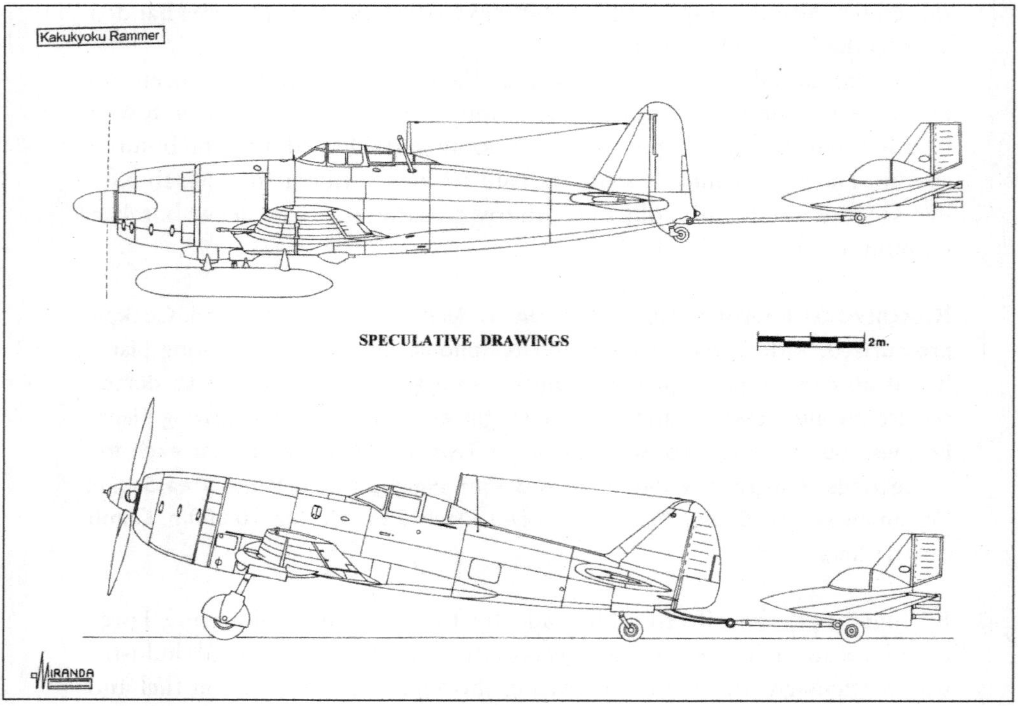
Kakukyoku Rammer
SPECULATIVE DRAWINGS
2m.
MIRANDA

light alloys. Prior to the US embargo, the IJA normally used 91-octane fuel, then the lower grade 87-octane fuel was introduced, to great detriment of aircraft performances and numerous engine maintenance issues.

Once the Allied forces were established in the Philippines and in Okinawa, Japan was cut off from the oil fields of the Dutch East Indies. The last tanker reached Japan in March 1945. At the end of the war the quality of fuel went down to 85 octane, because the gas was mixed with oil extracted from pine tree roots. The scarce 95-octane fuel captured from the Allies was reserved for the use of some elite units, such as the IJA 21st Hikodan, whose Ki.84 fighters performed kamikaze escort missions, or the Shiden-Kai fighters of the IJN 343 Kokutai which protected strategic targets. In contrast, the Allies consumed between 40,000 and 70,000 tons of 100/150 Grade Aviation 44-1 fuel each month.

Availability of high-octane fuel let the American engines run hotter without detonation problems, but the Japanese had 87-octane only and had to use forced-air cooling fans to avoid the overheating of their supercharged engines.

The situation demanded a new type of engine, easy to build with cheap metals and capable of running on any fuel, so the Japanese aircraft industry was forced to consider the use of ramjets.

In 1938 the Kayaba-Seisakusho Works Corporation was sponsored by the IJA Aero-Technical Research Institute (Rikugun) to investigate the feasibility of tailless aircrafts. In January 1939 the HK-1 flew for the first time, a tailless glider with a 25-degree swept wing.

The following prototype, the K2, had wingtip fins and flew by early November 1940. The K3 was a cranked rear-swept flying-wing with three pairs of control surfaces on the trailing edge. It was destroyed in 1941, being unable to recover stability during a flat spin.

At that time, Japan was already preparing for war and the IA cancelled the Kayaba programme to concentrate its efforts on the production of the Ki.43 and Ki.44 conventional fighters. In 1943 the IJA No. 2 Aeronautical Technology Research Institute, in collaboration with Kawasaki, built the Ne 0 ramjet engine based on the Sänger designs. The Ne 0 was 2.10m long with a chamber combustion of 60cm in diameter.

During ground tests conducted in July, the ramjet produced 60kg static thrust and at the end of that year was tested in suspended flight under the fuselage of a Kawasaki Ki.48-II bomber. Early in 1944, the IJA ordered from Kayaba the design of the Katsuodori, a ramjet point interceptor powered by an advanced version of the Ne 0 with 750kg thrust.

The new engine, called Kayaba Model 1, had a combustion chamber 1m in diameter and could run with heavy kerosene or crude pine root oil that the local chemical industry produced as ersatz fuel. The Katsuodori would have had a very similar airframe to that of the German project Heinkel P.1078 C German of February 1944, with 35-degree rear-swept wings built in wood/plywood, with vertical fins mounted in the wingtips, containing 2,000l of fuel. The circular fuselage was built of steel and contained the ramjet and cockpit with the in prone position.

The take-off was made on a detachable landing gear with the help of four Toku-Ro.1 Type 3 RATO detachable rockets, with 600kg peak-thrust and 20 seconds of life. The ramjet started at 367km/h and could run for 30 minutes. When the fuel ran out the Katsuodori landed like a glider on a retractable skid and a tailwheel. Kayaba had planned to manufacture its own version of the Ho-301, 40mm recoilless rocket-gun, modifying it to fire 30mm rounds.

In July 1944 the IJA decided to cancel the Katsuodori to concentrate on the manufacture of the Mitsubishi Ki. 200 rocket-fighter. To salvage the project, Kayaba adapted its design to accept the Ne 20 turbojet. The prototype was expected to be completed by the end of 1944, but the award of Ne 20 to the jet-fighter Nakajima J9Y1 Kikka forced its final cancellation.

KAYABA KATSUODORI TECHNICAL DATA: Wingspan: 8.99m. Length: 4.48m. Height: 1.85m. Wing area: 12.57sq.m. Maximum weight: 3,000kg. Maximum speed: 900km/h. Service ceiling: 15,000m.

With the appearance of Boeing B-29 bombers in the Japanese skies, the Imperial Japanese Navy (IJN) leadership decided to copy the Me 163 rocket-fighter using the German-supplied manuals as well as a Walter HWK 109-509 rocket engine. On 27 July 1944 a joint IJN-IJA commission formally ordered Mitsubishi to develop their own version of the Komet, denominated 19-shi-Experimental Interceptor Fighter, using reverse-engineered solutions. The final project was presented to the IJN in August 1944 and the mock-up was inspected in September.

The prototype, denominated J8M1 Shusui flew for the first time on 8 January 1945, with water ballast, towed aloft by a Nakajima B6N1 Tenzan bomber. The first powered flight test took place on 7 July 1945, with the prototype being destroyed because of engine malfunction.

J8M1 MODEL 19 TECHNICAL DATA: Wingspan: 9.5m. Length: 6.05m. Height: 2.7m. Wing area: 17.73sq.m. Maximum weight: 3,870kg. Maximum speed: 888km/h. Service ceiling: 12,000m. Climb rate: 230 sec. to 10,000m. Armament: two Type 5, 30mm cannon with 400rpm and 53 rounds per gun.

The version of the IJA received the Kitai number Ki.200 and differed from the J8M1 in having a shorter fuselage, with no side windows behind the

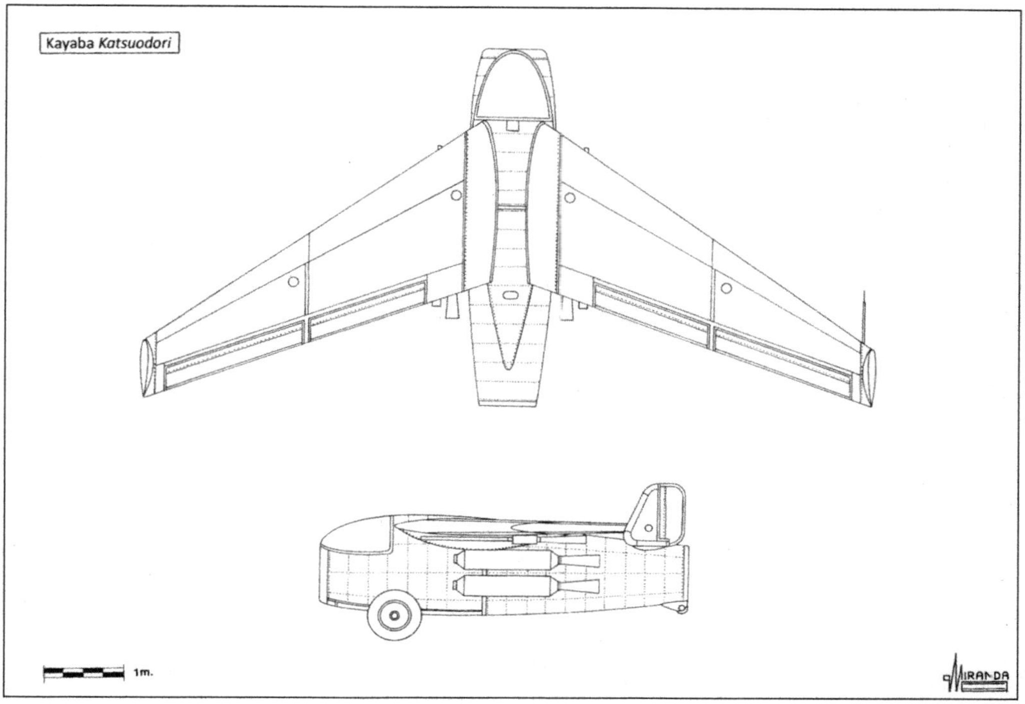

Japanese Rocket-Fighters

295

Kayaba *Katsuodori*

1m.

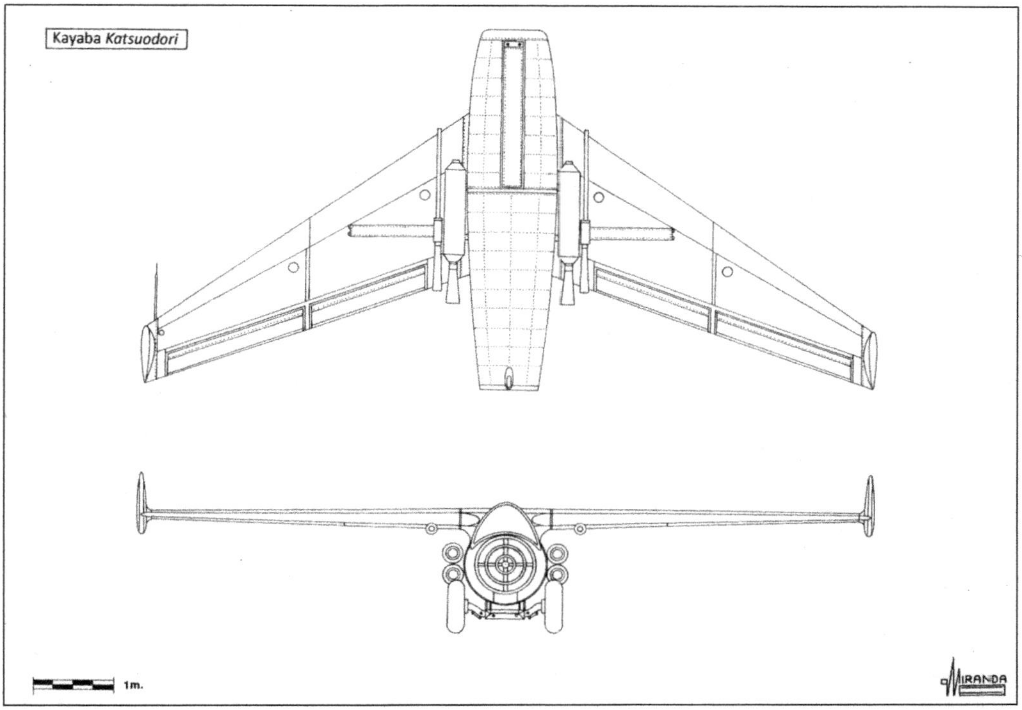

Kayaba *Katsuodori*

1m.

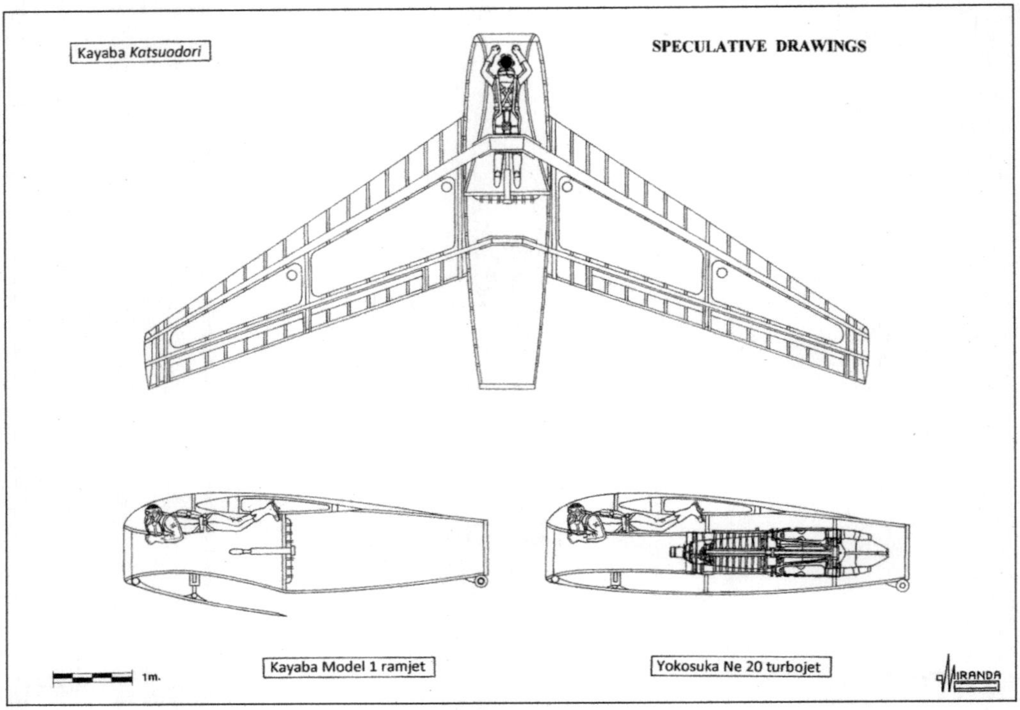
Kayaba *Katsuodori*
SPECULATIVE DRAWINGS
1m.
Kayaba Model 1 ramjet
Yokosuka Ne 20 turbojet
MIRANDA

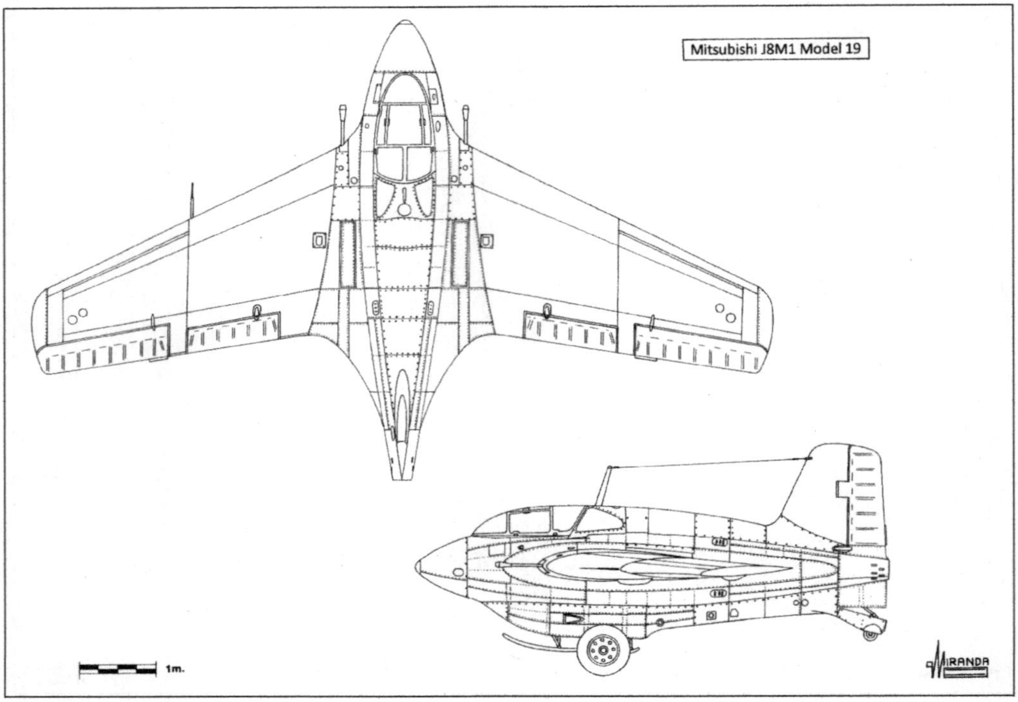
Mitsubishi J8M1 Model 19
1m.
MIRANDA

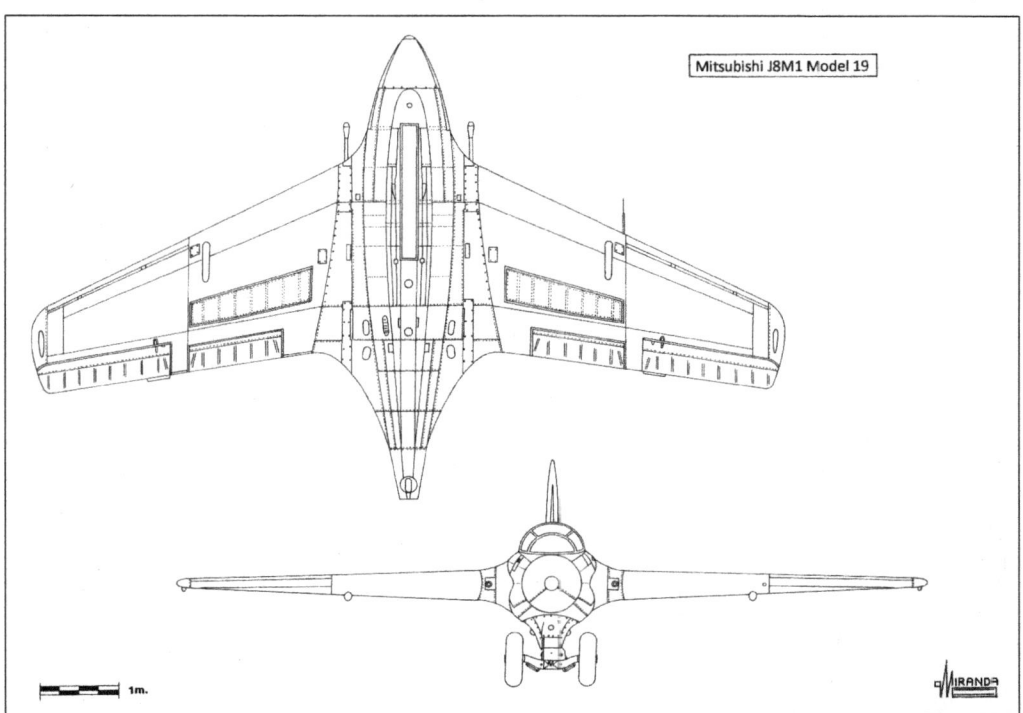

cockpit. The trolley attachment was advanced 30cm to improve stability during take-off. Internally, the hydraulic system and propellant piping were modified to make them safer. The armament was replaced by two Ho-155-II cannon.

Kı. 200 TECHNICAL DATA: Wingspan: 9.5m. Length: 5.95m. Height: 2.7m. Wing area: 17.73sq.m. Maximum weight: 3,000kg. Maximum speed: 800km/h. Armament: two Ho-105-II, 30mm cannon with 450rpm and 53 rounds per gun.

Both versions were powered by a Yamakita-Matsumoto Toku-Ro.2 (KR 10) 'hot' bi-propellant rocket engine, with 1,500kg peak-thrust.

In Japan the T-Stoff propellant was called Ko-Stoff and the C-Stoff, Otsu-Stoff. Both were colourless liquids easy to confuse, which was the cause of several accidents. It was manufactured at Edogawa Kagaku and Mitsubishi Kasei facilities.

The Shusui fuselage was built in light alloy and steel. It contained a cockpit (with armoured-glass screen and steel seat-plates, radio and oxygen equipment), 106 ammunition rounds, five propellant tanks with 1,159l of Ko-Stoff, one Toku-Ro.2 rocket engine with 2.48m length, one retractable skid with 1.8m length, one retractable 200 x 75 tailwheel, the detachable undercarriage dolly with two 700 x 200 wheels and attachment points for two detachable Toku-Ro.1 Type 3 RATOG rockets, with 600kg peak-thrust and 20 seconds of life.

The 27-degree rear-swept wings were built in wood/plywood, with fixed leading edge slots in the 40 per cent span, flaps and ailerons with metallic structure and fabric covering, metallic drag flaps, four propellant tanks with 536l of Otsu-Stoff and two 30mm cannon. The tailfin was built in wood/plywood ant the rudder with metallic structure and fabric covering.

Before the end of the Second World War, Mitsubishi manufactured six J8M1 prototypes and one Ki.200. Full-scale production was commissioned by Mitsubishi, Fuji Hikoki and Nissan Jidosha, a joint manufacture of 155 aircraft by March 1945, 1,300 by September and 3,600 by March 1946. These fighters would then be used to activate ten IJA Hikosentais based in Tokio, Nagoya-Osaka and Manchuria. The 312th Kokutai would be the first unit of the IJN to use the Shusui.

The design of the J8M2 Shusui-KAI Model 21 finished in July 1945. It was a modified version of the J8M1 with one of the cannons and its ammunition being replaced by two propellant tanks to extend the engine endurance from 5.5 to 7 minutes. The J8M2 was a dead-end design, because the Japanese lacked the operational experience acquired by the Luftwaffe with the Komet armament.

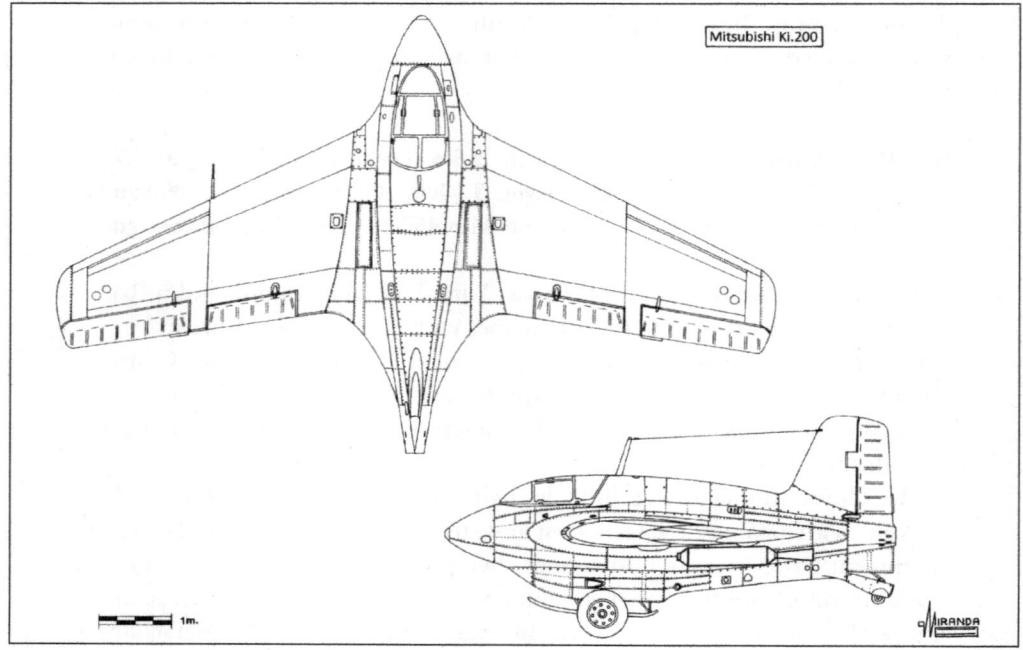

J8M2 Shusui-KAI Model 21 technical data: Wingspan: 9.5m. Length: 6.05m. Height: 2.7m. Wing area: 17.73sq.m. Armament: one Type 5, 30mm cannon with 400rpm and 53 rounds.

The J8M2 was modified again as Model 22, widening the fuselage diameter from 120 to 130cm, which allowed an 8 per cent increase in propellant capacity and the use of two cannons. The wingspan and overall length were also slightly increased.

J8M2 Model 22 technical data: Wingspan: 10m. Length: 6.428m. Height: 2.7m. Wing area: 18.66sq.m. Armament: two Type 5, 30mm cannon with 400rpm and 53 rounds per gun.

Data of the HWK 109-509 C rocket-motor was provided to the Japanese who used this information to build their own version: the Toku-Ro.3 (KR 20) with 1,600kg from the main chamber and 400kg from the auxiliary chamber.

Early in 1945 the IJA Rikugun Institute started the design of the Ki.202, a rocket-fighter with enough propellant capacity for 10 minutes and 28 seconds of powered flight. The final design was projected for February and the prototype completion was scheduled for August. To save fuel, the Ki.202 was to be launched by a rocket cart system, as the Ohka 43-Otsu. The semi-recessed landing gear was not detachable.

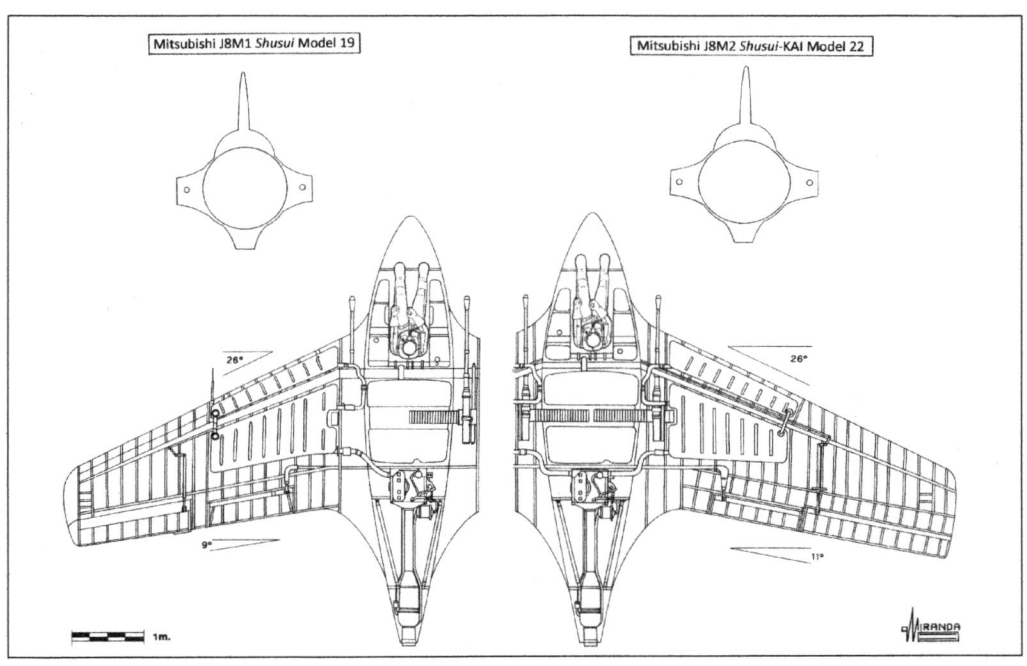

KI.202 TECHNICAL DATA: Wingspan: 9.75m. Length: 7.71m. Height: 2.74m. Wing area: 18.39sq.m. Maximum weight: 5,015kg. Maximum speed: 900km/h. Climb rate: 207 sec. to 10,000m. Armament: two Ho-155-II, 30mm cannon with 400rpm and 80 rounds per gun.

The Yokosuka MXY8 Akigusa was a tailless training glider developed by the First Naval Air Technical Arsenal (Kugisho) for the future pilots of the Shusui. The MXY8 was an unpowered version of the J8M1 built entirely of wood/plywood with a loaded weight of just 1,037kg.

During the first flight tests, performed in December 1944, the prototype was towed to altitude by a Kyushu K10W1 trainer proving satisfactory handling characteristics.

Two other prototypes were built by Kugisho, one of which was delivered to the Army Aerotechnical Research Institute (Rikugun) for evaluation and served as the basis for the development of its own training glider Yokoi Kokuki Ku.13, with the same dimensions as the MXY8. The other served as a model for the construction at the Maeda Aircraft Institute, a series of sixty Akigusa units for the IJN. This version was provided with water ballast tanks, which simulated the weight of rocket propellants to achieve a more realistic training, and was operated by the 312th Kokutai.

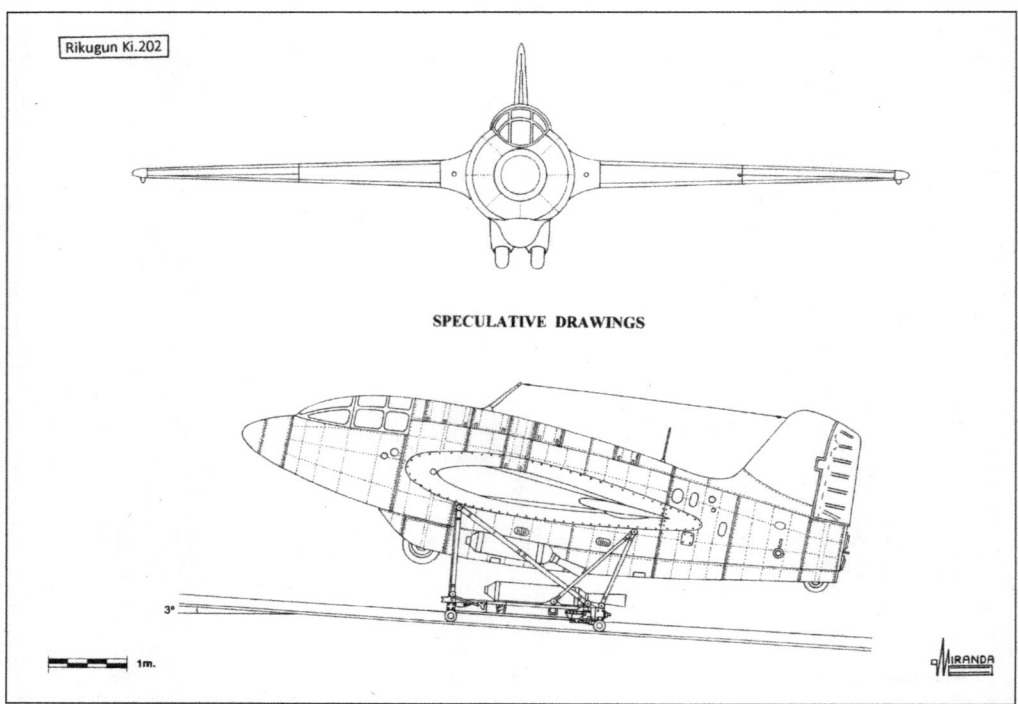

SPECULATIVE DRAWINGS

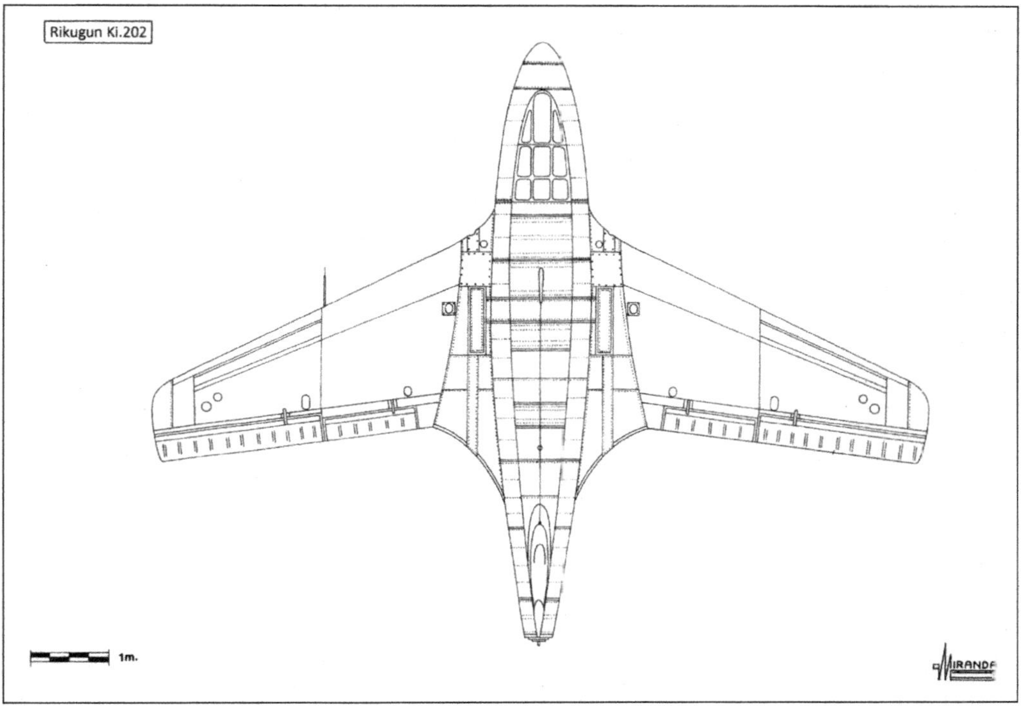

Rikugun Ki.202

1m.

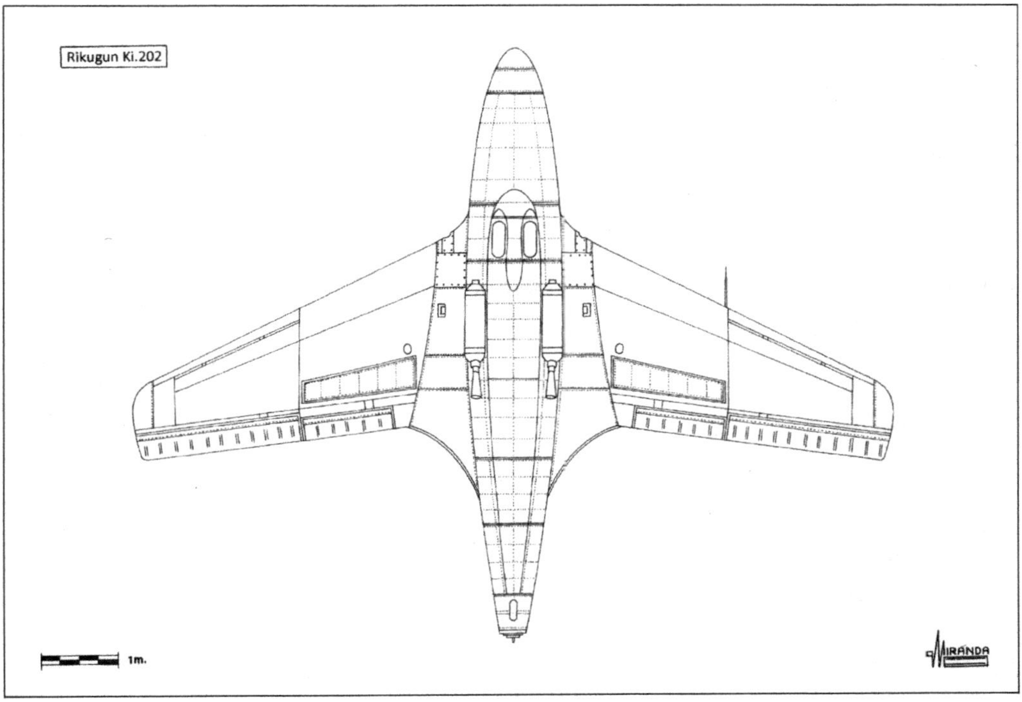

Rikugun Ki.202

1m.

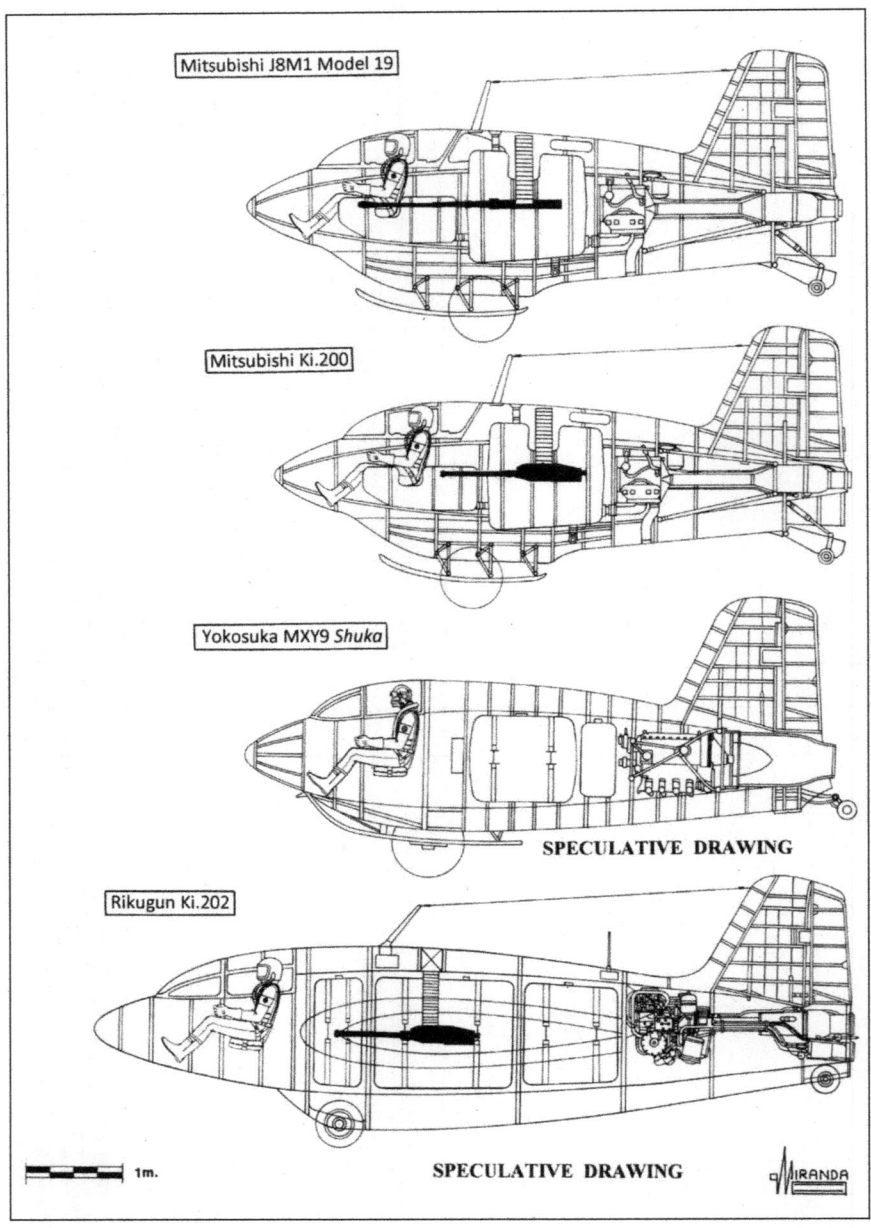

To avoid the rapid loss of altitude and increase flight time, a version of the Akigusa powered by a 105hp Hirth/Hitachi Ha-11 Hatsukaze II pusher engine, a driving two-bladed wooden propeller was designed, but its construction was rejected in favour of the more advanced MXY9 Shuka.